CHANGE AND CONTINUITY

Change and Continuity

Canadian Political Economy
in the New Millennium

Edited by

MARK P. THOMAS, LEAH F. VOSKO,
CARLO FANELLI, AND OLENA LYUBCHENKO

Carleton Library Series 248

McGill-Queen's University Press
Montreal & Kingston • London • Chicago

ISBN 978-0-7735-5740-6 (cloth)
ISBN 978-0-7735-5741-3 (paper)
ISBN 978-0-7735-5844-1 (ePDF)
ISBN 978-0-7735-5845-8 (ePUB)

Legal deposit second quarter 2019
Bibliothèque nationale du Québec

Printed in Canada on acid-free paper that is 100% ancient forest free
(100% post-consumer recycled), processed chlorine free

Funded by the Government of Canada   Financé par le gouvernement du Canada

Canada Council for the Arts   Conseil des arts du Canada

We acknowledge the support of the Canada Council for the Arts.

Nous remercions le Conseil des arts du Canada de son soutien.

Library and Archives Canada Cataloguing in Publication

Title: Change and continuity: Canadian political economy in the
new millennium/edited by Mark P. Thomas, Leah F. Vosko, Carlo Fanelli,
and Olena Lyubchenko.

Other titles: Change and continuity (Montréal, Québec)

Names: Thomas, Mark P. (Mark Preston), 1969– editor. | Vosko, Leah F.,
editor. | Fanelli, Carlo, 1984– editor. | Lyubchenko, Olena, 1990– editor.

Series: Carleton library series; 248.

Description: Series statement: Carleton library series; 248 | Includes
bibliographical references and index.

Identifiers: Canadiana (print) 20190102241 | Canadiana (ebook) 20190102446 |
ISBN 9780773557413 (softcover) | ISBN 9780773557406 (hardcover) |
ISBN 9780773558441 (ePDF) | ISBN 9780773558458 (ePUB)

Subjects: LCSH: Canada—Economic conditions—21st century. | LCSH:
Canada—Social conditions—21st century.

Classification: LCC HC113 .C53 2019 | DDC 338.971—dc23

This book was typeset by Marquis Interscript in 10/13 Sabon.

*For Wallace Clement, in acknowledgment
of his career-long dedication to advancing the field
of critical political economy in Canada*

Contents

Tables and Figures

TABLES

FIGURES

Acknowledgments

This book has its origins in a workshop on "Rethinking the New Canadian Political Economy" hosted by the Global Labour Research Centre (GLRC) at York University in December 2015. The co-editors would like to thank the GLRC for its support and assistance in organizing the workshop. We would also like to thank the following York University bodies for providing financial support for the workshop – Office of the Dean, Faculty of Liberal Arts & Professional Studies; Vice-President Research & Innovation; Provost & Vice-President Academic; the Department of Politics; and the Department of Sociology – as well as the Department of Politics at Ryerson University.

The preparation of this book benefited from the work of a number of individuals. We would like to thank Philip Cercone and the editorial team at MQUP for support throughout the publication process, as well as the anonymous reviewers for helpful comments that guided the revision of the original manuscript. We would also like to thank Alix Holtby, doctoral candidate in the graduate program in sociology at York University, for assistance in bringing the manuscript together and preparing it for submission.

The editors and publisher would like to thank the Faculty of Liberal Arts and Professional Studies, York University, Toronto, Canada, for the financial support it provided to this work.

Finally, we each thank our friends and family members for their ongoing support of our research.

CHANGE AND CONTINUITY

Canadian Political Economy in the New Millennium

Mark P. Thomas and Leah F. Vosko

In a contemporary Canadian context characterized by growing social and income inequality, the continuing consequences and legacies of settler colonialism, the spread of precarious employment, the ongoing effects of globalization, and the emergence of new social movements responding to such challenges, social scientists are pressed to develop innovative conceptual and analytic tools to both comprehend the changing political-economic landscape and to intervene effectively in public debates. For decades, the Canadian political economy (CPE) tradition has shaped a broad interdisciplinary body of critical social science research that is oriented toward understanding the dynamics of power in Canadian society and identifying processes that may generate progressive social change. Emerging out of a materialist approach to studying social relations, scholars within this tradition have worked continually to expand its boundaries, seeking new understandings of the social processes and social forces that shape society, their attendant conflicts and contradictions, and the potential for social change that could ensue. The CPE tradition has also itself been subject to transformation prompted by theoretical innovation and the exploration of new sites for empirical investigation, for example through the development of feminist political economy (FPE), the theorization of space and scale, attention to cultural processes, and a focus on the environment.

The essays in this volume assess the legacy of the CPE tradition for contemporary social science research, charting new directions for future scholarship in this vein, and offering critical insight into the dynamics of Canada's contemporary political economy, including on issues such as social and income inequality, the effects of neoliberalism on public policy, and the expansion and deepening of labour market insecurity. Like its immediate precursor (Clement and Vosko 2003), the central aim of this volume is to continue to push the boundaries of traditional CPE scholarship. Such scholarship, with its Marxist lineage, placed an emphasis on studying class relations (often construed narrowly as social relations surrounding production for surplus) within capitalist society to understand dimensions of social inequality and dynamics of social change (Clement and Drache 1985; Clement 2001b; McNally 1981; Panitch 1981). Over the course of the past several decades, such scholarship has been reshaped, in particular through FPE research and its analytic emphasis on the centrality of gender, as well as increasingly race, Indigeneity, citizenship, sexuality, ability, age, and other social relations, to expand and deepen understandings of inequalities, power dynamics, and social conflict and contradiction in the constitution of capitalism (Clement and Miles 1994; Stasiulis and Yuval-Davis 1995; Vosko 2002; Porter 2003; Sharma 2006; Bezanson and Luxton 2006; Corman and Luxton 2007; also Armstrong and Armstrong [1984] 2010). Through FPE scholarship, the CPE perspective has evolved to approach the study of the interactions between wide-ranging social relations not as abstract categories, but in all of their complexities and interconnections and in a manner that recognizes the historically and socially situated character of social location.[1]

Reflecting this approach, Clement (1997) asserts that the key assumptions guiding contemporary research based in this tradition are that: (i) social relations are shaped by relations of economic production and social reproduction; (ii) the organization of production and social reproduction are not just "economic" relations but are fundamentally social, cultural, and political relations; (iii) social relations are "historical and dynamic"; (iv) tensions and contradictions within society produce resistance to the social order; and (v) human agency plays an important role in shaping social, political, and economic relations. Armstrong and Armstrong ([1984] 2010, 5) thus aptly describe the focus of contemporary CPE scholarship as attending to "the complex of institutions and relations that constitute not only what are conventionally referred to as the political and economic systems but also the social, physical, ideological, and cultural systems." Building on this body of work and pushing its insights further to encompass a holistic approach to political economy, contributors resist any false narrowing of the conceptualization of class, viewing it as made (Thompson 1968) through social relations of gender, race/ethnicity, Indigeneity, ability, age, citizenship, etc. We consider this to be both a point of departure for this collection and a central contribution of CPE in the new millennium.

Moreover, as CPE has not only engaged in developing a critical analysis of contemporary social issues through this framework, but has also sought to explore the capacities for social science research to foster social change (see Clement and Vosko 2003), the volume as a whole aims to influence public debate and contribute to the dynamics of social change in progressive dimensions, that is, in the interest of social justice. Thus, as with earlier volumes in this series (Clement and Williams 1989; Clement 1997; Clement and Vosko 2003), in offering critical social science research that reveals underlying dynamics of power and inequality, our collective intervention has been produced through a methodology that is *itself* change-oriented and premised on a critique of the status quo. Finally, aiming to offer insight into the salience and continued relevance of CPE, the text approaches this tradition in a way that recognizes its analytical and methodological heterogeneity, as well as the plurality in topics and issues explored by its proponents, and takes such plurality as a key strength that allows for intellectual growth in numerous directions. Although there are many routes that contributors could have taken to their chosen topics, the essays herein reflect a diversity of influences and concerns that all engage, in a variety of ways, with a political-economic analysis of contemporary social relations. We see this approach as reflective of CPE's wider commitment to understanding tensions and challenges, and to recognizing the productive potential of contradictions, but by no means suggest that the volume reflects the full the breadth of CPE.

Arising from a lineage of CPE scholarship established through the series of volumes published by McGill-Queen's University Press under the editorship of Clement and Williams (1989), Clement (1997), and Clement and Vosko (2003), the essays comprising this current volume offer theoretical innovation by drawing from, and often bridging, insights from contemporary feminist theory, critical race theory, and citizenship studies to enhance and expand the lens of CPE and the ways in which this lens can both enrich and be informed by other approaches. Through a materialist lens grounded in political economy, contributors engage with topics and themes such as shifts in (im)migration policy, the persistence of settler colonialism, contemporary social movements, and resource development and extraction, as well as pressing issues including precarious employment, the experiences of people with disabilities, the renewal and revitalization of workers' movements, and Indigenous women's struggles to continue to engage in production for subsistence. In pursuing the theme of "change and continuity," the text explores the legacy of CPE scholarship in terms of its continued relevance to understanding Canada's contemporary political economy, and also points to

new theoretical directions that will give the field analytical resonance
in the new millennium.

CPE IN THE NEW MILLENIUM

In an earlier volume in this series, Clement and Williams (1989) note
that CPE scholarship bears the influences of both classical political economy and Marxist thought. In the first chapter of this volume, Clement
revisits the historical development of CPE, outlining its evolution through
the twentieth century. According to Clement, as CPE developed, though
it retained the materialism it derived from early political economy and
variants prominent in Canada, in particular from socialist feminist interventions rooted in this context, the analytic lens of contemporary CPE
has expanded considerably. The contributions of FPE scholars are particularly notable here, especially those adopting integrated conceptions
of class to encapsulate the broad array of socio-economic relations that
shape the organization of capitalism (for a review of FPE scholarship in
Canada, see Vosko 2002; see also Vosko, this volume). At its foundation,
the political economy method embraced by scholars working in the CPE
tradition retains an orientation that is dialectical, materialist, and change-
oriented or driven. It is dialectical in the sense that it creates, and engages
in, spiralling conversations between the epistemological paradigms and
the methods themselves (Leckenby and Hesse-Biber 2007, 270–1). It
seeks to interrogate multiple dimensions of social phenomena with the
aim of articulating the effects of adopting different approaches and
methods. Consequently, scholars writing in this tradition tend to build
on moments when events, developments, and insights speak to one
another, traversing but not transcending epistemological viewpoints that
hold insights and perceptions separate and apart from one another. At
the same time, while many authors writing in this tradition are open to
multiple approaches and methods, CPE is materialist. That is, in the most
basic sense, it assumes that most phenomena, including consciousness,
flow from material interactions and conditions. This materialist stance
helps explain the debt to history and/or historically grounded analysis
in the CPE tradition. At the same time, CPE is holistic in the sense that
it accounts for the interconnectedness or more precisely the integration
and often inseparability of multiple dimensions of social location, including socio-economic class, gender, race, age, citizenship, Indigeneity, disability, and sexuality, among others, in its materialist approach to social
relations. Moreover, as discussed above, CPE is change-oriented in the
sense that scholars seek to engage in a dialogue between theory and

practice/praxis as a means of both identifying patterns and processes of change through empirical investigation, and also fostering progressive social change through scholarship that contributes to the public good.

This orientation to CPE scholarship was captured and developed through the three aforementioned previous volumes in this series. In the first volume (Clement and Williams 1989), contributors mapped out the core elements of what was emerging at the time as the new Canadian political economy (NCPE), a tradition that had at its core Marxist concepts and assumptions, but that was also deeply informed by the field of political economy that developed through the economic historian Harold Innis, and his understanding of Canada's role as a staples economy in uniquely conditioning the trajectory of its economic development. In the second volume of the series (Clement 1997), the scope of NCPE was expanding analytically, in particular through feminist and anti-racist scholarship that located questions of social reproduction, racialized divisions of labour, and settler colonialism more centrally in its analysis. The most recent volume (Clement and Vosko 2003) addressed the question of social change, outlining both the political-economic basis of social change present in many spheres of Canadian society, and at the same time positing the role of political economy scholarship in contributing to social change.

THEORETICAL CONTRIBUTIONS OF THIS VOLUME

Against the backdrop of these broad premises and through importing the foregoing analytical tools, contributors in this volume advance a series of theoretical contributions and insights that take CPE into the new millennium. Without pigeonholing the diverse scholarship the CPE tradition reflects and engenders, these contributions, innovations, and insights move beyond the disciplinary and thematic, as well as methodological, boundaries of the NCPE. In particular, the following five thematic contributions define the text: tensions and contradictions as sources of challenge and change; the continuing importance of context; continuity through change; centring the margins and destabilizing the centre; and the reorganization/realignment of state structures.

Tensions and Contradictions as Sources of Challenge and Change

A defining feature of CPE is the notion that tensions and contradictions are sources of challenge and change. This orientation has guided empirical studies of Canada's political economy, as CPE scholars have sought to locate processes of social change within the tensions generated by highly unequal political-economic conditions, including those stemming from global processes (e.g., globalization) and international influences (e.g., US hegemony). Critical scholarly interventions identifying silences and omissions within CPE have prompted new currents of thought. The initial chapter of the volume takes up this point. Through a review of the CPE tradition, Clement highlights contradictions that have driven the intellectual currents of CPE forward and contributed to the transformation of this perspective itself.

Tensions created through Canada's integration into the global economy are notable in a number of chapters. Sharma, for example, takes as her point of departure what appears as a central contradiction characterizing the contemporary Canadian labour market: namely, the simultaneous presence of anti-immigration discourses in Canada alongside the increase in the number of people entering Canada through temporary foreign worker programs. She then explores how this tension is productive for Canadian and global capitalism in the current phase of neoliberal globalization, whereby citizenship and immigration policies become a way in which capitalist social relations at the global scale come to be operative within individual nation-states, and whereby those without Canadian citizenship status (including migrant workers) are subject to interacting processes of oppression including racism and labour exploitation.

The global trend of financialization – defined by McBride (this volume) as "a process whereby financial markets, institutions and actors gain influence over economic policy and economic outcomes" – has created further economic and political tensions, in particular through the instability and inequality created by forms of financial deregulation that accompany financialization (for interventions in previous volumes in this series, see Coleman and Porter 2003; Helleiner 2003; see also Helleiner 2014; Porter 2014). Although, as McBride suggests, these tendencies were less pronounced in Canada than in the US, looking across the chapters herein, it is still possible to link tensions and instabilities associated with financialization to social change through the rise in anti-austerity movements documented in particular in Wood's chapter in Part Five of the volume. Mills and Tufts also highlight the tensions associated with the interconnected processes of globalization and financialization. They point to how Canada's resource sector has become increasingly globally integrated and financialized since the 1980s, producing an increase in foreign ownership within Canada's resource industries, and making Canada (through the Toronto Stock Exchange) a global leader in mining finance capital. In this context, emerging pressures of global competition have led resource companies to adopt aggressive tactics vis-à-vis labour to increase shareholder value, which creates new challenges for workers and unions in the industry. From a different vantage point, Albo and Fanelli, in their investigation into the dynamics of "neoliberal urbanism," explore a contradiction between the increasing growth of urban centres on which capitalist accumulation depends and through which financialization is organized, and the pressures for services – including physical and social infrastructure – that the growing population within those centres presents.

Uniting these contributions is an emphasis on contradiction as a means of transformation, not merely of being trapped in a dilemma or series of dilemmas, but rather highlighting that dilemmas themselves – especially those that are most profound/deep – can open space for transformative possibilities. This is the case too for Graefe who, in seeking to understand global processes of capital mobility and their dynamics in Quebec, calls for a political analysis that sees the nation state as torn between two contradictory directions: the adoption of global standards of economic competitiveness and the reproduction of national legitimacy. Using this lens, Graefe is able to study the interventions of a broader range of actors in Quebec, as well as the capacities of institutions – including community organizations, women's organizations, and the student movement in Quebec – to carry forward their demands and to protect past social gains by pushing the state in terms of its reproduction of nationality.

Tensions and contradictions also prompt new forms of labour organizing as discussed by Ross and Thomas, whereby the absence of unions in workplaces characterized by highly precarious forms of employment has produced new forms of worker organizing and new kinds of worker organizations – such as worker centres – in a variety of contexts. As Black explores, the unionization of amateur athletes is also shaped by contradiction, where despite common understandings of sport that do not see it as "work," amateur athletes across North America – including the major junior hockey players in the Canadian Hockey League – face conditions that are compelling them to unionize.

Finally, regarding the ongoing transformation of the CPE tradition itself, Wood points to the productive potential of tensions between the CPE perspective and other approaches to social movement scholarship, suggesting that bringing these strands of scholarship into dialogue with one another generates insight into the materialist basis of contemporary social movements.

The Continuing Importance of Context

A second insight common to many of the chapters in the volume is that context matters. This orientation reflects the broad thrust of historical materialism (Marx and Engels 1970), insofar as it pushes political economy scholars to pay close attention to the particularities of historical moments – as well as the legacies set in place through historical developments – that may shape material conditions and social relations. The orientation to context also reflects the influence of economic geography scholarship within CPE, with its emphasis on the variegated nature of capitalist social relations according to space and scale.[2]

At one level, several contributions show that/how context shapes outcomes. For example, Smith's case study of the agro-food migrant worker housing dispute in southwestern Ontario's Norfolk County in late 2011 illustrates the weight of settler colonialism's legacy manifest in a local context in the present day. Likewise, looking at the theme of the regulation of employment standards (ES) in the province of Ontario, Vosko shows how the parameters of who is exempt from social minima provided under the province's *Employment Standards Act (*ESA*)* (or subject to special rules therein) reflects an outmoded understanding of what are deemed to be "normal" workplaces/workplace contexts, not to mention which groups are deemed "ideal" or "typical" workers. In this case, homecare employees, whose numbers are growing in the face of demographic change, and who perform personal support work (often for clients with disabilities and seniors) are deemed "exceptional" on account of the historical devaluation of so-called "women's work" on the market, with processes of racialization also tied to this devaluation. These employees' exceptionality under the ESA, as Vosko shows, means that they are only entitled to the minimum wage for a maximum of twelve hours per day and exempt from ESA provisions related to hours of work, daily rest periods, time off between shifts, weekly/bi-weekly rest periods, eating periods, and overtime; moreover, if homecare employees are employed by a Community Care Access Centre or an entity under contract with one (in what is effectively a triangular employment relationship) they are also exempt from the ESA's temporary help agency rules. Here the context of "occupational group" to which an employee belongs affects access to rights and protections, contributing to a more precarious employment experience for those in homecare.

At the same time, both Smith's and Vosko's insights into the significance of context give meaning to Sharma's examination of temporary migrant worker programs and their function for the Canadian labour market, illustrating some of the particular ways in which migrant workers experience conditions of work and living (e.g., both through a lack of effective ES coverage and enforcement and through inadequate housing). They also support Clement's depiction of how and why CPE has evolved as an (intellectual) tradition, specifically through efforts to place greater attention on the many ways in which workers may experience marginalization within capitalism.

Finally, drawing attention to interconnections between global and local contexts, Wood's examination of anti-austerity protest movements in Toronto and Montreal transcends the "global-local" dichotomy that is sometimes present in global social movement scholarship by showing the localized strategies of protest movements taking on the globalized politics of austerity – and hence challenging macro-level processes of financialization that give rise to the simultaneous withdrawal and reconfiguration of collective responsibility – in two of Canada's major urban centres.

Continuity through Change

As a prominent thread running across the contributions to this volume, the theme continuity through change captures the ways in which, the highly dynamic and fluid nature of capitalism notwithstanding, there nonetheless remain core social relations persisting across time and space that continue to shape Canada's contemporary political economy. For instance, Stanford, after documenting the structural shift in Canada to *becoming* "undeveloped," suggests that this shift has ideological roots: namely, a return to the classical political economic model of comparative advantage from the previous post-war era of national industrial development. This empirical demonstration of continuity through change enables Stanford to illustrate that Canada's renewed reliance on natural resources, specifically petroleum extraction in the 2000s, has contributed to deindustrialization. Reflecting on how interconnected processes of globalization and financialization have also prompted transformation in Canada's resource sector in considerable ways, Stanford again reveals patterns of continuity through change. Specifically, he notes that historically, staples production in Canada – with its roots in settler colonialism and its orientation towards exports to Europe – was *always* deeply connected to the global economy and, as such, there is a long history of foreign capital in its development. Nevertheless, Stanford argues that as processes of globalization and financialization have become more pronounced in recent times they have reshaped business models within the extractive industries.

Another example of continuity through change is demonstrated by Hall, who explores how the legacy of settler colonialism continues to impact the economic development of Indigenous communities engaged in struggles for both economic self-sufficiency and political autonomy. Additionally, Sharma and Smith both demonstrate how contemporary temporary foreign worker programs accord migrant workers a highly marginalized status while they work and reside in Canada, and Vosko illustrates how exemptions under ES legislation applicable to occupational groups (e.g., homecare employees, many of whom are racialized immigrant women) have racialized and gendered effects – reflecting, in part, Canada's role in global migration patterns, and how the state's longstanding racist treatment of immigrants and migrants from non-Western European countries continues to condition the immigration experience.

Finally, continuity through change also characterizes the experiences of contemporary workers' movements, with the shifting labour market defined by both declining employment in areas of traditionally high levels of unionization (manufacturing), as well as growth in low-wage services. In this changing context, workers' movements must develop innovative strategies to foster organizing in workplaces that are not traditionally unionized, and to better include workers who have often been left outside the boundaries of organized labour – in particular racialized and im/migrant workers – in order to confront continuing processes of labour exploitation.

Centring the Margins, Destabilizing the Centre

Common to many contributions to this volume is a preoccupation with understanding un(der)explored phenomena. Tracing a trajectory back to Marx's approach to political economy (1976), this preoccupation is akin to his determination to reveal the underlying social relations obscured by the surface appearance of things in capitalism, such as the so-called "fair" exchange between worker and employer of labour power for a wage, something that could only be revealed when one sought to enter the "hidden abode of production" (Marx 1976, 279). In the vein of contesting "common sense" understandings of social phenomena, contributors herein seek to push the boundaries of this exercise by using the analytical tools of political economy to contest both dominant social relations and analytical silences in the CPE tradition. In so doing, marginalized groups are brought to the centre of the analysis, as are the multiple and intersecting social relations that simultaneously reflect and produce marginalization.

Such phenomena are captured by LeBlanc Haley's examination of a new definition of "mental illness" in Ontario wherein "Mad people" are constructed as potentially productive citizens (i.e., capable of labour force participation and thus contributing to the economy) in the neoliberal era. LeBlanc Haley seeks to both centre the experiences of "Mad people," and also problematize the neoliberal thrust of current government policy. Likewise, in her examination of the marginalization of Indigenous people through the development of a Canadian economy, Hall shines a light on a gap characterizing both the new CPE tradition and the FPE perspective: namely, the failure to situate northern Indigenous women's labour (an activity that arguably demands greater analytical attention) within a mixed economy – that is, to attend to their contribution to local subsistence. Vosko also addresses the question of how marginalization takes shape, and by bringing to the centre of analysis a topic that has received limited attention in CPE scholarship – the regulation of ES – destabilizes the ways in which employment law is built on normalized assumptions that serve to exclude certain groups of workers from ES protections. From a different angle, Mills' and Tufts' critique of CPE's overemphasis on the national scale shows how the sub-national level is vitally important with regard to resource extraction and resource development. Pointing toward a larger critique of methodological nationalism that runs through some CPE, Mills and Tufts offer a reminder that "Canada" is far from a unified space – geographically, economically, politically, and socially – and that political economy scholarship should question the emphasis of the national scale central to much of its analysis.

In a complementary chapter, through what is also effectively a critique of methodological nationalism albeit along different lines, Lyubchenko's exploration of the explanatory capacity of FPE outside the Canadian context illustrates how this analytical variant of the CPE approach can contribute to centring the margins in other international contexts. Indeed, Lyubchenko's study of the Maternity Capital benefit in Russia demonstrates how an FPE lens illuminates the ways in which contemporary transformations within the Russian gender contract are integral to, rather than a side effect of, post-Soviet market transition.

The Reorganization/Realignment of State Structures

An enduring feature of CPE is that the institutions of the state still matter, especially as they interact with modes of accumulation. In the current global period of neoliberal capitalism, state structures have been profoundly reorganized/realigned to enhance market processes, with deep and multiple effects. This theme runs through many of the chapters in this volume and serves as a direct challenge to the neoliberal "free market" discourse that – invoking a version of Adam Smith's notion of the "invisible hand" – so often proclaims the economic virtues of a non-interventionist state. Rather, as McBride's chapter shows, neoliberal states remain highly active in the regulation of contemporary economies in a variety of ways; moreover, interventionism has become much more overtly aligned with the interests of capital in the neoliberal era. Illustrating the contradictions of neoliberal state institutions in the era of financialization, McBride notes that in the years following the 2008 crisis, economically powerful states engaged in a variety of private sector bailouts – in particular in banking and manufacturing sectors, as well as through the absorption of private sector debt – while at the same time aggressively implementing austerity measures to contain public spending.

A number of chapters provide additional examples. In their chapter on long-term residential care (nursing homes), Armstrong et al. show that neoliberal restructuring led provincial and territorial governments to turn to marketization and corporate ownership and, through funding cutbacks, to pressure nursing homes to contract out services. Noting how these tendencies are shaped by the global context, these contributors show how the inclusion of nursing homes in transnational free trade agreements exacerbates these tendencies. In his study of the political economy of cultural industries, Mirrlees suggests that the Canadian state plays a strong and active role in the cultural industries and highlights a peculiar kind of neoliberal intervention existing within the so-called "free market." Other chapters demonstrate the multiple ways in which state institutions enact forms of regulation that either fail to protect workers (Vosko) or actively work to support their marginalization (Sharma, Smith). As Albo and Fanelli demonstrate, state structures are also important at the urban scale, as cities internalize the different scales and temporalities of accumulation and state power. This is why, in their view, neoliberalism as a political economic practice should not be read as a juxtaposition of (less) state against (more) market, but rather as a particular kind of state suited to ensuring market-like rule. For all of these reasons, in her discussion of anti-austerity protests Wood also illustrates how the state remains central to movements of resistance against neoliberalism.

ORGANIZATION OF THE COLLECTION

This collection is organized into five parts, each of which engages with the preceding crosscutting themes in a variety of ways. Part One – The New Canadian Political Economy: Trajectories of Feminism, Anti-Racism, Citizenship, and Belonging – historically and conceptually situates the current volume within the CPE tradition, and also explores contemporary processes and intellectual developments that require CPE to continue to expand its scope of analysis and rethink its conception of political struggle.

Wallace Clement leads the collection with a review of the history and evolution of the field, focusing on the uniqueness of each of the volumes in this series vis-à-vis the specific historical conjuncture in which each appeared. Since its revival in the 1970s, motivated by a left-nationalist critique of an earlier staples tradition, the scope of CPE was broadened by different forms of class analysis, Indigenous studies, and anti-racist/ colonial as well as feminist political economy, all of which sought to recognize broader social factors of production and social reproduction and move towards more rigorous accounts of human agency, work, state policy, and social change. Contemporaneously, CPE has benefited from the rise of comparative intersectional analysis, as well as a renewed interest in staples theory. According to Clement, a critical staples approach represents a sense of continuity through change and provides analytical value in strategizing Canada's national energy requirements. Clement expresses confidence that nation building in Canada can be achieved with a wider sense of solidarity around issues of class, gender, the environment, and decolonization.

Leah F. Vosko's chapter on employment standards in Ontario – which legislate minimum regulatory protections for the majority of non-unionized employees – shows that the tools of FPE are useful in pursuing applied research on deteriorating conditions of work with the spread of precarious employment. FPE, especially through its attention to social reproduction and intersectional approaches as well as to the importance of context, is instructive not just when ES are formally violated, but when they are evaded, eroded, or abandoned through more informal means related to the differential treatment workers receive depending on their (often intertwined) social and occupational location. As a way of centring the margins, this discussion reveals the gendered, racialized, and citizenship-bounded dimensions of ES exemptions and special rules, the individualizing dynamics of neoliberal governance evident in "self-help" and "settlements" to resolve conflicts with the employer, and the overall exclusionary criteria that shape access to labour protection in Ontario. The "ES Enforcement Gap" conceptualization shows how an FPE approach can help identify a progressive policy agenda aimed at establishing universal social minima for those workers outside the ranks of organized labour.

In "The Political Economy of Belonging," Nandita Sharma's analysis of the recent categorization of "temporary migrant worker" in Canada reveals: a) the historical continuity of colonialism within Canada's immigration policies; and b) how national borders exist not only as a boundary between nation-states, but also within nation-states. The contradictory, simultaneous presence of anti-immigration discourses in Canada alongside the increase in the number of people entering Canada without permanent resident status is productive for capitalism in the securing of a low-wage, highly exploited migrant labour force. Consistent with the theme of tensions and contradictions as sources of challenge and change, in calling for a politics of "No Borders" this chapter opens space for a social justice that rejects nationalism and nation-states. This rejection is necessary in light of the inherent hierarchical social order that stems from the attachment of social, political, and economic rights to conditions of citizenship.

Questions of strategic nationalism flow from Part One into Part Two. Reflecting the volume's theme of continuity through change, chapters in "Regions and Resources" further explore the relevance of critical staples theory. They also highlight the need to address its gaps in light of the revival of, and recent changes to, Canada's natural resource industry. Part Two also probes developments at the level of regional politics, exploring the creative tension between the reproduction of Quebec's national legitimacy and its shift to neoliberalism after the 1970s.

Jim Stanford argues that Canada's renewed reliance on natural resources in the 2000s, specifically petroleum extraction, adopted with the election of the Harper Conservative government in 2006, is an ideological and structural shift to the classical political economic model, which largely benefits the powerful interests of domestic and foreign resource investors and Canadian political elites. He constructs an empirically rich account of the boom-bust cycles in staples industries in connection to the value of the Canadian dollar, which has been declining since 2013, and consistent with the ongoing reorganization or realignment of state structures. Looking forward, Stanford favours a state-led transformative project: a national energy policy that would consciously create economic linkages from the resource sector and diversify Canada's economy.

Suzanne Mills and Steven Tufts suggest that a more fluid staples theory is required to account for forms of uneven economic development at the sub-national level in Canada. Northern and Indigenous communities, which are located close to resource extractive industries, are most susceptible to the cyclical dynamics, stifled economic diversification, and environmental degradation associated with resource development. Another example of centring the margins, their chapter argues that a revised staples theory must be premised on the acknowledgement of Indigenous territorial rights and non-wage economic activities, as well as Indigenous communities' engagement with new forms of labour mobility in extractive sectors, environmental activism, and public policy development.

Shifting from the political economy of resource extraction to the political economy of regions, Peter Graefe contends that the neoliberal project in Quebec under the Parti Québécois took a specific form of competitive nationalism as a way to link a commitment to the rules of global capitalism with a set of national-progressive values. This unique tension opened space for a range of institutions including community organizations, women's organizations, and the student movement to tie their demands to the reproduction of national legitimacy. Graefe calls for a political analysis that sees the nation state as torn between two contradictory directions – the adoption of global standards of economic competitiveness and the reproduction of national legitimacy – and views this contradiction as a source of challenge and change.

Most contributors to this volume acknowledge the profound impact of the reorganization/realignment of state structures in accordance with neoliberal principles, and set their analysis of neoliberal restructuring against the background of the post-war Keynesian welfare state. Stephen McBride's chapter opens Part Three – "State, Capital, and Institutions" – with a historical overview. While the post-war era is often deemed the "golden age of capitalism," McBride rightly asks: golden age for whom? He argues that those who benefited most from this regime were White, male, unionized workers. Rather than an overnight ideological switch, the neoliberal turn was a protracted political conflict over a twenty-year period in which a gradual orchestration of cutbacks reduced expectations on the part of the Canadian public. Thus, while the "laissez-faire" neoliberal state has remained interventionist, the nature of that intervention has changed.

Part Three also shows the continuing importance of context by addressing the historical and ongoing structures of settler colonialism in Canada in relation to the process of capitalist accumulation. Adrian A. Smith looks at the case of the agro-food migrant worker-housing dispute in Ontario's Norfolk County in 2011, examining what he calls "the structures and struggles of living together" between agro-food migrant workers and the settler population in Ontario's Norfolk County to show how the processes of global capitalism and settler colonialism interact. The residents of Norfolk County understand themselves as the rightful occupants of the land in relation to the seasonal migrant workers, a conceit that conceals the continued settler colonial practices of dispossession. Smith embeds law and legality within the material social relations of the settler colonial capitalist state of Canada and, by doing so, not only expands the CPE tradition but also critiques settler colonial and socio-legal studies for neglecting the insights of critical political economy and reifying culture and discourse.

Rebecca Jane Hall makes the question of social reproduction, which Smith raises in his case study, a central component of her chapter. Hall's contribution identifies a gap in both the CPE and FPE traditions, which take capitalist production as their point of departure. To counter this starting point by, once again, centring the margins, Hall's discussion situates northern Indigenous women's labour within a mixed economy, with their social reproduction oriented toward the demands of capital as well as local subsistence. The imposition of a colonial gendered division of labour, as seen in the case study of the diamond mine industry in the Northwest Territories, leads to the continued surveillance by the Canadian state of Indigenous people, Indigenous women in particular. Hall powerfully argues that decolonization includes challenging the gendered ways in which the demands of capital infringe upon Indigenous self-determination.

Examining the complex and contradictory interaction between global capitalism, Canadian capitalism, and the Canadian state, Tanner Mirrlees applies a critical political economy approach to the study of the ownership, production, and distribution of cultural goods and services as commodities in Canada. Mirrlees' chapter highlights a central contradiction: that historically the Canadian state has pursued a policy of protectionism in the cultural sphere, attempting to shelter cultural industries from global capitalist ownership via financial subsidies and the enforcement of copyright laws. The contradiction lies in the fact that such practices go against Canada's ostensible commitment to the free trade rules of neoliberal globalization. Today, Canada's state-capitalist cultural policy is becoming less viable with the rise of digital technologies and the growth of US-based digital companies, opening space for the reimagination of the Canadian cultural regime in the global digital age in a way that could better express public interests.

Further exploring the reorganization/realignment of state structures, Part Four – "Social Services Restructuring" – addresses such restructuring in the specific context of neoliberalism. In their study of senior nursing homes, Pat Armstrong, Hugh Armstrong, Jacqueline Choiniere, and Tamara Daly show the health care implications of the emergence of the neoliberal regulatory state. While the demand for medical and psychiatric care has increased in recent decades, provinces and territories have failed to expand the number of publicly funded nursing home beds, instead turning to marketization and corporate ownership, in line with the project of neoliberal restructuring. At the same time, an explosion of new auditing and management techniques has restructured the daily lives of residents and placed greater pressures on the predominantly female labour force.

Constructed at the intersection of CPE and disability studies, Tobin LeBlanc Haley's contribution centres the margins by drawing attention to the re-positioning of "Mad people" (a reclaimed term) as productive members of society in the neoliberal era. This redefinition has been a source of liberation and oppression, as well as a key site of struggle. Following a history of psychiatric deinstitutionalization as a result of reduced funding (1960–70s) in Ontario, which led to the realignment of social policies and programs providing for the treatment, housing, and income of people with disabilities, "Mad people" have been encouraged to do the work of daily social reproduction alongside service providers. While admittedly an improvement over the previous practice of complete exclusion from the processes of production, ultimately these policies and programs functioned as a cost-saving mechanism for the neoliberal state. LeBlanc Haley traces this privatization of responsibility for "Mad people's" well-being to the neoliberal drive to eliminate supports for subsistence.

The practice of service downloading from the federal level of government onto provinces and municipalities has contributed to a fiscal and a revenue crisis for major Canadian cities, producing enormous tensions. Placing municipalities at the centre of their analysis of neoliberal restructuring, Greg Albo and Carlo Fanelli show that since the 2008 recession, Canadian urban centres – Toronto, Montreal, and Vancouver – have experienced a new phase of austerity, including tax shifting for economic competitiveness, privatization of city assets, reduction of social services, as well as precarious new workplace arrangements. The contradiction between increasing urban growth – on which capitalist accumulation depends – and the growing urban population's demands for services presents an important source of tension, which may contribute to dynamics of change.

The re-emergence of CPE in the 1970s was motivated in part by the anti-imperialist, feminist, civil rights, and anti-Vietnam War movements in the streets and on university campuses. Part Five of this volume – "Contestation" – further explores the ways in which tensions and contradictions are sources of challenge and change. Lesley Wood's chapter, "Protest Patterns: CPE as an Analytical Approach," outlines the history of CPE engagement with social movements as a methodology for understanding the reproduction of social relations under contemporary capitalism. Wood's intervention is a comparative study of anti-austerity protests in Toronto and Montreal between 1995–2015, where, for instance, a lower level of protest activity in Toronto reflects the particularly harsh imposition of neoliberalism by the Ontario provincial government in the late 1990s. Wood argues that the dialectical CPE approach can advance contentious politics scholarship, which often neglects an analysis of capitalism. The chapter explores how the emergence of a wide range of social movements signifies the presence of political economic contradictions and crises, as well as how the features of political economy shape social movements.

Like Wood, Simon Black brings the CPE tradition in conversation with another body of literature – critical sports studies – to better understand new forms of labour contestation. "Playing Left Wing: Political Economy of the CHL and the case for Unionization" examines professional sport through the lens of a political economy of labour, seeing it not only as a site of cultural production and capital accumulation, but also of alienation, exploitation, and resistance. Generally non-unionized, minor, and development league athletes rely on ES as their principle source of labour protection. With reference to Vosko's discussion of employers' formal and informal violation of ES, Black reveals that the CHL deliberately misclassifies players to deny them basic forms of labour protection. By documenting various forms of organized resistance amongst athletes, this chapter shows the increasing interplay of sport and the broader political economy of precarious employment.

With the aim of understanding how changing employment conditions are producing changes in worker organizing, in "Work and Workers' Movements: Organizing in Precarious Times," Stephanie Ross and Mark P. Thomas outline the changing landscape of work in years following the

2008 financial crisis. In this context, employers engaged in aggressive bargaining tactics and Canadian federal and provincial governments continued to alter the post-war labour rights regime, which included the right to organize, bargain, and strike. Weakened unions, however, have remained attached to the post-war settlement, compromising their capacities to contest attacks by employers and governments and to engage in new organizing amongst the significant number of non-unionized workers. These combined processes have prompted the rise of extra-union movements by groups that have been marginalized both in the workplace and within the formal labour movement. Ross and Thomas conclude with a call for CPE scholarship to account for the ways in which policies and practices promoting precarious employment are remaking not just the world of work but also workers' organizations.

The volume concludes with a chapter from Olena Lyubchenko, who examines the potential for the analytic lens developed in the book to be extended beyond the context of Canada through a case study of Russia's Maternity Capital benefit, a cornerstone of the new family policy in that country. Lyubchenko argues that issues and debates critical to recent FPE literature in Canada are relevant to current social science scholarship on post-Soviet transition and changing gender relations in contemporary Russia. Through an application of core FPE concepts, and resonating with Part Five's focus on contestation, Lyubchenko challenges dominant policy narratives to illustrate the ways in which the Maternity Capital benefit, which is promoted as a new developmental social policy and family policy initiative under the Putin administration, in fact both privatizes social reproduction and makes the family a site of profit for financial capital.

CONCLUSION

The publication of this volume marks thirty years since CPE scholars came together to re-envision the political economy tradition in its application to understanding the dynamics of contemporary Canadian capitalism (see Clement and Williams 1989). Through change and continuity, CPE today remains as forcefully relevant as ever, questioning long-held assumptions that have guided generations of scholars and charting new pathways to exciting arenas of critical inquiry. As captured in its title, the text aims to understand the specificities of the contemporary context of neoliberal capitalism, as well as the ways in which longstanding social relations continue to shape the present. In the spirit of the CPE tradition, and continuing a theme in this series (see Clement and Vosko 2003), at the heart of this volume is an emphasis on denaturalizing contemporary capitalism through a holistic approach to studying social relations, not only to better understand the present context, but also in order to contribute to the long-term struggle for a social justice that aims at nothing less than a total transformation. As diverse as the contributions to this volume are, the analytical framework that melds these works together is threefold: a broadly interdisciplinary body of thought open to change and theoretical innovation; a commitment to exploring wide-ranging registers of social oppression and inequality in all their forms; and an emphasis on dialectical relationships with an eye to understanding social totalities and social change.

In this sense, the essays of this volume go beyond analyses that isolate particular effects of capitalism, and rather stress the constellation of social, political, and economic forces that both constrain and potentially create new avenues for social change. In so doing, the collection advances a conception of the socioeconomic that captures the ways in which the tensions, contradictions, and conflicts of contemporary capitalism are organized through complex and overlapping social relations, such as gender, ethnicity, race, Indigeneity, ability, age, and citizenship status, among others. Contributors aim to identify and encourage the forces for progressive transformation at work in the contemporary context, which reflects CPE's orientation toward dynamics of social change. With the publication of this fourth volume spanning three decades in the continued evolution of this body of research, we hope that readers will continue to discuss and debate the CPE approach both as a means for critical social science research and as a vehicle for social change.

NOTES

1 For a broader discussion of this general approach that extends beyond debates within CPE, see, for example, Glenn 1992; Brand 1999; Brenner 2000; Picchio 2003; Bannerji 2005; Acker 2006; Hoskyns and Rai 2007; Bonacich et al. 2008; Lan 2008; Federici 2014a.

2 For a broader discussion of these general insights beyond CPE, see Harvey 2010b; Massey 1995; Peck 2005; Smith 2008.

PART ONE

The New Canadian Political Economy: Trajectories of Feminism, Anti-Racism, Citizenship, and Belonging

Locating the New Canadian Political Economy

Wallace Clement

Canadian political economy (CPE) represents a rich and diverse tradition of scholarship. The 1920s through the early 1950s were the classic period, with staples production and issues of space, natural resources, and transportation (in their international and regional geographic contexts) made central by the work of Harold Adams Innis and W.A. Mackintosh. The tradition then entered the doldrums, experiencing a revival in the early 1970s, focusing on responses to concerns about US domination over Canada's communications, culture, and economy, often viewed within a "dependency" paradigm. During the 1980s the new Canadian political economy (NCPE) tradition began to broaden and deepen these concerns, expanding the traditional focus on the economy and politics into wider social, cultural, and ideological domains. By the 1990s, this tradition of study embraced issues of gender, race, and ethnicity; Indigenous peoples; popular culture; and the environment. Broadly there has been a shift from territory as an organizing principle of national development (characterized by Donald Creighton's 1937 Laurentian thesis) to the social construction of the interdisciplinary subject located in its material base. The best of NCPE today fully incorporates the social and cultural with the political and economic. These dimensions compound the explanatory power and insight of an evolving NCPE.

There are several elements that compose the evolution of CPE as a tradition. These include the Canadian foundations of Harold Adams Innis (1956) in particular, but also notably Stanley Ryerson (1973), H. Claire Pentland (1981), and Vernon Fowke (1957). The international elements, including Mel Watkins' collected essays *Staples and Beyond*

(2006) and Kari Levitt's *Silent Surrender* (1970), have focused our attention on foreign ownership and control. The comparative perspective has
looked more to the class, power, and social dimensions – such as Wallace
Clement's *Continental Corporate Power: Corporate Elite Linkages
between Canada and the United States* (1977), Gordon Laxer's *Open
for Business: The Roots of Foreign Ownership in Canada* (1989), and
Wallace Clement and John Myles' *Relations of Ruling: Class and Gender
in Postindustrial Societies* (1994). The holistic turn introduced by the
NCPE, most notably through feminism, cultural studies, and environmental studies, was part of the resistance to the limitations of CPE. An
example of NCPE in a comparative setting is Vosko et al. *Gender and
the Contours of Precarious Employment* (2009). Each of these evolving
moments in this tradition build and deepen our understanding and ability
to explain Canada's development and place in the world.

Following upon the observations and movements associated with US
foreign ownership flagged by what came to be known as "*The Watkins
Report*" (Government of Canada 1968), the decade of the 1970s was
notable for three impressive scholarly collections: *Close the 49th parallel
etc.* edited by Ian Lumsden (1970), *Capitalism and the National Question
in Canada* edited by Gary Teeple (1972), and *The Canadian State: Political
Economy and Political Power* edited by Leo Panitch (1977a). This pro-
digious foundational output was crowned by the founding of the journal
Studies in Political Economy (SPE) in 1979 (now with nearly a hundred
issues published). It was the combination of class and nation that defined
the "new" Canadian political economy. There was a nationalist element
and a socialist element (sometimes Marxist, other times Social Democratic)
that instantly produced a tension within the tradition of the NCPE. These
elements were manifest in these four defining documents. The Watkins
Report made the transition from neo-classical economics to a nationalist
one in the era of the modern multinational corporation and branch plants
(see Watkins 2006). This nationalist theme dominated the Lumsden collection, expanding the concerns of nationalism from the economic to the
social and cultural spheres. The Teeple collection combined the class and
national questions creatively, highlighting the core tension and being
attentive to the twin draws of the national and the international. In
Canada, the national is always about its combination with the international. The Panitch collection shifted the focus into debates about the
nature of the state, informed particularly by European debates between
Ralph Miliband and Nicos Poulantzas as proponents of instrumental
and structural accounts.

Two notable volumes highlighted feminist scholarship in Canada in the next decade. Roberta Hamilton and Michèle Barrett's collection, *The Politics of Diversity: Feminism, Marxism and Nationalism* (1986) consolidated a multitude of important feminist pieces written in Canada but clearly informed by international debates, especially foregrounding the domestic labour debate, debates on class and gender, heritage issues, social reproduction, and subjectivity. The following year Heather Jon Maroney and Meg Luxton edited *Feminism and Political Economy: Women's Work and Women's Struggle* (1987), a collection of original articles in the political economy genre. It is organized around the themes of the women's movement, gendered divisions of labour, women's work, and state policies. They make the following address to scholars working in the area: "To feminists we argue that a political economy framework, particularly marxism, offers an important way to understand the situation of women. To those working within political economy we insist that without an analysis of sex/gender systems their analysis is flawed and incomplete" (ix). This was a warning that profoundly transformed the shape of NCPE as it moved forward.

THE STAPLES TRADITION EVALUATED

To launch the second decade of renewal, Leo Panitch, at the peak of his powerful insights, authored a key intervention in SPE on the twin dynamics driving the emerging tradition entitled "Dependency and Class in Canadian Political Economy" (1981). One of his main insights was to see "domination and exploitation as other than one-way streets." American imperialism was just as much about civil society as a means of securing hegemony through popular culture such as mass media, advertising, and mass education and a means of reproducing this regime, as were the more traditional concerns like fractions of capital and continental labour that had received the lion's share of attention. Rather than entirely dismiss the work of Innis as some Marxists had done, Panitch had this to say: "if Canadian political economy has much to learn from Innis today, this pertains less to his geographic determinism in the framework of unequal market exchange and more to his appreciation of imperialism as a contradictory phenomenon" (28). As an example, Panitch quotes from Innis's *Political Economy in the Modern State*, which contends that Canadian staples exports were: "a source of disturbance to the economies of other countries ... wheat production ... brought a revolution in British agriculture and led European countries to impose barriers or to undergo revolution. Pulp and paper production ... facilitated the rapid growth of advertising in the United States and contributed to the problems of industrialism and destruction of stable public opinion" (Innis 1946, ix–x). "Disturbances" were created in both Canada and the receiving countries as the "markets of Europe were bombarded in turn with such staple products as fur, timber and wheat and the United States with minerals and newsprints" (x). Innis located Canada within the global political economy as part of the complex transformations underway throughout the system of states. The staples approach proved to be an impressive lens through which to view Canada's history of development, albeit limited in some key respects for the ambitions of this new wave of political economists.

Recall that staples are defined as natural resources developed for export in a low-processed form. They undergo further processing or inputs to production outside their place of origin, such as beaver pelts manufactured into top hats. Staples tend to be produced in cyclonic fashion, subject to booms and busts dependent upon external markets, thus causing domestic and international distortions in patterns of development (Clement 1988b). For example, beaver top hats were in fashion in Europe between 1550 and 1850 when they were replaced by silk hats, undercutting the Canadian fur market.

Staples typically require extensive state-sponsored transportation networks (ports, canals, railroads, roads, pipelines, power grids, etc.) to support their export. In the classic staples tradition, commercially traded staples were the focus: fish, fur, square timber, placer gold, and wheat as a transition staple. Industrial staples, which boomed following the Second World War, are organized by multinational corporations and include minerals, precious metals, pulp and paper, lumber, energy (oil and gas), and frozen fish as inputs to industrial production.

Between 1946 and 1957 the Canadian manufacturing industry transformed from 35 per cent foreign owned to 56 per cent. For mining and smelting, the increase was from 38 per cent to 70 per cent. This rapid transformation was the result of a conscious policy by the US presidential commission known as the Paley Report: it was called *Resources for Freedom* and released as five volumes in 1952. *Resources for Freedom* identified twenty-two critical resource commodities the United States needed for the "security" of its military-industrial complex. Canada was the major source for thirteen of these resources, which were then duly stockpiled in the United States over the following decades (Clark-Jones 1987; Clement 1989, 43–4). Canada flourished in an unprecedented resource boom based upon an "artificial" economy manipulated by a political/military agenda that paid well but distorted development. Markets are political and social constructions. There is no greater example of why the "political" is a crucial part of political economy. And why the character of the export market itself is a crucial part of the overall explanation.

The point about the staples approach is to examine linkages or the allocation of benefits from the values associated with staples production. This was the key insight of Mel Watkins' classic revival of Innis' work in the essay, "A Staple Theory of Economic Growth" (1963). Backward linkages include the inputs into production; forward linkages are the transformations that occur to the raw material; final demand linkages are consumer goods for those associated with extraction. The essential point of the staples thesis is that a context of uneven power between those supplying the raw materials and those buying the resources produces what are known as "leakages." Leakages involve losses following from the capturing and creation of value associated with the linkages. For example: backward linkages include the source of the equipment and supplies which surrender their value in production; forward linkages include the processing of the raw material into final products thus adding value; and final demand linkages are the production of consumer goods such as appliances, clothing, and automobiles used by those producing staples. To the extent that these beneficiaries are controlled or located externally, leakage of value occurs. This means the leakage of capital and of jobs used in production, especially when the inputs to production and the processing of resources into manufactured goods occurs outside the country. A "staples trap" means being locked into a system of production dependent upon external markets with minimal local inputs adding value and minimal diversification of the economy. Canada became trapped in the emerging post-war American empire, both as a supplier of resources and consumer of imported products.

This was the material foundation for what came to be known as "left-nationalism," best exemplified through the intellectual career of Mel Watkins. I have reviewed the origins of this position in Clement's introduction to Watkins Staples and Beyond (2006), which claims that Watkins "embraced socialism before he embraced nationalism" (xvii). His nationalism comes out of anti-imperialism, as evident in his 1970 piece where he characterizes Innis as a "liberal nationalist," but goes on to claim that "Innis' anti-imperialism argues powerfully for the necessity of a Canadian nationalism of the left" (205–6). An important tracing of debates surrounding left-nationalism and NCPE is provided by Chris Hurl and

Benjamin Christensen (2015) based upon thirteen oral histories from those engaged in the NCPE turn. They differentiate the tendencies of an "Indigenous" approach and a neo-Marxist one that produced some creative tension within NCPE (183). They claim: "these two intellectual groupings overlapped and worked to establish a shared infrastructure to generate ideas" (184). For an elaboration of NCPE thought around these dimensions, see Suzanne Mills and Steven Tufts in this volume. For a sophisticated critique of nationalism and sovereignty in practice around citizenship, see Nandita Sharma in this collection.

As noted, the classic staples tradition tended not to examine social factors of production as part of the explanation for how development occurs. For example, I introduced a paper on Innis' writings on mining by saying "the staples tradition provides the raw material; class, the explanation" (Clement 1983b, 172). I went on to argue "Innis has a great deal to say about the forces of production in mining – capitalization, markets and technology – as they are conditioned by various minerals. He has much less to say about the social and political relations of production, particularly how the forces of production condition relations between classes" (173). The main advantage of class analysis in this case is its ability to mount a convincing account of social change dynamics through transformations in the relations of production. A second paper demonstrates mining's transformations in terms of the movement from simple commodity production to capitalist relations of production. This was followed by the transformation from the formal to the real subordination of labour based upon an explanatory theory of property relations (Clement 1983c).

An excellent example of the implications of bringing gender to the fore in staples production is provided by feminist analyses of the fur trade by Jennifer Brown (1980) and Sylvia Van Kirk (1980). They each demonstrate that the labour process in the fur trade included Indigenous women in two crucial respects. First, preparing the furs for trade. Men trapped, women created the pelts. Second, Indigenous women sustained the *Voyageurs* (indentured French servants) who transported the furs by providing food and shelter. Indigenous women were also crucial in the creation of an entirely new people, the Métis, who went on to occupy key intermediate roles in the fur trading enterprise and have become a central part of Canada's Indigenous heritage. Revealing social relations of production is crucial to understanding the deeper and nuanced gendered impact of the fur trade, thus recovering the complexity of what transpired and its implications. Ron Bourgeault (1983) goes further and locates the fur trade in a wider political economy that considers class, sex, and race, including the transformation of Indigenous labour under mercantilism into capitalist relations of production.

A seminal piece by Patricia Marchak entitled "Canadian Political Economy" did a masterful job of capturing the essence of the revival of this tradition: "Canadian political economy began with the 'crisis' of a nation, Canada; it now moves on to the impact of a world crisis on that nation. Staples theory was insufficient to explain Canadian underdevelopment, but its insights provided valid aids in explaining why Canada, still overwhelmingly dependent on staples exports and dependent on US markets, suffers a more prolonged and deeper economic crisis than more advanced world economies" (1985, 695). Marchak directly located the revival of political economy in the core of property rights and power relationships, which were embedded in culture and social relations. It was precisely this aspect of the staples approach that was required for its explanatory power to grow. As Paul Phillips noted, "What the staples approach largely ignored was the social (as contrasted to the technical) relations of production" (1989, 93). That is where NCPE thrived.

The NCPE developed as much within as between disciplines. For example, there are two articles chronicling the NCPE's influence within Canadian sociology: the classic piece just mentioned by Pat Marchak (1985), and my own, in 2001, for a collection on Canadian Sociology for the Legacy for a New Millennium. Each article demonstrated the transformative power of NCPE within Canadian sociology. Other disciplines were more resistant to the new tradition. Obviously, economics itself had turned away from political economy – but not all economists, many of whom found homes in interdisciplinary spaces such as public administration, social work, and law and legal studies. The traditional disciplines of anthropology, geography, and history were all places where the impact has been notable. Interdisciplinary programs such as labour studies, Canadian studies, and women's and gender studies tended to be open to its insights. Of equal relevance, however, were the transformative impacts of these various traditions back onto Canadian political economy itself.

PRECEDING VOLUMES

The consolidation of NCPE may be examined around the collective contributions to the three volumes I helped edit that precede this one:

The New Canadian Political Economy (edited with Glen Williams).
    1989. Montreal: McGill-Queen's University Press, 333.
*Understanding Canada: Building on the New Canadian Political
    Economy.* 1997. Montreal: McGill-Queen's University Press, 408.
Changing Canada: Political Economy as Transformation (edited
    with Leah F. Vosko). 2003. Montreal: McGill-Queen's University
    Press, xxxii, 498.

The first volume could have been called *Remembering the Roots*. There
was a self-conscious connection with the classic tradition of political
economy associated with such diverse authors as Karl Marx, Adam Smith,
John Stuart Mill, and David Ricardo. In Canada, there was a resurrection
of the pioneering work associated with the staples tradition, including
most notably Harold Adams Innis (1894–1952) and W.A. Mackintosh
(1895–1970). Neither approach was associated with the then-popular
dependency literature, which had roots in the Marxist tradition and was
represented by A.G. Frank (1966) and Johan Galtung (1971). Several
key Canadian figures were, however, variously associated with socialist
thought: H. Clare Pentland (1914–1978), C.B. Macpherson (1911–1987),
and Stanley Brehaut Ryerson (1911–1998). Recollecting the contribution
of these roots in combination with the emerging literature of the 1970s
and 1980s was the remit of the first volume, *New Canadian Political
Economy*. Its claim was "connecting the past with the future" (Clement
and Williams 1989, 4). In the introduction to this collection it was maintained that "political economy at its strongest has focused on processes
whereby social change is located in the historical interaction of the economic, political, cultural, and ideological movements of social life" (2).

   In this first volume, there was recognition of the need to refocus as
well as update the classical political economy. Isabella Bakker, for example, argued: "the new political economy must recognize the importance
of sex/gender systems as a necessary part of its theory of other social,
economic, and political structures. Building on this 'materialist' base,
feminism and political economy begin to establish a new common ground
that offers a powerful set of conceptual and practical tools" (1989, 112).

   Understanding Canada, the second volume, sought to move beyond
the roots of Canadian political economy as a tradition by building upon
that tradition and its new links to "current questions, puzzles, and problems." As noted in the introduction: "The new political economy seeks
most of all to prevent the political and social aspects of life from being
marginalized by a strictly economic logic. Its goal is to reveal the political

agendas of economic practices and to assert the importance of the social" (Clement 1997, 5). There was clearly a project of revealing the importance of human agency behind the collection and making it clear that the economy is not the only determinant of outcomes: "For political economy the economic provides the context, but the political, ideological, and cultural write the text of history and specify the particulars of each nation and the possibilities for the future. The script is one in which human actors have significant freedom of action within the limits of the structures that political economy seeks to identify" (5). The essay by Maroney and Luxton, "Gender at Work: Canadian Feminist Political Economy since 1988," speaks of a "breaking through of the political and theoretical ghettoization of women's issues," most notable in the transformative impact of gender's encounter with racialization (1997, 85–6). This represents a notable advance over the limitations they identified a decade earlier (1987).

There is a clear connection now made between both the forces and relations of production. The collection's strength was its breadth: it opened the scope of Canadian political economy to include the struggles of Indigenous peoples and the ways many settlers and migrants were incorporated into the labour force as unfree labourers; it questioned Canada's place in the world by challenging the nation state as a sole unit of analysis; it imagined Canada's foreign policy in alternative ways; questions about Quebec's nationhood were posed; the displacement of the welfare state through regulations was revealed; cultural identities and new communications technologies were explored; popular culture and leisure industries were examined; and, finally, the collection also highlighted the importance of social space and the environment. These were new terrains of contestation, and taken together they pushed the scope of political economy's boundaries.

HOLISTIC FRAMINGS

Feminism was the primary engine pressing Canadian political economy to transcend the economic and find itself embedded in various levels of abstraction. A key element of the debate was captured by Patricia Connelly, in an early SPE intervention entitled "On Marxism and Feminism" (1983). This early advocacy for intersectional analysis anticipates the kind of holistic framing that characterized the next era. It means the full incorporation of the social and cultural into the political and economic, which demonstrates that these approaches are not incompatible, but on the contrary can be combined to produce a deeper analysis. A new era of recovering complexity had begun for the NCPE.

Leah Vosko's outstanding SPE essay "The Pasts (and Futures) of Feminist Political Economy in Canada: Reviving the Debate" (2002) built a key bridge into this era of holistic analysis. Vosko provides an insightful location and account of feminism's transformation of CPE since the early 1970s, identifying four phases of engagement. This transformation began with the work on gender-blindness, such as Meg Luxton's *More Than a Labour of Love* (1980) where daily and intergenerational reproduction is foregrounded.

Next came the discussion over "levels of analysis," connecting the work of women and modes of production, highlighting the seminal intervention by Patricia Connelly, as mentioned, concerning the sexual division of labour and modes of production where she advocates for the study of social formations within specific historical contexts where ideological and material conditions meet. Vosko identifies this aspect as a key "turning point" for Canadian feminist political economy, leading to the third phase of what she calls "theoretically grounded, applied case studies." Connelly asked: "how do we develop a coherent and integrated perspective with which to analyze the oppression of women in capitalist society?" (1983, 155). She advocated for analysis that is conducted at the level of the "social formation," and claimed that "the general characteristics defined by the capitalist mode of production become specified by the historical circumstances of particular societies" (157). Connelly presses for a political economy wherein the mode of production is specified in concrete forms of politics, social relations, and ideological struggles. "At this level the focus is on how the relations of production intersect, combine and conflict with the relations of gender in different classes and in different historical periods within one society, and in different societies" (158).

The fourth phase is characterized by intersectionality and invokes class, gender, sexuality, and race/ethnicity in the context of capitalism's transformation. A key marker here is the SPE #51 collection edited by Gillian Creese and Daiva Stasiulis, which elevated the analytical importance of culture and ideology alongside the economic and political. These insights were transformational for feminist political economy. They identified "the multiple and contradictory intersections," noting for example, religion, region, dis/ability, and ecology (Creese and Stasiulis 1996, 5).

The blind spots of classical political economy derived from its primary focus upon the structures of production relations and the political supports for those structures. We now acknowldege that such structures require social and cultural supports. Production requires reproduction not only in the daily and intergenerational senses but also the ideological justifications required to sustain hegemony. It was no longer acceptable to simply "add on" women, the environment, culture, and heritage. They had become an integral part of the account *and* explanation.

This was the backdrop for the third collection, *Changing Canada: Political Economy as Transformation* (Clement and Vosko 2003), for which Leah Vosko was co-editor. Its distinctiveness is based on the introduction of the concept of applied political economy, characterized by informed intellectual engagement. It advocates for a transparent understanding in order to direct or promote social change. There is a double sense of transformation used here: social change and changes to the tradition of political economy. Engagement was core to both identifying important issues and how to connect the knowledge and understanding gained from addressing these issues. A strong example is the chapter by Joyce Green addressing some fundamental tensions. She claims: "Advanced capitalism is essentially colonizing civil society and state sovereignty" (52). Unlike British colonial rule where withdrawal is possible, "The colonial relationship in Canada and in other settler states is, first and foremost, between Indigenous and settler populations, both of which are permanently resident in one territory" (53) hence ruling out eviction since the "separation of colonizer and colonized is politically and practically impossible" (53). Her key insight is that "decolonization, however, is possible. Rather than separation, decolonization requires the inclusion of colonized peoples in institutions of power" (2003, 52–3). This is indicative of the nuanced yet forceful direction characteristic of this volume and the engagement of its authors.

Another notable illustration is the chapter by Carroll and Coburn (2003) on "Social Movements and Transformation" identifying the mutual implications of social movements and the political economy tradition. They identify political economy as a transformative practice, open and engaged. There are a multitude of outstanding pieces organized into five parts: "Political Transformations," "Welfare State Restructuring," "International Boundaries and Contexts," "The New Urban Experience," and "Creative Sites of Resistance."

Mel Watkins contributed chapters to each of the three volumes (1989, 1997, 2003). In the third one he frames his discussion around Karl Polanyi's movement (economic growth) and countermovement (protections, including unions, welfare states, social movements, and dissent in general) as articulated in *The Great Transformation* (1944). It is

worthwhile briefly highlighting some of Polanyi's contribution in this
way. Polanyi's "double movement" is about human agency confronting
and resisting the forces of capitalist modernization. The duality includes
responses to capitalist transformations and an understanding of those
transformations themselves. It is the social construction of the economic
and the social implications of the economic, including resistance. Counter
movement is foundational to taking charge of transformations by confronting them and directing them. They suggest that politics matter but
so do social movements and struggle located in civil society. It is reminiscent of a kind of Gramscian counter-hegemony. Market forces of
capitalism tend to produce forms of disintegration that in turn produce
responses based on resistance, including creating new forms of organization supportive of a social economy. This is what we meant by the expression "applied political economy."

COMPARATIVE INTERSECTIONAL ANALYSIS

NCPE has benefited from the insights of comparative intersectional
analysis in the post-*Changing Canada* era. I will illustrate with three
papers. In "Revealing the Class-Gender Connection: Social Policy, Labour
Markets and Households" (Clement 2004, 45), I outlined a comparative
analytical framework, emphasizing the importance of households and
generations to the class-gender nexus as it relates to transformations in
work: "how work is rewarded, organized, distributed and even recognized
is rapidly changing." This is explored comparatively through five gender-
arrangement models examined in six countries. The intersections triad
"focuses on the practices of social welfare, paid work and unpaid work
as located in citizenship entitlements, markets and households" (48). The
triad of labour markets, social policy, and households forms the core of
a relational analysis, based on the insights of property relations. The
claim is that "the three sites of labour markets, welfare states and households are not studied as institutions, policies or practices. Rather it is the
matrix of relations between these sites that yield our understanding of
class, gender and generation" (50).

This beginning has been extended in two further papers with my
colleagues (Clement, Mathieu, Prus, and Uckardesler 2009, 2010). These
papers focus on how precarious lives are created in a new economy
characterized by processes associated with post-industrialism, the knowledge society, new technologies, and precarious employment. This is done
in a comparative context using an intersectional framework. One

dimension of intersectional analysis includes the social characteristics of class, gender, generation, heritage, and ability. A second includes individual's lives embedded in the work-family nexus. The third aspect is the intersections between states, markets, and families located over the levels of the national, sub-national, and local. A main contribution is to extend the notion of precarious employment into the context of precarious lives.

There are multiple entry points into the political economy of precariousness. A rich notion of intersectionality is required to fully achieve our analytical ambitions. Using comparative data, we explore the prospects and limitations of intersectionality over time and space. Political economy remains the context for this research (see Albo 2010), but taking account of intersectionality involves delving deeper into the nature of social relations as influenced by their political, economic, and cultural contexts. We claim a key to understanding "the new economy is the puzzle of a co-articulation of regimes of social inequalities with technological changes, population dynamics, and macroeconomic policies ... the processes of the new economy are related to each other contingently, rather than deterministically ... contingent upon the relative power and organizing capacities of people and the political representation of socio-economic interests in the state" (2010, 60–1). This is an ambitious but promising direction for NCPE.

THE ANALYTICAL VALUE OF STAPLES INSIGHTS TODAY

There has been a resurgence of discussions about staples production. Jim Stanford attributes the resurgence to changes in material conditions: Canadian manufacturing had a resurgence in the 1980s and 1990s, accompanied by a decline in foreign investment with 1996 as the watershed year whereby Canadian foreign investment exceeded foreign ownership in Canada for the first time. There has subsequently been a "reversal" whereby the traditional staples pattern has been reasserted through "structural regression" (Stanford 2008, 9–10). Part of the resurgence is an extension of Innis' original staples approach based upon backward, forward, and final demand linkages to also include "fiscal linkages" (such as economic rents). Watkins says, "Adding fiscal linkage to the other linkages actually increases the likelihood that resource development will have positive effects on the regional economy ... But if fiscal linkages are not exploited for domestic, typically regional, advantage, the risk of the staples trap remains" (2007, 218).

Thomas Gunton (2014, 46) focuses on these fiscal linkages, asking: "How much rent is generated by the staple, and where does the rent go?" For fiscal linkages to benefit Canadians, "Maximizing the contribution of the staple requires collecting rent and distributing its equity to the owners of the staple, in the case of oil and gas, this is the public in the producing regions" (46). It seems there has been considerable fiscal leakage. Gunton cites André Plourde (2010) who "estimates that the private sector retains between 38 per cent and 65 per cent of the rent even under the new more aggressive Alberta royalty scheme." Over 47 per cent of profits in oil and gas were foreign controlled and most leaked (2014, 46). Intracompany transfers further confound royalty collection. Under the title "Why Linkages Matter" Jim Stanford says: "By the turn of the (twenty-first) century, raw and barely processed resources account for well under half of Canada's total merchandise exports – the lowest in our history. Early in the new century, however, the logic of staples dependence reasserted itself. Inflated global commodity prices (especially for oil, some minerals and agriculture) sparked major inflows of capital into expanded staples production in Canada" (2014a, 65; also see Stanford in this volume "Staples Dependence Renewed and Betrayed: Canada's 21st Century Boom and Bust").

A creative response to this new discussion has been provided by Gordon Laxer in "Alberta's Sands, Staples and Traps" (2014), contending that the "carbon trap" is also an "intellectual trap." There is a double edge to the original staples approach. He concludes that it is "hard to beat its explanatory power regarding how Alberta Sands oil got to be Canada's latest staple, impeding broader development. But with its Keynesian, consumptionist premises, the staple theory (in that original incarnation) can also be an intellectual trap, that hinders our transition to a low carbon future" (2014, 57). He is supported by Brendan Haley who identifies the carbon trap as a barrier to "transforming towards a low-carbon economy" by introducing a major rigidity to a sustainable, responsible approach to bitumen (2014, 77).

The environmental and sustainability dimension of energy capture has demonstrated itself to be fundamental. By failing to secure the environmental legitimacy of the oil sands, the transportation and market for this product has been jeopardized. So-called "dirty oil" has lost its lustre. A fuller response to this industry would include: being environmentally responsible in extraction and transportation practices, processing the product within Canada, and marketing it within Canada to displace foreign-imported oil and make Canada energy self-sufficient. None of these logics have guided the development of the oil sands or other energy reserves. Instead, the crude staples export model has dominated and now failed, especially suffering from the classic boom-and-bust cyclonics of staple production. The focus has been on the export of low-processed raw materials rather than on self-sufficiency and maximizing domestic refining. Think about the pipeline debates that haunt Canadian discussions today. The federal government supports pipelines to export bitumen, not ones to displace foreign oil imported to the east coast.

There remains much that could be learned from a critical staples approach to Canada's natural resources. This includes strategizing Canada's own energy requirements by avoiding staple exports of oil, gas, and hydro while importing petroleum to the east-coast market. Such considerations include securing the national market, responsibly transporting the energy, sustainably producing the energy in environmentally responsible ways, and processing the resources beyond their most elementary state. Canada should be extending its forward linkages in refining and processing its energy in order to re-establish gains it had made in backward linkages for inputs to production such as heavy equipment manufacture.

Moreover, this new staples economy is embedded in a different context, one Travis Fast identifies in "Stapled to the Front Door: Neoliberal Extractivism in Canada" (2014, 33). He claims: "the relative re-internationalization of the domestic economy, particularly the resource sectors, has to be read alongside the relatively successful and continued internationalization of Canadian capital ... while Canada's economy is indeed staples dependent, it would be simplistic to describe Canadian capital as dependent, especially in the light of the leading role played by Canadian-based capital in NRE [natural resource extraction] industries in other countries." This is a position I have long supported (1977). We should be asking "nation-building for whom?" not in a narrow nationalist sense but in a wider sense of international solidarity around class, gender, and the environment, as well as in the sense of decolonization for Indigenous peoples.

THE CONTRIBUTION OF NCPE

What is the continued relevance of Canadian political economy and what is the main contribution of the new Canadian political economy? Its contribution is to reveal what other social science approaches have concealed and to evolve this capacity to extend its scope and depth. It has striven to push the boundaries and establish new sites of investigation.

Political economy by its very nature troubles exclusively economic explanations. It is a holistic analysis that has broadened its scope of factors considered within the whole.

From the outset, classic political economy in Canada included space and time as key dimensions. It relied upon international markets, technology, and geography to account for changes. This traditional Canadian political economy concealed too much. The new Canadian political economy aims to reveal the social, cultural, and environmental factors as part of its explanation for change, claiming they are essential to more fulsome explanations and understandings. These factors are not simply consequences. Making these matters visible and demonstrating that they matter to how we understand and explain is the major contribution of this tradition. The tensions and contradictions evident through social relations are the dynamic relationships necessary for transformations. Attending to these has assisted in recovering the complexity and dynamism of understanding social change, particularly compared to the narrowness of purely economic accounts. Human agency, struggle, and resistance reminiscent of Karl Polanyi's "double movement" have aided in this development. Feminism and environmental movements have also contributed enormously to this tradition. Attention to the cultural and ideological in terms of creating consent and legitimization have also been a key part of this complexity, making it evident that the meanings people attach to practices matter.

This is a tradition that has grown and flourished because it continues to expand its scope of relevance and deliver insights more clearly than ever before. Applied political economy has the potential to mobilize and guide social change. It can transform how we formulate our understandings and actions. At its core, Canadian political economy emerged in order to make sense of contemporary issues with an orientation toward enhancing social change for the betterment of the social condition. As it has matured and become more sophisticated, new domains have emerged and are evident in the present collection. How effectively this bridging of analysis and action is accomplished is the challenge for the next generation of Canadian political economists.

2

Feminist Political Economy and Everyday Research on Work and Employment: The Case of the Employment Standards Enforcement Gap

Leah F. Vosko

Since only 30 per cent were unionized in 2017, the majority of Canada's 15.6 million employees rely on employment standards (ES) (Statistics Canada 2017).[1] Legislating minimum conditions in areas such as wages, working time, vacations and leaves, and termination and severance of employment, ES are especially important to workers in precarious jobs characterized by low income, a lack of control, and limited access to regulatory protection, and are particularly common among women, (im) migrant, and racialized workers, observations true not only to the Canadian context at multiple scales (i.e., the federal and provincial levels) but to other jurisdictions characterized by declining rates of unionization (e.g., Australia, Britain, and the US) (on the importance of ES in the foregoing cases, on Australia, see Landau and Howe 2016; on Britain, see Pollert 2009; and, on the US, see Weil 2010; Gleeson 2016).

Historically, scholars working in the tradition of the political economy of labour in Canada have paid scant attention to ES. This neglect flows partly from the focus on unionized workers and on central institutions of labour market regulation (Fudge and Vosko 2003). Given the changing nature of employment, however, recent years have seen growing interest in ES, particularly in their scope. This mounting attention owes a debt to the sustained interventions of a group of feminist scholars, working to expand the new Canadian political economy (NCPE). Beginning in the 1980s, such scholars examined and assessed the substance of these social minima versus other sources of labour protection because of their critical importance to equity-seeking groups. In the process, they illuminated the gendered, racialized, and citizenship-bounded employment norms that shape, and are shaped by, the inequitable levels of protection available to workers in different forms of employment.

This chapter contends that the tools of feminist political economy are also instructive in revealing, understanding, and contesting the erosion of normative goals and workplace objectives surrounding ES regulation as it is occurring through constraints on workers' access to these entitlements. Indeed, adopting a feminist political economy approach to studying regulations and policies on the day-to-day application and enforcement of ES further discloses inequities that are reproduced in often hidden ways. The analysis unfolds in three parts, beginning with a review of a feminist political economy approach, articulating its central tenets, and considering the insights it has offered to the study of ES. Against this backdrop, section two examines constraints on workers' access to and realization of protections that are often obscured. Using Ontario as a case study, it considers several aspects of ES regulation distant from public scrutiny and their effects: exemptions and special rules and the introduction of "self-help" reforms and settlements in the enforcement process. The chapter concludes with some brief reflections on the utility of feminist political economy in pursuing everyday research on work and employment, including inquiries into ES regulation.

FEMINIST POLITICAL ECONOMY AND THE STUDY OF EMPLOYMENT STANDARDS

A distinctly Canadian variant of feminist political economy, both a "holistic theory" and a framework for action (Maroney and Luxton 1987, 86), emerged in the late 1970s and early 1980s to bridge the "new Canadian political economy" (retrospectively labelled, Clement and Williams 1989) with liberal and socialist feminism. In this period, CPE imagined itself as advancing an interdisciplinary, historical, and comparative approach to studying "social relations as they relate to the *economic* system of production" (Clement and Drache 1978, 5, emphasis added). This approach understood society as "a totality which includes the political, economic, social, and cultural" (Clement 1997, 3; on the evolution of this approach, see Clement in this volume). As Luxton (2006a, 12–13) contends, CPE's all-encompassing perspective predisposed it "to integrat[ing] fully the study of women, gender, sexuality, race and class," as well as social relations of inequality such as age and ability, and also citizenship. Yet given CPE's general inattention to these social relations, in practice it has been largely left to feminist political economy to pursue such integration (on the hesitancy to adopt "gender" as an analytic category in studies of work and employment, as well as an integrated analysis, more broadly, see for e.g., Armstrong and Armstrong 1983; Fudge and Vosko 2003).

Much could be said about Canadian feminist political economy's parameters, its evolution, and its areas of emphasis – indeed, volumes have been devoted to reflecting on its core concepts and defining debates (see for e.g., Maroney and Luxton 1987; Andrew et al. 2003; Bezanson and Luxton 2006). As an approach, Canadian feminist political economy is dialectical, materialist, and praxis-oriented. In light of these inclinations, and its parting of ways with variants of liberal feminism oriented to legislative/regulatory change as a means to an end, much scholarship in this tradition begins with the assumption that, rather than an impartial umpire, the state is a "contested terrain" (Maroney and Luxton 1987, 87) – that is, inseparable from social relations. Hence conflict is central to understanding power and change therein (Gabriel 1996; Findlay 2015, 38). Because of its debt to socialist feminism, Canadian feminist political economy is also marked by a contribution to analyzing "women's work" (both paid and unpaid).

Chronicling writings in Canada's premiere political economy journal, *Studies in Political Economy*, elsewhere I argue that feminist political economy scholarship emanating in Canada might be characterized as moving through four overlapping phases (Vosko 2002). First were the early debates that raised the issue of gender blindness in the tradition of political economy. Subsequent inquiries explored questions related to "levels of analysis," specifically how to explain sexual inequality under capitalism and where to locate "women's work" (paid and unpaid) in the economic system. A third phase involved developing applied works, including a large body of scholarship on the welfare state and law. And a fourth phase, crystallizing in the 2000s in response to salient critiques from Aboriginal and anti-racist feminism (Bannerji 1991, 2000; Dua and Robertson 1999), addressed more deeply interactions between gender, Indigeneity, race, and ethnicity in shaping relations of production characterizing late capitalism (see for e.g., Abele and Stasiulus 1989; Arat-Koç 1989; Das Gupta 1996; Bakan and Stasiulus 2005; Kuokkanen, 2008).

Since the publication of my review essay, arguably a fifth stage has emerged characterized by a focus on neoliberalism (for another take on neoliberalism and its manifestations, see McBride in this volume). Through engagements with post-structuralist analyses of governmentality, feminist political economists studying developments in Canada are crafting approaches to understanding neoliberalism, its citizenship and gender regimes, and its central projects (see for e.g., Brodie 2007, 2010); emergent work seeks to reveal paradoxes and tensions inherent in neoliberal governance and its false gender neutrality through identifying neoliberalism's manifestations and mutations in different sites and at various scales (see for e.g., contributions to Braedley and Luxton 2010). Simultaneously, scholars continue to sort through field-defining dichotomies – such as the public/private divide – in the context of neoliberalism, alongside identifying particularly neoliberal forms of privatization (Armstrong et al. 1997) and associated racialized gendered strategies (e.g., reregulation, reprivatization, commodification, familialization, individualization, delegation, and depoliticization) and their challenges to feminism (see especially, Cossman and Fudge 2002; Arat-Koç 2012).

Several analytical commitments cutting across these phases are especially relevant to the study of ES: foremost is the persistent concern to highlight the narrow economism (Seccombe 1974) characterizing the political economy tradition – that is, feminist political economists' determination to reveal and theorize the relationship between production for surplus and social reproduction considered, initially, in light of domestic and subsequently international divisions of labour (i.e., taking account processes and patterns of migration) (on the domestic labour debates, see for e.g., contributions to Fox, ed. 1980; Luxton 1982; on international divisions of labour, see for e.g., Arat-Koç 2006). Another pertinent feature of feminist political economy is its abiding commitment to seeing contradictions as sources of change, and hence to using productive tensions as a means of understanding continuity through change and identifying critical sites of contestation (e.g., in the analysis of state policies and their effects) (Armstrong and Armstrong 1983; MacDonald 1991; Porter 2003). Also germane is the enduring emphasis on theorizing action or praxis as a means of transformation (Clement and Vosko 2003) (e.g., in the identification of community unionism, and associated institutions, such as workers' centres as sites for linking (paid) workplace concerns to social and economic problems, connected to processes of social reproduction) (Cranford et al. 2005).

Informed by such analytical commitments, feminist political economists studying ES in the 1980s and 1990s made key contributions to understanding their nature and organization (on CPE's contributions related to labour market change, see Ross and Thomas in this volume). Reflecting the early emphasis on gender blindness and locating "women's work", (paid and unpaid) in the economic system, inquiries focused first on "bringing women into" the ambit of labour protection and, where applicable, examining their degree of access to minimum ES. The pivotal study was "Labour Law's Little Sister: The *Employment Standards Act* and the Feminization of Labour" (1991a) by Judy Fudge, which used the case of Ontario to expose the inferior protections provided to workers covered exclusively by ES as compared to collective bargaining legislation. Fudge's analysis also revealed that, at that time, women were disproportionately represented in this group.

Until the publication of "Labour Law's Little Sister," to the extent that gender was addressed in the NCPE literature on work and employment, most studies focused on women's absence and/or marginal presence in unions and limited access to collective bargaining structures (see for e.g., Briskin and Yanz 1983; Briskin 1989); around that time, there was also considerable focus on specific "topics relevant to women," such as employment equity, occupational segregation, and equal pay (e.g., Armstrong and Armstrong 1984; McDermott 1991; Bakan and Kobayshi 2000). In contrast, early studies of ES drew attention to the fact that minimum standards legislation operates as the poor cousin of collective bargaining laws; they pointed to the bifurcated (and deeply gendered) structure of labour law and policy (e.g., Fudge 1993; ILGWU/Intercede 1993) and linked the formulation of ES to the process of feminization, at the time associated with an inferior floor of labour protections (see for e.g., contributions to Jenson et al. 1988). Feminist political economists working in labour history, such as Jane Ursel (1992) and Joan Sangster (1989), demonstrated simultaneously that gendered exclusions and partial exclusion from ES were rooted in legislation and regulations dating to the *Factory Acts* that targeted women and children. Such interventions provided means for revealing that a majority of workers for whom ES are the principal source of labour protection are women, presumed to be responsible for social reproduction (or the unpaid work required to produce a supply of workers for the labour force) and to be dependent on a male breadwinner. Using feminist political economists' formative insight about the necessary and integral relationship between production for surplus and social reproduction, they opened space for paying greater attention to not only non-unionized workers but to unpaid work and how it shaped women's patterns of labour force participation and the protective regime to which they were subject.

Building on this new area of inquiry, feminist political economists studying ES went on to explore the quality and character of different forms of employment. Studies on part-time and temporary forms of paid employment as well as on self-employment – highlighting their often inferior terms and conditions vis-à-vis full-time permanent employment – were the empirical outcome of such investigation (e.g., Vosko 2000; Hughes 2003; Cranford et al. 2005; contributions to Pupo, Glenday, and Duffy 2010). Also emerging from this area of inquiry were comparative studies examining different forms of employment characterized by high levels of insecurity, and probing the shape of particular forms of employment, such as part-time work, in different locales and industrial and occupational contexts in relation to the variation in ES regulation (see for e.g., contributions to Vosko, MacDonald, and Campbell 2009). Studies of ES in historical perspective also arose in the early 2000s; foremost was Mark Thomas' *Regulating Flexibility* (2009; see also Thomas 2010), which highlighted enduring gendered exclusions and began to expose racialized patterns linked, via continuity through change, to employer demands for neoliberal forms of labour "flexibility."

This wave of scholarship used the lens of feminist political economy – specifically its contributions to intersectional theorizing, its engagement of discourse analysis, and its understanding of state policy as always already contested – to make visible the normative model of employment underpinning access to the full range of labour protections – namely, the standard employment relationship (or the SER), where the worker works full-time and continuously for one employer on their premises under direct supervision, normally in a unionized situation, and has access to a social wage (Muckenberger 1989). It also revealed how the flipside of the SER (Vosko 2000) or forms of employment deviating from this norm, often treated as a catch-all and associated with the imprecise moniker "nonstandard work," were more properly identified with gendered and racialized precariousness due partly to the low floor (relative to that offered by collective bargaining) of rights protections provided under ES.

Subsequently, feminist political economists linked insights into the form and functions of the SER and its deviations to previous efforts to disclose which workers are disproportionately reliant on ES. Empirically, revealing the SER's false gender neutrality, this body of scholarship also demonstrated that this employment model took the native-born male industrial worker as its central subject (Fudge and Vosko 2001a, 2001b; Cranford and Vosko 2006; Vosko 2006b). In making this contribution, scholarship showed that the employment norm was gendered, racialized, and shaped by national citizenship and immigration status (Vosko 2010; Fudge 2012). It began to disclose how not only sex/gender but also international divisions of labour, which shape international migration for employment, affect patterns of social reproduction and influence employment norms.

USING THE TOOLS OF FEMINIST POLITICAL ECONOMY TO APPREHEND GAPS IN THE APPLICATION AND ENFORCEMENT OF EMPLOYMENT STANDARDS

The identification of the SER and its gendered, racialized, and citizenship-based exclusions are indispensable in understanding deteriorating terms and conditions of employment under neoliberalism, including those flowing from the lowering of the bottom of the floor of labour protections tied to ES. Feminist political economists studying ES have shown the persistent inadequacies of these social minima; foremost, they have produced studies demonstrating how the narrow scope of ES leaves large segments of the labour force ill-protected, particularly workers in occupations and sectors characterized by large shares of women, racialized, and migrant workers (e.g., domestic work and agriculture). In light of mounting evidence of deteriorating terms and conditions of employment among workers for whom ES are a primary source of labour protection in Canada as a whole (HRDC 1997, 41; FLSRC 2006), the insights of feminist political economy are equally critical to studies of ES enforcement. Its attempt to offer a holistic theory – one that is at once interdisciplinary, historical, and comparative – plus a framework for studying social relations vis-à-vis production enables the study of how workers are deprived of protection not only when laws are inadequate (e.g., their scope is too narrow) or are broken, but when they are avoided or eroded through subtle practices often linked to disparities in treatment on the basis of workers' social location (e.g., gender or national citizenship status).

In the remainder of this chapter, I explicate how the tools of feminist political economy help animate and operationalize a multi-dimensional conception of the "ES Enforcement Gap."[2] Presented in figure 2.1, the gap is a multi-dimensional cross-sectoral conceptualization of workplace protections depicting deficiencies in the application of social minima.

Adopting this conception calls for investigating not only formal violations of existing legislation, but interrelated practices of erosion, evasion, and abandonment. While the definition of violation is relatively straightforward, *erosion* entails the weakening of normative goals and policy objectives, including those of universality, social minima, and fairness

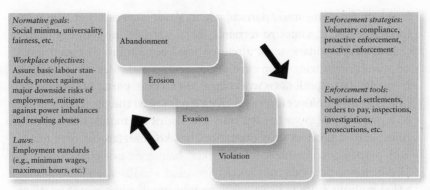

Figure 2.1 The enforcement gap (Vosko et al. 2019)

that motivated and framed the development of the *Employment Standards Act* (ESA) historically (Vosko, Noack, and Thomas 2016), and, if left unchecked, may lead to their non-application. *Evasion* involves the adoption by employers of "strategies to evade core workplace laws," such as the misclassification of employees as independent contractors (Bernhardt et al. 2008, 6). Widespread workplace violations and evasions of protective labour law can lead to not only their erosion but also their abandonment – that is, to practices that contravene societally agreed upon understandings of decent work with the knowledge that the enforcement of accordant standards will be left unchecked.

In the balance of this section, I use two illustrations,[3] reflecting the process of erosion, to highlight the utility of a feminist political economy approach in comprehending gaps in the application and enforcement of ES enforcement and their consequences: the cases of exemptions and special rules and the move to "self-help" in the claims-making and resolution process under Ontario's ESA.

Exemptions and Special Rules: Eroding Norms and Policy Objectives

In the face of an increasingly complex patchwork of exemptions and special rules shaping workers' access to ES in Ontario, feminist political economy's insights help illuminate the fraying margins of labour market regulation and how their weakening exacerbates the already disadvantaged position of workers presumed to have alternative means of subsistence/survival outside the wage (e.g., women, young people, and migrants) (Picchio 1992; Peck 1996, 31; Vosko 2000, 40, 42). In the process, they highlight how the state, particularly its policies directed at managing these margins, is contested terrain.

In Ontario to date, scant attention has been paid to divergent levels of protection flowing from exemptions and special rules for individuals in specified occupations or workplaces, on account partly of the assumption that all employees in the province who need the protection of the ESA are covered by its provisions. The list of exemptions and special rules, itself a product of contestation, has however grown over time – with particular consequences for workers belonging to socially marginalized groups.

Exemptions from the ESA fall into four broad categories: first, there are those that relate primarily to an employee's industry or sector of employment, which include the constellation of special rules and exemptions relating to professional/white-collar employees, agricultural employees, construction employees, and liquor servers. A second category of exemptions addresses those related to the organization of working time in specific occupations. Although these exemptions tend to be occupationally specific, they are addressed in the following clusters: namely, irregular working hour occupations; long working hour occupations; combined long and irregular working hour occupations; and continuous working hour operations. A third category of exemptions relates to (covered) employees' status within their workplace, regardless of their labour force locations. The main clusters in this category relate to managerial/supervisory status, and job tenure, including short tenure and temporary agency employees. The final category of exemptions covers those associated with characteristics that are inherent to an employee, such as student status (Vosko, Noack, and Thomas 2016, 11).

Common examples of exemptions include the exclusion of farm employees[4] from ESA provisions around minimum wage, hours of work, daily rest periods, time off between shifts, weekly/bi-weekly rest periods, eating periods, overtime, public holidays, and vacations with pay; individuals in supervisory roles from provisions on hours of work, overtime, time-off between shifts, weekly/bi-weekly rest periods, and overtime; students under eighteen years of age and working fewer than twenty-eight hours a week while attending school from the normal minimum wage (i.e., as of January 2018, such students could be paid $13.15 rather than the established $14.00 minimum wage); employees who regularly serve liquor in licensed establishments from the normal minimum wage (i.e., as of January 2018, they were only entitled to $12.20 rather than $14.00); and homecare employees who provide homemaking or personal support

services from the minimum wage after twelve hours of work in a day and
from ESA provisions related to hours of work, daily rest periods, time off
between shifts, weekly/bi-weekly rest periods, eating periods, and overtime.
The outcome of ongoing lobbying by employer associations, such exemptions are the result of piecemeal amendments to the ESA since its introduction in 1968, most of which were established by government to allow
for more flexible regulations for businesses in competitive environments
(LCO 2012, 41; for a complementary analysis of the dynamics behind
the neoliberalization of the social services sector, see McBride in this
volume). For example, the Canadian Restaurant and Foodservices
Association has long lobbied the provincial government to maintain
the lower minimum wage for liquor servers and students and the Ontario
Federation of Agriculture, Ontario Greenhouse Vegetable Growers, and
the Ontario Fruit and Vegetable Growers' Association recently pressed
for a separate minimum wage for farm workers in light of an increase
to the minimum wage and proposals for indexing minimum wage to
inflation (Antonacci 2014). Consistent with feminist political economy
analysis of the deteriorating margins of the labour market that result
in poor protections for workers in precarious jobs, these exemptions
contribute to affording the weakest protections where employees need
them the most (i.e., the greater the deviation from the SER, the lesser
the protection). This tendency is acutely evident in exemptions and
partial exemptions from core ESA provisions to which homecare employees
are subject.

ILLUSTRATION: THE CAP ON HOMECARE EMPLOYEES'
ENTITLEMENT TO THE MINIMUM WAGE AND THEIR
EXEMPTION FROM PROVISIONS GOVERNING
WORKING TIME
Using an intersectional lens to capture how gender interacts with other
social locations as they relate to ES coverage reveals how exemptions
and special rules applicable to occupational groups comprised of employees otherwise disadvantaged in the labour force can reinforce precariousness among those who require ES protection most. Homecare
employees providing homemaking and personal support services in
private homes, an occupational group comprised of fully 90 per cent
women, many of whom are racialized and born outside of Canada, are
a case in point (Statistics Canada 2011–2016; see also Lum, Sladek, and
Ying 2010; Brookman et al. 2016, 4). Their situation affirms feminist
political economy's early insights into the devaluation of forms of work
for remuneration associated with so-called "women's work" in the

market and subsequent recognition of processes of racialization tied to this devaluation.

Homecare employees have faced exemptions from minimum wage and working time standards since at least 1976 (Ministry of Labour 2017). Despite their typically long hours of paid work, homecare employees are only entitled to the minimum wage, and for a maximum of twelve hours per day. They are also exempt from ESA provisions related to hours of work, daily rest periods, time off between shifts, weekly/bi-weekly rest periods, eating periods, and overtime, and if they are employed by a Community Care Access Centre or an entity under contract with one, they are also exempt from the ESA's temporary help agency rules.

Official rationales advanced for such exemptions have changed over time. The Women's Bureau of the Ontario Ministry of Labour described the initial rationales as related to the difficulty of enforcement, the assumption that the work may involve "personal tasks" in addition to work tasks, and the lack of recognition of the tasks of domestic employees as "real work" (Archives of Ontario 1975, as cited by Vosko et al. forthcoming). Saturated by gendered norms of paid and unpaid work, such rationales reflected the feminized character of homecare work undertaken in private households.[5] According to the Ontario Ministry of Labour's ESA Exemption toolkit on Homemakers, Domestic Workers and Residential Care workers (2017, 8), it was also originally assumed that, since homemakers worked in private residences away from the employer's premises, "the employer has little ability to monitor the employees' hours of work and it may be difficult to use transitional methods (such as timesheets) to effectively monitor working hours," rationales questionable given the growing use of technology in governing working time (e.g., practices of surveillance and Taylorization are common under the marketized, fee-for-service homecare work model) (Vosko et al. forthcoming).

Departing from an emphasis on enforceability, contemporary rationales for the continued exemption of homecare employees offered by employer representatives relate increasingly to their need for so-called flexibility. They advance the notion that ES provisions governing working hours are out of sync with homecare delivery in Ontario, specifically, that flexibility in scheduling is necessary to accommodate the needs and preferences of clients located in homecare workers' dispersed worksites (Homecare Ontario 2015). Yet this employer-centred flexibility comes at a significant cost for workers in homecare.

For this occupational group, exemptions and special rules exist alongside their high levels of precariousness on several dimensions. For example, the cap on homecare employees' entitlement to the minimum wage, together with their exemption from provisions for overtime pay, reflects and reproduces their already limited earning potential. Considering the 2011–16 period, 53 per cent of homecare employees reported that their wages were lower than two-thirds of the median hourly rate of full-time employees – a share of low-wage work well above Ontario employees as a whole that is consistent with the devaluation of work undertaken in private homes (Vosko et al. forthcoming).[6] At the same time as homecare employees lack many of the ESA's key provisions, their capacity to engage in meaningful collective action is hampered by the use of contracting in homecare services in Ontario. In the publicly funded homecare system, Local Health Integration Networks (LHINS) control the terms of homecare employment by way of their contracts with service provider agencies. For the purpose of collective bargaining, however, service provider agencies rather than these LHINS are considered the employer, limiting the potential for collective bargaining and, where unions manage to gain certification, impeding collective agreements in making substantive gains for homecare employees, as agencies are constrained by the terms of their contracts with LHINS (Vosko et al., forthcoming).

In all of these ways, exemptions and special rules applicable to homecare employees under Ontario's ESA heighten precariousness for an occupational group comprised principally of women, many of whom are racialized and born outside of Canada, that already confronts substantial labour market insecurity. Engaging in work that has traditionally been diminished by its characterization as "women's work," homecare employees typically earn low wages and face profound barriers to collective bargaining. Research on work and employment looking through the lens of feminist political economy suggests that a simple analysis considering to whom ESA provisions governing minimum wage and working time apply – i.e., one inattentive to the history and evolution of such exemptions and special rules and to the composition of the workforces affected – is inadequate. In the case of homecare employees, it neglects to disclose fully the differential levels of protection experienced by employees in particular (occupational and industrial) contexts tied to social relations of gender and race as well as to immigration status and their effects.

"Self-Help" in Claims-Making and Resolution: Eroding Laws

Feminist political economy also increasingly generates influential analyses of the depoliticizing and individualizing dynamics of neoliberal governance.

A wealth of studies, whether their focus is social, fiscal, or anti-violence policy, reveal the ways in which policy frameworks characteristic of this era conceptually erase inequalities of gender, race, and socioeconomic class through privileging notions of individual responsibility and self-reliance. In her analysis of the paradoxes and tensions inherent in neo-liberalism that underpin its false gender neutrality, Brodie (2007, 103) describes neoliberal governance as a "disciplinary and dividing practice that places steeply rising demands on people to find personal causes and responses to what are, in effect, collective social problems."

Such insights into the features and effects of neoliberal governance, informed as they are by feminist political economy, help to illuminate the erosion of ES enforcement in Ontario, particularly evident since the province's adoption of a "self-help" approach in claims making and the expanded use of "settlements" as a means of resolving complaints.

ILLUSTRATION: REQUIRING AGGRIEVED EMPLOYEES
TO ATTEMPT TO RESOLVE WORKPLACE PROBLEMS WITH
THEIR EMPLOYERS AND THE EXPANSION OF SETTLEMENTS
Indicative of a model of self-help reflecting the soft-law or compliance orientation of contemporary ES emblematic of new governance (Vosko, Grundy, and Thomas 2014) that places greater responsibilities on the shoulders of claimants to resolve what are increasingly conceived as "disputes," Ontario's 2010 *Open for Business Act* (OBA), enacted on the heels of the Great Recession, established a requirement for aggrieved employees to first seek to resolve their complaints with the employer before gaining access to the Ministry of Labour's claims system. As a result of this measure, which remained in place until 2018, a claims processor engaged by the Ministry of Labour could refuse a complaint if a complainant could not demonstrate efforts to address their claim with the employer, without reasonable grounds, and there was no right of appeal. There were several formal grounds for release from this require-ment, many of which were tied closely to the social location of the claim-ant, including if a complainant was a young worker, a live-in caregiver, had difficulty communicating in the language of their employer, had a disability inhibiting communication with their employer, or if the reason for seeking the exemption was related to a ground under the Ontario Human Rights Code. An exemption was also possible in cases where the complainant feared their employer.[7]

Despite these limited grounds for exemption from the self-help require-ment, from fiscal years 2011–12 onwards (i.e., to 2014–15), the first full year for which this requirement was in place, more than four out of five complainants (85 per cent) reported that they had either contacted or attempted to contact their employer (Vosko et al. 2017).

Concomitantly, the volume of ESA complaints received by the Ministry of Labour decreased. Between 2008–09 and 2012–13, the number of complaints submitted annually dropped substantially (see figure 2.2), although it levelled off at about 15,000 per year starting in 2012–13. Notably, the absolute number of non-unionized Ontario employees increased during that time period; thus whereas in 2008–09 there was one complaint submitted for every 175 non-unionized employees in Ontario, in 2014–15 there was one complaint submitted for every 285 non-unionized employees (Vosko et al. 2017 (Figure 2)).

In addition to the self-resolution mandated as a condition of accessing the complaints system, another key trend in ES enforcement in Ontario from 2008–09 to 2014–15 was the expanded use of settlements whereby, rather than the full investigation of claims, the parties reach an agreement independently or through the assistance of an ESO (a "facilitated settlement"), which accounted for 4 per cent of complaint outcomes in 2008–09, and 15 per cent of complaint outcomes in 2014–15 (Grundy et al. 2016 (Figure 4)). Yet, overall, settlements tended to yield a smaller percentage of the total claim amount compared to those assessed by an ESO; in 2014–15, almost 40 per cent of facilitated settlements settled for less than 50 per cent of their total claim, whereas fewer than 30 per cent of non-facilitated settlements settled for less than 50 per cent, indicating that the involvement of ESOs may produce resolutions that are overall less favourable to complainants (Vosko et al. 2017, (Figure 6)).

The turn to a self-help mandate, broadly speaking (i.e., despite the removal of the requirement that aggrieved employees seek to resolve their workplace problems with their employer before being permitted to make formal complaints to the Ministry of Labour), and the increase in settlements reflect the erosion of the historical intent of ES to serve as social minima. The shift from law enforcement to dispute resolution between individual parties, evident in both sets of neoliberal reforms, negates the unequal power relations of the employment relationship and may amplify the risk that potential complainants face in attempting to remedy an ES violation. There are grounds for believing that the self-resolution requirement increased the risks that aggrieved employees had to bear in the complaints process and served as a deterrent to filing a complaint. For example, whereas in 2008–09, reprisal claims were only included in 6 per cent of all complaints, the proportion of complaints with a reprisal component grew in subsequent years, increasing to 8 per

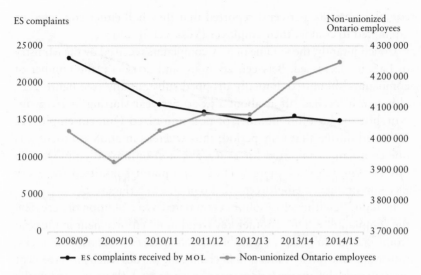

ES complaints   Non-unionized
                                                                 Ontario employees

25 000   4 300 000

20 000   4 200 000

                                                                 4 100 000
15 000

                                                                 4 000 000

10 000

                                                                 3 900 000

5 000   3 800 000

0   3 700 000
       2008/09 2009/10 2010/11 2011/12 2012/13 2013/14 2014/15
          —•— ES complaints received by MOL   —•— Non-unionized Ontario employees

Figure 2.2 ES complaints submitted to the Ministry of Labour, relative to the number of non-unionized employees in Ontario, 2008/09 to 2014/15

cent in 2010–11 and slightly more than 10 per cent in 2014–15, a development amounting to a 70 per cent increase in the share of complaints that had a reprisal component (Grundy et al. 2017; see also Vosko, Noack, and Tucker 2016, Appendices).

With regard to settlements, research investigating developments in ES in other jurisdictions in Canada and beyond indicates that they can also be marked by the same power imbalances of the employment relationship, whereby employees are subject to pressure to "agree" to substandard terms from employers, many of whom have independent legal and human resources representation throughout the settlement process. For example, in her California-based study of the complaints process, Gleeson's (2016, 57–9) analysis of the steps potential complaints must follow in order to proceed with a wage and hours claim shows that even after a lengthy process of establishing their coverage under the federal *Fair Labor Standards Act*, and even after filling out claim forms etc., complainants (and their employers) are expected to appear at a settlement conference at the agency office in the presence of a Deputy Commissioner; in this context, she reveals the precariousness of the claims of complainants already marginalized in other ways, such as undocumented workers facing labour standards violations. Commenting on the remarkably similar formalization of the ES settlement process in British Columbia,

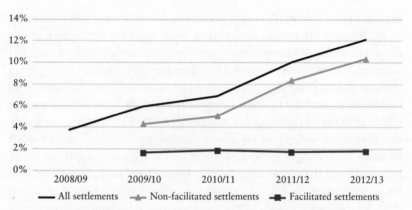

Figure 2.3 Use of settlements to resolve complaints, overall and by type, 2008/09 to 2014/15 (n=120,893)

Fairey and McCallum (2007, 22) thereby conclude that "because of imbalance in the power relationship between employees and their employers the new formalized mediation and settlement agreement process effectively places employees in a more vulnerable position, receiving less protection than was previously the case" (for further examples outside Ontario, see contributions to Vosko et al. 2019, on the British, Australian, and Quebec cases by Clark, Hardy, and Howe, and Gesauldi and Vallée respectively).

Although administrative data on the Ontario case do not allow for disaggregation by sex, immigration status, and other social markers, as studies drawing principally on qualitative and policy research otherwise show, aggrieved workers do not experience the effects of the erosion of ES occasioned by such individualizing procedural reforms equally; those historically disadvantaged in the labour force, for whom the ESA was originally to provide a floor of protections and for whom advice and (increasingly privatized) legal representation is largely inaccessible, face particularly severe consequences. For example, as Thomas' (2009) research investigating individualizing tendencies in ES enforcement in the 1980s prior to the introduction of the OBA shows, reports of violations experienced by workers of Chinese heritage prompted the Chinese National Council to underscore these inequalities in a letter to then Ontario Minister of Labour noting that, among other examples "language is considered a major factor, since most of the workers have difficulties to express in English and they believe the chances of getting an interpreter or meeting a Chinese speaking [employment standards] officer is very low" (Chinese National Council as cited by Thomas 2009, 105). Similarly, as qualitative interviews undertaken with workers in the late 2010s illustrate, those with precarious immigration status, such as migrant workers, recent immigrants, and refugees are often hesitant to engage in the complaints process. The reflections of one employee, a refugee from Colombia concerned to secure (upward) mobility in the labour market and cognizant of the need for solid employment references, exemplify this hesitancy: "when you are new in the country, you don't want to start to make problems or to be a problem ... I work and I apply for many jobs and I put that experience [on my resume] because it's important to have experiences in Canada to take another job" (Vosko et al. 2019, n.p). As these examples – along with analyses of administrative data – show, the contemporary movement towards "self-help" and settlements are all the more important because, as feminist political economists have long demonstrated, the population of workers coming under the jurisdiction of the ESA has gendered and racialized contours and is affected profoundly by national citizenship boundaries. In other words, developments in the application and enforcement of ES highlight the continuity of social inequalities.

CONCLUSION

A uniquely Canadian variant of feminist political economy has forged a holistic, interdisciplinary, and dialectical approach to studying work and employment, and, in particular, to understanding challenges pivotal to workers' realization of basic employment rights and entitlements. Its attentiveness to gendered, racialized, and citizenship-bounded employment norms has generated important insights into the historical evolution and substance of ES, and the often-inferior rights and protections they provide to many precariously employed workers for whom these social minima are the principal source of labour protection.

The insights of feminist political economy are also indispensable for understanding how and why inequitable levels of protection persist not only in formal legislation (i.e., in the official provisions of the ESA), but in ES implementation, that is, how inequities are reproduced and exacerbated, in often subtle ways, through regulations and policies on application and enforcement, underlining the formative assumption that state processes are contested terrain (i.e., themselves riddled with power relations). As this chapter has attempted to show, the ESA's special rules and exemptions and the adoption of an individualized self-help enforcement model, which may appear neutral on the surface, have implications for historically disadvantaged groups of workers and reproduce unequal power relations that come into full view through the adoption of an integrated approach as developed and applied by feminist political economists studying ES. In identifying new arenas of investigation related to gaps in the application and enforcement of ES, a feminist political economy approach thus helps point the way to developing a research agenda centred on regulatory effectiveness, aimed, for a start, at securing fulsome, universal, fair, and enforceable social minima for all workers on the job. At the same time, as ES are an increasingly important site of struggle, with the rise of living wage movements, anti-wage theft movements etc., often spearheaded by workers' centres and other types of organizations historically at the periphery of the organized labour movement (see Ross and Thomas in this volume), this approach also offers practical tools for resistance movements advocating progressive state reforms through re-regulating ES. Such reforms obviously do not represent ends in and of themselves but, rather, means of opening up new terrain for mobilizing, and mobilizing support for, those for whom such standards are the principal source of protection.

NOTES

I am grateful to Rebecca Casey, John Grundy, Heather Steel, and Mark Thomas for their comments on earlier versions of this contribution.

1 The research for this chapter was funded by a partnership grant, titled "Closing the Employment Standards Enforcement Gap: Improving Protections for People in Precarious Jobs," funded by the Social Sciences and Humanities Research Council of Canada (SSHRC). Access to data from the Ontario Ministry of Labour's (MOL) Employment Standards Information System (ESIS) was acquired under a unique data-sharing agreement with the MOL. I am grateful to this Ministry and its staff for engaging in this agreement and for supporting the larger research partnership from which this article emanates. The views set out in this chapter nevertheless represent those of its author and do not necessarily represent the views of the MOL.

2 This conception originated in a collaborative research project in Ontario, for which I serve as principal investigator, "Closing the ES Enforcement Gap: Improving Protections for People in Precarious Jobs," involving participants from university and community sectors.

3 The data cited below draw on findings reported in several studies emanating from "Closing the ES Enforcement Gap" in which I participated as lead or

co-author. I refer to select findings: my aim in this contribution is to demonstrate *how* a feminist political economy approach can inform analyses of the ES enforcement gap, as well as to make visible how this lens shaped the original research design for studying the day-to-day application of ES and helped make sense of early findings, rather than to offer a comprehensive empirical analysis.

4 Farm employees are employees employed on a farm whose employment is directly related to the primary production of eggs, milk, grain, seeds, fruit, vegetables (including mushrooms), maple products, honey, tobacco, herbs, pigs, cattle, sheep, goats, poultry, deer, elk, ratites, bison, rabbits, game birds, wild boar, and cultured fish (i.e., they do not include employees engaged in harvesting and Horse Breeding and Boarding).

5 As explained further by the Women's Bureau of Ontario (1976 as cited by Vosko et al. forthcoming): "the fact that the majority of domestic workers are women has also influenced their status … employers have often undervalued the domestic work performed since it falls into the realm of traditional women's work which is commonly done by family members without pay."

6 In 2014, Ontario announced a PSW Wage Enhancement Initiative to increase the minimum wage for personal support workers in the publicly funded home and community-care sector by $4.00 over three years, raising it from $12.50 in 2014 to $16.50 by 2016 (Ontario 2014). Despite such increases in hourly wages, many homecare workers still earn wages below two-thirds of the median hourly wage for full-time employees (Vosko et al. forthcoming).

7 Indeed, in this period, fear was the most commonly cited reason claimants offered for not contacting their employers. More than two out of every five claimants who did not contact their employer indicated that they were afraid to do so. This fear was particularly pronounced amongst claimants who were still working for their employer at the time that they filed a claim. Among this group, more than 65 per cent of those who did not contact their employer indicated that they did not do so because they were afraid (Vosko, Noack, and Tucker 2016, 23).

3

The Political Economy of Belonging: The Differences that Canadian Citizenship and Immigration Policies Make

Nandita Sharma

In preparation for writing this chapter, I looked through my well-worn copy of Wallace Clement and Glen Williams' 1989 edited volume, *The New Canadian Political Economy*. Upon re-reading their introduction, wherein they boldly say that "exploitation and struggle are the hallmarks of life in Canada," I felt the same sense of relief I had back when I was an undergraduate student. The sense of relief came from feeling *heard*. Some twenty years before beginning university, I had moved from India to Canada with some small part of my family (all the Canadian state would permit). It was 1969 and I was five. My father was admitted to Canada through its new Immigration Points System because he was a mechanical engineer and capital needed workers like him. Upon arrival, our lives were re-organized through the exploitation of my parent's (and soon enough, my brother's and my) labour and the struggles we had to wage just to be seen as human. My father's engineering degree was not accredited, my mother's racialized/gendered labour market status as an "immigrant women" landed her a succession of "3D" jobs – dirty, dangerous, and demeaning – and every day, someone, from somewhere, shrieked "Paki go home" at us. Canada was indeed a place of exploitation and struggle.

Seeing that stated in print, and in a text used in a university classroom, made a difference to me. Reading the articles on the political economy of labour, the political economy of gender, the political economy of colonialism, and the political economy of racism reinforced the lessons I had learned in the Canadian Farmworkers Union and the British

Columbia Organization to Fight Racism, which I supported. Most of all, having lived almost my entire life in the then-working class, east-side neighbourhood in Vancouver, the essays in *The New Political Economy* connected the lessons I learned from my father, a life-long anti-imperialist, to the specific character of how capitalism was *done* in Canada. Alongside Frances Abele's and Daiva Stasiulis' article, "Canada as a 'White Settler Colony': What about Natives and Immigrants?" I found Roxana Ng's article, "Sexism, Racism and Canadian Nationalism" in the Society for Socialist Studies' classic text, *Race, Class, Gender: Bonds and Barriers* published the same year as *The New Canadian Political Economy*. I also found Himani Bannerji and Dionne Brand.

And I also re-discovered a Marxism that anti-racist feminists had "stretched" to encompass the integrally related processes of exploitation and *oppression*. I felt a great sense of excitement. Our oppression as non-Whites in Canada was deeply connected to our subordinated positioning in its nationalized labour market. Canada's globally operative policies of selectively admitting immigrants from the Third World while fostering a sharply honed idea that we were "disrupting" – if not "destroying" – it, was part of how the Canadian labour market was made more competitive for capital investors. I thus took to heart what Clement and Williams wrote in 1989 (7): "political economy at its strongest has focused on processes whereby social change is located in the historical interaction of the economic, political, cultural, and ideological moments of social life, with the dynamic rooted in socio-economic conflict." For my PhD dissertation, completed under Roxana Ng's supervision, I studied the disjuncture between the official *discourse* of "being Canadian" – "lovers and defenders of freedom," "hard work paying off," etcetera – and the *reality* of Canada's ever-growing "temporary" and "foreign" labour force of "migrant workers" working on farms, in houses, factories, hotels, fast-food chains, and retail stores in Canada. I wondered how it was that they could be seen as a "foreign workforce." In my study of how "migrant workers" were *produced* by the dual processes of Canada's immigration policies and the culture of racism in Canada, I took seriously the post-structuralist insight that representational practices did not float above or below the exploitation of our labour power but right *through* the heart of the process.

However, I had to challenge – and reject – some of the assumptions deeply embedded in Canadian political economy, when trying to locate "migrant workers" in Canada and as a significant part of the labour force available to employers in Canada. First and foremost, I had to reject its methodological nationalism (Wimmer and Glick Schiller 2002). To best understand the work done by Canadian citizenship and immigration policies, I found it crucial *not* to take the nation-state as the unit of analysis from which an inquiry of capitalist society begins. Nor could I take on board the nationalism evidently dominant in the Left in Canada, a nationalism that argued for making the Canadian state "more progressive" through strategic interventions that would contest the exclusionary politics of immigration. I did not reject assisting people to become Canadian permanent residents or citizens (something required to gain access to the plethora of rights and entitlements reserved for those so categorized); but I did not – and do not – see the obtainment of Canadian citizenship as the horizon of our political possibility. If it was not already so, the very existence of a workforce of "temporary foreign migrant workers" – as well as all other "immigrant workers" in Canada – makes it evident that the political economy of capitalism, of sexism, of racism, of colonialism, does not begin nor does it end in the territories controlled by the Canadian nation-state.

Instead of living in a "national society," we live in a society that is global in scale and in scope. Starting with the colonization of what is now "Canada" by the British and French imperial-states, the very existence of the Canadian nation-state is a product of global processes, including the White Canadian nationalism that transformed Canadian territory from a colony of the British Empire to a nation-state. Moreover, the Canadian nation-state is part of not only the governance but the governmentality of the global capitalist system. Despite nationalist rhetoric, global flows did not end with the formation of the Canadian nation-state. Such flows were directed and regulated by it, always for the ultimate advantage of one or another segment of the class that owned and controlled capital. Indeed, the nation-state, as Benedict Anderson (1991) long ago pointed out, represents a particular style of ruling – one that crucially depends on differentiated categories of national belonging and not-belonging. State categories ranging from "Indian" to "Canadian citizen" to "immigrant" to "temporary foreign worker" to "illegal" are embodiments of the "accumulation of differences" that Silvia Federici (2004, 63–4) has shown always accompanies the accumulation of capital. These state-constructed categories operate as both labour market categories and ontological categories of being "human" in today's world. In short, they are representational practices carrying great material force.

Citizenship and immigration policies of nation-states provide an important entry point to this understanding because they lay bare the fact the "national societies" (and nationalized labour markets) that regard the regulation, restriction, exclusion, and even expulsion of "noncitizens" as a virtue by many "citizens" are carved out artificially of not only our shared planet, but also the global capitalist system that binds us all to one another. Citizenship and immigration policies are best treated as a key interface between a globally operative set of capitalist social relations and the regulatory work of the equally global system of nation-states.

With the biopolitical production of "national citizens" and their quintessential others – "migrants" – nation-states not only create a specific category of labour power – "migrant workers" – they also cheapen the price that employers have to pay for it. The nationalism that normalizes the Canadian state to so many, including on much of the Left, does the important political work of organizing the disorganization of the direct producers of wealth. From the start, Canadian nationalism has been the mechanism through which racism and sexism have been made "common sense" in Canada. Racism and sexism have always been about cheapening the price of some people's labour; but they have also been about producing political adherence to the nation-state by those who imagine themselves as the "real Canadians." Rejecting methodological nationalism thus allows us to see that the making of labour markets as national labour markets is a response by power against the struggles of the workers of the world. The making and the hegemonic normalization (and reification) of racialized and sexualized/gendered differences has been – and remains – central to the absence of a formidable radical Left in Canada.

Having said that, the importance of nationalism (and therefore racism and sexism) extends far beyond seeing how it organizes discrimination, a process that can be overcome by extending civil rights, i.e., the rights of "citizens." Instead, it has been shown that the institution of citizenship is fundamentally incapable of meeting the demands for social justice made by those who find themselves categorized as "migrants," or as Bridget Anderson (2013) has shown, even the demands of those categorized as "citizens." National citizenship regimes extend "rights," it is true, but they do so in a nefarious way: the citizenship rights granted to some very much depend on the denial of such rights to most others. No "nation" – and no nation-state – encompasses all the world's people – and none want to. Yet at the same time no nation-state in the world exists without the presence of people said to be "foreigners" there. This process of limiting the "imagined" political community of the "nation" is precisely one of the particularities of nation-states (Anderson 1991).

The creation of "foreigners" that is central to every national citizenship regime ensures competition throughout the system as well as the legitimacy for the inequalities that result. National citizenship regimes also contain workers in nationalized labour markets and naturalize their separation from workers in other national containers. This has not always been the case, however. While human mobility into and out of what we now call "Canada" has been a part of its history long before French or British imperialism, the movement of people to Canada in response to the violent imposition of capitalist social relations in England, Ireland, and, as capitalism spread, other European states – as well as, soon enough, other European colonies too – was crucial to the profitability of Canada as a colony. Not all these movements were movements of workers, of course. Canada was founded as a French and a British colony after all. Nascent entrepreneurs moved too, as did the colonial officials of the British imperial-state.

The organization of these disparate groups into a single "White Settler" colony under the rule of an imperial-state was reliant on the politics of separation. Such politics have, of course, been crucial to how capitalism has been done from its start in the English countryside in the sixteenth century (Linebaugh and Rediker 2000; Wood 2002; Federici 2004). And it was no less violent when it was mobilized in the colony of Canada. Here, people who had made a life for themselves prior to the arrival of the French or British empires were dispossessed of their land, displaced from their social, political, economic, and cultural systems, and those who survived were made subordinate in every imaginable way to imperial rulers. They were re-named, re-located, and brought into capitalist social relations and placed in the negative, subordinated half of the binary of European colonizer/colonized Native.

The proliferation of state-categories were crucial for the separation and containment of exploited and oppressed people who were racialized as either "European" (later "White"), "Indian," "Eskimo," "Negro," or "Asian." These forms of state-identities were added to the earlier categories, such as vagabond, idiot, and whore in an ever-expanding grid of hierarchically organized value and worth in and out of the paid labour market. Making Whiteness a superordinate value worked to ensure that Whites would be separated from other direct producers. Rulers represented Whitened workers as the co-beneficiaries of Empire and, later, of Canadian nationhood. So much so that the production of White, male, and quintessentially "Canadian" workers as a "high wage work force" became seen as an essential(ized) aspect of a specifically

"Canadian" political economy, something that certain political economists have talked about far too uncritically (Panitch 1981). The separation was not only between those categorized as White or as non-White.
Instead, with the fine-tuning of not-Whiteness, "Natives" were separated
from "non-Natives" (even as these "non-Natives" were often co-imperial
subjects of, especially, the British Empire). Such a separation would
come back to haunt politics as the separation between "the Indigenous"
and "immigrants" came to the fore from the late 1980s onward (see
Sharma and Wright, 2009, also see Smith in this volume for a slightly
different analysis that does not fully deconstruct the state category of
"native" or "Indigenous").

Crucially, immigration policies were not utilized to enforce these
hierarchies, however, until the late nineteenth- and early twentieth-
centuries. Until this time, there were no regulations and restrictions
governing entry to the British White Dominion of Canada. Indeed, the
formulation of immigration restrictions was *central* to the creation of a
nationally sovereign Canadian state (Mongia 1999). Looking at this
history will, I think, illuminate the disjuncture that exists between the
global scale of society that we actually inhabit and the national spaces
in which rights are recognized and differentially allocated in the global
market for labour power.

I will begin by historicizing Canada's first immigration restrictions and
regulations in the early twentieth century to de-naturalize the link between
state sovereignty and border controls and to challenge the nation-state
centrism of much of Canadian political economy. I will continue with a
discussion of the significance of the massive shift that has taken place in
the kinds of immigration statuses allocated by the Canadian state since
the start of the period of neoliberalism in the late 1960s and early 1970s.
I will focus on the largest of all state-categories of "migrants" to Canada
– "temporary foreign workers" – to show how national borders exist not
only at the boundary between nation-states but also *within* "Canadian"
space and *within* the "Canadian" labour market. It is a nationalist sen-
sibility that allows for the oxymoron of a "foreign workforce" living and
labouring *in* Canada.

CANADIAN NATIONAL SOVEREIGNTY AGAINST "THE MIGRANT"

Immigration controls were not part of the recognized sovereign rights of
imperial states. Imperial states, unlike the nation-states that replaced

them, operated largely under what Radhika Mongia has usefully conceptualized as "logics of facilitation" in regards to human mobility (2019). Empires were generally uninterested in limiting the movement of people *into* their territories. Far from it: facilitating human movement into vast imperial territories was necessary for the profitability of imperial ventures. European imperial-states were wholly reliant on capturing people categorized as "natives," transporting enslaved people, mostly from Africa, pressing people into service, sentencing people to penal transport, and moving people largely out of Asia as "coolie" labourers working under contracts of indenture. Moving these people into and throughout imperial space – as well as enforcing their stasis once with a series of controls on their free mobility *out* of the Empire – were structural elements of European imperialism (Potts 1990, 204).

This imperial logic towards human mobility – informed by an imperialist logic of expropriation and exploitation – was challenged by those who wished to nationalize the sovereignty of imperial-states by carving out separate nation-states, which they would rule. Unlike imperial-states, nation-states operated under what Mongia (2018) terms the logics of constraint. Indeed, I would argue that we can date the nationalization of state sovereignties by their implementation of immigration controls. Their reliance on such controls for making the "nations" that legitimated their power, however, did not mean that nation-states were against people moving into their territories. Instead, immigration controls were used as significant ways to mark the limits to hegemonic ideas of national belonging. Indeed, it is no exaggeration to say that the implementation of immigration policies marked the creation of a separate, Canadian national sovereignty (Mongia 2007). The logics of constraint produced a new logic of expropriation and exploitation, one dependent on the identity of national citizen and, hence, the identity of "migrant."

Efforts to restrict entry into the British colony of Canada began in the late nineteenth and early twentieth centuries. Advocacy for such controls took place in the context of a growing racist clamour in the "White British Dominions."[1] Whiteness – first invented by imperial states and circulated throughout the Empire – had become the quintessential category of societal membership and its absence was used to justify efforts to regulate and restrict the mobility of those human beings negatively racialized as being "not White." On the west coast of British Columbia, this took place after the completion of the transcontinental railroad that extended the reach of the Canadian state. Those governed by Canada as "Indians" were not spared either. White workers demanded that these colonial "natives" be further removed from centres of waged activity through their placement on segregated "reservations." In each of the "self-governing" but not yet sovereign White Dominions, racism became central to creating and continually reinsuring the political legitimacy of a specifically Canadian state.

However, until 1914, the British imperial office in London insisted that the movement of co-British subjects not be regulated and restricted (other than "coolie" labourers, the first group to face restrictions on their free mobility within the Empire). From an imperial perspective, co-British subjects (who were not "coolies") were free to move within the Empire, of which Canada was still very much a part. The idea of a shared imperial space for all of its subjects was not only a part of the accumulation strategies of British imperialism, but also crucial to its governmentality. Formally, and despite clear hierarchal distinctions between subjects, each British subject was declared to equally have the right to move freely about the Empire.

However, in 1914, in a direct attempt to nationalize its sovereignty, the Canadian government denied entry to *non*-"coolies" from British India arriving on the west coast aboard the passenger ship the *Komagata Maru* (Mongia 2007). In the context of the Canadian government's ongoing efforts to manifest a "White Canada" policy, the entry of the ship's passengers was restricted in order that "society be defended," as Michel Foucault once put it. Canadian officials deemed the 376 passengers from British India as "undesirable" for inclusion as citizens of the "Canadian nation."[2] In doing so, they cited the Canadian government's 1910 *Immigration Act*, which had created a separate Canadian citizenship to distinguish those British subjects who were domiciled in Canada from those who were not.[3] Thus, in contrast to the imperial office's distinction between subjects and aliens, the Canadian government enacted a new distinction between "Canadian citizens" and "migrants." We live with that legacy to this day.

For the Canadian government, the issue was not the entry of persons per se. In the year prior to the arrival of the *Komagata Maru*, over 400,000 people had arrived in Canada, mostly from various points in Europe, including many non-British subjects (Ali 2013, 43).[4] "The people of Canada want to have a white country," Sir Wilfrid Laurier declared in Parliament in October of 1914 (Mongia 1999, 550).[5] The people aboard the *Komagata Maru* were co-British subjects, but what they were not was White, and it was this "lack" that defined them as ineligible to move to Canada. That Canada's first attempt to nationalize its sovereignty took place against co-British subjects marked an important shift in Canada's relationship with the British Empire.

The 1914 *Komagata Maru* incident was, of course, not the first effort by the Canadian government to restrict the entry of persons deemed "undesirable" for national membership. In 1885, the Canadian government had imposed a special "head tax" of $50 on all workers (not all people) from China in an effort to discourage their immigration (by 1903 the head tax was increased to $500). In 1908, at the insistence of the Canadian government, a "Gentleman's Agreement" was signed in 1908 between Imperial Japan and the British imperial office to limit the number of Japanese subjects allowed free movement to Canada. That same year Canadian officials, in ongoing efforts to bypass the demands of the British imperial office, passed an order-in-council – known as the "continuous journey" regulation – that aimed at restricting immigration from British India.

However, none of these measures challenged the imperial distribution of sovereignty over Canada. Instead, each of these measures was an indirect effort to restrict the entry of various negatively racialized people. Lacking a separate sovereignty, Canada was unable to explicitly restrict the entry of Chinese or Japanese subjects, or the entry of co-British subjects from British India. Each of these measures was deliberately unspecific about both its intent and effect. This obfuscation was necessary if such restrictions were to be approved by the British imperial office. London was especially concerned with not offending the large numbers of "natives" within its imperial army, many of them from British India.

The *Komagata Maru* incident of 1914 was important, therefore, not because it was a continuation of efforts by Canada to define its "nation" through racist immigration policies, but because it was a break in Canadian government compliance with British imperial concerns. While the ostensible legal rationale was that its passengers had violated the "continuous journey" stipulation, the BC Court of Appeal, in a unanimous ruling against Munshi Singh, one of the passengers, went further. It asserted that "as a self-governing dominion in the British Empire ... Canada had the right to determine who got in" (quoted in Kazimi 2012, 7).

It was in the aftermath of the *Komagata Maru* incident and in the political context of the start of the First World War that the British imperial office conceded that the White Dominions could legally distinguish between British subjects with regard to their entry into Dominion territories. The 1914 *British Nationality and Status of Aliens Act* accepted that Dominion legislatures and governments should not be prevented "from treating differently different classes of British subjects" (*British Nationality and Status of Aliens Act* 1914, 26 (1) cited in Anderson 2013, 38). The expulsion of the co-British subjects from British India who arrived in Canada on the *Komagata Maru* thus marked the start of a distinct Canadian national sovereignty and the end of a broader definition of imperial subjecthood (Mongia 1999). Less than ten years later, in 1923, a year after Canadian Prime Minister Mackenzie King asserted that the Canadian Parliament would no longer follow the British imperial government's decisions in foreign affairs, the Canadian government passed the 1923 *Chinese Immigration Act* banning outright the entry of persons from China. Significantly, it was only when the Canadian state asserted a distinct national sovereignty that it could pass an act of exclusion, one that explicitly, instead of implicitly, denied entry to a negatively racialized group.[6]

Canada's entry into the then quite small club of nation-states was part of a broader trend towards the nationalization of numerous state sovereignties in the years between the two world wars. Recall that after the First World War, several empires – the German, Austro-Hungarian and Ottoman Empires – had collapsed and their territories were either subsumed into other imperial states (especially by the British) or had been carved into new nation-states. Eric Hobsbawm characterized this interwar period as an era in which the "national economy" emerged. Karl Polanyi (1994) saw this nationalization of "economies" and "cultures" as a crucial part of a "great transformation." Polanyi (1944, 202) argued that during this time "protectionism everywhere was producing the hard shell of the emerging unit of social life ... The new crustacean type of nation expressed its identity through national token currencies safeguarded by a type of sovereignty more jealous and absolute than anything known before." Crucial to the nationalization of state sovereignties during the "fragile peace" of the inter-war years was the growth of a paper trail of national identification documents. These were crucial to the implementation of national border controls against free human mobility. Some of these measures, particularly those that made possession of passports and other state-issued identification cards mandatory, provided the framework to record, monitor, and restrict people's movement across state borders, but also to regulate the existence and the movement of "foreigners" within states. Indeed, during the interwar period, the "jealousy" of nationalized sovereignties was increasingly felt within nation-states. It is not a coincidence that it was in this context of making a "Canadian nation" that the forced sterilization of impoverished people, women categorized as

Native, and people incarcerated in psychiatric institutions began in Canada in 1928.

With the start of the Second World War, as the militaries of both imperial- and nation-states wantonly crisscrossed the globe, regulations and restrictions on people's movements, both within states and across state borders, intensified, and so did the intensification of racist criteria for "national belonging." This history is well known. Canada constructed prison camps for "enemy aliens," including the internment of over 22,000 "Japanese" people (14,000 of whom were in fact British subjects). Canada also contributed to the Holocaust with its "one is too many" guide to the entrance of Jewish people trying to flee Nazi Germany (Abella and Troper 1998).

The nationalization of state sovereignty altered fundamentally the way capitalism was done. The nationalist transformation of "classes into masses," which Hannah Arendt (1951) famously discussed, worked to replace whatever class consciousness might have existed (and it certainly did in many quarters) – and hence class struggle – with a national consciousness and "national" struggles. Nationalism obfuscated not only the gross inequalities within any said "nation," but also the similarities that exist across national divides. Most significantly, I would argue, nation-states, unlike imperial states, were – and remain – far more subject to penetration by more powerful states than were imperial territories whose territories would be defended by the entire might of imperial-states.

The creation of a world of nation-states is thus the source of the hegemony of the United States. It was able to use its financial and military power during the Second World War to extract a promise from Winston Churchill that imperial monopolies over British colonies would come to an end. It is not for nothing that the United States insisted that the right of "national self-determination" was inserted into the founding Charter of the United Nations. The hegemony of nationalism and of the nation form of state power is also the source of the infamous "uneven development" or "neo-colonialism" much talked about in the post-Second World War period of postcolonialism. While governing under the fantasy of "national sovereignty" – and certainly organizing their "societies" as "national," mainly through policies that distinguish between "citizens" and "migrants" – no nation-state is impervious to the machinations of other nation-states. The world of nation-states is no less immune to the actual practices of colonization – expropriation, exploitation, and denigration of the colonized – than European empires were in the age of imperialism.

Just as each nation-state exists in a *world* of nation-states, similarly nationalism posits distinct and discrete spaces for "national subjects" and "foreigners," and both always already exist in the *same* space. This fact is nowhere more evident in Canada than in its "temporary foreign workers program" or, officially, the Non-Immigrant Employment Authorization Program (NIEAP). This program – which brings in the largest number of people in any category of (im)migration to Canada – also reveals the wholly ideological character of immigration controls, which is this: such controls do not work only to restrict the entry of people (although they also do this with ever more murderous effect). Instead, the main work of immigration controls is to produce "(im) migrant workers" who can be restricted in their enjoyment of the rights and entitlements reserved for those constituted as the state's "citizens." Canada's temporary foreign workers program also reveals just how productive anti-immigrant politics is for capital.

Contrary to much journalism on the subject, my past research shows that starting in 1976, the majority of all people migrating to Canada with a stated intent to enter the paid labour force were given the status of "temporary foreign worker" (53 per cent or 69,368 people) (Sharma 2006).[7] By 2004, this had jumped both proportionately as well as numerically so that 65 per cent (228,677) were given the status of "temporary foreign worker" while only 35 per cent (124,829) came with the rights of permanent residency. By 2008 the number of individuals entering as "temporary foreign workers" surpassed 300,000 (NOII 2015, 11). Since the mid-1970s, Canada has had a permanent and expanding system of "temporary foreign worker" recruitment. Indeed, the precarity of people classified as such has been intensified (see Vosko in this volume). In 2011, Canada announced the "four in and four out" rule, which bars people from renewing their work permits after their fourth year of work in Canada. It is not a coincidence that this rule was passed just when there was an increased effort to organize and even unionize temporary foreign workers, especially those in the agricultural sector – by Justicia for Migrant Workers[8] and the United Food and Commercial Workers Union (UFCW).

The NIEAP also demonstrates the central importance of the politics of representation in the political economy of capitalism. Starting in 1973, over the period when the Canadian state considerably expanded both the scope and the scale of its temporary foreign workers programs, official discourse has consistently pointed to immigration as a serious problem for "Canadians" (Sharma 2006, chapter 4). Anti-immigrant discourse,

far from excluding new (im)migrants coming to Canada, has enabled
national states to re-organize their nationalized labour markets to *include*
a group of temporary foreign workers who are made vulnerable to
employers' demands through their subordinated status as "temporary,"
as "foreigners," and as legally enforced unfree workers. The simultaneous
presence of anti-immigration discourses and increases in the number of
people entering Canada as non-citizens without permanent, full status
is thus not at all contradictory, but rather very much part of the nationalist logics of capital accumulation.

Such nationalist logics, while rhetorically deployed in the defense of
the "White working class" (for whom anti-immigration politics are enormously popular), work to increase competition within nationalized labour
markets through a process of "differential inclusion" of people into
Canada. In the current historical juncture, when people are moving across
state territories at historically unprecedented levels,[9] nationalism, with
its legitimization of the subordination of those classified as foreigners, is
a motor force for neoliberal capitalist globalization. While legally organized racism (discrimination against negatively racialized people) or
sexism has mostly been defined as being against the "values" of "multi-
cultural" and "liberal" states, such as Canada, nationalism continues to
provide a legal avenue for the making of sharp distinctions amongst us.
This is a crucial aspect of the work that nation-states do for capital. And
it is evident in the very structure of the NIEAP: expanded in the early
1970s, this program of recruiting unfree "foreign" workers, while presented as a protection for citizen-workers, is mostly a protection for
capital and for employers, each of which is insistent that the state facilitate
the creation of a group of "migrant workers" who can be legally and
socially denied the rights and entitlements won by workers with Canadian
citizenship (and permanent resident status) a few decades earlier. The
classic politics of "define and rule," as Mahmood Mamdani cogently
refers to it in an earlier era of imperialism, was no less helpful for this
late state of capitalist development (i.e., neoliberalism) than it was when
Canada was formed. But, it did not – and does not – have to be this way.
Workers of the world have united in the past and continue to do so
against all odds.

One very important challenge to the right of national states to accord
differential citizenship and (im)migration statuses to persons is the emergence of a politics of No Borders. Such a politics coalesces around a
struggle against the current international system of nation-states and its
denial of free movement. An essential understanding of such a politics is

that the border control practices of national states are not only a *reflection* of people's unequal rights (e.g., citizens are not generally denied entry into nation-states while non-citizens are) but are also *productive* of this inequality. By demanding that every person have the self-activated freedom to move, the concomitant freedoms to stay (i.e., not be displaced) and to return, No Borders theorists/activists have re-politicized the very legitimacy of (im)migration restrictions and, hence, nation-states.

As Anderson, Wright, and I (2011) discussed in our article "Why No Borders?," a politics of No Borders goes beyond the nationalist approach, which demands "more numbers" of "immigrants" or "more rights" for those so classified (e.g., when labour unions occasionally realize the importance of showing solidarity with (im)migrant workers, including at times the illegalized and those on temporary labour contracts). While this marks a real step forward in practical politics, unions (especially in the "rich world") have not given up on their nation-state-centrism and their advocacy of restrictive border controls. This is because they have not challenged borders and the institution of national citizenship itself. Thereby, while unions are sometimes willing to accept some small groups of (im)migrants into the nation-state, most people wanting or trying to move to Canada continue to be seen as a threat to labour solidarity.

In a related move, sometimes in alliance with organized labour or para-labour formations and sometimes not, some "immigrant rights" movements have focused on "fixing" the immigration system, on seeking legal and legislative reforms, on making it more "fair and just." Still other projects have focused primarily on the many problems with the post-Second World War international refugee regime, while also often reinforcing unsustainable divisions among various categories of migrants ("refugees," "illegals," "economic migrants," and so on). In the Canadian case, demands for legalization (or regularization) of undocumented and precarious-status workers (including failed refugee claimants) have featured prominently (see Wood in this volume). State-led and controlled regularization programs, often centred on recognizing a person's contributions to a workplace, have typically been tied to further tightening of the borders (and therefore have served to further reproduce states of illegality). Such movements, however, often also reproduce some of the same limits around who counts as a worker. In particular, they are unable to encompass gendered unpaid reproductive and domestic labour, not to mention paid sexual labour.

Thus, at the same time as acknowledging the importance of labour organizing within a migrant justice context, we must not forget the production of gender, sexualities, families, and households, as well as the production of labour relations, that is a function and consequence of borders. Moreover, we must keep in mind another border: that between the "public" and the "private," a central divide within the institution of citizenship. That divide simultaneously devalues and genders labour and means that only certain types of work are regarded as work, as much rich feminist scholarship on social reproduction, the welfare state, the institution of wage labour, and citizenship and immigration has elucidated. Most problematically, the divide between "national citizen" and "foreign non-citizen" is retained.

Yet despite such politics, the fact is that no set of border controls has ever worked to fully contain people's desire and need to move. In this sense, it can be argued that an everyday practice of refusing the border has existed as long as borders have. A contemporary politics for No Borders can, nonetheless, be said to have emerged in the mid-1990s. It is marked by the re-politicization of the very legitimacy of (im)migration restrictions and the distinctions made between "national" or even "regional" or "continental" (e.g., "European") subjects and their foreign-ers. What distinguishes a No Borders politics from other immigrant-rights approaches is their refusal to settle for "fairer" immigration laws (higher numbers, legal statuses, and so on). The rejection of borders and the differences they make among people (as labourers and lovers, as comrades and classmates, etc.) comes from a shift in standpoint from one centred on citizens and "their" organizations or "their" state to one that begins from the standpoint of migrants themselves. The initial organizations of a movement for No Borders were led by migrants who insisted that they were legitimate political actors within national polities and did not want or need citizens' groups to act as a cover for their activities. Such acts of autonomy brought back to people's attention that, in the struggle for liberty, freedom, democracy, livelihoods, and more, one needed to act with, and not against, those defined as (im)migrants and foreigners.

Far from reaffirming the significance of citizenship, those in the No Borders movement not only call into question the legitimacy of the global system of national states itself, but with it the related global system of capitalism (Balibar 2000; Anderson, Sharma, and Wright 2009). The No Borders movement thus redefines equality by positing it as a relationship between co-members of a global society and not one between "citizens." The related rights to move, stay, and return are seen as necessary to the creation of this equality. Such rights are seen as operational only at a global scale and against the "nation."

By way of conclusion, I would argue that the work to be done by the *new*, new Canadian political economy is to go against "Canada" and towards our fellow workers. I argue that a politics of No Borders affords us many new opportunities for praxis; but this requires us to listen to the theorizing of those who reject borders and the entire apparatus of nation-states, global capitalism, and bounded imaginations that give them support. To not do so is, in fact, to acquiesce to the enormous and always hierarchical differences organized through the institutions and relationships made by borders, nation-states, and capital, differences often further ensconced by current social movements that advance the rights of only one or another particular state category of persons, be they "citizens," "immigrants," "refugees," or others. No Borders movements offer us a "line of flight" away from the struggle of differentiated rights and towards the recognition of a common right of movement, livelihood, and full and equal societal membership for all.

NOTES

1 The "White Dominions" were those British colonies that had been organized as "White settler colonies." They formed a union of formerly separate British colonies (in Canada, for instance: Upper Canada, Lower Canada, the West, and so on) and secured a certain amount of autonomy and "responsible government" for themselves, though sovereignty still rested in the British Crown headquartered in London. They had separate governments, civil service, treasury, and armed forces. Canada became the first "White Dominion" in 1867 (with the passing of the UK Parliament's *British North America Act*). Australia became a "White Dominion" in 1900, followed by South Africa in 1909, and New Zealand in 1907. See Evans et al. 2003.

2 A 1902 Royal Commission to Investigate Chinese and Japanese Immigration into British Columbia had earlier declared that all "Asians" were "unfit for full citizenship ... obnoxious to a free community and dangerous to the state" (Canada *Archival reference no.* R1082-0-0-E).

3 Canada's *Immigration Act* of 1910 designated as Canadian citizens those British subjects who were born, naturalized, or domiciled in Canada. It declared that all other British subjects required permission to land. Later, a separate status of "Canadian national" was created under the *Canadian Nationals Act* of 1921. A Canadian national was a person who was defined as being a Canadian citizen by the 1910 act, the wives (but not husbands), and any children (but only those fathered by a Canadian national) who had not yet landed in Canada.

4 Ali Kazimi, *Undesirables: White Canada and the Komagata Maru, An Illustrated History* (Vancouver, Toronto, Berkeley: Douglas and McIntyre, 2012), 43.

5 "Official Report of a Debate in the Canadian House of Commons on Asiatic Immigration," *Proceedings A*, October 1914, no. 1, as cited in Mongia, 1999.

6 The 1867 *British North America* (BNA) *Act*, which created the "White Dominion" of Canada, still viewed Canada as a colony of the British empire. The BNA act was subject to section 2 of the 1865 *British Colonial Laws Validity Act* (*An Act to remove Doubts as to the Validity of Colonial Laws*, 28 and 29 Victoria, c. 63) that unequivocally stated that no colonial (Canadian) law could supersede a British Imperial statute. It was in 1931 when the British Parliament enacted the Statute of Westminster that removed the Canadian government from the *Colonial Laws Validity Act*. Yet, even then Canada was not fully sovereign, for it could not amend the BNA act that brought it into being. It was not until the 1982 *Constitution Act* that the "supreme law" in Canada would be those that met the criteria established by a separate Canadian constitution.

7 Only 47 per cent (61,461 persons) were given the rights of permanent residency.

8 For more information on Justicia for Migrant Workers, see: http://www.justicia4migrantworkers.org/. For more information on the UFCW's work with "migrant workers" in Canada, see http://www.ufcw.org/?s=migrant+workers+in+canada&x=0&y=0.

9 The United Nations estimates that in 2013 there were 232 million international migrants. See: http://esa.un.org/unmigration/documents/world migration/2013/Full_Document_final.pdf#page=7 (Accessed 18 January 2016).

PART TWO

Regions and Resources

4

Staples Dependence Renewed and Betrayed: Canada's Twenty-First Century Boom and Bust

Jim Stanford

INTRODUCTION: CANADA'S STRUCTURAL U-TURN

The dramatic expansion of petroleum extraction (and, to a lesser extent, other minerals) after the turn of the century sparked a fundamental structural transformation of Canada's economy. Booming investment in new petroleum projects in northern Alberta was the most important driver of this growth. There were many seemingly positive economic and fiscal effects from the resource upswing: including new jobs, incomes, exports, and tax revenues. But many challenges and risks were also experienced as a result of the mostly unbridled expansion of resource extraction: macroeconomic, fiscal, environmental, and geopolitical.

The surge in extractive industries, beginning early in the 2000s, was sparked by a global upsurge in prices for energy, minerals, and other commodities. This upsurge in turn reflected the impact of China's rapid industrialization on global demand for basic materials – as well as, in the case of energy, continued geopolitical risks arising in the Middle East. Gung-ho analysts confidently declared that this latest upswing in the commodities roller coaster reflected some new and lasting structural forces: a so-called "super-cycle" in which endless Chinese growth and depleting reserves would inevitably push prices higher and higher. (Remember, every speculative bubble – whether dot-com stocks in the 1990s, US housing securities in the mid-2000s, or even Dutch tulip bulbs in the 1630s – always finds willing economists to ratify the exuberance on the grounds of supposedly "real" or rational economic factors.) Canadian policy makers, for the most part, also rushed to endorse this significant structural swing in the national economy. The resource-celebrating consensus culminated with the election of the Harper Conservative government in early 2006, signifying a national endorsement of the rush into extraction, and a westward shift in the loci of both economic and political power in Canada. In one of his first major international speeches (prior to a G8 summit meeting in St Petersburg in summer 2006), Harper declared Canada to be a new "energy superpower." And his government would put major emphasis in coming years on facilitating and accelerating the energy boom: including streamlining or eliminating regulatory barriers to new extraction projects, trying (without success) to build new export pipelines, liberalizing foreign investment inflows into resource industries, and reducing business taxes.

Of course, as a resource-rich and relatively sparsely populated country, Canada (since being colonized by European settlers, at any rate) has always depended on resource extraction and export as a leading force in economic development. The first "staples" export consisted of timber harvested and exported back to Iceland by Viking settlers at L'Anse aux Meadows. Successive waves of resource development, always oriented toward export markets, motivated parallel episodes of settlement, transportation development, infrastructure, and governance. Fish, furs, timber, wheat, minerals, and now petroleum were the industries that led the way through these successive chapters of Canadian economic history.

Staples-driven accumulation and development always reflected differing regional features and impacts (as explored by Mills and Tufts in this volume). Not surprisingly, the specific regional characteristics of each staple and its associated infrastructure shaped its ultimate economic, social, and environmental impacts. Similarly, successive staples cycles had differential gendered and racialized impacts, depending on the nature of the product and the production process, the organization of both paid and unpaid work in staples-dependent communities (see for example, Neis and Williams 1997; Cohen 2007; Mills 2012), and the demographic, political, and legal status of Indigenous populations in staples-producing regions (Notzke 1994; Abele and Stasiulus 1989; Markey et al. 2000). Of course, staples-led accumulation also carried particular implications for class relations and struggles; the position of working people in staples industries implied a unique combination of potential power (given the often concentrated nature of production) and vulnerability (in light of the geographical isolation of many resource communities, providing employers additional opportunities to exert control over their workforces). Union organizing and struggles in resource industries and resource communities have thus played a central role in the history of the Canadian labour movement.

Two important dimensions of staples-driven development also help to explain their influence on Canada's economic, political, and social trajectory. First, all waves of staples expansion were oriented fundamentally toward export markets, and hence imparted a globalized dimension to Canada's economic development from the beginning. This global dimension is reflected not only in the physical sale of staples commodities into foreign markets (with resulting requirements for export infrastructure, transportation systems, and trade arrangements). It is also evident in the important role played by foreign capital in the development of all staples industries, the strong links between foreign capital and domestic business elites, and the extent to which this globalized orientation shaped the whole direction of politics and policy development. From the first shipments of raw lumber from Newfoundland back to Iceland at the beginning of the second millennium, to the obsession with building new bitumen export pipelines in the modern era, globalization has always centrally shaped the corresponding development of Canadian staples industries. The evolution of globalization in the neoliberal era, to incorporate more far-reaching aspects and dimensions than just facilitating international trade (such as more general requirements and restrictions on government policy governing business ownership, regulation, intellectual property, and more), means that this global influence has become even more far-reaching as Canada continues down its staples-dependent path.

Secondly, the influence of financial capital is also critical in understanding the nature of Canada's staples-driven political economy. In contrast to resource-exporting industries, in which foreign-owned capital has always been crucial, the financial sector in Canada has been traditionally dominated by Canadian investors and companies. This strong domestic financial capacity dates back to before Confederation, and has been reinforced by interventionist and protectionist measures to ensure the viability and profitability of domestic financial firms.[1] Here, too, the ascendance of financialization means that the influence of the (largely Canadian-owned) financial sector on staples developments has also become more far-reaching and multidimensional. The financial sector is not just a source of funds to underwrite real capital investments. It now strongly influences the structure of resource business models (emphasizing more elaborate and financialized ownership and management structures), enforces a focus on short-term financial gains as the top priority of business management, and serves as a convenient mechanism for extracting surplus from resource operations. And more often in the current era, the main emphasis of corporate managers is to return cash flow generated from operations back to financial investors through dividend payouts, share buybacks, capital gains, and other streams, rather than reinvesting that surplus in expanded real activity.[2] Like the more aggressive and intrusive influence of globalization, the rise of financialized business models and pressures under neoliberalism has also influenced how modern staples projects and industries in turn shape the overall development of Canada's economy and society.

The important, multi-dimensional influence of resource industries on the economic, social, and political development of Canada is a historical fact. But Canadians have been traditionally concerned, and rightly so, with the potential downsides of this resource dependence. Historians, economists, and political economists (led by W.A. Mackintosh 1967; Harold Innis 1930/1977; and Mel Watkins 1963[3]) described how each successive wave of staples-led development shaped the resulting pattern of economic, political, and social development – and not always for the better. They warned that Canada could become caught in a "staples trap," in which the dominance of a particular form of resource extraction and export undermined the country's capacity to develop a full-fledged, diversified economy.[4] The trajectory of staples dependence is always tied closely to political-economic structures and fissures within Canada, including a leading role for incoming foreign direct investment, and the vested interests of domestic elites (focused especially in the resource and finance sectors) who dream of profiting from the next great staples cycle. In modern times, these traditional concerns with resource dependence have been supplemented by environmental concerns about the non-sustainability of an economy rooted in extraction (Haley 2011).

Throughout the upswing of the post-2000 energy boom, there remained ample reason for Canadians to be concerned with the risks and costs associated with renewed staples dependence. These include:

- A stunted role in world trade: Canada became pigeonholed as a supplier of raw resources to other countries, to the detriment of other value-added activities (like manufacturing and tradable services).
- Greater regional and national exposure to the inevitable ups and downs of resource prices and profits.
- Poor innovation and productivity performance associated with the growing concentration of economic activity in resource extraction, and the corresponding decline of manufacturing.

- Massive costs, usually subsidized by government,[5] of the economic infrastructure required for resource extraction and export (including railways, ports, and pipelines). This expensive infrastructure becomes a sunk cost that in turn compels even faster extraction and export of resources to amortize the required large investments.
- An unbalanced political culture, in which super-profitable resource companies exert disproportionate influence over economic and social policy.
- Growing influence of foreign companies, which have invested huge amounts of capital in resource extraction and export and wield tremendous influence as a result.
- The environmental consequences (both local and global) of irresponsible management of non-renewable resources. Chief among these concerns today, of course, is the threat of global climate change.

However, even as Canadians continued to debate the relative merits and demerits of renewed resource dependence, the global commodities party ended as quickly as it began. Commodity prices (like other financial variables) had slumped dramatically, but temporarily, during the 2008–09 world financial crisis and recession. A more lasting downturn in world prices for oil, most minerals, and other staple commodities, however, began in 2014 – and proved more consequential to the future trajectory of resource-based industries. Oil tumbled by more than half (from $100 USD per barrel to less than $40) within months, followed by a slow and unsteady recovery. Prices realized for Canadian oil production are even lower, due to a price discount of $15 per barrel or more that is applied against heavier Canadian crude varieties in the over-supplied US mid-continental regional market (which is the destination for most Canadian production). The price downturn, layered on top of an already sluggish macroeconomic environment, had painful effects for a national economy that was once again unduly dependent on leadership from the resource sector. Canada slipped into a shallow, short recession in 2015, led by dramatic reductions in capital spending by resource companies. There is little reason to believe that commodity prices and resource investments will ever regain their feverish levels experienced during the 2000s. Global economic growth remains uncertain, most countries (including China) are taking strong measures to reduce fossil fuel consumption, and OPEC's ability to reliably restrain production and support oil prices is uncertain. In this regard, the more restrained global resource prices that have prevailed since 2014, and which have been associated with a marked slowdown in the pace of Canadian energy development, are not a temporary anomaly.

Canadians are thus relearning a lesson that should have been obvious from even a cursory review of our economic history: namely, that resource-driven booms are no foundation on which to erect a stable, diversified, and sustainable national economy. The collapse of this latest staples cycle coincided again with political change in Ottawa: the Harper Conservatives were defeated soundly in the 2015 election (and the failure of their petro-fueled economic strategy was a key factor in their loss), replaced by a more moderate but still business-oriented Liberal majority. This new government faced a challenging economic context. Oil prices and resource activity remain weaker than in the 2002–14 period. New bitumen developments have been thrown into question by low prices, infrastructure constraints (in particular the economic and policy uncertainty stalling the construction of several proposed export pipelines), and the evolution of environmental policy (with both the federal and Alberta governments moving ahead with carbon-pricing mechanisms with major implications for the energy industry). The Trudeau government also tried to diversify Canadian exports, both sectorally (restoring a more activist industrial policy approach to support manufacturing and other non-extractive industries) and geographically (by pursuing trade agreements with overseas markets, most importantly the EU and East Asia). These efforts were hampered, however, by global economic insecurity, the election of Donald Trump (and his aggressive trade interventions), and the poor capacity of Canada's business sector for innovation and creativity in sectors other than its traditional concentration in resources and finance.[6]

In short, the most recent staples expansion didn't last long at all: for barely a decade, from 2002 through 2014 (and even that interrupted by a global financial crisis). Enormous profits were earned for a while (particularly in the petroleum industry), and political and policy discourse were both predictably influenced by expansive but ill-founded promises of a prosperous, staples-dependent future. But the boom ended quickly, leaving Canadians once again seeking a more balanced and sustainable path of economic and social development.

The remainder of this essay is organized in the following sections. The next section reviews empirical evidence regarding the post-2000 resurgence of staples dependence and associated deindustrialization of exports, and the resulting national specialization at the lower rungs of the value-added ladder. Even within energy-related activity, Canada has specialized in raw bulk extraction, foregoing opportunities to expand value-added activity in downstream (refining) or upstream (machinery and equipment) activities related to resource production. The third section considers the broader risks and consequences of Canada's renewed resource dependence: including stagnant productivity and innovation, cyclical instability, and environmental degradation. The concluding section introduces some broad potential directions for economic policy to regulate and limit resource developments, enhance value-added linkages and spin-offs, and support greater diversity and sustainability in the overall economy; it also explores the impacts of the more recent weakness in global petroleum and mineral prices for the doctrine of extractivism in Canada, and the political prospects for alternative policy directions.

DESCRIBING RENEWED STAPLES DEPENDENCE AND DEINDUSTRIALIZATION

Canada's renewed reliance, since the early 2000s, on extraction and export of unprocessed resources (and petroleum in particular) is visible across a wide range of statistical indicators. Together they paint a clear picture of a national economy that fundamentally shifted direction, both quantitatively and qualitatively, beginning shortly after the turn of the century.

To counteract the acknowledged risks and limits of staples dependence, mainstream Canadian economic policy from Confederation was typically preoccupied with measures to regulate resource industries and nurture a more diverse "value-added" economy. Instead of simply extracting and exporting raw resources as fast as possible, and then using the resulting export revenues to pay for necessary imports (of manufactures and other value-added products), it was commonly accepted that Canada should diversify into a greater range of value-added industries. This would contribute to greater prosperity, productivity, and stability, and expand the range of vocations available to Canadians. Examples of policies aimed at promoting secondary and tertiary development included the early National Policy of tariffs to support domestic industry, the Canada-United States Auto Pact of 1965, various sector-focused strategies to develop key industries (like aerospace and telecommunications equipment), and the limits that were placed on incoming foreign investment from the 1960s through the 1980s (especially in resource industries).

For some decades after the Second World War, those strategies paid off. The share of Canada's merchandise exports that consisted of unprocessed or barely processed resources declined, eventually out-weighed by valuable exports of automotive products, aerospace products, and other technology-intensive, high-value products. By the end of the century it was no longer accurate to describe Canada as "a hewer of wood and drawer of water." Foreign ownership relative to Canadian GDP also declined (reaching a historic low in the mid-1980s). With the surge in global commodity prices after the turn of the century, however, this historic structural progress in building a more diversified, developed, and autonomous economy began to unravel.

This historic about-face is illustrated vividly by the dramatic U-shape of figure 4.1. It calculates the share of total Canadian merchandise exports accounted for by unprocessed or barely processed resource-based products (including agriculture and fishing, forestry, basic minerals, and energy). That share declined steadily during the postwar era, so that by 1999 barely 40 per cent of Canada's total exports originated in these basic resource-dependent sectors. That year Canada ranked as the fourth larg-est assembler of motor vehicles in the world – an astounding achievement for a small country. And Canada punched above its weight in several other high-value, technology-intensive sectors as well (including com-munications technology, aerospace, and pharmaceuticals). Business inno-vation (measured, for example, by business research and development spending as a share of GDP) reached its highest level ever. It seemed that Canada could be poised to escape its staples-dominated history.

After 2000, however, that progress was reversed – and dramatically. World commodity prices surged, whetting the appetites of investors for Canada's resource riches – especially petroleum. At the same time the prospects for Canada's value-added industries dimmed, for various rea-sons. The 9/11 terrorist attacks produced a short-lived recession in the United States, and a more lasting change in national consciousness there (including a thickening of the Canada-US border, and a renewed "America-first" attitude on the part of political leaders). Companies that had led the way in Canada's value-added transformation (from the North American-based automakers to Nortel Networks to Bombardier) faltered. The oil-fuelled take-off of the Canadian currency (which appreciated by 65 per cent in five years, beginning in 2002) made Canadian-made prod-ucts and services unnaturally expensive in the eyes of the rest of the world. Foreign capital surged into Canada; an unprecedented frenzy of takeovers of iconic Canadian firms (Stelco, Inco, Falconbridge, Alcan, Algoma, IPSCO, and more) added a stunning $112 billion to the stockpile of inward foreign direct investment in just the first two years of the new

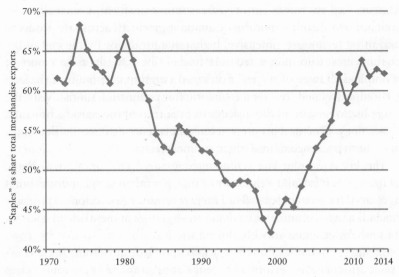

Figure 4.1 Composition of Canadian exports

Harper government (2006 and 2007). Of course, once the commodity price cycle turned down, most of those takeovers went sour – culminating in widespread restructuring and downsizing at all of the acquired operations (perhaps most dramatically at the former Stelco operations, now owned by US Steel, which eventually ceased steel production entirely in Hamilton, Canada's traditional steel heartland).

By 2014 those four staples sectors (agriculture, forestry, minerals, and energy) once again accounted for close to two-thirds of total merchandise exports. In essence, Canada structurally "undeveloped" over the first fifteen years of the new century. There is much debate in Canadian political-economy scholarship over whether Canada continues to play a subsidiary and dependent role in global capitalism, or whether it now qualifies (thanks in part to outgoing FDI on the part of Canadian-based mining companies and banks) as an "imperialist" power in its own right.[7] There is no doubt, however, that the renewed reliance on extraction and export of unprocessed staples to other, more technologically advanced economies over the last fifteen years represents a qualitative step backwards in Canada's economic development. Much like a less developed country (although, to be sure, with more income, more democracy, and more productivity), Canada has become once again primarily reliant on extracting non-renewable resource wealth to pay its way in global exchange.

Canada exports this wealth to others who transform it, manipulate it, and add value to it – and then Canada imports it back in the forms of advanced (and more expensive) products and services.

An interesting project based at Harvard University, called the Economic Complexity Observatory, has developed a quantitative index of the level of complexity and development of different countries, on the basis of a composite measure of each country's exports, imports, production, and technology. Canada's absolute score and relative ranking on this index have both plummeted: from the sixth most technically complex economy in the world in 1980, to twenty-ninth by 2010. The rapid expansion in staples extraction and export is not the only factor in this trend.[8] But it is clear that growing dependence on raw resource extraction is reshaping Canada's entire economy and reducing its stature in the world as a source of knowledge, innovation, and productivity.

Figure 4.2 describes a resulting Jekyll-and-Hyde dichotomy in Canada's international trade performance. Since 2002, when the petroleum boom took off, Canada has generated a large and growing trade surplus in energy products. That surplus reached $85 billion in 2014. However, Canada's trade performance in all non-energy products deteriorated even more rapidly than petroleum exports grew. Canada had traditionally enjoyed a large trade surplus in non-energy merchandise until early in the new century. In other words, until then Canada's export portfolio had been diversified, generating positive net export earnings across a wide range of goods (both energy and non-energy). But the two lines diverged as the energy export boom kicked into high gear. Canada quickly slid into a deficit in non-energy merchandise (by 2006), and that deficit grew steadily (reaching $80 billion in 2014), offsetting almost all of the surplus in energy products. When services trade, tourism, and investment income are also considered, then net exports of energy are too small to offset the negative balances on other current income flows; the result is that Canada has been mired in a large and now-chronic current account deficit since 2009. It seems that the more energy Canada exports, the less of everything else Canada exports. In fact, total exports have hardly grown at all since 2006 – and declined significantly as a share of total GDP (from a peak of 39 per cent of GDP in 2000 to around 31 per cent since 2015). By this measure, curiously, Canada's economy has both "undeveloped" in structural terms (with the reassertion of the leadership of resource extraction over the national economic trajectory), but has also disengaged from global trade (with a larger share of output now arising from sectors, including low-productivity private services, which are not heavily engaged in international trade).[9]

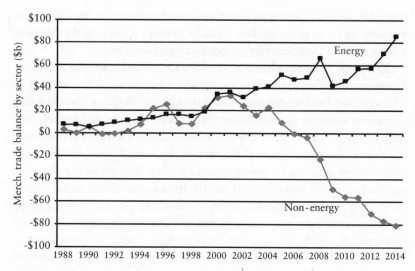

Figure 4.2 Trade balances by sector

The deterioration in aggregate measures of trade performance, even as the energy boom gathered momentum, reflected several underlying factors. One key factor was the dramatic increase in the Canadian dollar, which made Canadian-made products and services seem very expensive to foreign customers. Net outflows of investment income (resulting in part from the growth of foreign investment in Canada) produced another chronic drain on national expenditure.

Even within the broad category of energy exports, Canada's trade has become deindustrialized, as the economy moved further and further toward the primary end of the economic continuum. Most petroleum-producing jurisdictions, in an effort to capture more of the value-added potential of their non-renewable resource, invest heavily in developing upgrading, refining, and petrochemical facilities. Typically, strong policy interventions support this value-added activity: for example, through requirements for domestic processing, limits on exports of unrefined resources, the use of fiscal subsidies to encourage downstream investments, and even the direct allocation of public equity capital to refining and petrochemical projects. Even in Canada this was a traditional priority – illustrated, for example, by Alberta's effort (under then-Premier Peter Lougheed) to nurture a domestic petrochemical industry in the 1970s. In recent years, however, the importance of adding downstream value to petroleum output has largely faded from the radar screens of policy makers. And the integrated global producers who account for a large share of Canadian petroleum output naturally prefer to refine petroleum in their own refineries (most located in the United States). In this way, corporate decisions regarding what is cheapest or most profitable can easily diverge from broader cost-benefit calculations about what produces most value for Canadians.

As a result, the refining and petrochemical end of Canada's petroleum business has lagged far behind the extraction end. In fact, there has been little or no growth in petroleum refining and processing at all – despite the dramatic expansion in petroleum extraction. With the take-off in global petroleum prices (and the Canadian exchange rate) in the early 2000s, real GDP in the petroleum products sector declined by 10 per cent, even as the extraction boom accelerated. This decline could get worse, given the fragile prospects facing Canadian refineries in several locations (including BC, Quebec, and Newfoundland), where security of supply and other challenges jeopardize long-run viability. Some new investments are being made in upgrading (largely in Western Canada), but not enough to reverse the overall trend. Therefore, the stagnation – at best – of Canada's petroleum products sector continues, even as production of raw petroleum has exploded.

The stagnation of downstream activity is also apparent in Canada's poor international trade performance in that end of the petroleum business. Changes in regional patterns of energy supply and demand within North America have resulted in Canada becoming a major importer of refined petroleum products (both from offshore and from the United States). Petroleum product imports have exploded fivefold (in nominal dollars) since 2004, mostly destined for consumers in eastern Canada. Canada's exports of refined products, on the other hand, grew slowly over the same time (and this growth only reflected higher prices, not increased real quantities). By 2014, Canada actually imported more refined petroleum products than it exported. How ironic that Canada, a major global source of petroleum supply and supposed "energy super-power," should be a net importer of refined petroleum products. Meanwhile, the Canadian upstream industry continues to pump as much unrefined product into foreign markets as possible (for now, almost exclusively to the United States), and hence the realized prices of those exports are suppressed by regional supply gluts and the lower quality of the product.

Canada's failure to maximize the value-added potential of petroleum production is evident upstream, too, as well as downstream. The petroleum industry is heavily reliant on foreign suppliers for enormous inputs of value-added inputs, services, and technology to the resource industry itself. Hence most of the economic stimulus resulting from resource investments leaks out of Canada's economy through imports of machinery, equipment, and supplies.[10] Input-output studies indicate that the dominant supply chain feeding new resource projects in northern Alberta runs north-south, much more than it runs east-west. For example, according to the Canadian Energy Research Institute, the spin-off economic benefits from bitumen production in Alberta are five times larger in the United States than in Canadian provinces outside of Alberta (see Clarke et al. 2013, 80–1; Honarvar et al. 2011).

THE RISKS OF STAPLES DEPENDENCE

There are many reasons why the renewed reliance on resource extraction after 2000 should have already been a concern for Canadians and policy makers, even when oil prices were sky-high and the industry was booming. But once the short-lived global commodities bubble collapsed, and the national economy faced the resulting downsizing in resource industries, the risks of staples dependence should have been all the more apparent. It would be a lost opportunity if the popping of this latest commodity bubble should only leave Canadians hoping for the reinflation of the next one.

For example, Canada's poor national innovation performance has long been a source of national and international concern,[11] and Canada's ranking on this score continues to deteriorate. Business investment in research development has declined by one-third as a share of GDP since the turn of the century – precisely as the petroleum boom gathered momentum. The private sector invested just 0.8 per cent of GDP in research and development in 2013 (down from 1.3 per cent in 2001). That's the lowest research and development intensity since Statistics Canada began collecting this data. Canada now badly underperforms other industrial countries (and even some emerging market economies) in research and development spending, and the decline in that spending (relative to GDP) has been bigger in Canada over the last decade than any other OECD economy.

The petroleum-driven restructuring of the Canadian economy was an important cause of the deterioration of overall innovation performance since 2000. Petroleum companies and other resource-extraction businesses do conduct research and development, but significantly less as a share of the industry's GDP than the rest of the economy. Hence, the expanded relative importance of extraction activities will automatically be associated with a decline in overall innovation effort. The related contraction of the manufacturing sector (discussed further below) has a similar effect, since manufacturing is the strongest source of research and development spending. The manufacturing sector in Canada typically invests around 4 per cent of GDP in research and development activity, versus only 0.6 per cent for the petroleum and mining industries, so a reorientation of Canadian economic activity from manufacturing toward resource extraction will inevitably produce poorer research and development outcomes. That lack of innovation in turn reinforces economic reliance on the simple extraction of raw resources (since the less is invested in innovation, the less competitive are Canadian firms in markets for value-added products).

The impact of the resource boom on national productivity performance is another drawback of resource dependence. Productivity in resource extraction tends to decline over time, as the most readily available reserves of desired minerals are depleted – requiring more capital and labour effort to exploit less lucrative deposits.[12] (This effect can be offset to some extent by progress in extraction technologies.) The tremendous effort (including expenditure of energy) required to extract bitumen is an extreme example of this fundamental depletion problem in resource industries. Since the turn of the century, Canada's labour productivity has grown at the anemic rate of 0.6 per cent per year: ranking twenty-ninth among the thirty-four countries of the OECD, equal to less than half the average rate of productivity growth of the industrialized world. Resource extraction is certainly profitable (especially when global commodity prices are high), but its productivity declines over time – and this poses significant long-term economic risks to any country that places growing emphasis on this category of activity. So, as the composition of the economy shifts in favour of resource industries, which experience diminishing returns, overall composite productivity performance suffers accordingly.

The unplanned, "gold rush"-like approach to investment in new resource projects (especially in northern Alberta) has further undermined productivity. Mammoth, helter-skelter capital spending, with little attention paid to infrastructure, bottlenecks, and labour supply planning, regularly produces huge cost overruns and other logistical and operational problems in those new projects, and negative outcomes in terms of realized productivity. Research by Sharpe (2013) confirms the negative impact of growing resource dependence on national productivity. Average labour productivity in mineral and oil and gas extraction has been declining since the turn of the century at the rapid pace of over 5 per cent per year, giving this sector the dubious distinction of making the largest negative contribution to Canada's overall productivity performance. The growing share of national output accounted for by pure extraction activities thus has been an important factor in Canada's poor overall productivity record.

Undue reliance on the export of a small number of unprocessed commodities also poses substantial risks to economic stability, in the event of negative shifts in global demand, technology, or prices for those products. Indeed, the past history of Canada's staples-driven economic development features many examples of industries (and regions) wiped out by changes in global demand for the products concerned. In some cases the staples industry disappeared because of the exhaustion of supplies. But in other cases the decline reflected changes in foreign technology and tastes, which undermined demand for the staple export in ways that Canada had no control over – thus necessitating a painful restructuring.[13] To take a vivid example, Canada no longer exports beaver pelts, and not because we ran out of beavers. Rather, foreign demand for the product disappeared due to changes in taste and technology. Foreign appetite for other staple exports, including petroleum, is equally unpredictable. For many reasons (technological, environmental, and geopolitical) the strength of global demand for Canada's petroleum output should never have been taken for granted – even when oil traded for over $100 per barrel. This risk cannot be eliminated by merely trying to diversify the destinations of exports of raw petroleum (as advocates of new export pipelines suggest). The downturn in world oil prices after 2014 was one early sign of a fundamental shift away from petroleum-reliance in the world economy. Environmental, economic, and technological factors will all drive further changes in the intensity of petroleum demand, with the end result that a large proportion of existing petroleum reserves will never be produced.[14]

Indeed, the environmental constraints on extractivism constitute another set of reasons to question the resource-driven restructuring of Canada's economy since 2000. Resource policies (and, indeed, all economic policy) must now be evaluated in light of the overarching need to limit and reduce greenhouse gas pollution. The environmental problems associated with bitumen production in particular are well known, including both localized effects (tailings ponds, water pollution, and land reclamation issues) and emissions of greenhouse gases (since bitumen production is itself very energy intensive, it releases more carbon dioxide in extraction and processing than conventional oil). The rapid expansion of bitumen production has been by far the largest single source of new greenhouse gas emissions in Canada this century. Unless offset by dramatic reductions in emissions from other sectors, environmental constraints will inevitably curb future growth in petroleum output and hence threaten the value of sunk capital. Under an NDP government elected in 2015, Alberta implemented a new climate policy that taxed carbon emissions and imposed a cap on emissions from the bitumen industry (although that limit is high enough to allow substantial growth in production). The Alberta policy is underpinned by federal climate policy, which pledges to step in with its own carbon price to cover emissions in any province that refuses to implement its own. Despite strong challenges to both policies from the energy industry and conservative politicians, it seems clear that one way or another, environmental constraints will inevitably become more binding on future resource expansion.

Another set of concerns related to the rapid expansion of resource extraction and export since the turn of the century relates to the collateral damage that was experienced by other sectors of the economy. The most important channel for these negative spillover effects on other tradable industries was through the exchange rate. For various reasons, the rapid expansion in petroleum production and export was associated with the dramatic appreciation of the Canadian dollar, also beginning in 2002. That badly undermined Canadian production and exports of non-resource tradable products – including manufacturing, of course, but other tradable industries as well (such as tourism and tradable services[15]).

Other non-extractive industries were crowded out by the post-2000 resource boom, through a process that could be termed "resource-led deindustrialization." There are many potential channels for this effect,[16] but the impact of resource exports on the exchange rate was clearly the most important. It involves two causal factors working in sequence. First, the expansion of natural resource exports (and petroleum in particular) pushes up the value of the exchange rate. Second, that exchange rate appreciation in turn causes contraction in the scale of production and export of non-resource-based tradable industries – including, but not limited to, manufacturing. (Other tradable industries affected by exchange rate appreciation include services exports and tourism.) In neither case does the causal relationship need to be exclusive: that is, other factors may also contribute to the rise in the dollar and/or the contraction of manufacturing. To confirm the phenomenon of resource-led deindustrialization merely requires that both factors are relevant.

In other work (Clarke et al. 2013) I have reviewed in detail numerous published studies examining the link between petroleum exports and the decline of manufacturing in Canada since 2002. I consider each study's findings regarding each of the two causal relationships described above: the impact of the petroleum boom on the value of the Canadian dollar, and the impact of the higher Canadian dollar on manufacturing activity in Canada. Of the reviewed studies that address either hypothesis, all but one confirm that the run-up in oil prices, and the corresponding expansion of investment, production, and exports in Canada's petroleum industry, were significant factors (not necessarily the only factors) in the sharp appreciation of the Canadian dollar after 2002. And all but one of the relevant studies also confirmed that the appreciation of the Canadian dollar was a significant factor (again, not the only factor) in the contraction of Canadian manufacturing. The strong majority of research, therefore, supports the existence of both causal relationships that together drive this process of resource-led deindustrialization. In the intense debates that surrounded Canadian energy, industrial, and environmental policy during the years of the boom, this seemingly obvious finding became controversial in public discourse; petroleum lobbyists and sympathetic researchers denied that the bitumen expansion was having negative side effects for other Canadian industries (see, for example, Cross 2013). However, the evidence is strong that the relative and absolute erosion of manufacturing during this period (as well as other non-resource export industries) was clearly exacerbated by the over-appreciation of the Canadian currency, which in turn was clearly driven by resource industry developments. Neoclassical economic purists, with their faith in the virtues of "comparative advantage" specialization, might embrace and celebrate this development, but most Canadians (who hope for a bigger role for their country in world trade, beyond extraction of non-renewable resources) would not.

The precise "transmission mechanism" linking the petroleum boom to the exchange rate merits further discussion. Casual observers might assume that the impact is experienced through a generalized improvement in trade performance (measured by the current account balance), thanks to vibrant petroleum exports. But this is clearly not the case. As noted above, Canada's overall trade balance deteriorated markedly during the petroleum boom and remains mired in a deep and chronic deficit. Including services and investment income, Canada's current account deficit now regularly exceeds 3 per cent of GDP (leading to an annual accumulation in international indebtedness of equal proportion).

In fact, the link between petroleum and the exchange rate is not experienced through trade flows, but rather through capital and asset markets – and this is another channel through which the impact of modern financialized practices accelerates and exacerbates the negative side effects of staples-led development.[17] Speculative financial traders internalize (rightly or wrongly) the assumption that the Canadian currency is a "petro-dollar," and hence determine their short-term financial bets in light of their expectations of changes in petroleum markets. This belief can become self-fulfilling, and during periods of exuberant expectations it can push the dollar far higher than real fundamentals would justify. The transmission mechanism between the booming petroleum industry and the Canadian currency also reflects longer-run capital inflows associated with foreign direct investment in Canada's oil patch. Indeed, the historic surge in incoming FDI (focused on resource-related industries) in 2006 and 2007 was associated with the most dramatic upswing in the dollar. Continuing foreign investment in the oil patch reinforced this overvaluation.[18]

Canada represents a rare opportunity for private energy companies to invest in new sources of petroleum supply: over 80 per cent of the world's oil reserves are owned by state-owned enterprises, and over half of the remainder is located in Canada (Hussain 2012). This unique private access to a strategic non-renewable resource is another factor explaining the intense interest by foreign investors in ownership of Canadian petroleum assets (at least when they were bullish about the future trajectory of oil prices). A better understanding of the precise ways in which the petroleum expansion has translated into a rising Canadian dollar can also inform policy responses to the problem. For example, if incoming FDI in petroleum assets was a key factor pushing the dollar to high levels, then limits on foreign takeovers of resource assets and resource companies would help to break that link and moderate the currency's upswing during times of rising resource prices and profits. Evidence in support of this proposition was provided after 2013, when the Harper government announced partial limits on foreign investment by state-owned companies (especially from China) in the bitumen industry; this policy shift quickly contributed to a softening of the Canadian currency.

A bigger factor behind the sharp decline in the Canadian dollar after 2013 (with the currency retreating to more traditional levels, in the mid-70-cent US range), however, was the negative shift in investor expectations about Canada's general economic recovery, the "normalization" of monetary policy by US monetary authorities (with the phasing out of quantitative easing and gradual increases in interest rates), the collapse in global commodity prices (and expectations of future price levels), and a realization by investors that Canada's bitumen expansion faces many risks and constraints (economic and otherwise). The softer dollar (which soon fell below its purchasing power parity benchmark, around 80 cents US, after 2015[19]) will assist many export industries, but cannot automatically bring back non-extractive production and jobs lost during the dollar's upswing. Moreover, many firms worry the dollar would shoot upward again in the future (if and when oil prices strengthen further). Given the inaction of Canadian policy makers (including the Bank of Canada) during the dollar's rapid appreciation after 2002 this is a reasonable concern, and it may serve to inhibit any rebound in investment in manufacturing and other trade-sensitive activities, despite the downturn in the dollar.

Many other industrial countries also experienced a loss of manufacturing output and employment after the turn of the century, but Canada's decline was faster and deeper than most. Moreover, the decline in other non-resource export industries in the era of over-valuation (including tourism and tradable services) confirms this was not solely a manufacturing issue. All trade-sensitive industries were damaged by the sharp currency appreciation that was so clearly a side effect of the petroleum expansion.

CONFRONTING RESOURCE DEPENDENCE

Effective policy responses to Canada's latest cycle of staples boom followed by bust, with its legacy of overinvestment, deindustrialization, and regional and sectoral imbalance, would need to address the full range of drawbacks associated with unrestrained resource dependence identified above. Three broad classes of response can be envisioned:

i)   Policy could aim to directly regulate and restrain the expansion of resource industries (for both environmental and economic reasons), thus directly avoiding some of the negative side effects catalogued above. This approach requires a political willingness and capacity to challenge the powerful interest of resource investors in expanding resource production.

ii) Policy could also aim to strengthen forward and backward linkages from resource extraction to other value-added sectors (including, in the case of petroleum, more domestic content in machinery and equipment and other specialized inputs, as well as more domestic processing of the produced resource rather than immediate export of raw output), and hence support (rather than undermine) broader economic development goals. "Less extraction and more value-added" summarizes this strategy.

iii) Finally, a whole suite of policy measures could be invoked to support and nurture other strategic sectors in the face of any future renewal of resource-led growth: in particular, targeted measures would help to protect and nurture non-resource industries that produce high-value, innovation-intensive exports, and moderate the negative side effects of a future resource boom.

A useful example of the first strategy listed above is Norway's effort to regulate the pace, environmental effects, and distributional impacts of its petroleum industry (which similarly experienced strong growth during the global commodity upswing). Through a combination of public ownership of much of the petroleum industry, the collection of higher resource royalties from private producers (and the successful investment of those royalties through long-run public investment vehicles), and strong interventions to support non-energy industries (with the goal of replacing the petroleum industry in the future), Norway constitutes a strong counter-example to the less interventionist Canadian approach (Campbell 2013). Norway has been more successful in translating petroleum wealth into a strong fiscal situation, well-funded public services, and the accumulation of public assets (including through a trillion-dollar sovereign wealth fund) that can be mobilized to support future diversification efforts. On the other hand, even in Norway some of the negative side effects of extraction-led development are visible, including currency overvaluation, weak performance of non-energy exports, and growing greenhouse gas emissions.

Within the second category of policy responses above (strengthening value-added linkages attached to resource industries), several different policy strategies can be considered. Active efforts could be undertaken to boost Canadian content in the machinery, capital, and services that are purchased as inputs to resource projects. Given the enormous capital investments in new projects (especially bitumen), the industrial spin-offs to other Canadian sectors have so far been surprisingly small. Enhancing those spin-off benefits requires planning, regulation, and encouragement – rather than simply assuming that a rising bitumen tide will automatically lift all boats. Exports of raw petroleum might be discouraged or limited through regulation, and/or through constraints on the capacity of export infrastructure.[20] Instead, policy would encourage (or even mandate) more made-in-Canada upgrading, refining, and petrochemical activity, to add as much value as possible to the non-renewable resource downstream – and avoid driving down received export prices through excess shipments of lower-grade bitumen. On the other hand, there are drawbacks to the strategy of adding more domestic value to the petroleum supply chain that should also be considered. By broadening domestic linkages to resource projects, it could be argued that the economy's overall dependence on resource production is enhanced, not weakened (Watkins 2014 makes this argument). Environmental issues associated with resource-focused value-added activity (such as the operation of petroleum refineries, for example) are another concern (Haley 2011).

The third category of policy response identified above, consisting of proactive efforts to prioritize and nurture other strategic export sectors, has traditionally been termed "industrial policy." In a modern context, however, the broader term "sector development policy" (Stanford 2012) may be preferable, reflecting that proactive interventions should not be limited to large-scale industrial facilities, but rather can target other sectors as well – including exportable services industries, smaller-scale technology operations, and other forms of tradeable, innovation-intensive activity). Successful sector development strategies rely on the capacity of an active, empowered state to identify strategic sectors, direct and facilitate innovation and investment (Mazzucato 2013), and then both encourage and compel private firms to undertake a broader and richer range of activities than unconstrained businesses would otherwise pursue (Amsden 2007).

There are many successful international examples of sector development strategies in recent years, which should spur a reinvigoration of Canada's recent reluctance to engage in targeted sector strategies. The successful state-managed industrialization experience of several Asian and Latin American economies, on the strength of proactive and interventionist policy, confirms that innovative, productivity-enhancing growth does not occur spontaneously as a result of market forces. Instead, the "visible hand" of government intervention, in various shapes and forms, is necessary for sustained quantitative and qualitative economic progress. The successful industrial evolution of Korea and other export-oriented Asian economies is especially compelling. These countries relied on state planning, subsidized capital, strong domestic supply networks and innovation clusters, effective export promotion, and effective limits on imports to nurture high-value export industries. China has also adopted and revised many of these tools in its current effort to restructure its economy away from reliance on labour-intensive exports, toward a more innovative, consumer-driven, sectorally diverse development path; strong regulations on incoming foreign investment, and powerful efforts to promote the emergence of Chinese-owned global "champion" firms, are key features of the Chinese approach to sector development. Recent research highlights the importance of innovation networks and geographically concentrated "eco-systems" of medium-sized technology-intensive firms for successful sector strategies in modern high-tech manufacturing and services. This analysis suggests that policy should focus on connecting the various players in the innovation process, strengthening the domestic presence of growing innovative firms, and facilitating stronger connections between public innovation activity and commercial applications. Successful examples of this "network" approach to sector development include the "Top Sectors" strategy in the Netherlands, the "Catapults" program in the UK, and the National Manufacturing Institutes in the United States. More direct and powerful policy levers are still regularly invoked in many countries as well – including mandated domestic investments and domestic content in strategic sectors, active trade interventions, and public ownership.

Canada's own economic development experience also reinforces the conclusion that active policy strategies are necessary for attaining a more desirable sectoral mix – and for diversifying the economy beyond resource extraction. Most of the relatively rare high-tech industries that have been successfully established in Canada owe their success to an earlier willingness by policy makers to be proactive, rather than *laissez faire*. These success stories include the auto industry (built here on the basis of strategic trade policy, investment supports, and other tools), aerospace (which relied on public investment, public procurement, and trade policy), and telecommunications and ICT (first established on the strength of public research support and procurement, and sustained more recently thanks to effective leveraging of public educational and innovation services). Nevertheless, despite these success stories active sectoral strategies largely fell out of favour after the 1980s, when signing free trade agreements became, by default, Canada's primary industrial strategy. Revitalizing a more proactive approach to sector development policy will be essential for attaining a more balanced, prosperous, and sustainable economic structure.

There is a rich and diverse catalogue of policy levers that could be invoked as part of an overall strategy to foster the domestic development of strategically important, technology-intensive, export-oriented sectors.

Specific policies with modern relevance include subsidies and financial incentives for capital investment in targeted sectors; direct public participation in key innovation programs (what Mazzucato 2013 calls "mission-oriented innovation"); strategic trade interventions to boost exports or limit import penetration in key sectors; mandated public procurement strategies to maximize market opportunities for domestic producers in key sectors; public equity ownership of key firms or projects; expansion of high-quality physical and scientific infrastructure to benefit key industries; and more. Any strategy to develop a successful suite of non-resource tradable sectors will also require active measures to manage the macroeconomic side effects of resource expansion. These would include measures to maintain the Canadian dollar at levels that are compatible with Canadian export success. Fiscal measures to spread the benefits of resource production more widely throughout the country would also be important in regulating the economic and social effects of staples industries.

Of course, it requires more than just an inventory of potentially effective policy levers to achieve a shift in economic trajectory away from the narrowly focused extractivism of recent Canadian economic history. Politics, not just policies, play a crucial role in determining economic direction. In other words, political struggles and pressures will determine the nature of state intervention: on what issues, and in whose interests. Adoption of a more interventionist approach to limiting and regulating resource development, and sustaining and nurturing non-resource export industries, requires the mobilization of a sufficiently powerful constellation of political constituencies to force the state to confront and regulate the logic and power of the staples-dependent accumulation model. We must therefore consider the alignment and balance of political forces that would influence whether future state policy leans against the logic of extractivism, or in fact reinforces and accelerates it.

Some of the key constituencies that have traditionally mobilized for economic diversification and regulatory limits on staples development have included: the labour movement and its allies;[21] sections of the Canadian business class that identified their interests with domestic industrial and economic diversification;[22] and the political constituency associated with Canadian "nationalism." Nationalism has proven especially diverse and contradictory in its orientation and demands. Some streams of nationalist politics in Canada were developing a vision of a more well-rounded and capable Canadian capitalism, while others concluded that a more fundamental break from the logic of profit-driven accumulation was required to achieve a meaningful reorientation of national economic priorities. A nationalist critique of staples dependence can therefore be found in left, centrist, and even right-wing variants.[23] A common concern shared by all incarnations of nationalism is a desire to wean Canada's economy from undue reliance on staples production and export, and simultaneously from the traditionally extreme dependence on foreign capital in those industries. However, in light of the increasingly global consciousness and orientation of Canadian business leadership, the scope for a narrowly nationalist critique of staples-led development (as opposed to more thorough-going critiques that incorporate class, racial, and environmental considerations) would seem to have diminished. Unlike the heyday of Canadian anti-staples nationalism (in the 1960s and 1970s), Canadian business elites today are more uniformly aligned with the imperatives of global capitalism, in part due to the extending and multidimensional impact of globalization and financialization. This has clearly reduced the prospects for any kind of cross-class Canadian "coalition" to mobilize for constraints on export-oriented resource developments.

Some proponents of a more narrowly "extractivist" economic strategy actually celebrate Canada's renewed focus on raw resource extraction as an efficient reflection of our natural "comparative advantage." For them, there is nothing wrong with Canada becoming increasingly dependent on the extraction and export of raw resources. Government should not interfere with the drive to extract and export non-renewable resources (like petroleum), since the profit-seeking activity of the resource industry is presumed to reflect the real benefits and opportunity costs of various potential uses of scarce Canadian capital, labour, and ingenuity. Merely extracting the resource, in this worldview, is all the "value-added" that is required. For example, Tombe (2015) argues that raw resource exports themselves constitute value-added activity: "The value you're adding is in extracting the resource itself. It has no value a kilometre below the surface, but it has value when it's brought to the surface. When you take resources from below the surface and move it up to the surface and ship it [sic] to where the demand is, that is creating value" (cited in Smith 2014). This approach implies that unexploited natural resources are valueless and hence "wasted;" it is preferable for Canada to focus on extraction (if that is what market forces indicate the economy should specialize in), allowing other nations to do the associated work of converting those raw resources into value-added products and services.

Most Canadians would reject this stunted vision for Canada's economic future. Indeed, the majority of Canadians intuitively appreciate the risks

– economic, environmental, geopolitical – of becoming a mere source of raw materials for other, more industrially and technologically advanced economies, which then process those resources and sell us back the (more expensive) finished products. Most Canadians want something bigger for their country: an economy based on talent, innovation, ingenuity, productivity, inclusion, and sustainability. And the vision of building a more diversified, value-added economy might generate more interest and support in coming years, in light of Canada's recent experience with the downs (not just the ups) of resource cycles. Challenging the economic and political power of resource companies and the investors (both Canadian and international) who own them, and exposing the drawbacks of an economy focused so strongly around resource extraction, will be a daunting intellectual and political task. But the damage caused by Canada's latest failed ride on the resource rollercoaster should create new space within which that challenge can be mounted.

NOTES

This chapter extends and updates previously published work (Stanford 2014a, 2014b). The author thanks without implication the editors, and Wallace Clement, Fuyuki Kurasawa, and Greg Albo for helpful comments.

1 Those protections continue today, such as the prohibition on foreign takeovers of major Canadian banks, and the implicit guarantee of major bank lending by the Bank of Canada.

2 As noted by John Kay, who headed a recent UK commission on the financial industry, "In a paradoxical way, the function of equity markets today is not to enable savers to put money into companies. It's to enable them to get it out." See Milner (2013).

3 As Clement (this volume) describes, these early analyses of the dynamics of staples-led development constituted the crucial initial stimulus for the school of "Canadian Political Economy."

4 See Watkins (1963) for the classic statement of the dangers of the "staples trap." The commentaries compiled in Stanford (2014a) reflect on the lasting relevance of this analysis for Canada's present economic juncture.

5 As McBride explains in this volume, even under neoliberalism the state continues to play an active (and expensive) role in facilitating capital accumulation, including by subsidizing the extensive infrastructure required for staples exports.

6 As discussed below, Canada's already-poor record of business investment in research and development has deteriorated even further in the current decade, ranking as the worst of any major industrial country.

7 See, for example, Klassen (2009) and Kellogg (2015).

8 The successful industrialization of many emerging market economies in recent years is another factor that has affected relative economic complexity in Canada and some other OECD countries. But the fall in Canada's relative ranking has been comparatively steep; by 2010 Canada ranked by far the lowest of any G7 economy according to this measure, and within the lowest quarter of all OECD countries.

9 The shift of production from tradeable to non-tradeable sectors was partly a response to the impact of exchange rate appreciation on the competitiveness of Canadian exports, as discussed further below. The share of exports in total GDP is not a complete or precise indicator of "globalization," however. Gross export values include the value-added embodied in imported inputs (the value of an imported engine, for example, in a Canadian-assembled and exported motor vehicle). And globalization, of course, exerts its influence through many complex channels, not just merchandise trade.

10 There are some cases of relatively stronger and more sophisticated upstream linkages in Canadian resource industries; for example, Canadian firms have become leaders in the technology of heavy oil and bitumen extraction and processing (a specialization that may become worthless in light of the coming global transition away from fossil fuel reliance).

11 See Council of Canadian Academies (2013) for a useful overview of the evidence and causes.

12 See Stanford (2011) for more discussion of this relationship between resource extraction and productivity.

13 Haley (2011) discusses the dimensions of these risks, and highlights the continuing relevance of this problem – especially regarding environmental factors that will inevitably affect the demand for Canadian staples in the future.

14 For example, see Ashim et al. (2015) and Leach (2014).

15 International tourist visits to Canada plummeted dramatically in the 2000s, when the high Canadian dollar made Canada a very expensive destination. Exports of tradeable services (such as banking, transportation, and business services) also declined as a share of GDP during this time.

16 If capital and labour markets were constrained on the supply side, then a resource boom could crowd out other sectors simply by bidding up the price of those inputs and facilitating their reallocation away from other sectors. That type of restructuring would hardly be a problem, however, since owners of capital and labour (even in declining sectors) would experience rising incomes, and no difficulty finding alternative employment. In Canada's recent experience, it is clear that neither employment nor investment were constrained by supply, and the impact of the resource expansion on other sectors has been experienced through other, less benign channels.

17 Economists have long recognized that the exchange rate is a primarily financial variable, not predictably determined by factors in the real economy.

18 Estimates suggest that foreign investors own over 70 per cent of the equity in
Canada's bitumen production, including both Canadian subsidiaries of foreign
firms and foreign minority ownership of Canadian-based bitumen producers.
See Forest Ethics Advocacy (2012).

19 An exchange rate of around 80 cents (US) equalizes the purchasing power
parity (PPP) of the Canadian currency, and hence is a better indicator of true
relative costs in Canada. When the exchange rate trades above PPP bench-
marks, domestic costs look "too high" – and vice versa when exchange rates
trade below that level. PPP values are frequently understood as a long-run
centre of gravity for market exchange rates, which are dominated by financial
market pressures.

20 The still-unsuccessful efforts of the federal and Alberta governments, alongside
the petroleum industry, to facilitate and construct a new bitumen export pipeline is the most potent manifestation of this problem. Bitumen opponents hope
the barriers to pipeline construction will stop future expansion of bitumen
production, although the industry has developed other channels (including
more expensive and dangerous railway freight) to ship bitumen to US markets.

21 As Ross and Thomas (this volume) discuss, cross-sectoral alliances between
trade unions, community organizations, and other constituencies of civil
society are essential for the successful exercise of workers' power under
neoliberalism.

22 As described by Kellogg (2015), however, since the implementation of the
1988 Canada-US free trade agreement Canadian business elites have increasingly defined their interests as part of a globalized community of capital, and
at the same time have been increasingly focused on their own outward foreign
direct investment opportunities (especially in the mining and banking
industries).

23 An example of the latter would include the negative reaction of many
Canadian conservatives to major purchases of Canadian bitumen assets in
recent years by state-owned firms from China and other Asian economies –
a reaction that surely reflects racialized as well as economic motivations. In
response to that reaction, even the staunchly pro-petroleum government of
Stephen Harper introduced restrictions on some foreign takeovers of petroleum properties and companies.

5

Innis's Ghost:
Canada's Changing Resource Economy

Suzanne Mills and Steven Tufts

INTRODUCTION: RESOURCES MATTER

Resource industries and the staples they rely on continue to be a central feature of Canada's political economy. Resource industries include activities involved in the extraction, transportation, and minimal processing of natural resources, which are aspects of nature that are useful to humans. In this chapter we focus on non-agricultural resource industries involved in the production of staples, where staples include unprocessed commodified nature produced primarily for export. Staples theory was conceived in the first half of the twentieth century to explain the political economy of resource industries. Since this time, Canada has undergone considerable economic diversification and social transformation. This shift has prompted some authors to modify staples theory and others to critique its continued application to Canada (Mills and Sweeney 2013; Howlett and Brownsey 2008). Debate surrounding staples has, despite the efforts of some theorists, retained a national focus. Authors questioning the continuing relevance of staples theory and resource industries to Canada have cited the relatively small share of resource production to the country's overall GDP, the development of a home market, an increasingly urbanized population, and the role of Canadian capital internationally (Howlett and Brownsey 2008; Kellogg 2015; Gordon 2010). Others have maintained that staples theory continues to explain Canada's political economy – citing the strong ties between commodity prices, domestic markets, and currency valuations as well as the resource development orientation of federal and provincial governments as evidenced by policy decisions affecting labour, the environment, and taxation (Stanford 2008; Watkins 2007). By focusing on a national scale, however, the debate about whether staples theory is still relevant has overlooked significant changes that have occurred within the Canadian nation state. In other words, many critics of staples theory (and even some of its proponents) are themselves trapped in a methodological nationalism that often privileges the nation state at the expense of subnational analysis.

We suggest that staples theory has its greatest explanatory power at the sub-national scale. Although all regions in Canada have some connection to staples, theories about resource development have heightened relevance outside of the St Lawrence corridor and particularly in northern and Indigenous communities proximal to resource production. At the turn of the twenty-first century, over seven million people in Canada lived in 1,900 communities where 30 per cent or more of the local economic base was linked to a single resource value chain (see Rothwell and Bollman 2011, appendix c). It is in these regions where economies are most susceptible to the cyclical dynamics of resource production, stifled economic diversification, and staples-oriented political leadership. The persistent significance of resource industries and staple-driven policy to Canada's internal dynamics is particularly apparent when examining Canada's relationships with First Nations, Métis, and Inuit peoples, inter-provincial and inter-regional labour flows, and environmental policy and activism. These sub-national dynamics are critical aspects of Canada's political economy and are usefully informed by a staples tradition.

Despite several critiques of staples theory, such as those discussed by Clement (this volume), the Canadian political economy literature in this tradition has yet to engage fully with colonialism's role in resource development as well as Indigenous resistance to and participation in development, the increasing use of long-distance commuting in resource extraction, and shifting environmental policy and activism in relation to resource development. Though these new developments are influenced by changes at multiple scales, from the home and community to global commodity markets, their effects are most apparent in resource communities and regions.

We begin this chapter with an overview of some of the key developments of staples theory before summarizing the continuing debate about the significance of staples development to Canada's economy. Arguing that this debate was largely located at the scale of the nation state, we then draw on the writings of Hayter and Barnes (1990) to suggest that staples theory holds greatest relevance at a sub-national scale of analysis. We do not, however, discount the continuing importance of national and global scales, since this would simply replicate the same limitations of previous depictions of the nation as the only meaningful political expression of state power and belonging for a people (see Wimmer and Schiller 2002). Similarly, we do not privilege global connections that are the focus of much research in migration studies (Levitt and Jaworsky 2007). Instead, we focus on how staples theory influences economic development and politics at local and regional scales, with the understanding that resource development is subject to global economic processes as well as state regulation and within-state dynamics.

We therefore draw on literature that is on the boundary of what is understood to be mainstream Canadian political economy to argue that staples theory continues to be a relevant approach to understand the political economy of northern and hinterland regions in Canada, albeit with revision. A revised staples theory would involve greater acknowledgement of territorial rights and non-wage economic activities in the case of Indigenous communities, a better understanding of labour mobility in extractive sectors, as well as the ways that environmental activism can be mobilized to influence public policy.

STAPLES THEORY AND CANADIAN POLITICAL ECONOMIC THOUGHT

Staples theory was first conceived to describe the development of the Canadian political economy in the early twentieth century, though it is closely aligned with international development theories such as the resource curse hypothesis. Harold Innis (1930), an economic historian considered to be a founder of staples theory, highlighted how the peculiarities of staples (such as fish, fur, and wheat) production came to shape Canada's economic and political development. In his study of the fur trade, Innis emphasized how patterns of fur production influenced the development of transportation corridors, political boundaries, and Canadian economic policy as well as its close relationship with Britain. Innis' analysis of staples development was more pessimistic than that of other staples researchers such as W.A. Mackintosh (1964), who viewed staples production as a pathway to national development. According to Innis, Canada's continued reliance on staples production prevented it from industrial development akin to that in the United States. What Innis first characterized as a "discrepancy between the centre and the margin of Western civilization" (1930, 385) was later coined as the staples trap. This is the notion that an overreliance on the export of staples creates rigidities that pose barriers to more diversified industrial development. Drache (1982) further expanded on Innis's formulation by describing these rigidities in detail, suggesting that in the case of most staples, development is limited by the dependence on externally set prices; fluctuating demand; the need for large capital investments in transportation; and production infrastructure (fixed costs). Such rigidities often lead to monopoly tendencies and to a dependence on government assistance for transportation and communications. Both Innis and Drache argued that these factors, and the geographic division of labour that ensued, made Canada economically reliant on the United Kingdom and the United States, which in turn provided these countries with a measure of political control over the settler colony.

After a period of inattention, left leaning political economists, who observed stagnating development of industrial capital in Canada through the twentieth century, rediscovered staples theory (Watkins 1963, 1982; Drache 1982; Clement 1983). Watkins (1963) consolidated early writings on staples theory and honed the theory by articulating the spread effects that would allow economies initially reliant on staples to diversify. He posited that the character of the staple, the local population, and the political context would determine whether the linkage effects were sufficient for economies to avoid a staples trap (Watkins 1963, 151). This included the question of whether inputs for staples production were supplied locally (providing backward linkages) or imported; whether staples outputs stimulated investment in other value-added industries or cognate industries (forward linkages); and whether income from resource development was spent domestically fostering the growth of consumer goods industries (final demand linkages) or leaked. Last, Watkins (1963) argued that Canada's growth continued to be dependent on staples and that staples theory, in particular a resource-export orientation, could help explain lagging growth in manufacturing relative to the US economy.

Later writings through the 1980s sought to re-articulate staples theory in light of Canada's more developed post-war economy, drawing attention to the influence of international trade and to class relations resulting from staples development. Unlike Innis, these authors were influenced by Marxist political economy and sought to intervene in debates about Canada's participation in a Free Trade Agreement (FTA) with the US (Drache 1982; Clement 1981, 1983). Both Drache (1982), and Watkins (1982) called for the continued application of Innisian thought to

Canada's now more industrialized economy and to argue against Canada's participation in the FTA. By uniting Innis' work with that of contemporary political economists, Watkins (1989) described how the early importance of staples in Canada's economy created a continued dependence on foreign investment and ownership that hampered growth, despite several advances that Canada had made in its trade relationship with the US through tariffs and agreements such as the auto-pact. Accordingly, he argued that the pending FTA with the United States would "exacerbate the staples bias of the Canadian economy" (1989, 32).

Like Watkins (1982), Clement (1983) also adopted a nationalist framework, yet critiqued Innis for neglecting the importance of class structure to Canada's economy. Clement argued that the class structure of resource production had changed with the industrialization after the Second World War. He proposed that notwithstanding the industrialization of resource production that had spawned industrial labour relations in some city centres, Canadian capital and manufacturing continued to be stifled by foreign ownership, specifically the dominance of external, predominantly US firms. Clement termed Canada "a mature branch-plant society" whereby "foreign domination has distorted the Canadian economy and hence its class structure" (1983, 55). According to Clement, this translated into underdeveloped service and financial sectors since research and development, corporate headquarters, and marketing functions of resource industries were predominantly located outside of Canada.

Though Clement intervened in debates at a national scale, he was also concerned about uneven development within Canada, arguing that postwar development had favoured the golden triangle of manufacturing in southern Ontario and Montreal while the remainder of the country continued to rely on resource production. Feminist critics of staples theory also drew attention to sub-national scales, applying a gendered analysis to understandings of working-class resource-based communities (Luxton and Corman 2001; Maroney and Luxton 1987). In fact, early work from feminist political economists that brought social reproduction seriously into discussions of economic development in Canada were among the first to adopt a more local perspective as the home was considered in processes of industrial restructuring in resource communities (see Luxton 1980).

Since the 1980s Canada's resource sector has become increasingly globally integrated and financialized. Each of these trends can be understood to be evidence of the continued relevance of staples theory. Resource industries have largely responded to the financial risk resulting from greater international competition for commodities and fluctuating markets through consolidation. Mergers and acquisitions in a number of resource sectors have resulted in greater industry concentration globally and in several cases, Canadian companies have been acquired by larger transnational corporations based in the United States or elsewhere (Ericsson 2012). Adopting a staples theory lens, the increased power of mammoth transnational corporations hinders the ability of states and communities to capture resource rents and foster forward and backward linkages. In mining, for example, Dansereau (2006) argues that global concentration of ownership has served to harmonize production and labour practices globally – with the result that mines are more highly capitalized and have much reduced labour forces, which in turn reduces final demand linkages.

Financialization accentuates Canada's dependency on resource production in two ways. First, financialization has increased the amplitude of price peaks and troughs, increasing the speed and magnitude of development. This poses problems for states trying to harness forward and backward linkages. Second, financialization has accentuated "Dutch disease" whereby the Canadian dollar is so heavily influenced by the price of oil that when the oil industry booms, other industries (notably manufacturing) suffer as the cost of exports rise.

The defense of the relevance of staples theory remains persistent. Stanford (2008) and Watkins (2007) have argued that staples continue to be a central feature of the Canadian economy. Instead of evolving past the mature stage, they suggest that Canada's economy has regressed to an earlier stage of staples production. They describe how staples are increasingly extracted for export as raw commodities rather than being processed for local consumption and harnessed for economic diversification. In the case of oil, Watkins suggests, the flow of Alberta oil to the United States rather than to Canada's eastern provinces has maintained high oil prices that have caused declines in domestic manufacturing. Both authors also focus on the role that foreign capital plays in capturing and exporting economic rents (or "super-profits") that would otherwise be invested regionally – or at least domestically. In particular, Stanford (this volume) emphasizes that the unprecedented resource boom led to foreign takeovers, currency overvaluation, and crises in the domestic automotive assembly and parts manufacturing sector. He also describes how many regions of Canada have been led back into the staples trap(s) that policy makers sought to escape since the 1960s.

CRITIQUES OF STAPLES THEORY:
METHODOLOGICAL NATIONALISM
AND THE QUESTION OF IMPERIALISM

Despite support for staples thought in Canadian political economy, scholars and public commentators have questioned the continued importance of staples. Some have dismissed the relevance of staples theory, characterizing Canada as a "post-staples state" (Howlett and Brownsey 2008, Parkinson 2016). The post-staples state features severe cost and supply pressures that have led to the contraction of once-important natural resource industries, growth in metropolitan shares of employment and population, and economic diversification in both urban and rural areas (Cashore et al. 2008). Others, however, have criticized staples theory's prioritization of the nation as a unit of analysis and the positioning of the Canadian state as a dependent, peripheral nation given the role of Canadian mining capital in resource imperialism (Kellogg 2015, Gordon 2010).

McNally (1981) criticized the nationalist tendencies of new Canadian political economy (NCPE) theorists of the 1970s and 1980s who drew on Innis to support their positions about neoliberal trade agreements (CUFTA and NAFTA). Staples theory was integrated with the dependency theory emerging from the Latin American Marxists, and was arguably also infused with a robust post-war Canadian left nationalism (Kellogg 2015). For Marxists firmly entrenched in the MELT (Marx, Engels, Lenin, and Trotsky) traditions, the new CPE of the 1980s was frustrating. McNally (1981), for example, viewed the nationalist framework governing Canadian political economic thought as theoretically obstructive to an internationalist, working-class project that recognizes the universality of capitalism as an economic system.

Indeed, if staples theory sought to explain the subordination of the Canadian resource economy and state to large powers (France, Britain, and the United States), how can the theory explain the presence of Canadian mining companies operating in the Global South and the Canadian imperialist state's pressure to secure access to foreign resources? In answering these questions Gordon (2010) dismantles rigid left nationalist political economy and questions the application of staples theory to Canada. Specifically, he argues that viewing Canada as a subordinate country with little economic or political power no longer holds (if it ever did) as Canada is now an imperial actor. First, as others have argued for some time, the ratio of foreign direct investment to domestic production has not increased substantially since the 1970s. Nationalist staples theorists of the 1980s predicted this stasis, as did economic geographer Burgess (2002, 2007). Second, the Canadian state and military resources are no longer peacekeeping but aimed at stabilizing markets for investment and production (see Gordon and Webber 2007). Third, these are orchestrated by a strong concentrated Canadian bourgeoisie acting independently of US empire to extract resources (and surplus value) in Canada and abroad (see also Carroll 1986).

Gordon's argument that Canada is now a major player in staples production is further underscored by looking at how Toronto's Stock Exchange, which resulted from a merger of the Toronto Stock Exchange with the Standard Stock and Mining Exchange in the 1930s, has become a leader in global resource finance. Today, over half of the world's public mining companies are listed on Toronto's exchanges and the TSE is touted as the largest source of mining finance capital (Marshall 2017). Financialization has also heightened cost pressures on mining companies, leading them to adopt aggressive tactics in both domestic and international operations to increase shareholder value (de los Reyes 2017). The concentration of resource finance in Canada challenges any positioning of the country as a minor "staples" player. It also reasserts the uneven regional development in Canada as financial flows from the periphery to the centre concentrate power in the metropolitan core.

An even more targeted attack on the staples thesis as a theoretical foundation of the left nationalist Canadian political economy (CPE) is the work of Paul Kellogg (2015, 10), who argues that "Those who apply the simple 'staple trap' analogy to Canada almost always fail to interrogate the analogy from the standpoint of Canada's hugely privileged place in the world economy – a world economy that is extremely hierarchical. The economies at the top of the hierarchy benefit from, and aggressively work to sustain, the conditions that trap poor countries into dependency on staples – and Canada is very much ensconced at the top of the hierarchy of nations, not at the bottom. It is one of the architects of the current world system, not one of its victims."

For Kellogg, the staples thesis is only relevant in those nations that are truly dependent upon imperial powers and have failed to accumulate capital in the same manner as advanced capitalist economies. For example, while the oil sands may be central to Alberta's economy, the production and distribution of the resources are qualitatively different from other oil producing nations (e.g., Mexico). Kellogg is also correct in his assertion that a left nationalism that sees Canada as solely subordinate to the

United States and calls for a national resistance flirts dangerously with right-wing nationalist politics.

Burgess (2007), Gordon (2010), and Kellogg's (2015) interpretations are important interventions. They all confront a tradition in CPE that emphasizes the role of superpowers (e.g., the United States) in global systems of accumulation (see Panitch and Gindin 2012) at the expense of more polycentric views of power and the ways second-tier states such as Canada reinforce imperialist systems of domination. Arguing for the continued relevance of staples theory does not refute or dismiss the claims of those challenging mainstream CPE. Critiques of a vulgar staples thesis often have merit. For example, there is the much-debated issue of the Canadian bourgeoisie and the role of staples elites. It is argued that dependence on staples has limited the development of a coherent, strong, and independent Canadian ruling business class. Yet Canada's wealthiest people are drawn from a diverse range of global sectors beyond resources, including food production, finance, technology, communications, and industry (Canadian Business 2017). Further, multinational mining companies and the Canadian state have been linked to some of the most notorious documented global corporate malfeasance (see Gordon 2010; miningwatch.ca). However, Canadian imperialism can be linked to staples-led development. Staples theory dictates that institutions developed to support staples production shape the future trajectories of economic development, so it can only be expected that mining capital from Canada (developed in tandem with foreign investors) would eventually expand abroad and implement the business acumen and coercive state support that was first exercised domestically. While this does challenge some of the dependency integrated into staples thought through traditional CPE, it is not necessarily incoherent with staples-led economic development.

Our major concern, however, with both traditional CPE influenced by staples theory and its critics is the failure to escape a focus on the national scale as the unit of analysis: the impact of staples on Canada's national economy, Canadian capital's foreign investment in other nations, and the nation state's imperialist ambitions. Again, one of the major commonalities of both the critics and the supporters of mainstream CPE and staples theory is their methodological nationalism. Indeed, staples theory itself can be understood as a "grand narrative" focusing on national economic development. But why must staples theory be applied only to the level of the "nation" and national hierarchies? The staples thesis has different relevance when its scale of analysis shifts. Kellogg (2015) concedes that staples theory is perhaps relevant to the experiences of nations in the Global South, but it is also just as relevant to resource-dependent communities in Canada that have been systematically underdeveloped by state policy and foreign capital (Mills and Sweeney 2013). It is to this issue, which some economic geographers have raised for over two decades, that we now turn.

STAPLES AT THE SUB-NATIONAL SCALE

The authors recognize that resource development continues to be important in some regions but that it has changed qualitatively. Resource governance has become more complex as Indigenous peoples have gained a greater say over development in their territories. This greater influence has been the result of political actions, advances in Aboriginal rights jurisprudence, and participation in environmental assessments (Abele 2014). Additionally, the spatial organization of labour in resource industries has shifted from the construction of resource-based towns to the use of long-distance commuting. This shift has important implications for the ability of resource regions to harness forward and backward linkages. Last, environmental political interests and the evolution of environmental regulation have also gained influence in development trajectories (Hayter and Barnes 1990).

A focus on the sub-national scales of analysis recognizes the importance of these developments building on the work of institutional Hayter and Barnes (1990, 1997), who rekindled interest in staples theory to write about how the forest industry in British Columbia was changing through the 80s and 90s. These writers felt that staples theory continued to resonate with resource communities despite the dramatic restructuring of the forest industry in northern BC. Barnes (1996) emphasised the relevance of staples theory to understanding regional economies, characterizing Harold Innis as a "local hero." His use of "local" to characterize Innis was deliberate, and meant to emphasize Innis's ability to "model" economies in a way that accommodates the particular: "In the case of Innis, he was always interested in working-out ideas that would help make sense of the particular local formation of Canada. In doing so, he necessarily eschewed appeal to universal principles, for they were only the misnamed ideas of metropolitan powers and had been foisted upon the colonies" (Barnes 1996, 208). Innis invoked the "particular" at the scale of the nation state in order to explain economic development in Canada as unique relative to universal models. He was admittedly less concerned with the region, but he did in fact challenge explanations that dismissed particularity such as the Western, metropolitan global theories. Staples theory introduced, intentionally or not, that different scales of analysis are crucial to understanding economic development in place. Again Barnes (2005, 110) articulates this with respect to local community experience:

> In Innis's staples theory, as I will argue, staples goods have buried with them particular spatialities and temporalities that are realized when they are extracted and sold. Single industry towns that specialize in such staples are thus at the interface of those geographies and histories. They are borderline communities connected to the spatial and temporal relations produced by the staples on which they depend. Second, precisely because of this borderline status, single industry towns are borderline in a second sense. The confluence of these different geographies and histories makes single industry communities notoriously unstable, acutely sensitive to change. They are liminal communities, drawn faintly, and with the continual prospect of permanent erasure (and represented by the hundreds of ghost towns scattered among Canada's resource margins).

Staples theory is inherently a local theory, and its strength lies in an ability to understand economic development as a process that plays out unevenly over space, despite universal laws of accumulation. Many critics of staples theory hold it static in time and space, when it was perhaps meant to evolve much in the way it did with Innis' accounts of successive rounds of staples development. Staples theory as a local knowledge can perhaps be more fluid and responsive than its critics claim. Allowing innovations in staples theory to emerge from above and below the national scale of analysis is therefore necessary to its continued relevance.

An analysis that incorporates staples-influenced thinking is especially relevant to understanding changes in Canada's resource political economy. Staples production, especially extractive industries, is dynamic – as Innis himself noted when he identified the cumulative effects of successive rounds of staples development. Staples theory can assist our understanding of how these changes play out at multiple scales. We present three such changes: Indigenous political economy; restructuring the temporal and spatial relations of resource workers; and environmental resistance.

INDIGENOUS PEOPLES
AND RESOURCE DEVELOPMENT

Although Innis's first writings acknowledged the critical role played by Indigenous peoples in the development of the fur trade, since this time, the literature inspired by his work has given scant attention to the multiple roles that Indigenous peoples play in the contemporary resource economies of Canada's hinterlands as resource users, workers, business owners, and stewards of territories and resources. In the late 1980s, Abele and Stasiulis (1989) lodged a scathing critique of Canadian political economy for its theorization of Canada as a White settler society and its treatment of Indigenous people as small populations that were largely assimilated or excluded from capitalist development.[1] Since this time a small group of scholars have centred Indigenous peoples in their understandings of the political economy of resource development (for example see Hall this volume; Abele 2009; Kuokkanen 2011). This literature offers a useful corrective to staples theory by questioning the privileging of capitalist enterprises and wage work over traditional economies and by drawing attention to how questions of jurisdiction and Aboriginal rights can encumber capitalist development. In turn, we suggest that staples theory continues to hold relevance for northern Indigenous communities, who often leverage Aboriginal rights jurisprudence and the politicization of relationship to territory to gain influence over the allocation of resource rents and the trajectory of development.

Throughout his work, Innis demonstrated that he was cognizant of Canada's position as a settler colony and to how relations between North American Indigenous peoples and settlers shaped its economic development. Writing about the fur trade, he suggested that transportation routes to the interior and bases of supplies in the south shaped the present political and economic geography of Canada, and that "without Indian agriculture, Indian corn, and dependence on Indian methods of capturing buffalo and making pemmican, no extended organization of transport to the interior would have been possible in the early period" (1930, 389). Although Innis acknowledged the unequal relations of exchange between the British Imperial and Indigenous peoples, he accorded Indigenous peoples a strong position in history, stating that the "Indian and his culture were fundamental to the growth of Canadian Institutions" (1930, 392). The central importance that Innis ascribes to Indigenous peoples during the fur trade era, however, waned when he theorized the contemporary period (Abele and Stasiuli 1989).

Though relationships with nature are central to northern Indigenous economies, they are structurally different from those of resource-based communities. The latter are characterized by largely non-Indigenous residents, more men than women, high youth outmigration, and few employment opportunities for women. In contrast, research about northern Indigenous communities has highlighted strong social connections, a more even gender balance, sharing, and the importance of non-capitalist economic activities to livelihoods (Abele 2009). A continued reliance on subsistence harvesting in northern Indigenous communities has also led researchers to adopt the term "mixed economies" to denote northern economies, which were equally reliant on subsistence harvesting and wage work (Elias 1997; Usher et al. 2003). Usher, in particular, describes how subsistence and wage activities are interdependent at the level of the household since wage income is often required to purchase tools and equipment needed to participate in subsistence harvest. More recently, scholars have sought to broaden understandings of northern economies by using the term "social economy." Using a social economy lens avoids the dualisms of the mixed economy model and encompasses a broader array of activities important to community well-being including voluntary activities and entrepreneurship. These authors emphasize the centrality of economic activities outside of large-scale resource production (Abele 2009; Southcott and Walker 2009). Abele (2009, 38) describes the social economy as "part of the social productive system that lies outside the direct ambit of government programs and large businesses. It includes small business, not-for-profits, co-operatives, family based production, traditional or non-commodified production and volunteer support to others."

Both commercial and subsistence harvesting activities, which are centrally important to Indigenous livelihoods, continue to be threatened by the industrialization of resource extraction (Tough 1996). Indigenous knowledge, which encompasses use of resources and stewardship of lands, has therefore been central to Indigenous struggles for resource protection and has fuelled resistance to resource development (McGregor 2009). Much of the literature documenting Indigenous peoples' relationships to resource development has highlighted the negative impacts of resource development for northern communities, as well as Indigenous resistance to resource capital through protest and litigation (Blomley 1996; Gibson and Klinck 2005; Dylan et al. 2013). These challenges were underpinned by articulations of rights to territory and self-determination and culminated in multiple court decisions recognizing and defining Aboriginal rights.

Both the Berger inquiry and the James Bay Hydro Electric Project galvanized Indigenous resistance to resource development through the 1970s (Southcott et al. 2018). The Berger inquiry halted the immediate building of the Mackenzie pipeline, while resistance to the James Bay Hydro Electric Project did not halt the construction of Phase 1 of the James Bay Hydro Electric Project. It did, however, result in the signing of a comprehensive land claim, The James Bay and Northern Quebec Agreement (1975),[2] which included support for hunting and trapping and provisions for future consultations. These projects foreshadowed the evolution of jurisdictional landscape in northern Canada, which has accorded Indigenous peoples greater leverage over resource development decisions in their territories. In some cases, Indigenous peoples have successfully used legal and political mechanisms to halt planned resource development projects.[3]

The threat of Indigenous opposition is strong enough to compel most resource companies operating in Canada's north to voluntarily negotiate private agreements such as Impact and Benefit Agreements (IBAs) with local Indigenous groups to secure their investments. In negotiating benefit agreements, companies seek assurance from Indigenous communities that they will allow development to proceed unimpeded. From a political economy perspective, these agreements allow Indigenous communities to capture a share of resource rents resulting from development through direct transfers, employment, royalties, and business opportunities (Huskey and Southcott 2018). Few authors to date, however, have examined how the share of rents captured locally compare with those captured by provincial/territorial and federal governments and those accumulated by large resource firms.

Notwithstanding the aforementioned legal and policy shifts, several authors argue that the agency of Indigenous peoples to influence resource capital continues to be limited (Parlee 2015; Hall 2013; Caine and Krogman 2010; Kuokkanen 2011). While acknowledging the agency of Indigenous peoples, Kuokkanen (2011) suggests that traditional economies and systems of Indigenous governance have been undermined by global capitalism, particularly large-scale resource extraction. Others have suggested that processes governing consultation between Indigenous groups and resource companies are built on a terrain of unequal relations where the collusion between resource capital and the Canadian state effectively stifles Indigenous voices and influence over resource development (Caine and Krogman 2010; Hall 2013). Moreover, even when Indigenous groups do participate in development, many authors argue that the resource development often has negative social, cultural, and economic outcomes for Indigenous communities (Parlee 2015; Holfmann 2008). According to Huskey and Southcott (2018) the trappings of staples development apply to Indigenous communities who may be even less likely to capture resource rents that spur forward and backward linkages than non-Indigenous communities because of the colonial process that limited their access to lands and funds indirectly spurring outmigration of educated community members. As several authors have demonstrated, the power of transnational resource capital continues to exceed that of local Indigenous nations and to shape local adaptation to resource development. In the context of northern Indigenous communities, staples theory therefore remains salient.

RESOURCE WORKERS AND MOBILITY

Since the early 1990s, many mining and oil and gas firms have adopted long-term commuting arrangements to manage the labour needs for operations in remote locations (Storey 2001). The use of mobile workers is not a new phenomenon in resource industries. Rather, the cyclical character of resource industries creates temporal and geographical fluctuations in production that require different numbers of workers to be in different locations at different times. The use of long-term commuting does represent a shift, however, in that now workers travel thousands of kilometres on rotation schedules that often last only a couple of weeks to work in large extractive operations. As such, the use of long-distance commuting by firms is understood as a shift from the construction of single-industry towns that took place over the course of the twentieth century.

Although Innis's work acknowledged the mobility of workers in resource industries early on, later writings in political economy both within and outside of the staples tradition often focused on industrialized resource workers, particularly those living in resource communities or company towns (Bradbury 1979; Bradbury and St Martin 1983; Clement 1981). Single industry towns epitomized the staples trap since their dependence resources (and often one dominant firm) largely stymied broader economic development and created a staples-orientation in governance. Since towns were seldom able to leverage resource rents to stimulate the provision of other commodities or services, the closing of a mine or mill often led to economic decline and outmigration (Bradbury and St Martin 1983).

The organization of work in resource towns often resembled that of industrial manufacturing, and for a time the most privileged class of resource workers was able to enjoy relatively high wages, employment security, and workplace democracy through unionization. As Dunk (1991) and others note, however, these jobs were predicated on a White working-class masculinity constructed in opposition to women and Indigenous peoples. Notably, Indigenous men and women were often clustered in seasonal and more precarious forms of resource work. For example, in forestry Indigenous peoples are over-represented in tree planting, forest-fire fighting, and logging (Mills 2006). Although jobs in industrialized resource industries were stable relative to other forms of resource work, they remained vulnerable to the fluctuating production cycles that characterize primary commodities.

The resource-town model began to break down through the late 1980s. Increasing global competition led resource firms to rationalize production. This was partially achieved through technological developments leading to increases in labour productivity, which in turn had the effect of drastically reducing workforces and shortening the lifespan of many types of mines (Storey 2001). Storey (2001, 2010) also argues that governments gradually increased environmental regulatory requirements and reduced subsidies for the creation of resource-based towns. Firms began to see the costs of building towns as prohibitive and so looked to other models. Long-distance commuting emerged as a cost-effective alternative (Dansereau 2006). Using a long-distance commuting model also had the advantage of reducing the lag time from discovery to production and allowing extraction to respond more quickly to market signals.

An emerging literature has sought to describe long-distance commuting and examine the effects of long-distance commuting on workers, their families, and communities. Gender relations have figured notably in this literature, since long-distance commuting for resource work reinscribes a distinct set of gender relations: it is predominantly men who move for work (Hann et al. 2014; Dorow 2015). The health and safety of long-distance commuters has also been an area of recent research. Scholars have connected long-distance commuting to poor mental health, substance abuse, cardiovascular disease, sexually transmitted diseases, and higher rates of injury and fatality among workers (Temple et al. 2011). The negative effects of long-distance commuting are not limited to the workers themselves, and also extend to their families and communities (Markey et al. 2015). Haslam McKenzie and Hoath (2014) found that long-distance commuting was linked to domestic violence, high indebtedness, and high worker turnover while providing few economic benefits for source communities. Others have cited the difficulties that this model has posed for union organizing and representation since the spatial control of the worksite provide employers with an additional and powerful labour control mechanism (Russell 1999; Storey 2001). Not all descriptions of this model are negative, however. Markey et al. (2015) note that long-distance commuting has helped sustain forest-based communities that would otherwise have entered a period of decline after the closure of local mills.

In this respect, the long-distance commuting model challenges the bounded notion of place that forms the basis of the staples trap model by allowing workers to seek new work in other locales without relocating. Mobility therefore makes it possible to avoid community decline resulting from a boom-and-bust cycle – provided that the decline is localized. With increasing global integration in commodity production and the tendency for commodity prices to move in consort, however, it is unlikely that mobility will help workers avoid the precarity of resource work arising from the staples trap. Mobility, instead, increases the geographic spread of economic decline resulting from mine and mill closure.

Adopting mobile labour regimes in staples industries has also made it possible for employers to simultaneously bring in temporary international migrants and to employ Indigenous residents from remote communities. The resource industry's use of chronic labour shortages discourse has made employing international temporary migrant workers in addition to provincial migrants a more politically tenable strategy. The use of migrant workers in oil extraction in particular was a result of both the expansion of the Temporary Foreign Worker program to include lower skilled occupational classifications and employer appetites for workers who were malleable and less prone to resistance. Simultaneously, many firms have also promoted long-distance commuting arrangements to support local employment. In pre-project decision-making processes, companies often suggest that long-distance commuting will allow for more economic benefits to flow into northern communities since it allows Indigenous workers to retain residence in smaller communities while working on rotation. There is presently a debate as to whether long-distance commuting has benefited northern communities, however. Reports, often commissioned by communities, have suggested that long-distance commuting has dual effects, bringing wealth into communities and alleviating poverty among some households, while also leading to rising outmigration, economic inequality, poor health outcomes, and inflation (Pauktuutit et al. 2015, Nunatsiavut Government et al. 2015).

Staples theory can therefore enliven understandings of long-distance commuting by calling attention to how innovations in transportation and global price cycles are influencing the Canadian political economy in northern regions. Again, new mobilities that change the structure of traditional resource dependent communities do not erase the local.

Instead, a more nuanced understanding of local communities as interdependently linked to sites of extraction and sources of mobile labour is required. Perhaps more importantly, how can workers and communities in places such as Alberta and Newfoundland scale-up action to improve labour power and form coalitions to challenge their mutual dependency on staples?

STAPLES AND ENVIRONMENTAL RESISTANCE

The challenges of staples-dependent communities and of the environmental impacts of staples-friendly economic policy continue to shape resistance even with recent changes in federal government. During the decade rule of a Harper Conservative government, Canada's image in the global environmental movement diminished significantly. In 2011, the federal government weakened several environmental laws in Canada, including replacing the *Canadian Environmental Assessment Act* with diluted legislation that accelerated the review process, reduced the scope of assessments, and reduced the number of projects requiring review (Johnston 2015). Furthermore since 2006, in response to the resource industry lobby, Canada lowered its Kyoto commitments to reducing its greenhouse gas emissions, then repealed the *Kyoto Implementation Act* and ultimately withdrew from Kyoto altogether (Matthews, Glenn, and Artero 2013). Labour legislation was also altered to accommodate the oil boom in this period allowing companies in the oil patch to use temporary foreign workers and tap into an international labour market. The election of Prime Minister Justin Trudeau's Liberals, plus provincial elections such as Notley's NDP government in Alberta in 2015, did bring some hope to environmental activists, but it was fleeting. Trudeau was accompanied by over 300 delegates from Canada to the United Nations Framework Convention on Climate Change in Paris (COP21), signalling change explicitly with his statement "Canada is back" (CP 2015). While the principles Trudeau introduced differentiated the approach taken to climate change from the previous conservative government, it has signalled little in terms of concrete action (Goldenberg 2015). In fact, some have argued that Trudeau's policies will simply transfer Canada from the staples trap to a "carbon trap." Haley (2011) invokes staples theory to explain how Canada has not only been unable to transition to "green energy," but "low-carbon" fossil-fuel dependent innovations have also been stunted. He does, however, optimistically note that "Canada's diverse geography and its decentralized political structure produce a variety of sociotechnical systems relatively disconnected from the oil sands trajectory" (Haley 2011, 125).

Here, the socio-technical systems that have dominated energy policy can be disrupted at the subnational scale. In 2018, the federal government announced the $4.5 billion government purchase of the Trans Mountain pipeline from Kinder Morgan Canada. The project required significant investment to build a new line as well as pumping stations beside the older line from Edmonton to Alberta. The project was approved after an environmental assessment in 2016, but faced significant opposition by local Indigenous communities, environmental activists, and the B C government. This opposition led Kinder Morgan to stall construction and the federal government to take over the project as part of an attempt to develop the oil sands for markets in Asia. Similarly, while the election of an N D P government in Alberta brought hope to environmentalists that oil sands development may be slowed down, fossil fuel dependence remains deeply rooted. Gordon Laxer (2015a) notes that Alberta's oil sands industry is not greatly affected by the N D P's climate plan. In fact, Laxer argues that Alberta's plan may impede Canada's ability to meet carbon emission reduction targets.

It is clear that staples-led economic and environmental policy remain persistent. Further, Canada's location in the North American economy must also be understood. Stevis and Mumme (2000) found that N A F T A led to a convergence of environmental policy based on market principles and "weak ecological modernization." Huque and Watton (2010) similarly argue that Canada is converging with the United States in terms of environmental policy as it increasingly involves the private sector, tends toward voluntary forms of regulation, and shifts to marketization (e.g., cap and trade systems). In this manner, the influence of a superpower over a staples economy remains present. At the same time, the "excessive" decentralization of environmental policy to provinces, cities, and communities as part of a regulatory strategy makes it difficult to coordinate efforts that require global scales of enforcement (see Paehlke 2000). Again, a rigorous staples theory requires analytical work that analyzes how multiple scales of (de)regulation reinforce one another.

The environmental movement in Canada is focused on climate change as an existential challenge. Global warming indeed changes everything as Naomi Klein asserts. However, the role fossil fuels (as staples) play in our economy mediates environmental resistance. Although it could be argued that climate change activism is more developed in some jurisdictions, on the whole, environmental movements in Canada have been muted. In their study of environmental justice in Toronto, Keil et al. (2009) find that there is more happening than we recognize as environmental justice is integrated into other struggles (e.g., food security, accessible public transit). Staples production in Canada, however, shapes environmental resistance and the strategic focus in particular ways. Fortunately, there is some evidence that social movements focussed on the economic and environmental consequences of staples production (especially fossil fuels) recognize that multiscalar campaigns are required.

The obvious example is the targeting of pipelines carrying bitumen by climate change activism. How to keep oil in Canadian ground is the strategic question challenging the environmental justice movement. Anti-pipeline battles against Keystone xl, Northern Gateway, and Line 9 are inevitably tied to oil sands extraction. But staples theory can, in part, explain some of the tactics used by anti-pipeline activists. Laxer (2015b) advocates for a "transition" of pipeline development away from exports to the United States to projects that would simply move cleaner oil to the east in a manner that would be phased out over thirty years as cleaner energy is developed. Here, the strategy is based on "breaking" the dependence on oil exports (again staples) to the US empire and creating energy self-sufficiency. Anti-Keystone xl activists based in Canada took the struggle to Washington as First Nations activists joined major anti-Keystone demonstrations in 2013 and 2014. Indeed, a defining aspect of anti-pipeline activism has been solidarity with Indigenous groups fighting for resource rights and claims for sovereignty over the territories where pipelines are established. Multiscalar strategies are in place bringing voices from local Indigenous communities in Canada to pressure imperialist and metropolitan decision makers. One could argue that staples thinking – a clear recognition of the economic relationship staples economies have with metropolitan centres – has influenced anti-pipeline activist tactics.

At a deeper level, staples theory may inform mainstream anti-extraction protests and alternatives. Building on earlier anti-capitalist critics of Innis and traditional cpe, Angus argues in his 2010 edited collection that the key to environmental resistance is a class-based strategy that establishes strong red-green alliances to form ecosocialist alternatives (see also Sandberg and Sandberg 2010). This differs significantly from emerging blue-green alliances in Canada that advocate for more "green" work and just transition for workers in staples extraction to other forms of work (e.g., green energy). Again, for many critics of traditional cpe, the issue is not so much the unsustainability and volatility of staples production (as Innis and his followers note) but rather the systemic problems with capitalism itself that must be addressed if climate disaster is to be averted on a global scale. Still, any resistance group must address and understand how workers and communities unevenly depend on staples.

It is the multiple scales of both analysis and action that must be considered carefully with staples theory. As capitalism is inherently uneven (and must be so), staples theory is one way of understanding the same unevenness and resistance to resource extraction. The failure to understand Canada's complex resource economy at a sub-national scale and how climate change mitigation and adaption itself has uneven and contradictory implications for communities and workers will impede abilities to organize the mass movement needed for systemic change.

CONCLUSION

In this paper we have argued that a staples approach to Canadian political economy is still relevant despite the significant changes to Canada as an advanced capitalist economy. Specifically, we suggest that staples theory is most applicable at sub-national scales of analysis. While an orthodox application of Innis' staples theory is undoubtedly problematic, if the theory is allowed to evolve and applied to scales beyond the national it offers useful insights to understand the Canadian political economy. We therefore suggest that Canada's economy constitutes a neo-staples economy, one whereby staples continue to shape social relations within the state, but in forms that deviate significantly from earlier formulations.

While Canada may be a second-tier imperialist power, that power itself has emerged out of staples-led development. The Canadian state and resource capital have expanded extractive operations into the Global South as an outgrowth of domestic staples production. An imperialist Canada also uses finance and telecommunications vehicles to advance its interest abroad, but it can be argued that these too are related to staples development (e.g., mining capital, communications infrastructure developed to bring resources to market). At the very least, we can consider Canada's imperialism as "staples led" – as it continues to be dominated by larger powers.

We chart three innovations in the political economy of natural resources that call for staples theory to be revised. First, a political economy of resources needs to account for the history of colonial relations and the increasing participation of Indigenous peoples in resource development. In particular, new writing needs to take into account the central role played by Indigenous peoples in resource governance and in the harnessing resource rents locally through employment, subcontracting and royalty commitments. Additionally, new understandings of resource economies need to consider the dramatic shift in the organization of work that has taken place across Canada. Last, staples remain at the forefront of environmental policy and social movements (e.g., Oil sands, Line 9, Keystone, clear-cutting etc.). Other "environmental justice" movements do occur, but are marginal compared to the attention climate change and extractive industries receive. It may, however, be premature to label environmental justice movements in Canada a specific "staples environmentalism."

Staples theory provides an important starting point to understanding the uniqueness of the political economy of resource development. As such, staples theory continues to hold relevance for both Indigenous communities and the source regions of southern long-distance commuters. Innis brought an understanding of the particular to economic development that challenged universalist models (Barnes 1996). Staples theory in its crudest formations and applications is not as relevant as it once was. Nevertheless, Innis' ghost continues to haunt Canadian political economy.

NOTES

1 Abele and Stasiulis do recognize some exceptions to their critique, including the work of Asch (1977) and Watkins (1977b).

2 Signatories include the Government of Quebec, the James Bay Energy Corporation, the James Bay Development Corporation, Hydro-Québec, the Grand Council of the Crees (of Quebec), the Northern Quebec Inuit Association, and the Government of Canada.

3 Three examples of projects that were not approved because of resistance from First Nations are: Meares Island, Prosperity Mine, and Kemess North.

6

Political Economy and Quebec Capitalism

Peter Graefe

In the growth years of Canadian political economy, there was a parallel tradition in Quebec studying capitalism and the state. This tradition largely fell off the map in the 1980s, only to start to re-emerge in the twenty-first century. This chapter briefly considers the strengths and limitations of the work from the 1970s in order to retrieve elements for making sense of the contested trajectory of capitalist development in Quebec. It employs the idea of the neoliberalization of Quebec society as a reconnaissance (following McKay 2000) to bring together the political economy of capital and the state with parallel literatures on alternative strategies for development coming out of studies of the women's movement, the community sector, and community economic development actors.

THE POLITICAL ECONOMY TRADITION IN QUEBEC

Given the relatively late development of the social sciences in francophone Quebec, there was no "pre-history" of departments of political economy, as for instance at University of Toronto. Both political science and economics only really came into their own as academic disciplines in Quebec in the 1960s (Salée 1999).

As Mills (2010) has shown, Montreal in the 1960s was a place of significant debate and exchange about colonialism in its various forms, and third worldist ideologies worked their way into political and social analysis. This work provided a useful starting point for fusing nationalism with the overturning of other social hierarchies. Where French Canadian nationalism often had Conservative and masculinist overtones, the new Quebec nationalism of the Quiet Revolution[1] could spark and engage with other radical imaginaries, such as second-wave feminism, Black power, and anticapitalism. The young left intellectuals who tried to build on this, such as Jean-Marc Piotte or Gilles Bourque, tended to gravitate to France for further studies. Indeed, through the late 1960s and early 1970s, many of the budding critical academics passed through Paris, picking up the structuralist Marxism of Louis Althusser and Poulantzas. This produced a particular form of political economy. The humanist influence in English Canadian neo-Marxism, which drew on E.P. Thompson, Raymond Williams, or even Ralph Miliband, was far less present. Also noticeably absent was the tradition of Harold Innis, which remained out of phase with the interests and perspectives of the Quebec academy, both in Innis' day and with the re-engagement with his work by the new Canadian political economy in the 1970s (Salée 1999). Beyond the work of Albert Faucher and Maurice Lamontagne (e.g., Faucher and Lamontagne 1953) on Quebec's economic development, there was hardly an echo of the staples approach.

It is a fool's errand to try and capture the breadth and complexity of the production of these years. One is struck by the relative confidence that the transformation of a range of social relations is at hand, with the bigger question being whether these changes had revolutionary implications or would simply reinforce the capitalist system. True, there was plenty of scepticism about the Parti Québécois and the labour movement, particularly as the decade wore on. This reflected an understanding of the Quiet Revolution as the result of a multi-class compromise, which brought together Quebec-based capital with the working class and elements of the new middle class in a project of economic modernization and welfare state building (Coleman 1989; Gagnon and Montcalm 1990). As this "revolution" stretched into the late 1970s, the difficulty of the working class or other relatively subaltern groups like the women's movement to extract gains from this compromise became a sore point (e.g., see the chapters in Léonard 1978).

This chapter follows one major debate around which others were clustered – namely, the debate about the character of Quebec capitalism. It was led in the conceptual language of the time, which emphasized national fractions of capital. It had a particular interest in the nature of the Quebec bourgeoisie – specifically that fraction of the capitalist class based in Quebec and whose field of accumulation was largely centred in Quebec – and its relations with other fractions of capital active in Quebec, such as those with a pan-Canadian or continental field of accumulation. It was these debates that Coleman (1989) surveyed when he covered Quebec for *The New Canadian Political Economy*.

The critical analyses of the 1970s tended to start from the conception of a power bloc in Quebec made up of Quebec, Canadian, and foreign (mainly American) fractions of capital. Even while recognizing that American imperialism hovered above this power bloc, most of the analyses dealt with the conflict between a Quebec bourgeoisie, centred on developing its Quebec accumulation base, and a Canadian bourgeoisie, for whom Quebec was only part of a larger accumulation base. Since Quebec and Canadian capital occupied many similar industrial fields, they were often in direct competition (see Bélanger and Fournier 1987).

At the time, there were various readings of this conflict. For some, it was a question about managing American imperialism, with the Quebec bourgeoisie using the post-Quiet-Revolution nationalist upsurge to improve its standing in the imperial chain. As such, the post-1976 Parti Québécois government's economic development strategies were considered evidence of a Quebec bourgeoisie using a sovereignist government to renegotiate its place in the networks of big American and Canadian capital. In this view, the PQ was not seeking to launch an autonomous development strategy, but to increase the benefits for Quebec capital in encouraging the use of local sub-contracting (Bélanger 1981–82; Bourque 1984). This came at a time when Canadian capital was hard-pressed to fight back as it had to be working on other fronts trying to stifle the plans of other regional bourgeoisies, particularly those in Western Canada (see Ferland and Vaillancourt 1981; Fournier and Villeneuve 1981). For its part, American imperialism backed the Canadian bourgeoisie due to their joint economic and military (NORAD, NATO) interests built after the Second World War (Paquette 1978).

A more extreme reading came from Pierre Fournier. In his view, a Quebec bourgeoisie had consolidated itself by bringing together parts of the cooperative sector, the state sector (the Caisse de dépôt, Hydro-Québec, and a variety of investment bodies) and the private sector. This bourgeoisie used the provincial state to defend its interest and extend its accumulation base at the expense of Canadian capital. In the constitutional disputes of the time, the PQ could be seen as representing the interests of the cooperative and state elements of that bourgeoisie. By increasing the powers of the Quebec state, the PQ could enhance the state's ability to favour Quebec capital (Fournier 1978; Fournier et al. 1981). The project of sovereignty-association, put forward in the 1980 referendum, could be seen as an autocentric and relatively autonomous development strategy for Quebec capital (at least with respect to Canadian capital – the place for American capital was more or less safeguarded in the view of Fournier et al. (1981)), and the considerable efforts taken by Canadian capital to ensure a victory of the No side provided confirming evidence that these were the stakes. The division between the Quebec and the Canadian bourgeoisies was so palpable that it extended right down to business organizations, with the Montreal Board of Trade and the Conseil du Patronat representing big Canadian and American capital, and the Montreal and Quebec Chambers of Commerce being closer to Quebec capital (Fournier 1976).

With the advantage of hindsight, some problems can be identified in this analysis. First, it exaggerated the conflict between the different fractions of the Quebec bourgeoisie. The emphasis is understandable given the very tangible division between the francophone and Anglophone business communities. The politicization of francophones' historic inferiority and the efforts made by Quebec governments in the 1960s and 1970s to reverse this historic disadvantage also underlined the importance of this cleavage. But forty years later, this period instead looks like the start of the integration of these fractions under the hegemony of American and Canadian capital.

For instance, Coleman and Mau (2002) suggest that the ethnic division between the Montreal Board of Trade and the Montreal Chamber of Commerce started to decline after the PQ's 1976 victory, when they worked together to counter the flight of capital and head offices. With the departure of the more intransigent members of the Anglophone business community and the growing influence of francophone executives, the Board and the Chamber merged in 1992. The near merger of the Conseil du Patronat and the Chambre de Commerce du Québec in the early 2000s is another sign of the convergence in the view of capital in Quebec. The divisions noted by Fournier in the 1970s no longer seemed so insurmountable.

In a similar vein, federal and provincial policies encouraged changes in the corporate network. Thirty years ago, Bélanger and Fournier (1987) underlined how the emphasis on bilingualism and multiculturalism had an impact on the nomination of representatives of Quebec capital to corporate boards for Canadian firms. While often a limited form of representation, it nevertheless constituted a concession to Quebec capital that had an effect in reducing conflict. This seems to be confirmed in Carroll's data (2004, 103): the percentage of francophones in the corporate elite directing firms based in Quebec increased from 12 per cent in 1976 to 31 per cent in 1996. Similarly, provincial language laws requiring firms to use French as the language of work opened senior management jobs to francophones even in firms owned by Canadian and American capital (Coleman 1984).

The exaggerated account of fractional conflict within Quebec was mirrored in the analysis of conflicts between different regionally based bourgeoisies in Canada, missing the more fundamental recomposition of these groupings around a common neoliberal and free trade consensus. In other words, the analysis ignored what was happening in the global political economy both in terms of national economic management (with the shift from Keynesianism to neoliberalism) and in terms of the organization of production (with the creation of global production chains and financialization). The analysis also had a weakness in its methodological nationalism. By emphasizing competition between national capital fractions trying to reproduce national spaces of accumulation, it missed the peculiar character of post-war American imperialism. The Americans rebuilt the global economy by penetrating the different social formations of Western Europe and Japan in a manner to align their capitalist classes around institutions and productive systems promoted by American capital. To follow Nicos Poulantzas or Robert Cox, these were "internationalized" in the post-war period in the sense of accepting the responsibility to create the internal conditions necessary for accumulation internationally (see Panitch and Gindin 2003–04).

Had the analysis followed this line, it might have offered a way to overcome an overemphasis on national fractions of capital, and to instead try to capture relationships between global processes of capital mobility and territorially rooted nation states. Individual capitals have increased their direct integration into global economic calculations, with even domestically oriented firms needing to make decisions based on international options and constraints. These decisions are nevertheless made complex by the fact that production takes place in a specific national context and according to the laws and policies of that state. Even where the realization of investment or reproduction of capital takes place in the international arena, accumulation still depends on fluctuating exchange rates and national trade policies (Bryan 1995; Rude 2005).

National states are therefore pulled in two potentially contradictory directions. First, the adoption of global calculations by multinational and exporting firms creates a powerful bloc of actors who want the state to manage the national economy so that exchange rates and balances of payments support the internationalization of the circuit of capital. But this internationalization also reinforces international competition and thus the need to find new comparative advantages. Second, states must also reproduce the nation as a lived political reality, and to do so, they need the legitimacy that comes from maintaining living standards (Bryan 1995). States can be conceived of as torn between assuring the global circulation of capital, on the one hand, and of trying to attract investment through favouring domestic competitiveness, on the other. In other words, there is an ongoing tension between nationalism and internationalism.

This calls for a different kind of political analysis. First, rather than starting from the "nationality" of capital, it suggests looking at how individual capitals identify their interests in terms of exchange rates, trade policies, competition policies, and domestic fiscal policies. It is then a question of how these capitals organize themselves through the state to create hegemonic projects, assembling the specific interests into a common development project. Second, one needs to trace the political process that tries to reconcile the internationalization of the state with its nationality and the reproduction of a national community. In other words, beyond the development of hegemonic projects within capital, there is the question of how capital redefines national projects, faced with other projects of national development held by other social actors. This invites an expansion of the scope of analysis to a broader range of actors and concerns, and indeed to unequal social relations beyond those of class and nationality that were central to the work of the 1970s.

This new analysis begins with a relatively blank slate, in part because the earlier analysis of class fractions more or less ended with the 1982 referendum, or with the publication of Fournier and Bélanger's *L'entreprise québécoise* in 1987. Apart from an update of the latter book in 1998, and a bit of research on financial networks, there was little development of this tradition until several pieces were published in *Nouveaux cahiers du socialisme*, beginning in 2009 (e.g., Beaulne 2009, 2013).

The reason for the decline of this analysis, and of political economy analysis more broadly, is threefold. First, it is easy to see how the nationalist surge of the 1960s and 1970s created hopes for political transformation, particularly through the PQ and the sovereignist project. The failure of the 1980 referendum, the use of draconian back-to-work legislation on public sector workers in 1981, and the Patriation of the Constitution without Quebec's consent (but with limited public outcry in 1982), all contributed to a general morosity on both the activist and the intellectual left (Beaudet 2011).

Second, many critical academics who worked with structuralist Marxist analytical categories in the 1970s jettisoned these commitments in favour of post-structuralism. It is not so far as it might first seem from Althusser's

ideological state apparatuses interpellating subjects to Foucault's governmentality. This led to a blossoming of work on nationalism, citizenship,
and identity in the late 1980s and 1990s, but this work was at best loosely
linked to an analysis of capitalism in Quebec, or political economy more
generally. There was a big missed opportunity here in the jump from
structural Marxism to post-Marxism, namely the chance to consider how
a materialist political economy analysis might illuminate and be informed
by identity politics. For instance, in mobilizing Quebecers to support its
project for sovereignty the Quebec nationalist movement had to juggle
many competing conceptions of what defined the Quebec nation, and
how Quebec sovereignty would lead to a renegotiation of unequal social
relations, such as race/ethnicity, gender, or class. Most Quebecers would
not support sovereignty if it was simply about changing the flags. They
wanted to know how it would enable them to live better. A materialist
political economy could provide a lens to understand the negotiation of
claims to inclusion or exclusion in national identity as rooted in power:
nationalist leaders had to open the possibility of a more equitable renegotiation of society, but always within a reading of what was "realistic"
in terms of the existing distribution of power. This nationalist mobilization
nevertheless also transformed the political economy by enabling the mobilization and expression of different paths to development that were taken
up in varying degrees in state policies (Rioux Ouimet 2017; Graefe 2015).

This is related to a third point, namely the foregrounding of other
social relations, and particularly those related to immigration and cultural
diversity. Given the importance of the unresolved national question, the
contestation of these relationships took on a complicated geometry, leading to proposals on how they might be expressed or managed in order
to meet some standard of justice. The contribution of scholars who still
kept a foot in the realm of political economy was to criticize the silences
of the more mainstream debates on this topic: did they pay sufficient
attention to the economic circumstances of various communities and the
manner in which they affected the inclusion, participation, and equality
of groups? Did they continue to marshal a nationalist frame that under-
played histories of dispossession of the first peoples and racialization?
Did they recognize diverse identities, but mostly instrumentally – that is,
in order to serve the Quebec national project rather than democratic
equality? In *Understanding Canada*, Salée and Coleman (1996) surveyed
these debates.

The decline of the "national fraction" analysis of Quebec capitalism
is a good thing to the extent that it opened spaces for voices that were

lost in its big-picture posturing about imperialism. After all, behind this late 1970s debate were other contributions, trying to understand feminist pressures on the state and the PQ government, or relations between the labour federations and big picture development strategies. Moreover, an overemphasis on how Quebec francophones are subjects of imperialism made it hard to unpack how these francophones sustained colonial relationships with First Nations communities. In a sense, the strength of the nationalist imaginary meant that even many critical academics had a hard time integrating Indigenous demands for sovereignty and self-government ahead of the resolution of the national question pitting Quebec against Canada (for a fuller discussion see Salée 2003).

In the process, much less was said about the co-construction of aboriginal organizations and demands, as the flexing of the Quebec's state economic capacity (for instance in developing the James Bay hydroelectric project) and political potential (in making claims for greater autonomy in Canada) ran into the "internal" limits of Indigenous claims to territory and self-governance. By making the language of "nation" common currency in Canadian political discourse, and in placing Canada's form of regime in question, Quebec nationalism transformed the field of political opportunities for Quebec's and Canada's first peoples. If questions of sovereignty were going to be debated, the protection of historic rights required new organizations and representations to assert claims of aboriginal sovereignty and nationality (see Bourque and Duchastel 1996; Jenson and Papillon 2000; Rousseau 2008).

However, the net effect of the decline of "national fraction" analysis was less an opening to these voices than it was a deradicalization of the academy and a thinning out of political economy analysis. Nevertheless, the social movements continued to be objects of study – especially the women's movement, the labour movement, and the community movement. These were joined by the anti-globalization/alter-globalization movement, especially after the 2001 Summit of the Americas in Quebec City, and the student movement, especially following the 2005 student strike and the 2011 Maple Spring (Dufour 2013; Dufour and Savoie 2014).

If one route out of structuralist Marxism was post-structuralism, the other was the *Régulation* school, where the influence of Robert Boyer and Alain Lipietz was particularly strong. This fed into the economic sociology of the CRISES research group, which looked for a non-neoliberal mode of regulation built around positive-sum capital-labour compromises in the workplace and local and regional development. This contributed to the idea of Quebec's socio-economic exceptionalism: that there was a Quebec model of development that differed from the surrounding North American neoliberalism through the much greater adoption of labour-employer partnerships in the workplace, the involvement of a wide range of stakeholders in development decision-making, and the use of the "social economy" to find innovative solutions to social exclusion. This formed the basis of the "counterparadigm" of social and economic development for which Daniel Salée and William Coleman (1996) provided an even-handed assessment in *Changing Canada*.

The *Régulation school*-inspired analysis also fed into the work of the GRETSÉ, which was more interested in a political sociological analysis of state form (from Fordism to post-Fordism, or from Liberal State to Welfare State to the Neoliberal State) and particularly the restructuring of social protection in post-Fordist times. Over time, this approach became anchored in fairly standard institutionalist and comparative welfare state literatures. One example is the debate over the causes of Quebec's exceptionalism in terms of tracing a lower social inequality path than the other Canadian provinces (see van den Berg et al 2017; Noël 2013).

NEW PATHS

Scholars have continued to work in the broad field of political economy, but without institutions to gather their work together into joint research programs. As a result, the output is fragmented in the topics and thematics covered. The creation of a left policy think tank, IRIS, in 2000 and the subsequent launch of the activist-academic *Nouveaux cahiers du socialisme* in 2009, are promising events in terms of creating institutions that might reduce that fragmentation of political economy work on Quebec.

The remainder of this chapter will propose a reconnaissance of more recent developments in the field. Ian Mackay (2000, 620) has proposed the term reconnaissance as a manner of taking stock of a field in a broad sense, without melting analyses into a uniform synthesis. It provides a way of treating individual studies as "sightings": while irreducible to a single narrative, they can nevertheless form part of the map of a more general argument. Here, my aim is twofold. First, the reconnaissance provides a manner of tracing some lines of connection through diverse contributions, providing a partial synthesis of what recent work on Quebec political economy has contributed. But it also traces out new paths for pursuing a political economy analysis of Quebec.

The reconnaissance I propose is to read work since the 1980s as involving the "neoliberalization" of Quebec society, which provides a way to return to the earlier interest in capital and the state but with changes that respond to earlier shortcomings. It starts from this paper's earlier critique of the use of national fractions in economic analysis, and the need to replace this with an analysis of how capital organizes to align the state with the global political economy, on the one hand, and how other forces react to this realignment of the state or try to shape the state with their own alternative development projects. This provides a closer alignment with the global political economy by considering the strategies of capitalists and groups of capitalists, including how they change over time as the economic structure of global capitalism changes. It also allows for a richer understanding of the politics of hegemony and consent as the mobilization of identity claims intersects with debates about development and in the process shapes the social and economic strategies of contemporary Quebec.

By posing this as a process of neoliberalization is not to posit a necessary *telos*, but to recognize the material and discursive pressures on social and economic management pushing for a redeployment of the state from the Keynesian emphasis on sustaining demand that marked the 1960s and 1970s, towards an emphasis on structural competitiveness and the recommodification of labour. The general outline presented in the chapters by McBride and Thomas and Ross is applicable here, but each political community has its particularities shaping neoliberalization, affecting which parts of the preceding Keynesian period are retained and what possibilities for alternatives are developed. This process can be captured through juxtaposing two paths, namely an analysis of the "social movement from above" that pressed for the adoption of a neoliberal state form in Quebec, as well as the "social movement from below" that both contested this first movement and proposed alternatives (Cox and Nilsen 2014).

It should be noted that this approach shares a shortcoming reflected in most of the work being surveyed, namely that it takes the Quebec state for granted, and thereby erases important questions related to contested national claims, be it the claims of First Nations communities against the Quebec and Canadian states, or the unresolved status of Quebec's place in Canada. Through the 1990s and after, scholars with a critical view of unequal social relationships grappled with these questions (see Salée 2013 for an overview). With the exception of Bourque and Duchastel's 1996 book, few studies have connected a critical analysis of constitutional questions with the sustained study of neoliberalism.

SOCIAL MOVEMENT FROM ABOVE

With the adoption of neoliberalism in the United States on the heels of the 1979 Volcker shock and the election of President Reagan in 1980, the idea that the Quebec State might plan and manage investment in a manner of creating an autonomous development model moved from the highly improbable to the unthinkable. The point at which the Quebec capitalist class fully threw its lot in with a neoliberal trajectory has not been studied. However, for the employers' associations, the adoption of a neoliberal program in a strict sense dates from the early 1980s. Whereas their pre-budget briefs used to be a time for discussing macro-economic targets to sustain high levels of employment, by the early 1980s they called for a redefinition of the state's role in the economy. The unemployment and budgetary crisis that came with the early 1980s recessions made the Lévesque PQ government receptive to this call (see Graefe 2004). While the Quebec story has its own particularities, it is similar to the one that McBride provides for Canada as a whole, both in its timing and in the messy entanglement of neoliberal emergences with Keynesian holdovers.

The employers' associations promoted streamlining the state to prioritize the international competitiveness of firms and to discipline inflationary social demands. Moving from budgetary policy to trade policy, where firms themselves would be disciplined by competition, opinions were divided, and work was needed to build a unified business consensus. It was mainly manufacturing interests focused on the domestic market that opposed broadly liberalized trade. At a very general level, there is a divergence between the CPQ's "unequivocal but prudent" support for free trade, and the very tortured support offered by the Canadian Manufacturer's Association based on the necessity to ensure access to the American market. In the latter case, this position was the result of export-oriented manufacturers using their trade association to try to convince domestic manufacturers about potential benefits.

The Quebec Chamber of Commerce, in turn, put forward a discourse to rally small and medium size businesses. Its representatives underlined the popularity of free trade among surveyed members, as well as the support of the Chamber and its affiliates at each step of the process. This discourse situated free trade as the obvious choice for a class of entrepreneurs who saw themselves as dynamic risk-takers who could achieve their full potential on a continental stage.

The work to create a consensus on free trade also took place through the state. New state-run export consulting organizations, for instance, played a preponderant role in gathering SMEs behind this strategy. Darel Paul (2004) observes how these organizations failed in increasing the SME's share of international exports but succeeded in propagating the ideology of trade liberalization in a potentially protectionist small business milieu.

As such, since the beginning of the 1980s, there was near unanimity around the neoliberal project among the leading representatives of employers. The desire to promote this project further is seen in the creation of new ideological instruments in the 1990s and early 2000s, such as the Institut économique de Montréal (IEDM), a free market think tank, and the Institut sur les partenariats public-privé, as well as in the increased free market tilt of the economic visions of the Quebec Liberal and the Action démocratique du Québec parties. The idea that there is a class fraction in Québec that would have an interest in leading an autonomous development project, an important idea in the 1970s accounts discussed above, is not credible faced with the quasi-unanimous adoption of neoliberalism as the path to development by employers' organizations, their think tanks, and their political parties.

This program "denationalized" Quebec capital, in the sense that the national bourgeoisie (to use that problematic concept) backed a neoliberal project and so gave up its role as the cornerstone of an autonomous development path. This project was also "denationalizing" in making preferential treatment for Quebec capital illegitimate. This did not mean that the institutions built during the Quiet Revolution to favour Quebec firms, such as the Caisse de dépôt, suddenly disappeared. They continue to play a role in developing and reproducing a corporate elite in Quebec, and to give Quebec a different economic profile from other Canadian provinces – for instance in having many more sources of public venture capital. Their capacity to draw on a nationalist legitimacy allows them to persist in their role, and the firms that benefit from these state institutions have every interest in maintaining them, provided that their role remains discreet and does not interfere with their integration in the global economy (see Rioux-Ouimet 2012, 2017).

But this analysis of the neoliberalization of the Quebec political economy requires some further specification at a different level of resolution. To consider the changing role and positioning of the Caisse de dépôt is to point to the importance of strategy and institutional diversity that shape the process of neoliberalization. The Quebec of 2015 is not the Quebec of 1980. The intervening years have witnessed the financialization of the economy that has been observed across the Global North. At a banal level, this is seen in the decline in manufacturing, on the one hand, and the growth of the financial services sector and the residential construction sector, on the other. The related process of service sector dualization is visible in the rise of non-standard and precarious work, which now accounts for about 37 per cent of all jobs. Even in the years of growth between 1996 and 2009, part-time work grew more quickly than full-time work (Graefe 2011). It is also visible in earnings polarization, which has moved up as in the rest of Canada, with the bottom 70 per cent of families providing more hours of work for very limited increases in income (Couturier and Schepper 2010).

This banal analysis nevertheless misses the main point of financialization, namely the manner in which finance comes to discipline the productive economy as a whole. Pineault (2014) has suggestively argued that Quebec is caught in a stagnation-austerity trap. Despite relatively low rates of overall economic growth, the financial sector continues to grow and profit. The manufacturing sector is in tighter straights but is willing to go along with this model as it includes significant wage repression in the export sector. In other words, the internalization of the imperative of competitiveness by workers means there is very little pressure bidding up wages. Slow growth nevertheless undermines the state's revenue base, leading to continued public sector austerity and attempts to chip away at the welfare state, for instance through the recourse to user fees (e.g., higher tuition fees), the normalization of private alternatives (e.g., in health care), or the private delivery of public infrastructure and services (e.g., through public-private partnerships; see Albo and Fanelli this volume).

This situation poses a real challenge to those workers who achieved a middle-class lifestyle through sharing in the fruits of growth. When the remaining prospects for growth in this stagnation-austerity trap come from either the marketization of public services, or the acceleration of mining and forestry in the north, the capacity to sustain this lifestyle and some semblance of ecological balance becomes doubtful (see also Pineault 2012). Pineault's reading is a provocative one and points to a range of questions requiring more study. How does the process of financialization roll out over space and time, including the development of new linkages between the financial sector and the state around policies for the financial industry, as well as around trade, labour markets, and taxation? Why do the Charest and Couillard governments invest such political capital in northern resource development, given the massive public subsidy (e.g., building roads) and the very modest royalties extracted (but see Hurteau and Fortier 2015)?

MEETING THE SOCIAL MOVEMENTS FROM BELOW

This big picture story about the insertion of Quebec capitalism into global neoliberalism, and of the state's role in facilitating it, used the example of the Caisse de dépôt to broach the issue of reconciling global capitalism with the reproduction of nationality. However, the need for an economy that reproduces a community by providing resources to meet societal expectations and demands is yet broader. One of the popular solutions to this tension is to invoke the necessity of competition. States can give a nationalist spin to their efforts to create conditions of domestic production that will allow for a competitive rate of profit. The idea of competitiveness gives global processes a national interpretation, by linking the fate of a country's citizens to the success of their national economy in attracting mobile capital.

This was certainly part of the appeal to the Parti Québécois in the early 1990s, as it provided a way to link a commitment to the rules of global economic competition with a set of progressive values. They argued that competitiveness required an inclusive Quebec where all resources were mobilized and no one was left behind. This "competitive nationalism" succeeded in rallying the left behind the sovereignist option in 1995 and was congruent with the "progressive competitiveness" being mooted by the labour federations. For the latter, the idea was that the negotiation of workplace flexibility, in conjunction with inclusive stakeholder decision-making around regional development and labour market policy, could lead to innovative approaches in the workplace and beyond. This innovation, in turn, could allow firms to compete on the high road, without cuts to jobs or to pay and benefits.

Critics of progressive competitiveness nevertheless remind us that not all countries can be successful at the same time. Indeed, the logic of competition means that even the "winners" will have to work ever harder and engage in forms of "competitive austerity" (Albo 1994) to keep up (such as the wage repression in manufacturing noted by Pineault [2014]). In the process, progressive forces are likely to sacrifice their legitimacy in agreeing to a series of increasingly one-sided deals that favour capital. Students of the Quebec labour movement recognized this dynamic at the 1996 Social and Economic summits, where the unions agreed to balanced budgets (and by extension public sector program and employment cuts), in return for more or less empty job-creation promises (see Piotte 1998).

However, one should not be too quick to see this period as a pure recuperation of the labour movement, or indeed of other movements. As

Wood's chapter in this volume observes, there is a strong tradition of large-scale protest in Quebec, in which the labour movement continues to have an important role. Researchers on state-social movement linkages have underlined the particular form these take in Quebec (see Haddow 2015; Laforest 2007; Noël 2013). There are a range of institutions, ranging from local and regional health care boards, through to local and regional development bodies, to peak level labour force training tables, where one finds the representation of a range of stakeholders. This includes the representation of community organizations and women's organizations to an extent unseen elsewhere in Canada. The result is a particular form of insider-outsider politics, where social movements are able to find relays within the state to carry their demands and protect past gains. The term "conflictual concertation" is sometimes used to capture the creative tension between the potential for cooptation, and the capacity to challenge and question government plans (Jetté 2008; Masson 2015).

One of the important wars of position over the past decade has been precisely over this form of decision-making. The post-2003 Charest Liberal government and the post-2014 Couillard Liberal governments showed a strong desire to break from this "corporatism" (Boismenu et al. 2004). After all, conflictual concertation both slows the neoliberal roll back of the welfare state while providing a channel into the state for the ideas of these movements. To date, important elements of this structure of representation have been maintained despite attempts by a frustrated right to take them apart (e.g., Haddow 2015). On the other hand, the relative lack of interest by the short-lived Marois PQ government (2012–14) in reviving this form of concertation does raise questions about its longer-term viability (Graefe 2012).

If concertation provides a door into the state, what ideas are movements trying to push through that door? A lot of the opposition is generated from a basic social democratic understanding of the importance of social rights and of the role of social programs in ensuring those rights. As the hope of a "win-win" progressive competitiveness is ground down by the stagnation-austerity trap, this social democratic understanding becomes an important centre of gravity in protests against austerity. It may be augmented by ecological reflections about the non-advisability of extractavism or even "growth for growth's sake" as a response to the current stagnation (Pineault 2014; see also Stanford this volume).

This "social rights" perspective has been enriched by the insights of movements around globalization and global justice. These have had a particular influence in Quebec due to the twin processes of the women's movement acting as the organizational hub of the first World March of Women in 2000, and the organizing around and against the Summit of the Americas in Quebec City in 2001 (Dufour 2013). The influence of this movement is an important piece of the puzzle explaining the origins of Québec Solidaire, a new left party launched in 2006 (see Dufour 2009; Boudreau 2015). Global linkages have given a greater depth of economic critique to the women's movement (e.g., Dufour 2008), as well as inspiring new strategies in the labour movement for dealing with new employment categories (see Noiseau 2014).

The ideas being fed into the state are not solely reactive or defensive, however. Part of the success of progressive movements in Quebec has been to push the state in terms of its reproduction of nationality. Here, the most important actor has been the feminist movement, in developing an economic vision centred around fulfilling basic needs, so as to combat violence and poverty (see Masson 2006, 1999/2000). This has taken a variety of forms, running from improved labour standards, through to supporting community-based "social infrastructures" that fill unmet needs, to improved parental leave and child care policies. As a result, even as Quebec's political economy is neoliberalized along many dimensions, on other dimensions there are social democratic alternatives such as expanded family policy, improvements to labour standards, and the early adoption of a law against poverty (see Dufour 2004; Noël 2013).

The discussion of these social movements from below does have an "institutionalist" taste, as it stresses the ability of movements to find a foothold within the state and to successfully play the game of engaging the state without being coopted. On this front, the causes for success lie in the capacity of organizations to form "civic networks" on a sectoral and cross-sectoral basis, thus providing an organizational basis for mobilization and for making it harder for the state to play interests off against each other (see Laforest 2007). This organizational capacity in turn reflects wins made by the women's and community movements in the 1970s to secure forms of base funding to community organizations, as well as ongoing state funding for sectoral representative and advocacy organizations (Garon and Dufour 2010; see also Boudreau 2015). In the case of the student movement, its success is also built on a unique form of legal recognition – based on an industrial relations model – that provides a unique framework for contestation and strikes compared to the situation in the other provinces (Pineault 2012).

The point in stressing the institutions is not to claim that they are the prime cause for the more contentious politics in Quebec or the capacity to sustain a higher degree of redistribution in Canada. Clearly, effective and energetic organizing coupled with a protest tradition interact with these institutions to produce sustained contestation. However, there is sometimes a fetishization of Quebec protests in the rest of Canada – seeing them as proof that what is needed is a radicalization of discourse and a will to take radical actions – that ignores the institutional infrastructure that sustains movements between protest cycles, that enables linkages at moments of mobilization, and that provides the necessary structure to make protest actions endure long enough to affect social debates and discussion (see Dufour and Savoie 2014).

The relative "denationalization" of capital discussed above may have different knock-on effects in other movements. Blad (2011), for instance, argues that as neoliberalism increasingly puts the economy off limits as a place to exert national identity, the state comes to invest more in developing national identity in the cultural sphere. There is some evidence that the neoliberal turn has complicated relationships between the nationalist movement and other social movements, effectively splitting the nationalist coalition in two. On the one side, many progressive actors have played down the national question and adopted a fairly open definition of the nation, while on the other side the more traditional nationalist organizations have regrouped around a narrower definition based on the historic French Canadian community living in Quebec (see also Dufour and Traisnel 2014). Recent debates on reasonable accommodations and on secularism have provided windows for many who have been left behind by neoliberalism to express their discontent through a particular form of republican nationalism. Dressed in the language of protecting the secular nature of the Quebec state and gender equality, this nationalism has succeeded in federating militant secularists and republican feminists with conservative nationalists and Islamophobes. This nationalism is not appreciated by Quebec capitalists, who fear it will interfere with their desire for a cosmopolitan space of freely flowing investment and high-end human capital. But it is perhaps even more complicated for the progressive social movements, as it disorganizes the linkages between nationalism and progressive goals that proved crucial to challenging the state and capital over the past half century.

CONCLUSION

The study of Quebec's political economy has had enduring interest as part of the study of Canadian political economy for two reasons. On an empirical level, the presence of a left nationalist upsurge post-1960, and its role in shaping social movement struggles and electoral politics over the ensuing fifty years, has its own interest. In many ways, the Quebec left has been a pace-setter for welfare-state building and social democratic innovation in Canada. With large social mobilizations like the Common Front strikes of 1972 and the Maple Spring of 2012, as well as the potential reshaping of the Canadian political community with the 1980 and 1995 referendums, there has been plenty of potential for social transformation. On a theoretical level, the presence of a parallel community of critical scholars in Quebec with a different set of academic touchstones and traditions has provided some opportunity for analytical innovation. Nevertheless, the particular manner in which Canadian political economists engage with questions of nationalism and diversity cannot be divorced from the pressure that Quebec nationalism has placed on social movement and class politics in Canada.

From the reconnaissance attempted in this chapter, two ideas seem to stand out. First, for those actively studying Quebec, there may be value in trying to make sense of particular political conjunctures against a backdrop of a more general neoliberalization of Quebec, and the tension involved in reconciling the internationalization of the state with the reproduction of the nation. Where once nationalist demands and possibilities of social transformation were linked, as at the time of the 1980 and 1995 referendums, they now seem disarticulated. The progressive competitive nationalism of the 1990s appears to have eroded the progressive sheen on the nationalist project, as promises of social change remained unrealized due to new global realities. While the left remains nationalist, it is no longer so easily organized into the PQ's sovereignist politics and turns elsewhere such as Québec Solidaire. In turn, the dominant nationalism of the PQ moves to mobilize less around socioeconomic inclusion, and more around appeals to ethnic identity, such as with the Values Charter.

Second, for those looking at Quebec from elsewhere for inspiration, the ability of progressive actors to navigate insider-outsider tensions with stakeholder institutions may be a key point of interest. Whether in the institutional politics of the women's movement, or the relatively flat mobilization structures of the Maple Spring's student movement, there is a degree of strategic reflection on the importance of organizational structures in blocking austerity and in proposing alternatives that deserves greater outsider attention (Graefe and Rioux 2017).

NOTE

1 The Quiet Revolution refers to the post-1960 period in Quebec. In its narrow-
est meaning, it describes the 1960–66 period when the Liberals under Jean
Lesage were in power, but it is often extended through to the end of the first
PQ government in 1985. The Quiet Revolution is marked by the rapid decon-
fessionalization of Quebec society and the development of the Quebec state
as a primary lever for the advancement of the rights and status of francophones in Quebec. Modern Quebec nationalism dates from this time, as do
major parts of the Quebec welfare state, and various state institutions built to
favour the concentration and expansion of francophone-owned business interests. See Mills (2010) and Gagnon and Montcalm (1990) for a fuller
discussion.

PART THREE

State, Capital, and Institutions

7

From Keynesianism to Neoliberalism: The State in a Global Context

Stephen McBride

One of the prevailing images of the post-Second World War era is the establishment of a policy regime known as Keynesianism or the Keynesian Welfare State (KWS) and, from the mid-1970s, its gradual displacement by an alternative regime – originally termed neo-conservatism or, more commonly today, neoliberalism.[1] Though the term policy regime (Wilson 2000) refers to the ideas and policies, institutions, and interests that are applied to and involved in the governance of a particular society at a particular time, discussion often focuses primarily on the ideational level. Indeed, much of the discussion of the transition from Keynesianism to neoliberalism features the replacement of one policy paradigm (Hall 1993; Skogstad and Schmidt 2011) by another. However, it is reasonable to associate the concepts of policy regimes and policy paradigms with particular configurations of social forces and institutional structures that are consistent with implementing them.

This link between ideas, institutions, interests, and underlying structures is perhaps better captured by the Marxian concept of social structures of accumulation (Kotz, McDonough, and Reich 1994; O'Hara 2006). A social structure of accumulation is: "the complex of institutions which support the process of capital accumulation" (Kotz, McDonough, and Reich 1994, 1). If a particular social structure of accumulation – "the ensemble of economic, political, and ideological institutions which serve to reproduce capitalist relations of production" – can no longer perform that function, then crisis results, and can only be resolved by constructing new institutions that can (McDonough 1994, 80). This is cast in rather functionalist terms. In the account that follows here, the politics

– including the actors involved in creating a new set of economic, political, and ideological institutions adequate to reproduce capitalist relations of production – will receive due attention.

An image often associated with the shift from Keynesianism to neoliberalism is that of a change from state-interventionist in the Keynesian period to "laissez-faire" in the neoliberal era. However, it seems more accurate to acknowledge that whilst the state's role may have changed, it retains a central and active role in both periods, rather than positing activism in one and withdrawal in the other. With respect to globalization Janine Brodie argued that states had acted as its "midwives" (Brodie 1996, 386); the same is true of neoliberalism. Underlying its central role is an ongoing concern with orchestrating conditions conducive to capital accumulation (McCormack and Workman 2015; McBride and Whiteside 2011b).

Notwithstanding the eventual triumph of neoliberalism, elements of the Keynesian welfare state clearly linger today, albeit in a different institutional and political context from that in which they were created. However, assuming the readership of this book is primarily university students born since 1990, for most readers the Keynesian era itself is beyond living memory and personal experience and it will be useful to begin by reviewing the period by outlining briefly its characteristics, social and institutional bases, and some of its strengths and weaknesses.

THE KEYNESIAN ERA[2]

The Great Depression of the 1930s was a global crisis in which Canada, because of its dependence on commodity exports (prices of which plummeted), was arguably one of the worst affected countries. The gross national product fell by 42 per cent between 1929 and 1933, while unemployment peaked at around 30 per cent and remained in double digits until the outbreak of Second World War. The welfare state was hardly developed, most responsibility for "relief" rested at the financially strapped provincial and municipal levels, benefits were at poverty levels, and whole categories, such as single unemployed males, were excluded altogether unless they entered "relief camps."[3] Orthodox economic theory and government policy continued to rely on a faith in small government, austerity and balanced budgets, and the power of market forces.

A British liberal economist, John Maynard Keynes, fearful of the ability of the capitalist system to survive such an economic crisis, developed an alternative theoretical perspective intended to save capitalism from itself by modifying its operation. His ideas grew in influence during the depression and war years and became the new policy orthodoxy in much of the Western world after 1945. Underpinning the Keynesian analysis of the Great Depression and its policy contribution in the post-war period was the theoretical demonstration (see Keynes 1936) that markets do not always achieve equilibrium at full employment levels. When they do not, there is underutilization of labour expressed in high unemployment rates, together with high rates of unused capacity of other factors of production. Whilst orthodox economists, then and now, consider that in the long run markets always "clear," this argument gave rise to Keynes's famous riposte that in the long run we are all dead. As a result, more immediate action was needed than waiting for markets to clear.

Given that markets got "stuck" and could stay stuck in sub-optimal condition, with unemployment at unacceptably high levels for prolonged periods, Keynes's explanation focused on a systemic condition to which capitalism was prone – insufficient aggregate demand[4] rather than alleged individual characteristics of the unemployed, as neoliberal labour market theory is prone to do. The solution was for the state to compensate for the lack of aggregate demand by adjusting its spending and taxation levels (fiscal policy), and/or interest rates (monetary policy), and by establishing a set of "automatic stabilizers"[5] for the economy through social policy. The generation of additional demand[6] would enable production and employment to resume and be maintained at full employment[7] levels.

In this schema the state's role was active but not, from a private sector perspective, overly interventionist. Investment decisions remained largely in private hands and although new sets of rules were established to make "industrial relations" (i.e., relations between labour and capital) fairer than they had previously been, in countries like Canada it remained largely a matter for business and unions to settle between themselves without extensive state intervention.[8]

The international context after the Second World War provided scope for national Keynesianism. Western powers and elites were concerned about an ideological and political rival in the shape of the USSR, and about working-class power in their own countries. The international financial architecture they established, the Bretton Woods system, constrained international capital movements to some degree and allowed space for national social policies and economic management. The term "embedded liberalism" (Ruggie 1983) was widely used to describe this regime and was contrasted with laissez–faire and doctrines of sound

finance that had dominated pre-war international economic policy
(Helleiner 1994). Still, Keynesianism was not a one-size-fits all policy
regime. It was applied to different degrees and in different ways (and
sometimes hardly at all) depending on national conditions, institutions,
and the balance of class and political forces.[9] In the Canadian case, its
application was less than whole-hearted (Campbell 1987; McBride 1992).
Its implementation was affected by the openness of the Canadian economy, resulting in a blend of staples-derived export dependency and
Keynesianism (Wolfe 1984). The *relative* weakness of Canadian working
class and left organizations, when compared to European ones, was
associated with the very gradual development of welfare state programs
and institutions that remained liberal or residual rather than emulating
the more comprehensive versions found in much of western Europe
(Esping-Andersen 1990).

That said, Canada's gradually expanding social safety net came to
include universal family allowances, a variety of cost-shared federal-
provincial programs for social assistance and welfare, a *Canada Pension
Plan* (CPP) established in 1965 (with a parallel *Quebec Pension Plan*, as
Quebec opted out of the national plan), the *Medical Care Act* (1966),
providing for universal public coverage of hospital and doctors' services,[10]
and a variety of regional development programs. Unemployment insurance had become a federal responsibility by 1940 and from an initial
coverage of 42 per cent of the workforce, achieved almost complete
coverage of the labour force after the 1971 *Unemployment Insurance
Act*, with reasonably generous income replacement rates and flexible
qualifications criteria based on regional variations in unemployment. The
1971 act also introduced publicly provided and paid maternity leave.

Some of the impact of these changes can be tracked by increased government spending, which rose from around 26 per cent of GDP in 1950
to 46 per cent in 1984. The trend was similar to that in other Western
countries, and began in the pre-Keynesian era, an indication that shared
structural factors were at work as well as the new ideas. However, the
expansion after the Second World War was more dramatic and was
generally attributed to the new policy regime. Level of spending is not
the entire story. The Keynesian period was exemplified by the expansion
of the "social wage," broadly defined as material benefits and services
provided to citizens through public expenditures in areas like health,
education, pensions, housing, and social welfare. Spending is part of the
equation, but the sense of real benefits being extended in terms of both
coverage and generosity accounts for the optimism of the period. People

at the time knew that things were better than they had been in the pre-Keynesian past. They assumed, wrongly as it turned out, that this trajectory of gradual improvement would continue into the future.

As was the case elsewhere in the Western world, an expanded social wage or welfare state was accompanied by a healthy labour market. The Canadian commitment to full employment was not that forceful discursively. The 1945 *White Paper on Employment and Income* promised only to deliver "high and stable levels of employment" (Canada 1945). Correspondingly, neither was the practice of the Canadian state particularly robust. Canada's unemployment was higher than the OECD average for most of the period 1945–85 (Campbell 1987; McBride 1992). However, much of the policy discourse did revolve around employment issues that enjoyed high priority, and it can be reasonably argued that between the end of the Second World War and the mid-1970s the Canadian labour market was relatively secure and exhibited relatively full employment. "Relatively" here is in comparison to the preceding situation in the earlier twentieth century and the subsequent situation in the 1980s and beyond. Security refers to the low unemployment levels, increased protection due to unionization, and the low incidence of part-time or temporary work as compared to full-time, ongoing work.

Whether this adds up to a "golden age" is debatable. If the Keynesian full employment era was one of a standard employment relationship (Vosko 2000, 24) featuring ongoing employment with a single employer, full-time work with reasonable hours, often in a unionized environment, these attributes were more commonly found amongst White, male workers. The Keynesian labour market was a gendered and racialized one. And, on some indicators – labour force participation, employment, and unemployment rates – the situation today actually looks better for women than it did in the mid-1970s, or not much different. For women there were significant improvements in all three indicators; for men, the reverse was true. However, in other areas there has been a dramatic across-the-board deterioration since the heyday of Keynesianism. Then, for those who had work but became unemployed, unemployment insurance coverage was more comprehensive and more generous. Protections at work were stronger as union density, especially in the private sector, was higher. The availability of full-time, full-year work was greater and increasingly has been replaced by precarious and insecure employment for many (Lewchuk et al. 2013; Ross and Thomas this volume). Arguably, the quality of work was higher. And Canada was a more equal place, in terms of distribution of income, than it subsequently became (Veall 2012).

The social base of the Keynesian welfare state is generally depicted in terms of a tacit class compromise or social contract between business and labour. Certainly, labour's influence had increased during the Second World War and as a result of the post-war strike wave in industrial centres like Hamilton and Windsor. This, and the mid-1940s' electoral strength of Canada's social democratic party, the CCF, indicated to capital and to the Liberal prime minister, Mackenzie King, that a social compromise, including stealing some policy ideas from the left, would be an intelligent strategy. The Keynesian era was also that of the height of the Cold War. Part of the tacit compromise seems to have been that the Canadian left, and trade unions in particular, become more moderate and distance themselves from association with communism. That done, in a series of internecine battles within Canada's labour movement (Abella 1973; Avakumovic 1975), and with ongoing ideological adaptation by the CCF and subsequently the New Democratic Party (Evans 2014) relations between capital and labour stabilized into an arms-length, generally tolerant accommodation of interests, punctuated by strikes and lock-outs certainly, but conducted within the regulatory system established at the end of the war.

Institutionally, Canadian federalism posed difficulties to the implementation of Keynesian policies as many key areas of social policy and labour jurisdiction were under provincial jurisdiction whilst taxation powers were primarily federal. The Rowell-Sirois Royal Commission[11] had probed these problems and their recommendations – in combination with Keynesian economic theories and wartime centralization – restructured what had been a very decentralized federation. In the post-war period, under what sometimes was referred to as "cooperative federalism," the Canadian state managed to create shared-cost programs in social policy. With the development of an economic crisis and the rise of neoliberalism from the 1970s the degree of cooperation declined, partly in response to what the provinces viewed as federal unilateralism in changing financial guarantees and offloading responsibility and costs onto the provinces and municipalities (Prince 1999; Albo and Fanelli this volume). Whilst cooperative federalism was in effect, however, the building of national standards in a variety of social policy areas on which all Canadians could rely, regardless of the relative wealth of their province, conferred real material benefits and fostered a new Canadian identity in which social provision, moderate redistribution of incomes, and regional equalization all featured. With the rise of neoliberalism, the capacity of Canadian institutions to deliver such outcomes was also constrained by the conditioning frameworks of new international economic agreements and institutions (see Grinspun and Kreklewich 1994; McBride 2010). Although they rarely dealt explicitly with social policies, trade and investment agreements, pressures from international credit rating agencies and monetary organizations, and "best practices" recommendations to make labour markets more flexible all served to embed neoliberal priorities and render Keynesian ones illegitimate.

CRISIS OF THE KEYNESIAN POLICY REGIME

As with its rise, the fall of Keynesianism was an international phenomenon in which national states like Canada were active participants. For many, the repudiation by the American state of the Bretton Woods system of fixed exchange rates unleashed a period of volatility in the global political economy to which states scrambled to adapt. In fact, the gradual increase in the structural power of finance in the 1960s and 1970s may indicate that "embedded liberalism" was less embedded than is commonly thought. State interests also played a role. American hegemony was once expressed through the Bretton Woods arrangements but as these came under challenge from competitors in Europe and Asia, the US state sought new strategies. In the new order of mobile capital, free trade, and deregulated capitalism there was less room for accommodating subordinate classes through union recognition and generous social programs. In both the United States and the United Kingdom the introduction of neoliberalism was associated with aggressive measures against organized labour in the early 1980s. Examples include the firing of air traffic controllers by President Reagan, and Prime Minister Thatcher's waging of an internal war against the National Union of Mineworkers.

In Canada, the political consensus and class compromise surrounding Keynesian policy also began to unravel in the 1970s. Its demise stretched from roughly 1975 to 1995. The opening shot was the Bank of Canada's 1975 conversion to monetarism, expressed as "monetary gradualism" and outlined in the Bank's *Annual Reports* from 1975. Through targeting a non-inflationary increase in the money supply, the bank indicated that monetary policy would no longer play a supportive role to fiscal policy in sustaining full employment. Rather, monetary policy would focus on control of inflation, even if that had detrimental effects on employment. The shift to neoliberalism was partly crisis-driven but, like any crisis, the one of the 1970s needed definition and interpretation. Ideas about the crisis, and what to do about it, mattered. Without being overly reductionist it is clear that the ideas that prevailed were those that reflected concerns among Canadian capital, and their counterparts elsewhere, about how capital accumulation processes could be maintained and potential threats to capital's hegemony from labour and potentially from the state itself could be averted. The post-war period had its share of minor fluctuations in the business cycle. But the first serious economic problems that emerged were in the early 1970s – the United States removed the dollar from gold convertibility in 1972. The international monetary system henceforth became less predictable, capital searched more energetically for cheaper production sites, and a process of "de-industrialization" began in the advanced industrial states. This was compounded by the oil crisis and inflation. Unemployment began to drift upwards and, with it, a "fiscal crisis" of the state was proclaimed (O'Connor 1973) as state revenues and expenditures (at existing tax rates) were declared incompatible. There were steady downward pressures on programs as the neoliberal solution to the crisis gathered strength.

At the ideational level Keynesianism was declared a failure, partly because it was tolerant of budget deficits that, whatever their role may have been in the past, were now seen as counter productive. Keynesianism also failed to anticipate the simultaneous appearance of inflation and unemployment. According to some versions of Keynesianism a country might expect one or the other but not both at the same time. Given the inability of governments to escape this awkward combination of economic problems, new policy options were advanced. In many countries, including Canada, these included wage controls to rein in inflation.[12] Arguably, such measures were designed to maintain the Keynesian consensus on full employment and adequate social programs. But they were denounced from the left for interfering with free collective bargaining and for acting more on prices than on wages, and from the right as representing an unacceptable degree of state interventionism in the economy. The consensus in effect dissolved, and the outcome of the battle over alternatives was acceptance and implementation of neoliberal ideas.

The process of transition was protracted. With the benefit of hindsight, it amounts to a twenty-year period of sustained pressure in a neoliberal direction punctuated by efforts to find alternatives. Such alternatives included trying to alleviate inflation through wage controls (McBride 1983) rather than interest-rate induced recessions and high unemployment, and a nationalist industrial policy, as with the National Energy Program, seen as an alternative to continentalism and letting market forces work their way, as represented by free trade with the United States

(Clarkson 1985). The length of the transition period is an indication that Canadians were reluctant converts to the tenets of neoliberalism and the state's gradual orchestration of the change was a necessary feature.

With the exception of a brief interlude in 1979–80,[13] the Liberal Party under Pierre Trudeau was in office from 1968–84 (and these governments had been preceded by minority Liberal governments in the 1960s). From 1984 until 1993 the Progressive Conservatives under Brian Mulroney[14] formed the government, to be followed from 1993 by Liberal governments under Jean Chrétien and then Paul Martin. The transition from Keynesianism to neoliberalism began under Trudeau, though contestation and a search for alternatives was most apparent in that period, and was completed under Chrétien and his then Finance Minister, Paul Martin. The 1984 Mulroney Conservative government intensified a rhetoric of deficit control, instituted deregulation and privatization, and negotiated a free trade with the United States. All this heralded a new, and non-Keynesian approach. However, the key moment came later when the Chrétien Liberal government produced its 1995 budget, which firmly established the primacy of deficit reduction over maintenance of the social safety net. That budget produced such significant change that is has been depicted as marking one "bookend" of the Keynesian era (Kroeger 1996, 21).

The gradualism of the process[15] can be attributed to a number of factors. First, the process was initially one of trial and error accompanied by uncertainty about whether the mid-1970s crisis was a passing episode or something more systemic. Certainly much of the political elite and even some of the economic elite lacked a clear blueprint of where they wanted to go and many probably favoured the Keynesian world to which they were accustomed, perhaps rejuvenated by new industrial policy initiatives and temporary wage control policies. Second, there was a recognition that the preferences and expectations of Canadians needed to undergo a period of adjustment and to become habituated to a different and, as far as the state was concerned, reduced set of expectations. This could not be accomplished overnight and a prolonged and complex political struggle occurred.

When Prime Minister Trudeau mused in a 1975 year-end television interview that "we haven't been able to make it work, the free enterprise system" his remarks set off a firestorm of criticism (English 2009, 291–8). Business spokespersons were quick to accuse Trudeau of wishing to move Canada towards a socialist state or an authoritarian dictatorship. Clearly, this was hyperbole. However, the context was one in which the federal government had just introduced wage and price controls, a far more interventionist measure than the limited fiscal and monetary policy adjustments typical of the Keynesian era. Labour had been vociferous in its opposition to the move and the degree of interventionism had occasioned business disquiet. Faced with the economic crisis of the mid-1970s, fissures began to merge or deepen between and within political parties and between different state institutions. The Liberal cabinet was deeply divided between Keynesians (including Trudeau) and monetarists,[16] and important sectors of the bureaucracy, including the Department of Finance and the Bank of Canada, were monetarist (English 2009, chapter 10).

These divisions heightened as the era wore on. Almost twenty years later the 1993 Liberal election platform[17] exhibited extreme ambiguity in an effort to keep both factions of the party – business liberals who favoured neoliberalism and Keynesian-inclined social liberals – inside the same tent (Clarkson 2005, 169–76). Behind the conflicts in political parties and institutions, and the growing strength of neoliberalism, lay a powerful array of interests in which a reorganized Canadian business sector played a key role.

The transition period was complicated by various expressions of the national question in Canada. The country faced an existential challenge from sovereignist movements in Quebec that made the straightforward application of a neoliberal vision for a small state stripped of many of its redistributive functions risky. And it is worth recalling that in the late Keynesian period the role of the state became entwined also with a burst of (English) Canadian nationalism that found both cultural and economic expression. A series of reports (Watkins 1968; Gray 1971) created increased awareness of and, in many circles, concern about the level and consequences of foreign ownership in the Canadian economy. A series of policy responses followed, including the creation of the Foreign Investment Review Agency (FIRA) to screen proposed foreign investments and the establishment of a state-owned oil company, Petrocan. Eminent political scientist Donald Smiley (1975) considered that a new National Policy might be in process, one that would be based on an industrial strategy and regaining ownership and control of key economic sectors. As late as 1980, with the introduction of the National Energy Program (NEP) and various other projects such a vision remained in the realm of practical politics.[18] Yet it faced, from the beginning, an alternative based on free trade with the United States, and therefore on continentalism rather than economic nationalism, and a preference for the neoliberal nostrums of a small state, fiscal conservatism, and a less regulated economy.

On these points there may have been initial division within Canadian capital. Increasingly, however, it came to define its interests in continental, or even global terms, and nationalism consequently had little appeal. For some, this was the product of the historic weakness and dependency of Canadian capital, which defined itself as a junior partner of its stronger American counterpart (Niosi 1985; Laxer 1989). More convincingly, for others it was the policy of a mature and highly concentrated Canadian capitalist class that had outgrown its traditional weaknesses and was much more assertive about its needs and wants (Carroll 1986; Richardson 1992). Rather than rely on a relatively small internal market, big players in Canadian business increasingly favoured an export-led growth strategy (Cohen 1991). The price of access to large external markets involved opening up the Canadian market to increased foreign competition. An additional perceived benefit of free trade, from this perspective, was that the rules embodied in free trade agreements would act as constraints on state activism.

Armed with a developing agenda and faced with crises and challenges, the most powerful business organizations in Canada initiated a reorganization of the structure of business representation and used it first to win over virtually the entire business community (which in the mid-1970s was still somewhat divided), and then to extend its reach to the broader society. In 1976 the Business Council on National Issues (BCNI) was founded.[19] It consisted of the CEOs of the top 150 companies in Canada and included, as ex-officio members, the heads of the other main peak business organizations, the Chamber of Commerce and the Canadian Manufacturers Association. This gave it both a powerful representative role but also the capacity to integrate business opinions and, *de facto*, act as an executive committee of Canadian business organizations (Langille 1987). The BCNI spearheaded an "attitude adjustment" in the ranks of business (Bradford 1998) and both directly, and through a bevy of corporate financed think tanks, set about doing the same in the broader political culture.

In the political arena, the significant breakthroughs for the neoliberal program were the election of the Mulroney government in 1984 and the release of the MacDonald Royal Commission Report in 1985. Chaired by a former Liberal cabinet minister, the commission's message was very clear: free trade with the United States and, more generally, greater reliance on market forces and a limited role for the state (Bradford 1988). The internal processes that led to the final report prioritized certain types of evidence – economic orthodoxy leading to continentalist conclusions

– and certain types of interest – business, leading to neoliberal outcomes (Inwood 2005). Once published, the report legitimated the trend towards neoliberalism although significant public resistance continued: witness the hard-fought 1988 election, which turned into a referendum on free trade. Although the Conservatives achieved a majority of seats and hence held onto the government, the parties opposing the agreement gained a majority of votes cast. Similarly, in the 1993 election won by Chrétien's Liberals, it seems that concerns about unemployment were the key to victory: "the Liberal Party won a mandate to increasing employment and fostering economic growth, while no party received a mandate for deficit reduction or cuts to social spending" (Clarke et al. 1996, 141). With the 1995 budget, the government delivered the reverse of these priorities, and the Keynesian era, and the popular aspirations that went with it, could be declared to be over.

How are we to understand the role of the Canadian state during the Keynesian era, during the transition to neoliberalism, and in the neoliberal period itself? There is a lengthy and sometimes vibrant tradition of debates on "theories of the state" in both international and in Canadian political economy literature (Aronowitz 2002; Barrow 1993; Panitch 1977a; McBride and Whiteside 2013). This is not the place to re-engage with those debates. However, the following observations can be made about the transition from Keynesianism to neoliberalism.

First, from its inception the Canadian state has been concerned with ensuring that the accumulation needs of capital operating in Canada are met (Panitch 1977b). This is a constant factor regardless of the policy regime or social structure of accumulation that might be in place at a particular time. Second, the accumulation needs of Canadian capital have been met in different ways in different time periods. The profile of state activities is not a "one-size-fits-all" phenomenon; rather, it is an evolving portfolio of measures taken on behalf of capital's interests (Albo and Jenson 1989). The state, therefore, can be seen as responding to the needs of capital but not only to capital. Its activities may be swayed by pressure from other factors and actors including subordinate classes and/or social movements, institutional or political conflicts within the state itself, from other states, and by unanticipated events.

During the Keynesian period one useful way of categorizing state functions, or activities[20] was by whether they were primarily targeted at accumulation, legitimation, or coercion (O'Connor 1973; Panitch 1977a; McBride 1992). It can be conceded that particular activities or policies may cross over these categories, performing two or more at the same time, and that it is hard, though far from impossible, to apply the typology empirically.[21] Nonetheless, the relative shifts between these activities and the patterns revealed can be helpful in describing the state's role. In the transition from Keynesianism to neoliberalism for example, it seemed that the concrete or material legitimation activities[22] of the Canadian state were partly displaced by symbolic or ideological forms of legitimation, backed by increased reliance on coercion (McBride 1992). Similarly, the means of ensuring accumulation changed from the light interventionism of the Keynesian state, predicated on sustaining adequate domestic demand and a high wage, full employment economy, to an export-led strategy, in which domestic labour conditions were increasingly seen as obstacles to competitiveness, rather than contributors to national economic growth. As a result, a drive to make labour markets more flexible (for employers) was part of the neoliberal package. In that context, the state focused on opening foreign markets for Canadian exporters and investors through free trade agreements and constraints on domestic labour to contain labour costs.

If these agreements opened new markets and opportunities for profitable investment so too did the sale of public assets and other forms of privatization, such as public private partnerships or P3s (Whiteside 2015). Similarly, deregulation of finance, especially in the United States and other international centres, unleashed innovations in financial products and investment instruments that eventually triggered the 2007–08 financial crisis. Before the crisis, however, along with real estate they absorbed large pools of capital in essentially speculative activities. All these activities represented "fixes" to the over-accumulation of capital/shortage of profitable investment opportunities that features in David Harvey's (2006) account of crisis.

This phase of neoliberalism has been widely referred to as "financialization," a process whereby financial markets, institutions, and actors gain influence over economic policy and economic outcomes at the expense of participants in the real economy of production and distribution of real products (see Clark 2016, 125–6). David Harvey (2003, 147) has suggested that financialization promotes high levels of personal and national indebtedness, which creates conditions of servitude for debtors. State de-regulatory changes have permitted this process – depicted as "privatized Keynesianism" by Colin Crouch (2011) – which allows for consumption even in the absence of real growth. Financial deregulation is inherently unstable, is associated with escalating levels of inequality, and has led to series of crises in the neoliberal era (see

McBride and Whiteside 2011) culminating (so far) in the crash of 2007–08. The crisis that ensued was the result of dubious financial innovations and intense speculation in toxic financial instruments, the value of which, on the eve of the crisis, exceeded the real economy many times over (Clark 2016, 125–6).

Since the crisis, the role of the state in capitalist societies generally has evolved to match the needs of a system embroiled in crises. This evolution includes rescuing leading capitalist sectors like banking and auto, and unorthodox measures such as transferring bad private sector debts to the public accounts, bailouts, quasi-nationalizations, and other asset guarantees.

Canada's avoidance of some of the worst effects of the crisis has been attributed to a financial sector that is more concentrated and centralized than the US banking system, subject to tighter state regulation, and which has had a more conservative managerial culture. Because of this conservatism, Canadian banks did not become over-leveraged against their asset base to the extent that US and many European banks did. Similarly, sub-prime mortgages had not developed very strongly in Canada. Few Canadian mortgages were sub-prime and there was much less of a tendency to "securitize" mortgages and sell them on to third parties. However, Canada may have been fortunate in the timing of the crisis. The Harper government had begun to introduce forms of deregulation that encouraged risk-taking behaviour – such as reducing the down payment requirements on house purchases and to extended amortization periods (Campbell 2009; Ireland and Webb 2010). This deregulatory thrust was discontinued once the crisis broke and Canada avoided the need to nationalize banks as happened elsewhere (Loxley 2009). Even so, major financial commitments were made to support banks if they needed to borrow money, and it has been estimated that Canada's banks received $114 billion in cash and loan support in the immediate post-crisis period. In other areas, Canada showed the same symptoms of financialization as other Western states – "privatized Keynesianism" with higher levels of individual debt as "compensation" for greater inequalities, together with labour market and public sector restructuring (Peters 2014).

Adoption of new accumulation policies by the Canadian state did not happen automatically but rather, as we have seen, through a protracted political conflict involving business organizations and allied think tanks, professional experts (particularly economists whose version of social science achieved hegemony amongst political and bureaucratic decision-makers), the media, other instruments of ideological persuasion, and the political party elites. Albeit to different degrees and at different speeds, all these actors moved to neoliberal positions between 1975 and 1995.

It may be doubted whether such neoliberal fixes can permanently offset capitalism's recurrent tendency to crisis. But, for the moment, the policy regime or social structure of accumulation seem durable enough and neoliberalism has been reconstituted and reinforced in the wake of the crisis (McBride 2015).

CONCLUSION

The transition from Keynesianism to neoliberalism was a response to structural pressures but these did not dictate how the transition would occur. The process was conditioned but not determined by similar processes occurring in other states. Keynesianism represented a class compromise, which was tacit in Canada and more explicit in some other countries. The nature of the compromise was extending to the working-class material concessions, in the form of an enhanced social wage, full employment, and increased labour rights, and guaranteeing conditions that did not threaten capital accumulation.

As conditions changed, Keynesianism and capital accumulation came to be perceived by capital as mutually exclusive. Effectively, the postwar compromise was repudiated by capital. The effects of the repudiation and the construction of a new neo-liberal regime of accumulation included decreased labour rights, precarious and insecure employment, and a reduced social wage subject to greater conditionality. The latter was accomplished by making qualification for benefits more difficult, or receipt of benefits more conditional.

The transition from one to the other was not and could not have been achieved by edict. Rather it resulted from a lengthy and complex political adjustment, the outcome of which was unclear when it was originally launched. The specifics of the transition were domestically driven but took place in an international context in which major states and international organizations were pushing neoliberalism and its globalization dimensions in the form of new generation trade and investment agreements. International pressures assisted the transition. Sometimes these took specific form, as with the US hostility to the nationalist and interventionist National Energy Program; at other times, they took a more general form as with the ethos of the Washington consensus expressed in many different fora. Domestically a key part of the exercise was the habituation of the Canadian public to a lower set of expectations and to the view that there was no alternative. This was accomplished by think tanks, official pronouncements of politicians and opinion leaders from business, the espoused certainties of the economic profession, and a media that, by and large, did not deviate from the neoliberal script.

The neoliberalization of the major political parties in Canada meant that the public had few choices.[23] A widespread condition of democratic malaise was noted, along with sporadic outbursts of protest, met by more coercive policing than had been common in Keynesian times. When a perceived choice did exist, as in the 2015 federal election[24] in which the Liberals espoused a greater tolerance for budget deficits in the name of infrastructure investment and job creation, the alternative seemed well received by the electorate. Such events apart, however, neoliberalism appeared to have been reconstituted in the years since the financial crisis, a reminder that while crises can be implicated in a transition from one policy regime to another, there is no guarantee that such a transition will occur.

NOTES

1 Generally, neoliberalism is conceived of as an array of free market, anti-state economic doctrines whilst neoconservatism, which shares those ideas, adds a concern for traditional values, gender roles, lifestyles, and family structures, and greater attention to law and order and an aggressive defence and foreign policy stance (see Nieguth and Raney 2012).

2 References to selected sources are provided in this section. However, further discussion and fuller references may be found in McBride 1992; McBride and Shields 1993, 1997; McBride 2011, 2005; and McBride and Whiteside 2011.

3 For a brief but very informative account see: http://www.thecanadianencyclo pedia.ca/en/article/great-depression/.

4 Aggregate demand can be defined as the total demand for goods and services in an economy. It is composed of consumer spending, investment spending, government spending (both on consumption and investment), and net exports.

5 Measures designed to offset fluctuations in economic activity without new intervention by the government. For example, spending delivered through programs like unemployment insurance kick in automatically during an economic downturn as more people come to rely on them.

6 Not only directly but through "multiplier" effects, where an initial increase in expenditures triggers additional expenditures by those who receive the original expenditure as income, and so on. Thus, the impact of the original change will be greater, by some multiple, than its original value.

7 Full employment can be defined as existing where all eligible people wishing to work can find jobs at prevailing wage rates. The figure will never be o per cent because some proportion of people is always changing jobs, some employment is seasonal, and so on. In Western Europe after the Second World War actual rates of unemployment of less than 3 per cent – which proved quite achievable until the 1970s or even later – were considered to be full employment. In North America rates tended to be higher, but still well below those that were typical of the 1970s and beyond.

8 In the neo-corporatist countries of parts of Western Europe the state played a more active role (Berger 1982).

9 Amongst the literature capturing this variety see Esping-Andersen (1990) on varieties of the welfare state and Hall and Soskice (2003) on varieties of capitalism extant in the broadly Keynesian era.

10 Other services such as home care, extended care, pharmaceutical benefits, and dental care were not included.

11 The Royal Commission on Dominion-Provincial Relations, which reported in 1940.

12 Clearly there were also international influences related to business' preferred strategy for constraining wage costs to maintain competitiveness in US and global markets.

13 During which Progressive Conservative Joe Clark was prime minister.

14 Except for June to November 1993, when Kim Campbell succeeded Mulroney as prime minister.

15 See Armstrong et al. and LeBlanc Haley, this volume.

16 Monetarism is an important component of neoliberal economic doctrines. In the early stages of the move way from Keynesianism the conflict was often depicted as one between Keynesianism and monetarism (e.g., Hall 1993 on the UK).

17 *Creating Opportunity: The Liberal Plan for Canada*, popularly known as *The Red Book*.

18 The consequences of abandoning these efforts and of returning to strategies of resource dependency are explored in Stanford, this volume.

19 It later became known as the Canadian Council of Chief Executives (CCCE) and, in 2016, changed its name once more to the Business Council of Canada.

20 I prefer the use of the term activities to distance the analysis from the criticism often levelled at this type of state theory for its alleged "functionalism" as explanation. Identifying state policies using these categories can help interpret how the state is acting without implying an explanation that the state *must* act in these ways.

21 A point that can be made of other useful ways of categorizing policy processes or outcomes. For example, discussing policy paradigms and the issue of policy change, see Schmidt, 2011.

22 So described, because through such measures as social programs, free health care, and unemployment insurance, they conferred concrete or material benefits on subordinate classes in capitalist society.

23 The exhaustion of the social democratic alternative and its role in actively promoting neoliberalism and austerity has been widely noted (see, for example, Evans 2014) and was highlighted in the way the New Democratic Party was outflanked on its left by the federal Liberal Party in the 2015 election, and by the provincial Liberals in the Ontario election in 2014.

24 And arguably in the 2014 Ontario and 2015 Alberta elections.

8

Toward a Critique of Political Economy of "Sociolegality" in Settler Capitalist Canada

Adrian A. Smith

The conventional point of departure for the study of law and legality in Canada remains an acceptance of the legitimate authority of the Canadian state and its law. Simply put, Canada is taken for granted. But what would it mean to trouble, destabilize, or downright *unsettle* this foundational assumption – especially given that it informs not only the study of law but the so-called Canadian political economy tradition as well? After all, political and legal shifts, twists, and turns notwithstanding there is a great deal that is troubling about "Canada" in its foundational relations with Indigenous peoples (e.g., Green 2003; Manuel and Derrickson 2015; Gordon 2010; Alfred and Corntassel 2005; Coulthard 2014). And the troubles persist with respect to relations with so-called foreign, non-resident, and resident peoples (Smith 2015a; Sharma 2006; Choudry and Smith 2015, Bunk House; Satzewich 1991; Abele and Stasiulis 1989). Given this stubborn persistence, Canada's taken for granted authority requires a great deal of work. The ensuing analysis addresses the work and workings of Canada as a settler colonial capitalist entity with an emphasis on the role of law and legality – that is, with a view to the socio-spatial practices (namely, work and labour) of ordinary people in everyday life, or what below I term "material-legality."

Since the 1960s, the field of socio-legal studies (or law and society) has provided both a growing venue as well as evolving sets of theories and methods to conceptualize the role of law in society, legality's standing in relation to the social. Its relative success is a quite different matter. While enjoying considerable interest in both Canadian and wider scholarly circles, much of socio-legal studies adopts a largely one-sided focus on law's constitution of the social. Far less is understood about how the social interacts with law (but see Feenan 2013; D'Souza 2010). And, with certain notable exceptions (e.g., Knox 2009–10, 2009; D'Souza 2011), in its current manifestations much too little exists in the way of a sustained commitment to emancipatory praxis. Working toward detaching the study of law and legality from the "sociologizing" disciplinary trajectories of socio-legal studies,[1] trajectories that even to certain of its stalwarts appear to have run their course (Silbey 2013, 2005), I embed law and legality instead within an account of the material processes, practices, relations, and conditions of settler colonial capitalism, or, to adopt Marx's path-breaking framing, a critique of political economy. Employing an anticolonial (e.g., Fanon 1963; Coulthard 2014) and antiracist (e.g., Bannerji 2005, 1995; Camfield 2016; Gordon 2007; Bakan 2008) historical materialist approach, I pursue a critique of political economy necessarily for the reason elaborated by Marx that capitalism amounts to a starkly unequal, exploitative, dehumanizing, and ecologically destructive way of organizing human relations within and against which we must vigorously struggle to secure its replacement. But political economy critique also registers here in the way that Canadian political economy, the tradition to which readers of this volume instinctively if not invariably would turn to fashion a new way forward, generally has not dealt well with law and legality (but see Bartholomew and Boyd 1989; Fudge 1991; Fudge and Cossman 2002). Its adherents have tended to treat these as essentially formal and not properly contextualized phenomena especially in not taking seriously enough settler colonialism and what the colonial relation means for claims of legitimate authority of the Canadian state and legality (Smith 2015c; Pasternak 2014).

That said, a turn to the emergent field of settler colonial studies (e.g., Wolfe 1999, 2006; Veracini 2010) and sub-disciplinary engagements with law offers a helpful – but ultimately circumscribed – analytical interrogation of the colonial relation. The effect is circumscribed to the extent that it seemingly downplays or neglects the insights of the critique of political economy, especially pertaining to: (a) the capital relation and its core productive *and* social-reproductive dimensions, understood in gendered and racialized class terms; and, (b) the necessity of an explanatory framework forged on the unity of the whole – a *raison d'être* of political economy critique.[2] Ultimately, I contend, the historically specific open-ended structural relations and processes of settler colonial capitalism inform what is meant by "socio" and what is meant by "legal" (or

"legality"). "Sociolegality," which takes on general and specific understandings and configurations within a given historical context, emerges
out of socio-spatial practices undertaken not just by official actors and
their activities but more profoundly through the daily activities of ordinary people.[3] In other words, sociolegality contains a material productive
and reproductive dimension or core. I link this under-acknowledged facet
of sociolegality, what I refer to as material-legality, to the ongoing work
and labour of settler colonial capitalism in the territory now known as
Canada. Material-legality informs assertions of authority and belonging
within the Canadian settler state.

The analysis opens with a discussion of settler colonialism as concept
and lived existence aiming to show that contemporary accounts displace,
misplace, or forestall consideration of the embodied socio-spatial practices of settler colonial capitalist relations, understood in materialist
terms. Work, labour, and the capital relation are essential to appreciating
the processes of primitive and dispossessive accumulation at the core of
settler capitalism. Interrogating socio-legal studies, the second section
levels a critique at a dominant contemporary incarnation, a "cultural"
approach to the legal consciousness of ordinary people. While supporting the focus on legal consciousness of ordinary people (see also Smith
2015a, 2005), I argue that the leading approach is conceived to view
peoples' strivings and struggles as non-material and, as such, material-
legality must be dislodged from sociolegality or socio-legal studies and
set within a (renewed) historical materialist account and emancipatory
praxis. In the final section I redeploy the borrowed concept of "structures
of living together" (Ricoeur 1992; Deneulin 2008) as a heuristic tool to
capture the cumulative effects of the structural relations and processes
of settler colonial capitalism. As an open-ended conceptual framing,
structures – and the concomitant struggles – of living together assist
with apprehending concrete social relations in totality and, through their
interplay, derive meaning and significance. The structures and struggles
of living together provide the context from which sociolegality emerges
and to which material-legality gives real (materialist) meaning. Drawing
on my recent study addressing a dispute over migrant worker housing
(Smith 2015a), I sketch these structures and struggles in the southwestern
Ontario agrarian community of Norfolk County. In contrast to the
growing focus on fossil-fuel-indebted resource extractivist approaches
to capitalist accumulation, the discussion centres on the successive layers
of agro-food extractivism within the settler colonial capitalist context
of what we now call Canada.

SETTLER COLONIALISM
AND ITS INNER WORKINGS

An examination of "Canada" must begin with the troubling acceptance of the *Canadian* state's legitimate authority and, in this regard, with the recognition that law assumes a pivotal role. Emergent understandings and practices of settler colonialism, including its socio-legal dimensions in Canada, offer an important corrective. Ongoing contestations over the legitimate authority of the Canadian state and law in relation to Indigenous peoples and territories, while necessarily mounted from within dominant settler traditions, have also spawned politics of "resurgence" and even "refusal" (e.g., Coulthard 2014; Simpson 2008; Alfred and Corntassel 2005), as well as initiatives that seek to retrieve and reclaim pre-existing and contemporary Indigenous legal orders, practices, and traditions (see Indigenous Law Research Unit 2012; Borrows 2002). At core, these accounts contest how assertions of Canadian sovereignty could have erased Indigenous governance authority within the settler colonial formation (McNeil 2013; Pasternak 2014).

Until recently, scholarly practice treated settler colonialism as either distinct from or a subset of colonialism (Veracini 2013a). Colonialism has been understood as an expansionary process or form of domination of a group over native lands and labour. However, recent interventions such as the work of historical anthropologist Patrick Wolfe (1999, 2006) enforce a sharp division or distinction between colonial and settler colonial formations. Famously characterizing settler colonial invasion as "a structure not an event" (1999, 2), Wolfe's formative account takes settler colonial structure as "not primarily established to extract surplus value from indigenous labour" but for "displacing" Indigenous peoples from or "replacing them on" the land (1999, 1). In contrast to colonialism's dependence on "native labour," therefore, settler colonialism "is first and foremost a territorial project" that prioritizes not "extracting an economic surplus from mixing their labour with it" but displacement and replacement of natives on a given land (Wolfe 2008, 103). "Territoriality," on this account, forms "settler colonialism's specific, irreducible element" (Wolfe 2006, 388).

Although "not an event," settler colonialism is anything but uneventful. As a (trans)formative structural relationship of domination and authority expressed in national-territorial terms, or through an emphasis on control or sovereignty over territory, it functions on an obfuscation of its necessarily violent means carried out to secure and enforce authority over a native or Indigenous population. But *carried out by whom?* Lorenzo Veracini draws an essential distinction between "the settler" and "the migrant" emergent within three formations of displacement, metropolitan, colonial, and settler colonial (2013b, 2733). Under the metropolitan formation, "the Indigenous element" receives sovereign privilege over the "exogenous" or migrant. Under the colonial formation a reversal occurs in that the settler "is the exogenous invader who travels with a sovereign charge" (and, by extension, the postcolonial represents an inversion but not a negation or supersession). In settler colonial formations the settler "simultaneously subject[s] indigenous people and exogenous 'others,'" based on an uneven and "somewhat inconsistent logic" of "exogeneity" and "indigeneity" (2013b, 2733). Settlers and their descendants undertake continuous multi-generational settlement that, through differential incorporation or inclusion (e.g., Satzewich 1991; Sharma 2006), is linked with the periodic introduction of immigrant and migrant populations. Both sets of introduced populations, settler and descendant on one side im/migrant on the other, more or less "inheri[t] the blame, and possibly the guilt, but have no alternative identity, no other homeland" (Bateman and Pilkington 2011, 3). Settlement, as it were, represents a sort of guilty pleasure in settler colonialism.

SETTLER COLONIAL THEORY'S DISPLACEMENT AND REPLACEMENT EFFECT

Veracini concedes that the metropolitan-colonial-settler colonial distinctions "remain purely analytical categorizations" that "in reality ... intertwine and overlap in various ways in the context of shifting patterns of relations" (2013b, 2733). That said, one must question the sorts of explanations that these analytical distinctions undermine. Here, it appears, the emphasis on the settler colonial relation negates any sustained interrogation of the capital relation. While settler colonialism indeed marks the displacement and replacement of natives in a given territory, to claim the irreducibility of territoriality in settler colonial formations without confronting productive and reproductive forces is to engage in a displacement and replacement of another kind. In other words, the claim that territorial displacement-replacement drives settler colonialism has its own displacement and replacement effect. I posit that work and labour form an integral yet displaced dimension of the terrain of analysis and struggle. Territoriality is not a thing but rather an actionable spatial and legal claim of authority set within the relations of private property, dispossession, commodification, and exploitation and carried out through socio-spatial practices of work and labour situated within – and as a formative element of – capitalist relations.

The displacement and replacement effect is evident in several respects. A common approach within settler colonial studies is to provisionally delay or forestall the question of labour. Seminal efforts such as Cole Harris' privilege land dispossession in the first instance, treating land as "the principle resource" (2004, 179), but then turn around and bring labour in through the back door. As Harris almost immediately goes on to note: "The initial ability to dispossess rested primarily on *physical power* and the supporting infrastructure of the state" (2004, 179, my emphasis). Similarly, to the extent that settler colonialism is characterized as an "expropriated land base" driven by "settlers' interest in land as livelihood" (Harris cited in Wolfe 2008, 104), expropriation and livelihood stand in for processes, practices, and ways of being or living more properly associated with conceptions of work and labour – chiefly social relations of production and reproduction.[4] Hence work and labour within the capital relation are distant frames in settler colonial accounts.

We can therefore trace the displacement of work and labour in leading conceptualizations of settler colonialism. Early conceptualizations of settler colonialism as a total economic force have been replaced by postcolonial (and similarly situated) theoretical accounts in which "economic categories have disappeared virtually without trace" (Foley 2011, 26). The jettisoning of work and labour from "bourgeois social thought" (Amin 2013, 13) follows from a rejection of the orthodox Marxist view that the dispossession of Indigenous peoples from land occurred *solely for the purposes of securing surplus labour*, and from the now well-entrenched retreat from class analysis, politics, and struggles in the academy and certain social movements (see Wood 1995). Postcolonial analysis exhibits very real limits to be sure. But we must also concede that the problem rests not merely on the side of those engaged in the jettisoning. Marxist orthodoxy showed itself doggedly unaccepting of the qualitative multiplicity of work and labour. Forceful interventions have sought to remedy the deficiency by accounting for racialized and gendered dynamics of capitalist social relations of production and social reproduction in anti-essentialist terms (e.g., Bannerji 1995, 2005; Weeks 2011; Luxton 2006b).

Following these correctives, we can conceive of work and labour in fundamentally different terms. If pivotal forces driving settler colonialism are primitive accumulation and its continuation as dis-possessive accumulation (see Harvey 2003), then it is crucial to acknowledge that the very practices, processes, and relations of dispossession, of divorcing people from land, of pushing them toward market dependence, and of transforming existing ontologies of lived existence or survival, are not only themselves about the creation of capitalist work and labour, but also call forth work, labour, and the capital relation. Dispossession is but another, more general way of framing the ongoing work and labour of settler colonialism. A key dimension of the work of settler colonialism is the work of displacement and replacement of Indigenous peoples in territory to which those peoples toil(ed) and dwell(ed). Therefore, work, labour, and the capital relation matter to how we characterize settler colonialism, and how we conceive of the sites, forms, and aims of resistance to prevailing structural relations and processes. The structures and struggles of settler colonial capitalist formations are constituted by work and labour practices and relations of subsistence or survival.

A second dimension of the displacement and replacement effect relates to law and legality. Displacement owes something to the presumed distinction between "socio" and "legal." The socio-spatial practices of work and labour displaced within characterizations of unfolding settler colonial dispossession necessarily entail the work and labour of claiming and keeping – and these are legal constructs. Socio-spatial practices unfold within the historically specific and open-ended set of structural relations and processes of settler colonial capitalism. Much of the focus on contemporary capitalism places great emphasis on dispossessive accumulation through fossil-fuel and mining-based natural resource extraction or extractivism (but see Petras and Veltmeyer 2014, chapter 3). Yet agricultural work and labour assumed – and, I argue, continues to assume – a crucial place within settler colonial capitalist dispossession, especially the claiming and keeping of territory and land, and the resources that run with it. Christopher Tomlins (2010) discusses the work of early English colonizers in peopling, planting, and keeping mainland North America. "Labour was essential to colonizing," notes Tomlins, "because labour constructed the means of keeping – labour transformed the face of the land" (2010, 12). As a "legal notion," keeping is the process through which "law would determine who kept what." The characteristic practices of planting, and of agricultural work and labour more broadly, proved integral to dispossession and appropriation in law and to the determination of who kept what.[5] Or, to put it differently, work and labour are necessary to the legal recognition and expression of private property ownership within settler colonial capitalist relations.

But there is still more that can be added. Work and labour exist as a means of claiming and keeping evident in the practices of early English, French, and other settlers who cleared the lands of "North America" transforming it from "waste" into "productive" space, a transformation that in Lockean-liberal terms justified private property ownership. Notwithstanding whether European settlers saw North America as empty or unpeopled, or as peopled by "savages," for territoriality to work as the irreducible element of settler colonialism there must be re-peopling, there must be human practices of clearing, claiming, and keeping – *a population from the metropole planted, an Indigenous population supplanted*. Planting and supplanting are processes of racialized valuation requiring hard work and labour. The racialized dynamics of settler colonialism were imposed through pre-existing ideas and practices of difference, but also derived meaning from the content of the activities, practices, and relations of settler colonial capitalism. In this latter respect, the work and labour of early settlers framed the racialized formation and formulation of social relations in the ever-expanding North American settlements. A pivotal dimension of the story is racialized undermining, of the socio-spatial (i.e., traditional) practices and ontologies of Indigenous peoples, and of introduced "foreign" populations.

Given my focus on law and legality, I turn to address how socio-legal studies has contributed to the neglect of settler colonial capitalist work and labour.

SETTLING ON LAW: CULTURE, MATERIALISM, AND LEGAL CONSCIOUSNESS

The emergence of socio-legal studies in the 1960s marked an attempted redress of the tightly bounded professional study of law and its practice(s). Concerned with the role or place of law in society, socio-legal studies engages in a deep questioning of doctrinalist treatments of "law as comprising only of a set of legal norms, separate from society" (Feenan 2013, 10). It has sought to replace elite-driven and flattened formulations of law through the deployment of interdisciplinary – and in certain cases transdisciplinary – theoretical and methodological insights. Socio-legal studies ultimately produced two dominant framings on the law-society relation. The first regards law as either autonomous from or determinative of the social world. The second proposes that a chasm or gap separates law in or on the books from law in action and that this gap is either "socially dysfunctional" or "legitimating" (Tomlins 2007, 46). While space precludes the recounting of these debates here, it is helpful to appreciate that a materialist socio-legal studies gained considerable traction from the mid to late 1970s and extended well into the 1980s (e.g., Stone 1985; Balbus 1977; Hay 1975). That account, associated with socialist or "capital M" "Marxian" theories, adopted structural-functional and instrumental explanations of "law's overall social role" and relative autonomy (Tomlins 2007, 46–7; also see Tucker 1984; Comack 2006, 34–42). Critics argued that it suffered from determinism and functionalism that severely circumscribes its explanatory utility (e.g., Ewick and Silbey 2002, 151).

In its place, scholars have inserted a constitutive or cultural perspective on law around which a certain level of consensus formed in line with the belief that law and society are co-constitutive: "The legal is as much social as the social is legal" (Tomlins 2007, 47). For these proponents, the law-social constitution marks the temporal transition from an "autonomy paradigm" to a "mutuality paradigm" (Tomlins 2007, 47). This has been furthered, not undercut, by a shift in emphasis to the legal consciousness of ordinary people (Silbey 2005a). A central strand of contemporary socio-legal analysis (Ewick and Silbey 1998, 1992; Silbey 2005a), the study of ordinary peoples' legal consciousness provides a lens through which to advance the investigation of law and legality because it emphasizes lived experience and the ways in which law is invoked, not invoked, revised, and resisted in everyday life. "This research," according to Silbey, "pays close attention to language and discourse tracing the residues of legal concepts and meanings in everyday social transactions" (2005b, 332).

While it is true that discourse (and ideology) addresses human participation in the construction of consciousness of how law shapes existing social relations, this understanding of legal consciousness ignores material dimensions of socio-spatial practices of everyday life. In one sense, socio-spatial practices fail to register as materialist phenomena informing and informed by law. Recognition that socio-spatial practices are embodied falls in line with an unwillingness to separate language and body. As David McNally (2001, 10) forcefully asserts, "the question of language is a question of the body" and "all body questions are questions of life and work – and the prospects for their liberation" (14). In another sense, a crucial task is "to continue to emphasize the directly coercive features of a legal regime that distinguish law from other discourses" (Fudge and Tucker 2001, 7). For law's "distinctiveness as discursive practice" rests on a foundation of coercive force and violence. And so the discursive dimensions of legal consciousness ought not be divorced from law's material impact on people and relations. It is on these bases that we might deploy the concept of material-legality, situated within an historical materialist treatment of legal consciousness, to inform the critique of political economy. In this, I take Indigenous epistemologies (e.g., Henderson 2002) and "new materialism" (e.g., Edwards 2010) not as gospel but as an invitation to *renew* the ontological dimensions of historical materialism, "insist[ing] upon the openness, contingency, unevenness, and complexity of materialization as an ongoing process within which social actors and theorists are irremediably immersed" (Coole and Frost 2010, 28).[6] While I can only begin the renewal process here, it is my hope that readers will appreciate the potential for deepened analysis. In what follows I take material-legality as socio-spatial embodied practices central to agro-food extractivism – carried out to clear, claim, and keep.

THE STRUCTURES AND STRUGGLES OF LIVING TOGETHER IN CONTEMPORARY "CANADA"

In this final section the discussion shifts to situate the preceding account of sociolegality within the specific socio-historical processes of national state formation in what is now known as Canada. These processes are constitutive of, to renovate a borrowed phrase, the structures and struggles of living together (Smith 2015b), which signifies the cumulative effects of the relations, practices, and processes of living together within the constitution and perpetuation of "Project Canada" (Green 2003), a definitive centuries-long socio-historical project of settler colonial capitalism. The contemporary work of empire-building abroad, set within capitalist imperialism, of which Canada's Seasonal Agricultural Workers Program or SAWP forms an example, is firmly rooted in the foundational civilizing mission of colonization (Smith 2015; see also Gordon 2010). With the arrival of settlers and the displacement and dislocation of Indigenous peoples from traditional territories, the production of aboriginality (Alfred and Corntassel 2005), the relegation of Indigenous peoples to reserve lands and more, the founding mission of Project Canada captures the clearing of space for settlement and the claiming and keeping of land.[7] To these initial and ongoing accomplishments of capitalist extractivism, we must consider the introduced immigrant and migrant populations. I take the opportunity afforded by a dispute over migrant farm worker housing in southwestern Ontario's Norfolk County to sketch the structures and struggles of living together.

MIGRANT LABOUR AND SETTLEMENT
IN SOUTHWESTERN ONTARIO

In late 2011, Norfolk Select Potato Company made an offer for purchase of an abandoned school building to convert it into housing for migrant workers employed through the SAWP. Migrant worker "bunk houses" typically are located on or near the employing farm facilities. In the proposal, workers would be housed some distance away from the farm operation in the tiny community of Windham Centre. Norfolk Potato's offer was made conditional on a Norfolk County zoning by-law amendment, which, according to the provisions of Ontario's *Planning Act*, can only be taken by the municipal council after a public consultation process, including a notice period, an opportunity to provide comments, and a public meeting on the application.[8] In examining the written responses of Windham Centre residents, I argue elsewhere that their overwhelming opposition is evidence of a legal consciousness of the political and legal configuration of Canada's SAWP. The opposition re-inscribes and extends the unfree, racialized, and migratory labour relations and conditions in which migrant workers toil and dwell (Smith 2015b; Satzewich 1991). Residents perpetuate growers' control not merely of labour power but in fact over racialized labouring bodies.

With respect to structures of living together, the SAWP, a political-administrative apparatus designed to produce labour unfreedom by mobilizing workers to cross national state territorial borders, by then heavily circumscribing labour market and spatial mobility while in Canada and by upholding "precarious migratory status" (Goldring, Berinstein, and Bernhard 2009) (and an explicit denial of permanent residency) of those categorized as migrant labour (see Smith 2013), constructs a fundamentally skewed cohabitation arrangement whereby the migrant is always already the outsider in everyday existence. The contemporary planning regime, a product of political-legal administrative design, while organized around the facilitation of local agency and governance, constructs locality in a specific and insular way such that migrant labour necessarily remains excluded from land-use decision-making processes. Through these interlocking regimes – residents' understandings about the first given expression and application through the second – we see how residents are engaged in asserting their political-legal authority over migrant workers.[9] Racist devaluation of the labouring bodies of a so-called foreign population underwrote residents' opposition characterized by spatial dimensions in which settlers police the boundaries of local and national community and belonging at their property fence line.[10] In these structures of living together residents' assertions of authority, their "propertied citizenship," takes form representing the cumulative effects of private property ownership in single-family dwelling homes, as well as one's political-legal status as rightful claimant of the national state and by extension of this particular local. If the planning regime constitutes the local through a privileging of insularity, it too is constituted through the profoundly exclusionary practices of opposing residents. And because those residents convey and reproduce devalued understandings of racialized labouring bodies within global capitalism, the migrant housing dispute and the wider SAWP rests at the local and global interface – the constitutive actions of residents forming the connective tissue. We might extend this insight by thinking through, in the context of wider settler colonial capitalist relations, the way in which residents cast themselves as rightful occupants and migrant workers as foreign invaders.

A deepening of the "Bunk House" analysis requires an excavation of longer-standing structures and struggles of living together in Norfolk County and wider territory – a process I can only sketch out here. Situated on the north shore of Lake Erie, Norfolk County forms a prime and fertile tract within Ontario's agricultural belt (Niewójt 2007). Reaping initial rewards for early settlers, and then later perceived by foresters as a "wasteland" (McQuarrie 2014), the climatic conditions and sandy soils proved favourable for the intensive growth of horticultural crops, most notably tobacco but also ginseng, blueberries, and of course potatoes, among others, on the Norfolk sand plain. Flue-cured tobacco production took root in the mid-1920s, expanded considerably over the next decade and notwithstanding periodic ebbs and flows, including reaching its height for a nearly thirty-year period from the 1970s onwards and then declining considerably during a period of transition away from tobacco through a state buyout regime launched in 2008 (The Canadian Press 2008), remains a livelihood for a sizeable number of growers (Daniszewski 2011), as well as local and migrant workers. Tobacco production exemplifies a "reclamation of 'wasteland'" and as such "became a source for a celebration of (capitalist) human ingenuity and its power to overcome natural obstacles" (McQuarrie 2014, 45). To the extent that "tobacco interests remade the agricultural wasteland of foresters" (McQuarrie 2014, 35), it is due to the interventions and exertions of workers and labour. Deploying varying sources of labour, from unemployed and "transient workers" (Reid-Musson 2014) to youth, European immigrants, and later Polish veterans of the Second World War (Satzewich 1989, 1991), and since the mid- to late 1960s migrant workers predominantly from the Caribbean (Satzewich 1991), Norfolk tobacco production has served as a key driver of political and economic dynamics of the region.

In an earlier period, enslaved people fleeing slavery in the United States found their way to present-day Norfolk County among other communities in nineteenth-century southwestern Ontario. Earlier still, United Empire Loyalists fleeing the Thirteen Colonies during and after the American Revolution populated the county in the mid- to late 1700s. Loyalists, granted a range of benefits for their support in the war effort, received land grants, and engaged in farming practices. Over an even longer historical span, the Attawandaron or Neutrals are understood to be the first human inhabitants of the area. They harvested Nicotiana rustica, used in trade and ceremonies, as well as maize, squash, and beans on traditional territory encompassing present-day Norfolk County. Armed with "digging sticks and shell hoes" (Niewójt 2007, 358–9), the Neutrals' agrarian existence in the area is said to have ended by the middle of the seventeenth century when famine, disease, and inter-nation conflict, especially with the neighbouring Haudenosaunee, led to their demise. But of course, the claim of demise fits the settler claim of Attawandaron territory as barren and unpeopled wasteland.

Here, again, the planning regime's insular locality figures prominently, but now in extending the erasure of Indigenous communal life, the work and labour of subsistence agriculture – or in a phrase, social reproduction. But if it is settler locality that reigns, we must not neglect the work and labour of settler colonial capitalism. Such an accounting would put a different spin on the established understanding that migrant farm labour prove "structurally necessary" for contemporary agricultural production (see Smith 2013). For Windham Centre residents – like growers – need migrant labour and their harvesting work to maintain the structural relationship of settler colonialism – and they need it in this way to prevent counter-claims posed by migrants and others. In this respect, the continuing work of displacement and dispossession of Indigenous peoples and territory occurs not solely through settlers and their progeny but also through the deployment of racialized unfree migrant labour. This produces a rather strange juxtaposition at the heart of Project Canada: of the foreign (racialized unfree migrant labouring) "other" and the Indigenous "other." It may not be that we should conflate processes of migration and colonialism (Sharma and Wright 2009), or of imperialism, but that we must contend with, and fundamentally trouble, the contradictory relations and sources of authority in which *we* all exist.

Here, then, the work of early English settlers joins with that of contemporary migrant farm workers. Just as the work and labour of early settlers informed law; the continuation of settler colonialism – that is, "the settler-colonial present" (Coulthard 2014) – also demands the enactment of material-legality. Except now, in terms of contemporary agro-extractivism, the continuing work of settler colonialism is increasingly performed by migrant farm workers. The peopling and keeping of the territory now known as Canada occurs through the deployment of migrant farm workers – migrant worker material-legality. Migrant farm labour (as a categorical imperative of settler colonialism) and the work to which that particular labour is assigned in the ongoing settler project, undercuts the claims and very existence (i.e., the survival) of Indigenous peoples and communities to belong on terms of their own choosing. Here we see that, in the structural relationship of settler colonial Canada, the migrant other and Indigenous other are linked through the undertaking of agricultural work in service of settler capitalist accumulation; the work of survival of the former is deployed to undermine the work of survival of the latter. Settler colonialism, therefore, is a negation of the traditional practices and authority of Indigenous communities through material-legality, which, in turn, undermines the work, labour, and authority of migrant farm workers within transnational familial relations.

CONCLUSION

History does not happen by itself. Whatever history there will be, it will have been made by the acting subjects themselves. The future is made in the present; it is as much a present-future as a future-present.

Bonefeld 2010, 66

In problematizing "Canada" as taken-for-granted in the study of law in the territory now known as such, this chapter traverses toward a critique of the political economy of sociolegality. I have sought to confront the ongoing historical production of Canada as settler colonial capitalist formation. The history of these structural relations and processes does not just happen. Acting subjects make and re-make historical circumstances, even if not as they always please. As such, it is not just a peoples' history of the territory that becomes a necessity, but a peopled one in which work and labour represent formative and ongoing socio-spatial practices of living together, authority, and belonging in settler capitalism.[11] The chapter undertakes an essential – but not essentializing – accounting of work and labour, which, through an anticolonial and antiracist historical materialism, pays heed to the complex and contested activities of ordinary people, and to longstanding Indigenous and Marxist-feminist materialist insights, that a great deal of social life is embodied work and labour, but that there must be more to life than (just) capitalist work – or even a more *just* capitalist work.

The foundational colonization of Indigenous peoples and traditional territory, consolidated and fortified through the system of reserve lands and reserve peoples, has been followed by other large-scale civilizing missions (Smith 2015c). The work and labour of settler colonialism, in its early or initial deployments, incorporates the socio-spatial practices of clearing, claiming, and keeping (Tomlins 2010). Just as these practices undermine(d) traditional ways of life of Indigenous peoples, they continue through such regimes as the Seasonal Agricultural Workers Program in which so-called foreign labour is produced in racialized terms as structural necessity and outsider threat in service of settler capitalist accumulation (Smith 2013). Within settler colonial capitalist formations such as Canada, agricultural work of this nature not only engages law, it forms the very content upon and through which law derives meaning and becomes lived existence. Here we begin to see that "the social" constitutes "the legal" through the performance of work undertaken by racialized migrant agricultural labouring bodies. These socio-spatial practices – what I refer to here as material-legality – structure living together and assertions of authority and belonging.

If this amounts to an intervention to restore work and labour to its rightful place within accounts of settler colonialism, it is not meant as a re-inscription of "the economic" in productivist, anti-social reproductivist, and white-washed accounts of social life. It instead signifies a renewed materialist commitment to accounting for the qualitative multiplicity of settler capitalism's work and labour, informed by insights on social reproduction, and by an anticolonial, antiracist, and antiwork emancipatory praxis (see Weeks 2011). In this respect, resistance struggles in support of migrant justice and Indigenous self-determination hold potential as transformative re-articulations of law and legality, authority, and belonging. The material-legality insight also imposes an obligation on present-future settler-working class exertions to reconfigure and transform work, labour, and social life by attending to the exploitative, commodifying, and dispossessive dynamics apparent within structures of living together. Ongoing struggles of living together must contain prefigurative commitments, to contesting processes of racialized valuation – and even more acutely racist devaluation – of Indigenous and migrant labouring bodies and their practices of survival; and to that which we all hold in common (Sharma and Wright 2009), if in differential ways across space, place, and time: social reproductive work.

And so a critique of the political economy of sociolegality within settler capitalism reveals the indispensability of a politics of retrieval, renewal, and refusal – retrieval of the work and labour that underwrite sociolegality in the settler Canadian state; renewal of working class movements (Camfield 2011) or the "next new left" (Sears 2014) through interrogative struggle of "internationalism from below" (Featherstone 2012) attentive to racialized, colonized, and gendered class dynamics; and a refusal to make settler colonial capitalism work.

NOTES

1 Tomlins (2007, see especially the conclusion) calls for something like a "non-sociologized" understanding of law. While I find this call provocative and somewhat consistent with my argument, it is not my aim to echo it here. My claim instead is based on a desire to retrieve "material-legality" from its encasement within prevailing accounts of sociolegality through a critique of political economy driven by a commitment to contesting and replacing intertwined relations of capitalism and settler colonialism.

2 The concept of racialization employed here views it as both an embodied process and process of re-embodiment contingent on signifying and classifying people based on perceived phenotypical traits. Analytically speaking, it marks the preparation for the assignment of value to labouring bodies, which I refer to as racialized valuation, which is preliminary to but subsuming of racism or the process of devaluing labouring bodies (racist devaluation). As a rule, I avoid using the concept of "race," which is indicative of a static and analytically unaccountable understanding in that it appears to occur without a subject, and is definitive.

3 The prominent theorist of settler colonialism, Lorenzo Veracini, has produced a number of informative and forceful interventions on settler colonialism. Their importance notwithstanding, a critique could be levelled at the general abstractedness and decontextualized (perhaps ahistorical would connote too strong a characterization) of these accounts. Perhaps one way of thinking about Veracini's "purely analytical" account of settler colonialism, discussed

below, is that settler colonial capitalism is a historically specific generality and, as such, we can derive general or open-ended understandings from its essential logic and contours, but specificities may (and, in fact, do) differ across space and time so that socially contextualized, richly historical accounting remains necessary. To provide a crude example, the logic and contours of settler colonialism in Australia, Canada, New Zealand, and the United States may prove generalizable, but it is left to historically specific contextualizations to sort through the intricate details.

4 Along similar lines, but with a well-developed recognition of the social reproductive dimensions of the analysis, Glen Coulthard (2014, 4) discusses efforts to "overtly uproot and destroy the vitality and autonomy of Indigenous modes of life," and the "undercutting [of] Indigenous political economies and relations to and with land" – "Indigenous modes of life" and "political economies and relations to and with land" are in effect coded characterizations of work and labour.

5 Of course the work of keeping and claiming includes the work of lawyers, justices of the peace, and a range of agents of the Crown, among other officials or "insiders."

6 I find the intervention less compelling when it is couched as "new" or "new critical" materialism because of the evidentiary basis on which "newness" is proclaimed. Newness, while squarely falling within academic fashion, is a tired and highly problematic form of distinction that provides a temporal marking which encourages ahistoricism. For instance, Indigenous epistemologies and praxis captures longstanding alternative accounts of materialist relations. As James (Sákéj) Youngblood Henderson (2002, 45) puts it: "autochthonic ecologies taught our peoples that everything is interrelated and all life forms and forces are in a process of flux or circular interaction. The belief that the ecological order is connected through relationships with the keepers of life is the premise of our worldviews. By knowing our relationships with the natural order, our shared relationships can sustain harmony and balance. Coming to know is not located outside one's self but is founded upon the interconnectedness and interdependent relationship one has with the sources of life. Understandings come through connecting with the sources of life through intuition and through experience. Through millenniums of observation and relationships with a certain ecology order, our teaching emerged."

7 Quite importantly, Amar Bhatia undertakes an analysis of treaties as integral features of the structures of living together.

8 In opposition, local residents of the community in which the former school facility is situated, organized a letter writing campaign and a petition with ninety-three signatures. Virtually all respondents expressed unequivocal

opposition to the application, expressing fear that a decision to approve the application would unleash "armies of offshore labour" in their otherwise tranquil community (see Smith 2015a).

9 Much has been said about reforming Canada's migration regime. Given the racialized, unfree, and migrant labouring plight of workers in the SAWP, re-making migrant labour through the provision of a pathway to citizenship in the SAWP and greater inclusiveness in the by-law amendment process, would likely not have undermined residents' production of migrant labour.

10 It is in this broader respect that we might say residents seek to police workers, understood in the broad sense as Marx deploys it (see *On the Jewish Question*), through the deployment of the police force or monitoring and supervision by growers, or both.

11 We must also see here that a focus on human relations notwithstanding, an accounting of the role of non-human relations is pivotal to the development of a critique of political economy of sociolegality in Canada. Settler capitalism in Canada has relied upon what Jason Moore (2015) terms "cheap natures" – cheap labour, food, energy, and raw materials.

9

A Feminist Political Economy
of Indigenous-State Relations
in Northern Canada

Rebecca Jane Hall

> *this river is a woman*
> *forever*
> *returning*
> *twisting north*
> *a snake carved*
> *into prairie grass*
> *hiding everywhere*
> *eroded with age*
> *etched into her edges and newly born*
> *every day*
>
> Vermette 2014, 7

Persistent violence against Indigenous women in Canada has extended from overtly genocidal state policies to more insidious forms in the age of liberal recognition of Indigenous peoples by the state (Coulthard 2014). Indigenous and feminist scholars and activists (Maracle 1988; Anderson 2003; Sisters in Spirit 2010; Kuokkanen 2011; Simpson 2014; Hele, Seyers, and Wood 2015) locate Indigenous women's bodies at the frontline of violent processes of colonial dispossession and decolonizing resistance in Canada.[1] This is a contemporary and corporeal violence: it has not, as Tuck and Yang (2012) remind us, moved to metaphor, and it demands understanding and response. More than a product of colonial processes, targeting Indigenous women's bodies, lives, and labour is itself a colonizing strategy (Smith 2005). Engaging Indigenous and feminist scholarship with Canadian political economy (CPE), this chapter discusses the insights that emerge when Canadian state interventions targeting Indigenous women and the social reproduction they perform are considered an integral part – rather than a side effect – of historical and ongoing processes of settler colonialism.

Over the past forty years, scholars have addressed previous gaps in CPE literature in the acknowledgment of the dispossession of Indigenous peoples as the foundation to the development of the Canadian capitalist economy. However, for the most part, analysis has focused on the dispossession of land and the uneven incorporation of Indigenous peoples into capitalist relations of production. Comparatively, there has been limited CPE engagement with state interventions into Indigenous social reproduction and the gendered nature of these processes. In response, this chapter takes a feminist political economy (FPE) approach to expand political economic analyses of Canadian state/Indigenous relations to include social reproduction and subsistence labours and to look at the ways in which these relations are gendered – intersecting but distinct projects. This chapter examines ways in which – and the reasons why – state projects of restructuring have targeted social reproduction performed by Indigenous women with a consistent intensity. This theoretical inquiry will be rooted in an analysis of the modern political economy of the Northwest Territories (NWT), a space in which Canadian State attention to Indigenous social reproduction arrived late, but with great force.

The chapter begins with a brief review of key decolonizing interventions into northern studies, Indigenous studies, and gender studies that have called attention to the colonial nature of the political economic development of the Canadian state. Theorizations of social reproduction developed in FPE literature are then used as an avenue for addressing the inattention to Indigenous women's bodies and labour as a key site of de/colonizing struggle. Social reproduction, as it is used in this chapter, refers to "the processes involved in maintaining and reproducing people, specifically the labouring population, and their labour power on a daily and generational basis" (Bezanson and Luxton 2006, 3. See also LeBlanc Haley this volume). The NWT case study follows, and compares the recent history of northern state/Indigenous relations at the site of social reproduction with contemporary iterations of these relations.

THEORIZING SETTLER COLONIALISM
AND THE NORTHERN MIXED ECONOMY

For those concerned with settler colonialism, study of the NWT provides an illuminating glimpse of the colonial contradictions woven into the fabric of the Canadian tapestry. The north provides a symbolic reference point for that which is deemed Canadian: for many southern Canadians, life in the north was first given flesh by authors like Farley Mowat and Pierre Burton (Coates 1985), who wove tales of harsh climates and hard men, frontier narratives told with honky-tonk flourish. Ray Price (1974) described the NWT as the "new yet ancient land," evoking images of a wild empty space ripe for adventure. Frontier rhetoric extends to the contemporary, in both culture and politics. However, while the imaginary of the north is central to the consolidation of Canadian identity, the materiality of Indigenous dispossession and exploitation inherent in northern development has been consistently obscured – dismissed as a relic of the past, or as a deviation from the general path of Canadian development. Indeed, the frontier narrative denies the long and storied state presence in the north and its role in the development of the northern mixed economy (Abele 2015). Rather, in the "frontier" account, mascu-linized White settler labour carves out a capitalist economy upon a rugged empty space. The colonial violence of exploiting and restructuring existing Indigenous socio-economies is reframed as perseverance in a hostile environment, subsistence socio-economies are trapped in anachronistic space,[2] and Indigenous women and men are relegated to the role of bit-players or symbolic markers, rather than living, labouring actors.

Since the first settler accounts of what is now Canada, Indigenous peoples have offered an alternative narrative; however, it was not until the mid-twentieth century that, compelled by anti-colonial movements within Canada and around the globe, these voices began to be heard in academic spaces (Battiste 2011). Since then, a scholarship has emerged tied together not by discipline – it is energetically interdisciplinary – but by a commitment to decolonizing the people, processes, and institutions that make up postsecondary education and research in Canada (Battiste, Bell, and Findlay 2002) and internationally (Smith 1999; Dei 2005). This work challenges the colonial basis of Indigenous studies (Smith 1999) that is research on, replacing objectifying studies with research by or research with (Dei 2005). Indigenous activists and scholars have exposed the dispossession and exploitation inherent in the Canadian settler econ-omy and elevated the experiences, socio-economies, and ontologies of

Indigenous peoples and communities. Intervening in the field of CPE, Howard Adams broke new ground with his work tracing the development of the Canadian economy from the point of view of Indigenous peoples, theorizing economic and racial subordination from the fur trade through the 1885 Métis struggle to residential schools and modern liberation struggles. Challenging the dismissal of colonialism as a past mistake, he linked historical processes of colonization with modern poverty in Indigenous communities (1989) and with the ongoing and contradictory processes of engaging Indigenous communities in extractive projects (1995).

As with other disciplines, settler CPE scholarship has been mixed in the extent to which it has included, listened to, and incorporated decolonizing voices. As Sharma argues in this volume, methodological nationalism in CPE has, among other things, obscured the colonial relations through which the Canadian nation-state was established; in particular, the new political economy was concerned with Canada's past as a European colony being replicated by a dependency on the US (see Clement, and Mills and Tufts this volume), rather than the ongoing internal colonialism of Indigenous peoples. However, from the 1970s onwards, in northern Canada, engagement between the new political economy, Indigenous political economists, community-based researchers, and activists (noting these are not discrete categories), led to a new body of literature on northern political economy challenging "frontier" understandings of northern development (see, for example, Watkins 1977a; Bourgeault 1983; Abele and Stasiulus 1989; Adams 1995; Abele 1997; Kulchyski 2005; White 2006; Abele 2009; Coulthard 2010). For example, inspired by the northern Indigenous calls for recognition and campaigns against the Mackenzie Valley Pipeline in the NWT,[3] Mel Watkins (1977b) took a new approach to Innis' staples theory and argued that Canada's reliance on staples for its economic development was made possible by its exploitation of Indigenous populations. Like Watkins, Abele and Stasiulus called for attention to Indigenous peoples as actors in contemporary relations of production, rather than survivors from a "doomed" way of life (1989).[4]

Indeed, in the face of persistent colonial interventions from the fur trade onward, the northern mixed economy is triumphant evidence to the contrary. Far from disappearing, Indigenous modes of life (Coulthard 2014) have interacted with settler society to build place-based (Coulthard 2010) socio-economies that encompass both Indigenous and Western cultures, and capitalist relations of production and ongoing subsistence production (Asch 1977; Usher and Wenzel 1987; Brody 2002; Kulchyski

2005). Subsistence labour – that is, place-based labour (Coulthard 2014) oriented towards communal needs – is an alternative to the totality of capital; this labour prioritizes the intergenerational well-being of community and land (Kuokkanen 2011). Literature on the historical and contemporary northern mixed economy offers insights on the role of settler dispossession in building the northern political economy, the ongoing and active role of Indigenous peoples in developing northern socio-political structures, and the multi-scalar role of the Canadian State in these processes. However, in articulating settler processes of dispossession, CPE literature has tended to focus on the appropriation of land and resources as these are related to capitalist production. There is a gap, then, in analysis of the long and devastating history of state interventions into Indigenous social reproduction, from residential schools to forced relocations to contemporary racialized processes of foster care and the settler patriarchal ideology that contributes to structuring these interventions.

GENDERING INDIGENOUS-STATE RELATIONS IN THE NWT

This is not to say there is not ample scholarly and activist literature outside of CPE identifying the gendered nature of colonial processes, and the targeting of Indigenous women's bodies and reproductive capacities, both social and biological. Indigenous women – some who identify as feminists and others who do not[5] – have long pointed to the violence with which their bodies and subjectivities have been attacked (Anderson 2003; Smith 2005), linking the structural and corporeal violence directed at Indigenous women's reproductive labours with the pursuit of political and economic resources and power. For example, Sylvia Maracle asks: "Why was it primarily men who were occupying formal positions of leadership [in Indigenous communities]? When the treaty parties came to us, the Europeans didn't bring their women. In turn, they didn't want to deal with the women who were the leaders of our families, clans, communities and Nations." (2003, 73) Maracle is pointing to the patriarchal power relations and ideological assumptions of the settler state and the ways in which they have come to shape negotiation, legislation, and policy since first contact (Deerchild 2003, 101). For example, through the *Indian Act* (1876) an Indigenous woman's status became contingent on the status of her husband. Thus, if she married a non-Indigenous man, she lost her status, and if she married a man outside of her band, she lost membership in her band (Gehl 2000). Loss of status also applied to her children.[6]

Loss of status was just one way the social reproduction of Indigenous communities was hampered. Residential school was the most explicit attempt to eradicate Indigenous social reproduction, but its racist and violent targeting of Indigenous communities – and especially Indigenous women – continued through, for example, the forced sterilization of Indigenous women in the 1970s (Anderson 2003, 176) and the ongoing overrepresentation of Indigenous children in protective services (Blackstock 2007). Indigenous women scholars (Maracle 1988; Smith 2005; Simpson 2014) have demonstrated that, rather than an indirect consequence of processes of colonization, violence against Indigenous women is a direct tool of patriarchy and colonialism (Smith 2005, 2), undermining women and their central role in protecting and reproducing Indigenous peoples, both materially and ontologically. This is a tactic that links colonial and racist state-building and capitalist processes across borders and time (Davis 1981; McClintock 1995; Hill Collins 2006). Incorporating this insight is crucial for an approach to CPE that is feminist, decolonizing, and inclusive of what is unmistakably a key site of settler colonialism in Canada. When analysis stops at the site of capitalist production, the continuities of gendered and racialized violence aimed at terminating Indigenous social reproduction are obscured.

In politicizing and denaturalizing social reproduction, FPE theory opens the space for grounded explorations of the relationship between the state and its varied and, never minimalist and sometimes activist, role in social reproduction (Jenson 1986; Vosko 2002; Bakker and Gill 2003). Jane Jenson (1986), and Leah Vosko (2002) add that analysis of the state's relationship with social reproduction must not be general, but rather must historicize and particularize state relationships with social reproduction. This includes not just the question of why various states approach social reproduction differently, but why and how the social reproduction of different groups within a state are approached unequally. Thus, analysis of the state and social reproduction must attend to the racialized and colonial ideological and material relations through which social reproduction struggles play out (Vosko 2002; Federici 2004; Bannerji 2005; Ferguson 2008; Sharma this volume). Historically, attention to race has been a gap in FPE analysis. Increasingly, however, FPE has incorporated an intersectional feminist approach (Crenshaw 1997), attending to the ways in which race and gender, among other aspects of identity, shape the material conditions of capitalist production and social reproduction (Vosko this volume).

The concept of social reproduction, as it has been developed by feminist political economists, is a means of bringing the insights of Indigenous women scholars into conversation with northern political economy for a more fulsome analysis of Indigenous/state relations. Developments in the field of FPE have established the inextricable relation between social reproduction and capitalist production (Vosko 2002). A relational approach to social reproduction and capitalist production elevates the ways in which social reproduction can be both paid and not, capitalist and not, inside of the state and outside. These are sites of mutability and tension that articulate in processes of colonialism targeting Indigenous social reproduction, and in decolonizing Indigenous resistance. However, social reproduction is largely a concept developed in opposition and in relation to capitalist production. Within FPE, there has been little attention to forms of non-capitalist labour, including subsistence labour, and non-Western, non-nuclear forms of organizing social reproduction, such as those found in northern Indigenous communities. Indeed, in the NWT mixed economy, subsistence production operates alongside social reproduction and capitalist production. In this regional socio-economy, then, social reproduction cannot be approached simply as it relates to capitalist production. Rather, social reproduction is located relationally with subsistence and capitalist production, navigating the ideological and material tension between the two. Locating social reproduction at this site of de/colonizing tension helps to explain the continuity of colonial intervention into Indigenous women's social reproduction.

Thus, in what follows, the insights offered from Indigenous and anti-racist feminisms, northern political economy, and FPE are combined in order to move beyond the notion that capitalist relations of production are total (Kuokkanen 2008) and, rather, approach northern Indigenous women's labour as enacted within a mixed economy that persists through capitalist and non-capitalist economies and systems of meaning. Social reproduction is located as a site of gendered, racialized, and de/colonial struggle: a site of reproduction both for the demands of capital, and for the local, place-based pursuit of maintaining and strengthening Indigenous socio-economies. In turning to the empirics of the case of the NWT mixed economy, an examination of the modern history of state restructuring and social reproduction in the NWT is followed by an examination of contemporaneous trends in these processes.

TWENTIETH-CENTURY STATE INTERVENTIONS INTO NORTHERN INDIGENOUS SOCIAL REPRODUCTION

In Canada, settler interventions into Indigenous processes of social reproduction are as old as settler colonialism itself. While the early settlers relied upon the pre-existing Indigenous social relations to support the early fur trade, the fur trade disrupted Indigenous social reproduction (Bourgeault 1983). Moreover missionaries, whose goal was to interrupt and intervene into Indigenous modes of life, accompanied fur traders. Missionaries set up the first residential schools, but almost as soon as the Canadian state was born, it took over these institutions and their violently interventionist project. Residential schools operated in Canada with the explicit mandate of "civilizing" the Indigenous population.[7] "Civilizing," in this instance, meant replacing community and family bonds with strangers who abused, imposed racial hierarchies upon, and punished children for any attempts to reproduce their own community – whether by speaking their own language, carrying on their religious practices, or telling the stories of their communities (Martin-Hill 2003). It also meant denying Indigenous children the opportunity to learn subsistence knowledge and skills and build the kinship and community relationships necessary for reproducing their local socio-economies. Instead residential schools focused on training children for the settler workforce.

As Canada's political economic geography is concentrated along the 49th parallel, prior to the mid-twentieth century Indigenous people living in the NWT had been exempt to some extent from the colonial social restructuring tactics that the Canadian state had pursued in southern Canada. As Philip Blake, speaking in his home community, stated to the Mackenzie Valley Pipeline Inquiry, "For a while it seemed that we might escape the greed of the southern system. The north was seen as a frozen wasteland, not fit for the civilized ways of the white man. But that has been changing over the past few years" (Blake quoted in Watkins 1977a, 6). However, after the Second World War political and economic interests converged in a newly interventionist approach to social reproduction in northern Indigenous communities (Abele 2009). The Second World War highlighted the potential importance of resources and land in the North, and the presence of US military in the sub-Arctic and Arctic – soldiers originally stationed there as a response to Pearl Harbour were retained in smaller numbers during the Cold War – posed a threat to Canadian sovereignty (Abele 1987).

At the same time, the post-war reconstruction effort moved political economies around the globe toward welfare state development. In Canada, the growing state assumed a greater role in social provisioning (Mahon 1984). While welfare policies around state responsibility for social reproduction did not extend to northern or southern Indigenous communities in materiality or ideology (Shewell 2004), the combination of intensified extractive development in the north and high-profile cases of starvation in Inuit communities put pressure on the Canadian state to extend so-called "charity" to northern Indigenous communities (Southcott and Walker 2009, 15). The global and domestic political appetite for charitable intervention combined with the new international political interest in demonstrating Canadian sovereignty and the economic imperative to intensify northern resource development led to a state restructuring project in fast-forward – a profound, and sometimes violent, colonial process of restructuring and resistance that continues in northern Indigenous communities to this day.

At the outset, this restructuring project was framed as social policy, rather than economic policy, and targeted social reproduction in northern Indigenous communities rather than attempting to recruit Indigenous people as a capitalist workforce. Indeed, while capitalist extractive projects have consistently relied upon Indigenous expertise, land, and resources, Indigenous people initially engaged in these projects in a time-limited fashion that did not fundamentally disrupt their structures of social reproduction and subsistence (Watkins 1977b; Asch 1977). Compared to many Indigenous communities in southern Canada, attempts by the Canadian state and private capital to proletarianize Indigenous communities in the NWT (and, indeed, Nunavut and the Yukon)[8] have been a much more recent project.

Instead, from the end of the Second World War to the close of the twentieth century daily and intergenerational social reproduction of Indigenous people in the NWT constituted the primary site of Canadian state intervention. At that time, Canadian state initiatives targeting Indigenous social reproduction in the NWT were structured through the triadic relationship between welfare payments, relocation, and mandatory education. As government schooling was made mandatory for Indigenous children, welfare payments were made dependent on children's attendance. And access to welfare payments – as well as new social services – became dependent on relocating to permanent settlements. In the case of settlements adjacent to a town with a government school, permanent relocation also came with the incentive of keeping one's family together while sending children to the mandatory school. This collusive web, in the context of new limits on subsistence activities as a result of extractive development operating concurrently in the territory, explains the speed with which state-dictated structures of social reproduction took hold in NWT Indigenous communities.

The push for Indigenous peoples to settle permanently in communities – rather than continue nomadic subsistence production, living in different camps at different times of year and moving flexibly based on the needs of the community, the climate, and the status of the land and animals – was not a simple or immediate effort, nor should it be construed as a complete process, given that Indigenous people all over the north continue to go out on the land in varying forms. As described by Wilf Bean, northern federal employees were charged with convincing Indigenous people to abandon their traditional hunting camps and nomadic lives (Watkins 1977a, 131). This convincing was made possible by tying welfare payments to the new permanent communities; in other words, Indigenous peoples were forced to reside in designated permanent communities as a condition for receiving their payments. It is important to clarify here – particularly given the racialized and colonial tropes that critique Indigenous peoples for their reliance on welfare – that payments to northern Indigenous communities did not come about as a government response to poverty, but as treaty payments distributed in accordance with negotiations with the Federal State and northern Indigenous peoples (YK Dene First Nations Elders Advisory Council 1997; Zoe 2005; Shewell 2004). At this time, the market value for furs had diminished and increased extractive development and corresponding settlement was creating new strains on subsistence production; as a result, many northern Indigenous peoples had begun to rely upon treaty payments as a crucial component of the resources required to meet their daily needs (Coates 1985, 192–3).

In this context, the insistence upon permanent residence as a condition for treaty payments (YK Dene First Nations Elders Advisory Council 1997) – re-imagined as state charity – had a profound impact. Although some families continued to travel to the barrens annually up until the late 1970s, the move to permanent communities marked a major shift toward sedentary lifestyles, one that proved particularly detrimental to the hunting of small game and gathering of local plants (subsistence activities traditionally assigned to women) as permanent settlement led to over-use of these resources (Irlbacher-Fox 2009). At the same time that subsistence labour was made more difficult, Indigenous communities, newly living in government homes and in government towns, experienced a new proximity to Canadian state surveillance of their social reproduction, a surveillance that would persist in contemporary times. Indeed, Thobani (2007) argues that mid-twentieth century Canadian welfare state social policies were characterized by racist norms that targeted Indigenous and other racialized women, and their households and communities. She writes: "In the welfarist national imaginary, Native families were deficient; Native mothers deviant and a menace to their own children; and the nation the caring benefactor of these children" (109).

In this vein, the push toward permanent settlements was directly tied to residential schools. In the immediate sense, some families moved to permanent settlements in order to send their children to mandatory schools while keeping the family together. In the longer term, children who attended residential schools were more likely to remain in towns, as they had been separated from subsistence education and indoctrinated into settler modes of life. Residential schools arrived late to the NWT – not until the 1950s – but when they did arrive, they did so with devastating force. From 1954 to 1964, the federal government opened five large public schools to which children from around the Territory were flown.[9] The goal was to put every school-age child in the NWT in a school by 1968; and, indeed, "[a] far higher percentage of the Aboriginal population in northern Canada attended residential schools than was the case in the rest of Canada. According to the 2001 Statistics Canada Aboriginal Peoples Survey, over 50 per cent of Aboriginal peoples forty-five years of age and older in the Yukon and the Northwest Territories attended a residential school" (GWT 2013, 20). The impact of the violence endemic to residential schools – ideological, structural, corporeal, and socio-cultural – and the ways in which the residential school experience continues to manifest cannot be overstated (Kakfwi 1977; Milloy 1999). Maria Yellow Horse Brave Heart (2003) and Julie Christensen (2014) link analyses of the impacts of residential school trauma to longstanding experiences of colonial trauma: a "collective emotional and psychological wounding that occurs over the lifespan and across generations" (Christensen 2014, 811).

Residential schools were, arguably, the most violent arm of the overall aim to restructure Indigenous social reproduction toward capitalist production. Given the limited opportunities for wage labour in the NWT at the time, especially in smaller communities, many Indigenous people felt they were being trained in schools for jobs that did not exist, while at the same time they were being separated from the education they would have received in their home communities through engagement in subsistence labour (Kakfwi 1977). Traditionally, the whole community took part in educating children by including them in all parts of camp life. Phoebe Nahanni explains that, "within the domestic unit, each member of the family performs tasks which were learned by observation or taught to members of the family" (1992, 57). These intricate learning processes – intimate and intimately tied to the land – were violently dismantled, and rebuilding the intergenerational learning that was lost as a result is an ongoing decolonizing project in the north (Irlbacher-Fox 2009).

Just as social reproduction was being restructured toward the needs of capitalist accumulation, the prevailing patriarchal gender order attached to the capitalist economy – that is, that capitalist production is a male responsibility and social reproduction is a female responsibility – was imposed upon Indigenous communities, albeit in contradictory and incomplete ways. Social service programs targeted the mother as the person solely responsible for the child, administering treaty payments under two assumptions: first, that social reproduction was undertaken in Western-style nuclear family arrangements; and, second, that social reproduction was the woman's responsibility. In most northern Indigenous communities, while women are often responsible for meeting the immediate needs of young children, children are seen as the responsibility of the entire community and their care and teaching is approached in an interdependent manner (Nahanni 1992; Harnum et al. 2014). However, erroneous though they may be, state assumptions about the feminized responsibility for care intensified the colonial tendency to target social reproduction through the labours and bodies of Indigenous women, a violent implication that continues to colour northern Indigenous women's experiences of social reproduction.

CONTEMPORARY STATE INTERVENTIONS INTO NORTHERN INDIGENOUS SOCIAL REPRODUCTION

The last residential school closed, disquietingly recently, in 1996, but the Canadian state has continued to target Indigenous women, their bodies, and their labours, and to interrupt northern Indigenous social reproduction. Rates of violence against Indigenous women are devastatingly high and, as Cindy Blackstock (2016) notes, there are more Indigenous children in state care through child welfare than there ever were in residential schools. While there are evidently violent colonial continuities that run through past and present Canadian state approaches to northern Indigenous social reproduction, the contemporary iterations of these relations are characterized by the political economy of the day. Notably, as a result of domestic and international Indigenous organizing, it is no longer politically acceptable to explicitly punish Indigenous modes of social reproduction collectively (e.g., through mandatory schooling and mandatory relocations). Punitive measures now are – ostensibly – individualized, targeting those who are not meeting Canadian norms regarding social reproduction. Furthermore, with the erosion of the welfare state and the advent of neoliberalism, employment has become the central preoccupation of federal Indigenous social policy. In the context of the north, where the primary industry is resource extraction, this preoccupation manifests itself as "responsible extraction."

Contemporaneously, the primary expression of struggle at the site of Indigenous social reproduction is state surveillance and discipline respecting the care of children, most notably involving the apprehension and placing into foster care of Indigenous children from individuated homes – labelled by some as the "new residential school" (Christensen 2014; Blackstock 2016). In the NWT, home to the last active residential school, there is significant overlap between the "old" and the "new" eras of intervention. In 2012, in the NWT, 1,042 children received services from Child and Family Services. Of these, 372 children received voluntary services aimed at mitigating child protective concerns, while the other 670 children received other forms of "protective services" (i.e., they were either taken from their families and placed under the temporary care of the Director of Child and Family Services – 266 children – or were removed under some other form of protective services) (Auditor General 2014). Given that 95 per cent of the 1,042 children receiving services are Indigenous (Auditor General 2014), the 670 children under protective services and the 1,042 receiving all services represent 3 per cent and 5 per cent, respectively, of the approximately 22,000 Indigenous people (GNWT Bureau of Statistics 2015) living in the Territory.[10]

These numbers are devastating, not just in terms of the children they represent, but in terms of their indication of an ever-present possibility of surveillance, judgment, and apprehension in Indigenous homes. Child apprehension also serves as a stick to discipline Indigenous women and men into model "Aboriginal (Canadian) Citizens." In practice, the surveillance and judgment lands at the feet of Indigenous women. Women who have been separated from their children are given criteria they must meet before any reunifications. In continuity with the racist settler logic that informed Canadian state programs, Indigenous women are made responsible for social reproduction, while at the same time ideologically connected to symbols of "bad mothers" through violent colonial tropes denigrating Indigenous women and non-Western structures of care (Martin-Hill 2003). Those who do not meet the criteria are "bad parents," or, most often, "bad mothers." Kim Anderson (2003) locates the contemporary surveillance of Indigenous women's childcare in a long history of attacks on the social reproduction of Indigenous communities. She writes: "There is always the threat of someone coming to judge one's parenting, someone coming to take the children away, someone scheming to erase us permanently. The political, social emotional and practical response to these issues has been to reproduce in spite of it all" (Anderson 2003, 176).

On the face of it, the intense surveillance of and intervention into social reproduction in Indigenous households is a racialized, colonial contradiction to the observed Canadian state neoliberal retrenchment of social services. In the context of shrinking budgets for social service provision and a political climate encouraging a so-called "small state," one might suggest that the state activist approach to intervening in northern Indigenous social reproduction is an institutionalized ideological relic, an anomaly that can only be historically and not contemporaneously explained. However, as McBride writes, in this collection, the state's role under neoliberalism is better understood as having shifted, not diminished. Indeed, feminist theorists have demonstrated that the Canadian state has a long history of targeting particular mothers along racialized and class lines (Dua and Robertson 1999; Thobani 2007), one that has not waned in lean neoliberal times but has instead been reconfigured through an intensified concentration on individualized responsibility for childcare that lands at the feet of mothers (McKeen and Porter 2003; McKeen 2007).

It is clear, then, that while Canadian state interventions into northern Indigenous peoples' social reproduction is newly articulated in individualistic terms, apprehension of children by the state persists in a social restructuring enacted along racialized and gendered colonial lines, carrying with it continuities from the interventions of the mid-twentieth century. Ideologically, the shift from group-apprehension in residential school to individualized apprehensions meets liberal demands for Indigenous recognition and multiculturalism (Coulthard 2014), while at the same time striving for a hegemonic nation-state norm in household and care structures.[11] And materially, the surveillance and disciplining of Indigenous social reproduction is structured to support the new, or newly intensified, project of integrating northern Indigenous people into capitalist wage labour. Indeed, while during the welfare state period interventions into Indigenous social reproduction were structured toward the reproduction of capitalist social relations, they were largely motivated by concerns for Canadian sovereignty: asserting state sovereignty over northern Indigenous people, while using these bodies to assert Canadian sovereignty to other states interested in the north. Conversely, in the neoliberal era, state interventions in northern Indigenous social reproduction are primarily driven by an active interest in northern economic development – particularly resource extraction, which has, from the fur trade onward, been a pillar in the NWT mixed economy – and efforts to incorporate Indigenous people into this development.

An examination of the northern diamond industry and its need for available and flexible labour power exemplifies the capitalist imperative for state efforts to feminize and individualize social reproduction in northern Indigenous communities, including attempts to orient these labours towards the demands and norms of capitalist production. As the primary economic driver in the NWT since the first diamond mine opened in 1998, the northern Canadian diamond industry targets Indigenous people as potential workers. The diamond mines operate through a Fly-In/ Fly-Out (FIFO) work structure, wherein diamond workers are flown to the mine site for fourteen-day shifts, and then flown home for two weeks of "rest." This mode of work is structured through the assumption that the worker has no social reproduction responsibilities of his (and it is most often *his*) own. While traditional Indigenous structures of social reproduction oriented toward subsistence are built on gendered interde- pendence and inter-household links (Usher, Duhaime, and Searles 2002; Irlbacher-Fox 2009; Mills and Tufts this volume), settler modes of social reproduction and production individualize and feminize responsibility at a household level. In this way, Indigenous men are free to take up work at the mines – an industry that benefits significantly from a loyal, local workforce. Hiring Indigenous workers satisfies new norms for "respon- sible development" while saving on worker transportation costs for the mines and providing the mines with workers with local expertise. The state has a strong interest in the diamond industry's success: until devolu- tion of resource rights to the Territorial government in 2014, the Federal government was reaping royalties from the success of diamond operations of approximately $1.6 billion annually (Canada 2014).[12]

Feminizing the responsibility for social reproduction – and enforcing this ideological structure through gendered enactments of government policy – is a two-sided sleight of hand that facilitates Indigenous partici- pation in the diamond mines, as well as the appearance of "responsible development." By feminizing social reproduction, not only are Indigenous women made responsible for daily and intergenerational reproduction but Indigenous women's engagement with capitalist labour and subsis- tence labour is also obscured. In this way, a Western, capitalist typology of women caregivers and male breadwinners obscures the inter- and intra-household social relations of subsistence. According to the new extractive approach, subsistence production – referred to as "traditional activities" in industry documents and understood primarily as hunting, fishing and sometimes trapping (GNWT 2014) – is divorced from its relational, community quality, as well as from its very specific relation to the land (see Mills and Tufts for further discussion of the relationship between northern subsistence and resource extraction). Rather, subsistence is reframed as recreation or cultural activity that can be undertaken in a worker's "time off." By redefining subsistence in masculinized, individualized terms, the ways in which interdependent Indigenous relations of social reproduction are disrupted by the FIFO diamond-mining regime is masked. Thus, not only does feminizing and restructuring social reproduction meet the needs of capital insofar as men are "freed" to engage in wage labour as social reproduction is subsumed, but it simultaneously undermines the social reproduction of the mixed economy and makes this continued colonization invisible.

Thus, the current approach to northern Indigenous social reproduction, ostensibly individualized and focused on Indigenous employment, demonstrates the capitalist imperative for state interventions into Indigenous women's lives and labours. In feminizing responsibilities for care and enforcing a sedentary nuclear approach to production, state interventions into Indigenous social reproduction in the twentieth century helped to make the current masculinized emphasis on Indigenous employment possible. Past and present social policies targeting Indigenous women's social reproduction are linked by a continuity of gendered and racialized violence explained, at least in part, by the location of social reproduction as a site of tension between capitalist production and subsistence in the mixed economy, a threat to the imagined and desired totality of the Canadian capitalist economy.

CONCLUSION

This chapter approached Canadian state interventions into Indigenous women's social reproduction as part of an ongoing – and contested – project of appropriating Indigenous labour, land, and resources for the Canadian settler economy. To be sure, Indigenous/state relations north of the 60th parallel are distinct from relations in southern Canada in timeline and in political geography. However, the observations that social reproduction – as it sits on the boundary between that which is capitalist and not – is a key site of social restructuring (Federici 2004), is generalizable. Indeed, by approaching the physical dispossession of land, the proletarianization and capitalization of Indigenous workers and resources, and the restructuring of social reproduction performed by Indigenous peoples as interrelated processes, colonial continuities across these spheres of analysis – and through time and space – become apparent. Consequently, decolonizing the Canadian state's approach to Indigenous women's social reproduction requires not only policy and ideological intervention, but must also challenge the gendered ways in which the demands of capital continue to infringe upon Indigenous self-determination at the levels of ontology, production, *and* social reproduction. At the same time, a focus on social reproduction elevates the incomplete and mutable character of Canadian state social restructuring and, most significantly, the ways in which Indigenous resistance has shaped, and is continuing to shape, daily and intergenerational reproduction through transformative and creative acts.

NOTES

1 "Bodies," in this discussion, are approached not as an "object of inquiry," but rather as a "social category of analysis" (Fonow and Cook 2005). That is to say, this analysis includes the ways in which bodies and their productive and reproductive capacities are socially interpreted and interrupted, incorporated into political and economic relations, exploited, and/or subjected to violent exclusion. In this piece, the focus is on how Indigenous women's bodies are a site of de/colonizing struggle because of their symbolic and material relationship (Anderson 2003) to the reproduction of Indigenous "modes of life" (Coulthard 2014).

2 Anne McClintock describes "anachronistic space" in the following: "Since Indigenous peoples are not supposed to be spatially there – for the lands are 'empty' – they are symbolically displaced onto what I call anachronistic space ... According to this trope, colonized people – like women and the working class in the metropolis – do not inhabit history proper but exist in a permanently anterior time within the geographic space of the modern empire as anachronistic humans, atavistic, irrational, bereft of human agency – the living embodiment of the archaic 'primitive'" (30).

3 The Mackenzie Valley Pipeline was a proposed plan to transport natural gas 1,700 km from the Beaufort Sea across the fragile Arctic Tundra to northern Alberta. Vehemently opposed by northern Indigenous people, their organizing attracted the attention of the federal government and led to an inquiry by Justice Thomas Berger. In 1977, after in-depth local consultation, Berger advised the government to halt progress on the pipeline until northern land claims had been settled. This led to a ten-year moratorium and a new

precedent for consultation with Indigenous communities prior to the development of extractive projects.

4 See also Abele (1997).

5 As Joyce Green notes (2007), "feminist" is not a term widely taken up by
Indigenous scholars and activists, partly because of an exclusion of Indigenous
women from (largely White) feminist movements.

6 The gender discrimination in the act was doggedly challenged by Indigenous
women in the courts in the 1970s and early 1980s, and was finally repealed
in 1985.

7 Indeed in 1879, responding to a recommendation for residential schools, John
A. Macdonald agreed, saying: "It has been impressed upon me as head of the
Department that Indian children should be withdrawn as much as possible
from the parental influence, and the only way to do that would be to in central
training industrial schools where they will acquire the habits and modes of
thought of white men" (Miller 1996).

8 When discussing the history of the Northwest Territories, I am also referring
to Nunavut, as they were not separated until 1999.

9 The administration of these schools was moved from the federal government
to the territorial government in 1967.

10 22,000 is the number of all Indigenous people in the Territory, not of
Indigenous children. As such, the percentage of Indigenous children who
are receiving services would be significantly higher.

11 While I am pointing to the colonial continuities in foster care, I would be
remiss to deny the myriad and contradictory ways in which policy is enacted
on the ground. Most often, front-line child service workers are northern
women, many of whom take up a number of supportive and progressive
roles in the community.

12 This figure is based on federal government stats on mineral export government
revenue from the NWT. Revenue from the diamond mines is not separated
from other minerals; however, 99.8 per cent of revenue accrued was from the
diamond industry.

10

A Political Economy of the Cultural Industries in Canada

Tanner Mirrlees

In the thick of the 2015 Canadian election campaign, Liberal party leader Justin Trudeau promised voters that if elected prime minister, he would reverse a decade of Conservative cutbacks and reinvigorate support for the cultural industries. The 2016 Budget of Prime Minister Trudeau's Liberal Government notes that "our cultural industries represent a key sector of our economy" and also, that "investing in the Canadian cultural sector helps to create jobs, strengthens the economy and ensures that the unique Canadian perspective is shared with the world" (Morneau 2016, 184). In September 2017, following months of cultural policy consultation, review, and analysis, the Department of Canadian Heritage Minister Mélanie Joly unveiled the "Creative Canada" strategy. The Liberal Government increased the Federal subsidy to the Canada Media Fund in support of the Canadian cultural production sector, added $125 million to a Creative Export Strategy to shuttle Canadian cultural commodities into markets around the world, and allocated $300 million to developing infrastructure for new urban "creative hubs" where "creators can build their entrepreneurial skills, create, collaborate and innovate" (Leblanc and Mayaz 2017). This federal budgetary discourse and policy expresses how in twenty-first century Canada, "culture" is primarily valued by politicians, cultural policy makers, and the corporations that make it for its benefit to the "economy." This discourse's affirmative use of the "cultural industries" concept, blunt reduction of culture's value to the cash nexus, and casual framing of culture as instrumental to economic returns, suggests that culture is in no way autonomous from capitalism.

The relationship between culture and economy is dealt with much more critically in political economy of communication (PEC) research on the cultural industries published in previous volumes in this series (Magder 1989, 1997; Mosco 2003; Kurasawa 2003). A cursory review of these chapters highlights some of the PEC's key concerns and focal points. Some PEC researchers focus on the importance of public communication to an educated citizenry and functioning democracy (Magder 1997), and the threat to public communication and democracy by private ownership (Mosco 2003). PEC researchers also highlight the concentrated ownership of the communication and cultural industries by a handful of big companies (Magder 1989, 283–5; Magder 1997, 348–9; Mosco 2003, 288–9, 294–5, 307), and show how the structure of the market, media ownership patterns, and much of the cultural industries' dependence on advertising revenue influences what types of cultural products get produced and circulated to audiences (Magder 1989, 289–94; Magder 1997, 341–6). Furthermore, PEC researches examine the commodification of culture, or, the conversion of ideas, stories, and symbols into copyrights (Mosco 2003, 291–2), the transformation cultural work and labour (Magder 1997, 339) and the unpaid work of the "audience commodity" for network TV (Magder 1989, 285–6; Magder 1997, 349–50). Additionally, PEC researchers have shown how the cultural industries in Canada are protected and promoted by the Canadian state's cultural policies, laws, and regulations (Kurasawa 2003, 474; Magder 1989, 290–2; Magder 1997, 354) in a global neoliberal context in which United States cultural imperialism and a US-centred neoliberal policy framework that extols the privatization, de-regulation, and liberalization of the cultural industries continues to influence Canada as a whole (Kurasawa 2003, 471–5; Magder 1989, 288–90; Magder 1997, 347; Mosco 2003, 296–300, 307). Significantly, PEC researchers shed light upon sites of resistance to the corporatization of culture and identify social struggles in and around the cultural industries (Magder 1989, 1997; Mosco 2003; Kurasawa 2003).

By building upon some of these key concerns and focal points in the PEC research tradition, this chapter aims to offer a clear and broad overview of the cultural industries in twenty-first century Canada. It clarifies the meaning of the cultural industries, conveys the value of the PEC approach to analyzing these industries, considers how capitalist and state power influence their workings, and situates Canada's cultural industries in a global context by illustrating the continuing power of US cultural imperialism. To this end, the first section defines the cultural industries, delineates the "core" cultural industries and describes why they matter to contemporary capitalism, politics, and culture. The second section reviews the central tenets of the PEC approach to the cultural industries. The third section highlights the capitalist logics of the cultural industries, the fourth shows how these are supported by the Canadian state, and the fifth highlights continuity and change in US cultural imperialism with regard to the current dominance of US-based digital media giants in Canada. The conclusion addresses emerging sites of struggle within and against the cultural industries.

THE CULTURAL INDUSTRIES IN CANADA: WHAT'S IN A WORD?

During the Second World War, the critical theorists Max Horkheimer and Theodor Adorno (1995) coined the concept of the "culture industry" to both highlight the capitalist system's incorporation of culture into its circuits of accumulation and critique the for-profit production, distribution, and marketing of all the world's cultural forms – high and low – as standardized commodities. For these thinkers, the culture industry was a pejorative, a Marxist fighting word. Throughout the 1970s and 1980s, though, PEC scholars such as Nicholas Garnham (1987/1995) and Bernard Miège (1989) moved beyond what they saw as a pessimistic, idealist, general, and one-sided culture industry concept and called for empirical studies of the complexity, contradictions, specific workings, and plurality of actual "cultural industries" around the world. Since the early 1980s, Canadian communication studies scholars have analyzed the specificity of the history, policy framework, market structure, and technologies of the cultural industries in Canada (Audley 1983; Dorland 1996; Wagman and Urquhart 2012). And for the past two decades, cultural industries research has boomed worldwide, criss-crossing disciplines and borders and appearing everywhere from the curricula of undergraduate and graduate programs in communication and cultural studies to United Nations Educational Scientific and Cultural Organization (UNESCO) symposia to World Bank "development" projects (Hesmondhalgh, 2007).

What are these cultural industries? Druick (2012) says that the types of companies and sectors that get bundled together into definitions of the cultural industries change over time and continue to change with new "cultural" types of firms and sectors emerging. Hesmondhalgh (2007) defines the cultural industries as "those institutions (mainly profit-making companies, but also state organizations and non-profit organizations) that are most directly involved in the production of social meaning" (12) in the form of texts. The "core" seven sectors – advertising, broadcasting, film and TV, music, publishing, digital games, and the Internet – "deal primarily with the industrial production and circulation of texts" (12) that "are open to interpretation" (13). In this chapter, I define the capitalist cultural industries in Canada as all of the companies currently operating in Canada that take part in the production, distribution, and exhibition of copyrighted cultural products and services for the market (with the goal of private profit) instead of for social need using capital goods (technology) and human labour power (manual and mental skills). The core sectors of these cultural industries produce, distribute, and exhibit texts in a variety of forms – print, electronic, digital – that represent and convey meaning about the world. The meanings given to these texts, in their contexts of production by workers and reception by audiences, may be as complex and contradictory as the society they are assembled from and responsive to. Table 10.1 narrows the scope of the cultural industries in Canada to eight specific sectors and cross-references them to the North American Industry Classification System's (NAICS 51) codes.

WHY DO THE CULTURAL INDUSTRIES MATTER?

The cultural industries matter to capitalism. Once caricaturized by conservatives as a drain on public resources with little to no shareholder return and idealized by modernists as naturally set apart from the instrumental rationality of market considerations, culture is now lauded by its boosters as substantively functional to twenty-first century capitalist development in Canada. As a 2007 report from the Conference Board of Canada commissioned by Canadian Heritage entitled "Valuing Culture: Measuring and Understanding Canada's Creative Economy" declares: "the cultural sector helps drive the economy." Indeed, the cultural industries prop up capitalist development in many ways. They contribute to about 3 per cent of Canada's Gross Domestic Product (GDP), or $47.7 billion, a sum double the GDP of Canada's agricultural, fisheries, and forestry sectors combined; they are sources of employment, with approximately 600,000 people paid to work in them; they are agents of trade abroad and feed ancillary service markets at home (Nesta 2016; Leblanc 2016). Cowan (2015) opines that in a period of worldwide capitalist slump, the cultural industries "could be an ideal gateway to a long-term strategy improving Canada's competitiveness and capacity for innovation, leading a more certain, sustainable future economy." In June 2016, Mélanie Joly (2016), Minister of Canadian Heritage, appeared at

Table 10.1
The core cultural industries in Canada

Sector-NAICS codes	Description	Examples
Advertising 5418 5419	Companies engaged in creating and coordinating advertising, marketing, and PR campaigns for the clients that pay them across print and digital publications, radio and TV broadcasts, in-cinema, indoor and outdoor display, and via websites.	BBDO Canada DDB Leo Burnett
Broadcasting 5151	Companies that own and operate radio and TV broadcasters. These firms produce, license and transmit programs, and generate revenue from the sale of air time to advertisers.	CBC/Radio-Canada CTV Corus Québec
Film and TV 5121	Companies that produce and/or distribute copyrighted films and TV shows for exhibition. These companies generate revenue by selling the rights to distribute and exhibit content to TV broadcasters, theatres, and digital streaming services.	Canadian Motion Picture Park Downsview Park Film Studios Mel's Cité Du Cinéma
Music 5122	Companies that produce, publish, and distribute copyrighted music or sound recordings in a variety of forms (records, CDs, digital).	Sony Music Canada Universal Music Canada Arts & Crafts
Publishing 511	Companies that produce, publish, and distribute copyrighted newspapers, magazines, and books in print, audio and digital forms.	Torstar Random House of Canada Maclean's
Video Games 511212 541515	Companies that develop, publish, and sell copyrighted video games.	Capcom Vancouver Rockstar Toronto, Ubisoft Quebec
Telecommunications 517	Companies that sell telecommunications services (telephone, mobile), Internet access, and/or video entertainment services (cable TV) over networks (wired, wireless, or satellite).	Bell Canada Rogers Communications Telus
Internet-Web 51913 5181	Companies that provide Internet and Web services and related products, such as search engine, advertising, web page hosting, social networking, video sharing, and streaming.	Google Facebook Netflix

the Economic Club of Canada – a forum for sharing ideas with Canadian corporate elites – and spoke of the cultural industries as an economic driver and culture as the fuel of a new "industrial revolution."

The cultural industries also matter to the cultures of Canada, as they are materially and ideationally interwoven with the heterogeneity of the identities, customs, beliefs, and practices that constitute the ways of life of the many people residing across Canada. The cultural industries' products carry "texts": captivating news stories, TV show and filmic fictions, ad-scripted lifestyles, and personalized messages about daily happenings pulsing through social media. The texts of cultural products do not simply reflect the world as it is, but react to, represent, and shape the world as well, showing and telling readers, viewers, listeners, and prosumers what it means to be an owner or a worker, citizen or serf, a man or a woman, racialized majority or minority, conservative or a socialist, old or young, a Canadian Us or an American Them. Although many texts are designed to sell in mass and niche markets and their exchange value is realized through market transactions, they may socialize the wider culture by constructing and normalizing certain ways of being, thinking, and acting. They take part in imagining, differentiating, and clashing over the meanings of multi-cultures inside and outside of Canada, and the monolith of "Canada" as well. Cultural texts are not "superstructural" fluff, but very much part and product of the "base" of capitalism. Nonetheless, these texts may affirm or contest the ruling ideology of the corporate class and the reigning "nationalist" ideology of the state, as well as other ideologies such as classism, racism, sexism, ableism, militarism, and imperialism. They may even address the central conflicts, hopes, and fears of the society, or at least the viewers they target, while staging struggles for hegemony between rival blocs (Kellner 1995, 20; Kurasawa 2003, 469).

The cultural industries furthermore matter to democracy in Canada. Essential to democracy, whether representative or deliberative in form, is a citizenry that is informed about and able to join with and meaningfully participate as members of interested publics in making the decisions that shape their lives and communities (McChesney 2008). The cultural industries are a significant source of the texts that may orient citizens to or disorient them about the happenings of the world. They thus weigh heavily upon the quality of citizenship and democracy in Canada, and elsewhere. The cultural industries sell cultural products to consumers in markets that tell people what topics and issues to think about (what matters) and how to think about them (why it matters). The cultural industries may serve democracy by giving citizens what they need to realize their potential as publics willing and able to exercise sovereignty over their own destinies, or, they may degrade democracy by deluding, distracting, and duping the many on behalf of the few. When they over-supply texts that manipulate the perceptions and understandings of what's actually happening in the society, and under-supply texts that engage, inform, and educate, democracy suffers.

The significance of the cultural industries to contemporary capitalism, cultures, and democracy in Canada is clear, but there is a need to move from blanket claims about why the cultural industries matter and idealist debates about what they do or do not do or should do to the difficult work of actually doing research on them. In this regard, the PEC has great theoretical and methodological value.

A POLITICAL ECONOMY OF THE CULTURAL INDUSTRIES IN CANADA

In general, the PE of the cultural industries in Canada is the study of the capitalist and political power relations that shape the conditions and characteristics of the ownership, production, distribution, and exhibition of cultural goods and services as commodities in society. The PE approach to the cultural industries, however, is not essentially or exclusively "Canadian." It has a long and transnational history, with key works produced over the past six decades by a large number of scholars working in and across many countries (Hardy 2014a, 2014b). Presently, PE is a well-attended section at the annual International Association of Media and Communication Research (IAMCR) conference, is taught across borders in communication and media studies programs, is a key topic area for many scholarly journals, and there is even a new journal, *The Political Economy of Communication*. PE is also associated with variants of Marxism, but it is open to heterodoxy too.

Unfortunately, the PE approach has long been woefully misrecognized and wilfully caricaturized by its motley bunch of opponents as totalizing, economistic, ideological, simplistic, and monolithic (see Meehan and Wasko 2013, for a rejoinder). Fortunately, the PE approach's suppleness, dialectics, self-reflexivity, complexity, and diversity of contributions has been carefully documented and defended (Meehan and Wasko 2013), and its strengths and weaknesses judiciously evaluated (Hardy 2014a; 2014b): "This has been a decade of flourishing output, exciting synthesis and developments that leave the caricature image of PE far in the shade"

(Hardy 2014a, 190). The PE's vitality is demonstrated by the abundance of definitions of what it is and what it does (see, for example, Babe 2009, 4; Garnham 1987, 25; Hardy 2014b, 4; Mosco 2006, 25; McChesney 2008, 12; Wasko 2014, 260; Wasko, Murdock, and Sousa 2011; Winseck 2011, 11). Instead of summarizing these definitions, I now discuss five common tenets of a PE approach.

This PE approach is holistic in that, instead of treating the cultural industries as part of a bounded or closed economic sphere, it links and connects the economic to the political and the cultural. Neoliberal ideology represents the cultural industries as part of laissez-faire markets and nothing more, with media firms dutifully and reflectively giving sovereign consumers whatever cultural products and services they want, when they want them, wherever and through whatever platform they freely choose. Yet the cultural industries are not an island. They are part and product of society; they shape and are shaped in significant ways by the capitalist mode of production (the economic sphere), the state and civil society (the political sphere) and culture (the sphere of discourses, ideas, and meanings). The PE approach highlights the interdependencies of the economic, the political, and the cultural to show how the cultural industries are influenced by and influencing of the larger and smaller power relations that criss-cross all of these spheres.

In addition to being holistic, the PE approach is attentive to the histories and geographies of the cultural industries. PE tries to understand "what's going on now" and "what came before" in the cultural industries, striking a delicate balance between present and past knowledge that captures the dialectic of change and continuity. PE is also attuned to the geographical dimensions of the cultural industries and grapples with their "uneven" and "combined" developments in a world system. The cultural industries do not develop simultaneously everywhere, but asynchronously, in certain places and at different paces, unevenly, sometimes not at all. This historical-geographical focus enables comparative research on the different temporalities and landscapes of the cultural industries, at local, municipal, regional, and national levels, and highlights how these developments converge with and diverge from those happening worldwide.

This PE approach is also concerned with normative questions about the role and effects of the cultural industries in society. What is a good society? A democracy where citizens exercise self-governance or a plutocracy where rich and powerful elites make all the decisions for everyone else? One torn asunder by classist, racist, and sexist inequalities or one where social bonds of egalitarianism and human dignity are paramount? One in which the value of possessive egotistical individualistic consumerism prevails or one where the value of the interdependency of all supports social recognition and redistribution? Most PE scholars support a good society defined by deliberative democracy, egalitarianism, social justice, and solidarity (Hardy 2014a; McChesney 2008). Self-reflexive, open, and honest about their commitments, PE scholars judge the cultural industries and their texts with regard to their service to or sabotaging of a good society.

If and when PE scholars find the cultural industries to be failing a good society, they don't accept this situation as inevitable or unchangeable but instead channel their discontent into rabble-rousing critique. When PE scholars critique the cultural industries, they do so with the belief that these industries and the wider society don't have to be the way they are, and ought to and can be different – better in some way.

The PE's imperative to understand the cultural industries as accommodating of or antithetical to a good society, and the critique of the cultural industries that stems from research that demonstrates the latter, "place its practitioners under an obligation to follow the logic of their analysis into practical action for change" (Wasko, Murdock, and Sousa 2011, 2). Praxis, the idea that scholars ought to try to understand the world, and by doing so, change or transform it for the better, keeps researching, writing, teaching, and communicating about the PE of the cultural industries lively. It is a useful deterrent to idealism, elitism, cynicism, and dispassionate ivory-tower disinterest. While administrative researchers often seek to understand to conserve or change things on behalf of powerful public authorities and private interest groups (like reigning governments or media corporations or the lobbies and think-tanks that they pay to push their interests), PE researchers challenge monopolies of knowledge with counter-knowledge about the cultural industries that may be translated into public opinions, policies, and practices that work toward a good society.

Having outlined a PE approach to the cultural industries in Canada, the next sections explain how capitalist logics shape the cultural industries, how the state facilitates and legitimizes the "business" of the cultural industries, and how US cultural imperialism may persist in the global age.

THE CAPITALIST CULTURAL INDUSTRIES IN CANADA

The cultural industries are part and product of the wider Canadian national and global capitalist economy in which companies possess private ownership powers, a class division between owners and waged workers exists, and products and services are made for markets with the goal of making their owners profit.

Private ownership. There is some public ownership of the cultural industries – the CBC, Radio Canada, National Film Board, and SaskTel-in Canada – but private companies are the most significant owning entities at the present time. Not so long ago, private companies tended to operate in a single sector of the cultural industries and were kept separate by cross-ownership regulations. A telecommunications firm like Bell, for example, stuck to selling phone services, while a TV firm like CTV focused on attracting viewers to ads. Throughout the 1990s, companies that previously operated in one sector merged and converged with firms in many other sectors. Big Canadian companies resultantly grew even bigger through horizontal integration (acquiring ownership over the means of producing, distributing, and exhibiting one type of product for one market segment) and vertical integration (acquiring ownership over the means of producing, distributing, and exhibiting many different types of products for many different market segments). Concentration helps companies centralize resources and take advantage of economies of scale and scope, but it also gives them opportunities to abuse market power, constrict the source diversity of cultural goods, control the content, and constrain public access (Winseck 2015).

What companies currently own the lion's share of the cultural industries in Canada? Are markets concentrated or competitive? Winseck (2016a) says "lots of people, and powerful vested interests especially, offer up lots of opinions and assertions related to the issues of ownership and concentration, and there is an appalling lack of evidence to ground our understanding one way or another. We need – and deserve – better." The Canadian Media Concentration Research Project (CMCRP) (http://www. cmcrp.org/), directed by Winseck at Carleton University, is by far the best source of knowledge on this topic. The CMCRP "offers an independent academic, empirical and data-driven analysis" of a "profoundly important question: have telecom, media and Internet markets become more concentrated over time, or less?" The CMCRP analyzed "the state of competition in the mobile wireless market, Internet access, broadcast, pay and streaming TV services, Internet advertising, advertising across all media, newspapers, browsers, online news sources, search, social media, operating systems, in Canada over the period from 1984 until 2017." This "network media economy" is distinguished by significant vertical and diagonal integration – Bell, Telus, Rogers, Shaw, and Quebecor accounted for 73.4% of this $80 billion economy. The CMCRP findings are available at: http://www.cmcrp.org/media-and-internet-concentration-in-canada-1984-2017/.

Class division. In the privately owned cultural industries, there exists a class division between the owners and the workers. The "owning class" refers to chief executive officers (CEOs) and majority shareholders of companies. In 2014, the average pay to Canada's top one hundred executives was $8.96 million, 184 times more than the average wage in Canada (Mackenzie 2016). The CEOs of the top cultural industry companies were paid an even higher sum. In 2014, Bradley Shaw (Shaw Communications) received $13.3 million; George Cope (BCE) earned about $11.5 million; Pierre Dion (Quebecor) took home $10.8 million; Joe Natalie (Telus) enjoyed $9.4 million; and Guy Laurence (Rogers Communications) got $8.9 million (Mackenzie 2016). This largely White and male owning class occupies the commanding heights of the cultural industries in Canada. While owners live off the profits generated by the cultural products and services sold by their companies, most workers live off the money they're paid to create or circulate these commodities.

What, then, is it like to work in the cultural industries? Over the past decade, the "blind spot" of work in the cultural industries has been illuminated by research on the objective conditions and subjective experiences of cultural workers (Brophy and de Peuter 2014; Cohen 2008, 2012, 2015a, 2015b, 2016; Deuze 2007; de Peuter 2014; de Peuter and Cohen 2015; Hesmondhalgh 2007, 2008, 2010; Huws 2003, 2007, 2010, 2014; Maxwell 2016; Meehan and Wasko 2013; Mosco and McKercher 2008; Ross 2004, 2009, 2013). Cohen (2016b) says that researching the conditions of work in the cultural industries matters because such a focus enables scholars "to examine the capitalist social relations that shape" it, and "by looking at how cultural products are produced, we gain a much better understanding of why, for instance, we are surrounded by particular media messages." The old Fordist cage of a routinized, standardized, and alienating waged "job for life" has been blasted open by new post-Fordist "spirits of capitalism" (Boltanski and Chiapello 2005), and these afford some workers in the cultural industries opportunities for flexibility, innovation, the expression of subjectivities and passions through the texts they create, as well as recognition by networks of peers. But capitalist power relations often thwart the prospect of good quality work in the cultural industries. A recent study by the Mitchell and Murray (2016, 37) found that the highest incidence of precarious work in the province is in the "arts, entertainment and recreation sector": 57.7 per cent of workers toil in non-standard employment. In addition to being a site of precarious work and class division, the Canadian cultural industries are troubled by racial and sexual discrimination, as non-White people and women often face structural, institutional, and ideological barriers to entry and representation (Radheyan 2017a, 2017b). For example, while Telefilm works toward gender parity in Canadian film, and almost half of Telefilm-supported Canadian cultural productions for 2017 had a female producer, director, and screenwriter (SimonPillai 2017b), women only directed about 16 per cent of the major big budget Canadian TV shows and films (Simonpillai 2017a). Also, numerous Canadian artists cite "everyday racism," which keeps them out of the TV and film productions (CBC News 2017).

The profit-motive. In the cultural industries, companies produce and sell cultural products and services in markets with the goal of making a profit, as this is what they are primarily organized and obligated to do. In general, profit is the difference between what a corporation spends to bring a cultural product or service to market (costs) and the amount it gets in return for the sale of these in the marketplace (revenue). All of the companies in the cultural industries pursue profit, but each company generates revenue in different ways relative to the sector they are in and the specific role they play within it. Take TV. TV production studios manufacture copyrighted TV texts; distribution companies buy the licensing rights to finished TV texts from TV studios and lease the use of these texts to exhibitors (TV broadcasters, cable TV channels, digital TV streamers, and so on). Exhibitors buy the rights to exhibit TV texts over specific times and territories and get paid by consumers (via subscription fees) and/or by advertisers (which pay for ad space and time). All of these TV-involved companies pursue profit; TV studios make revenue by selling textual content rights to distribution companies; distribution companies generate revenue from selling to exhibitors; exhibitors take revenue by selling subscriptions to consumers or selling access to consumer attention to advertisers. This is a rough sketch, but the basic TV profit-making model outlined above is quite different from that of a telecommunication firm, and a telecommunication firm's model is different from say, Google, which commoditizes its users' data to suck up ad revenue. The cultural industries uniformly pursue profit, but accumulation is a variegated process.

Furthermore, the companies in the cultural industries try to "risk-minimize" and "profit-maximize" by devising ways of selling more cultural products and services to more consumers while incurring less costs to produce and circulate them. Companies may try to squeeze maximal value from workers in the division of labour by employing hard Tayloristic managerial strategies that standardize, intensify, and speed up the labour process (Huws 2010) and "humane workplace" strategies aimed at getting workers to self-manage their own exploitation (Ross 2004). Also, they may try to keep labour costs to a minimum to reap high profits. Apropos post-Fordism's flexible accumulation (Harvey 1989), companies may do this by: organizing non-standard employment regimes (short-term contracts, freelancing, and task-based work) (Cohen 2016a; de Peuter, 2014; Ross 2009); harnessing unpaid sources of labour like interns (de Peuter, Cohen and Brophy 2015; Perlin 2012); crowdsourcing tasks to networks of digital prosumers (Howe 2004; Scholz 2013); outsourcing jobs to lower paid workers in other places (Miller et al., 2005; Mirrlees 2013); and automating creative tasks (Carr 2014; McChesney and Nichols 2016; Steiner 2012). In the cultural industries profit is paramount, and knowledge about how it is made and at what social cost is important.

THE STATE OF THE CULTURAL INDUSTRIES IN CANADA

Capitalism is the base of the cultural industries in Canada, but these industries are also shaped by the state, "an institutional complex claiming sovereignty for itself as the supreme political authority within a defined territory for whose governance it is responsible" (Hay and Lister 2006, 1). In the early twenty-first century, the Westphalian state system persists, and states still define the "national interest" in their respective territories and pursue it vis-à-vis the cultural industries with cultural policy and regulation. Generally, cultural policy refers to the policies that bear upon "the conduct of those institutions and organizations … whether public or private, which are involved in the production and distribution of cultural goods and services" (Bennet and Mercer 1996, 8). Regulation is a tool employed by the state to try to compel the cultural industries to heed and comply with its cultural policy. Contrary to the notion that neoliberalism's mantra of privatize, deregulate, and liberalize has weakened the state vis-à-vis the economy, and opposite to the idea that cultural markets naturally operate according to laissez-faire principles, the Canadian state plays a strong and active role in the economy by cementing the private interests of the cultural industries in markets: it facilitates their profit-making with an industrialized cultural policy and regulatory regime and legitimizes this to the public with corporate nationalism.

For the past five decades, federal cultural nationalist policy has supported the industrialization of culture (Edwardson 2008). In the

post-Second World War era, the 1951 Massey Report recommended that
public cultural institutions foster an elite Canadian public culture distinct
from the massifying market influence of US-based globalizing cultural
industry, but still opened the door to the industrialization of culture
(Edwardson 2008). The decade of Trudeau mania (1968–79) saw the state
shift away from fostering a uniquely Canadian modernist high culture
differentiated from a threatening American mass commercial culture to
building Canadian-owned and market-oriented cultural industries capable
of profiting off of their own cultural commodities (Edwardson 2008). In
the 1980s and 1990s, the state continued to support the "industrialization
of culture" and its internationalization as a matter of national security
(Pennee 1999). In the early twenty-first century, the state reduced "the
primary function of cultural policy" to adjusting "existing infrastructures
to the needs of internationally competing, profit-generating domestic
cultural industries" (Milz 2007, 101), and at present, policy makers
routinely trumpet culture's commercial value.

In the early twenty-first century, a wide array of state agencies and
instruments secure the cultural industries by protecting their property,
subsidizing their operations, regulating in their favour, and boosting
them abroad.

The Canadian state secures the cultural industries' profit by recognizing and enforcing copyright – the exclusive legal right to produce, reproduce, publish, or perform an original cultural work. Copyright is essential
to cultural commodification – the transformation of cultural use-values
into exchange-values – because it is this right that is most often sold and
bought by firms in markets. The Canadian Intellectual Property Office
(CIPO), an arm of Industry Canada, Canadian Heritage's Copyright
Policy, the Copyright Board of Canada, and others administer and enforce
Canada's copyright regime, and abiding the *Copyright Act*, these state
ministries and agencies solidify, promote, and protect the copyrights of
the core cultural industries in Canada. The Royal Canadian Mounted
Police (RCMP) even secures copyright, recording all copyright infringe-
ment allegations and investigating each criminalized case with help from
the CIPO's Copyright Enforcement Guidelines. The Canadian state legally
secures copyrights and backs them with coercion.

The Canadian state also supports the cultural industries in Canada
with subsidies or in liberal parlance, "investments," whether directly in
the form of transfers of public monies to firms as grants or indirectly,
with tax credits. Soon after being appointed Minister of Canadian
Heritage in 2015, Mélanie Joly asserted that "investing in arts and culture

is so key to our government" and "content development is the core of the creative economy that we know will be our future economy" (cited in Burke 2016). Indeed, the Canadian Federal Government operates a vast network of organizations that allocate billions in funds to large and small cultural producing individuals and companies.

The public broadcaster, the CBC/Radio-Canada, is a major source of Canadian cultural goods. The Canada Council for the Arts, which "champion[s] and invest[s] in artistic excellence so that Canadians may enjoy and participate in a rich cultural life" allocates millions to writers, publishers, musicians, and new media firms. Its CEO Simon Brault notes that "art is serious business for Canadians!" (Patch 2016). Telefilm Canada's driving goal is "to stimulate demand for and access to Canadian productions – in Canada and everywhere, from big screens to those still being invented, and every platform in-between." The National Film Board is a treasure trove of Canadian films. The Canada Cultural Spaces Fund (CSF) puts millions into the construction and renovation of Canada's "cultural infrastructure" to "improve physical conditions for artistic creativity and innovation." The Canada Media Fund (CMF), administered by Telefilm, "fosters, promotes, develops, and finances the production of Canadian content and relevant applications for all audiovisual media platforms." The Canada Book Fund (CBF), Canada Interactive Fund (CIF), Canada Music Fund (CMF), and Canada Periodical Fund (CPF) further support an assemblage of cultural goods.

Adding to the largess supplied by these federally administered organizations are provincial-level cultural industries support agencies. For example, the Government of Ontario's Ministry of Tourism and Sport, with its Ontario Media Development Corporation being "the central catalyst for the province's cultural media cluster," offers a variety of grants and tax credits to the cultural industries. In 2013, Ontario allocated a record $343 million in subsidies, most of which went to film and TV studios shooting in Ontario with its production services Tax Credit and the Computer Animation and Special Effects Tax Credit (Campbell 2014). Federal and provincial subvention agencies combine with municipal agencies, like the City of Toronto Arts and Culture Services agency or the Toronto Film and Television Office, to further support the business of culture.

In addition to subsidizing the cultural industries, the Canadian State regulates (some of) them. The Canadian Radio-Television and Telecommunication Commission (CRTC), established by Parliament in 1968, describes itself as "an administrative tribunal that regulates and

supervises broadcasting and telecommunications in the public interest."
Though mandated to serve the public interest by promoting compliance
with the 1993 *Telecommunication Act* and the 1991 *Broadcasting Act*,
the CRTC often supports the private interests of the cultural industries.
The CRTC ensures that the companies operating in Canada are controlled
by a Canadian owning class by prohibiting foreign companies from owning more than 10 per cent of a telecom firm and 20 per cent of a broadcaster. The CRTC has supported the concentration of ownership in the
cultural industries by approving a slew of mergers and acquisitions that
let the biggest companies grow bigger. Furthermore, the CRTC compels
broadcasters to daily exhibit national cultural products, and by regulating
into existence a captive market for such products, it supports a TV and
film production sector. Additionally, the Canadian tax code (Line 8521)
encourages Canadian advertising companies to feed the profits of the
cultural industries by letting them deduct 100 per cent of their ad costs
so long they buy ad space and time from Canadian publications or broadcasters. This gets Canadian ad firms to pay Canadian magazines and TV
networks to deliver the attention of their readers, listeners, and viewers
to ads for their clients' goods and services. CRTC-mandated "simultaneous substitution" (the replacement of the signal of an American TV channel
with a Canadian one that's scheduled the same TV show at the same time)
keeps Canadian viewers watching Canadian TV ads to keep hundreds of
millions of ad dollars pumping through the system.

With its business-supporting national cultural policy and regulation,
the Canadian State has secured the profit interests of cultural industries
within the territory of their key operations. At the same time, Canadian
foreign policy has protected and promoted these industries' profit
interests globally.

The Canadian state has pursued bi-lateral, multilateral, and regional
free trade agreements with over fifty countries, but it fiercely protects the
cultural industries from all of these. The Global Affairs (2016) website
stipulates: "While we are seizing the opportunities of global and regional
economic integration, preserving and promoting domestic flexibility
related to culture is a core objective for Canada in all international trade
negotiations." Indeed, the Canadian state has flexibly exempted the cultural industries from the Canada-United States Free Trade Agreement
(FTA), the North American Free Trade Agreement (NAFTA), the General
Agreement on Tariffs and Trade (GATT), and the World Trade Organization
(WTO). In the fall of 2005, for example, delegates from over 180 countries
(led by Canada) approved the UNESCO Convention on the Protection

and Promotion of Diversity of the Cultural Expressions (CPPDCE), which exempts "culture" or more properly, the cultural industries, from free trade agreements (Mirrlees 2013, 142). The CPPDCE says it aims to promote Canadian and global cultural diversity, yet it also protects the territorial market power of the cultural industries against stronger US firms. Nonetheless, the Canadian State's recent signing on to the Trans-Pacific Partnership (TPP), a US-led multilateral free-trade agreement covering twelve countries, unsettles its prior commitment to the *l'exception culturelle*. The TPP explicitly "prevents the government from developing policies to support Canadian content on digital platforms" (Geist 2016), "enshrines a neoliberal interpretation of culture that is at odds with Canadian and international standards for the promotion [and protection] of cultural diversity" and primarily benefits the US cultural industries (Maltais 2016).

However, while trying to exempt the Canadian cultural industries from free trade, the Canadian state boosts Canadian cultural exports. Indeed, Global Affairs and Canadian Heritage collaborate to strengthen the cultural industries globally by opening markets, increasing cultural exports, and providing cultural trade expertise. A piece of the Liberal government's budget entitled "Showcasing Canada's Cultural Industries to the World" allocates $35 million to "support the promotion of Canadian cultural industries abroad" and to "help Canadian foreign missions promote Canadian culture and creativity on the world stage" (Morneau 2016, 186). Furthermore, the Minister of Canadian Heritage is consulting "on how best to continue to support Canadian cultural exporters as they contribute to inclusive growth" (Morneau 2016, 186). Additionally, a government of Canada (2016a) webpage entitled "Strengthening Canadian content creation, discovery and export in a digital world" says "there is work to be done to ensure that Canada – and Canadian content – is poised to succeed in the face of increasing global competition and alongside the rapid evolution of new technologies that are changing the ways content is watched, read, experienced and discovered." Hinting at a global digital cross-platform cultural export strategy, it notes that these "technologies and the global platforms that have emerged have given rise to new ways of distributing and discovering content, with the potential to reach new markets for Canada's high-quality cultural exports."

In sum, the Canadian state tries to defensively protect the cultural industries in the territory of Canada against the US cultural industries but offensively promotes Canadian cultural capitalism around the world.

US CULTURAL IMPERIALISM IN CANADA:
CONTINUITY AND CHANGE
IN THE GLOBAL DIGITAL AGE

US cultural imperialism refers to the processes by which the US territorial state facilitates and legitimizes the business interests of large and small-scale American ICT, cultural, and media corporations as they compete to control the ICT and cultural industries and markets within and across other national territories (Mirrlees 2016a). US cultural imperialism is not just the global dominance of US ICT and cultural industries; it is the processes by which the US-based ICT, cultural, and media corporations go global and are backed by the geopolitics of the US territorial state, which supports the US ICT and cultural industries – strategically, legally, and diplomatically – across borders. The idea that Canada's security is threatened by US cultural imperialism has long been a staple in Canadian policy and public opinion. From the 1949–51 Royal Commission on National Development in the Arts, Letters, and Sciences, led by Vincent Massey, to the 2005 UNESCO CPPDCE, to the present day, the US empire's cultural industries have been framed as a threat to Canada and the industries charged with telling and selling "our stories" and linking geographically distanced and often quite different citizens visually and sonically together as one national community. In response, Canadian capital and the state allied via a corporatist policy framework to "protect," "defend," and "secure" the Canadian cultural industries – and to some extent, partial and selective imaginings of Canadian culture – against US cultural imperialism.

In the early twenty-first century, the US is still an empire, and the US-based globalizing cultural industries are a significant source of US capitalist, military, and cultural-ideological power worldwide (Mirrlees 2016a, 2016b). The 2017 *Forbes Global 2000* ranks the world's biggest corporations in four metrics (sales, profits, assets, and market value), and the US is at the top of the global ICT and cultural industries. The US is home to five of the world's top five broadcasting and cable companies (Comcast, Walt Disney, Charter Communications, Time Warner, and Liberty Global); two of the top five advertising firms (Omnicom Group and Interpublic group); three of the top five communications equipment firms (Cisco Systems, Corning, and Harris); four of the top five computer hardware firms (Apple, Hewlett-Packard Enterprise, HP, and Dell Technologies); three of the top five computer service firms (Alphabet, IBM, and Facebook); three of the top five computer storage device firms

(Western Digital, SanDisk, and NetApp); three of the top five Internet and catalogue retail firms (Amazon.com, eBay, and Liberty Interactive); three of the top five printing and publishing companies (Thomson Reuters, S&P Global, and Nielsen); two of the top five recreational game firms (Activision-Blizzard and Electronic Arts); two of the top five semiconductor firms (Intel and Qualcomm); four of the top five computer software and programming firms (Microsoft, Oracle, VMware, and Adobe Systems); and two of the top five telecommunication firms (AT&T and Verizon Communications) (Forbes 2018). Furthermore, globalizing Hollywood studios continue to rule the world entertainment market, annually producing and distributing the highest grossing global flicks (Box Office Mojo 2018). Also, the US is home to seven of the world's top ten most visited web sites: Google.com (#1), YouTube.com (#2), Facebook.com (#3), Wikipedia.org (#5), Reddit.com (#6), Yahoo.com (#7), and Amazon.com (#10) (Alexa 2018).

Clearly the US ICT and cultural industries are gargantuan, and currently are larger, wealthier, and more powerful than Canada's. For example, the Forbes Global 2000 list shows seven of the world's top ten Broadcasting and Cable TV companies to be based in the US: Comcast (#35), Walt Disney (#71), Time Warner (#156), Time Warner Cable (#227), CBS (#425), Viacom (#479), Dish Network (#517), and Liberty Global (#591). Four of the top Canadian media companies hold prominent places on the Forbes Global 2000: Bell (#308), Rogers Communication (#565), Telus (#616), and Shaw (#1357). But these do not rival the US giants. An asymmetrical economic and cultural power relationship between the US and Canadian-based cultural industries exists, as there is no cultural trade reciprocity between these two countries. In 1986, Canada's cultural trade deficit with the US was about $1.5 billion (Magder 1989, 288); by 2008, it had grown to $2.4 billion. In 2015, Canadian-made films took a mere 1.9 per cent of box office revenues in Canada; US films took 80.6 per cent, while other foreign films took 17.5 per cent (Government of Canada 2016b). In that same year, the top ten TV shows broadcast by American and Canadian TV networks were all owned by US-based firms. *The Amazing Race Canada* was the top TV show of the year in Canada; though produced by Canadian firms, it is a format controlled by US firms (Tenuta and Potter 2015; Nielsen 2015).

The spread of the Internet and World Wide Web, the flow of smartphones, tablets, and laptop computers, and the growth of US-based digital giants – Google, YouTube, Facebook, Netflix, and others – have rocked the foundations of Canada's state-capitalist cultural policy and regulatory regime and presented new challenges. Indicative of an emerging US-centred "platform imperialism" (Jin 2013), the top ten most visited websites in Canada are American owned: Google.ca, Google.com, YouTube.com, Facebook.com, Amazon.ca, Reddit.com, Wikipedia.org, Twitter.com, Live.com, Netflix.com (Alexa 2018). These American giants reign over Canada's digital cultural marketplace, collecting an immense amount of data about Canadian users, monetizing it, and using it to extract billions in revenue from advertising companies. Year after year, Google and Facebook take in the most digital ad revenue (Taylor 2016), and nearly half the total Web advertising revenue generated in Canada flows into US coffers (Nordicity 2016). Furthermore, a lot of Canadian data "boomerangs" to the US, where the biggest data firms are headquartered and this exposes the digital lives of Canadians to US NSA surveillance (Clement and Obar 2015). Netflix has captured nearly 5.2 million Canadian subscribers to its digital video streaming service. With just over 700,000 subscribers combined, Bell Media's Crave TV and Rogers and Shaw's Shomi don't come close to rivalling Netflix's market power in Canada (CBC News 2016). Moreover, digital video broadcasters like the Google-owned YouTube and Netflix do not remit value-added taxes (HST) or pay income taxes to the state, and due to the Harper administration's "New Media Exemption Order," these companies do not contribute a percentage of their revenue to the Canada Media Fund (Anderson 2016). In effect, the current political economy favours the power and prosperity of US digital giants at the expense of monies that might support Canadian culture.

Given the above, concerns about US cultural imperialism in Canada are not unreasonable. One wonders how the US state and corporate class would react if the situation were reversed and the United States was swamped with Canadian cultural goods, with stories about and images of Canada filling the American mediascape, and the US digital marketplace basically run by Canadian-based data-surveillance firms. While it is tempting to still conceptualize Canada as the "world's most dependent 'developed' country," one that suffers total "cultural submission" to the US's "Consciousness Industry" (Smythe 1981), the continuing power of the US empire does not mean that Canada is a weak victim. As discussed earlier, Canada is home to strong capitalist cultural industries, backed by the Canadian state. Yet, much of Canada's state-capitalist cultural policy and regulatory regime was formed prior to the digital age, and it has served the cultural industries well, at home and abroad. But today, it is ill equipped to mitigate US platform imperialism and digital dominance. Canadian Heritage recognizes this, and in 2016 reviewed existing policies, regulations, institutions, and programs pertaining to this regime. Leading up to the review, Department of Canadian Heritage Minister Mélanie Joly said: "everything's on the table" (Leblanc 2016). Yet, after months of consulting with Canadian cultural owners, lobbies, and workers, Joly launched "Creative Canada" in 2017, and this "barely moved the dial on cultural policy" especially as related to digital media governance (Taylor 2017; Yakabuski 2017). Around the world, states are starting to bring globalizing American digital media giants conducting business within their territories in line with their media-cultural policy and regulatory framework. For example, across the European Union, Netflix, Amazon Prime Video, YouTube, and other digital streaming services must subsidize and dedicate 30 per cent of their output to TV shows and films made in Europe by European firms (Rankin 2018). Many in the Canadian cultural industries would like the Canadian state to compel Netflix and YouTube to contribute to the Canadian Media Fund and abide by Canadian content quotas, just as other broadcasting firms operating in Canada do (Wynoch, 2017). But Joly's Creative Canada strategy did not let that happen. There are many good reasons to reimagine the Canadian cultural regime in the global digital age, but there are even better reasons to ensure that the concrete form this reimagining takes will be democratic as opposed to elitist and express the public interests Canadians have in achieving a good, equitable, and just society as opposed to one that just re-solidifies the private interests of the American and Canadian corporations that preside over the ICT and cultural industries in Canada today.

CONCLUSION: SITES OF STRUGGLE IN THE CULTURAL INDUSTRIES

The role of the PEC researcher is to hold a mirror to the power of the Canadian corporate class and state to influence the cultural industries in order to understand the social dimensions of this arrangement, and also, to shed light upon the sources of hope – the individual and collective responses and potentially resistant social moments and movements that may interrupt, transform, and reach beyond the present arrangement. Any PEC scholar worth their salt will identify, engage with, and learn

from the many emerging sites of struggle in the cultural industries. These
include but are not limited to:

- *Struggles over the precarious conditions of work in the cultural
  industries.* These include union-organized campaigns. The Canadian
  Media Guild (http://www.cmg.ca/en/) and Unifor (http://www.
  unifor.org/) are on the frontlines of struggles in the cultural
  industries to unionize cultural workers, represent the interests
  of already unionized cultural workers via battles and collective
  bargaining with employers, and press the state to establish and
  enforce employment standards. Struggles also include those by
  non-unionized cultural workers that are "experimenting with
  organizational forms and collective activities" in response to non-
  standard, insecure, and often poor working conditions (de Peuter
  and Cohen 2015, 305). Some of these non-union worker
  experiments include "mutual aid" (e.g., the establishment and
  provision of health insurance and benefits, self-organized
  co-working spaces, and worker-run cooperatives) (de Peuter and
  Cohen 2015, 309), policy from below (e.g., the *Urban Worker
  Strategy* and the *Status of the Artist Act*) (de Peuter and Cohen
  2015, 311) and fights over the meaning of cultural work that
  "attempt to interpellate cultural workers into a counter subjectivity,
  that of resistant, autonomous workers" (de Peuter and Cohen 2015,
  315). Cultural Workers Organize (https://culturalworkersorganize.
  org/) is a stellar source of knowledge about cultural labour politics
  in Canada.
- *Struggles over the juridical, policy, and regulatory framework of the
  state that aim to reform the cultural industries.* For communication
  and media reformers, the cultural industries are shaped by
  capitalism, but make possible the changing of capitalism too,
  meaning struggles in and over the cultural industries may be a key
  way of engaging with and contesting capitalist power in society
  more broadly. Media reform is a democratic priority (Hackett and
  Carroll 2006; Hackett 2008). Instead of just hoping for or waiting
  for a total cultural industries revolution to happen, reformers often
  work across partisan divides and propose reforms that make
  meaningful changes. Some reformist initiatives include bringing
  communication and cultural resources out of market control and
  putting them into public hands, breaking up media oligopolies and
  diminishing concentrated ownership, enabling universal public
  access to the means of retrieving and imparting cultural goods,

widening the communicative commons by narrowing the private enclosure of culture and information, protecting privacy rights to personal data in an age in which the corporate and state surveillance of the Internet is near total, and challenging American-sponsored cultural free-trade agreements to protect and promote what's left of cultural autonomy and diversity. A global media reform movement has been growing for some time (Hackett and Carroll 2006; Hackett 2008; Freedman et al. 2016), and in the Canadian context, progressive proposals are being developed (Winseck 2016b) while OpenMedia.ca remains on the frontlines of reforming the corporate-controlled Internet.

- *Struggles over the mediatized representation of reality by mainstream media corporations and alternative and activist media organizations.* The texts of the mainstream corporate controlled news media (e.g., the Postmedia chain, the Torstar chain, CTV, or Global News) may fail to represent, under-represent, or simply mis-represent the world in the service of the powerful, and in response, independent or non-corporate media organizations (e.g., *Briarpatch Magazine, Canadian Dimension, The Tyee*, Rabble.ca, The Real News Network) are playing a vital role in producing and circulating texts that give expression to voices, views, and stories marginalized by mainstream media corporations. The Internet, Web, and social media are being used by a plurality of groups that create, tweet, upload, like, share, and comment upon their own texts in hopes of shaping public opinion about the causes and consequences of inequality, oppression, war, and ecological calamity. Through digital media platforms, many organic intellectuals are crafting texts that aim to win the consent of others to their group's worldview and project. The Media Action Research Group is a useful source of knowledge about activist media (http://www.mediaactionresearch.org/) and many independent media organizations are currently in operation (http://www.lib.sfu.ca/help/research-assistance/format-type/alternative-news).

- *Struggles over the connotative meaning given to socially resonant signs* like nation, security, society, democracy, capitalism, socialism, the environment, rich and poor, man and woman, Black and White, common sense, the good life, and so on. The late Stuart Hall (1982, 70) showed how "signs" are part of "what has to be struggled over," for they are part of the "means by which collective social understandings are created – and thus the means by which consent for particular outcomes can be effectively mobilized." In politics,

signs continue to be a real material force, and that is why they are
fought over by a plurality of actors and groups. Tactical media
experiments like culture jamming (e.g., *Adbusters*) and pranking
(e.g., The Yes Men) appropriate, re-contextualize, and radically
reframe the corporate or governmentally produced meaning given
to signs for brands and whole nations with the goal of revealing the
workings of power and agitating to change it (Kurasawa 2003).

- *Struggles over the interpretation of popular cultural texts.*
  Intellectuals in thrall to hegemony may read films, TV shows, and
  video games to simply affirm or maintain the ideological status quo,
  but counter-hegemonic intellectuals may generate readings that
  reveal or redeem the oppositional elements of widely circulating
  texts as part of a radical cultural pedagogy. Interpreting how
  popular texts may take a position for or against the dominant
  ideologies of the day or say something in-between, and sharing
  these interpretations with others, may inspire critical or oppositional
  forms of consciousness in society. As Kurasawa (2003, 484)
  reminds, popular culture "offers potential resources and spaces for
  individual and collective creativity in the formation of a politics of
  resistance in everyday life."

- *Struggles in higher education* over the role, content, and goals of
  communications and cultural studies curricula, the type of research
  academics undertake (administrative or critical), and the political
  side collectives of academics and the knowledge they produce take
  in the key battles over the past, present, and future of the cultural
  industries, in Canada, and worldwide.

The struggles for and against inequality, oppression, environmental sanity,
war, and imperialism are also cultural struggles being taken up by a
plurality of actors in and through the cultural industries. Newspapers,
magazines, ads, songs, TV shows, films, video games, and websites are
significant spaces where many of the central social struggles to maintain
or transform the existing political economy of twenty-first century capitalism are waged and staged, legitimized and de-legitimized, won and
lost. In this regard, the PEC remains a vital and useful theoretical and
methodological approach that encourages and enables scholars to participate in such struggles to understand and change the cultural industries,
and change the world, for the better.

PART FOUR

Social Services Restructuring

Caring for Seniors the Neoliberal Way

Pat Armstrong, Hugh Armstrong, Tamara Daly,
and Jacqueline Choiniere

Canadian political economy exposes the contested terrain that produces health services. Struggles over power within medicine have a long history (Naylor 1986), with gender, class, and unions all playing a role (Armstrong and Silas 2014; Coburn 1987). As Swartz (1977, 316) points out, "the idea of health insurance grew out of the problems industrial workers experienced in gaining access to medical care" and because of the "realization that 'distress breeds a dangerous temper.'" At the same time, the experience of the Second World War encouraged support for greater state involvement as did the pressures from multiple communities (Armstrong and Armstrong 2010). For feminist political economists, health services bring together all the issues related to women's work. More than one in five employed women work in health services, where the overwhelming majority of workers are women, but they have historically worked under the direction of men. Although nearly 60 per cent are unionized (Laxer 2015), much of the work remains precarious (Armstrong and Armstrong 2009). A disproportionate number of those at the bottom of the wage and power hierarchy are from racialized and/or immigrant communities. Even more women do unpaid care work, demonstrating both the integral relationship between production and reproduction and the persistence of ideas about women's natural caring skills (Grant et al. 2004). Health services also provide a telling example of the ways neoliberal strategies are blurring the lines between public and private spheres and the ways in which privatization plays out in the lives of women as workers and as those in need of health care.[1]

Beginning in the late 1950s, Canada socialized the costs of first hospital and then doctor care. According to the preamble of the *Canada Health*

Act (Canada 1985, 1) that clarified the federal commitments, the Parliament of Canada recognizes that "continued access to quality health care without financial or other barriers will be critical to maintaining and improving the health and well-being of Canadians." The socialization of costs dramatically improved access to care for the poor and the old. Women in particular benefited both as workers and as patients. At the same time, doctors' incomes grew and many hospitals emerged from debt (Armstrong, Armstrong, and Scott-Dixon 2008). Medicare worked for many, becoming and remaining Canada's most popular social program. Unfortunately, federal governments in the following years have not moved beyond doctor and hospital care, despite the recommendations of many government-supported investigations. Instead, successive governments have introduced neoliberal reforms that have reduced access to health services while simultaneously reducing the quality of care and of work in care.

In large measure because public care has enjoyed such widespread support, neoliberal strategies have most frequently been offered as a way to save the public health care system. Public services were represented as wasteful and inefficient, individuals as too dependent on the public purse. Taxes, unions, and regulations were seen as stifling the innovation necessary for person-centred care, and choice was defined in terms of the individual's right to buy. Competition, private sector investment, user fees, and managerial strategies taken from the for-profit world were promoted as essential ways forward to making the necessary cuts to public investment in care. It is a form of privatization by stealth.

The aging population in particular has been singled out as a threat to public care; a threat that can be solved only with neoliberal solutions. There is no question that there will be more people requiring health care services as a result of population aging. However, there is no reason to see this aging as a disaster waiting to happen. Population aging accounts for only an estimated 1 per cent of the annual growth in health care spending. As Grignon (2013) put it in the *National Post*: "The yearly increases in total health-care spending in Canada – approximately $10 billion per year nowadays – does not result from aging per se, but the costs of treatment, including diagnostic tests, drugs and doctors, for all patients, young and old. It's not that we have too many seniors that will break the bank, but how those seniors, and others, are treated in the health system that affects the bottom line." Moreover, the aging popula-tion is wealthier and healthier than past generations, so they are less likely to need care. In addition, seniors make enormous contributions to the unpaid care of other seniors, thus lowering the costs of public care. The real crisis is about access to services and treatment within services but, as we argue here, neoliberal strategies are not the solution.

This chapter uses the particular case of long-term residential care (LTRC), or what are most often called nursing homes, to explore the consequences of both the failure to extend Medicare and the application of neoliberal approaches to health services. It focuses on shifting responsibilities and accountability strategies as well as on market approaches to ownership and work organization. As with most doctor and hospital services, provinces and territories have the primary responsibility for funding and regulating nursing homes, although municipalities also play a role. According to the Canadian Institute for Health Information (CIHI 2014a), "nursing homes serve seniors and others who do not need to be in a hospital but who do need access to twenty-four-hour nursing care not generally available in home care programs or retirement homes."[2] The 143,000 people who live in the 1,360 Canadian nursing homes are served by the equivalent of 126,000 full-time workers (CIHI 2014a), most of whom are women and many of whom are from immigrant and/ or racialized groups. The actual numbers employed are higher, given that a significant number have part-time or casual work. Although this population especially needs public protection and support, nursing homes are not explicitly covered in the *Canada Health Act*. It is thus generally understood that the principles of accessibility, universality, comprehensiveness, portability, and non-profit administration that apply to hospital and doctor services do not apply in nursing homes. Nursing homes are frequently ignored in debates about and reports on health services. Romanow's (2002) *Report on The Future of Health Care in Canada*, for example, made no mention of nursing homes. But they have not been ignored in practice. As is the case throughout the world, corporations see dependent seniors as a promising source of profits and governments see corporations as a source of provision and as a model for change, albeit with country-specific variations.

Nor are nursing homes explicitly mentioned in the "free trade" agreements in place or currently being negotiated. Primarily about "strengthening investor and intellectual property rights, and creating global market rules that bind the future policy options governments might pursue" (Ruckert et al. 2015), agreements such as the Trans Pacific Partnership (TPP, now re-branded as the Comprehensive and Progressive Agreement for Trans-Pacific Partnership, or CPTPP) would make matters worse for nursing home residents and workers, in part by increasing the number of countries whose corporations could sue Canadian governments over policies that are potentially damaging to their investments and .in part by requiring governments to involve corporations in discussions of any policies affecting them. TPP would also extend the reach of patent protection, raising the price of brand-name prescription drugs and limiting access to cheaper generic drugs.

SHIFTING RESPONSIBILITY
AND THE RIGHT TO BUY

The shift to private responsibility for care in relation to nursing homes is not entirely obvious in part because it is hidden by gendered practices and by the structural changes outside them that alter the need for care. Unlike doctor and hospital services, nursing home care has never been without fees. There is general agreement that nursing home care should be affordable for everyone who needs it and that everyone should have a little left over after they pay their fees. However, this often requires demonstrating that residents cannot pay for it out of other income, including the federal, universal Old Age Security program, and the means-tested Guaranteed Income Supplement (MacDonald 2015).

The association with "home" continues as a justification for fees. As Duckett (2012, 132), a former health services manager in Canada and Australia, explains, "part of the service there directly substitutes for a home (that would otherwise be paid for by the resident as rent or capital) and for the food, light, and power that would normally be paid for by the individual. But some services – health care provided by nurses and other staff such as personal care workers – are not a substitute." This justification dates from a time when nursing homes primarily cared for the frail elderly. But those days are long gone. Based on neoliberal assumptions about state and individual responsibilities, private sector approaches, as well as concerns about debts and deficits, the federal government dramatically cut transfers to the provinces.

Beginning in the 1990s, federal cutbacks and subsequent provincial ones significantly reduced access to health services. "Hospitals were particularly affected at that time by fiscal restraint measures, as federal and provincial/territorial governments focused on reducing or eliminating budget deficits. This was a period of hospital consolidation, restructuring and bed closures. Chronic care and rehabilitation hospitals were closed and acute care was redefined to include only those requiring immediate medical intervention. There was systematic shifting from inpatient to outpatient care, especially to day surgery procedures and ambulatory clinics in hospital settings" (CIHI 2014b, 48). By 2011, Canada had only 3.3 hospital beds per 1,000 population compared to the average of 4.9 in the thirty-four countries reporting to the Organization for Economic Cooperation and Development. As a result, seniors who were previously cared for without fees in acute, chronic care, and psychiatric hospitals had to find care elsewhere (OECD 2011, Table 4.3.1). These neoliberal reforms combined with governments' failure to provide a sufficient supply of beds and appropriate staffing mean significant variations among provinces that create inequities related to income, geographical location, and gender.

Nursing homes are often the best or only option for those requiring twenty-four-hour support. Yet, the share of provincial resources spent on nursing homes covers a wide range. "Public spending on [long-term residential care] LTRC as a share of health dollars ranges from 5.1 per cent in British Columbia (BC) to 15.8 per cent in Nova Scotia" (MacDonald 2015, 84). Although investment varies, everywhere the number of beds available has not expanded to meet the demand. Indeed, many jurisdictions have actually cut beds. For example, "in the 1990s, the Alberta government reduced the number of [long-term care] LTC beds by over 40 per cent." "Between 1999 and 2009, the number of LTC beds per Albertan aged seventy-five and over decreased by 20 per cent" (Parkland Institute 2013, 15). The total number of residential care beds in BC was cut by 2,529 between 2001 and 2004, although 1,065 "assisted living" beds (for individuals in their own apartments but needing limited personal support) were added (Cohen et al. 2005, Table 6).

The result of bed shortages is long waits for care, even as the criteria for entry have tightened so that only those with the most complex care needs are eligible. In Nova Scotia, "there were approximately 1,284 people waiting for long-term care beds in April 2007. That increased to approximately 1,740 clients in April 2010 – an increase of 35.5 percent" (CBC 2011), with some waiting more than a year. In Ontario "median wait times from home were as low as sixty-eight days in 2004/5 and have increased over the decade. From hospital, median wait times for long-term care home beds rose by sixteen days to sixty-five days from forty-nine days in the last four years" (Health Quality Ontario 2014, 72). Those who apply from the community can wait much longer, even years. The main option, as BC's Fraser Health Authority's website suggests, is a private facility: "Depending on individual circumstances, private pay residential care may be the right option for either temporary or permanent care. There are many private pay residences to choose from, each offering a variety of services and features. Some residences have both publicly subsidized and private pay rooms. It is important to know that choosing to pay privately on a temporary basis does not guarantee you will be transferred to a subsidized bed in the same building" (Fraser Health 2011).

According to Sun Life Financial (2012), as of October 2012 those private pay homes in B C ranged in price from $2,275 to $9,500 a month, with admission based on ability to pay. Moreover, such facilities can make people leave if they cannot pay or if their care needs increase significantly. In other words, access to the alternative facilities is based primarily on income rather than on need and those most in need may be excluded. Such costs are particularly problematic for women and other equity seeking groups because they are the least likely to have employment pensions and are more likely to have received low pay if they had paid employment. At the same time, they are the most likely to need nursing home care because lower-income people lack alternatives and women live longer than men. Moreover, access is not secure even with higher incomes because you can be made to leave if your care needs are too great.

If seniors get into a nursing home, they frequently face significant care gaps as a result of the neoliberal strategies discussed later in this chapter. Female relatives in particular are often expected to fill this gap by providing unpaid care. Increasingly, those with enough money privately hire personal companions to provide individual care within the nursing home (Daly, Armstrong, and Lowndes 2015). Not part of the nursing home staff, these workers are most often women from immigrant and racialized groups who have few, if any, protections. Their growing presence provides a clear indicator of both care gaps and inequality.

In sum, by reducing access to hospitals and by failing to provide either enough beds or enough staff in publicly funded nursing homes, governments are forcing seniors to pay for care, putting care beyond the means of many and shifting care work to those privately paid or unpaid for the job.

MARKETS IN CARE

Historically, hospitals in Canada have been owned by non-profit and charitable organizations or by municipalities. Before neoliberal restructuring, however, there were a significant number of privately owned nursing homes. These were frequently converted houses and mainly owned by individuals or families. "Few homes provided much more than room and board 'with practically no nursing care of a skilled type'" (Struthers 1997, 176). As neoliberal hospital reforms and an aging population increased demands for residential care, governments in many jurisdictions developed affirmative action plans to promote corporate ownership of both homes and of services within non-profit homes. The result was a transformed landscape and renewed questions about the quality of care.

Ontario and BC have taken the lead in promoting for-profit ownership of facilities but the Atlantic Provinces have been close behind (Berta et al. 2006). When the Ontario Conservative Government decided to license 20,000 new nursing home beds and retrofit another 16,000 to meet safety, fire, and privacy standards, it introduced a competitive bidding process that favoured large corporations (McKay 2003). To make the investment attractive, the government offered to pay $10.35 per day for the next twenty years, at a total of $75,555 per bed in capital subsidies and additional operating costs as well as per diems for every resident to cover food, nursing care, supplies, and programs (McKay 2003). At the same time, it removed the regulations requiring at least one registered nurse on every shift and a minimum of 2.5 hours of nursing care per resident per day. It also allowed owners to increase the proportion of beds that could be charged extra fees. The requirement to have enough capital to enter a formal bidding process based on considerable expertise in markets and to meet new standards for physical structures all made it difficult for charitable or non-profit homes to compete even for the retrofit money. As a result, two-thirds of the 20,000 new nursing home beds were awarded to for-profit nursing home chains. The top five municipal and charity-based nursing home operators were awarded 2,049 new beds while the top five for-profit corporations such as Leisureworld (now called Sienna) and Extendicare were allocated 6,573 new beds (McKay 2003). Today the majority of beds in Ontario are owned by for-profits (CIHI 2015, Table 1.1), virtually all of them corporations.

There are similar patterns in BC. With the contracting conditions favouring large ownership, the number of corporate-controlled beds for all types of residential care facilities in BC increased between 1990 and 2004 by 599 per cent, or from 552 to 3,856 (Cohen et al. 2005, Table 8). Not all provinces have followed this pattern but the latest data from CIHI (2015, Table 1.1) indicate that the largest share of facilities is owned by for-profit facilities and those facilities tend to have the highest number of beds.

Even these data hide the extent to which corporations operate within non-profit, government, and charitable homes. Some governments such as in BC have actively pressured homes to contract out services, while others have done so indirectly by failing to provide sufficient funding. Neoliberal notions of cost savings found in for-profit firms prompt these homes to follow the government's lead. International corporations such as Sodexo have taken over food, laundry, cleaning, and even care work within organizations that are counted as non-profit. Daly (2015, 50) has documented this marketization, showing that "perhaps most surprising, was the number of nonprofit and public beds managed by for-profit companies." Almost a third of the residents lived in a nonprofit or charitable home in Ontario that was managed by a for-profit company.

This marketization has happened in spite of considerable research demonstrating that for-profit care is often inferior care. Much of this research has been done in the United States, which has moved farthest in for-profit care. Perhaps it could be dismissed on those grounds. However, research on BC (McGregor et. al. 2006), published even while Ontario was surging ahead with marketization plans, showed that hospitalization rates were higher from for-profit facilities compared to non-profit ones, confirming for Canada what foreign research had shown. Several years later, research on BC showed that nursing staff levels were lower in for-profit homes than in non-profit homes (McGregor et al. 2010, 1). As the authors point out, "nursing hours per resident-day is considered to be one reasonable measure of nursing home quality." Lower staffing levels may also explain why for-profit nursing homes have more verified complaints than do not for profit ones (McGregor et al. 2012). Based on their survey of the literature, McGregor and Ronald (2011, Preface) argue that "In spite of US and Canadian research finding a link between for-profit ownership and inferior quality in residential long-term care for seniors, and the fact that vulnerable seniors are more likely to receive the quality of care they require in nonprofit facilities, the for-profit sector in Canada is expanding at the expense of the nonprofit sector." Rates of death and hospitalization are also significantly higher in Ontario's for-profit nursing homes than in non-profit ones (Tanuseputro et al. 2015).

In sum, governments in Canada have followed neoliberal marketization strategies that have left a very large proportion of beds and of services within nursing homes operated for profit by international corporations that are protected by international trade agreements and responsible first to their shareholders. It is not surprising that as a result access to care and the quality of care have declined and inequities have increased.

REGULATING AND ACCOUNTABILITY?

Neoliberalism is usually portrayed as opposed to regulation and bureaucracy, often labeled as red tape. But neoliberalism in practice is much more complicated than that. Long-term residential care provides a telling example of how regulations and auditing can expand under neoliberalism and do so in ways that often support rather than undermine corporate interests.

The nursing home industry in North America is highly regulated. Many regulations have been a response to scandals resulting from neoliberal reforms. In their examination of scandals publicized by the media in Norway, Sweden, the United Kingdom, the United States, and Canada, Lloyd et al. (2014, 3) report that "for-profit ownership of care homes, large nursing home corporations and conflict around the role of the state were identified as major themes in the emergence of scandals." Indeed, the exposure of abuse has been a major factor in nursing homes becoming as regulated as the nuclear industry in both the United States and Canada (Banerjee and Armstrong 2015, 8) even as neoliberalism has gained hold. For example, the BC Ombudsperson (2012, 227) reported a wide range of problems with nursing home care but her solution was a host of regulations to fix specific problems at the workplace level. For instance, she recommended that claims that residents' calls were ignored should be addressed by introducing technology to measure and record responses to residents' bells. Such regulation seems to run counter to calls for a free market and a reduction in red tape.

At the same time, some for-profit owners have welcomed the introduction of regulations. Struthers (1997, 177) reports that back in the late 1950s when the Ontario government began offering significant financial support for care, the private sector rushed in: "Rapid expansion of the business intensified demands from established operators for provincial licensing and regulated standards within their industry to prevent unfair competition." In those days, the operators were mainly small but when the large corporations moved into the market their interests were similar. Twenty years later one of those corporations made it clear that some regulations could benefit them. "Leisureworld has significant opportunities for acquisitions in the fragmented LTC industry. With the regulatory burden becoming more onerous for smaller industry participants, larger companies with scale are positioned for continued growth" (quoted in Daly 2015, 49).

We can understand this contradiction, in part at least, in terms of the nature of the regulations that have been introduced and the forms of accountability as well as in terms of the sanctions – or lack thereof – that result. Most of the regulations have focused on the work of care, and thus on the workers. The regulations in most Canadian jurisdictions require detailed care plans, and in Ontario for example, set out very specific requirements for such things as how residents must sit at the table, when they should eat, and how much they must drink. Such a focus on process and outcomes supports employers in their control over workers, something that fits well with neoliberal approaches. The employer's control is supported by the government's requirement that these processes and outcomes be recorded regularly, usually on a daily basis and often more frequently than that.

Power (1999) talks about the "audit explosion" that involves the proliferation of rules, using technologies to monitor both the work and what are assumed to be direct consequences of work, and the expansion of offices to oversee this reporting. According to Power, this trend reflects a more general one replacing the welfare state with the regulatory state, but it is regulation of a particular sort. The imposition of RAI-MDS offers a specific example. Developed in the United States, the Resident Assessment Instrument-Minimum Data Set is mandated for use in Ontario and many other jurisdictions. According to CIHI (2010, 3), "The RAI-MDS 2.0 is a comprehensive assessment that documents the clinical and functional characteristics of residents, including measures of cognition, communication, vision, mood and behaviour, psychosocial well-being, physical functioning, continence, disease diagnoses, nutritional status, skin condition, medications, and special treatments and procedures."

The data collected in RAI-MDS are intended to provide a basis for funding, for accountability to both governments and the public, and for resident-focused care, among other purposes (Fries and Fahey 2003, 1–2). Although RAI-MDS is credited with improving some outcomes such as a reduction in bedsores and falls, the kinds of detailed data collection and monitoring it promotes have severe limitations (Armstrong, Daly, and Choiniere 2017, especially 353–6). One major issue relates to the accuracy of the data. In Ontario the data must be input by either a Registered Nurse (RN) or a Licensed Practical Nurse (LPN), but those who know what actually happens are the personal support workers

(PSWS) who provide most of the care. The data put in are thus usually second hand. The PSWS are usually not included in the development of the care plans, raising questions about the link between plans and care. Questions have also been raised about the accuracy of the data in terms of how much consistency there is in measuring pain, for example, and the ways in which the measurement of issues such as falls can negatively shape care, encouraging nursing homes to put most people in wheelchairs even if they can walk with help. Moreover, as Kontos et al. (2010, 359) point out, RAI-MDS assumes that standardization improves care and thus "restricts the care plan to standardized interventions." Using this tool as a basis for funding may also encourage employers to exaggerate the needs of residents in order to qualify for more government funding, prompting even more questions about data accuracy.

RAI-MDS is just one example of this focus on measurement and auditing that can apply to everything from the size of windows in residents' rooms to the width of corridors. Complying with such regulations requires technology and capital; both of which are more readily available to large corporations. But this is not the only reason for corporations to be less resistant to such regulations than theory might suggest. The emphasis on process and outcomes has left larger structural conditions virtually untouched. Most obviously, Ontario has not provided regulations on minimum staffing levels even though there is considerable research demonstrating that staffing levels are critical to both quality care and workers' health. Nor has the government introduced limits on foreign and corporate ownership of nursing homes, even though the research shows how important such ownership is to ensuring that the money goes to care rather than to profits. Such conditions have a profound impact on the very processes and outcomes that the audit process is intended to protect. Indeed, the audit process takes precious staff time away from care without clear evidence of benefit, especially for workers, an issue expanded on in the next section. At the same time, there is little evidence that effective sanctions result when employers are found in violation of the rules (Armstrong, Armstrong, and Kehoe-MacLeod 2015). Indeed, the combination of free trade agreements and foreign ownership makes it difficult for governments to enforce regulations effectively.

In sum, the emphasis on performance measurement is more than a set of rules: it is a way of thinking imposed on workers and managers that tends towards reductionism without expanding control for residents and workers or increasing accountability to the public. Without naming the process neoliberal, Tuohy (2003, 196) warns "there is a risk that some important dimensions of leadership capacity and indeed of democratic government, as well as some distinctive features of decision making in the health care arena, will be eclipsed."

NEOLIBERAL CARE WORK

Nursing homes have never been great places to work. In the past nursing homes primarily housed frail elderly women and other women were hired to look after them, based on the notion that any woman knew how to do what was considered to be basic domestic and caring work. Those with the economic means were mainly cared for at home and few with complicated care needs survived into old age. With public hospital care, those with medical needs were treated in acute, chronic, or psychiatric hospitals. With the extension of some public funding to nursing homes came the unionization of workers in the sector, promoting improved wages, working conditions, and job security. But this improvement has not continued under neoliberal strategies supporting hospital cutbacks, corporate ownership, contracting out, the application of for-profit management strategies throughout the system, and the auditing culture.

Hospital cutbacks have shifted a great deal of medical and psychiatric care to nursing homes, just as more people with medical and psychiatric issues have been surviving into old age. Meanwhile, provinces and territories have failed to expand the number of funded nursing home beds to meet the growing demand and have had to introduce more stringent criteria for entering them. As a result, each resident has required not only more care but also more complicated care. However, most governments in Canada have not put adequate minimum staffing requirements in place to deal with rising resident needs. Nor have they increased funding enough to provide adequate skills training.

Work has intensified in the wake of these reforms. In Ontario, where reforms have gone the farthest and international corporate ownership is the strongest, 63 per cent of personal support workers surveyed said they have too much to do all or most of the time. This compares to 30 per cent in Denmark (Armstrong et al. 2009, Tables 6 and 7) where staffing levels are higher and international corporate ownership very limited (Bertelsen and Rostgaard 2013, 142). Canadian direct care workers on the day shift said they cared for nearly twenty residents during the week whereas Danish workers said they looked after six (Armstrong et al. 2009, Table 4). Such staffing levels mean that, even when they work unpaid overtime and forgo their breaks, these workers say they leave many tasks undone. This is especially the case with non-medical tasks such as chatting, taking residents out, walking with them, and providing emotional support (Armstrong et al. 2009, chapter 5). The mainly female labour force is expected to adapt and to fill the care gap. This expectation is partly dependent on gendered assumptions that the required care remains the sort traditionally done by women in the home and that women feel responsible for making sure care is there (Baines 2004). Asked about whether they managed to take the breaks that are set out in their contracts, more than half the RNs and LPNs surveyed in Canada said they missed half or more of their breaks (Armstrong et al. 2009, Figure 10). One nurse spoke for many when she wrote into the survey that "We arrive thirty minutes early and leave thirty minutes late to get the work done" – all unpaid time (Armstrong et al. 2009, 69).

The intensity of this work takes a toll on workers' health and spills over into their home life. Among the Canadian care aides on the survey, two out of five reported feeling inadequate all or most of the time (Armstrong et al. 2009, Table 19), 43 per cent said they almost always finish their work feeling mentally exhausted (Figure 23), while 60 per cent indicated they were almost always physically exhausted (Figure 24). A third almost always finished the day with back pain (Figure 25). All these indicators were significantly higher in Canada compared to Nordic countries, even though the resident populations are quite similar. What differs is greater privatization, lower staffing levels, and more reporting requirements in Canada. Not surprisingly, in Canada absences due to illness and injury are also highest in this sector and, within it, highest for those who provide direct care all the time.

A family member interviewed for our ethnographic study of LTRC[3] nicely summed up the problem: "Well, the only thing is that there's not enough working hands, right? I don't know if I'm right or not now because I know that how the government assigns the staff ratio is that they give only one and a half hour[s of] care per resident per day. So basically that's not enough. That's not enough. And so I can see the care aides they are rushing all the time." Privatization, especially in the form of contracting out, puts jobs, security, pay, and benefits at risk. Cohen and Cohen (2004, 4) have documented what the contracting out of services in the health support sector to one international corporation meant for BC workers: "Wages have been cut almost in half, and these workers have no pension, long-term disability plan, parental leave or guaranteed hours of work. They do not know from one week to the next how many hours they will work, when those hours will be scheduled, or what their take-home pay will be."

The contracting out process meant not only the loss of gains that women had made under pay equity but also that women would now be paid less than men. When the B C Government passed Bill 29 – the *Health and Social Services Delivery Improvement Act* that allowed unions and pay equity rights to be eliminated through contracting out – the unions contested Bill 29 all the way to the Supreme Court. They won a landmark victory affirming their right to collective bargaining but not to the pay equity gains (Supreme Court of Canada 2007). This affirmation of the right to collective bargaining was fundamental to protecting workers' rights. Unions have launched campaigns to resist privatization and demand adequate minimum staffing requirements, among other things. In part because they face such powerful interests, in part because there are so many jurisdictional differences, in part because there are multiple unions negotiating separately, they have not had much success in preventing many of the consequences Cohen and Cohen identify. It is women who mainly feel these consequences, given that women make up the overwhelming majority of both residents and workers in nursing homes.

It is not only for-profit companies that have undermined workers' rights to secure and decently paid work. In keeping with the neoliberal push to reduce public spending, governments have promoted for-profit practices and failed to fund sufficient staffing and other resources. As a result, all homes have embraced corporate practices, albeit to varying degrees. With deteriorating conditions of work, employers have turned to immigrant labour and to those from racialized communities – in other words, to the least powerful. Families too have turned to these groups, hiring private companions to cover the care gap.

At the same time as the heavier medical and social needs of residents have intensified labour, the new auditing demands have added to the workload. Listen to this health care aide: "Too much documentation. Too much ... you don't even have time to do certain things but you have to do documentation ... but what are you going to do? You have to do it ... You have to run from binder to binder. You have a restraint. You have what you're taking care of in the morning. You have to do that. You have the snack book. Like we give the dessert out we've got to put that in documentation, you know. It's a lot of writing." But additional workload is not the only consequence. Because in Ontario only R N s and L P N s can actually input these data recorded by those who do much of the direct care, divisions within the workforce are more rigid. The nurses are taken away from care work and often hidden away in offices. Moreover, the auditing system does more than structure hierarchy; it also tends to structure the work in ways that undermine workers' right to base care on their knowledge, as this nurse practitioner explains. "It's weird. It almost is robotic mechanical. Yeah, that's really how I want to describe it. It's robotic mechanical nursing care. If this happens then you do this. If this happens then you do this. The computer is thinking for you and the humanity is lost in it ... The thing is people are feeling inca-pacitated to make their own clinical judgments without having the 'I don't know everything about it but the indicator came up.' You shouldn't need to have the computer tell you what the problems are with your person. It just seems ridiculous to me because you're the one telling the computer so then the computer can then tell you."

In sum, neoliberal restructuring has emphasized inequalities among those who provide care while auditing adds to the workload, taking time away from care. Neoliberal management techniques, combined with the lack of formal staffing requirements and adequate resources, have intensi-fied the work. Increasingly families turn to private means, creating further inequalities, and employers turn to the most vulnerable to carry out the necessary care work.

CONCLUSION

There is a lot of money to be made from the growing number of seniors. One way Canadian governments have been supporting this search for profit is by reducing the number of hospital beds and by failing to make up for this loss by funding more nursing home beds, let alone by expand-ing the number of such beds to deal with the growing demand. This failure has left lots of space that allows for-profits to move in, offering alternatives such as retirement homes for those with enough money to pay. More direct forms of support include competitive bidding for publicly funded care that favours corporate providers and the contracting out of services within non-profit and government homes. Although the number of regulations has expanded in part as a response to scandals, the failure to provide regulations that address larger structural issues such as staffing and ownership tends to favour large corporations while limiting govern-ments' ability to enforce the regulations that are important to the health of both residents and workers. The auditing culture that is represented as a way to ensure accountability takes time away from care without clear evidence that it improves quality. Work has intensified as a result of the failure to legislate staffing levels. At the same time, residents' growing needs resulting in large measure from neoliberal reforms, the failure to provide enough nursing home beds, and the application of for-profit managerial approaches to work organization add to this intensification. Nursing homes provide just one example of what neoliberal reforms mean for workers and residents, and for the public at large who seek to maintain democratic control over care. Although Nordic countries have resisted many of these privatization moves and have helped ensure better conditions of work and care, marketization has begun there as well (Meagher and Szebehely 2013).[4]

NOTES

This paper is a product of a seven-year team project on "Re-imagining Long-term Residential Care: An International Study of Promising Practice" funded by SSHRC (File #412-2010-1004: pi Pat Armstrong), with additional funding from the European Research Area in Aging project for a study on "Health Aging In Residential Places," funded in Canada by CIHR.

1   For a general introduction to the concept of neoliberalism, see Harvey (2005). For its discussion in the Canadian context, see McBride (this volume). For a discussion of ways in which it is used to inform measurement in health care, see Armstrong (2013).

2   This criterion also distinguishes nursing homes from assisted housing, supportive housing, and other forms of congregate living. Labels differ across jurisdictions, in Canada and abroad. This is also the case for the staff providing most of the paid care in nursing homes: those called health care aides in BC are called personal support workers or PSWs in Ontario. Nurses include both registered nurses (RNs), and assistive nurses, in Canada called licensed practical nurses (LPNs) or registered practical nurses (RPNs).

3   Between 2013 and 2015, our research team visited twenty-five nursing homes in Canada and in five other countries, conducting over 500 interviews and compiling more than a thousand pages of field notes. Teams of twelve to fourteen spent a week observing and interviewing in at least one site in each jurisdiction and visited another site for a day in the same location.

4   It should be noted that in this chapter "privatization" is used broadly and taken to include several forms, one of which is marketization. Meagher and Szebehely treat "marketization" separately as being about market mechanisms, whether or not for-profit ownership status in involved. This difference in usage does not significantly affect the analysis here, which relies heavily on Canadian evidence. The increased sway of neoliberal thinking and practices is to be found to varying degrees throughout the six countries examined in our "Re-imagining" project, and indeed beyond (Harvey 2005).

12

Mad (Re) Production: Defining "Mental Illness" in the Neoliberal Age in Ontario

Tobin LeBlanc Haley

The new Canadian political economy (CPE) literature, and especially the feminist political economy (FPE) strand, continues to carve out space for issues of gender, race, citizenship status, age, and ability in analyses of the history and current organization of Canada's economy (see Vosko in this volume for greater discussion of the trajectory of CPE especially and FPE). Despite this commitment to understanding and challenging the precise contours of marginality in Canada, sustained attention to the experiences of consumers/survivors/ex-patients/Mad people (c/s/x/m)[1] is relatively limited. This absence is surprising considering the recent scholarship from CPE and other Canadian policy scholars on governmental promotion of employability (McKeen and Porter 2003), and specifically, employability and associated challenges for people with disabilities in Canada (Tompa et al. 2006; Malhorta 2009; Hall and Wilton 2011) At the same time, there is an increase in attention by governments to issues of mental health (e.g., Anti-Stigma Campaigns and the At Home/Chez Soi pilot and research project)

Similarly, while Canadian disability studies is attentive to unemployment, low welfare rates, and attendant economic hardships experienced by people with psychiatric diagnoses (e.g., Chouinard and Crooks 2005; Prince 2016; Galer 2018), there is little attention to the economy as an integrated whole. Therefore, work on disability and employment, and work on disability and state care are often siloed, despite both interventions remaining attentive to the material hardships caused by or exacerbated by neoliberal policy-making. A feminist political economy intervention, attentive to all aspects of production (for surplus and social reproduction) builds bridges between disability literature focussed on employment and disability literature focussed on care, while taking seriously critiques of the biomedical model, pathologization, and the long history of psychiatric oppression within and outside Ontario.

A central component of Ontario's attention to mental health is a focus on employment, especially on challenging the view (long perpetuated through the provincial mental health care system) that people with mental illness labels are unable to participate in the processes of production (both production for surplus and social reproduction). For people with psychiatric labels, recognition of the capacity for participation in production is an important departure from the myth that they are solely what Tronto (1993) calls care-receivers. Previously, people labelled "mentally ill" were classified in the policy arena as the "deserving poor" (see Teeple 1995; Woolford and Nelund 2013; Grey at al. 2015) – people unable to reproduce themselves independently of state services due to their diagnosis, and in need of significant state support and intervention. Indeed, people with psychiatric diagnoses were forcibly excluded from the labour force and from recognized socially reproductive work through practices of institutionalization, and in the period from deinstitutionalization to today, through inaccessible workplaces and discrimination.

To put this another way, people with psychiatric diagnoses have been historically excluded from the labour force and from access to resources for social reproduction on the basis of diagnosis and attendant institutional practices. More recently, the Ontario government has been crafting social policy and practice, often mobilized at the point of care, which disciplines people with psychiatric diagnoses to align themselves with the processes of production within which people with disabilities experience high levels of low pay and precarity (Canadian Survey on Disability 2012).

Given the changing landscape of mental health care in Canada – and especially the repositioning of people with psychiatric diagnoses, and in particular those facing socio-economic marginalization, as productive within mental health care policy and practice – a CPE/FPE intervention that seeks to make sense of the logic and effects of these changes is both timely and long overdue. In this chapter, I argue that the tools of Canadian FPE, with the focus on understanding Canada's economy as an integrated whole, can be employed and expanded to shed light on the experiences of people labelled mentally ill under neoliberalism and the emerging contours of Mad oppression in Canada. Additionally, this chapter shows how the current pressures on people labelled "mentally ill" to perform "productivity" within an economy that marginalizes and impoverishes them acts as a resolution to the existing contradiction between perceptions of this community as unproductive, rooted in an earlier phase of capitalism, and advances the broader contemporary goals of privatizing responsibility for the work and resources involved in maintaining life. These novel insights appear consistent with CPE/FPE insights into the privatization, downloading, and individualization of support services (Fudge and Cossman 2002; Brodie and Trimble 2003), increasing rates of precarious employment (see Vosko 2010 for greater discussion of precarious employment), and the erosion of citizenship entitlement (Peck and Tickell 2002; Harvey 2005; Brenner et al. 2009; Wacquant 2013). What is needed, however, is a close study of the specific logic and effects of this recent development in the area of mental health.

Before beginning this analysis, it is essential to point out that the perceptions of people with psychiatric diagnoses as unproductive are mistaken. At question here is not whether people with psychiatric diagnoses (or any disability label) are productive or not, but rather how productivity among people with psychiatric diagnoses is being taken up in the current policy arena and in mental health care practice.

People with psychiatric diagnoses have historically been engaged in work that is forced and unpaid, (see Fernando 1991; Reaume 2004, 2009). More recently they have been called on to do a great deal of peer support work within mental health care facilities and programs (Fabris 2013; Haley 2018).[2] The assumption that people with psychiatric diagnoses are unproductive is a myth, related to a perception that those carrying a label of mental illness cannot consent freely to sell their labour power and keep up with workplace demands (i.e., the demand to secure surplus value). At the same time, the construction of people with psychiatric diagnoses as unable to engage in socially reproductive work is linked to the long history and present of eugenic and neoeugenic policies and practices that operate with the goal of eliminating enminded and embodied difference by controlling biological reproduction, as well as parenting and other care activities among people assigned disability labels (Haley 2017). Consequently, people with psychiatric diagnoses have been and are routinely denied access to the resources needed to complete the daily and intergenerational work of social reproduction.

Yet, as I argue in this chapter, the current repositioning of people with psychiatric diagnoses as productive in policy and practice, and the attendant pressures to obtain labour market attachment and independence in the activities of daily life, is not a resolution to the poverty, isolation, and state scrutiny that beset mental health care today. Nor will maintaining low levels of income support and disciplinary supports for daily life address the economic and social marginalization disproportionately experienced by people assigned psychiatric labels.

Using the province of Ontario as a case study, I show how the government-led project of repositioning people labelled "mentally ill" as productive in policy and social programs is neither wholly progressive, nor is it about simply fostering labour market attachment, thereby reducing the availability and usage of state-provided income supports and replacements and expanding the pool of available workers. It is also about the regulation of everyday life in a way that furthers and legitimizes a neoliberal approach to public supports for social reproduction for people labelled "mentally ill," and indeed for all people in this late phase of capitalism.

Ontario is a particularly useful case study, as the landscape of employment for people labelled as disabled is undergoing a dramatic change in the province. Notable examples include the recent decision to close sheltered workshops (see Ministry of Community and Social Services 2015), the continued growth in social enterprises in non-profit organizations and through programs like Working for Change, and the roll out of a mental health care strategy that places work and independence from state supports at the centre of well-being (Open Minds, Healthy Minds 2011). With the recent election of the Ford Conservatives, it is possible that Ontario will see an abrupt change to these recent trends, or perhaps the attempts to promote labour market attachment and independence among people with psychiatric diagnoses will continue or be intensified. In either case, it is important that the current landscape be documented and analyzed to preserve the often erased history and experiences of c/s/x/m people in Ontario and to lay the ground work for understanding the new policy landscape that may emerge under Ontario's new leadership.

This chapter proceeds in three parts. Part one explains the theoretical framework employed here, highlighting the specific insights FPE brings to the question of changing mental health policies, specifically the question of people labelled "mentally ill" as productive in both production for surplus and social reproduction. Parts two and three consider recent developments in the province of Ontario, illuminating how an FPE approach sheds light on precisely how and why the repositioning of people with psychiatric diagnoses as productive in the areas of employment and social reproduction is taking place. Specifically, part two provides a hitherto absent critical history of the government's current mental health strategy. Part three involves an exploration of the articulation of this new understanding at the ground level through the case study of high-support housing sites.

High-support housing is a form of congregate living operated largely as non-profit organizations where residents have their own room or apartment in a dedicated building or wing of a building. As the name suggests, high-support housing involves intensive supports for people deemed "seriously mentally ill," which include medication administration, coordination of medical appointments, money management, cooking, cleaning, laundry, and in some cases, cognitive behavioural therapy. Supports are provided by both "clinical" and "non-clinical" staff who are on-site twenty-four hours a day, seven days a week. Rent is typically paid through income provided by Ontario Works or the Ontario Disability Support Program.

In essence, high-support housing are sites where the room, board, and "treatment" once provided in the institution are now provided in a common space located in the community. To put it another way, high-support housing programs are spaces where the income support, housing, and "treatment" policies and programs that constitute community-based mental health care coalesce. High-support housing is one of three housing models that make up Ontario's supportive housing network, comprised of approximately 22,000 units (there is no official count to date), including approximately 1,200 high-support units (Suttor 2016). These homes are sites where the policies of the mental health care system intersect, and where the new understandings of what it means to be "mentally ill" (more compatible with the neoliberal project) are being mobilized and are readily observable.

Although the current redefinition of mental illness in mental health policy is a new neoliberal policy technique, it is the latest in a long line of government strategies since deinstitutionalization to eliminate, or at least reduce, state responsibility for the cost of mental health care. The policy techniques may have changed, but the desired outcome of cost reduction via increased dependence on the labour market for the resources for life and reduction in social supports for social reproduction remains the same. There is continuity through change in the area of mental health care. Therefore, there is a need to ask precisely why and how this shift in understanding of "mental illness" is taking place, if and how this alignment of productivity and recovery is articulated at the ground level, and if and how it relates to the broader neoliberal restructuring of mental health care and supports services in Ontario. It is insufficient to accept the prevailing logic that greater inclusion of people with psychiatric diagnoses in the contemporary labour market, demands for independence, and a reduced presence of the state is uniformly progress. Expanding the FPE literature to consider questions of productivity and madness sheds light on the logic and effects of recent changes.

A FEMINIST POLITICAL ECONOMY OF SOCIAL REPRODUCTION FRAMEWORK

Identifying the appropriation of demands for c/s/x/m autonomy over daily life as a means of entrenching neoliberal social policy is not a novel insight. Rather, this appropriation is identified by Mad and critical disability scholars as fundamental to the past and contemporary forms of Mad oppression, and a key site of struggle (see for example Costa et al. 2012; Howell and Voronka 2012; McKeown et al. 2014). I hope very much that this chapter will contribute in a small way to this ongoing project of Mad liberation and to the reclaiming of what mental illness and recovery mean. What is novel about this chapter is its close attention to often neglected questions of productivity and the relationship people with psychiatric diagnoses have to production, including social reproduction, and the close reading of how the redefinition of people labelled mentally ill as productive in the policy arena, the same arena that forcibly excluded people with psychiatric diagnoses from production, is about the retrenchment of services for this particular group, and all people, under neoliberalism.

In analyzing the repositioning of people with psychiatric diagnoses as productive in mental health care policy and practice, this chapter advances an FPE of social reproduction analysis that draws on insights from critical disability and Mad Studies scholarship. Whereas some critical political economists locate social reproduction outside the economy, an FPE approach defines the capitalist economy as consisting of the interrelated processes of production for surplus and social reproduction (Vosko 2002). Whereas production for surplus involves the creation of value through participation in wage labour, social reproduction is the socially necessary, and highly feminized, work that contributes to the production of value through the consumption of resources needed to reproduce the population on a daily and intergenerational basis (Laslett and Brenner 1989; Bakker and Gill 2003; Luxton 2006b; Steans and Tepe 2010).

Despite being socially necessary to capitalism, social reproduction exists in tension with surplus production (Bezanson 2006; Cameron

2006; Rioux 2015). The rate at which capitalists pay their workers, provide benefits, and pay taxes for state services exists in an inverse relationship to production of surplus. The higher the wages, the more generous the benefits and the more robust the supports offered by the state, the greater the quality of life of the worker and her family, but the more surplus value the capitalist must forgo. The organization of social reproduction changes across time and place reflecting the rate of the state's involvement in the provisioning of social supports, the prevailing economic ideology, and, ultimately, the balance of power between labour and capital (Katz 2001; Bakker and Gill 2003; McKeen and Porter 2003; Vosko 2006a; Brodie 2010). In the specific context of neoliberalism, "the contested political rationality that weaves foundational commitments to market logics, individualization, economic calculations of efficiency, and multiple sites of authority into new public policies and regulatory fields and onto existing ones" (Brodie 2010, 1588), employer-provided and public supports for social reproduction are generally reduced. The reduction in supports pushes increasing amounts of this work into the private sector – and largely onto women.

In this chapter, however, I am not focusing on the gender dimensions of increased demands on people with psychiatric diagnoses to perform this work. Instead, I focus on their general repositioning within mental health policy and practice as capable of doing the work of production for surplus and social reproduction and examine how this privatization of responsibility for well-being at the level of the individual is related to the neoliberal impulse at the level of the state to eliminate supports for social reproduction. Such analysis includes, but also moves FPE beyond, traditional sites of engagement such as the labour market, the household, the pressures on caregivers, and the lack of services for service users. This intervention also demonstrates that similar to how social reproduction has been understood as naturally female work – valueless and hidden within the home and other sites of care – the work of social reproduction done by people with psychiatric diagnoses has been concealed and constituted as having no value through medicalized discourses of therapy and recovery.

Finally, this intervention opens up space for consideration of how social reproduction has become a sort of workfare among people who access supports for this socially necessary labour, training them not only for the workplace but for independence in social reproduction – that is, in all processes of production. When high rates of low pay and precarious employment among people with psychiatric diagnoses are not attended to, policy and practice that focus on work and the independent

completion of activities of daily living are part of the hollowing of the
category of the deserving poor via a focus on labour market attachment. By paying attention to the relationship people labelled mentally
ill have to the economy as an integrated whole and not simply production for surplus, we can see and make sense of the full thrust of the
changing mental health care system in Ontario. In examining the
intensified demands for independence in surplus production, and
especially social reproduction, this chapter contributes to the project of
challenging the myth that people living with mental illness labels are
unproductive, while simultaneously critiquing inclusion in the prevailing
patterns of production as necessarily progressive policy making. It also
contributes to expanding the analysis of FPE into new areas of state-led
interventions in the processes of social reproduction (see for example
Hall in this volume). There may indeed be an inclusion of a sort taking
place; but it is inclusion in an economy characterized by precarious
employment relationships and minimal state supports, dynamics that
are experienced disproportionately by marginalized peoples, including
people with disabilities. To celebrate this kind of inclusion legitimizes
this arrangement of production for everyone.

TOWARDS PROVIDING OPPORTUNITIES
FOR INDEPENDENCE

Under capitalism, states have developed numerous techniques for
addressing human needs (McKeen and Porter 2003) and, specifically, for
managing tensions between the capitalist imperative of unfettered
accumulation and the resources required for social reproduction (Vosko
2006a). The rate at which states provide supports typically aligns with
the prevailing economic ideology. For example, greater support was
provided during Keynesianism than under neoliberalism today (McBride
and McNutt 2007, McBride in this volume) where the focus of policies
is employability rather than decommodified supports (those acquired
outside of employment relationships and/or purchased using wages)
(McKeen and Porter 2003).

It is in this context that the evolution of Ontario's current approach
for addressing the problems of poverty and isolation is best considered.
This approach is clearly articulated in the recent mental health care
strategy "Open Minds, Healthy Minds (2011)," which is focused on the
inclusion of people with psychiatric diagnoses in the labour market and
on developing the skills pertinent to performing activities of daily living

independent of state-provided or supported services. In this strategy, the Ontario government posits that a psychiatric diagnosis, while still defined as illness or impairment, no longer precludes participation in the labour market or the ability to exercise autonomy over and complete the activities of daily living independently from the state. Recovery is measured vis-à-vis rates of both labour market attachment and the use of state supports, and a relationship of mutual benefit is being established between the well-being and autonomy of people with psychiatric diagnoses and the provincial government's goals of cost-saving and economic growth in the area of mental health care specifically, and in social services generally. This strategy states that through early intervention, a focus on children, the development of workplace programs, streamlined and personalized access, and reduced stigma, "we" (all Ontarians) will be able to decrease the use of costly services like hospitals, and create more inclusive, happier, and therefore more productive workplaces, and reduce absenteeism. The ultimate objective of Open Minds, Healthy Minds is to reduce the social, personal, and economic costs of mental illness through the incorporation of greater numbers of people with psychiatric diagnoses into processes of production, and meeting this objective involves, rather than withdrawal from the lives of people with psychiatric diagnoses, substantial amounts of intervention. This intervention, as is demonstrated in this chapter, is enacted through the policies and practices of service provisioning that make up mental health care systems.

The need to reposition people labelled mentally ill as productive within policy and practice ultimately finds its roots in the psychiatric deinstitutionalization that took place in Ontario in the 1960s and 1970s. At that time, the provincial government dramatically reduced funded days of care with little consideration for the needs of deinstitutionalized ex-patients/survivors (Marshall 1982; Dear and Wolch 1987; Simmons 1990). This laissez-faire approach to deinstitutionalization was, for the provincial government, a cost-saving mechanism rolled out under the flag of ending this particular form of psychiatric oppression (Simmons 1990). As deinstitutionalization took place, there was little expectation of or supports for ex-patient participation in production. Welfare programs provided access to (some of) the resources to survive and an increasingly defunded and downloaded set of social programs providing (some) support for daily living, most infamously the supports offered in Toronto's boarding home system. While indeed a victory for the c/s/x/m community, and one this community and allies worked tirelessly for, the end of psychiatric institutionalization was a way for the provincial government to save money. At the same time, supports for daily living provided under Ontario's particular brand of Keynesian social policy were slowly eroded in the period following deinstitutionalization, and ex-patients, once institutionalized and hidden from public view, experienced visible poverty, homelessness, substandard housing, and incarceration.

Following a number of high-profile deaths in Ontario's board and care homes (*Mayor's Action Task Force on Discharged Psychiatric Patients* 1983, 1984) and increased media attention to the conditions former patients faced (Hartford et al. 2003), the municipal and provincial governments were forced into action, leading to what can be understood as a period of debate over the best strategies for "managing" the deinstitutionalized psychiatric population. It is important to note that this debate over mental health strategies was occurring alongside debates about the correct path for welfare reform across all levels of government as neoliberalism gained popularity throughout the Western world. The longstanding sequestration of "mental patients" from production, together with the erosion of decommodified supports, was creating a significant problem for provincial and municipal governments in the province.

The wholesale efforts to include people with psychiatric diagnoses in the processes of production as an attempt to deal with poverty and homelessness was still about fifteen years away. Instead, the provincial and municipal governments continued to reform how resources necessary for everyday life were being provided by the state (see for e.g., Building Community Support 1988; Putting People First 1993). The focus was on downloading administrative and some fiscal responsibility to non- and for-profit community organizations, reducing and freezing welfare payments, and tightening eligibility programs. It is this period that is often understood as the "rejuvenation" of the categories of deserving and undeserving poor. At this time, people with psychiatric diagnoses, specifically those experiencing poverty, were largely considered deserving poor, requiring state services (and control). While there was some discussion of opportunities for employment whenever possible, the focus was still on privatizing social supports.

In the mid-1990s, a more concerted effort to encourage people with psychiatric diagnoses to take responsibility for the work of social reproduction and the acquisition of necessary resources began to emerge. This shift occurred under the Harris government during the "common sense revolution," a period when the provincial government sought to entrench neoliberal principles across social services and the labour market. In 1999-2000, the provincial government developed, as part of their mental health strategy, Making it Happen (1999), a policy framework for increasing labour market attachment among those with so-called serious mental illnesses (SMIS) entitled Making it Work (2000). This framework focussed on employment as a key determinant of mental and physical health. An assessment of the severity and duration of illness based on the amount of services used was directly related to this focus on employment as a health determinant. While the strategies from the previous two decades, Building Community Support (1988) and People Putting People First (1993), considered inaccessible labour markets, the focus here was more on cultivating and streamlining private sector service provisioning and promoting community, family, and individual responsibility for the problem of homelessness caused by deinstitutionalization. Previous strategies were focussed on the rates of income replacement and supports for social reproduction. Making it Work attempted to reposition people with psychiatric diagnoses – and in particular those accessing social assistance – as productive, to download responsibility for material needs not just to the private sector but to the individual, and by extension, I argue, to reduce the number of people with psychiatric diagnoses occupying the category of the deserving poor.

While the Harris government was replaced by the Liberals nearly fifteen years ago, the general trends towards welfare-state retrenchment, and the specific focus on getting people with psychiatric diagnoses into the labour market, arguably deepened, with the government stressing the role that private businesses and families play in building recovered and resilient communities and downloading the message of productivity and recovery to the Local Health Integration Networks[3] and other non-profit organizations that now provide much of the mental health care services in the province. The focus on labour market inclusion and independence in social reproduction arguably crystallized with the release of Open Minds, Healthy Minds. Alongside the continued downloading, privatization, and individualization of services for mental health care in the province, this strategy proposed a symbiotic relationship between labour-market attachment, reduced service use, economic growth, and the well-being of people with psychiatric diagnoses.

This new approach to mental health policy is framed as a "recovery approach" to care, focusing on providing people with the opportunities to "access the social determinants of mental health" (12) and individuals' resiliency to deal with the ups and downs of everyday life (7, 9). Broadly defined as access to education, employment, income, and housing, the rates at which Ontarians can access these social determinants and reduce their use of costly social services correlates directly to how their sickness and recovery is defined, and to how success in mental health care provisioning is measured in the province generally.

Open Minds, Healthy Minds represents the newest understanding in mental health care policy of what it means to have a psychiatric diagnosis and what recovery looks like; but this understanding has been building over the last thirty years. In this paradigm, people with psychiatric diagnoses are *accurately* recognized as having the capacity for productivity, but are positioned as an economic burden due to the high cost of mental health care services and the unemployment and homelessness they disproportionately experience. The responsibility for mitigating this "burden" lies with the individual, and mental health care policies and programs should be constructed in such a way as to promote (greater) independence from the state regarding both participation in employment and in performing activities of daily living such as cooking and cleaning. This mitigation of current or potential public "burden" is, according to the most recent policy documents, recovery. Those who remain on social assistance and/or who use high-cost mental health care services (like hospitalization or Assertive Community Treatment) at a high rate are labelled as SMI, and continue to receive services, but are indeed seen as burdensome. Those people with psychiatric diagnoses who obtain independence from state services are perceived and celebrated as recovered/recovering and are the protagonists of recent anti-stigma public education campaigns that seek to eliminate discrimination to provide greater opportunities for achieving the social determinants of health (see Costa et al. 2012).

The shift in Ontario towards tightening access to income supports and replacement and supports for social reproduction among people with psychiatric diagnoses, and the positioning of the state as the facilitator and benevolent partner in participation in all aspects of production, is congruent with national and international trends. The Mental Health Commission of Canada, a non-profit organization created by the federal government in 2006 on the heels of the national report on mental health Out of the Shadows at Last, also aligns employment with recovery, reduced service use, and cost saving. In the last twenty years, Canada has signed the Copenhagen Declaration of Social Development (1995), which promotes, alongside free trade, working towards full employment for so-called "disadvantaged groups" (including people with disabilities). We are also witnessing a global preoccupation with employment and "mental illness," in particular the preoccupation with absenteeism and lost productivity due to employees who are assigned a psychiatric diagnosis (with depression commonly being used as an example) (WHO 2010; Evans-Lacko and Knapp 2016), while at the same time the global labour market is recognized as a site of debility (Puar 2017). These developments point to a need for comparative analyses of mental health strategies under neoliberalism with specific focus on the impact on those excluded from the labour force. Such an analysis is, unfortunately, beyond the scope of this chapter. Instead, this chapter will now examine how this shift in what it means to be mentally ill, and the focus on inclusion in social reproduction, is present not only in social policy but also in the everyday lives of people with psychiatric diagnoses.

LIFE IN THE HOMES

To examine how the repositioning of people with psychiatric diagnoses in policy as capable of production for surplus and social reproduction is articulated at the ground level, I now turn to an examination of data from twenty-three interviews with residents living in high-support housing in Ontario and fifteen service providers working in or with these sites.[4] It should be noted that the high-support housing community in Ontario is very small, with an estimated 1200 units in the province (Suttor 2016). Therefore, I do not name the sites I visited or state the precise number of sites visited, and I have changed some distinctive patterns of speech (indicated by the use of closed brackets). Instead, I will specify that I visited more than one and less than five of these sites. These measures are necessary to protect the confidentiality of residents and service providers.

I first examine the articulation of the understanding that residents are capable of participating in the labour market. I then move on to consider how people with psychiatric diagnoses are positioned as capable of participating in work involved in social reproduction, specifically daily maintenance or the activities involved in residents' daily survival. This exploration of the repositioning of people with psychiatric diagnoses vis-a-vis production, demonstrates how the welcome recognition of resident capacities for work and the activities of daily living is being mobilized to reduce state supports and enact pathologization in new ways.

It should be noted that I am not focusing here on intergenerational daily maintenance or other aspects of social reproduction (biological reproduction, reproduction of the working class, see Bakker and Gill 2003) because the policies, programs, practices, and institutions that constitute the mental health care system are organized around sustaining individuals on little more than a day-to-day basis. Intergenerational daily maintenance responsibilities/work, such as childcare, are neglected, limited, and, in some cases, prohibited. While these restrictions provide insights into the form intergenerational social reproduction may take among people with psychiatric diagnoses under neoliberalism, it is not the focus of this study, but rather is considered elsewhere (Haley 2017).

Labour Market Attachment

For the most part, the people I interviewed work with or are considered SMI, that nebulous category indicating a high rate of service use. For this group, the expectation of labour market attachment by service providers is relatively low, as is the expectation of recovery as defined in social policy and by non-profit organizations. Despite service providers expecting a low level of productivity, the notion that residents can and should achieve labour market attachment and perform the activities of daily living using as few state resources as possible in order to demonstrate and secure wellness still permeates the lives of those considered the "sickest."

While most of the residents worked prior to entering the homes, typically in precarious employment relationships, I did not find that there was a high demand for labour market attachment among this group. What I did find, however, is that the repositioning of residents as able to work and the equation of unemployment and high rates of service use with illness penetrated these spaces.

Within the homes, wellness is not measured solely in relation to the absence of psychiatric symptoms, but also in relation to the ability to maintain labour market attachment or, at least, to volunteer outside the homes and to the ability to perform the activities of daily living, as will be discussed later. When asked if residents work, service providers spoke about unemployment as resulting from illness, describing anyone working as "doing well." Moreover, there was widespread agreement among service providers that those who are able to maintain higher degrees of independence should not be living in the homes, but rather should be stepped down to lower levels of care, which, they lamented, were not readily available.

Absent from the insights of service providers were considerations of how access to supportive housing allowed people to maintain labour market attachment, of the low rates of remuneration (Hall and Wilton 2011), and high rates of precarious employment among people with disabilities (Tompa et al. 2006). Nor was there consideration of the fact that the majority of people living in these sites have not had access to higher levels of education and worked in precarious employment prior to coming to live in these spaces. Service providers spoke about illness as the impediment keeping residents out of the labour force, and participation in the labour market as a (if not the) dominant indicator of wellness. Interestingly, among service providers working with those labelled SMI, full-time employment is rarely considered a realistic goal. There remains a sort of contradiction between new discourses of employability and low expectations of service providers. This contradiction is resolved by painting unemployment as evidence of a serious mental illness or incomplete recovery. Essentially, residents who do not attain labour market participation are considered the sickest of the sick, which locates the cause of poverty and unemployment in the body of the individual. In this context, only those who are considered the sickest and in need of substantial psychiatric intervention are unemployed. This obscures both the structural factors of unemployment, as well as the fact that the redefinition of mental illness is about removing supports *and* disciplining people not to use these supports lest they be a hindrance to economic growth due to their "mental impairment."

Many residents identified their lack of employment as a personal failing that needed to be addressed if they were to be responsible citizens who could live without the services for income replacement and, by extension, support services. This desire not to be constructed as burdensome due to a lack of access to basic necessities independent of the state is reflected in the following sentiment expressed by one resident discussing volunteer work. "It is sort of working for taxpayers' dollars anyhow. If you are working in the hospital, you are out delivering flyers or any job, it is like working for your own taxpaying money. It is not the same as living on anyone's taxpaying money but you are working for the taxpay[ers'] money. That would be a good thing don't you think so? I want to leave something to someone as everyone who is proper in life should do. Like the normal and proper is to have something to leave behind. Not just sit there because I am psychiatric, schizophrenic, and think that I would have to blame it on my illness that I couldn't perform that myself, like everyone else's life."

The majority of residents I interviewed expressed a plan to acquire full-time work once they were "well." Residents expressed the view that to be well is to be able to cope with the pressures of the labour market. Those who are able to acquire employment are seen as doing the best. They are treated, as Costa et al. (2012) point out, as the aspirational figure for everyone else. Residents, for the most part, want to move out of the category of the deserving poor, and see doing so as wellness. While residents' desires to work should be supported, and certainly access to work can improve quality of life, it is essential to ask why employment is the marker of wellness and what kinds of jobs residents are moving into, and to query whether it is truly inclusion or little more than an extension of precarious employment into the lives of people contending with punitive income support programs.

In the stories of residents, it becomes abundantly clear that the pressures created by low levels of income replacement are acutely felt. The mapping of wellness and sickness onto employment and unemployment respectively erases the influence of factors such as inaccessible labour markets, high rates of precarious employment, and a lack of resources for completing the work of daily maintenance. Moreover, it directly encourages residents to work in any job with little consideration for the hardships associated with being the working poor. In Ontario, minimum wage jobs do not provide a living wage nor (usually) benefits. This latter issue is especially relevant for people routinely medicalized and who can access (some) free pharmaceuticals under existing welfare programs.

Daily Maintenance

This focus on productivity in the labour market is coupled with a focus on productivity in the home. In addition to measuring wellness in relation to the ability to participate and cope with the pressures of the labour market, no matter one's class position, the day-to-day lives of residents also involve therapeutic work for the purpose of equipping them with the skills for "independence" in daily living or, to be more accurate, for independence from state supports for activities of daily living. The focus on wellness as involvement in the running of the home translates into residents doing a noticeable amount of the work of daily maintenance involved in running the housing sites. Sometimes this work is done in exchange for minimal amounts of money or for a cigarette, and sometimes as volunteer work. Residents reported sweeping, mopping, feeding, and cleaning up after house cats, taking out the garbage, and running errands for staff and housemates. Residents described this work as helping out and completing required chores.

I sweep the balconies upstairs. I help out, no pay.

I help out as much as I can. I do garbage at nights; they have got me doing a couple of chores. They've got a couple of things around the house certain people do.

I sometimes go [run errands] for [another resident]. She is unable to walk, so she buys me coffee to get things for her. Also, they give me the mail, and I give it to the places where it needs to be sent, and they give me five dollars for that. Sometimes we pick up food and bring it to [another housing site]; we get a little bit of money [from the organization] for that.

When asked about residents' daily routines, the staff confirmed the list of tasks described by residents and added that residents also clean the kitchen and watch more vulnerable housemates during outings. Staff described these tasks mostly as "volunteering," while compensated tasks were framed as work.

There is a lot of that [volunteering]. Cleaning, taking out the garbage, feeding the cats.

Some clean the litter, kitchen, dishwasher, and dust, but, not laundry, and some sweep. Some get paid right away, some save. It is not a lot; sometimes they want a cigarette or a coffee the same day. It is whatever they prefer. We trained [a resident] to do it [go get drugs from the pharmacy]. It is like their little job.

Staff also stated that, in addition to cooking and gardening, residents offer peer support to their housemates. This work was primarily described as volunteering and/or falling under the category of occupational and recreational therapy. As one staff member put it: "We do have a building committee where we have started groups, gardening groups and things to get everyone involved in the community and looking after the building. So in that sense it is not paid employment, it is volunteering."

Participation in the tasks of everyday life is understood by both residents and staff to indicate well-being, recovery, and resiliency. Those who can participate in this work are understood as doing well, and those who do not are understood as sick. The work within the homes is not, however, broadly framed as residents contributing to the running of their home and creating caring and supportive environment in a way that alleviates increased demands on service providers. Rather, this work is seen as therapeutic, as providing people with the skills for everyday living without state supports. What becomes visible through the analysis of the work involved in maintaining everyday life, is the emergence of a sort of social reproduction workfare that blends discourses of the burdensome unemployed resident with recovery as independence in everyday life.

Mental patients engaging and doing work in care sites as therapy is not new. What is new is that expectation and encouragement of independence in social reproduction through rewards of minimal compensation or the promise of greater autonomy over the everyday. At the same time, many of these tasks of social reproduction are being done by paid service providers who are themselves overworked (for a broader discussion see Haley 2018). Encouraging residents to do this work alleviates increased demands on service providers under neoliberalism. In this trend we can see further movement toward a system of care that seeks to remove as many people as possible from the category of the deserving poor, and, in the particular case of social supports for residents, proceeds under the guise of liberation.

CONCLUSION

From the building of the first asylums through deinstitutionalization in the 1960s and 1970s and the elimination of "universal" entitlement to social programs, people with psychiatric diagnoses in Ontario have been perceived as unproductive and remained firmly within the category of the deserving poor in social and public policy arenas. Within this context, the recent changes in Ontario appear like a progressive recognition of the capacities of people with psychiatric diagnoses to work and look after themselves, a victory for those advocating for real inclusion. There are indeed elements of the redefinition of mental illness that are an improvement over wholesale exclusion from the labour market. After all, labour market attachment can mean greater access to income, benefits, and social connections, and can provide a sense of well-being and personal fulfillment as well as some measure of autonomy over everyday life. Most importantly, residents interviewed here want to work.

Careful analysis reveals, however, that the greater incorporation of people with psychiatric diagnoses, and in particular those experiencing poverty, into the processes of production is part of a broader global trend toward the application of market principles to government, the workplace, the community, the household, and the conduct of individuals (Peck and Tickell 2002; Harvey 2005; Brenner et al. 2009; Wacquant 2010; Peck 2013). In short, the current repositioning of people with psychiatric diagnoses as productive within and outside the household is a neoliberal social policy strategy geared towards hollowing out the recently renewed category of the deserving poor. This shift in how mental illness is understood is an attempt to resolve the existing contradiction between perceptions of people with psychiatric diagnoses rooted in an earlier phase of capitalism and its incompatibility with the broader goals of neoliberalism, specifically the elimination of all social welfare supports through the eradication, or shrinking, of the category of the deserving poor.

The analysis of the repositioning of people with psychiatric diagnoses in policy must extend beyond the labour market if we are to fully grasp the techniques involved. The policy techniques aimed at including this particular group more fully in capitalist relations of production are enacted through the processes of care provisioning and involve the promotion of labour for surplus as well as social reproduction. To pay attention only to employability is to reproduce an incomplete understanding of production, as well as to miss the substantial amount of social reproduction people with psychiatric diagnoses are doing, and often being compelled to do, within sites of care. It is to miss a new form of workfare that specifically involves the activities of daily maintenance and to leave unanalyzed the erasure of the work of daily maintenance through the mobilization of medical and, specifically, psychiatric discourses.

As FPE continues to contend with neoliberalism (see Vosko this volume), new spaces and uses for FPE analysis are emerging (see Hall this volume). This chapter has made a small contribution to expanding FPE by considering its utility to questions of production and madness in this late phase of capitalism. There is a need for greater scholarly and activist work in this area if the struggle for well-paid work and access to the necessary supports for social reproduction are to include people with psychiatric diagnoses, and other people previously sidelined in FPE scholarship. Beyond carving out a kinder capitalism we must, when imagining and working towards a socialist economy, remain attuned to the materiality and nebulosity of saneism and ableism if we are to ever truly leave these forms of oppression behind.

NOTES

1 The terms consumer(s), survivor(s), ex-patient(s), and Mad people are used as self-identifiers by those with psychiatric diagnoses or experiences with the psychiatric system, and are typically associated with the psychiatric survivor and Mad movements (see LeFrancois et al. 2013). In my work, I use the inclusive c/s/x/m, people with a psychiatric diagnosis, people labelled as mentally ill, or people living with a label of mental illness. The purpose is to decentre the biomedical model and to recognize the multiplicity of ways people with psychiatric diagnoses identify. Indeed, identity is fundamental to a c/s/x/m politic

as c/s/x/m are political identities, each meaning something slightly different, but mobilized together to draw attention to a common experience of psychiatric oppression, violence, and discrimination by the state, the market, the family, and the community, to work together for material change in law and policy, and to imagine and work towards a Mad futurity free from the current social, economic, and political relations.

2 These patterns are not dissimilar to the experiences of people with intellectual disabilities (see Abbas 2012), another group of people who are currently largely excluded from CPE/FPE analysis.

3 Ontario is now divided into fourteen of these LHINS (previously the smaller and more numerous District Health Councils), which are non-profit organizations that have the "authority to manage their local health systems" (see *Local Health System Integration Act* and Public Information, Ontario Ministry of Health and Long-Term Care and Ontario's Local Health Integration Networks). A survey of the LHIN's *Integrated Health Services Plans* (IHSPS) for 2013–16 reveals a commitment to the redefinition of mental health by the Ontario government.

4 This research has been reviewed and approved by York University's Research Ethics Board.

13

Fiscal Distress and the Local State: Neoliberal Urbanism in Canada

Greg Albo and Carlo Fanelli

The "urban question," as it came to be called in the 1970s, is now a central focus of academic study, state planning, and political struggle alike (Castells 1977; Harvey 1973). It is impossible to disentangle these concerns with today's "urbanized world," in all its myriad of social forms, from meta-cities to ex-urban sprawl, from the political economy of capitalist development. In *The Communist Manifesto*, Karl Marx and Friedrich Engels early on provocatively implicated urbanization with capitalism – "The bourgeoisie has subjected the country to the rule of the towns. It has created enormous cities" (1848, 40). There is already here a sense that capitalism produces "urban space" – concentrated and intensified built environments for the production, circulation, and consumption of commodities; vast matrices of transportation and communication networks; enormous tracts of housing refracting class and social divisions; and complex organizational apparatuses for the production of infrastructure and social order. "Capitalist city" seems an unavoidable term to capture some sense of the economic contradictions and political tensions that are caught up in the urbanization process. The urban theorist Henri Lefebvre insisted that: "There is nothing more contradictory than 'urbanness.' On the one hand, it makes it possible to some degree to deflect class struggles ... On the other hand, the city and its periphery tend to become the arena of kinds of actions that can no longer be confined to the traditional locations of factory or office floor. The city and the urban sphere are thus the setting of struggle; they are also, however, the stakes of that struggle" (1991, 386).

The political economy of urban development now receives an equal measure of global attention and anxiety. With half of the world's population now living in urban locales, the UN-Habitat's *World Cities Report 2016* offers a glimpse of the world-historical transformations. The raw figures are, at times, difficult to fathom: over 500 cities of one million; one in three of the world's population living in slums; the urban conglomeration centred on Tokyo estimated at some thirty-five million; and meta-cities of ten million or more becoming something of a commonplace. If the most mesmerizing urbanization developments today are taking place in the Global South (with an astonishing variation in settlement patterns and urban forms), North America remains the most urban of the continents with Canada, by some measures, being more urbanized than the United States. The leading urban cores in Canada – Montreal, Toronto, and Vancouver – continue to grow demographically, spatially, and in density at generous clips. The Greater Toronto Area, Canada's meta-city, now has a population pushing toward some seven million, growing steadily at over one hundred thousand per year, with its urban armatures stretching hundreds of kilometres in all directions from the shores of Lake Ontario (table 13.1).

The territorial demarcation of the urban landscape is, in consequence, thoroughly blurred. The old division of rural-urban (which traditionally dominated both urban studies and Canadian political economy) has lost meaning from the *extension* of the urban across geographical space alongside the *intensification* of built space within urban centres. The thesis that capital accumulation produces urban space is, even if a general abstraction, foundational to any adequate understanding of cities (Beauregard 2018). It is, however, still necessary to investigate the particularities of the spatial and temporal forms and patterns of urban political economy today. This initially can be captured in the transition, as David Harvey (1989a) first termed it, from a postwar Keynesian "managerial urbanism" to the "neoliberal city" of the last decades. This is, on the one hand, a particular historically situated abstraction positing a socio-spatial shift from the "national-local" to the "global-national-local" as capital restructured its patterns of accumulation and reproduction. On the other, it is a set of specific contentions about the circulation of capital as it traverses and fixes urban space and the remaking of the modalities, apparatuses, and capacities of local states. The terms "neoliberal urbanism" and "urban austerity" (the latter term focusing on the mutation of the 2008 financial crisis into new urban policy mandates) identify the production of particular built environments and urban planning practices. This does not mean – as neoliberal rhetoric suggests – a withdrawal of the state from the "market" and the urban

Table 13.1
Canada's largest cities

Geography	Nominal GDP per capita 2009	Population size 2014
Toronto	48,532	6,055,724
Montreal	41,718	4,027,121
Vancouver	44,249	2,470,289
Calgary	61,246	1,406,721
Edmonton	59,695	1,328,290
Ottawa-Gatineau	55,506	1,318,122
Quebec	42,940	799,632
Winnipeg	42,522	782,640
Hamilton	37,057	765,228
Kitchener-Waterloo	43,989	506,858
London	41,319	502,360
Halifax	43,471	414,398
St Catherines-Niagara	33,137	405,906
Oshawa	28,918	384,143
Victoria	46,763	358,685
Windsor	36,194	333,937
Saskatoon	49,213	300,634
Regina	65,404	237,758
Sherbrooke	32,650	212,061
St John's	49,844	211,724
Barrie	30,892	200,416
Sudbury	42,138	165,690
Guelph	44,217	150,946

Sources: Statistics Canada, CANSIM, *Table 381-5000; Table 051-0056; Table 326-0022.*
Figures based on a census metropolitan area (CMA) formed by one or more adjacent
municipalities linked to a population centre (known as the core city).

political economy. Rather, the terms signal the need to investigate the specific forms of neoliberal urbanism in Canada; and the individual ways the apparatuses of each local state have been subjected to the fiscal disciplines of austerity.

URBANISM AND CAPITAL ACCUMULATION

Capitalist development pits urbanization and growth of the world market in a direct and contradictory relationship. This can be seen in Marx's theory of capital accumulation. The opening section of *Capital* points to the tension. The commodity as a use-value is always particular, worked up from specific resources by the concrete labours of workers embedded in particular social relations and communities. But the commodity as an exchange-value is universal and capitalists seek out the entire world market for its sale. Marx thus directly links local production and world trade: "The production of commodities and their circulation in its developed form, namely trade, form the historic presuppositions under which capital arises" (1867, 247). The particular and the universal, the local and the global, are different dimensions of a capitalist world market.

The dynamics of capital accumulation directly shape the built and natural environments of the urban political economy. The accumulation of capital leads to an intensification and concentration of the forces of production. The mass of fixed capital put in motion by any individual worker increases in its organic mass, technical complexity, and value. The growing organizational complexity of capital depends, in turn, upon a parallel process of "stratification." As the fixed capital required for factories and offices becomes increasingly intricate, and the technical labour required to staff these facilities also grows, government support for infrastructure, research and development, technical training, financing, and regulatory intervention becomes necessary. Government revenues and resources become progressively more mobilized in the interest of accumulating capital for the owners and senior executives of corporations. This is the idea that the accumulation of capital is the production of space as a built environment: capitalism is always urbanization. Harvey (1989b, 54) has argued that "it is through urbanization that the surpluses are mobilized, produced, absorbed, and appropriated and ... it is through urban decay and social degradation that the surpluses are devalued and destroyed." This ever-expansive capitalist logic is also a continual process of differentiation of labour processes, branches of production, working class skills, and state organization. Local capitalisms materialize from these particularities, not as isolated local economies and states, but as part of the value flows of the world market. Indeed, in the major urban centres financial capital emerges, in all its complexity and myriad forms, as the pivotal fraction of capital mediating the value flows of the world market and channelling capital into sectors of the national and regional economies; and, in turn, aggregating surplus capital and facilitating the internationalization of local and national capitals (Walker 2016). The power condensed and legitimated in the national state may ultimately set the political parameters, policy fields, and fiscal capacities of municipalities, but they cannot avoid operating within and through the local state (Gough 2014; Obeng-Odoom 2016).

It is here, in the processes of accumulation, that neoliberal urbanism needs to be situated (Brenner and Theodore 2002). Neoliberalism first appeared in the 1970s as a project to break working-class resistance to the restructuring of capital and the state. Its economic policy regime can be summarized as "market-expanding" in its regulatory focus on the market determination of distribution and allocation of output, the internationalization of capital, the monetization of the public sector, and self-regulation by market dependence for economic agents. As with any economic policy regime, neoliberalism forms within particular political strategies and is institutionally mediated within states. Neoliberal policy regulation is always, therefore, uneven and differentiated across political jurisdictions and governance scales, or "variegated" in the terminology common to urban geography (Hackworth and Moriah 2006; Peck, Theodore, and Brenner 2009b). Neoliberalism thus serves as a prelude to the fiscal retrenchment of cities and the urban, in turn, the terrain in which neoliberal practices are continually being re-invented.

Neoliberal urbanism speaks to the processes by which local states internalize the transformations of the state economic policy regime in their own forms, functions, and modes of administration and, in turn, produce the scales and spaces of neoliberalism. Local economic development strategies, for example, are re-ordered to cultivate locational competitive advantages for attracting investment, for forming financial niches (as with Toronto in the mining sector, Montreal in derivatives trading, and Vancouver in East Asia financial flows), encouraging tourism, and for building export platforms in the "new technology economy." As priority is given to the development departments of the local state, fiscal austerity tends to dominate the redistributive branches and agencies of welfare, housing, transit, and others. In contrast, empowering the policing branches of the local state serves both policy practices: "law and order" campaigns police the marginalized hit by the cuts in city budgets, while "property and security" is provided for the investors and the "creative classes" in the new economy. Neoliberal urbanism can never be reduced to a static policy manual for municipal administration; it is the social form of local rule, of urban governance, under the unrelenting pressure of fiscal constraints and austerity (Peck 2012).

NEOLIBERAL URBANISM IN CANADA

Neoliberal urbanism in Canada can, in some respects, be dated back to the 1970s with the end of the postwar "Fordist" boom and the political struggles to reorder the matrix of state policies. That more market-oriented policy practices began to break surface on the terrain of the local state in Canada is in retrospect not entirely surprising, given the openness to international capital flows and urban development of almost any kind. The federal government abandoned any overseer role in urban development in the 1970s, and housing policy reoriented to increased support for private sector mortgage markets and developers. The provinces also began to push for municipal amalgamations to bring a measure of rationalization to providing services to the sprawling "Fordist" suburbs result from the focus on the car and single-unit dwelling, and to bolster the attractiveness of cities for business investment (Filion and Kramer 2011, 203–7).

Through the 1980s state and industrial restructuring drastically increased the population dependent on welfare. Manufacturing deindustrialization both downsized workplaces and shifted many industrial plants to lower-tax, lower-unionized "greenfield" sites and ex-urban regions. At the same time, financialization led to a huge expansion of the speculative activities and bureaucracies associated with the banking and insurance sectors. With the North American free trade agreements and the increasing inter-penetration of Canadian and US capital, these economic developments intensified, while being steadily replicated across the world market. This led Toronto, Montreal, and Vancouver to stake their claim, as argued by Roger Keil and Stefan Kipfer (2003, 335–6), as "world cities" more "transnationalized" than other Canadian cities, with unique "pathways to urbanization."

In this context, neoliberalism consolidated as the policy framework through the 1990s. Under Prime Minister Brian Mulroney, the federal government began to limit fiscal transfers to the provinces in terms of equalization payments but also the funding of key social programs. The downloading process accelerated under the Liberals in the mid-1990s with the new Canada Health and Social Transfer withdrawing the federal government from direct funding of many programs as well as reducing overall transfer levels. In turn, provincial governments, freed from federal fiscal constraints and facing increased costs and less revenues, offloaded more programs and funding responsibilities onto the municipalities (table 13.2). This included their support to both cities and planning capacities of provincial municipal affairs departments.

The reorganization of multi-level governance became a pre-occupation of the Canadian state to try re-assign fiscal capacities and policy functions with a neoliberal policy regime oriented to international competitiveness as NAFTA was implemented (Andrew 2003; Donald 2005). The downloading of service provisions and responsibilities from federal and provincial governments to municipalities has been a central neoliberal policy and administrative strategy. It was a means to challenge universal non-market provision of social services, with democratic pressures to advance to higher standards, toward market provided services that are both priced and delivered at lower standards for the average user. This translated into specific policy objectives: the lowering of taxes; the withdrawal of government from providing services and pricing the rest to users as feasible; the lowering of public sector employment; norming public sector wages to lag private sector settlements; and the creation of new profit opportunities for business through privatization contracting-out, and monetization of the local state. Such new policy measures, with their new modes of urban administration, did not merely respond to the new world market configuration. They also shaped a spatial polarization in Canadian cities between inner-city gentrification and professional employment, and outer suburbs of aging residential blocks segmented by race, immigration settlement, and precarious service-sector employment (Kipfer and Keil 2002).

As a result of coping with one fiscal crisis after another across the scales of the Canadian state since the 1980s, a vast underfunding of infrastructure exists in Canada, particularly in housing and transit, but extending from urban forestry to social support facilities. In the leading cities, the shortfalls can be dramatic given the increasing demands from a booming population. With finance strapped from transfer cuts, and competitive pressures on the existing property tax base, municipal budgets increasingly depend upon development projects of all kinds to generate charges and to widen the tax base. Provincial states aided this process by deregulating municipal planning controls while leaving regional

Table 13.2
Municipal expenditure responsibilities, provinces and territories, 2008

	NF	PEI	NS	NB	QC	ON	MB	SK	AB	BC	YU	NWT	NU
General government services[1]	x	x	x	x	x	x	x	x	x	x	x	x	x
Protection of persons and property	x	x	x	x	x	x	x	x	x	x	x	x	x
Courts of law	x	x	x	x	x	x	x	x		x	x	x	x
Policing	x	x	x	x	x	x	x	x	x	x			x
Firefighting	x	x	x	x	x	x	x	x	x	x	x	x	x
Regulatory measures	x		x	x		x	x	x	x	x	x	x	x
Transportation and communication[2]	x	x	x	x	x	x	x	x	x	x	x	x	x
Public health	x	x	x	x	x	x	x	x	x	x	x	x	x
Hospital care		x			x	x	x			x			
Medical care			x	x		x	x				x		
Preventive care	x		x	x	x	x	x	x	x	x	x	x	x
Other health services	x		x		x	x	x	x	x	x	x	x	x
Social services	x	x	x		x	x	x	x	x	x		x	x
Social assistance						x	x	x	x			x	x
Other social services	x	x	x		x	x	x	x	x	x		x	x
Education	x		x	x	x		x	x	x				
Resource conservation and industrial development	x	x	x	x	x	x	x	x	x	x	x	x	x
Agriculture			x		x	x	x	x	x				
Other	x	x	x	x	x	x	x	x	x	x	x	x	x
Environment[3]	x	x	x	x	x	x	x	x	x	x	x	x	x
Recreation and culture	x	x	x	x	x	x	x	x	x	x	x	x	x
Housing	x	x	x	x	x	x	x	x	x	x	x	x	x
Regional planning and development	x	x	x	x	x	x	x	x	x	x	x	x	x

*An x denotes per capita expenditure larger than $10.
Sources: Statistics Canada, CANSIM, *Table 385-0024; Table 051-0005.*
[1] General government services includes expenditures on executive, legislative, administrative, and other services.
[2] Transportation includes expenditures on roads, snow and ice removal, parking, and public transit.
[3] Environment includes expenditures on water purification, sewage, garbage and waste collection, disposal, and other services.

planning and governance ineffectual. This "competitive city" politics is further promoted, as mapped out by Gene Desfor and his colleagues (2006), by new modes of neoliberal planning – marketization of the local state; discretionary implementation of urban design, zoning and density by-laws; business-dominated urban development corporations; subsidized knowledge industry clusters; and others. These market-expanding policies assist the developer-led boom in the inner cities in the name of densification and "smart growth," while also encouraging suburban subcentres to concentrate malls and offices and massive new housing tracts pushing against – and often breaching – "green belts" meant to border in development. Smart growth planning across Canada often looks just like more development for the assessment charges are crucial to cover the fiscal distress of municipal budgets.

This fiscal bind has led to many calls for a new urban agenda for Canada. In the early 2000s, then Prime Minister Paul Martin proposed a "new deal for cities." It was hardly visionary. It included some minor sharing of gas tax revenue to support public transport, and recycling commitments to social housing and public infrastructure. The quick ouster of Martin from office let even these modest proposals fall to the side. The Conservatives under Prime Minister Stephen Harper did next to nothing about urban issues, seeing this in strict constitutionalist terms as a matter of provincial jurisdiction. The Conservatives preferred one-off bilateral deals between the federal government and individual cities to support a specific project, such as spectacle architecture projects or world sporting events, or a public transit line here and an urban regeneration project there. None of this was remotely adequate to the build-up of problems from neoliberal urbanism (Boudreau, Keil, and Young 2009). As the case studies from Toronto, Montreal, and Vancouver below show, the asymmetrical distribution of fiscal powers and services responsibilities assigned to municipalities in the Canadian state system has led to demands for concessions from city workers, the deterioration of Canada's municipal infrastructure, and cuts to social services notably to the erosion of the affordable housing stock.

THE FISCAL CONSTRAINTS
OF URBAN GOVERNANCE IN CANADA

The Constitution Act of 1982 established both the exclusive and shared distribution of federal and provincial powers and responsibilities. Although judicial interpretation and economic developments would later weaken the strong federated model that confederation had envisaged, under Section 92(8) of the act, "municipal institutions" fell under the exclusive power of provincial legislatures. In this way, municipalities were understood to be "creatures" of provincial governments, which had the legislative power to create, modify, or eliminate a local government at will (Dewing et al. 2006). Each provincial government was – and remains – able to determine which powers a local government is entitled or responsible to execute, such as basic social services provisioning or forms of revenue generation. As well, legislation governing municipal employment falls under the purview of provincial private sector labour relations statues. Although specific responsibilities differ across the provinces, municipalities provide a range of services essential to the social, economic, and cultural well-being of municipalities. This includes general government services, policing, fire and emergency medical services, road and street maintenance, public transit, preventative health care, social assistance, water purification and supply, sewage and waste collection and disposal, recreation and culture, as well as regional planning and development. In some cases, this also includes courts of law, social assistance agricultural services, and social housing.

However, compared with governance structures across the Organization for Economic Cooperation and Development (OECD), Canadian municipalities are amongst the most restricted in terms of local autonomy and decision-making powers. This is particularly true when one considers the absence of relative fiscal independence with that found in other jurisdictions (table 13.3). Whereas property taxes account for 36 per cent of municipal revenues across the OECD, in Canada they account for more than half. The Nordic countries, Germany, and Switzerland receive over 90 per cent of their tax revenue from income taxes, while Hungary and the Netherlands collect between 50 and 75 per cent of local revenue from various sales taxes. The same is true in France, Japan, Korea, and the US where sales taxes comprise about 20 per cent of local revenue. Yet, income and sales taxes are largely prohibited across Canadian municipalities (FCM, 2012). The result is an asymmetric assignment of responsibility and power, with municipalities largely tasked with providing services in the absence of adequate fiscal capacities.

Despite a range of forms of revenue generation, Canadian municipalities remain largely dependent on transfers and revenue generated from taxing property and development. As a percentage of own-source property tax revenues, this ranges from a low of 53 per cent in Manitoba to a high of 76 per cent in Quebec. But municipalities' near singular dependence

Table 13.3
Municipal tax measures across Canadian provinces

	BC[1]	AB[2]	SK[3]	MB[4]	ON[5]	QC[6]	NB[7]	NS[8]	PEI	NFL[9]
Property tax	√	√	√	√	√	√	√	√	√	√
Business tax		√	√			√	√			√
Area/improvement/ service area/parcel	√	√	√	√	√	√		√	√	
Road pricing and taxes	√				√	√				
Equipment tax		√	√	√						√
Fuel tax	√					√	√			√
Hotel tax	√	√	√	√		√	√	√	√	√
Amusement tax					√	√				√
Sin tax					√					
Advertising tax					√	√				
Income/poll tax										√

Source: British Columbia Ministry of Community, Sport and Cultural Development, 2012.
[1] BC: Road pricing/taxes and fuel taxes in BC apply to Translink in the GVRD only.
[2] Alberta: Destination marketing fees are voluntary in Edmonton, Calgary, Lethbridge, Medicine Hat, Canmore, and Jasper.
[3] Saskatchewan: Destination marketing fee in Regina and Saskatoon only.
[4] Manitoba: Amusement tax applies to the City of Winnipeg only.
[5] Ontario: Road pricing/taxes, amusement tax, sin tax, and advertising tax apply to the City of Toronto only.
[6] Quebec: Road pricing/taxes and fuel tax apply to the Transportation Agency of Montreal. Amusement tax applies to the City of Montreal only.
[7] New Brunswick: Destination marketing fee in Saint John, Bathurst, Fredericton only.
[8] Nova Scotia: Hotel tax in the Halifax Regional Municipality only.
[9] Newfoundland and Labrador: Fuel tax, hotel tax and amusement tax apply to City of St John's only.

on property taxes is problematic for a number of reasons (tables 13.4 and 13.5). First, unlike income taxes, which are withheld at the source, and sales taxes, which are paid in small amounts with each purchase, property taxes generally have to be paid directly in the form of periodic lump sum payments. Because the ability to make these payments requires advanced savings or increases in debt, the saliency of property taxes disproportionately impacts low-income households and seniors, who may be asset rich but income poor. Second, unlike income tax, corporate tax, and sales taxes, property taxes do not increase in tandem with economic growth. This income inelasticity results in an improvised and politically driven process whereby annual increases are usually necessary in order to maintain the property tax base. Fiscal supports to cities thus often fail to match new demands on city budgets. The property tax system, under pressures from business and the logic of neoliberalism, has also seen a decline on business levies on commercial property and an increase on residential property taxes. By adding to the regressivity of the overall tax system, neoliberals in Canada have encouraged a property tax revolt at the municipal level.[1]

In the absence of broad-based consumption taxes such as on income and sales, transfers as a whole represent more than 20 per cent of local government revenues, and in some cases much higher. These transfers go towards covering the costs of programs administered locally, but a significant majority of provincial transfers are conditional, meaning they must go toward expenditures mandated by senior levels of government, although some are matching grants that require equal contribution from receiving governments. Despite a range of governance arrangements across the provinces and territories, municipal fiscal crises have been a chronic feature of Canadian urbanism for several decades as fiscal capacities could not keep up with increased demands for services, urbanization, and pressures related to amalgamation (Young and Horak 2012; Bradford 2007). These pressures have been amplified in the context of provincial and federal devolution, which have shifted the costs of social and physical infrastructure onto lower tiers of government. Although the federal government has no constitutionally prescribed municipal responsibilities, almost all of its decisions affect municipalities in one way or another. However, except for some grants, bilateral agreements, and emergency relief, the federal role in municipal affairs over the last thirty years have generally revolved around ad hoc agreements, selective activism, and targeted expenditures. An example is the *Building Canada Infrastructure Plan*, which provided a one-time $40 billion fund for municipal infrastructure between 2007 and 2014, with much of this support then being allocated to individual projects. But one-time fiscal injections (as opposed to dedicated revenue streams) will do little to reverse long-term trends, such as Vancouver's affordable housing shortage or the crisis of infrastructure in Montreal. This reflects the absence in Canada of a national policy for cities (unique among advanced capitalist states) or for urban funding of crucial infrastructure, transportation, housing, immigration, and anti-poverty initiatives.

After declining across the 1990s, per capita total municipal expenditures in Canada modestly increased in the 2000s, particularly as municipal responsibilities were realigned from government downloading, policy

Table 13.4
Municipal expenditures, provinces and territories, 2008 and 2013

Geography	Per capita municipal expenditure (2007$)		Municipal expenditure as % of provincial GDP		Municipal expenditure as % of total provincial-municipal expenditures	
	2008	2013	2008	2013	2008	2013
Newfoundland	759.4	1011.8	1.4	1.9	6.4	7.7
Prince Edward Island	535.4	543.2	1.6	1.6	5.3	5.2
Nova Scotia	1320.9	1447.4	3.6	3.8	14.2	15.0
New Brunswick	868.2	970.1	2.3	2.6	8.9	9.6
Quebec	1441.9	1578.5	3.6	3.9	13.8	14.3
Ontario	2109.1	2202.2	4.5	4.7	27.0	26.1
Manitoba	939.5	1333.6	2.2	3.0	9.9	13.3
Saskatchewan	1352.5	1405.5	2.5	2.5	12.3	12.3
Alberta	1771.2	1986.8	2.4	2.6	17.0	20.5
British Columbia	1391.6	1485.6	3.0	3.2	16.9	18.2
Yukon	1478.4	1748.4	2.4	2.7	5.9	6.0
Northwest Territories	2456.3	2752.2	2.5	3.3	7.7	8.1
Nunavut	4853.9	4267.8	10.2	7.7	11.4	9.4
Canada	1682.6	1813.9	3.5	3.7	18.4	19.0

Sources: Statistics Canada, CANSIM, Table 051-0005; Table 384-0038; Table 385-0037; Table 326-0022.

budgets expanded, and economic growth slowed. In contrast, per capita municipal revenues stagnated as intergovernmental transfers declined, and municipalities had to rely on own-source revenues, particularly property taxes but also "new revenue tools" such as increased user fees and new taxes. As a consequence, for some two-decades expenditure pressures on Canadian cities has been outstripping revenue sources, with a low-tax regime locked in across all scales of the Canadian state (FCM 2012, 2–14; Table 13.6). For the local state in Canada, this has precipitated continual bouts of labour conflict, an astonishing infrastructure deficit estimated at more than $1.1 trillion (Table 9), and a strain on local services – in some cases to a breaking point, as with all kinds of

Table 13.5
Distribution of municipal expenditures and revenues, provinces and territories, 2013

	NL	PEI	NS	NB	QC	ON	MB	SK	AB	BC	YU	NWT	NU	CAN
PER CAPITA MUNICIPAL EXPENDITURES ($)	1012	543	1447	970	1578	2202	1334	1405	1987	1486	1748	2752	4268	1814
MUNICIPAL EXPENDITURES TYPE:														
General public services	33.8	35.6	9.5	14.2	23.7	40.5	26.2	21.8	46.4	17.3	27.1	42.1	21.6	33.4
Defence	0.0	0.0	0.0	0.0	0.0	0.0	0.0	0.0	0.0	0.0	0.0	0.0	0.0	0.0
Public order and safety	9.5	19.5	23.3	28.8	15.6	7.7	25.3	21.1	14.3	24.0	11.4	4.5	3.0	13.2
Economic affairs	20.0	12.6	14.6	17.5	24.3	12.2	19.8	20.0	16.5	13.4	18.6	14.3	18.6	15.9
Environmental protection	12.1	4.6	12.1	14.2	15.0	6.3	2.3	9.2	4.0	11.4	14.3	4.5	3.0	8.5
Housing and community amenities	12.9	19.5	7.6	13.4	5.5	5.9	20.5	11.6	7.9	13.8	7.1	18.8	32.3	7.7
Health	0.0	0.0	6.3	0.1	1.2	2.5	0.4	0.0	0.0	1.2	0.0	0.0	4.2	1.7
Recreation, culture, and religion	11.7	10.3	11.5	11.8	11.4	5.4	5.1	15.8	9.2	17.9	21.4	15.0	16.2	9.0
Education	0.0	0.0	15.2	0.0	0.1	0.0	0.2	0.0	0.0	0.0	0.0	0.0	0.0	0.4
Social protection	0.0	0.0	0.0	0.0	3.1	19.5	0.2	0.5	1.7	0.9	0.0	0.8	1.2	10.1
Total expenditure	100	100	100	100	100	100	100	100	100	100	100	100	100	100

PER CAPITA MUNICIPAL REVENUES ($)	1409	780	1717	1435	2088	2732	1789	2172	3206	2026	2173	4490	5862	2414
MUNICIPAL REVENUE SOURCE:														
Own source														
Taxes on property	44.5	37.6	68.2	54.0	60.4	45.6	39.7	26.7	42.2	48.4	44.8	18.0	6.1	48.0
Taxes on goods and services	5.2	0.8	0.4	2.7	2.4	7.3	7.5	20.7	14.4	8.9	2.3	1.8	0.9	7.7
Other taxes	0.7	0.0	0.0	0.0	0.0	0.0	0.0	0.0	0.0	0.0	0.0	0.0	0.0	0.0
Property income	1.0	0.0	0.3	0.3	1.4	1.9	1.8	2.2	2.6	4.3	1.1	0.9	2.2	2.1
Sales of goods and services	20.9	23.2	21.2	22.9	20.6	20.8	25.8	29.9	21.2	34.1	23.0	18.4	31.6	22.7
Fines, penalties, and forfeits	0.2	0.8	0.7	0.2	2.1	0.9	0.8	0.9	1.4	0.0	1.1	0.9	0.0	1.1
Voluntary transfers (not grants)	0.0	0.0	0.0	0.4	0.0	0.2	0.0	0.0	0.0	0.0	0.0	0.0	0.4	0.1
Miscellaneous revenue	0.0	0.0	0.0	0.0	0.1	0.0	0.0	0.0	0.0	0.0	0.0	0.0	0.0	0.0
Total own-source revenue	72.6	62.4	90.8	80.5	87.0	76.7	75.7	80.4	81.8	95.8	72.4	40.1	41.2	81.8
Grants from general government units	27.4	37.6	9.2	19.5	13.0	23.3	24.3	19.6	18.2	4.2	27.6	59.9	58.8	18.2
Total revenue	100	100	100	100	100	100	100	100	100	100	100	100	100	100

Sources: Statistics Canada, CANSIM, *Table 385-0037*; *Table 326-0022*.

social housing. Urban austerity is the means by which these problems emerge, but the economic constraints that impose them cannot be resolved within the local political economy.

A new phase of austerity urbanism has emerged since the 2008 recession (Davidson and Ward 2014; Peck 2014). This has included tax-shifting for competitiveness, reductions to social services provisioning, contracting-out and privatization of city assets, concessions from unionized and non-unionized municipal employees, new forms of marketization such as the use of public-private partnerships, and a shift away from commercial property taxes to consumption-based levies. New workplace arrangements have also proliferated, including the use of part-time and short-term contracts, as well as casual and seasonal forms of employment, as the case of Toronto illustrates. This has often incorporated new restrictions on workers' rights to unionize and bargain collectively. Reductions to employee compensation have been an aim of urban austerity.

However, while total employee wage compensation by the local government sector amounted to 5.8 per cent of GDP in 1992, it has steadily declined since then, dropping to 4 per cent of GDP in 2007. It increased as a share of GDP during the 2008 recession (4.69 per cent of GDP) as the underlying economy itself shrank, but has since fluctuated, declining to 4.2 per cent of GDP in 2012 and rising to 4.93 per cent in 2014. Average weekly wages paid by municipal and regional governments rose from $622.67 in 1992 to $952.86 in 2012, a compound annual increase of 2 per cent a year. This works out to annual pay of $49,549 in 2012. However, average pay for those paid by the hour at the local government level was considerably lower averaging roughly $40,000 in 2012. In comparison, overall average weekly earnings increased at an annual average rate of 2.3 per cent since 1992, rising to $871 weekly in 2012 and $45,292 annually. Since 2000, local government wages have also increased at a slower annual rate than the overall average (2.5 per cent versus 2.9 per cent).[2] The efforts to reduce municipal workers' compensation stem not from overgenerous pay or out-of-control municipal finances, but reflect the neoliberal political project of harmonizing downwards the wages and working conditions of municipal workers while privatizing public services.

FLASHPOINTS OF URBAN AUSTERITY

Toronto: Toronto provides a vivid portrait of a local government seeking to extract wage and benefit concessions from workers, while reducing

Table 13.6
Intergovernmental grants as a percentage of municipal
expenditures, 2008 and 2013[1]

Geography	2008	2013
Newfoundland	58.3	38.2
Prince Edward Island	25.0	54.0
Nova Scotia	13.0	10.9
New Brunswick	33.7	28.8
Quebec	17.5	17.2
Ontario	25.6	28.9
Manitoba	39.8	32.6
Saskatchewan	45.3	30.3
Alberta	38.2	29.4
British Columbia	11.5	5.8
Yukon	38.0	34.3
Northwest Territories	137.6	97.7
Nunavut	66.5	80.7
Canada	25.0	24.2

Sources: Statistics Canada, CANSIM, Table 385-0037;
Table 326-0022.
[1] Intergovernmental grants refer to any grants received
by local governments from the federal or provincial
governments.

social services provisioning (Fanelli 2016). This was brought to a head
during the 2009 round of collective bargaining between the city of
Toronto and its civic workers represented by Canadian Union of Public
Employees (CUPE) Locals 79 and 416.[3] A number of issues were central
to this round of bargaining, including attempts to: weaken job security
provisions and seniority rights; limit transfers and promotion; impose a
freeze on cost-of-living; implement two-tier wages; increase the contracting-out of employment; and expand managerial control over the labour
process. The city contended that due to the recession and lower than
expected revenues, it was necessary to reduce municipal wages and benefits in order to meet its fiscal challenges (see table 13.7). Workers countered that there was little evidence to support such a claim – as reports

by KPMG would confirm – that the city's fiscal challenges were tied to overgenerous social services or excessive public sector compensation. After six months of bargaining without a contract, in June of 2009 both CUPE locals went on strike.

The locals were unprepared strategically and tactically, but also politically. There was a lack of experienced organizers leading the strike, workers had not been booked off ahead of time in order to inform the membership of the issues involved and prepare members for strike duties. Importantly, there was an absence of strike politicization and making the connection between the users and producers of public services. After thirty-nine days on strike, the city and unions reached an agreement. Economically, both locals managed to fight off major concessionary demands to freeze wages, implement a multi-tiered wage system and limit seniority-based promotion; and the locals gained an average annual 2 per cent wage increase over three years. But part-timers did not see any extension of benefits. The strike was, moreover, a political failure when it came to mobilizing sustained action and education, garnering public support as well as linking the defense of unionized workplaces with fighting for workers in non-unionized jobs, the underemployed, and unemployed.

Following on the heels of the strike, city council implemented a 5 per cent target for cuts across all departments, while moving forward with new tax and user-fee hikes. The next election saw the most fiscally conservative councillor in the previous term, Rob Ford, elected as the new mayor of Toronto. Ford used the 2009 strike to direct public anger and frustration toward so-called lavish union wages and wasteful city spending. While his term was turbulent to say the least, the 2012 round of bargaining did not see a repeat of the 2009 strike. It did, however, confirm that previous rounds had merely prepared the ground for even further austerity.

The new agreement included language that allowed the city to unilaterally make changes to shift schedules so long as employees are served notice. Job performance criteria could now be used to determine shifts and scheduling. The new contract removed a letter of agreement that provided protection to all permanent employees regarding contracting-out or technological displacement. Under the new agreement, the threshold of protection was reduced from covering all workers to only those with at least fifteen years of seniority (a decrease of coverage from 100 to about 68 per cent of employees). The city reduced the amount of coverage for health and dental benefits by some $20–35 million, and

Table 13.7
Distribution of municipal expenditures and revenues, Toronto, 2008 and 2014

	TORONTO			
	2008 (2007 $)	2014 (2007 $)	2008 (%)	2014 (%)
MUNICIPAL EXPENDITURES				
General government	650,889,648	710,042,705	8.3	7.6
Protection to persons and property	1,390,273,438	1,619,282,918	17.8	17.4
Transportation	1,763,558,594	2,508,599,644	22.6	27.0
Environmental services	589,008,789	817,797,153	7.5	8.8
Health services	360,129,883	382,109,431	4.6	4.1
Social and family services	1,752,232,422	1,704,430,605	22.4	18.3
Social housing	545,795,898	647,433,274	7.0	7.0
Recreational and cultural services	667,658,203	810,879,004	8.5	8.7
Planning and development	97,259,766	106,928,826	1.2	1.1
Total	7,816,806,641	9,307,503,559	100.0	100.0
MUNICIPAL REVENUES				
Property taxes	3,290,965,820	3,352,321,174	35.4	33.5
Municipal land transfer tax	161,858,398	400,003,559	1.7	4.0
Taxation from other governments	78,818,359	99,286,477	0.8	1.0
User charges	2,059,006,836	2,449,531,139	22.2	24.5
Government transfers	2,170,526,367	2,448,498,221	23.4	24.5
Government enterprise earnings	228,561,523	65,196,619	2.5	0.7
Investment income	161,811,523	240,750,000	1.7	2.4
Development charges	N.A.	117,903,025	N.A.	1.2
Rent and concessions	N.A.	379,830,071	N.A.	3.8
Other	1,138,202,148	455,235,765	12.3	4.5
Total	9,289,750,977	10,008,556,050	100.0	100.0
Annual operating surplus/deficit	1,472,944,336	701,052,491		

Sources: City of Toronto, *Financial Report: 2014*; City of Toronto, *Financial Report: 2008*; Statistics Canada, CANSIM *Table 326-0022.*

also eliminated post-retirement benefits of $54 million. Finally, in return for giving up a significant portion of their job security, workers received a one-time bonus of 1.5 percent, 0 per cent in 2012, 0.5 per cent in 2013, 1.75 per cent in 2014, and 2.25 in 2015.

This was, and in many ways remains, a significant defeat for civic workers. In the absence of a cohesive strategy from municipal unions and sustained political mobilization from community groups, CUPE was unable to challenge the growing precarization of employment. If this is to be reversed a number of initiatives must be placed front and centre. This includes struggles to contract-in services previously outsourced and a greater emphasis on improving the working conditions and employment security for the city's growing part-time labour force. Community-union campaigns against privatization that seek to enhance both the universality and quality of public services, from the transit system to parks to waste collection, will be essential to any feasible challenges to neoliberal urbanism as this cannot be done only within collective bargaining.

Montreal: Montreal best reflects the lack of fiscal independence and the severe crisis of infrastructure plaguing municipalities (table 13.8). An increasing number of studies have drawn attention to Canada's infrastructure needs (Canadian Chamber of Commerce 2013; CCPA 2013; Canada West Foundation 2013). Canada's municipal infrastructure deficit rose fivefold between 1985 and 2003 from $12 billion to $60 billion, reaching $123 billion by 2007. It is expected to reach $400 billion by 2020, and as much as $2 trillion by 2065 if present trends continue.[4] This includes everything from waste and water systems, to transportation and transit, waste management, community, and recreational and cultural infrastructure. As maintenance and new investments are delayed, the municipal infrastructure deficit grows as assets reach the end of their service life, and repair and replacement costs rise as infrastructure deterioration accelerates with age. Unlike other tiers of government, municipalities cannot run operating deficits. This puts pressure on municipal capital budgets, which do not face the same immediate demands for service provision as operating expenditures, making capital investments easier to delay. This is compounded by the fact that municipalities receive roughly eight cents of every dollar collected in total taxes across all levels of government. As such, it is not possible to finance municipal investments in infrastructure through property taxes alone.

In 1961, the federal government controlled some 23.9 per cent of the national capital stock, while provincial/territorial and municipal governments each had 45.3 per cent and 30.9 per cent. Between 1955 and 1977,

Table 13.8
Distribution of municipal expenditures and revenues, Montreal, 2008 and 2014

| | MONTREAL | | | |
	2008 (2007 $)	2014 (2007 $)	2008 (%)	2014 (%)
MUNICIPAL EXPENDITURES			percentage of total	
General administration	504,958,984	668,506,228	9.9	13.2
Public safety	895,950,195	962,900,356	17.5	19.1
Transportation	1,844,259,766	1,614,847,865	36.1	32.0
Environmental health	514,967,773	525,620,107	10.1	10.4
Health and welfare	126,056,641	119,417,260	2.5	2.4
Urban planning and development	231,656,250	190,623,665	4.5	3.8
Recreation and culture	548,153,320	551,555,160	10.7	10.9
Financing expenses	445,302,734	415,161,032	8.7	8.2
Total	5,111,305,664	5,048,631,673	100.0	100.0
MUNICIPAL REVENUES				
Taxes	2,613,351,563	2,709,651,246	54.6	48.5
Payments in lieu of taxes	220,730,469	223,271,352	4.6	4.0
Quota shares	N.A.	356,380,783	N.A.	6.4
Transfers	612,804,688	827,903,915	12.8	14.8
Services rendered	772,462,891	850,183,274	16.1	15.2
Fee collection	125,594,727	166,566,726	2.6	3.0
Fines and penalties	154,914,063	158,690,391	3.2	2.8
Interest	122,084,961	115,508,007	2.5	2.1
Other revenues	167,222,656	179,896,797	3.5	3.2
Total	4,789,166,016	5,588,052,491	100.0	100.0
ANNUAL OPERATING SURPLUS/DEFICIT	- 322,139,648	539,420,819		

Sources: Ville de Montréal, Annual Financial Report: 2014; Ville de Montréal, Annual Financial Report: 2008; Statistics Canada, CANSIM, Table 326-0022.

new investment averaged 4.8 per cent annually, roughly paralleling increases in population growth and the rate of urbanization. The two decades following this period, however, saw new investment grow on average just 0.1 per cent per year. As a result, 28 per cent of municipal infrastructure is now more than eighty years old, with one-third between forty to eighty years.[5] By 2002, the federal share of new infrastructure investment had dropped more than 70 per cent to just 6.8 per cent, while the municipal share rose to 52.4 per cent. As the most recent Canadian Infrastructure Report Card (table 13.9) shows, municipal infrastructure across Canada, along with the institutional frameworks that finance these assets, is in dire need of repair.

In Montreal, these concerns turned into tragedy with the de la Concorde overpass collapse in 2006 that killed five people and seriously injured six others. After the collapse, a commission headed by former Quebec premier Pierre-Marc Johnson found that nearly half of all bridges in the province were structurally deficient and needed replacement within five years. In March 2011, two engineering reports on Montreal's Champlain Bridge – one of Canada's longest and busiest bridges at 6 km in length and handling 160,000 daily crossings – said the structure was in a state of severe deterioration and that a partial or complete failure could not be ruled out. After the reports were released, the Archdiocese of Montreal erected a billboard at the entrance to the bridge advising motorists to "Faites votre prière." In 2011, a fifteen-metre-long, twenty-five-tonne chunk of concrete fell onto the Ville-Marie expressway where it collapsed on a vehicle, narrowly missing its occupants. Between 2010 and 2013 there were at least seven incidents of falling concrete, including major sinkholes and highway flooding. In light of major cracks discovered in the Turcot Interchange in early 2011, Transport Quebec identified another forty-seven locations in need of immediate repair (Riga 2013).

Many red flags concerning Montreal's deteriorating infrastructure had been raised prior to these events. A 2010 report by Montreal auditor-general, Jacques Bergeron, examined 555 pieces of infrastructure under local jurisdiction. He concluded that twelve were in critical condition, forty-four were deficient, thirty-eight were mediocre, and another eighty-one were rapidly deteriorating. Bergeron found that more than 30 per cent of Montreal's bridges, tunnels and overpasses needed work, with 65 per cent of the city's tunnels, roadways, and sewer systems more than half a century old (BVG 2010). Roughly 33 per cent of Montreal's water-distribution pipes have already reached the end of their service lives, with another 34 per cent of the water-pipe stock estimated to reach the same state by 2020. This has contributed to the loss of about 40 per cent of the clean water the city treats due to leaky conduits and has been singled out as one of the likely causes of major sinkholes across the city. Bergeron

Table 13.9
Canada's municipal infrastructure deficit[1]

Infrastructure	Extrapolated replacement value of all assets (billions $)	ASSETS IN VERY POOR AND POOR CONDITION	ASSETS IN FAIR PHYSICAL CONDITION
		Replacement value (billions $)	
Potable water	207	25 (12%)	35 (17%)
Wastewater	234	26 (11%)	56 (24%)
Stormwater	134	10 (7%)	21 (16%)
Roads	330	48 (15%)	75 (23%)
Bridges	50	2 (4%)	11 (22%)
Buildings	70	12 (17%)	20 (28%)
Sport and recreation facilities	51	9 (18%)	14 (27%)
Transit	57	9 (16%)	15 (27%)
Total	1,133	141 (12%)	247 (22%)
Replacement value per household	80,000	10,000	18,000

Source: *Informing the Future: Canadian Infrastructure Report Card* (2016), p.12.
[1] All infrastructure reported as in further declining condition based on anticipated reinvestment levels (except for transit as data is unavailable).

also drew attention to the ethical conduct of city officials citing widespread corruption and collusion for municipal contracts awarded for the development, rehabilitation, and replacement of facilities and infrastructure assets that were found to have squandered public monies amid a lack of oversight.

In his 2013 annual report, Bergeron argued that chronic underfunding of infrastructure was hastening the deterioration of these assets noting that road and sidewalk maintenance in Montreal was underfunded by $100 million in 2010 and 2011, and that the city must now spend $178 million annually just to keep up with maintenance. Bergeron wrote (2013, 12): "If nothing is done to remedy the situation the city could find itself in a critical position, in which the ensuing backlog would be difficult and very costly to address ... There is an undeniable link between the state of disrepair of the city's assets and level of quality and compliance of the materials used. Although this is not the only underlying cause of the precarious state of municipal infrastructure, it is reasonable to conclude that the lack of quality control with regard to the materials used could be one of the driving factors behind the poor condition of these assets. Furthermore, it is disturbing to realize that past infrastructure investments may have been made without a comprehensive quality control process in place to ensure the materials and installation adhered to strict standards." In November 2015, Montreal began diverting 8 billion litres of untreated sewage into the St Lawrence River. This was to complete repairs on an aging interceptor tunnel that feeds sewage to a treatment facility as well as to relocate a snow chute (Banerjee 2015).

The deferral of much-needed investments in infrastructure has exacerbated the deteriorating state of the built environment of Canada's cities. As capitalism develops, and existing infrastructure ages and new investments to support accumulation are required, ever-increasing portions of urban budgets have to be devoted to these purposes. The policy regime of urban neoliberalism in Canada runs completely counter to these forces and pushes one city after another into fiscal distress. The various forms of privatization and public-private partnerships have attempted to leverage increased funds for infrastructure, but only compound the underlying fiscal impasse. This can only be reversed by community-union led anti-privatization struggles seeking to restore and expand local planning capacities, and an extension of democratic inputs and control over the administration of public assets and common goods. But such an anti-austerity agenda cannot be limited to individual cities. Extra-local urban policies at the provincial and national levels to coordinate and finance a long-term public investment plan (taking advantage of historically low yields on bonds with long maturities) are also needed to break urban austerity and repair the dilapidated state of infrastructure.

Vancouver: Federal and provincial withdrawal from social services provisioning combined with the erosion of intergovernmental transfers lies at the heart of Vancouver's affordable housing crisis. Compounding these concerns is the general weakness and administrative fracturing of municipal governance. Lack of affordable housing often overlaps with many other social issues, including homelessness, addictions, lack of health and other social services, an absence of quality employment, and mounting local pressures (table 13.10). A number of authors have documented the historical development and transformation of social housing policy (Rose 1983; Hulchanski 2007; Pomeroy and Falvo 2013). The year 1993 is noteworthy in this regard as it marks the beginning of the end of Canada's national housing program. The federal government announced that, with the exception of on-reserve Indigenous housing, there would be no new commitments for social housing. Federal subsidies for existing units were set to end over the next thirty years as mortgages expired, with a steep drop-off expected around 2020 (Chisholm 2003). This was compounded over the decade by rent control liberalization, a near absence of private sector rental property development, and broad cuts to a range of welfare programs. As a consequence, while total population grew 6.9 per cent between 1990 and 1995, poverty rates in metropolitan areas grew by 33.8 per cent, with Indigenous populations experiencing urban poverty rates at twice the national average. The federal government's embrace of neoliberalism and cuts of the 1990s occurred alongside provincial and municipal fiscal erosion in British Columbia.

In 2001, the provincial Liberal government of Gordon Campbell reduced the minimum wage by $2/hour, cut funding for women's centres and social assistance, sold-off public assets such as BC Railway, and opened-up collective agreements so as to allow for the privatization of health, education, and social services. Non-profit organizations were urged to explore partnerships with the private sector in the absence of provincial funding for social housing (Isitt 2008). By 2004, there were more than 11,000 households on BC Housing's applicant registry. It is estimated that there are an additional 40,000 "hidden homeless" who sleep with family, in cars, or couch surf, and another 60,000 people at risk of becoming homeless because they spend more than 50 per cent of their income on rent (Social Housing BC n.d.). As Vert (2005, 64) notes: "The case of BC Housing is one where a federal withdrawal in turn prompted a provincial withdrawal in order to cope, fiscally speaking. From here, the impact goes directly to the municipalities."

Rapidly escalating real estate prices as a result of land-use deregulation, an influx of foreign capital investing in the housing market, and state divestment from social welfare have contributed to a chronic affordability crisis in Vancouver's housing market. Between 2007 and 2012, average monthly rent rose nearly 17 per cent from $898 to $1,047, while the average cost of a detached home rose from $700,000 to nearly $900,000. Rental vacancies dropped to 0.8 per cent as of October 2015, down from 1.7 percent in 2013, and compared to the national average of 3.3 percent (CMHC 2015). As a result, rents have increased on average by 3.9 per cent since 2014 and 9.3 per cent since 2012, with average rents totalling $1,144 (CMHC 2015). By the end of 2015, the average detached house price in Vancouver was $1,567,500, resulting in 52 per cent of all Vancouver houses costing greater than $1,000,000 (CMHC 2016). Meanwhile, the number of homes for less than $385,000 purchased by

Table 13.10
Distribution of municipal expenditures and revenues, Vancouver, 2008 and 2014

| | VANCOUVER | | | |
	2008 (2007 $)	2014 (2007 $)	2008 (%)	2014 (%)
MUNICIPAL EXPENDITURES			percentage of total	
General government	135,761,719	217,840,747	10.5	18.2
Utilities	220,608,398	154,565,836	17.0	12.9
Police protection	207,083,008	234,463,523	16.0	19.6
Fire protection	86,193,359	96,164,591	6.6	8.0
Engineering	193,489,258	163,040,925	14.9	13.6
Planning and development	69,950,195	22,760,676	5.4	1.9
Parks and recreation	209,839,844	160,361,210	16.2	13.4
Community and cultural services	175,379,883	93,699,288	13.5	7.8
Other	N.A.	55,670,819	N.A.	4.6
Total	1,298,305,664	1,198,567,616	100.0	100.0
MUNICIPAL REVENUES				
Property taxes, penalties, and interest	538,197,266	597,458,185	47.0	43.0
Utility fees	153,134,766	197,157,473	13.4	14.2
Other fees, rates, and cost recoveries	344,963,867	N.A.	30.1	N.A.
Program fees	N.A.	92,843,416	N.A.	6.7
Bylaw fines	N.A.	14,085,409	N.A.	1.0
License and development fees	N.A.	57,909,253	N.A.	4.2
Parking	N.A.	68,969,751	N.A.	5.0
Revenue sharing, grants, and contributions	24,380,859	248,616,548	2.1	17.9
Investment income	35,965,820	24,814,947	3.1	1.8
Rental and lease income	46,782,227	62,738,434	4.1	4.5
Sale of property	1,548,828	25,178,826	0.1	1.8
Total	1,144,973,633	1,389,772,242	100.0	100.0
ANNUAL OPERATING SURPLUS/DEFICIT	- 153,332,031	191,204,626		

Sources: City of Vancouver, British Columbia, *Annual Financial Report: 2014*; City of Vancouver, British Columbia, *Annual Financial Report: 2008*; Statistics Canada, CANSIM, *Table 326-0022*.

first-time buyers dropped from 12,000 to 8,563, with average first-time homebuyer house prices in Vancouver approaching $506,500 (BMO 2014). It should come as no surprise, then, that *The Economist* ranked Vancouver as the most expensive city in North America to live in, while *Demographia* ranked it the second-least affordable in the world (Huffington Post 2013, 2015). Wages in Vancouver grew by 36 per cent between 2001 and 2014, whereas house values soared by 211 per cent (VanCity 2015; CBC 2015; SCMP 2015).

The provisions of quality, affordable housing is, of course, a complex distributional issue of social policy and development planning not resolved at the local level. BC municipalities (as elsewhere in Canada) have generally preferred voluntary agreements and incentives for developers, rather than mandatory measures. But these neoliberal market measures to leverage private developers into low-cost housing have clearly failed, and the limited fiscal capacities of cities have allowed the social housing stock to deteriorate and homeless programs and shelters to become a policy of crisis management. This does not mean, however, that municipalities are impotent. Anti-poverty and community struggles directed at the local state can yield any number of practical reforms: regulatory changes providing for the legalization of secondary units; density and development agreements mandating affordable and rental housing; dedicated provisioning of land for supportive housing; prohibition on the conversion of rental suites and dedicated development levies that go into a fund for affordable housing; levies to discourage quick "flipping" and housing market speculation; limitations on foreign and domestic ownership of "investment" (non-primary residence) properties; and review of by-laws and building regulations to encourage new multi-unit dwellings (SPARC 2009). But ultimately these local struggles need to insist on a decommodification of housing, in general, in the forms of public, non-profit, and cooperative housing to address affordability. Here, any number of transitional reforms are possible, such as new regional-local coordination in housing policy and, more ambitiously, the re-ordering of federal and provincial financial policies for housing programs.

URBAN FRACTURES AND LOCAL LEFTS

These points of contention within Canada's three largest cities are illustrations of the fractures in the urban political economy of Canada. Neoliberal urbanism never takes a singular form, unfolding as a variegated social process, each city becoming its own terrain of experimentation in new modes of administration. A tally of these modes could easily be multiplied: the utter failure to sustain low-cost public transit; the vulgar monetization and commodification of public spaces; the lack of any coherent strategy to address the degradation of work conditions and wages for precarious and immigrant workers; the undermining of public planning capacities to control urban sprawl or match densification with adequate infrastructure; and too many others. If capitalism produces urban space integral to its "laws of development," neoliberal urbanism always internalizes the disjunctures and antagonisms between the global accumulation imperatives of capital and the historic "life-places" of workers and their communities.

In Canada, the asymmetries in fiscal capacities across the scales of governance refract into the urban political economy as a constantly shifting constraint on the parameters of local policy-making (Kalman-Lamb 2017). In a quite formal way, the essential extra-market functions that cities provide in the building of urban space are always in a position of financial constraint from the fiscal paternalism embedded in Canadian federalism and constitutionalism. There is, in a sense, a state of permanent fiscal crisis in municipal finances in Canada, leaving Canadian localities always to beg for "new deals" – as the Federation of Canadian Municipalities continues to do, under one name or another.

The neoliberal fiscal practice of downloading administrative responsibilities without parallel fiscal capacities to subnational and local states has been a particularly powerful incubator of urban austerity. Indeed, the general adoption of a fiscal regime of austerity across the scales of governance, in response to the continued economic turbulence from the financial crisis of 2008–10, has led to further closure of fiscal space at the local level (Fujita 2013; Phillips-Fein 2017). Neoliberal urbanism can be expected – as in the areas of employee relations, infrastructure, and housing used as exemplars here – to undergo even more innovation, policing, privatization, monetization, and defunding. The fiscal distress of local states in Canada, under the continual pressures of providing for the urbanization of capital accumulation, already is cause to all kinds of political contortions and grotesque social inequalities in an impossible effort to manage this contradiction of capitalist cities.

Canadian cities have been the stage for any number of campaigns of resistance to neoliberal urbanism – the "sanctuary city" project to protect undocumented workers; the "riders" campaigns for affordable public transit; the "Fight for $15" living wage mobilization; the "union-community" alliances to protect municipal services from cuts and privatization; the urban ecology movements insisting on cities address climate change by blocking pipeline expansion for transporting fossil fuels from the Tar Sands and the expansion of parks and green spaces; and many others. In municipalities across Canada, there have been a slew of petitions, disruptions of council proceedings, occupations, demonstrations, community watches of police, neighbourhood rallies – a part of the pattern of everyday urban life. But these have largely remained defensive reactions to the latest austerity initiative, and suffering battle fatigue from years of campaigning, with every gain under a threat from a new round of austerity, and every zone of failure open to right-wing populism (Kipfer and Saberi 2015).

In Vancouver and Montreal (and to a lesser extent Winnipeg), the Left has historically formed wider political groupings. But these have all been more citywide electoral pacts than political and campaigning organizations of the Left to develop an alternate agenda for urban space and to contest the capitalist city. In Toronto, the NDP has a quite loose municipal caucus, and it has been years since a socialist presence on city council making the anti-capitalist case and demanding a more radical local democracy has been heard. The local Left has all but dissolved as an active force contesting local centres of power. The last two decades or so of everyday urban politics in Canada has individual councillors attempting to leverage minor social measures out of the latest development scheme and condo complex, negotiating the trimming of municipal services on the least unfavourable terms, and supporting local – preferably green – entrepreneurs and markets. There is nothing in any of this that one can possibly conjure as the means to break with urban austerity.

The Left tradition has historically been quite different. Following from the Paris Commune, workers' councils, and "water and sewer socialism," it has focused on the reorganization, democratization, and decentralization of political and economic activity. The "urban revolution" was central, Lefebvre (1991, 54) argued, to any transformative prospects: "A revolution that does not produce a new space has not realized its full potential; indeed it has failed in that it has not changed life itself, but has merely changed ideological superstructures, institutions or political apparatuses." But this was never seen as a project isolated to single urban centres – a localism "in-itself" as the objective of political resistance. Instead, local bases of power and self-administration had to be integrated into revolutionary projects to transform national state power and to internationalize political struggles and alliances against the world capitalist market (Mayer 2009; Harvey 2012; Fumaz and Charnock 2017).

Any alternate politics in Canada today will have to produce new urban spaces – a right to good work and living wages, a new infrastructure of free transit and public spaces, social housing for all. But also: it will have to be project of "rebel cities" connecting across the networks and scales of the Canadian state.

The urban political economy of Canada raises crucial strategic agendas and research questions, sparking new lines of enquiry that parallel growing flashpoints in the urban political economy. The growth of meta cities with huge suburban environs raises, for example, issues of multi-level governance, the proliferations of specialized state agencies (often insulated from democratic accountability) and the coordination of urban policy and planning (Filion, Kramer, and Sands 2016; Keil 2018). These growth trends beg for a response from the Left in terms of re-asserting the societal imperatives for democratic forms of urban planning and new strategies for controlling capital flows and subordinating developmental logics to community and ecological needs. Indeed, just such an anti-neoliberal agenda is generating both new research and political experiments in the re-municipalization of public goods against privatizations and new practices of "commoning" and building "public spaces" in both cooperative and state-led administrative modes (McDonald 2018; Kalb and Mollona 2018). Cutting across all these developments is the need to pay close attention, for both research and political interventions, is the multiple forms urban labour and social movements are being re-made in organizational forms, collective and place identities, and political alliances (MacDonald 2017; Tomiak 2016; Boudreau 2017).

Canadian political economy has often had a pre-occupation with the national state, capital and trade flows, and the economic policies that formed Canada's place in the world market. This has focused much debate (and politics, too) on the degree of autonomy of the Canadian state to form policy alternatives independent of the American empire. The study of urban political economy has established that even as the accumulation of capital breaches scales of political governance to form a world market, this is also – and necessarily so – an urbanization process nested in other scales of political economy. Critical urban studies in Canada has, however, tended to juxtapose the urban to the global, eviscerating the regional and the national in abstract calls for a transnational urbanism of resistance. But even a cursory examination of urban austerity reveals that constituted state powers remain administrative obstacles and political forms that require strategic address not theoretical elision. If a radical politics of localism to challenge neoliberal urbanism is to emerge in Canada, it will do so from multiple cities in a national politics of transformation in its organizational capacities and internationalist in its commitments. New studies in the political economy of Canada, this essay concludes, will be crucial to bridging these divisions of political scale in research focus and activist ambitions in social struggles.

NOTES

1 In theory, development charges are fees that developers pay to municipalities in order to offset the costs of funding new capital costs and services resulting from growth such as water and sewer lines, new roads, and maintenance. In practice, however, neither property taxes nor development charges support long-term operations, ongoing maintenance, and replacement costs. Also, because most municipalities do not coordinate their development charges and land-use planning goals, this dynamic reinforces urban sprawl as a means of short-sighted revenue generation and individual city councillor attempts to trade off cash contributions or amenities from developers in return for allowing them to exceed height and density restrictions. This is in contrast to new planning orientations that support more compact development, wide-ranging building types, a closer mix of employment and residential use, and transit-friendly growth. The net effect is to reinforce expensive, low-density automobile-dependent sprawl, with denser development in the urban core often subsidizing single-family households in ex-urban areas.

2 Figures calculated from: Statistics Canada, CANSIM, 2013, 326-0020, 380-0063, 281-0027; 2016, 326-0022; 380-0074; 384-0038.

3 Traditionally made up of white- and pink-collar workers, Local 79 is the largest municipal local in Canada with a membership of 18,000, although various contingent, seasonal and part-time workers push estimates of membership upwards to 24,000. Local 416 is primarily made up of blue-collar workers and has approximately 6,200 members. Together, they work in areas of public health and education, child and elder care, parks, recreation, water treatment, Emergency Medical Services, as well as housing and court services, road maintenance, by-law and safety enforcement, building inspection, animal rescue, waste collection, and social services administration.

4 Broadhead et al. (2014, n.p.) suggest the Federation of Canadian Municipalities' "methodology likely underestimates the size of the municipal infrastructure deficit, as it fails to incorporate other types of infrastructure that are pillars of modern cities and communities. For example, affordable housing and safe shelter, low-carbon energy systems, and reliable information and communication technologies help mold municipalities into livable, resilient and

economically competitive places." This does not include infrastructure owned by other orders of government, nor does it include about $115 billion required for new municipal infrastructure needs.

5 Total public investment in infrastructure in Canada reached 3 per cent of national GDP in 2008, marginally surpassing the 2.9 per cent necessary to maintain current stock. World average expenditures on public infrastructure averaged 3.8 per cent of GDP per year. It is estimated that Canada requires at least 5 per cent annual investment in infrastructure to address the deficit (Brodhead et al. 2014).

PART FIVE

Contestation

14

Protest Patterns:
CPE as an Analytical Approach

Lesley J. Wood

Canadian social movements are erupting in ways that reflect an unstable and changing context. From the Black Lives Matter actions to the militarized clashes between the police and protesters at Toronto's G20; from Quebec's anti-austerity movement to Idle No More round dances and blockades challenging extractivist and colonial policies and arguing for nation to nation relations; from No One Is Illegal challenging immigration policy and its ties to capitalism and colonialism to mining injustice protesters and Queers Against Israeli Apartheid; Canadian movements have never been more globalized, have never been more intersectional, and have never been less dominated by the descendants of European settlers.

How do we understand such movements and their relationship to neoliberal restructuring and the austerity state? It is not surprising that Canadian political economy approaches to social movements are powerful, given the roots of the field. As Leah Vosko notes in this volume, Canadian feminist political economy is dialectical, materialist, and praxis-oriented. This holds true for CPE more generally. However, if one searches for "Canadian political economy" and "social movements" on Google Scholar for work done since 2011, one finds almost nothing. This is particularly unnerving, because while CPE's influence on social movement theory is declining in visibility, leading social movement scholars like Jeff Goodwin, John Krinsky, and Paul Almeida and others have called for an analysis of political economy within social movement theory.

The relative decline in CPE studies of social movements corresponds with the rising popularity of the contentious politics framework – an approach synthesized by Sidney Tarrow, Charles Tilly, and Doug McAdam (2001) that emerged in the United States and has spread internationally. Emerging out of studies of state formation in Western Europe, contentious politics approaches use a rigorous empirical analysis of the micro-relations of contention. It adopts a scholarly style critical of politically driven writing that uncritically evaluates movements. Its goal is to understand why and how contention varied across time and space. The approach uses the historical comparative method to identify recurrent processes and mechanisms that influence variation in tactics, targets, networks, and outcomes. The approach defines the social movement as a collective, sustained, non-institutionalized challenge that involves campaigns, public displays of worthiness, unity, numbers, and commitment, and a social movement repertoire that includes rallies, marches, petitions, and delegations. The approach is useful for comparing movements across time and space.

Over the past ten years there has been some convergence between contentious politics researchers and European scholars more influenced by the New Social Movements (NSM) tradition of Alberto Melucci, Jürgen Habermas, Manuel Castells, and Alain Touraine that see contemporary social movements as networks engaged in cultural transformation and struggles over meaning and symbols. Through the work of Bert Klandermans, Cristina Flesher Fominaya, James Jasper, and others, discussions of identity formation and culture have become more central to contentious politics research.

Nonetheless, in the recent past, the contentious politics approach has faced criticism. First, while Tilly and Tarrow's landmark historical works (Tarrow 1967; Tilly 1964, 1992, 1995) avoid this problem, many contentious politics scholars neglect any analysis of capitalism (Hetland and Goodwin 2013). While the roots of the approach emphasize economic and political transformation and its effect on the form of contention, too often the literature drops its dialectical emphasis and simply describes the relationship between the structure of a political regime and the repertoire of contention without examining the dialectical relationship between political economy and mobilization. Second, because the ultimate goal of research is a scholarly one, and the approach aims for value neutral social science, the approach can be politically disengaged from the movements themselves.

As dialectical, materialist, and praxis oriented, the Canadian political economy approach to social movements takes a different approach. It sees movements as part of ongoing struggle amongst political, economic, and cultural relations, and emphasizes the creation of counter-hegemonic knowledge. As other chapters in this volume illustrate, the object of analysis of Canadian political economy is the Canadian social formation as a historically specific configuration of economic, political, and cultural relations. The CPE approach looks at the reproduction of relations under capital and state. The main emphases of a CPE approach have been the way that resources, social class, and international trade are produced and reproduced within the colonial and capitalist state. This lens locates social movements within this larger set of dynamics – emphasizing their activity within larger systems of production and reproduction, and less as autonomous agents. Historical and dynamic CPE offers an approach to understanding social transformation that highlights the interactions amongst agents and forces of change (Clement 2001a). While recognizing that there are international political economists and world systems theorists involved in social movement research beyond Canada, this paper will focus on the role of Canadian political economy and social movements.[1] Overall, the tradition engages with social movements in three distinctive ways:

1 As part of a political project – for social spending, for the welfare state, against free trade, against corporate rule, against male domination and White supremacy
2 Methodologically – by offering a way of understanding social movements that emerge out of tensions and contradictions within society (Carroll and Coburn 2002)
3 As the object of analysis – working to understand the construction of a counter-hegemonic force and its implications for the strategy of particular movements

These different activities converge in a distinctive approach. While recognizing that I'm categorizing a broad set of authors and analysts as CPE, some of whom may not identify as such, I will review these three tasks one by one.

CPE AS A POLITICAL PROJECT

While there were earlier forays, Canadian political economy began to engage with social movements in earnest in the early 1970s. As socialist, anti-imperialist, communist, and social democratic peace movements, student movements, anti-Vietnam War movements, and feminist movements blossomed, there was a massive growth in social science programs in Canadian universities. Many graduate students and faculty drew on their movement experience, and their scholarly work influenced the movements themselves.

As Clement (2001a) points out, CPE scholars in early 1970s combined the Indigenous "staples" tradition with international development or anti-imperialist Marxist writings from Africa, Latin America, and European anti-colonial movements. By and large, they did this not in order to evaluate Canada as a colonizer as much as locate Canada as a colony of Europe and later a "branch plant" of the United States political economy. The approach fed a political project whose goals were to strengthen and differentiate the Canadian social democratic project from the US model, while critiquing the idea that Canada was a pluralistic democratic state. This analysis became part of an analytical and political project that worked to strengthen the social safety net, and to oppose neoliberal restructuring, free trade, and corporate rule, as well as male domination and White supremacy. The approach inspired and shaped institutions, departments, and research projects, including the Canadian Centre for Policy Alternatives, the Progressive Economics Forum, various programs in women's and gender studies, and in work and labour studies, as well as the Canadian Research Institute for the Advancement of Women, the Broadbent Institute, the Council of Canadians, anti-free trade organizing, and many national trade unions.

These bodies offered material support to social movements, particularly during the struggles against free trade in the 1980s and 1990s, and since that time in the global justice, anti-austerity, and feminist movements. An obituary for Abe Rotstein, a scholar of political economy at University of Toronto, reflects one way that Canadian political economists engaged politically:

> Abe became the editor of the then prestigious *Canadian Forum*. He founded the University League for Social Reform, which published a number of books. He was active in the teach-in movement on the University of Toronto campus against the American war in Vietnam. He supported Quebec's right to self-determination. He was a member of a federal government Task Force on Foreign Ownership. The task force, which offered policy recommendations to counter and regulate foreign ownership, included Ed Safarian and me from the University of Toronto. He was one of the founders of the Committee for an Independent Canada, which morphed into the Council of

Canadians, and of the Canadian Institute for Economic Policy
(Watkins 2015).

Through the years, the dominant CPE approach faced critiques from
others on the left. Some Marxists argued it paid too much attention to
the role of US imperialism as an explanation of Canadian political economy, rather than looking at capitalism more broadly (Smith 2000).
Indigenous and anti-colonial activists noted that Canada was not simply
colonized, but also operated as a colonizer within a global system.
Feminists argued that the conception of political economy must incorporate an analysis of gendered and racialized relations of production and
reproduction (Luxton 2006b). These critiques shaped the political engagement of CPE scholars and activists. Some of these interventions spawned
their own projects, like the Feminism and Political Economy Network
in southern Ontario. Through these interventions, CPE scholar activists
made significant contributions to social movements by contributing to
discussions of movement strategy, debates around priorities, facilitating
coalition work and recruitment, and pointing out contradictions and
opportunities. We see this in spaces like those offered by the Metro
Network for Social Justice, the Canadian Centre for Policy Alternatives,
the Workers Assembly, Public Interest Research Groups, and York
University's Global Labour Research Centre. Each has offered space for
reflection, popular education, and skill building. These spaces helped
movements to "name the moment" and to examine the dynamics of the
state and capitalism.

MOVEMENTS AS METHODOLOGY

When CPE scholars look at social movements, they usually begin with
a description of the economic and political context. Movements themselves are often used in order to better understand the reproduction
of relations under capital and state – with a particular emphasis on
the way classes, and class fractions are shaped, and the resultant struggles. Movements are seen as a "reflex of structural contradictions" – and
dialectical analysis of them is seen as part of a broader understanding
of the "architecture of power." This emphasis highlights the relationship between macro social and economic processes and mobilization.
This approach sees movements as response to tensions and contradictions within capitalism (and colonialism). This means that there is less
emphasis on comparing across movements, and more emphasis on

examining change in a single site. This approach has political justifications. As the anthology *Sociology for Changing the World* argues, the
role of the engaged scholar is not to study social movements as objects,
but to work from the inside, in order to better produce knowledge for
more effective forms of activism for changing the world (Frampton et
al. 2006).

Sometimes political economists analyze the connection between movement and political economy extremely systematically. US social movement scholars Roberta Ash Garner and Mayer Zald (1987) offer a
schema to this end. They highlight the entire swath of social movement
activity, the social movement sector in their comparison of movements
in the 1970s and 1980s in Italy and the United States. They highlight
the relationship between political economy and social movements by
looking at different characteristics of social movements in a particular
time and place. They point out that the size of movements, their degree
and nature of organization, what class their base supporters come from
and where they mobilize, whether and how they align with left-right
orientations, the autonomy of the movement from other institutions,
and the character of change in the movement over time can be usefully
mapped and analyzed. They explain why social movement activity in
the United States is much more personalized and tied to issues of identity
than in Italy by arguing that in the US, relations of reproduction (family,
school, etc.) are relatively autonomous from relations of production. As
well, they note that because universities are sites of "contradictory class
positions" in the United States, they are particularly important.

Although it includes a useful emphasis on the class composition of
movements, unemployment rates and the structure of the economy, Ash
Garner and Zald's (1987) examination of an entire sector is broader and
more schematic than most CPE analysts. However, such mechanistic
approaches fell out of favour by the mid-1990s. Instead, there were
attempts to get at the dialectic between "ruling relations" and resistance
more explicitly, and to move beyond seeing economic struggle as tied to
industrial workers. CPE scholars like William Carroll and R.S. Ratner
(2010) draw on Gramsci's analysis of hegemony and counter-hegemony
to think through the dialectics between political economy and mobilization in a way that paid attention to knowledge creation. They note that
the actions of the bourgeoisie to maintain control oblige the left to "conduct a war of position within civil society – to gain ground through
processes of moral-intellectual reform that prepare subordinate groups
for self-governance by creating post-capitalist sensibilities and values,

practical democratic capacities, and a belief in the possibility of a radically transformed future" (8). This emphasis on knowledge production and consciousness resonates with many. Carroll and Ratner and their collaborators work to understand the way that neoliberalism was not only transforming organizations and actions, but knowledge itself. In this vein, Aziz Choudry (2015) cites Allman (2010) when he explains that capitalism (or political economy more generally) is not external to human beings but is "the structured relations of human beings into which they enter routinely in order to produce their material existence. Forms of organization and physical structures, as well as the legal system that gives legitimacy to the structure, are created in order to 'cement' this structuring of human relations, but the real and material substance of the structure is the daily, sensuous activity of human being" (Choudry 2015, 22).

This suggests that to understand the effect of capitalism on social movement activity, we look not just at material production but also at the infrastructure of the state and capitalism – its legal, media, educational, and cultural components. A fine example of such work is Annette Demarais' (2007) monograph on the politics of food and the international peasant organization Via Campesina. Locating her analysis within a broader analysis of neoliberalism, she shows how rural activists and peasant organizations built a shared space and identity that allowed them to transcend the patterns of those who claimed to represent them – the church, conservative political parties, and NGOs. Other strong work looks at the way the petroleum and extraction economy affects the construction of a counter-hegemonic bloc by climate justice and environmental justice movements (Haluza-Delay 2014; McCreary 2014).

Also raising material questions of the forces shaping resistance, Dene scholar Glen Coulthard (2014) uses Marx and Fanon to explain how settler colonialism is shaping Indigenous struggle. He sees how modes of colonial thought have led Indigenous activists to repeatedly "commit to colonized to the types of practices and subject positions that are required for their continued domination" (16). As a result, he urges movements interested in serious transformation to push beyond the nation state. A similar conversation is underway in movements where the relationship between the state and the commons is being called into question. A panel on this topic held in downtown Toronto in 2015 included Harsha Walia, an immigrant justice organizer from Vancouver, and Desmond Cole, an anti-racist criminal justice activist and writer from Toronto. Both argued that Canadian social movements have held up the welfare state as the protector of the commons – an assumption that disregards the ways that the state is engaged in excluding marginalized communities. Instead, as Haudenosaunee panellist Dan Longboat argued, the commons needs to be understood as a relationship of accountability and responsibility amongst communities and individuals.

Another set of work that examines how political economy affects movements looks at the criminalization of and repression of activists. This work examines the way that changes in political economy effect changes in social movements and vice versa (Hall and De Lint 2009; Wood 2014). Such an approach can be productive in its emphasis on both the relations between political economy and movements and how they affect praxis and strategy. Shiri Pasternack's (2011) analysis of the state surveillance of Indigenous struggle illustrates this. She shows how the Indigenous sovereignist movement poses a particular challenge to capitalist accumulation by Canadian and international settler elites. Such insights show how movements signify contradictions and crises in the state and economy and how the features of political economy shape the response by movements. This approach differs from contentious politics theory whose goal is generalizable theory about the processes and mechanisms that shape them. While contentious politics scholars do recognize the way that relational ties, including those around resource extraction and economic exchange shape regimes and repertoires, there is often less attention paid to the dialectical and transformative nature of these relations.

Social Movements as an Object of Analysis

In 2002, William Carroll and Elaine Coburn argued that CPE approaches, while engaged with movements, do not examine the movements themselves as the objects of analysis. Nonetheless, Canadian political economy scholars have investigated key questions about praxis and mobilization over the past fifty years – with a particular emphasis on different manifestations of the labour movement and feminist movement (Carroll and Coburn 2002, 83; Vosko this volume). Because of the emphasis on the interactions between context and praxis, certain questions have garnered particular attention.

I will highlight two. First, how do activists produce knowledge and develop shared identities? Second, how do they build coalitions? These are used to answer the more general strategic question of how can movements make change most effectively? Or as Carroll and Ratner (2010) put it – "how can the balance of cultural power in civil society be shifted and space won for radical alternatives, unifying dissenting groups into a system of alliances capable of contesting bourgeois hegemony?"

The question of knowledge production in social movements spawned Hackett's (2006) work on media activism in an age of corporate, commercial media, and Prince's work on the effects of neoliberalism on the disability rights movement (2012). Janet Conway moves this conversation forward with her discussion of knowledge production in local social movements in Toronto and internationally. Of particular interest is her book *Praxis and Politics: Knowledge Production in Social Movements* (2010). Other recent work includes: Aziz Choudry and Dip Kapoor's 2010 book *Learning from the Ground Up* and Choudry's 2015 book *Learning Activism: The Intellectual Life of Contemporary Social Movements*.

The question of coalition building between movements that were working around questions of redistribution and movements that were highlighting struggles for recognition became a topic of debate. Since Carroll and Ratner's (1996) work on alliances and networks amongst organizations in Vancouver, there has been other solid work on such relationships – from Roger Keil (1994) and Rod Bantjes' (1997) work on coalitions between the environmental and labour movements, to Robert Hackett's (2000) work on media democratization movement, to Janet Conway's (2004) work on coalitions in Toronto. Coalitions within the labour movement have also been examined by Linda Briskin in her article, "Autonomy, Diversity, and Integration: Union Women's Separate Organizing in North America and Western Europe in the Context of Restructuring and Globalization," and by Stephanie Ross in her work on unions (2011) and on strategy in the global justice movement (2008).

ANTI-AUSTERITY PROTESTS IN MONTREAL AND TORONTO (2015)

Like other years, Montreal and Toronto activists filled the streets on 1 May 2015 to celebrate International Workers Day. The similarities and differences between these two events help to illustrate how a CPE analysis can be used. Toronto's march and rally was the tenth annual May Day, organized by an evolving coalition that consistently included the migrant justice organization No One Is Illegal, and the Ontario Coalition against Poverty. This year, the Latin American and Caribbean Solidarity Network joined the team. There were eight themes for the day: Indigenous sovereignty and self-determination; migrant workers' resistance to border imperialism; solidarity with working class struggle globally; anti-poverty and anti-austerity organizing; student strikes and academic labour battles against neoliberalization; environmental justice; militant rank and file labour movements; and gender justice. Black Lives Matter Toronto organizers criticized the event for neglecting anti-Black racism, which was then incorporated as an additional theme by the speakers. The tactics of the day were typical for Toronto. An unpermitted rally began at City Hall with ceremony led by Wanda Whitebird, a Mi'kmaq elder, who was followed by speeches and performances. The speeches targeted the Conservative federal government, alongside the Liberal provincial government, the Toronto city council, capitalism, and colonialism more generally. After the speeches, approximately 1000 people marched with drummers and banners across the downtown core to St James Park. There was little police intervention.

In Montreal, May Day 2015 was far more dramatic. It was part of a provincial day of action against the austerity policies of the Liberal government, and there were over one hundred actions planned throughout the day in the city (Murray and Sundaram 2015), including blockades outside of the National Bank, the World Trade Centre, and the CHUM Hospital. Although various unions had voted for a day long "social strike," the Quebec Labour Relations Board (the Commission des relations de travail) had declared it illegal. Nonetheless, some picket lines were formed outside of government offices, schools, and universities. Parents and teachers formed human chains around schools and daycares. At noon, there were "militant picnics" throughout the city, including one outside the elite Club 357C. There were numerous public meetings about austerity, more BBQs, kiosks, popular education, austerity workshops, and banner-making. Then at 4:00 p.m. there was a rally for all striking faculty at Cégep Ahuntsic (Murray and Sundaram 2015). An anti-capitalist march called by Convergence des Luttes Anti-Capitalistes (CLAC) hit the streets in the evening, with the Montreal police quickly declaring it illegal, using tear gas, and arresting eighty-four people. Fifty-seven were arrested under municipal by-law P6, which allows demonstrations to be declared illegal; the police charged the rest with criminal offenses (Murray and Sundaram 2015).

How do we understand these two events? In order to critically evaluate the possibilities of and limits of CPE, it is useful to use a concrete case. To this end, I will examine protests in Toronto and Montreal in 2015, with a more focused consideration of anti-austerity protests. I approach the material from two angles – comparing a political economy approach with the strategy of a contentious politics scholar.

As mentioned, the goals of the two approaches matter. For a CPE scholar, the goal is to understand how capitalism and the state are shaping movements in order to help those movements to challenge the capitalist state. For the contentious politics scholar, the goal is to better understand the variation within processes and mechanisms within contention, in order to understand how popular struggle operates. These different approaches can mean the work looks quite different – the former approach making the dialectic between movement and context central, and the latter highlighting the causal relationships within movements and particular regimes.

To represent the mobilizations in the two cities, I use event catalogue data in addition to statistical data on political economy, news media coverage, and field notes. These catalogues of events are commonplace within contentious politics approaches to social movements as tools for systematically capturing the variation of topics, actors, action, and stories in a particular time and place. The method was developed by Charles Tilly and his collaborators in order to examine the changing forms of contention in Great Britain from 1760–1834. They looked for evidence of "contentious events" – or public gatherings of more than ten people, which challenged the interests of authorities within newspapers, magazines, and parliamentary transcripts. That "Contention in Great Britain" project collected evidence of 8088 contentious gatherings. This project uses the same logic, but relies on the coverage of the major English language newspaper in each city (*Montreal Gazette* and *Toronto Star*). Clearly, such a filter misses many protests, and particularly strikes. It reflects the biases of news coverage and tends to cover violent or dramatic, local, comprehensible or odd protest events, while ignoring many smaller, day-to-day but otherwise important challenges (Gitlin 1980). Nonetheless, there are reasons to continue to use event catalogues to look for variation for an exercise such as this. The biases are relatively comprehensible and consistent across time. Protest events were identified by searching the two papers using the Lexis-Nexis newspaper database with the search terms of protest, protested, protesters, rallied, and demonstrated. Events were included in this dataset if they were public collective challenges that involved more than five people.

Such data gives us only one aspect of social movements. Protests are only one form of action. As Leanne Simpson (2011, 16) critiques social movement studies: "When resistance is defined solely as large-scale political mobilization, we miss much of what has kept our languages, cultures, and systems of governance alive." Recognizing the deep truth of such an insight, this sliver of contention shows us something about a particular aspect of contention in a particular kind of formation, in a particular place at a particular time. This is not intended to be a conclusive study of movement activity in the two cities during neoliberal restructuring, only a lens by which to explore the similarities and differences between a CPE approach and an analysis guided by contentious politics theory.

Event Catalogue Data

If we look at the size and number of protests in Montreal and Toronto in 2015 we see two cities with radically different levels and forms of protest activity.

Although Toronto (2001) has more than double the population of Montreal,[2] it had only half the number of protests in 2015. The protests in Montreal are larger, more likely to involve arrest, and have a higher number of arrests. Beyond size and level of mobilization, there are visible differences in the issues around which people mobilized in the two cities.

In Montreal, the most frequent topic of protest in 2015 was austerity (thirty events). These involved a spring mobilization including a two-week strike and anti-austerity mobilization (February–May) led by post-secondary student protests concerned about tuition. These also included regular protests by parents and teachers concerned about cuts to education and daycare, and an autumn mobilization around stalled contract negotiations with public sector workers (eighteen events). Other issues that generated more than two events were police brutality (four), immigrant rights (three), and the taxi workers' struggles around Uber (three). The largest mobilizations were the September 1 day of action against cuts to education, which involved 20,000 parents, teachers, and students, and a march of 40,000 public sector workers and their supporters around contract negotiations and austerity budgets on December 9.

In Toronto, the issue that generated the highest number of protests was Ontario's new sex education curriculum, which inspired seven conservative and religious protests. The other contentious issues that mobilized people more than twice were the taxi worker/Uber conflict (four), racist policing (three), and an anti-austerity movement (three) largely concerned with cuts to public sector jobs and a lack of social spending. The largest demonstrations were the March for Jobs, Justice and the Climate (10,000), and the University of Toronto and York's teaching assistant and contract faculty strikes (6000).

Both cities (like others around the world) are seeing protests around austerity, police brutality, and taxi-work. Why are these the main topics

Table 14.1
Protest activity in Montreal and Toronto in 2015

	Montreal	Toronto
# Events 2015	70	36
# Events > 1000 participants	13	6
# Events with arrest	11	0
# Arrests	402	0

of protest? Canadian political economists and contentious politics scholars would approach this task differently. We have discussed the different goals of the two frameworks, but would note that readers of this volume would not be surprised that Canadian Political Economists would likely frame the anti-austerity mobilizations of 2015 within an analysis of the current moment in the Canadian capitalist state, and internationally. They would be less likely to do a full comparison of the mobilizations but might note that anti-austerity mobilizations are in part a response to contradictions of a post-2008 global economic crisis, a neoliberal Conservative federal government, and Liberal provincial government. They might note the increasing gap between rich and poor, the role of neoliberal cuts to the public sector and social spending, and the offloading of the administration of urban crises to municipalities. They would recognize that this context is being shaped and is shaping organizations, leaders, and local histories.

The local economy would be important. As Albo and Fanelli note in this volume, in both cities there is "a state of permanent fiscal crisis in municipal finances in Canada," and the lack of investment in urban infrastructure. Both cities face instability because the requisite funds for education, health care, transportation, housing, and public services are not available, and – when people rise up – municipal police forces and governments must struggle to maintain control.

Given the similarities between the structural conditions of the two cities, CPE analysts who are interested in the formation of a counterhegemonic bloc through coalition building might highlight the powerful Front Commun coalition between the student movement, which had shaken the province in 2012, and the public sector unions. CPE scholars would likely note that Quebec has much higher union density (39 per cent) than Ontario (28 per cent) (Ross and Thomas this volume, 2011 figures). This figure measures the percentage of workers in a given area that are either members of or covered by the provisions of a collective agreement. Recognizing that much of the left in Anglophone Canada has abandoned May Day as an anti-capitalist workers' day of resistance, CPE scholars might also point to the role of Quebec nationalist ideology in facilitating coalition building around mobilization. The Montreal mobilization might be compared with the Toronto context. CPE scholars would likely note the lack of a broad anti-austerity coalition amongst anti-poverty activists, striking teaching assistants, and other public sector workers. They might celebrate the diversity of issues and groups being mobilized, but also bemoan the relative strength of conservative and religious mobilizations. As Albo and Fanelli note in chapter 13: "The local Left has all but dissolved as an active force contesting local centres of power." If sympathetic, they might also argue that Ontario had already lost many of the battles Quebec was facing around austerity during an earlier period of neoliberal restructuring.

In contrast, contentious politics scholars would pay close attention to the differences in tactics, forms of organization, and resources in the two cities – getting close to the action, and attempting to identify recurrent processes and mechanisms. They would definitely highlight the organizations involved in these mobilizations, their networks, and interactions. They would note who was mobilizing the sex education protests, and what tactics they used. They might compare the budgets spent by unions in Montreal and in Toronto. They might also look at the resources and skills used in recent years – possibly examining the diffusion of tactics or narratives from the Occupy and student movements. They might also highlight the way tensions between the local, provincial, and federal governments might affect political opportunities in the two cities – shaping the leverage of particular movements on particular issues.

Both approaches have their strengths and weaknesses. The contentious politics approach can analyze what tactics, forms of organization, and network structures are causing which effects in a systematic way, but CPE scholars will pay attention to the changes in political economy that might be making those tactics, forms of organization, and network structures possible. Contentious politics approaches are better at mapping variation, but CPE scholars will be more likely to answer the questions that activists ask. While contentious politics scholars are more likely to provide analysis that neglects the role of capitalism and economic fluctuations, CPE scholars can sometimes jump from detailed analysis of neoliberalism to a description of a movement with few intermediary steps.

CONCLUSION

Given that Canadian political economy is dialectical, praxis oriented, and materialist, it offers a dynamic and useful approach to studying social movements. However, the benefits of this approach are often missed. This is clear when one reads the table of contents of a recent book entitled *Protest and Politics: The Promise of Social Movement Societies* edited by Howard Ramos and Kathleen Rodgers. The volume examines a range of mobilizations in Canada – including immigrant mobilizations, environmental movements, the religious right, and the Quebec women's movement. Mostly, however, these writings neglect the role of political economy. Instead, they/we use the contentious politics approach to social movements partly because of the rich explanatory and comparative leverage, and due to its legitimacy in international scholarly networks.

But there have been persistent and growing complaints that contentious politics scholars often neglect the political economy that surrounds and influences movements. As I noted earlier, in 2013 in an edited volume entitled *Marxism and Social Movements*, Gabriel Hetland and Jeff Goodwin argue that "recent scholarship tends to overlook not only the direct and proximate effects of capitalist institutions on collective action, but also the ways in which capitalist dynamics indirectly influence the possibilities for protest, sometimes over many years or even decades, by, for example, shaping political institutions, political alliances, social ties and cultural idioms" (86). They are not alone. There is a clear revival of political economy and Marxist approaches to social movements underway in the United States and Europe. Other publications including *We Make Our Own History: Marxism and Social Movements in the Twilight of Neoliberalism* edited by Laurence Cox and Alf Gunvald Nilsen (2014), and Donatella della Porta's (2015) *Social Movements in Times of Austerity: Bringing Capitalism Back into Protest Analysis* suggest that perhaps an analysis of capitalism should be incorporated into the state-centred field of social movement studies. This is old news for Canadian political economists, who have long been doing this work, and indeed for Canadian scholars more generally. How can a Canadian political economy perspective help us to understand contemporary social movements and how can understanding movements make us rethink or refine our understanding of the broader political economy?

At a moment when movements are erupting in diverse and unconnected ways, we need to understand both what is happening and how to make those we admire more successful. CPE approaches to understanding and thinking beyond the current moment in capitalism, settler colonialism, and the state and how they are tied to social movements and their ability to build a counterhegemonic project offer a great deal. If combined with the rigorous comparative approaches that contentious politics scholars use, we will be able to better understand both how and why the twenty-first century movements are emerging from and transforming a more unstable, integrated, and volatile world.

NOTES

1 Social movement scholars in the United States using a world systems or political economy perspective include Christopher Chase-Dunn, Immanual Wallerstein, and Jackie Smith.

2 Toronto 2001 population of 2,481,494 and Montreal of 1,039,534.

15

Playing Left Wing:
Renewing a Political Economy of Sport

Simon Black

After watching a game of cricket, Karl Marx is said to have concluded that a revolution in England was improbable. If the masses could be so easily subdued by such a resolutely sedate game with its mores of bourgeois Englishness dripping from every rule and expression, then all was lost for the socialist cause.

Carrington 2009, 20

Echoing Marx, many contemporary writers and theorists on the Left are dismissive of sport as a space of struggle and progressive social transformation. For instance, in a recent essay, the British literary theorist Terry Eagleton channelled Marx himself, proclaiming, "it is sport, not religion, which is now the opium of the people" (2007, 26). For his part, French sociologist Marc Perelman (2012, 3) has condemned sport as "a stabilizing factor for the existing [capitalist] system" and calls for nothing less than its abolition. And Noam Chomsky (2002, 99) has argued that one of the basic functions sport serves in society is "occupying the population, and keeping them from trying to get involved with things that really matter."

If sport is merely "a conduit for dominant ideology" (Carrington 2009, 21), why should the new Canadian political economy (NCPE) – with its emphasis on the dialectic of structure and agency, stability and change (see Clement, this volume) – be concerned with it? Simply put, because contra the likes of Eagleton, Perelman, and Chomsky, sport matters as a site of contradiction, tension, and social change. Yes, with its emphasis on competition and commercialism, professional sport in particular has a role in sustaining ideology and reproducing the culture of capitalism (see Young 1986). And from the local playing field to the grand stage of the Olympics, sport reflects and contributes to normative configurations of gender, race, class, and ability (Field 2015, 5). But, to return to Marx, if we are interested in not only interpreting the world of sport but also changing it, this line of critique only gets us so far.

Sport can also be understood as "contested terrain" (Whitson and Gruneau 1997) upon which class conflict plays out in both odd and familiar ways, where hegemonic gender norms and identities are disrupted, a space in which racism, colonialism, and the politics of empire are open to contestation (e.g., Abdel-Shehid and Kalman-Lamb 2011). As Ben Carrington argues, the Left needs more engaged analyses of sport that appreciate its "protean, dialectic nature as a site of everyday domination *and* resistance; a space of joy and creativity *and* routine mechanized existence" (2009, 16, emphasis in original). For it is only through such analyses that "we develop ways to conceptualize sport's potential for (embodied) emancipation and freedom but without any final guarantees as to its political effectivity" (Carrington 2009, 16).

Thankfully, the NCPE tradition has been home to such an approach (e.g., Whitson and Gruneau 1997). Scholars working in this tradition have interrogated the deep interconnections of sport, popular culture, the economy, and the state, understanding sport as neither "politically irredeemable" nor "strategically irrelevant" to social struggles and projects of social transformation (see Gruneau 1988, 14). This chapter hopes to build on this tradition.

I begin by locating NCPE scholarship in the development of critical Sport Studies. In the late 1970s and 1980s, Canadian-based scholars such as Bruce Kidd (1979, 1982), Rob Beamish (1982, 1985), David Whitson (1984), Hart Cantelon (Cantelon and Gruneau 1983), and Richard Gruneau (1981) furthered a neo-Marxist perspective on sport, which influenced the field of Sport Studies (see Carrington 2009). Much of this work blended cultural studies and political economy approaches, analyzing sport as a popular cultural form, its ideological capacity, and the degree to which it reproduced relations of domination.

With the exception of Beamish, an analysis of sport as labour was not central to this scholarship. Yet while professional athletes, like entertainers, have a role in producing and shaping popular cultures of consumption, they are "first and foremost workers engaged in labor processes that are tightly controlled by their employers and the corporations employing them accumulate the profits" (Beamish 2007). Canadian political economy scholarship has been particularly strong in the study of work and workers' organizations (e.g., Phillips 1997; Fudge and Vosko

2003; Gindin and Stanford 2003; Ross and Thomas this volume; Vosko this volume). In the conclusion of the first section, I argue for a renewed engagement between the NCPE and sport through a political economy of labour.

Towards this end, in the second half of the chapter I present a case study of the Canadian Hockey League (CHL), the world's premier major junior hockey competition. While the majority of athletes at the elite level of team sport in North America – i.e., the major leagues – are unionized, many athletes in minor and development leagues are not.[1] Like other non-unionized workers, these athletes must rely on employment standards as their principle source of labour protection (see Vosko this volume). However, the CHL has intentionally misclassified players as either independent contractors or student-athletes, denying them basic forms of labour protection, including the minimum wage. By no accident, major junior hockey players' circumstances parallel that of athletes in revenue-generating college sports in the United States.[2]

But while the CHL is a site of exploitation, it is also a site of resistance. In recent years, CHL players have launched class-action lawsuits against the league and its teams, claiming systematic violation of their rights as employees. Furthermore, labour advocates have pushed state regulatory bodies to investigate wages and working conditions in the league. Finally, there have been a series of efforts to organize a union, the most recent of which is led by Canada's largest private sector union, Unifor. I briefly review these strategies of resistance and assess their effectiveness.

In conclusion, I locate labour struggles in major junior hockey in the context of a growing revolt among working athletes across a wide range of sports; a revolt that mirrors the recent upsurge in labour and social movement activism (see Ross and Thomas, this volume). Often caricatured by the media as a world of millionaire athletes and billionaire team owners, some see professional sport as far removed from the everyday struggles of working people and indeed as a distraction from – in Chomsky's words – "things that really matter." As this chapter demonstrates, the working lives of many professional athletes – who are struggling with economic insecurity, employment precarity, and bad bosses – are not all that dissimilar from that of the broader working class.

CRITICAL SPORT STUDIES AND THE NEW CANADIAN POLITICAL ECONOMY

The field of critical sport studies encompasses the multidisciplinary study of sport through the lens of critical theory – including Marxist, feminist, critical race, queer, and postcolonial theory – understanding sport as "a site of social, economic and racial inequalities emerging from larger histories of patriarchy, colonialism, and capitalism" (Abdel-Shehid and Kalman-Lamb 2011, 2). As an academic field, critical sport studies has its roots in the 1960s New Left and academic interest in popular and working class cultures (see Carrington and McDonald 2009). This section provides a brief overview of the development of critical sport studies and the place of CPE scholarship within it.[3]

Prior to the emergence of critical sport studies, the radical critique of sport was heavily influenced by the critical theory of the Frankfurt School (see Carrington and McDonald 2009). Scholars working in this tradition condemned sport "as ideological, divisive, alienating, and exploitative" and "the culturally and historically specific expression of physical culture under the conditions of capitalism" (Carrington and McDonald 2009, 2). Perhaps with the exception of the Trinidadian Marxist, C.L.R. James – who stood outside of this tradition and whose powerful exegesis of the role of cricket in the colonial Caribbean, *Beyond a Boundary* (2005 [1963]), claimed sport as a site of resistance – Marxist critiques of sport were overwhelmingly structuralist in nature, leaving little room for the agency of either athletes or fans.

With the Gramscian turn in Marxist thought and the establishment of the critical sociology of sport within the academy, scholars became increasingly concerned with exploring the limits and possibilities of resistance within sport (Carrington and McDonald 2009, 3). It is during this phase in the development of critical sport studies that academics based in Canada played a formative role. According to Carrington and McDonald, the likes of Rob Beamish (see 1981, 1985), Hart Cantelon (see Cantelon and Gruneau 1982), Richard Gruneau (see 1981, 1983), and I would add the former Canadian Olympian Bruce Kidd (see 1979, 1982), contributed to producing a "sophisticated and complex materialist theory of culture as the basis for a (neo-) Marxist perspective of sport ... highlighting the rootedness of sport within social relations of power, its ideological potency, its alienating effects" while also theorizing its potential as a vehicle for progressive social transformation (Carrington and McDonald 2009, 3)

A brief review of the contributions of Bruce Kidd illustrates the intersections of critical sport studies and CPE. Kidd's book *The Political Economy of Sport* (1979) and subsequent article, "Sport, Dependency, and the Canadian State" (Kidd 1982), built on the left-nationalist critique of Canadian "dependency" pioneered by the likes of Mel Watkins and Kari

Levitt. For Kidd, sport was one element of popular culture through which US imperialism secured and reproduced hegemony. Kidd argued that "the subordination of major professional sports in Canada resided in the interests of the United States and in structures of dependency," undermining sport, and more particularly hockey's role in the formation of an independent Canada and an independent sports culture not guided by the interests of US capital (Booth 2015, 410).[4] Kidd's contributions were part of a broader debate on the relationship between sport, culture, and the capitalist state, which included the voices of others in the new Canadian political economy (NCPE), including Wallace Clement (see Clement 1982).

More recent work from Whitson and Gruneau (1997, 2006) and new voices such as Ammirante (2006, 2009), have continued to apply the analytical approach of the NCPE to the critical study of sport. In a contribution to an earlier volume in this series, Whitson and Gruneau (1997) examine the political economy of North American major league sport. They begin by putting the restructuring of major league sport since the mid-1970s into historical context, tracing the commercialization of sport from the period of early industrial capitalism and urbanization, through to the rise of powerful cartels and the formation of US-based major league monopolies in the 1920s, and then on to the post-war expansion of the sports industry with the advent of television and mass consumption.

In the contemporary period of globalization and transnational capitalism, North American major league sport has expanded into new markets, now reaching global audiences, and has become fully integrated with industries that produce and promote popular cultural goods and consumption styles, what Whitson and Gruneau (1997, 380) call "the real integrated circus." Reflecting broader trends in capitalism, sports franchises are now typically owned by large, integrated corporations, which have interests in related leisure and entertainment businesses (Whitson and Gruneau 1997, 377–80).

Insofar as they address class dynamics within the production of major league sport – i.e., the relationship between team owners and players, Whitson and Gruneau focus on the question of the ideological framing of labour disputes. In the case of lockouts and strikes, fan anger – stoked by the media – tends to be equally directed at "big business" and "big unions" who are seen to be "pursuing their own interests over the 'good of the game'" (Whitson and Gruneau 1997, 378). Furthermore, populist anger at the actions of "greedy" players, Whitson and Gruneau note, "seems easily extended to tacit condemnation of trade unions in general" (Whitson and Gruneau 1997, 380).

As this brief summary suggests, Whitson and Gruneau analyze the restructuring of major league sport in North America through a political economy of popular culture, exploring its place in a new phase of capitalist accumulation in which the "production of images and the marketing of pleasures have become so significant that political struggles centred in and through popular culture may now be as crucial as the more traditional struggle against class domination at the workplace or in state policy" (1997, 362–3).

A Critical Political Economy of Sport Labour

As Donnelly (2007, 4716–18) observes, it is now commonplace to refer to professional sports as a business, but "perhaps some resentment about the salaries of some professional athletes in some sports … is related to the sense that sport is not work." Yet while commodity sport is consumed as spectacle, it is spectacle produced by the concrete labour of athletes who sell their capacity to work to owners or promoters in return for a wage (Beamish 1985). And despite the unique aspects of sport labour – e.g., production cannot be mechanized to increase rates of profit – like most workers in a capitalist society, athletes are alienated from both the process and the product of their labour, i.e., the sporting contest (Beamish 1985; Robidoux 2001). A political economy of professional sport must therefore analyze sport as both cultural commodity – sold to spectators, sponsors, and various media – and as a way of making a living, i.e., as work. Whereas to accomplish the former, Whitson and Gruneau analyze sport through a political economy of popular culture, to accomplish the latter we must analyze sport through a political economy of labour.

Such an approach is not new. Scholars such as Rigauer (1981) and Beamish (1985) developed an understanding of sport heavily influenced by Marxist critiques of labour within capitalist social relations. And more recent contributions in this area have explored among other things: the ways scientific management has been applied to coaching and training regimes (e.g., Robidoux 2001); the changing nature of sports labour markets in an era of neoliberal globalization (e.g., Ammirante 2006, 2009); labour relations in major league sport (e.g., Schiavone 2015); how racism and processes of racialization shape professional athletes' experiences of the workplace (e.g., Valentine and Darnell 2014); and the gender pay gap in sport (e.g., Zill 2015). There is also an emerging body of feminist research on how the work of social reproduction, done primarily by women, facilitates the participation of men and children in sport (see Thompson 1999).

Notable exceptions aside, critical political economy has left the analysis of sport labour to the field of sports economics. This is problematic on two counts: first, while some sports economists employ a radical perspective, like its parent discipline, the field is dominated by mainstream, non-critical approaches.[5] Second, sports economists overwhelmingly focus their attention on major league sport, overlooking the minor and development leagues in which the vast majority of working athletes ply their trade earning "only a small fraction of what is earned by their professional peers, even though they generate revenue for teams" (Abdel-Shehid and Kalman-Lamb 2011, 11). While professional athletes in the major leagues were once highly exploited and had little control over the conditions of their work, unionization and collective bargaining has balanced the owner/player power relationship and today's major league players receive a fairer share of the revenues they generate for their teams and leagues (Beamish 2007). Yet few minor and development leagues are unionized, leaving athletes in these leagues reliant on employment standards as their principle source of labour protection.

Scholars working in the tradition of the political economy of labour in Canada have observed that under neoliberalism, employment standards have become an increasingly important site of struggle (see Ross and Thomas this volume and Vosko this volume). As the following case study of major junior hockey illustrates, exploring professional sport through a political economy of labour can break down the perceived divide between the working lives of professional athletes and that of the broader working class.

EMPLOYMENT STANDARDS, LABOUR STRUGGLES, AND THE POLITICAL ECONOMY OF MAJOR JUNIOR HOCKEY

The Canadian Hockey League is an umbrella organization that represents sixty teams and just over 1,300 players in three Canadian-based major junior hockey leagues: the Ontario Hockey League (OHL), the Western Hockey League (WHL), and the Quebec Major Junior Hockey League (QMJHL).[6] Teams are located in small to midsize cities in nine Canadian provinces with eight teams located in five American states. Major junior hockey is the highest level of junior hockey competition, which is played by young men between the ages of sixteen and twenty.

The CHL self-classifies as an "amateur student-athlete development league" (see CHL 2014). This classification requires deconstructing. First, while some major junior hockey players are enrolled in high school or online education programs, a player need not be a student to play in the CHL. Second, as the "world's premier development hockey league" (CHL 2014), the CHL claims to supply more players to the NHL than any other league, including the US college hockey system. However, while the CHL may advertise itself as the "Gateway to the NHL," fewer than five per cent of the league's players go on to play in hockey's elite league (Campbell 2007). Third, the CHL's amateur status is an illusion: CHL franchises are private, for-profit businesses and players work under the control and direction of their clubs in return for compensation.

In fact, the CHL is a significant site of capital accumulation. While the lowest average per game attendance across its three leagues is around 2,000, the Quebec Remparts pull in crowds of 14,000 – larger than four NHL teams (Slawson 2016). Other teams such as the London Knights and Calgary Hitmen regularly see crowds of 8,000 to 9,000. And while tickets are reasonably priced compared to the NHL, like a major league sports franchise, CHL clubs rely on multiple sources of revenue beyond ticket sales. In addition to premium seating (such as corporate boxes), teams make money from: in-stadium food concessions; team merchandise, such as jerseys, hats, and other memorabilia; video game rights (the CHL has a deal with the popular video game company Electronic Arts); various corporate sponsorship deals; major events, including the World Junior Championships, the Mastercard Memorial Cup, and the CHL Top Prospect Game; kickbacks from NHL clubs when a major junior player is drafted and/or signs a professional contract; and finally, revenues from a multimedia platform deal with a cable television channel (see McKiven 2014).[7]

Whereas many NHL franchises are owned by large, integrated corporations with diverse interests in related leisure and entertainment businesses (Whitson and Gruneau 1997), with the exception of the Quebec Remparts, CHL clubs tend to be owned by local capitalists with connections to the community in which the team is based. However, as the history of major league sport makes clear, even civic-minded, locally based team owners are governed by the logic of profit maximization (Ammirante 2009). While it is difficult to determine exact team revenues (as all but one of the CHL's clubs is privately owned), CHL franchises have sold for as much as $10 million and mid-to-large market teams are estimated to be valued at approximately $8 million (Westhead and Cribb 2014). The Quebec Remparts recently sold to media conglomerate Quebecor for between $20 million and $25 million (Westhead 2015a). As league commissioner, David Branch, has stated, the CHL "is not as profitable as many people think, but we are not going to cry poor" (as quoted in Westhead and Cribb 2014).

The CHL as a Site of Employment Precarity

You were always abiding by the team's rules, even when you weren't at the rink … If you wanted to go out on a Thursday night and knock a few back, well you better do it before 10 p.m. because there's a curfew. You're always under the thumb of the boss, the coach. Hey, that's part of the game; you always need that figure, that power structure to keep things on track. But it was a job, a full-time job, make no mistake about it.[8]

CHL players work on an average thirty-five to forty hours per week and occasionally up to sixty-five hours or more (Lum 2014). This includes travel to and from away games (which ranges from between two and ten hours depending on the location of the opposition), time spent practicing and training, team promotional activities, and participation in games three times a week with seventy-five games per season (Curtis 2015).

Under a player's contract with their club and the league (called the "standard player agreement form" or "standard player contract"), a player is obliged to report to training camp, attend practice, games, and promotional events, and must follow the direction of the team's general manager, assistant general manager, coach, and assistant coaches. Players are supervised in the rink and at home, with curfews imposed during the regular season. The clubs also reserve the right to use a player's name, signature, statistical record, biographical information, and image likeness in promotional material and on team merchandise (Walter v. Lewiston 2014).

In return for their services, clubs provide players with room and board, travel expenses, and weekly stipends or "allowances" ranging from $35 to $150 per week.[9] In addition, players are compensated with an "education package" in the form of scholarship money to be used at a Canadian college or university of their choice. They are also covered under a limited medical and injury insurance policy. Finally, CHL clubs are obliged to provide players with training facilities and necessary hockey equipment.

Former players, labour advocates, and sports journalists have all criticized the CHL's compensation and benefits package on a number of grounds (see McKiven 2014; Black 2015; Lum 2014). First, the education package comes with a sunset clause that sees scholarships expire thirty months after a player's twentieth birthday (Curtis 2014). It is often the case that players who are not drafted to the NHL will look for a career in the minor leagues or in Europe. These players lose a year of scholarship money for every year they play pro hockey. Furthermore, if a player embarks on even a short pro career, their scholarships are likely to expire before they are ready to enrol in post-secondary education (McKiven 2014). And because of the amount of time and dedication devoted to travel, practice, promotion, and playing, it is difficult for players to maintain the good grades and enrolment necessary to move on to post-secondary education (see Walter v. Lewiston 2014). In fact, only 20 per cent of CHL players complete post-secondary (Lum 2014).

Second, unlike other workers employed by a CHL franchise – from the general managers and coaches, down to the concession stand workers and Zambonis – the young men upon whose labour the league rests – i.e., the players – receive no hourly wages, no overtime pay, no holiday pay, and no vacation pay. As three class-action lawsuits filed against the CHL on behalf of former and current players allege, by issuing stipends to players of as little as $35 a week and not providing for overtime, vacation, or holiday pay, the league and clubs violate minimum-wage laws and other employment standards in every Canadian province and American state in which they operate (Klein 2014).[10]

This gets to the crux of the matter: CHL players' employment status. Prior to 2013, the standard player contract referred to the relationship between a player and club as one of "independent contractor" (Walter v. Lewiston 2014). However, given that players are providing services to their club for a wage (i.e., the weekly stipend) and are under the control and direction of that club, there is a general consensus among labour lawyers that major junior players meet the legal definition of employees (Cribb 2015). There is also legal precedent to support this view. The case of *McCrimmon Holdings v. Canada (Minister of National Revenue)* (2000) centred on whether the Brandon Wheat Kings – a CHL franchise in the Western Hockey League – was responsible to pay certain assessments issued pursuant to the *Employment Insurance Act* and the *Canada Pension Plan* on the grounds that its players were employees acting under contracts of service (see Walter v. Lewiston 2014). Government lawyers argued that the weekly stipends were remuneration for services and thus insurable earnings. The Wheat Kings countered that players' relationship to the club was one of students engaged in private education and that remuneration was nothing more than an allowance paid to a student participating in a hockey program that offered scholarships for a university education (Walter v. Lewiston 2014).

In its ruling, the Tax Court of Canada concluded that the relationship between a club in the WHL and a player is one of employer-employee: "The business of the Wheat Kings is simply the business of hockey. It is a commercial organization ... carrying on business for profit. The players are employees who receive remuneration, defined as cash, pursuant to the appropriate regulations governing insurable earnings" (in Walter v. Lewiston 2014, 7).

Despite this ruling, the WHL, OHL, and QJMHL continued to use the term "independent contractor" in the standard player contract and failed to pay wages in accordance with the applicable employment standards legislation (Walter v. Lewiston 2014, 7). Facing growing public scrutiny, the CHL's three leagues redrafted player contracts in 2013, removing references to "fees" (weekly stipends are now termed "allowances") and all language referring to the status between player and club as one of "independent contractor." The new contract, which all players are required to sign, refer only to "the player" and "the club."

Since 2013, spokespeople for the CHL, including the league's commissioner, publicly refer to players as "amateur student-athletes."[11] While the term does not appear in the new contract, the use of this language is strategic. As a legal concept, "student-athlete" has its genesis south of the border. The National Collegiate Athletic Association (NCAA) – the governing body of US college sport – adopted and mandated the use of the term "student-athlete" in 1954 to support the notion that athletes in receipt of athletic scholarships playing revenue-generating sports (i.e., NCAA Division I football and basketball) should be considered students rather than employees of their universities (McCormick and McCormick 2006, 84). Like in the CHL, the NCAA's adoption of "student-athlete" was in response to an unfavourable court decision which ruled that Division I football and basketball players were in fact employees of their universities and thus entitled to statutory benefits under state law (McCormick and McCormick 2006, 83).[12]

As McCormick and McCormick (2006) have argued, the term "student-athlete" is a myth invented by the NCAA to deny athletes' employee status, obscure the reality of the university-athlete employment relationship, and to avoid universities' legal responsibilities as employers (see also Branch 2011). NCAA basketball and football is big business, generating billions of dollars in yearly revenues for the NCAA, colleges, and universities. Collectively, these institutions "profited immensely from the vigorous defense and preservation of this myth" (McCormick and McCormick 2006, 86). The irony of the CHL's adoption of the term "student-athlete" is that under NCAA eligibility rules designed to preserve college athletics' "amateur" status, major junior hockey players are ineligible for NCAA competition on the grounds that the CHL is a "professional hockey league" and any player signed to a CHL contract is therefore in violation of the principle of amateurism (see McKiven 2014).[13]

In either its use of the term "independent contractor" or "student-athlete," it is clear that the CHL is engaged in employee misclassification and regulatory evasion (see Vosko this volume), avoiding the league and its clubs' legal obligations under employment standards legislation, while reaping healthy profits through the exploitation of unpaid teenage athletes. For major junior hockey players, what emerges is a picture of employment precarity (see Vosko 2006b): low wages; little control over the conditions of their work; a lack of regulatory protection and access to statutory benefits; and as is typical for professional athletes, little job security as players can be traded, let go, or demoted to a lower league at any time, all the while performing work in which occupational injuries – including career-ending injuries – are common.

Lawsuits, Advocacy, and Unionization: The CHL as a Site of Resistance

While the CHL is a site of exploitation, it is also a site of resistance. Former players, labour advocates, and unions are engaged in various strategies to improve wages and working conditions in the league. As mentioned above, three class-action lawsuits have been filed against the CHL (and its member leagues and clubs) on behalf of former and current players. Collectively, these class actions are demanding $190 million in back wages, overtime, and holiday and vacation pay as well as punitive damages to be paid to between 4,000 and 5,000 former players (Hune-Brown 2014). While the cases have yet to be certified, there is "strong consensus among labour lawyers and hockey agents that junior players do meet the legal definition of employees working for private, for-profit businesses" and that the class-actions will be successful (Cribb 2015).

In addition, labour advocates, including the president of Canada's largest private sector union, Unifor, have called for the relevant regulatory bodies to investigate working conditions in the CHL (Black 2015). However, in Washington State, where four teams are based, this strategy has had limited success. At the behest of a formal complaint, the state's department of labour launched a child labour investigation centring on the employment status of the teams' sixteen and seventeen year-old players. The state's child labour laws stipulate that sixteen and seventeen year olds can only work four hours per day on a school day and up to sixteen hours per week and that they are entitled to the same minimum wage as adults (Westhead 2015a). In response to the investigation, team owners lobbied state politicians to pass legislation exempting players from the state's *Minimum Wage Act*, *Industrial Welfare Act*, and *Industrial Safety and Health Act* (Cohen 2015). These efforts were successful, and the law was passed in May 2015.[14]

In response to a similar complaint in Ontario, the provincial government's Minister of Labour has ordered staff to research whether OHL players are considered employees under the province's *Employment Standards Act* and *Labour Relations Act* (Westhead 2015a). With the province's labour laws currently under review, union leaders and CHL player advocates are also lobbying Ontario's Minister of Labour and Minister of Sport to set up a provincial taskforce to study the treatment of junior hockey players (Allingham 2015). This demand dovetails with a coordinated campaign by trade unions and social movement groups urging the government to update the province's labour laws and employment regulation regime, which fail to protect precariously employed workers and make it difficult for workers to unionize (Ross and Thomas this volume).

Amidst the lawsuits and labour investigations, there are also ongoing attempts to organize a players' union, including a recent effort by Canada's largest private sector union, Unifor. Player advocate, Jamie McKiven (2014), has argued that a CHL players' union would "help to ensure transparency and proper dispersal of revenues to ensure players are receiving adequate benefits packages including: medical, mental health support, education packages, and expense reimbursements." At a minimum, a collective agreement would: establish and manage an education fund for the players; eliminating the unfair and arbitrary rules that currently restrict player access to the education package; set league minimum salaries; introduce a grievance procedure; grant players personality rights revenue from CHL events and team merchandise; and ensure players have access to adequate health care, including mental health supports (see CHLPA 2012; McKiven 2014).

However, in addition to the usual fierce opposition mounted by employers, there are barriers to collective action that are somewhat unique to professional sport. The short career span of professional athletes acts as a disincentive to organize and go on strike. With an average career length of between four to six years, a season lost to a strike or lockout means the loss of a significant chunk of a player's lifetime earnings. There is also the related question of union or class consciousness: typically players consider themselves to be athletes lucky to play the game they love, not workers pitted in class struggle with team owners (Robidoux 2001). Historically, union organizers in major league sport have had to convince players – in the words of Marvin Miller, the legendary director of the Major League Baseball Player's Association – "to think like steelworkers" (Miller 1991, 82). This problem is even more pronounced in minor and development leagues. As Robidoux (2001, 153) observed in his study of a minor league hockey players, "because the opportunity to play professional hockey is, for most players, a childhood dream, few [players] scrutinize their job and/or working environment." Support for a union could get a player blacklisted, quashing their chances to play in the major leagues. In the case of the CHL, there is also the pressure that many coaches and parents will put on players to keep the league union-free, and the politically conservative culture of hockey more generally (see Whitson and Gruneau 2006).

Despite these barriers there is evidence to suggest that CHL players are willing to stand up for their rights, to "play left wing." In 2015, in response to the firing of their beloved coaching staff, the OHL's Flint Firebirds walked into their team owner's office, threw their jerseys on the floor, and collectively quit (Kennedy 2015a). In response to what was effectively a player strike, the owner of the Firebirds rehired the entire coaching staff and apologized to the players. Reflecting on these developments, the respected hockey agent Allen Walsh mused: "The whole situation proves again the power players at any level have when they stand together. Without players, there is no game" (as qtd. in Kennedy 2015a). Indeed, the incident suggests that under the right conditions, these young athletes are capable of banding together and exercising their collective power to improve their working lives.

CONCLUSION

In this chapter, I have argued for a renewed engagement between sport and critical political economy with the aim of advancing a political economy of sport labour. Critical approaches to sport that are concerned only with its ideological capacity – sport's role in maintaining relations of domination and reproducing the culture of capitalism – obscure the tensions, contradictions, and possibilities for progressive social transformation within it. In contrast, the analytical approach of the NCPE helps us see sport as contested terrain, making room for the agency of athletes, and for social struggle and resistance. Furthermore, through the lens of a political economy of sport labour, the distance between the lives and struggles of working athletes and the broader working class is narrowed, possibly opening up the prospect of fan-athlete solidarity against the interests of capital.

In the major leagues, players' unions have made tremendous gains for working athletes. Whereas union density in Canada and the United States has steadily declined since the 1980s, a high percentage of working athletes in major league sport are members of a union. The creation of two new leagues in the 1990s, the Women's National Basketball Association and Major League Soccer, was quickly followed by the formation of players' unions. Yet as the case of the CHL illustrates, minor and development leagues, which are the primary source of labour supply for the "majors," are significant sites of exploitation and precarity. In baseball and soccer, this labour supply extends to the Global South. In addition to leagues like the CHL, in these sports athlete development also relies on highly exploitative academy systems, based in developing countries that have links to professional clubs in Europe and North America. Taking advantage of weak labour laws and state regulatory capacity, and the absence of players' unions, academies develop young talent at a fraction of the cost of minor and development clubs in the rich countries. In baseball, young men aged fifteen to nineteen train in Major League Baseball-affiliated academies in the Dominican Republic and Venezuela that routinely violate international human rights and labour standards, in what Gordon (2013) has called the MLB's "sweatshop system." Similarly, professional soccer clubs based in Europe are increasingly reliant on systems of athlete recruitment and development in Africa, which critics argue mirror the exploitative neocolonial practices of multinational corporations in the resource extraction sector, but in this case Europe is extracting African football labour "on the cheap" (Garcia 2018).

But as the old left-wing adage goes, where there's oppression, there's resistance. We are in a period "defined both by conditions of heightened precariousness *and* emergent forms of resistance on a scale not seen for many years" (Ross and Thomas this volume). In a development that rocked US college athletics, in 2014 Northwestern University football players filed a petition with the National Labor Relations Board to form a union (see Zirin 2014). The NLRB ruled that football players are in fact employees of their universities, not student-athletes, and have the right to unionize. The Northwestern case further illuminates the interplay of sport and the broader political economy of precarious work. As sports journalist Dave Zirin (2014) observed, "the universities are afraid that if the football players can unionize, then the graduate teachers, the custodial staff, the work-study students and the cafeteria workers will all say, 'If they can be a recognized union, then why not us?'"[15]

On another front in sport's labour wars, minor league baseball players have launched a lawsuit alleging that their parent league, Major League Baseball (MLB), has failed to pay them the minimum wage (Kennedy 2015b). These players are employees of MLB but are not unionized or covered under the collective agreement between the league and the MLB Player's Association. The lawsuit contends that minor leaguers earn between $800 and $2,000 per month, which amounts to less than the US federal minimum wage. In a move reminiscent of the CHL in Washington State, the MLB has responded to the lawsuit by lobbying lawmakers to have minor-league baseball players classified as "seasonal" workers, which would exempt them from hourly wage laws (Kennedy 2015b).

Finally, there are rumblings of triathletes, tennis players, and mixed martial artists (in the highly lucrative Ultimate Fighting Championship) forming unions. All this is to say that as fast food workers, home care providers, and Walmart employees take to the streets in the fight for better wages and working conditions, athletes may soon be walking out of sports stadiums and arenas to join them.

NOTES

1 The National Football League (NFL), Major League Baseball (MLB), National Basketball Association (NBA), the National Hockey League (NHL), Major League Soccer (MLS), and the Women's National Basketball Association (WNBA) are all unionized workplaces. Hockey players in the two largest minor leagues in North American professional ice hockey, the American Hockey League (AHL) and ECHL, are also unionized as are players in the Arena Football League (AFL), considered to be the NFL's de facto minor league. However, players in the NBA's Developmental League (D-League) and Minor League Baseball are not. And as I discuss in this chapter, nor are players in the NHL's premier development league, the CHL.

2 The term "revenue-generating college sports" refers to NCAA Division I football and basketball.

3 This history is informed by Carrington and McDonald's (2009) excellent historical overview of the development of Marxist approaches within sport studies and the growth of a Marxist-inflected cultural studies of sport.

4 According to Booth (2015, 410), "Kidd argued that once city-based teams such as the Toronto Maple Leafs were enmeshed in commercially sponsored competitions, they lost their power to enunciate a sense of Canadian national identity. As part of a commodity market, players represented the highest bidder rather than their local communities." With the NHL dominant by the end of Second World War, the Amateur Canadian Hockey Association had been reduced to, in Kidd's words, a "slave farm of hockey" with US-based NHL controlling rules, style of play, player development, and national team" (in Booth 2015, 410).

5 One only has to glance over the contents of an issue of the leading journal in the field, *Journal of Sports Economics*, to see this is the case. In relation, Carrington and McDonald (2011, 5) note the political consequences of the Marxist retreat from the political economy of sport: "Despite much theoretically innovative work within recent Marxist scholarship, sport has remained a marginal and often neglected subject matter … In fact it could be argued, somewhat provocatively, that the 'leading edge' work on sport and capital is being produced by professors of Economics, often found within business schools and departments of Marketing and Advertising. That is, the economic impact and social significance of sport have not been lost on those who seek to accelerate the effects of sports globalization."

6 Each club has a roster of twenty-five players. Players enter the CHL through an annual draft system in which they are drafted by their respective CHL club from their minor hockey clubs at the age of fifteen or sixteen.

7 In 2014 the CHL and Sportsnet announced a twelve-year multiplatform rights extension reported to be worth $5 million a year (Westhead 2014).

8 Gene Chirallo, former major junior player and employment lawyer (in Curtis 2014).

9 Allowances vary by member league and by players' age, with older players receiving a higher amount. Players are entitled to small bonuses based on team performance.

10 The CHL class action is actually three class actions: one in Toronto (against the CHL, OHL, and OHL teams), one in Calgary (against the CHL, WHL, and WHL teams) and one in Montreal (against the CHL, QMJHL, and QMJHL teams).

11 For instance, in a newspaper article on the lawsuits his league is facing, Branch stated: "Our players are some of the best amateur student-athletes in the world, and we are proud to provide them with the support, programs and tools to ensure they have the best player experience" (in Klein 2014).

12 The decision was in *University of Denver v. Nemeth* in which "the Colorado
    Supreme Court upheld a determination by the state Industrial Commission
    that Ernest Nemeth, a football player at the University of Denver, was an
    "employee" within the meaning of the Colorado workers' compensation stat-
    ute. Thus, the university was obligated to provide workers' compensation for
    his football injuries" (McCormick and McCormick 2006, 83).

13 Due to both the stipends CHL players receive and to the fact that some CHL
    players have already signed professional contracts with NHL clubs, making
    them professionals under NCAA regulations.

14 The law was reportedly passed against the legal advice of the state's assistant
    attorney general who argued that the players should be considered as employ-
    ees (Westhead 2015a).

15 While the ruling has since been overturned, the newly formed College Athletes
    Players Association, backed by the United Steelworkers union, have vowed to
    continue the fight until college athletes can collectively bargain for stipends,
    better health coverage, and limits on travel and playing time, which impede
    athletes' ability to earn decent grades and graduate from university (see CAPA
    2015).

16

Organizing in Precarious Times: The Political Economy of Work and Workers' Movements after the Great Recession

Stephanie Ross and Mark P. Thomas

Precarious employment is increasingly the "new normal" in Canada's labour market. Whether in the form of low job security, low wages, low control over the labour process, or a lack of regulatory protection from either collective agreements or labour and employment laws, growing numbers of workers are experiencing conditions of employment characterized by some degree of precariousness (Standing 2011; Vosko 2006b, this volume). Some groups of workers, including women, racialized workers, newcomers, people with disabilities, and Indigenous peoples, have always been more subject to these disadvantageous labour market conditions. However, precariousness has now spread to what have been considered "good jobs." These include industrial manufacturing jobs that were transformed through unionization, public sector employment that had some measure of protection from market booms and busts, and professions whose high skill content meant autonomy and irreplaceability, all of which have been eroded. Beginning in the 1970s, the relentless reorganization of employment normalized insecurity, albeit unevenly, across the Canadian labour market. The rise of temporary contracts, part-time work, and multiple job-holding, accompanied by the neoliberal re-regulation of labour and employment laws and set in the context of an increasingly integrated global economy, have normalized precariousness and contributed to a growing economic polarization in Canadian society (OCF 2015; PEPSO 2013).

These developments have had a significant impact on both the capacities of organized labour to improve working conditions and the collective capacity of the working class to organize against capitalism more generally. The unionization rate in Canada peaked in the mid-1980s, dropped dramatically in the 1990s, and has since stagnated. The geographic reorganization of production on a global scale, facilitated by the rapid development of global supply chains and implementation of free trade agreements, contributed to deindustrialization in Canada and decimated unionization in the manufacturing sector – a traditional area of union strength. In the public sector, union strength was weakened through waves of neoliberalism that restricted the right to strike, downsized public sector workforces, and sought to expose public sector workers to market forces. The private service sector, responsible for significant job growth in general and in precarious employment in particular, has proven highly resistant to unionization efforts.

Despite these challenges, new movements and strategies of resistance have emerged to counter these processes. Notable examples include the anti-austerity Occupy movement, the Fight for $15 and Fairness campaign to raise the minimum wage, and new associational forms such as community-based worker centres. These initiatives are largely taking place outside formal union structures, at a time when the labour movement is on the defensive and experiencing declining membership in some sectors, creating a shift in where the base of the union movement is located. At the same time, unions are themselves attempting to reorganize and reorient to the new conditions and politics of production.

Set in this general context, this chapter aims to explore the contemporary political economy of work[1] and workers' movements in Canada. As the general trajectory that began in the 1970s has been well documented (see Fudge and Vosko 2003; Phillips 1997; Stanford and Gindin 2003), we focus specifically on developments post-2008, the time of the so-called Great Recession and its aftermath. This period is of significance as it is defined both by conditions of heightened precariousness and emergent forms of resistance on a scale not seen for many years. Recognizing that wage labour within capitalism has always created conditions of precariousness for the working class (Palmer 2013), this chapter seeks to examine the particular conditions of precarious employment that are unique to the current conjuncture. Also recognizing the general dynamic of resistance that emerges as workers respond to conditions of alienation and exploitation within capitalist workplaces, the chapter seeks to reveal this dynamic in contemporary forms of precarious employment. Post-2008, how have jobs been transformed, what forms of resistance are emerging in response, and what are the implications for labour organizing?

A second aim of the chapter is to explore the ways in which the political economy perspective remains relevant to exploring these questions. In taking up this matter, the chapter also offers a reflection on the Canadian political economy (CPE) tradition in terms of its attention to questions of work, employment, and labour.[2] Specifically, what does CPE contribute in terms of helping us understand the contemporary social organization of employment, labour markets, and workers' movements? What new analytic directions do we need to pursue in order to explain the political economy of employment and workers' movements? In this regard, CPE is distinct from mainstream Industrial Relations (IR) and Human Resource Management (HRM) scholarship, two predominant fields of research on the changing workplace. In IR research, the shifting organization of work is often presented as a reality to adapt to or moderate through institutional regulation. With a tendency to see the postwar industrial relations framework – including labour and employment legislation, unions, and collective bargaining – as having provided "balance" between labour and employers, contemporary trends towards precarity are problematic insofar as they undermine that balance (see Godard 2017). Within IR, accounts of how the changing nature of work makes collective bargaining difficult are used to support policy recommendations for how to "restore balance," rather than to examine either the flaws in the previous system or the underlying shifts in class power that complicate a return to modified postwar institutions. Within the management-oriented HRM tradition, interest lies in developing strategies for employee/personnel (i.e., human resource) management, including through organizational change brought on with the implementation of new employment relationships (Thompson and McHugh 2002). For those working within this perspective, such trends are often lauded as providing employers with much-needed flexibility and global competitiveness, even as they present challenges for maintaining employee loyalty, morale, and productivity. Both IR and HRM scholars thus seek to develop solutions to manage the negative "side effects" of precarious employment without contesting the underlying social forces and processes that produce precariousness in the first place.

In contrast, we frame our response through a political economy perspective informed by an intersectional analysis that critically examines the underlying power inequalities in the organization of work. Grounded in the materialist approach of political economy outlined in earlier chapters of this volume, class remains a central concept and class relations are seen as definitive of the social context. Moreover, we adopt a materialist approach that aims to capture the holistic set of social relations that shape class, including but not limited to gender, racialization, and citizenship status (see Clement, Sharma in this volume). These intersections, grounded in the material context created by transformations in the organization of work, become particularly salient in our exploration of the new forms of worker organizing that have emerged in response to contemporary conditions of precariousness, particularly through organizing that is taking place within groups that have not only been marginalized in the workplace, but also within the formal labour movement. Political economy scholarship, we argue, must contend with both the limits and possibilities of these initiatives in terms of their capacities for social transformation.

The chapter proceeds in two main sections. First, we outline key dynamics contributing to the transformation of employment, focusing on: (i) the structure of the labour market; (ii) labour-management relations; and (iii) the neoliberal politics of precarious employment. These dynamics are described in relation to general tendencies that have been present for several decades and that include developments at the scale of the global economy, though emphasis is placed on the post-2008 period. Second, we consider the dynamics of worker organizing in this same period. Here, focus is placed on both the economic and political dilemmas faced by the labour movement itself, as well as forms of resistance aiming to counter precariousness in employment that have emerged in spaces where unions are either absent or have been unable to have a meaningful effect. The chapter concludes by considering the implications for the longer-term trajectory of the political economy of employment and workers' movements in Canada.

THE POLITICAL ECONOMY OF PRECARIOUS EMPLOYMENT AFTER THE GREAT RECESSION

By the early 2000s, many were already observing the significant fraying of the elements of the Fordist regime of accumulation and its expression in labour-management relations and state regulation. This erosion took place over several decades beginning in the 1970s, and can be attributed to the rise in employer power connected to processes of global economic restructuring, including the outsourcing of manufacturing and goods production through global supply chains, as well as the rise of neoliberalism in many Western capitalist democracies (Jackson and Thomas 2017).

The trends towards more precarious labour markets, aggressive employer strategies, and neoliberal state policies were thus already well underway by the time the Great Recession hit in 2008 – indeed, that recession was in part caused by the effects of those very dynamics (Albo, Gindin, and Panitch 2010). In that sense, 2008 was not a turning point for the fortunes of labour; rather, it is when the severity of the damage done to the strategic capacity of the union movement became undeniable.

Precariousness in the Labour Market

In the years preceding and certainly following the Great Recession, the political economy of work has been characterized by the spread of precarious employment into most sectors of the labour market. Rather than a dichotomy between "good" and "bad" jobs, precariousness in employment can be characterized as a condition that exists on a continuum and that is multiply determined through a combination of factors (Vosko 2006b). Precarious employment includes (but is not limited to) workers who are employed in a range of so-called nonstandard employment relationships, such as permanent part-time, full- and part-time temporary workers, solo self-employed, and self-employed employers. Moreover, conditions of precariousness are present even in sectors of the labour market that have traditionally been sites of more stable employment (PEPSO 2013).[3] A major factor in this context of precarious employment is unionization. While currently approximately 30 per cent of Canada's labour force is unionized, this is down notably from a peak of 38 per cent in 1984. Moreover, there are significant disparities that are telling in terms of the spread of precarious employment. For example, while approximately 71 per cent of public sector workers are unionized, this is only 16 per cent in the private sector. While 33 per cent of full-time workers are unionized, only 25 per cent of part-time workers have union representation. And while the unionization rate is relatively high in large workplaces (those with over 500 employees) at 55 per cent, in small workplaces (under twenty employees), the rate is only 15 per cent (Statistics Canada 2013c).

The growth of precarious employment should be set in the context of a larger global shift towards "flexibility," a process of restructuring labour markets, jobs and production methods, and human resource and industrial relations practices that began in the 1970s as employers sought to reorganize production on a global scale to counter a downturn in profitability (Harvey 1990; Moody 1997; Thomas 2009). Accelerating through the 1990s, "flexibility" entailed the growing use of nonstandard employment relationships in order to break apart job tenure and produce "numerical flexibility" in hiring practices through the use of temporary contracts. As well, "time flexibility," through both the growth of part-time labour and increased overtime hours, enabled production practices more tightly conditioned by demand cycles and resulted in an increasing polarization in working time (Basso 2003). Finally, "functional flexibility," integrated into work processes through lean production methods, involved multi-tasking, work intensification, and management-by-stress. Labour "flexibility" was promoted in the business community as a strategy to restore competitiveness following the breakdown of the profitability enjoyed in the postwar boom period. Over several decades, the spread of "flexible" work arrangements and "flexible" work processes – including through outsourcing arrangements ("fissuring") whereby corporations distance themselves from the employment relationship (Weil 2014) – produced a political economy of work increasingly characterized by rising insecurity, combined, quite often, with an intensified labour process. Thus, precarious employment became normalized in many/most sectors of Canada's labour market.

All workers did not experience these conditions in the same form, or on equal terms: they were highly variegated according to region, sector, and workers' social location (Thomas and Tufts 2016a; Vosko et al. 2003). In the core of the private sector manufacturing workforce, the geographic fragmentation of production processes facilitated by the rise of global supply chains and free trade agreements decimated the wages, working conditions, and job security of blue-collar workers. In the heavily unionized public sector, successive assaults by neoliberal governments ranged from downsizing and outsourcing to the abrogation of collective bargaining rights. In the fast-growing private service sector, part-time work, temporary contracts, and a lack of union protection quickly became the norm. Moreover, precariousness was conditioned by gender, race, and citizenship status, with groups already disadvantaged in the labour market over-represented in forms of precarious employment. As we outline further below, these factors are significant in understanding the dynamics of organizing as groups of workers seek to contest precariousness. In particular, for those workers who are not only marginalized in the labour market, but also in the labour movement, contesting precarious employment has necessitated the emergence of new organizing forms and strategies.

Labour-Management Relations in the Private Sector

The spread of precarious employment also required a major reorientation in capital's approach to labour-management relations, particularly in highly unionized sectors. The 2000s thus ushered in a renewed aggressiveness towards unions from employers in both the public and private sector. Although it has often been said that Canadian employers have been much less virulently anti-union than their US counterparts, indications abound of a shift away from the postwar consensus. While many private sector employers pursued restructuring of their labour processes and labour forces throughout the 1990s, few undertook full frontal attacks against their employees in the ways that US employers did in the 1980s, the latter demanding major concessions to work rules and worker compensation (Moody 1988). By 2008, however, the gloves were off: the recession gave employers in Canada both the pretext and the material conditions with which to impose concessionary deals on unionized workers, and lockouts became a more common tactic. The means to achieve these goals included companies' well-established global supply chains with multiple production centres; corporate diversification that minimized reliance on particular profit streams; and free trade agreements. Governments were content to abet employers in their search for dominance.

There was another wave of closures in manufacturing and resource sectors beginning in 2005. In the auto sector, both General Motors (GM) and Chrysler asked for government bailouts to weather the collapse of consumer demand after 2008. Both the US and Canadian governments required major concessions from unionized workers in return for such bailout money. At GM, this meant the introduction in the 2009 bargaining round of a second tier of Supplemental Workforce Employees (SWES), workers paid a lower wage and afforded more limited access to job security and union representation rights but working side by side with permanent seniority employees. Other employers, like US Steel and Air Canada, set their sights on breaking free of legacy costs in the form of defined benefit pension plans. Despite the employment guarantees they agreed to as a condition of being permitted to purchase the struggling Stelco, US Steel proceeded to lock out its employees for well over a year in 2009 and has since stripped its Hamilton facilities of all valuable production (Arnold 2012). Air Canada pushed its various employee groups to the brink of strikes in 2012 on the question of two-tier pensions (Stevens and Nesbitt 2014). However, the most extreme example of aggressive employer anti-unionism was Caterpillar's impossible demand for a 50 per cent wage cut at their Electro-Motive locomotive plant in London, Ontario. When CAW Local 27 refused, Caterpillar locked them out on New Year's Day 2012, and shuttered the plant a mere month later (Ross and Russell 2018).

Union responses to this shift in their employers' approach to labour relations varied widely. Some unions retained a modest ability to "deliver the goods" and make gains at the workplace, particularly those situated in those sectors of the economy growing through this period.[4] Other unions accepted concessions that they had previously resisted, such as tiered collective agreements and workplaces, hoping to minimize the damage and weather the storm. Still others, like USW at Vale and US Steel, CAW at Caterpillar, and unions at Air Canada, were more overtly resistant but unable to develop an effective strategy that would not only allow them to block employer demands but also delegitimize these kinds of demands. The Caterpillar conflict was a case of lost opportunity: while there was widespread popular revulsion against a corporation making record profits, and some spirited community mobilization, this was never generalized to foster a movement against similar tactics taking place in workplaces across the country. In private sector industries made mobile via globalization, many unions have had to confront the fact that they have nearly no meaningful strike power, though some unions in private services, for example in the hospitality sector, have been able to use strikes to greater effect (Tufts 2014).

Neoliberalism, Austerity, and the Politics of Precarious Employment

The heightened precariousness in Canada's labour market has been brought about through successive waves of the neoliberal re-regulation of labour laws and policies. Indeed, capital's labour "flexibility" strategies were actively enabled by governments through neoliberal labour market policies that both removed various forms of social protection and created new forms of regulation that exposed them to the vagaries of the market. Here we see "neoliberalization" (Peck et al. 2009a) as a process of creating openings for market forces. In the realm of labour relations, neoliberalization is enacted through the removal of labour rights and employment standards established in law, the broader re-regulation of labour markets through social and economic policy, and government employment practices vis-à-vis public sector workforces. While a general tendency that has reshaped Western labour markets for several decades (dating to the early 1980s in the United States and the United Kingdom), neoliberalization must be seen as an uneven process, with differential impacts across space and scale, as well as workers' social location (Peck et al. 2009a; Thomas and Tufts 2016a).

In the Canadian case, the uneven and spatially variegated impacts of neoliberalization can be seen through the variety of neoliberal policies and practices at municipal, provincial, and federal levels. Early neoliberal efforts that instigated the reshaping of work in Canada involve developments at the transnational scale, including the adoption of the Canada-US Free Trade Agreement in 1988, followed by the North American Free Trade Agreement in 1993, steps that deregulated cross-border trade, contributed to the realignment of industrial manufacturing across the North American region, and resulted in job losses in the heavily unionized automobile manufacturing industry (Jackson 1999). The dramatic federal budget cuts implemented in the mid-1990s through the Canada Health and Social Transfer significantly reduced transfer payments to the provinces, with direct implications for the funding of public services and compensation for public sector workers (McBride and Shields 1997). Labour market policy became driven by supply-side considerations, particularly with respect to training, with unemployed workers made individually responsible for "investing" in their "human capital" to compete for twenty-first century jobs. These initial phases of neoliberalization contributed to the normalization of precarious employment, ensuring that the public sector, whether as an employer or a provider of decommodified and redistributive public services, was neither a haven from developments in private sector workplaces nor a counterbalance to the effects of precarious employment on workers' lives. This shift was experienced in different ways by workers in the public and private sectors and varied by regional labour markets as well. Across the public and private (and particularly blue collar manufacturing) sectors, and despite the unevenness of neoliberalization, there was nevertheless evidence of growing insecurity in job tenure, as well as declining union strength.

Neoliberal governments also made labour and employment law reforms at the provincial level to further facilitate the spread of labour market flexibility. Given jurisdictional arrangements in the Canadian state, where the provinces retain primary responsibility for regulating labour and employment conditions for most workers, the actions of provincial neoliberal governments are particularly notable here. The labour law reforms of Mike Harris's Ontario government provide an early leading example, as that government altered the province's *Labour Relations Act* in 1995 to make certification more difficult, lower the threshold for decertification, and enable the use of replacement workers during strikes (Panitch and Swartz 2003). Reforms to provincial employment standards contributed to the trend towards precarious employment as well, with leading examples in Ontario and BC. In Ontario, in 2000, hours of work limits were increased from forty-eight to sixty, provisions for the averaging of overtime hours were introduced as a means to avoid overtime premium pay, and the minimum wage was frozen from 1996 to 2004. In BC, provisions to the province's employment standards (ES) legislation, introduced in 2002, included allowing for averaging agreements for overtime hours, changes to enforcement procedures that placed greater onus on individual workers to resolve complaints, and the exclusion of workers covered by a collective agreement even in cases where the agreement contained standards below the legislated minimum (Fairey 2007). While labour law reforms contributed to the erosion of union strength by impacting union capacities for organizing, ES reforms had the effect of lowering the floor of social protection for workers without union coverage (Thomas 2009). The erosion of ES also heightened racialized labour market inequality through minimum wage freezes, exemptions from legislated standards, and poor enforcement practices, all of which disproportionately impact jobs performed by racialized workers (Thomas 2010).

Neoliberalization has also meant a more aggressive approach to labour-management relations at all three levels of government. From the mid-1990s onwards, federal, provincial, and municipal public sector workers found themselves subject to renewed attacks through layoffs and wage freezes due to the cost-containment efforts of neoliberal governments (Ross and Savage 2013). Neoliberal labour relations strategies included increased use of back-to-work legislation, expansive essential worker designations, and the imposition of collective agreements. Given the state's normative role as a "model employer," these shifts in public sector labour relations demonstrated to the private sector what would be tolerated in labour relations in the rest of the economy.

Turning to the post-2008 context, neoliberalization intensified following the Great Recession with the adoption of austerity measures at the federal, provincial, and municipal levels in Canada. The politics of austerity reflected the strategy of neoliberal governments post-2008 to undertake further cost containment and instil labour discipline as a response to the global economic downturn, with significant impact on public policy, labour regulation, and labour rights (Albo et al. 2010).

Like neoliberalism more generally, austerity policies and practices were experienced unevenly across Western labour markets, and in particular targeted public sector workers through wage freezes, downsizing, and concessionary bargaining (Ross and Savage 2013). At the federal level, the government implemented back-to-work legislation to restrain collective bargaining efforts of air transport workers and postal workers, while provincial governments imposed similar restraints on teachers, health care workers, and civil servants (Camfield 2006, 2009). Municipal governments engaged in aggressive labour relations tactics with unionized municipal workers, including through both concessionary bargaining and the privatization of municipal services (Fanelli and Thomas 2011; Thomas and Tufts 2016a; Tucker 2014).

The processes of neoliberalization in general, and austerity in particular, perhaps drew an end to the period of "permanent exceptionalism" (Panitch and Swartz 2008, 2013), where in the years following the "postwar settlement" that established collective bargaining rights for workers in Canada, federal and provincial governments, as a strategy to contain labour struggles, often departed from the formal labour rights entrenched in law but without changing the legal framework of industrial relations. However, by the early years of the twenty-first century, government incursions into the rights to organize, bargain collectively, and strike were of a character that indicated that the pretence of "exceptionalism" was being dispensed with. This shift was exemplified by a move away from card-check certification in nearly every province. Other notable provincial examples include legislation that restricted the scope of collective bargaining (for example for teachers and health care workers) and imposed collective agreements in British Columbia, essential service legislation in Saskatchewan and Ontario that applied to transit workers, and Nova Scotia bills that forcibly merged bargaining units in health care, while the federal government restricted the right to strike of workers in its jurisdiction (as discussed above) and unilaterally removed sick days from collective agreements. Rather than being short-term measures for coping with a temporary fiscal crisis, post-2008 austerity policies aimed to consolidate the defeat of labour that had been cultivated over the earlier phases of neoliberalism. Ironically, only the Supreme Court of Canada – never considered to be a friend of labour – provided some relief against this onslaught, most notably through a series of rulings that revisited the disappointing Labour Trilogy and provided some constitutional protection for the rights to organize, bargain, and strike.

Overall, several decades of neoliberalism, combined with its most recent manifestation through the politics of austerity, served to significantly weaken the floor of labour rights shaping both employment conditions overall and the formal institutions of the labour movement. Moreover, these processes combined attacks on public sector workers and their unions with the dismantling of public services.

LABOUR'S STRATEGIC IMPASSE: WAITING FOR A NEW MOVEMENT TO BE BORN?

In conjunction with the results of collective bargaining, which have been decidedly mixed, the most commonly used indicator of the health of the labour movement is union density – the percentage of workers in a given area that are either members of or covered by the provisions of a collective agreement. By this measure, even after the Great Recession, the Canadian labour movement continues to be relatively healthy and stable, with overall density at 28.4 per cent in 2016 (Statistics Canada 2017a). Canada's union density has remained around 30 per cent over the past fifteen years (despite a more significant decline between the late 1980s and mid-1990s). However, relative stability in public sector employment, which remains highly unionized, masks some very troubling trends: a major decline in private sector union density, as well as a persistent inability to make significant inroads in particular industries that have relatively high levels of job growth, such as retail and other private sector services. There are signs that these private sector declines are slowly pulling the overall unionization rate down.

However, another important assessment of the labour movement's capacity lies in their political-strategic orientation. In a previous iteration of this collection, Gindin and Stanford (2003, 423) expressed a somewhat optimistic view of the political developments within Canada's progressive oppositional forces, of which the union movement was one. They noted three political developments: 1) the leadership of progressive forces had shifted from electoral/party politics to "coalitions of extra-parliamentary forces"; 2) the ideology of those extra-parliamentary forces was shifting; and 3) a series of political projects aimed at generating a new politics of the left in Canada was emerging.

Indeed, in the ten years leading up to that assessment, there was much to be optimistic about. For a brief period, the potential seemed to exist for both renewal of labour militancy and a reinvigorated political strategy for fighting neoliberalism centred around extra-parliamentary mobilization. The Ontario Days of Action, a series of eleven spirited and creative community-based mass walkouts between 1995 and 1998 that protested the Mike Harris Conservative government's neoliberal policies, were widely considered evidence of a political turning point (Moody 1997). This was followed in 1998 by a two-week illegal strike by Ontario teachers, who were protesting government policies on education funding. Elsewhere in the country, resistance came from striking hospital workers in Calgary, public sector workers in New Brunswick, and through general strikes involving teachers and hospital workers in British Columbia. These struggles were enveloped in a large wave of creative, audacious, and militant "anti-globalization" protests that drew the organized union movement together with a range of other allies fighting various aspects of the global economic order, including major protests at the 1997 APEC summit in Vancouver and the 2001 Summit of the Americas in Quebec City (Klein 2002; Ross 2003). At the same time, the New Politics Initiative emerged in 2001 in an attempt to move the NDP back to the left. A project reminiscent of the Waffle of the early 1970s, a group of activists both within and outside the NDP – including MPs Libby Davies and Svend Robinson, prominent feminist activist Judy Rebick, and Jim Stanford, a CAW economist and contributor to this volume – attempted to shake the NDP's acceptance of the neoliberal consensus and advocated the founding of a new party based on stronger alliance with those social movement forces mobilizing in the streets (New Politics Initiative 2001).

The élan of extra-parliamentary mobilization of the late 1990s and early 2000s was abruptly halted by the aftermath of 9/11. While there were always tensions in the union movement's relationship to the global justice movement and its repertoires, as evidenced in the oft-told story of the Quebec City marchers being told by union parade marshals to march away from the fence, 9/11 pushed many unions back to the more comfortable terrain of electoral politics. Despite a fragmentation in strategy – between steadfast NDP partisanship on the one hand, and strategic voting campaigns to block the worst manifestations of neoliberal government on the other (Savage 2012) – significant elements of the union movement have engaged in electoralism, as evidenced by the NDP's Orange Wave in 2011, the OFL's #StopHudak campaign in 2014, the election of Rachel Notley's NDP government in Alberta in 2015, and the anti-Harper 2015 Federal Election campaign. The Harper Government's pitiless, mean-spirited, and anti-intellectual version of neoliberalism pulled some professional public sector unions into overt electoral mobilizing for the first time in their history, including the Professional Institute of the Public Service of Canada, the Canadian Association of Professional Employees, and the Association of Justice Counsel. Even when successful in their own terms, however, these political mobilizations have not generated a substantial alternative to neoliberal policy approaches.

By the beginning of the 2010s, however, we have witnessed a significant revival of extra-parliamentary struggle, in part as an expression of utter frustration with the deepening of austerity as the policy response to the 2008 financial crisis. With the outbreak of the Occupy Wall Street movement in 2011, various unions provided financial resources and support to sit-ins and occupations of key public spaces such as the occupation of St James Park in Toronto, which received material support from some Ontario unions. Given that their message about the growing problem of income inequality meshed with longstanding warnings from the labour movement, the Occupy movement's targeting of the wealthy 1 per cent bolstered the efforts of Canadian unions in the post-Occupy political environment, for example through campaigns that opposed the privatization of public services and that connected inequality and corporate welfare (Tufts and Thomas 2014). Unions, especially those located in western Canada, also supported the Idle No More movement's blockages of key transportation corridors and flash mobs in malls to protest the Harper Government's neglect of Indigenous issues. Other key initiatives in this vein include Black Lives Matter and the environmental/climate justice movement. The 2010 G20 summit in Toronto saw a reconnection of organized labour to the global justice movement, with a major trade union presence in multi-day protests that drew tens of thousands into the streets. Importantly, all of these movements contained demands of an economic-material nature, but were nowhere led by the union movement. Indeed, although there have been strong statements of support from the elements of the official labour movement, at best they remain followers or passive supporters. Some may justify this in terms of the norms of being a good ally, but this may also be seen as an inability (or reluctance) to expand the labour movement's "culture of solidarity" in a more profound way (Swartz and Warskett 2012).

Some labour federations and district councils have made real efforts to prioritize struggles and campaigns that speak to both union and non-union workers' interests, including Campaign to Raise the Minimum Wage/Fight for $15 and Fairness, the Ontario Common Front, and the Canadian Labour Congress' campaigns on improving public pensions and established a national Pharmacare program. Despite these promising examples, however, most unions have generally remained focused on the defence of their members' interests defined in fairly conventional ways. This strategic and tactical conservatism is a product of both the conjunctural effects of neoliberal politics and a deeper structural constraint rooted in the nature of the legal framework of postwar unionism. Despite their willingness to engage in political contestation, unions remain attached to the forms of power bestowed upon them by labour law – mandatory union recognition, a legally supported certification system, and the Rand Formula's union security provisions – even though these very same powers come with an obligation to adhere to "responsible unionism" and forego more militant and inclusive organizing approaches and identities. Speaking of a much earlier context, Panitch and Swartz (2008, 21) argued: "The trade unionism which developed in Canada during the post-war years bore all the signs of the web of legal restrictions which enveloped it. Its practices and consciousness were highly legalistic and bureaucratic, and therefore its collective strength was limited." The institutional arrangements and practices that emerged out of the arrangements of the "postwar settlement" continue to shape the trajectory of union action in the present context, whether in the realm of organizing, representation, or mobilization. For Gindin (2013), Canadian unions now suffer from a deep and cumulative ideological and organizational crisis that has narrowed their ambitions, solidarities, and capacities.

The inability of unions to represent significant groups of workers via the legal certification model[5] has led to a flowering of new workers' organizations attempting to organize and represent workers in new ways. Sometimes captured under the banner of "alt-labour," many of these are part of a larger movement based in the US, whose own labour movement has been driven via desperation to take up new (or even old) strategies (Eidelson 2013). Perhaps the most important of these have been workers' centres, community-based organizations that use a combination of servicing, advocacy, political mobilization, and direct action to challenge both employers and governments (Fine 2006). Unhindered by the legal requirements or restrictions placed on unions, workers' centres possess different sets of capacities than do unions. Such organizations assist non-unionized workers in filing employment standards complaints, facilitate labour rights education, organize demonstrations and actions in response to workplace rights violations, foster coalition-based labour activism, and engage in political campaigns to pressure for legislative reform (Cranford and Ladd 2003). Because of the intersection between non-union status and other patterns of labour market inequality, workers' centres have also provided much needed representation for those marginalized by their gender, race, ethnicity, or citizenship status (Fine 2006; Hetland 2015). The workers' centre model is not without limitations, however. Such centres often must grapple with other legal restrictions, such as the charitable status prohibition on engaging in "political activity." They are also often dependent on external and foundation funding. Without the legal ability to collect dues that the Rand Formula provides unions, workers' centres' membership numbers are unstable (Black 2012).

Nevertheless, these organizations have won remarkable victories in the US. Many of their Canadian counterparts, such as the Toronto Workers' Action Centre, have similarly led successful campaigns to change employment standards legislation and to pressure for improved enforcement practices. Fight for $15 and Fairness is a highly notable example of precarious worker organizing, with workers in both Canada and the US having launched campaigns to establish a $15 minimum wage (Bush and Abdelbaki 2016; Ehrcke 2015). Building on the demands of the Occupy movement, and arising from the organizing activities of labour and community-based organizations including worker centres, Fight for $15 began with a day of demonstrations and walkouts undertaken by fast food workers in New York City in the fall of 2012. The following year, the campaign grew to a number of US cities and involved low-wage workers in fast food and retail services. The campaign was formally launched in Canada with a series of province-wide demonstrations on 15 April 2015, marking a national day of action, which was repeated in April 2016. Involving unions, labour federations, and workers' centres, the campaign is built through coalition-based organizing aimed at transforming the conditions of the low-wage labour market. Moreover, given that workers of colour are highly over-represented in low-wage work in both Canada and the United States, the campaign is informed by anti-racist principles and maintains aims of racial equity as well. The impact of the campaign is evidenced by recent minimum wage increases in Ontario, Canada, as well as at both municipal and state levels in the United States.

Another example of organizing against precarious work is evident in the efforts of the Toronto-based Good Jobs for All Coalition of labour, community, and social justice organizations and activists to contest the contracting out of municipal building cleaning services (Carson and Siemiatycki 2014; Thomas and Tufts 2016b; Vosko and Thomas 2014). In 2012, then-mayor Rob Ford sought to privatize cleaning services in an effort to reduce the labour costs of work performed by unionized municipal cleaners, many of whom are racialized, older immigrant women. Through a campaign that connected privatization to the insecurity of low-wage work, the Good Jobs for All Coalition built support within Toronto city council to defeat the contracting out initiative. As this campaign took place in the context of a larger austerity-driven attack on the public sector, the Good Jobs campaign acted to not only contest precarious work but also preserve public sector jobs and the provision of public services.

Organizing amongst migrant agricultural workers and their allies provides illustration of the intersection between struggles for workplace justice and struggles for migrant justice (as Sharma discusses in this volume). In Ontario, farmworkers, including migrant farmworkers employed in the Seasonal Agricultural Workers Program, have historically been exempt from labour relations legislation that facilitates freedom of association and collective bargaining. However, this exclusion has been contested (though unsuccessfully) through a campaign to win the legal right to organize and bargain collectively for agricultural workers in Ontario led by the UFCW. While migrant farmworkers in Ontario continue to lack collective bargaining rights, the UFCW has established community centres to provide services to migrant workers in communities where they are present. Moreover, the UFCW has undertaken organizing campaigns on farms in Quebec, Manitoba, and British Columbia leading to collective agreements for farmworkers in those provinces (Preibisch 2010; UFCW 2011). In addition, a number of migrant worker justice initiatives have emerged in the absence of unionization (Choudry and Thomas 2012; Hennebry 2012; Thomas 2016). This includes the work of both Justicia for Migrant Workers, a grassroots activist collective that promotes the rights of migrant farmworkers, and the Immigrant Workers Centre in Montreal, which provides education on labour rights for migrant and immigrant workers and engages in organizing campaigns. These initiatives demonstrate the variety of worker organizing strategies that have arisen through the interconnections between precarious work and precarious migration status, and also indicate a global dimension to labour organizing within Canada.

In the post-2008 period, the most innovative forms of worker organizing both within and outside the formal union movement are emerging from those who are not only marginalized within the labour market but also within the labour movement itself, including racialized workers and those without permanent status in Canada.[6] This dynamic raises important strategic questions for unions as they endeavour to confront the political economy of precarious employment. On the one hand, new forms of organizing are emerging to address the changing social relations of employment, particularly as they impact racialized and recent im/migrant workers who are often under-represented in unions. On the other hand, as precariousness spreads to those workers previously protected by unions and still reliant on the standard methods of labour regulation, it is unclear whether the kind of energy and inventiveness being developed outside the unions can find its way into the established structures of the movement. As such, while new forms of worker organizing seek to contest both precarious employment and existing/traditional forms and strategies of workers' organizations themselves, their impact remains an open question.

Moreover, this pattern of worker organizing points to the need for a political economy perspective deeply informed by an intersectional analysis. While the political economy of precarious employment is characterized by an intensification of class-based labour exploitation, political economy scholarship must direct analytic attention towards the holistic set of social relations that shape class, including but not limited to gender, racialization, and citizenship status. As this chapter has outlined, new forms of worker organizing that have emerged in response to contemporary conditions of precariousness are rooted in forms of labour exploitation that are shaped through multiple intersecting social relations.

CONCLUSION

In this chapter, we address political economy on two levels, both in reference to the analytical approach of the CPE perspective, and in terms of the material conditions and social relations that constitute Canada's political economy. In terms of the study of work and worker organizing within CPE, the new political economy of precarious employment, particularly in the years following the Great Recession, requires that political economy scholarship critically examine the ways in which the traditional organizations of labour face conditions that are not only remaking the world of work, but that are also generating pressures that may contribute to the remaking of workers' organizations themselves. This dynamic is of course not new; it was through workers responding to the transformation of work in the industrial era that gave rise to what was then the new model of industrial unionism. In the current conjuncture, political economy scholarship must be attuned to the ways in which the interrelation between changing patterns of work and workers' collective resistance may, once again, be generating new forms of worker organizing. This is not to say that unions should be written off as institutions of the past; rather, unions themselves are dynamic organizations. At the same time, political economy scholarship must also engage with the wide-ranging intersecting social relations that organize both work and workers' organizations, including those of class, race, gender, and citizenship status, among others. Understanding these dynamics of change is a key question for scholarship that aims to study the political economy of precarious employment.

In that regard, the implications of the rise of precarious employment for worker organizing are stark. In sectors of traditional union strength, labour has been put on the defensive through the combined processes of work reorganization, globalization, and neoliberalism. Job loss has contributed to declining rates of unionization while aggressive, concessionary bargaining has weakened the power of workers' organizations to counter the changing patterns of work. In the fast-growing private services sector, intense anti-unionism amongst employers, combined with conditions not conducive to unionization (small workforces, high turnover, nonstandard work arrangements), have reproduced low levels of union representation. Thus, a major element of the political economy of precarious employment in Canada includes a loss of union power and a growing number of workers without union protection. As well, the political economy of precarious employment includes many workers who are either not covered at all by minimum employment standards or are often unable to exercise their workplace rights because of their precarious status in the workplace, fear of employer reprisal, or job loss (WAC 2015), including workers from racialized groups and those with precarious status in Canada. Overall, these conditions create not just the necessity for worker organizing to counter an employer-led offensive, but for new forms of worker organizing in that context.

This context of growing precariousness in the labour market, along with the recent worker organizing initiatives raised above, presents many questions regarding the future of the labour movement and of worker organizing in Canada. Is the emergence of new organizational forms a sign of labour movement weakness or vibrancy? It could be argued that there are not as many of these initiatives in Canada because the traditional labour movement structures and methods still have the capacity to deliver the goods. However, given the rise of campaigns and strategies involving non-unionized workers, what is the potential for lasting relationships between unions and other worker organizations or campaigns that prioritize issues of non-unionized workers? Such initiatives have emerged unevenly in Canada, and also appear more vibrant and advanced in the

US (e.g., Fight for $15 and Fairness); does this signal the persistence of institutional barriers that may impede new forms of organizing here? There is also the question of the capacities of unions themselves to create new forms of representation.[7] As the political economy of work in Canada is reshaped through labour market change, globalization, the neoliberal re-regulation of labour and employment laws, and shifting approaches to labour-management relations, worker organizing and workers' organizations will need to consolidate traditional bases of strength while at the same time developing new strategies to not only resist these processes but also create a path towards more just and equitable work and workplaces.

NOTES

1 The chapter develops its analysis through a focus on paid work (the employment relationship) rather than all dimensions of work, notably unpaid and reproductive work.

2 For overviews of the study of work, employment, and labour within the CPE tradition, see Phillips (1989) and Maroney and Luxton (1997).

3 For detailed statistical overviews of precarious employment in Canada, see OCF (2015), PEPSO (2013), and Vosko (2006b).

4 Until 2015, the oil and gas industry represented one of these growth areas. Building and construction trades unions were able to extract both jobs and income for their members, particularly those from Canada's economically depressed regions. However, this industry has also been characterized by a boom-and-bust dynamic with significant personal and social costs borne by workers, their families, and communities (Gibson and Boychuk 2012). Moreover, the collapse in oil prices in 2015 has made it clear that the relative protection some sectors enjoy is ephemeral.

5 For an examination of the limits of the union certification model in Canada, see Warskett (1998) and Swartz and Warskett (2012).

6 One could argue that this continues a pattern from the 1970s and 80s, during which feminist activists generated significant dynamism within the labour movement as a result of their struggles to make union priorities, organizations, cultures, and solidarities more inclusive of women. See Maroney and Luxton (1997).

7 A recent example can be seen in the community chapter model developed by Unifor, which presents an exciting potential, but to date has produced no new chapters since the union's formation in 2013.

17

The Maternity Capital Benefit in Russia: Analyzing Neoliberal Transitions in Post-Socialist States through a Feminist Political Economy Lens

Olena Lyubchenko

In the previous volume, *Changing Canada: Political Economy as Transformation* (2003), Clement and Vosko called on scholars to challenge the Canadian political economy (CPE) tradition by transforming its theoretical and methodological underpinnings in light of emergent social contradictions and spaces of resistance. Theoretically grounded applied political economy paved the way, pointing to transformative directions in the analysis of Canadian society. While acknowledging that CPE must continually question its constructed boundaries and borders to curb the risk of methodological nationalism, most subsequent analyses have focused on social relations in Canada and their relationship to developments in North America and globally (e.g., Gabriel and Macdonald 2003; Coleman and Porter 2003; Helleiner 2003). These works have sustained the original intellectual framework of the CPE tradition, which was shaped by breakthrough analyses of Canada's "dependent industrialization" in relationship to the United States and its place within international political economy – for example, Kari Levitt's *Silent Surrender*, Ian Lumsden's *Close the 49th Parallel*, and Gary Teeple's *Capitalism and the National Question in Canada*.

In the spirit of the current volume's efforts to renew the CPE tradition and its explanatory power, as well as to proactively draw in new voices, I advance a new line of inquiry for CPE in the new millennium. Moving beyond a focus on Canada's political economy and its embedding within a larger international context, I pursue the internationalization of CPE's core insights and concepts. In particular, I apply the methodological and theoretical innovations of feminist political economy (FPE) that developed within the CPE tradition in Canada (i.e., from the work of scholars based in Canada albeit in conversation with similar scholarship originating in the Global North and Global South), to a post-Soviet context undergoing profound political economic changes. The spread of neoliberal capitalism and its concomitant "gender contract" – defined broadly as the normative basis upon which the exchanges between breadwinning and caregiving operate at an institutional level (see Fudge and Vosko 2001b; Vosko 2010) – to post-Soviet spaces calls for the internationalization of a corresponding critique. In line with Sharma (this volume), I argue that an FPE perspective that has illuminated the changing gender contract and social policy under neoliberalism, albeit how it is uniquely manifested in Canada, can be helpful in addressing its development in contemporary Russia. Also in line with the discussion by Hall (this volume), I suggest that contemporary Russian social policy constitutes an illuminating case study of how late capitalist relations of production and reproduction operate in different sites and contexts as well as at different scales, expanding FPE analyses of state-socialist relations undergoing free-market restructuring.

The Maternity Capital Benefit (MCB), introduced by the Putin administration in 2006 as a flagship of the new post-Soviet family policy in Russia, forms the case study of this chapter. This focus is pertinent to the development of FPE for multiple reasons. As a one-time limited voucher given predominantly to women who give birth to or adopt a second child, the MCB is meant to combat the falling national birthrate, while helping women financially take time out of the labour force. It thereby represents a pro-natalist interventionist tactic on the part of the state officially aimed at curtailing some of the most draconian free market reforms introduced in the 1990s. In practice, however, it appears to privatize responsibilities for social reproduction that were previously socialized by the Soviet state. Existing scholarship on the Maternity Capital Benefit (e.g., Rotkirch et al. 2007; Chandler 2009; Rivkin-Fish 2010; Avdeyeva 2011; Borozdina et al. 2016; Popova 2016) grapples with characterizing its concomitant gender contract and associated breadwinner model, concerns that are pivotal to the unique Canadian variant of FPE.

A feminist political economy analysis highlights the significance of social reproduction to accumulation as well as to the state's effort in constructing the heteronormative "family," offers a depth of perspective on neoliberal restructuring, and lends itself well to pursuing research in a holistic way, specifically to analyzing empirical data in a manner that avoids the false separation of the material from the discursive (e.g., Jenson 1986; Cossman and Fudge 2002; Vosko 2002, 2010; Bezanson and Luxton 2006). Applying an FPE lens in studying the post-Soviet transition in Russia thus illuminates how rather than a side effect of the free market transition, the transformation of the Russian gender contract, as reflected in the Maternity Capital Benefit, is integral to it. As post-Soviet Russia constitutes a unique new site for empirical investigation, in particular the mechanisms of transforming state-socialist political economy, it simultaneously offers insights into addressing theoretical dilemmas raised by feminist political economists in Canada. These insights create potential to make the approach more self-reflexive and internationally relevant.

In developing these overarching arguments, the remainder of this chapter proceeds in three parts. First, I introduce the FPE perspective briefly, building on Vosko's contribution to this volume, which details its development over time (see also Vosko 2002). Second, I apply key conceptual and methodological insights from FPE such as the notions of "social reproduction" and "gender contract" to the shifting gender relations and citizenship model of post-Soviet Russia. In this section, I describe how early FPE understandings of the sex/gender divisions of labour, as well as debates around locating women's work in the mode of production, grounded applied FPE case studies of women's oppression in different social formations. I describe the gender contract characterizing the Soviet era and show how FPE analysis contests, in part, the normative policy direction that the Soviet gender contract offered by revealing its limitations. Third, I sketch the broad contours of the post-Soviet gender contract and identify how key concepts from FPE shed light on its form. This discussion frames the ensuing case study of the Russian Maternity Capital Benefit as emblematic of the post-Soviet gender contract. Specifically, I demonstrate how the tools and concepts devised through FPE, especially insights around the neoliberal gendered citizenship regime, are instructive in studying the contemporary processes of neoliberal governance in Russia.[1] I conclude by pointing to how social reproduction is increasingly caught up in the circuits of finance capital, as demonstrated by the Maternity Capital Benefit, and how this is a promising avenue for FPE research taking place within and beyond Canada.

FEMINIST POLITICAL ECONOMY IN CANADA: A LENS FOR RESEARCH IN OTHER CONTEXTS

Debates in FPE among scholars in Canada have been at the forefront of theoretical innovation and transformation within CPE, although their utility goes well beyond the Canadian context (see Maroney and Luxton 1987; Bakker 1989; Vosko 2002; see Vosko this volume for a fulsome review of its currents over time).[2] FPE emerged in the late 1970s and early 1980s and was rooted in the Canadian women's movement, both in the mainstream women's organizations of second wave Canadian feminism as well as more radical socialist–feminist currents.[3] The post-war Keynesian welfare state and its ideal gendered citizenship model of the male citizen breadwinner with a dependent wife and children, which reinforced a particular organization of social reproduction, set the context of FPE's development. This was also the context of FPE's theoretical engagements within the "malestream" of CPE. Taking seriously the core insight from within CPE that "political economy is a holistic approach to understanding society from a materialist perspective" (Clement 1997, 3), the expanded FPE lens highlighted the multi-faceted nature of socio-economic inequalities and, in the process, what is defined as "materialist." As Clement and Vosko each discuss in this volume, the Canadian variant of FPE was one of the first scholarly traditions within the field of political economy to criticize the gender-blindness of its analysis and its neglect of the important role of women's unpaid labour in the material reproduction of capitalist societies (see also Vosko 2002). Interventions therein challenged the economism of the established CPE tradition that focused mostly on the relations of production, narrowly conceived (see Clement this volume). A limited understanding of class inherited from Marxist political economy – identified with the sphere of production for surplus and centred on the White male industrial worker-citizen as the subject of political economy research and of anti-capitalist struggles – came under criticism as a misguided conception that neglected the "totality" of social relations.

To better understand the workings of late capitalism and the multi-faceted nature of inequalities produced therein, FPE has aimed to show how class is intimately intertwined with social relations of not just gender, but importantly of race, ethnicity, Indigeneity, citizenship, ability, and age (see for e.g., Seccombe 1974, 1980; Connelly 1983; Bezanson and Luxton 2006; Abele and Stasiulus 1989; Arat-Koç 1989; Bakan and Stasiulus 2005; Hall this volume; LeBlanc Haley this volume; Armstrong et al. this volume; Vosko this volume). In light of these theoretical developments, capitalism as a mode of production has come to be studied as a historically, socially, and politically concrete formation, upsetting the false separation between the political and the economic (see Connelly 1983; Jenson 1986; Bannerji 1995; Wood 1995). Due to its normative orientation toward systemic social transformation, FPE has redefined the nature and parameters of scientific investigation. The FPE approach challenges scholars to think carefully about issues of evidence, record, and agency in social science research. The production, institutionalization, and reproduction of unequal power relations come into full view through the adoption of an integrated analysis and dialectical method of inquiry (Clement and Vosko 2003). To understand power relations and structures of domination and subordination, then, requires both an analysis of laws, policies, and institutions as well as recognition of the lived experience of social agents. In this way, researchers and their tools are necessarily internal to their objects of analysis (Fudge 2014; Vosko 2016).

Though FPE developed largely in the context of research focused on the political economy of Canada, its orientation toward a holistic understanding of political economy together with the key concepts of the FPE tradition are instructive for research outside this domain. In particular, analyses of women's work in historically concrete social formations, constituting the third phase of FPE in Canada, combined with analyses of neoliberal restructuring of the post-war Keynesian welfare state in Canada, constituting the fifth phase of FPE in Canada, offer insights useful for empirical research on the post-Soviet transition, late capitalist relations, and the ensuing transformation of gender relations in Russia (see Vosko 2002 and Vosko this volume for a discussion of FPE phases emanating in Canada).

In studying the Soviet/post-Soviet case, I bridge FPE and a body of scholarship on the restructuring of gender relations in post-Soviet Russia, and, to a lesser extent, Eastern Europe. To that end, I use the inclusive term "gender relations" to identify strategically the wide-ranging scholarship both in Russia (in particular, analyses by Borozdina et al. 2016; Zdravomyslova 2010; Chernova 2012; Rotkirch, Temkina, and Zdravomyslova 2007) and Western Europe and North America (in particular, works by Rivkin-Fish 2010; Cook 2011; Chandler 2009; Weiner 2009) engaged in gendering the transition between these two eras. My review of this wide-ranging scholarship is necessarily partial, and interpretation of debates therein may not correspond with the understandings of scholars involved in them. Russian scholarship gendering the transition emanates principally from the discipline of sociology and covers the extensive themes of family policy, welfare state restructuring, parenting, changing sexual relations, and women's health and reproductive practices. While it engages with literature on social policy focusing on the classification of breadwinner models (in particular, works by

Esping-Andersen 1990; Lewis 1992; Orloff 1993), specifically the discursive shifts, Russian scholarship on the transition neglects to acknowledge or engage with FPE. This lack of engagement represents a missed opportunity, as concepts and insights emanating from FPE shed light on the preoccupations of scholarship on gender relations in Russia and the phenomena it aims to explain.

At the same time, feminist political economists in Canada have paid little attention to the political economy of socialist or post-socialist societies, such as contemporary Russia.[4] Yet, such a focus is important for two historical reasons. First, the critique of women's unpaid work in the home as central to their subjection in patriarchal and capitalist societies was strongly espoused by female revolutionaries like Alexandra Kollontai and Inessa Armand in Russia, whose impact on the Marxist Feminist tradition remains largely under explored. Armand and Kollontai were influential in the construction of social policy initiatives in the early Soviet period that were later partially rolled back under Stalin (Fuqua 1996). Since then, there has been a lack of social reproduction analyses in Russia, especially in relation to neoliberal restructuring, creating an opening for an FPE contribution. Second, and relatedly, as some scholars have previously suggested, the very development of the Keynesian welfare state in North America and Western Europe, which became dominant when "organized workers' militancy was strong and, thus, employers and the state took the threat of revolt seriously" (Fudge and Vosko 2001a, 274), cannot be fully studied in a manner that is detached from the international context of the Cold War and the threat that actually existing communism posed in terms of offering a more universal and comprehensive social settlement (e.g., Palmer and Sangster 2017; Sangster 2005; Eley 2002; Pearson 2014; Goldstein 2014, among others). Currently, societies undergoing transformation like post-Soviet Russia make for promising empirical case studies for understanding what went wrong under state socialism and in testing the utility of FPE's core concepts in a different context. In so doing, the explanatory power of a variant of FPE emerging in Canada can be expanded and made more relevant to studies outside this domain.

THE UTILITY OF CORE CONCEPTS OF FPE: STUDYING THE SHIFTING GENDER CONTRACT IN POST-SOVIET RUSSIA

Central to the development of FPE scholarship within and beyond Canada is its expanded conception of the capitalist mode of production. FPE scholarship has highlighted that in modern industrial capitalist societies the family is the primary site of social reproduction. The separation of direct producers from the means of production and reproduction has led the family-sphere to be physically and ideologically separated from the sphere of capitalist production and exchange (Seccombe 1974; Maroney and Luxton 1987; Fudge 2014; see also Laslett and Brenner 1989; Picchio 1981; Federici 2004 for analyses in other contexts). This separation has rendered women's work in the home natural, commonsensical, and therefore invisible while the sphere of capitalist production and exchange has been identified as the most important site of economic analysis (Seccombe 1974; Fudge 2014; see also Laslett and Brenner 1989; Federici 2004). An expanded conception of the capitalist mode of production as developed in FPE includes both production for surplus and social reproduction – the mental, manual, and emotional labour involved in maintaining the existing and future generations of workers – as two components of an integrated process (Seccombe 1980, 1974; Maroney and Luxton 1987; Bakker 2003; Arat-Koç 2006; Fudge 2014; see also Laslett and Brenner 1989). FPE scholars show that production and social reproduction are fundamentally social, cultural, and political relations, shaped by historically contingent forms of human agency (Luxton and Braedley 2010, 19; Jenson 1986).

For feminist political economists, social reproduction is essential to the contradictions and forms of resistance that emerge under capitalism. A drive for profit leads to contradictions between social reproduction and capital accumulation mediated by the state through public services, labour legislation, supports provided by third sector organizations, etc. The household is the site at which the conflict between wages, public services, and historically given standards of living are internalized (Vosko 2006; Bezanson and Luxton 2006; see also Picchio 1981, 1992). Thus, the standard of necessity, or the basket of goods that sustain the worker, structured by different axes of social location, is determined in important ways by class struggle at the point of reproduction.[5] Struggles for redistribution and against the commodification of everyday life – important for inequalities of gender, sexuality, ability, and race – are seen as integral to anti-capitalist resistance more broadly (Vosko 2002).

This more critically oriented "supply-side insight" of FPE (Vosko 2002, 77) has shed new light on the relationship between the capitalist state and the household. Applied case studies in FPE show that social reproduction has been the subject of interest of the capitalist state from its inception, but differently in different social and historical contexts.

Jenson's (1986, 41) comparative study of sex-specific protective labour legislation in Britain and France reveals, for example, that: "the state's contribution [to the oppression of women] is variable; not only across social formation but also across time. The needs of capital for the reproduction of the labour force and the state's activities to create and maintain the nation are dependent upon the stage of capitalism as well as particular patterns of social relations." Thus, FPE's foremost theoretical contribution pertinent to the Russian case is the illumination of the ways in which sex/gender divisions of labour are productive for capitalist accumulation and are shaped by the state in specific historical conjunctures.

Since the late nineteenth century, but most profoundly in the post-war period, Western industrial democracies have been organized to various degrees according to a male breadwinner/female housewife gender contract. This was a subset of a larger "gendered citizenship regime" at the time that defined men as active, full citizens and women as passive and dependent citizens and therefore partly excluded from full citizenship rights (e.g., Jenson 1986; Mahon 2002; Brodie 2008; Vosko 2006, 2010). Ideally, a man's "proper family wage," usually attached to a standard employment relationship (SER),[6] as well as a cluster of state policies and the "social wage" or access to social benefits and entitlements, were to cover the majority of household costs and presupposed the unpaid social reproductive labour of an economically dependent wife and children (Fudge and Vosko 2001, 272, 278; Vosko 2006, 9; Cossman 2002, 175; Bakker 2003; Fudge 2014; Porter 2003; see also Laslett and Brenner 1989; Fraser and Gordon 1992).[7] An important conceptual tool – the "gender contract" – has been developed, which refers to "the normative and material basis around which sex/gender division of paid and unpaid labour operate in a given society" and captures "the relationship between social, legal, and political norms surrounding the exchange between breadwinning and caregiving, protection and freedom, and public and private responsibilities" (Vosko 2010, 6–7; Fudge and Vosko 2001; Fudge 2014). This important conceptual innovation shows how the organization of gender relations, often relegated to the sphere of the individual household, is not just a matter of a "traditional" worldview but serves a political economic purpose that is institutionalized through laws and policies. Thus transforming the gender contract requires more than an ideological awakening; it necessitates changing the structures and interests around work and production globally (Fudge 2014; Vosko 2010; see also Weeks 2011).

Soviet Russia and the post-Soviet transition therein, I suggest, forms a case study in the tradition of FPE scholars tracing the historical evolution of various sex-specific protective labour legislation in Western Europe and North America, which instituted gender contracts complementary to their industrial-capitalist regimes (e.g., Jenson 1986). Comparatively, the organization of a state-command economy, the employment relationship and the central underpinnings of the dominant gender contract looked very different in the Soviet era in Russia. Women engaged in full-time, full-year employment yet they were subject to deeply gendered (and indeed protective) laws, legislation, and policies imbued with biologically deterministic assumptions about the appropriate role of women in the labour force.

Contrary to non-Soviet case studies most often pursued in the FPE tradition, post-war state-socialism depended on women's full-time participation in the labour force and operated with the absence of the male breadwinner/female caregiver gender contract in a context of state-command economic development. The socialist state's promise of equality was achieved through women's full participation in the workforce and the simultaneous institutionalization of gender difference via sex-specific labour regulations that reinforced norms of female caregiving. The state instituted compensatory social provisions for women's universal employment and special rights associated with motherhood (Teplova 2007; Zhurzhenko 2001; Kaminsky 2011). In Russia, Soviet women received the "social wage" (including vacation pay, state-subsidized vacation, pensions, regular hours, sick days, disability insurance etc., alongside state-funded universal daycare) by virtue of their employment. Unlike men, however, women received the social wage by combining employment with motherhood (Teplova 2007; Zhurzhenko 2001). Mandatory dual roles of worker and mother were institutionalized through social and labour policies. The notion of the "gender contract" is helpful in revealing that while raising children to be Soviet citizens was recognized as just as "valuable" as formal employment, the activity was: a) viewed as biologically determined, because men did not receive special benefits attached to fatherhood; and b) only associated with the immediate years after the child's birth, covered by state provisions.

The Soviet SER and associated gender contract, however, presents more than just another national variation on the form of the breadwinner model. An FPE lens reveals its uniqueness as a case study of the relationship between gender equity and citizenship. Compared to the West, different structures of state policy and women's experiences with the state and economy – i.e., dependence on the individual male breadwinner through wife- and motherhood in the West as opposed to a direct relationship with the state through full employment officially equal to that of men and motherhood in the East – led to forms of patriarchy that "either officially support[ed] or supplant[ed] the conventional authority and practical power of the individual male as household head," respectively (Ferree 1995). The "public/private" dichotomy – historically central to feminist debates in North America due to women's official exclusion from the labour force and relegation to the private sphere of the family (Laslett and Brenner 1989; Vosko 2002) – was not experienced as strictly "masculine/feminine" by women in the Soviet Union, who participated en masse in the "public sphere." Soviet women's citizenship was not premised on "an abstracted individual, a disembodied market citizen," or an "honorary man" (Cossman 2002, 179) expressed through a "politics of access" to an inclusive, and even at times somewhat socially progressive citizenship in the "gender neutral" or "gender blind" Western liberal democratic state (Connell 1990; Ferree and Young 1993). Instead, the unique gendered citizenship regime in Soviet Russia was institutionalized through a notion of an "embodied" women's citizenship, premised on their dual roles of mothers and workers.

The gender contract instituted by the Soviet state in Russia, with its socialization of the costs of social reproduction as part of women's equal social citizenship, in part, represents a favourable normative policy direction in the vein of FPE analyses. However, FPE debates locating women's work within the mode of production and the rate of exploitation of women's labour both "inside" and "outside" of production for surplus (Vosko 2002) reveal this system's limitations despite mass women's employment, compensatory social policies, and the undeniably progressive formal legal achievements in gender equality that officially supplanted the old patriarchal structure of the family.[8] FPE's expanded supply-side insight helps highlight the contradictory relationship between the Soviet state's socially and politically "progressive" family law and the Soviet political economy that prioritized military competitiveness, industry, and innovation over standards of living. Thereby, it challenges the seemingly favourable normative policy direction that the Soviet gender contract appeared to offer. The particular organization of the state-socialist production system meant that the division of unpaid work between men and women resulted, potentially, in a triple-day oppression of women (previously suggested by Heinen 1990). Gender inequality was not based on non-standard employment and limited social citizenship rights for women (as it was generally in North America and Western Europe); rather, it was rooted in the very distance between official policy and standards of living, the quality and availability of services, and the quality and availability of consumer goods, which fell onto women to manage as the assumed natural caregivers. This distributional consumption dimension of gender inequality, particular to the mechanisms of Soviet socialism's political economy, is not fully captured by feminist political economists who have focused principally on capitalist relations of production and reproduction (for two exceptions, see Hall and LeBlanc Haley in this volume).[9] In a study of the Soviet context, an FPE analysis, which takes into consideration social reproduction and distribution as central aspects of political economic systems, is helpful in revealing important elements of state-command socialist economies; it also identifies new and different dynamics that FPE must account for in its analysis of gender inequality in similar transforming societies.

THE NEOLIBERAL GENDERED CITIZENSHIP REGIME AND THE POST-SOVIET GENDER CONTRACT

FPE scholarship is especially robust when it comes to articulating the content and effects of neoliberal restructuring of the post-war Keynesian welfare state in Canada (Bakker 2003; Fudge and Cossman 2002; Brodie 2008; Bezanson and Luxton 2006; Fudge 2014). In particular, feminist political economists have explored the material aspects of neoliberal restructuring intertwined with forms of neoliberal governance of the self in everyday life (see especially contributions to Braedley and Luxton 2010). Neoliberal restructuring, described as "a politically guided inten- sification of market rule and commodification," has produced a new gendered citizenship regime in Canada and elsewhere, one that downloads the costs of social reproduction onto the individual/family and away from a tax-starved welfare state (Brenner, Peck, and Theodore 2010, 184; Brodie 2008; Fudge and Cossman 2002; see McBride this volume). While the Canadian variant of the post-war Keynesian welfare state's commitment to social security was gendered, it socialized some of the costs of social reproduction and expanded social citizenship rights (Brodie 2008, 150; Cossman 2002; Vosko 2002; Bakker 2003; Luxton and Braedley 2010). Canadian social policy thus underwent a "politics of renaming," understood as the politics of "framing policy interventions in the language of individualization rather than gender orders or other systemic inequalities" (Brodie 2008, 154–5). The privatization of social problems has been justified through a political discourse centred on the self-reliant *homo economicus* and away from public goods and collective responsibility (Fudge and Cossman 2002; Bakker 2003, Luxton, and Braedley 2010). The definition of equality and freedom as the individual's right to freely compete on the market has become a rationalization for inequality and has ignored and hid the unequal social relations that shape labour markets, employment relations, and welfare states.

Women's entrance into the public sphere of employment in large numbers in Canada – a feminist demand – coincided with the deterioration of the SER in favour of more precarious forms of work and the feminization of employment.[10] This led to a decline of the family wage and a lower standard of living (Fudge and Vosko 2001, 272; Fraser 2009, 2016). The transference of social provisioning from public services to either the market or the family in order to reduce costs had "disproportionate and deleterious impacts on women, especially those marginalized by economic and social difference" in Canada and globally (Brodie 2008, 148; Fudge 2014, 7; Arat-Koç 2006; Vosko 2016). Newer FPE scholarship in the contemporary globally integrated neoliberal context has shown that the erosion of social citizenship in the Global North and labour migration from the Global South are two sides of the same coin, where citizenship status is intimately intertwined with gender relations (see for e.g., Arat-Koç 2006; Yeates 2012; Williams 2011; Vosko 2010; Fudge 2014).

In its conceptualization of the neoliberal gendered citizenship regime, the FPE perspective has moved toward a more complex approach that recognizes the inseparable discursive, normative, and instrumental dimensions of global political economy. Importantly, in revealing the contradictory nature of the neoliberal project, FPE retains its critical-materialist supply-side insight centred on social reproduction. As Brodie notes, "after two decades of the unfolding of the neoliberal project, it is increasingly apparent that the practice of neoliberalism is often contradictory, if not at times incoherent, and that the interface between neoliberalism and gender is far more complex, contested, and contextualized than formal logics might project or allow" (2008, 148). FPE scholars reveal that the current neoliberal breadwinner model espouses a tendency toward familialism and privatization, or both an intensification and erosion of gender difference (Bakker 2003; Fudge 2014). While a gender sameness discourse in public policy and law advocates for women's equal participation in the labour market, in practice it simultaneously privatizes and hides care work by placing the responsibility for social reproduction on the family unit and, by extension, women (Bakker 2003; Vosko 2006; Luxton 2006). More precisely, the neoconservative re-articulation of the familial ideology supports the neoliberal privatization project. Cossman (2002, 171) writes that "the current phase of reprivatizing the costs of social reproduction, while at times relying on some of the older 'stories' of gender and family, is resulting in a shift in the gender order, with new and contradictory claims being made on the family." Because of the seeming contradiction between ostensible gender neutrality (neoliberalism), on the one hand, and the re-articulation of old gender difference (neoconservatism), on the other hand, the privatizing project is producing not only an intensification and erosion of gender difference (Bakker 2003, 66), but placing additional pressure on the family unit and female caregivers (Cossman 2002). What the supply-side insight of FPE shows is that while neoliberalism glorifies strong female participation in the labour market on an equal footing with men, it nevertheless reproduces and even intensifies capitalism's systemic need for private social reproduction, and in so doing turns the neoliberal era's notions of gender neutrality and gender equality on their heads.

Issues and debates currently critical to FPE in Canada, such as privatization and familialization of the welfare state, are relevant to social science scholarship on post-Soviet transition, most of which aims to describe and categorize the post-Soviet welfare state model and its changing gender relations (e.g., Avdeyeva 2011; Popova 2016; Ashwin and Yakubovich 2005; Rivkin-Fish 2010; Chandler 2009; Rivkin-Fish 2010; Cook 2011; Borozdina et al. 2016). In comparison to Western liberal democratic states such as Canada, which experienced almost a half-century of social liberalism through the Keynesian welfare state, capitalist market relations were imported to Russia from the West in their latest neoliberal form during Shock Therapy reforms of the 1990s after the fall of the Soviet regime (Rutland 2013; Gerber and Hout 1998; Bohle and Greskovits 2012). In this decade, the state-socialist organization of social reproduction gave way to a market economy characterized by draconian fiscal policies of restraint and cutbacks in social spending. The extension of neoliberal policy ideas to the East warrants the application of parallel critique, which FPE offers. Applying an FPE lens to research on post-Soviet transition in Russia has the power to illuminate and explain how rather than a side effect of the free market transition, contemporary transformations within the Russian gender contract are an integral part of this transition.

In the context of Shock Therapy free market reforms in the early 1990s, some scholars have suggested that women's labour force participation would decrease at the expense of their maternal roles, as universal provisions that previously supported women's employment in Soviet Russia were eroded.[11] Women's withdrawal from the labour force for an extended period of time to take care of children, scholars argued, would establish a "neofamilial" breadwinner model, defined by a "male earner/female carer" model and a gendered public/private divide that would support the reproductive needs of the new market economy (Einhorn 1993;

Racioppi and O'Sullivan See 2009; Weiner 2009). This argument was underpinned by an assumption that the new free market regime would socialize some of the costs of social reproduction and provide for the dependent wife and children through the male family-wage, in light of large-scale privatization and deregulation. Whether scholars perceived the market transition as a loss of women's economic emancipation (Ferree and Young 1993; Young 2000) or a gain of women's democratic rights and freedoms (Weiner 2009), women's retreat from the public sphere of employment into the private sphere of the family in post-socialist states was the dominant prediction. Other, more recent studies benefitting from hindsight have steered away from such uniform arguments. They have shown that in the context of overall unemployment during the time of restructuring in the 1990s and well into the 2000s, women's employment rates remained high (and at times higher) in relation to men's as male-dominated sectors such as heavy industry, metallurgy, coal mining – very important to the Soviet economy and state finances – were slowing down (Avdeyeva 2011; Popova 2016; Ashwin and Yakubovich 2005; Rivkin-Fish 2010). Women's continued high levels of labour force participation reflect a feminization of employment of a particular sort and reveal how a continuity of Soviet gendered norms of labour law, following the free market changes of the 1990s, is possible in a new neoliberal form. The concept of the "feminization" of employment, defined as forms of employment associated with women characterized by flexibility and precariousness, in the West (thus "feminization"), is not transferable to the Soviet context in a straightforward fashion (Fudge and Vosko 2001, 272, 278; Vosko 2006, 9). Nevertheless, studies reveal that occupational and industrial segregation by sex, with women employed predominantly in the tertiary sector or less "labour-intensive" positions in commodities production or manufacturing was instituted though labour laws and policies as the state's way of protecting mother-worker citizens (Teplova 2007; Heinen 1990; on this aspect of the feminization of employment norms applied to the Canadian case see Vosko 2000). This pattern sheds light on processes of continuity through change, where contradictory Soviet social structures have been adapted to market relations to foster neoliberal governance in Russia.

THE MATERNITY CAPITAL BENEFIT IN RUSSIA FROM AN FPE PERSPECTIVE

First mentioned in the *Annual Address to the Federal Assembly* (Putin 2006) on 10 May 2006 by the Russian president Vladimir Putin, and coming into effect on 1 January 2007, the Maternity (Family) Capital benefit – a federal program – has become a flagship of the new Russian family policy in the post-Soviet era.[12] The official purpose of the benefit was to fight the declining national fertility rate by incentivizing women to give birth to more than one child, whilst compensating monetarily for women's losses in the labour force as a result of taking time out (Rotkirch et al. 2007, 351; Borozdina et al. 2016). As a large one-time voucher given to mothers having a second child, the Maternity Capital Benefit is intended for one of three potential uses: to fund children's education; to allow the mother to save for her retirement; and/or to improve housing. Originally totalling RUB 250,000, the value of the benefit in 2017 was approximately RUB 450,000 or USD $6500 (approximately). The initial ten-year project has been extended until 31 December 2021, with amendments for children that are born or adopted after 1 January 2018.[13] Mothers are identified as primary recipients, while fathers are only eligible to receive Maternity Capital in the context of the mother's death, loss of her legal status as a parent, or as a result of the mother's intentional criminal harm against the child in question (Chandler 2009, 18).

In introducing the Maternity Capital Benefit, Putin made the case for a new Russian developmental model, making a parallel between Roosevelt's New Deal after the Great Depression and his own presidency after the wild deregulated Shock Therapy reforms of the 1990s. Politically, the address also made reference to the power of the Russian oligarchs, who amassed astronomical wealth during the conversion of national Soviet state enterprises to private firms. It was this oligarchic power that Putin was going to curtail via new social policy:

> The changes of the early 1990s were a time of great hopes for millions of people, but neither the authorities nor business fulfilled these hopes. Moreover, some members of these groups pursued their own personal enrichment in a way such as had never been seen before in our country's history, at the expense of the majority of our citizens and in disregard for the norms of law and morality. "In the working out of a great national program which seeks the primary good of the greater number, it is true that the toes of some people are being stepped on and are going to be stepped on. But these toes belong to the comparative few who seek to retain or to gain position or riches or both by some short cut which is harmful to the greater good." These are fine words and it is a pity that it was not I who thought them up. It was Franklin Delano Roosevelt, the President of the United States of America, in 1934. These words were spoken as the country was emerging from the great depression. (Putin 2006)

In this way, Maternity Capital was introduced in the context of an alleged shift from a deregulated free market economy of the late twentieth century, which resulted in lower standards of living and a demographic decline, towards stronger state intervention in market economy though social policy. As a way to help women reconcile work and motherhood, Putin stated:

> Finally, and most effective in my view, is a measure to ensure material support. I think that the state has a duty to help women who have given birth to a second child and end up out of the workplace for a long time, losing their skills. I think that, unfortunately, women in this situation often end up in a dependent and frankly even degraded position within the family. We should not be shy about discussing these issues openly and we must do so if we want to resolve these problems. If the state is genuinely interested in increasing the birth rate, it must support women who decide to have a second child. The state should provide such women with an initial maternity capital that will raise their social status and help to resolve future problems. Mothers could make use of this capital in different ways: put it towards improving their housing situation, for example, by investing it in buying a house, making use of a mortgage loan or other loan scheme once the child is three years old, or putting it towards the children's education, or, if they wish, putting it into the individual account part of their own old-age pension. (Putin 2006)

Yet even from this address it is clear that while the loss of skills is the motivation behind introducing Maternity Capital, its spending options do not address this particular issue directly.

Scholars adopting an institutionalist perspective have revealed the Maternity Capital Benefit to be highly pro-natalist, putting the Russian welfare regime model further onto a neofamilial path (see for e.g., Rotkirch et al. 2007 Chandler 2009; Rivkin-Fish 2010; Avdeyeva 2011; Borozdina et al. 2016; Popova 2016). Maternity Capital, they argue, no longer aims to reconcile paid work and motherhood fully at the level of official state discourse, as has been the case in Soviet Russia and instead attempts to incentivize women's re-entry into the private sphere (Chandler 2009; Rivkin-Fish 2010; Avdeyeva 2011; Cook 2011; Borozdina et al. 2016). Most analyses point to the policy's aims and possible outcomes as contradictory, pulling the Russian welfare state in opposing directions.

Read widely as interventionist, conservative, nationalist, and even Soviet-style state feminist initiative, it is argued that the MCB reflects an ideological shift within the contemporary Russian state under the Putin administration, eschewing the wild deregulated capitalism of the 1990s (Rotkirch et al. 2007; Rivkin-Fish 2010; Cook 2011; Borozdina et al. 2016). At the same time, scholars acknowledge that the "neofamilial" interpretation – i.e., conceiving the Maternity Capital Benefit as a tactic to keep women within the home and further designate them as primary caregivers – stands in stark contrast to high levels of women's employment in the labour force on the ground (Rotkirch et al. 2007; Chandler 2009; Rivkin-Fish 2010; Avdeyeva 2011; Borozdina et al. 2016; Popova 2016). This distance between state discourse and practice is left unexplained.

FPE insights around the neoliberal gendered citizenship regime, more precisely, the re-articulation of the household's responsibility for care and simultaneous erosion of the family wage, along with the ostensible commitment to gender equality in the labour force, can illuminate important gendered dynamics of neoliberal restructuring in post-Soviet Russia and, in doing so, reveal important contradictions of the neoliberal project therein. In particular, "social reproduction as an analytic device could enhance [research on post-Soviet Russia] by locating institutional arrangements, policy choices and discourses within the power relations of the state/market/family" (Findlay 2012, 11). The Russian state's approach to family and women's work (paid and unpaid) must be connected to the contradictory ways in which the neoliberal project is unfolding in Russia. Currently, scholars are unable to highlight the paradoxical simultaneity of false gender neutrality and familialization implicit in neoliberal forms of governance (see Cossman and Fudge 2002; Bakker 2003; Braedley and Luxton 2010) and their (partial) legacies from the Soviet era.

An FPE perspective helps transcend the terms of the current debate on the Russian welfare state model (Cook 2011; Kravchenko 2012; Ashwin; Chandler 2009), which uses the degree of state intervention as a barometer for measuring the level of economic and political liberalization. Based on FPE analyses of the tensions and paradoxes inherent in neoliberal governance, the Maternity Capital Benefit, embedded in a range of work–family reconciliation policies, is characterized not by the withdrawal of the state from the market (as Cook 2011 suggests), but rather by a simultaneous withdrawal and reconfiguration of collective responsibility (Vosko 2002). In this instance, the direction of social policy and family policy is characterized by the state's adoption of a strong disciplinary, interventionist role to facilitate market relations (McBride and Whiteside 2011b). CPE analyses show that instead of deregulation, neoliberalism is a project of re-regulation, whereby the state works to extend the rules of market compulsion to all spheres of life, including social reproduction practices, through laws, policies, and institutions (see the introduction to this volume and McBride this volume; see also Brodie 2008, 2014).

State intervention through the Maternity Capital Benefit signifies a shift from a social citizenship model based on universal entitlements, as was common under the Soviet system, to a more fiscally austere and individualized approach based on cash-transfers (or their equivalent in vouchers) provided by the state as a subsidy for child-rearing and women's exit from the workforce. At the same time, the Maternity Capital Benefit is far from adequate and does not fully counter the need for women to work. Serving largely as leverage for loans, primarily new mortgages, the benefit does not reinforce a male breadwinner/female caregiver gender contract. Thus, the Maternity Capital Benefit – which appears to be neoconservative in its emphasis on the family and motherhood – is not antithetical to the overall neoliberal project (Cossman 2002). Rather, it privatizes the family's responsibility for childcare, placing it predominantly on the mother as the "natural" caregiver without substantive entitlements, at the same time as requiring women to continue to participate in the labour force in order to secure the means necessary for the social reproduction of their families. Here, FPE insights around the dual nature of the neoliberal gender contract, characterized by both gender neutrality and the intensification of gender difference, are especially valuable (Cossman 2002; Bakker 2003). Applying the lens of FPE shows how the neoliberal citizenship regime can utilize elements of the Soviet gender contract.

Studies of the Maternity Capital Benefit reveal it as a gendered and pro-natalist benefit, because through its provision, the state identifies mothers as primary caregivers, with fathers only eligible to receive the benefit in very rare circumstances (Rotkirch et al. 2007; Chandler 2009; Rivkin-Fish 2010; Avdeyeva 2011; Borozdina et al. 2016; Popova 2016). The prevailing scholarship has, however, neglected to capture the male irresponsibility discourse implicit in the design of the benefit as a voucher given to mothers and what this means about the extra work of social reproduction built into the benefit. By identifying women as the primary recipients and therefore caregivers, the state allegedly ensures that the Maternity Capital Benefit is spent "responsibly" and that it stays attached to the second child in question (for which it has been received). This goal is assured, for example, by the fact that the vast majority of divorce cases in Russia identify the mother as the primary caregiver, as the courts overwhelmingly grant custody to the mother. Mothers are identified not just as better caregivers to the child, but also as better managers of the benefit, as part of the household budget and overall spending (interview 2018c; 2018e; 2018g; 2018h; 2018i; 2018j). The gendered citizenship regime that was established in Soviet Russia – with the mother-worker gender contract between the mother and the Soviet state – is adapted in the neoliberal era to a new set of free-market policy initiatives. While the state no longer aims to socialize the costs of social reproduction (such as childcare, see Teplova 2007), it downloads the risk of social investment onto women who are expected to make the best use of the subsidy.

In connection, an integrative F P E methodology, which pays attention to both personal experiences and larger political economic structures and institutions, highlights powerful material interests behind the Maternity Capital Benefit. These dynamics, which drive Russian political economy in the current neoliberal era, are not discernable without such an integrative lens that is better able to capture the multi-faceted power-ful interests driving public policy. The lack of affordable housing for young families since the fall of the Soviet Union has not been addressed by the contemporary state directly in social policy terms, by providing affordable housing options. In some cases, particularly in St Petersburg, families remain in communal apartments that are relics of the Soviet era (on the history of the Soviet housing policy see Attwood 2010; Trumbull 2014; Khmelnitskaya 2014; Kravchenko 2014). While some initiatives have been made to provide new housing options at the level of municipal and provincial (oblast) governments, these housing options are often located on the periphery of the city, far from the neighbourhoods where parents work and children attend childcare/school (Interview 2018a; Interview 2018f). Instead, the M C B has become one way to address this issue through incentivizing mortgage loans for housing.

Based on empirical research, the overwhelming majority of families who obtain the Maternity Capital Benefit are motivated to get their first mortgage in order to invest the value of the voucher. In fact, many Russian women perceive this to be the real reason behind the introduction of the benefit and the only reasonable way to spend it, despite the very high interest rates of 14–17 per cent, which translate to around fifteen to twenty-five years of repayment (in particular, Interview 2018b; 2018c; 2018d; 2018j; 2018k). Just like the primary recipient – the mother, the form of the Maternity Capital Benefit – a voucher instead of a cash payment is intended for "responsible" and "unwasteful" spending via a mortgage. This particular finding, read through an FPE lens, reveals an intricate mechanism whereby state benefits, as opposed to being a direct form of universal social provisioning, are fed through the circuits of financial capital for private profit. In this way, the family becomes a direct site of financial accumulation. At the same time, the loss of state social provisioning reinforces the privatization of social reproduction.

Feminist political economists analyzing policies in the Global North and Global South engaging concepts complementing those adopted by FPE scholars in Canada, such as Lavinas (2014, 2017) and Federici (2014b), suggest that social policy has played a crucial role in advancing financialization and reducing the scope of citizens' rights and entitlements. Based on empirical research, the Maternity Capital Benefit serves as a case in point, and a new possible format of neoliberal social policy in former socialist countries, a variety of neoliberalism. In studying policies in Brazil similar to the Maternity Capital Benefit in Russia, such as Bolsa Família, Lavinas (2017, 5) argues that social policy serves as incentive to access financial markets through credit, facilitating an intense process of financial inclusion and supporting debt-financed spending at the expense of the provision of public goods and services.[14] Similarly, Federici (2014b, 233) suggests that with the dismantling of the welfare state "an increasing number of people (students, welfare recipients, pensioners) have been forced to borrow from the banks to purchase services (education, health care, pensions) that the state formerly subsidized, so that *many reproductive activities have now become immediate sites of capital accumulation*" (emphasis in original). In fact, this new financialization of reproduction is "not something superimposed on the real economy but is the 'real economy,' insofar as it is the direct organizer of people's labour," where credit is seen as investment and household members as entrepreneurs (Federici 2014b, 235). While promoted as a policy of state-regulation of the wild free market brought to post-Soviet Russia in the 1990s, the Maternity Capital initiative under the Putin administration serves the very same interests, under the centralized direction of the state. Underwriting the costs of social reproduction through credit works to further deteriorate the Soviet model of social citizenship, while using some of its gendered elements that instituted women's equality through difference in the labour market towards the privatization of social reproduction. Social inclusion through credit, whereby social policy is directly linked to finance capital has yet to be analyzed using the tools of FPE. However, read through an FPE lens, the operation of the Maternity Capital Benefit in post-Soviet Russia reveals the financialization of social reproduction as a strategy available to states under neoliberalism and thus an important focus of future research in Canada and beyond.

CONCLUSION

This chapter approached the case of the Maternity Capital Benefit – an emblem of contemporary family policy in Russia – using the core concepts of an integrated FPE perspective, especially as it developed in Canada. By applying an FPE lens to guide empirical research on neoliberal restructuring in Russia, which is characterized by the new debt-led consumption and financialization of social reproduction, this chapter has sought to question and extend the geographic boundaries of FPE. To understand how late capitalist relations of production are transferred to and come to operate in different political-economic contexts requires internationalizing, and therefore, expanding our critiques of late capitalist processes and associated gender contracts to probe developments in former state-socialist regimes undergoing free-market restructuring. The internationalization of the FPE perspective, specifically its application to transitioning and transforming societies like post-Soviet Russia, while encountering different historical social relations therein, simultaneously tests and expands the utility of FPE, making this strain of CPE relevant to empirical investigations beyond Canada. To that end, I sought to underscore the potential offered by greater dialogue between the sociologically-oriented critical scholarship on changing gender relations in post-Soviet Russia and the FPE scholarship, emanating in Canada, whose holistic political economic approach highlights blind spots in existing analyses of the contemporary Russian breadwinner model.

FPE's expanded view of the capitalist mode of production highlights an important relationship between the organization of gender relations, the state, and the market through the concept of the "gender contract." While family policy under the Putin administration in the form of the Maternity Capital Benefit is often read as an interventionist state strategy, using an FPE lens allows us to ask, and begin to answer, different questions than those addressed in scholarship preoccupied with the degrees of state intervention: namely, questions about state intervention to what ends and through what means? An integrated FPE analysis shows that a discursive shift within the contemporary Russian state towards greater state intervention through a politics of familialism, reflected in the Maternity Capital Benefit, is a continuity of the neoliberal project toward greater privatization of social reproduction and a contraction of social citizenship rights of the Soviet era, with material consequences for gender equality. The Maternity Capital Benefit, which is promoted as a new developmental social policy and family policy initiative under the Putin administration, not only privatizes social reproduction and holds women as the responsible carers and managers of the household, it makes the family a site of profit for finance capital. This finding points to an important future direction in FPE scholarship on how neoliberal social policy and family policy are built and indeed lived in former state-command socialist economies.

NOTES

1 The empirical part of the chapter draws on fieldwork research in St Petersburg and Moscow, Russia, May–August 2018. This research was reviewed and approved by the Human Participants Review Sub-Committee, York University's Ethics Review Board, and conforms to the standards of the Canadian Tri-Council Research Ethics guidelines. The author conducted twenty-two semi-structured interviews, using a set of open-ended questions, with male and female respondents who are either eligible, have received, and/or invested the Maternity Capital Benefit. All respondents were recruited via snowball sampling; all interviewees had the option of their responses to be treated as confidential (used only as background information), anonymous (information to be quoted but not attributed to the respondent by name), or "on the record" (information to be quoted and attributed to the respondent by name).

2 Some of these debates have occurred in, but go well beyond the CPE volumes (1987, 1997, 2003, and the current volume). In particular, see the journal *Studies in Political Economy*.

3 See Findlay (1988) and Brodie (2008) on the history of the official women's movement, including the RCSW and the NAC. See Luxton (2001) on the relationship between the official women's movement and what she calls the "autonomous women's movement" inside the second-wave in Canada.

4 Notable exceptions are Heitlinger (1987), writing about former Czechoslovakia, as well as a special issue of *Social Politics* edited by Mahon and Williams (2007) on *Gender and State in Post-Communist Societies*, which includes an incisive contribution by Teplova.

5 Here it is also important to acknowledge recent American scholarship, very close theoretically to Canadian FPE (and often written in collaboration with Canadian Marxist feminists) around developing Social Reproduction Theory

(SRT). See the collection edited by Tithi Bhattacharya: *Social Reproduction Theory: Remapping Class, Recentering Oppression* (2017). Bhattacharya and contributors make the case that if historically capitalism is the separation of workers from the means of subsistence, with market compulsion for survival, then struggles at the point of reproduction – redistributive and anti-commodification – are anti-capitalist. As SRT insightfully shows, the issues that intersectionality aims to articulate directly lead to struggles beyond the workplace toward struggles at the point of reproduction: different sections of global working people are produced differently at different historical moments (Bhattacharya 2017, 87).

6 SER stands for "a full-time continuous employment relationship, where the worker has one employer, works on the employer's premises under direct supervision, and has access to comprehensive benefits and entitlements" (Vosko 2010, 1; see also Deakin 1986, 1998).

7 It is important to note that "while there was considerable variation between women, and while many women's lives did not fit the postwar ideal, these gendered assumptions were integral to welfare state programs" (Porter 2003, 37; see also Fraser and Gordon 1994). As Fudge (2014, 11) shows, "married women's economic dependence on their husbands was actively constructed by law" where "employment and the family were sharply separated and regulated by their own distinctive technologies."

8 Central to the revolutionary program, and arguably a part of the institutionalization of the mother-worker gender contract in Soviet Russia, was the creation of Soviet family law, unprecedentedly progressive in terms of women's rights in comparison to its European and North American contemporaries. As Soviet historian Kaminsky (2011) shows, starting with the Code on Marriage, the Family, and Guardianship in 1918, with subsequent amendments, the law allowed for divorce, abolished the concept of illegitimate children, and recognized unregistered unions (i.e., common-law partnerships). Interestingly, social and legal historians note that in the era of Stalin's leadership, the earlier discourse of protecting Soviet women as a distinct population shifted towards the discourse of protecting Soviet families (Kaminsky 2011, 69).

9 In this way, I suggest that at a conceptual level, various differentiations within feminism, such as first world/third world feminism (Mohanty 2003) or White/Black feminism (Hill Collins 2000), etc., which have informed FPE scholarship, can also be illuminated by the dynamics and tensions between "Eastern" and "Western" feminism (Ferree 1995).

10 As it is applied to North American and Western European contexts, feminization of employment is used to refer to conditions of employment

resembling those conventionally (and historically) identified with women and other marginalized workers (that is, flexible, precarious, and lacking a "social wage" – i.e., access to social benefits and entitlements through paid work) (see especially, Vosko 2000; Vosko 2006, 9; on the notion of "more women's work in the market," see also Armstrong 1998).

11 Teplova offers some impressive data on childcare institutions for the ten-year restructuring period, 1990–2000: "According to the official Goskomstat data, the number of childcare institutions declined from 87,900 in 1990 to 53,300 in 2000, a practical collapse of the system of nurseries. The number of communities with state nurseries declined from 55.2 per cent in 1994 to only 34 per cent in 2000,7 and the proportion of children over three years old in those facilities dropped by more than 50 per cent from 9,009,000 in 1990 to 4,263,000 in 2000" (2007, 291–2).

12 This is an important detail, because provinces (oblast) also offer similar programs, separate from the federal Maternity Capital and smaller in value, often given to families after the birth of the third child.

13 The 1 January 2018 amendments include: monthly payments for families with "less than 150% of the able-bodied population's subsistence minimum per family member" until the child reaches 1.5 years old; funds made available for childcare and pre-school education after two months (previously available after three years); preferential mortgage interest rates for families with two and three children (Pension Fund of Russian Federation 2018). While the fieldwork research used in this chapter was conducted after the introduction of amendments to MCB, the data collected was based on the benefit's previous form and use (women whose children were born before 1 January 2018). These amendments and their effects will require further study with time in the context of changing social policies and political economy in contemporary Russia.

14 Building on Lavinas, Brazilian scholars located at Rio de Janeiro State University, like Ruas (n.d.), are further exploring the Bolsa Família policy using a social reproduction perspective, looking at what this perspective means for complex relations of racial inequality in contemporary neoliberal Brazil. In particular, they are analyzing how the introduction of Bolsa Família under Lula's populist-statist government (arguably parallel to Putin's government in Russia) represents a variety of neoliberalism, by way of using social policy to socially include poor and racialized women (and families) through credit and leading to a simultaneous erosion and intensification of gender and race difference.

References

Abbas, Jihan. 2012. "A Legacy of Exploitation: Intellectual Disability, Unpaid Labor, and Disability Services." *New Politics* 14, no. 1: 22–6.

Abdel-Shehid, Gamal, and Nathan Kalman-Lamb. 2011. *Out of Left Field: Social Inequality and Sports*. Halifax, NS: Fernwood Publishing.

Abele, Frances. 1987. "Canadian Contradictions: Forty Years of Northern Political Development." *Arctic*: 310–20.

– 1997. "Understanding What Happened Here: The Political Economy of Indigenous Peoples." In *Understanding Canada: Building on the New Canadian Political Economy*, edited by Wallace Clement, 118–40. Montreal: McGill-Queen's University Press.

– 2009. "The State and the Northern Social Economy." *Northern Review* 30: 37–56.

– 2014. "The Lasting Impact of the Berger Inquiry into the Construction of a Pipeline in the Mackenzie Valley. In *Commissions of Inquiry and Policy Change: A Comparative Analysis*, edited by Gregory J. Inwood and Carolyn M. Johns, 88–112. Toronto: University of Toronto Press.

– 2015. "State Institutions and the Social Economy in Northern Canada." In *Northern Communities Working Together: The Social Economy of Canada's North*, edited by Chris Southcott, 74–96. Toronto: University of Toronto Press.

Abele, Frances, and Daiva Stasiulis. 1989. "Canada as a 'White Settler Colony': What about Natives and Immigrants?" In *The New Canadian Political Economy*, edited by Wallace Clement and Glen Williams, 240–77. Kingston: McGill-Queen's University Press.

Abella, Irving. 1973. *Nationalism, Communism and Canadian Labour: The CIO, the Communist Party and the Canadian Congress of Labour, 1935–1956*. Toronto: University of Toronto Press.

Abella, Irving, and Harold Topper. 1998. "The Line Must be Drawn Somewhere: Canada and Jewish Refugees, 1933–1939." In *A Nation of Immigrants: Women, Workers, and Communities in Canadian History, 1840s–1960s*, edited by Franca Iacovetta, Paula Draper, and Robert Ventresca, 412–45. Toronto: University of Toronto Press.

Acker, Joan. 2006. *Class Questions, Feminist Answers*. Toronto: Rowman and Littlefield Publishers.

Adams, Howard. 1989. *Prison of Grass*. Saskatoon: Fifth House Publishers.

– 1995. *A Tortured People: The Politics of Colonization*. Penticton: Theytus Books Ltd.

"Affordable Housing Advocates Urge Action on Growing Crisis." 2015. CBC, 10 September 2015. http://www.cbc.ca/news/business/affordable-housing-rent-1.3222472.

Albo, Greg. 1994. "'Competitive Austerity' and the Impasse of Capitalist Employment Policy." In *The Socialist Register*, edited by Ralph Miliband and Leo Panitch, 144–70. London: Merlin.

– 2004. "The Old and New Economics of Imperialism." In *The Socialist Register*, edited by Leo Panitch and Colin Leys, 88–113. London: Merlin.

– 2010. "The 'New Economy' and Capitalism Today." In *Interrogating the New Economy: Restructuring Work in the 21st Century*, edited by Norene Pupo and Mark Thomas, 3–20. Toronto: University of Toronto Press.

Albo, Greg, Sam Gindin, and Leo Panitch. 2010. *In and Out of Crisis: The Global Financial Meltdown and Left Alternatives*. Oakland: PM Press.

Albo, Greg, and Jane Jenson. 1989. "A Contested Concept: The Relative Autonomy of the State." In *The New Canadian Political Economy*, edited by Wallace Clement and Glen Williams, 180–211. Kingston & Montreal: McGill-Queen's University Press.

Alexa. 2018. "World's Top Websites." Accessed 1 August 2018. https://www.alexa.com/topsites.

– 2018. "Top Ten Websites in Canada." Accessed 1 August 2018. http://www.alexa.com/topsites/countries/CA.

Alfred, Taiaiake, and Jeff Corntassel. 2005. "Being Indigenous: Resurgences against Contemporary Colonialism." *Government and Opposition* 40, no. 4: 597–614.

Allingham, Jeremy. 2015. "Canadian Hockey League Taking Advantage of Junior Players, says Unifor President." CBC *News*, 19 March 2015.

Allman, Paula. 2010. *Critical Education against Global Capitalism: Karl Marx and Revolutionary Critical Education*. Rotterdam: Sense Publishers.

Amin, Samir. 2013. *Three Essays on Marx's Value Theory*. New York: Monthly Review Press.

Ammirante, Julian. 2006. "Globalization in Professional Sport: Comparisons and Contrasts between Hockey and European Football." In *Artificial Ice: Hockey, Culture, and Commerce*, edited by David Whitson and Richard Gruneau, 237–61. Peterborough, ON: Broadview Press.

– 2009. "Manufacturing Players and Controlling Sports: An Interpretation of the Political Economy of Hockey and the 2004 NHL Lockout." In *Canada's*

Game: Hockey and Identity, edited by Andrew C. Holman, Montreal, 180–210. Montreal: McGill-Queen's University Press.

Amsden, Alice. 2007. *Escape from Empire: The Developing World's Journey through Heaven and Hell*. Cambridge, MA: MIT Press.

Anderson, Benedict. 1991. *Imagined Communities: Reflections on the Origins and Spread of Nationalism*. Revised Edition. London: Verso.

Anderson, Bridget. 2013. *Us and Them: The Dangerous Politics of Immigration Control*, Oxford: Oxford University Press.

Anderson, Bridget, Nandita Sharma, and Cynthia Wright. 2011. "Why No Borders?" *Refuge* 26, no. 3: 5–18.

Anderson, John. 2016. *An Over-the-Top Exemption: It's Time to Fairly Tax and Regulate the New Internet Media Services*. Ottawa: Canadian Centre for Policy Alternatives.

Anderson, John, James Beaton, and Kate Laxer. 2006. "The Union Dimension: Mitigating Precarious Employment?" In *Precarious Employment: Understanding Labour Market Insecurity in Canada*, edited by Leah. F. Vosko, 301–17. Montreal and Kingston: McGill-Queen's University Press.

Anderson, Kim. 2003. "Vital Signs: Reading Colonialism in Contemporary Adolescent Family Planning." In *Strong Women Stories: Native Vision and Community Survival*, edited by Kim Anderson and Bonita Lawrence, 173–90. Toronto: Sumach Press.

Andrew, Caroline. 2003. "Municipal Restructuring, Urban Services and the Potential for the Creation of Transformative Spaces." In *Changing Canada: Political Canada as Transformation*, edited by Wallace Clement and Leah Vosko, 311–34. Montreal: McGill-Queen's University Press.

Andrew, Caroline, Pat Armstrong, Hugh Armstrong, Wallace Clement, and Leah. F. Vosko, eds. 2003. *Studies in Political Economy: Developments in Feminism*. Toronto: Women's Press.

Angus, Ian. 2010. *The Global Fight for Climate Justice: Anticapitalist Responses to Global Warming and Environmental Destruction*. London: Resistance Books.

Antonacci, J.P. 2014. "Growers Call for Separate Minimum Wage for Farm Workers." *Norfolk News*, 23 April 2014.

Arat-Koç, Sedef. 1989. "In the Privacy of Our Home: Foreign Domestic Workers as a Solution to the Crisis of the Domestic Sphere in Canada." *Studies in Political Economy* 28: 33–58.

– 2006. "Whose Social Reproduction? Transnational Motherhood and Challenges to Feminist Political Economy." In *Social Reproduction: Feminist Political Economy Challenges Neo-Liberalism*, edited by Kate Bezanson and Meg Luxton, 75–92. Montreal: McGill-Queen's University Press.

– 2012. "Invisibilized, Individualized, and Culturalized: Paradoxical Invisibility and Hyper-Visibility of Gender in Policy Making and Policy

Discourse in Neoliberal Canada." *Canadian Woman Studies/Les cahiers de la femme* 29, no. 3 (Spring/Summer): 6–17.

Arendt, Hannah. 1951. *The Origins of Totalitarianism*. New York: Harcourt, Brace and Co.

Armstrong, Hugh. 2003. "Neoliberalism and Official Health Statistics: Towards a Research Agenda." In *Troubling Care: Critical Perspectives on Research and Practices*, edited by Pat Armstrong and Susan Braedley, 187–99. Toronto: Canadian Scholars' Press.

Armstrong, Hugh, Pat Armstrong, and Patricia Connelly. 1997. "Introduction: The Many Forms of Privatization." *Studies in Political Economy* 53: 3–9.

Armstrong, Hugh, Tamara J. Daly, and Jacqueline A. Choiniere. 2017. "Policies and Practices: The Case of RAI-MDS in Canadian Long-Term Care Homes." *Journal of Canadian Studies* 50, no. 2: 348–67.

Armstrong, Pat, and Hugh Armstrong. 1983. "Beyond Sexless Class and Classless Sex: Towards Feminist Marxism." *Studies in Political Economy* 10: 7–43.

– 1984. *The Double Ghetto: Canadian Women and Their Segregated Work.* Toronto: McClelland and Stewart.

– 1985. "Women." In *The New Practical Guide to Canadian Political Economy*, edited by Daniel D. Drache and Wallace Clement, 36–43. Toronto: J. Lorimer.

– 2009. "Precarious Employment in the Health-Care Sector." In *Gender and the Contours of Precarious Employment*, edited by Leah F. Vosko, Martha MacDonald, and Iain Campbell, 256–70. New York: Routledge.

– 2010 [1984]. *The Double Ghetto: Canadian Women and their Segregated Work.* Reprint, Don Mills, ON: Oxford University Press.

– 2010. *Wasting Away: The Undermining of Canadian Health Care.* Don Mills: Oxford University Press.

Armstrong, Pat, Hugh Armstrong, and Krista Scott-Dixon. 2008. *Critical to Care: The Invisible Women in Health Services.* Toronto: University of Toronto Press.

Armstrong, Pat, Hugh Armstrong, and Krystal Kehoe MacLeod. 2015. "The Threats of Privatization to Security in Long-Term Residential Care." *Ageing International* 41, no. 1: 99–116.

Armstrong, Pat, Albert Banerjee, Marta Szebehely, Hugh Armstrong, Tamara Daly, Stirling Lafrance. 2009. *They Deserve Better: The Long-Term Care Experience in Canada and Scandinavia.* Ottawa: Canadian Centre for Policy Alternatives.

Armstrong, Pat, and Linda Silas. 2014. "Nurses Unions: Where Knowledge Meets Know-How." In *Realities of Canadian Nursing: Professional, Practice and Power Issues*, edited by Margorie McIntyre and Carol McDonald, 158–80. New York: Walters Klumer.

Arnold, Stephen R. 2012. "Steel City Meltdown: Hamilton and the Changing Canadian Steel Industry." In *Boom, Bust and Crisis: Labour, Corporate*

Power and Politics in Canada, edited by John Peters, 84–102. Halifax: Fernwood.

Aronowitz, Stanley, and Peter Bratsis, eds. 2002. *Paradigm Lost: State Theory Reconsidered*. Minneapolis: University of Minnesota Press.

Asch, Michael. 1977. "The Dene Economy." In *Dene Nation*, edited by Mel Watkins, 47–61. Toronto: University of Toronto Press.

Ash Garner, Roberta, and Mayer Zald. 1987. "The Political Economy of Social Movement Sector." In *Social Movements in an Organizational Society: Collected Essays*, edited by Mayer Zald and John McCarthy, 293–317. London: Transaction Publishers.

Ashwin, Sarah, and Valery Yakubovich. 2005. "Cherchez la Femme: Women as Supporting Actors in the Russian Labour Market." *European Sociological Review* 21, no. 2: 149–63.

Attwood, Lynne. 2010. *Gender and Housing in Soviet Russia: Private Life in a Public Space*. Manchester: Manchester University Press.

Audley, Paul. 1983. *Canada's Cultural Industries*. Toronto: Lorimer.

Avakumovic, Ivan. 1975. *The Communist Party in Canada: A History*. Toronto: McClelland and Stewart.

Avdeyeva, Olga. 2011. "Policy Experiment in Russia: Cash-for-Babies and Fertility Change." *Social Politics* 18, no. 3: 361–86.

Ayres, Jefrrey. 2001. "Transnational Political Processes and Contention against the Global Economy." *Mobilization: An International Quarterly* 6, no. 1: 55–68.

Babe, Robert. 2009. *Cultural Studies and Political Economy: Toward a New Integration*. Lanham, MD: Lexington Books.

Baines, Donna. 2004. "Caring for Nothing: Work Organization and Unwaged Labour in Social Services." *Work, Employment & Society* 18, no. 2: 267–295.

Bakan, Abigail. 2008. "Reconsidering the Underground Railroad: Slavery and Racialization in the Making of the Canadian State." *Socialist Studies* 4 (Spring): 3–29.

Bakan, Abigail, and Audrey Kobayshi. 2000. *Employment Equity Policy in Canada: An Interprovincial Comparison*. Ottawa: Canada, Status of Women.

Bakan, Abigail, and Daiva Stasiulus. 2005. *Negotiating Citizenship: Migrant Women in Canada and the Global System*. Toronto: University of Toronto Press.

Bakker, Isabella. 1989. "The Political Economy of Gender." In *The New Canadian Political Economy*, edited by Wallace Clement and Glen Williams, 99–115. Kingston and Montreal: McGill-Queen's University Press.

– 2003. "Neo-liberal Governance and the Re-privatization of Social Reproduction: Social Provisioning and Shifting Gender Orders." In *Power, Production and Social Reproduction: Human In/security in the Global Political Economy*, edited by Isabella Bakker and Stephen Gill, 66–82. London: Palgrave Macmillan.

Bakker, Isabella, and Stephen Gill, eds. 2003. *Power, Production, and Social Reproduction: Human In/security in the Global Political Economy.* London: Palgrave Macmillan.

Balbus, Isaac D. 1977. "Commodity Form and Legal Form: An Essay on the 'Relative Autonomy' of the Law." *Law and Society Review* 11, no. 3: 571–88.

Balibar, Étienne. 2000. "What We Owe to the Sans-Papiers." In *Social Insecurity*, edited by Len Guenther and Cornelius Heesters, 42–3. Toronto. House of Anansi Press.

Banerjee, Albert, and Pat Armstrong. 2015. "Centring Care: Explaining Regulatory Tensions in Residential Care for Older People." *Studies in Political Economy* 95: 7–22.

Banerjee, Sidhartha. 2015. "Montreal Sewage Dump Now Underway Necessary, Mayor Says." *Toronto Star*, 11 November 2015.

Bannerji, Himani. 1991. "But Who Speaks for Us? Experience and Agency in Conventional Feminist Paradigms." In *Unsettling Relations: The University as a Site of Feminist Struggles*, edited by Himani Bannerji, Linda Carty, Kari Dehli, Susan Heald, and Kate McKenna, 81. Toronto: The Women's Press.

– 1995. *Thinking Through: Essays on Feminism, Marxism and Anti-Racism.* Toronto: Women's Press.

– 2000. *The Dark Side of the Nation: Essays on Multiculturalism, Nationalism and Gender.* Toronto: Canadian Scholars' Press Inc.

– 2005. "Building from Marx: Reflections on Class and Race." *Social Justice* 32, no. 4: 144–60.

Bantjes, Rod. 1997. "Hegemony and the Power of Constitution: Labour and Environmental Coalition-Building in Maine and Nova Scotia." *Studies in Political Economy* 54: 59–90.

Barnes, Trevor. 1996. *Logics of Dislocation: Models, Metaphors, and Meanings of Economic Space.* London: Guilford.

– 2005. "Borderline Communities: Canadian Single Industry Towns, Staples, and Harold Innis." In *Bordering Space*, edited by Henk van Houtum, Olivier Kramsch, and Wolfgang Zierhofer, 109–22. London: Ashgate.

Barrow, Clyde W. 1993. *Critical Theories of the State: Marxist, Neo-Marxist, Post-Marxist.* Wisconsin: University of Wisconsin Press.

Bartholomew, Amy, and Susan Boyd. 1989. "Toward a Political Economy of Law." In *The New Canadian Political Economy*, edited by Wallace Clement and Glen Williams, 212–39. Kingston and Montreal: McGill-Queen's University Press.

Basso, Pietro. 2003. *Modern Times, Ancient Hours: Working Lives in the Twenty-First Century.* London: Verso.

Bateman, Fiona, and Lionel Pilkington. 2011. "Introduction" In *Studies in Settler Colonialism: Politics, Identity and Culture*, edited by Fiona Bateman and Lionel Pilkington, 1–9. London: Palgrave Macmillan.

Battiste, Marie. 2011. *Reclaiming Indigenous Voice and Vision*. Vancouver: UBC Press.

Battiste, Marie, Lynne Bell, and L.M. Findlay. 2002. "Decolonizing Education in Canadian Universities: An Interdisciplinary, International, Indigenous Research Project." *Canadian Journal of Native Education* 26, no. 2: 82–95.

Baumann, Anja, and Matt Muijen, eds. 2010. "Mental Health and Well-Being at the Workplace – Protection and Inclusion in Challenging Times." *World Health Organization*. http://www.euro.who.int/__data/assets/pdf_file/0018/124047/e94345.pdf?ua=1.

Beamish, Robert. 1982. "Sport and the Logic of Capitalism." In *Sport, Culture and the Modern State*, edited by Hart Cantelon and Richard Gruneau, 141–97. Toronto, ON: University of Toronto Press.

– 1985. "Understanding Labor as a Concept for the Study of Sport." *Sociology of Sport Journal* 2: 357–64.

– 2007. "Sports and Capitalism." In *Blackwell Encyclopedia of Sociology*, edited by George Ritzer, 4660–2. Oxford, UK: Blackwell Publishing.

Beaudet, Pierre. 2011. "La radicalisation des mouvements sociaux dans les années 1970." *Bulletin d'histoire politique* 19, no. 2: 97–117.

Beaulne, Pierre. 2009. "La foire d'empoigne du capitalisme canadien." *Nouveaux Cahiers du socialisme* 1: 103–12.

– 2013. "Le capital canadien dans la tourmente." *Nouveaux Cahiers du socialisme* 9: 34–54.

Beauregard, Robert. 2018. *Cities in the Urban Age*. Chicago: University of Chicago Press.

Bélanger, Yves. 1981–82. "Le PQ et le renouvellement de la dépendance." *Conjoncture politique au Québec* 1: 25–40.

Bélanger, Yves, and Pierre Fournier. 1987. *L'entreprise québécoise*. LaSalle: Hurtubise.

Bennett, Tony, and Colin Mercer. 1996. "Improving Research and International Cooperation for Cultural Policy." Paper prepared for UNESCO on behalf of the Australian Key Center for Cultural and Media Policy.

Berger, Suzanne, ed. 1983. *Organizing Interests in Western Europe: Pluralism, Corporatism, and the Transformation of Politics*. Cambridge: Cambridge University Press.

Bernhardt, Annette, Heather Boushey, Laura Dresser, and Chris Tilly, eds. 2008. *The Gloves off Economy: Problems and Possibilities at the Bottom of America's Labor Market*. Ithaca, New York: Cornell University Press.

Bernstein, Stephanie, Katherine Lippel, Eric Tucker, and Leah. F. Vosko. 2006. "Precarious Employment and the Laws Flaws: Understanding Labour Market Insecurity in Canada." In *Precarious Employment: Understanding Labour Market Insecurity in Canada*, edited by Leah F. Vosko, 203–20. Montreal and Kingston: McGill-Queen's University Press.

Berta, Whitney, Audrey Laporte, Dara Zarnett, Vivian Valdmanis, and
    Geoffrey Anderson. 2006. "A Pan-Canadian Perspective on Institutional
    Long-term Care." *Health Policy* 79: 175–94.
Bertelsen, Tilde Marie, and Tine Rostgaard. 2013. "Marketization in Eldercare
    in Denmark: Free Choice and the Quest for Quality and Efficiency." In
    Marketization in Nordic Eldercare, edited by Gabrielle Meagher and Marta
    Szebehely, 127–62. Stockholm: Department of Social Work.
Bezanson, Kate. 2006. "The Neo-Liberal State and Social Reproduction:
    Gender and Household Insecurity in the Late 1990s." In *Social
    Reproduction: Feminist Political Economy Challenges Neoliberalism,* edited
    by Kate Bezanson and Meg Luxton, 173–214. Montreal and Kingston:
    McGill-Queen's University Press.
Bezanson, Kate, and Meg Luxton, eds. 2006. *Social Reproduction: Feminist
    Political Economy Challenges Neo-Liberalism.* Montreal: McGill-Queen's
    University Press.
Bhattacharya, Tithi, ed. 2017. *Social Reproduction Theory: Remapping Class,
    Recentering Oppression.* London: Pluto Press.
Black, Simon. 2012. "Community Unionism and the Canadian Labour
    Movement." In *Rethinking the Politics of Labour in Canada,* edited by
    Stephanie Ross and Larry Savage, 198–222. Halifax: Fernwood.
– 2015. "Unifor Faces Off against Major Junior Hockey." *Canadian
    Dimension* 49, no. 3: 53.
Blackstock, Cindy. "The Unequal Provision of Health and Social Services for
    First Nations Children Has Been Documented for More Than a Century. Is
    This the Moment When the Wider Public Will Demand Action?" *Policy
    Options,* 6 October 2016. http://policyoptions.irpp.org/magazines/october-
    2016/the-long-history-of-discrimination-against-first-nations-children/.
– 2007. "Residential Schools: Did They Really Close or Just Morph into
    Child Welfare?" *Indigenous Law Journal* 6, no. 1: 71–8.
Blad, Cory. 2011. *Neoliberalism and National Culture: State Building and
    Legitimacy in Canada and Quebec.* Leiden: Brill.
Blomley, Nicholas. 1996. "'Shut the Province Down': First Nations Blockades
    in British Columbia 1984–1995." *BC Studies* 111: 5–35.
Bohle, Dorothee, and Bela Greskovits. 2012. *Capitalist Diversity on Europe's
    Periphery.* New York: Cornell University Press.
Boismenu, Gérard, Pascale Dufour, and Denis Saint-Martin. 2004. *Ambitions
    libérales et écueils politiques: Réalisations et promesses du gouvernement
    Charest.* Outremont: Éditions Athéna.
Boltanski, Luc, and Eve Chiapello. 2005. *The New Spirit of Capitalism.* New
    York: Verso.
Bonacich, Edna, Sabrina Alimahomed, and Jake B. Wilson. 2008. "The
    Racialization of Global Labor." *American Behavioral Psychologist* 52, no. 3:
    342–55.

Bonefeld, Werner. 2010. "History and Human Emancipation: Struggle, Uncertainty and Openness." *Critique* 38, no. 1: 61–73.

Booth, Douglas. 2015. "Bruce Kidd, Sport History and Social Emancipation." In *Playing for Change: The Continuing Struggle for Sport and Recreation*, edited by Russell Field, 407–36. Toronto: University of Toronto Press.

Borozdina, Ekaterina, Anna Rotkirch, Anna Temkina, and Elena Zdravomyslova. 2016. "Using Maternity Capital: Citizen Distrust of Russian Family Policy." *European Journal of Women's Studies* 23, no. 1: 60–75.

Borrows, John. 2002. *Recovering Canada: The Resurgence of Indigenous Law*. Toronto: University of Toronto Press.

Boudreau, Julie-Anne. 2017. *Global Urban Politics*. Cambridge: Polity Press.

Boudreau, Julie-Ann, Roger Keil, and Doug Young. 2009. *Changing Toronto: Governing Urban Neoliberalism*. Toronto: University of Toronto Press.

Boudreau, Philippe. 2015. "La politisation comme composante active de l'évolution de la culture mouvementiste: étude du rapport à l'action politique de trois mouvements sociaux québécois, 1980–2009." PhD diss., Université d'Ottawa.

Bourgeault, Ron. 1983. "The Indian, the Métis and the Fur Trade: Class, Sexism and Racism in the Transition from 'Communism' to Capitalism." *Studies in Political Economy* 12 (Fall): 45–80.

Bourque, Gilles. 1984. "Class, Nation, and the Parti Québécois." In *Quebec: State and Society*, edited by Alain-G. Gagnon, 124–47. Toronto: Methuen.

Bourque, Gilles, and Jules Duchastel. 1996. *L'identité fragmentée*. Montreal: Fides.

Bradbury, John H. 1979. "Towards an Alternative Theory of Resource-Based Town Development in Canada." *Economic Geography* 55, no. 2: 147–66.

Bradbury, John H., and Isabelle St-Martin. 1983. "Winding Down in a Quebec Mining Town: a Case Study of Schefferville." *Canadian Geographer* 27, no. 2: 128–44.

Bradford, Neil. 1998. *Commissioning Ideas: Canadian National Policy Innovation in Comparative Perspective*. Toronto: Oxford University Press.

– 2007. "Placing Social Policy? Reflections on Canada's New Deal for Cities and Communities." *Canadian Journal of Urban Research* 16, no. 2: 1–26.

Braedley, Susan, and Meg Luxton. 2010. *Neoliberalism and Everyday Life*. Montreal and Kingston: McGill-Queen's University Press.

Brand, Dionne. 1999. "Black Women and Work: The Impact of Racially Constructed Gender Roles on the Sexual Division of Labour." In *Scratching the Surface: Canadian Anti-Racist Feminist Thought*, edited by Enakshi Dua and Angela Robertson, 83–96. Toronto: Women's Press.

Brave Heart, Maria Yellow Horse. 2003. "The Historical Trauma Response among Natives and Its Relationship with Substance Abuse: A Lakota Illustration." *Journal of Psychoactive Drugs* 35, no. 1: 7–13.

Brenner, Johanna. 2000. "Rethinking Women's Oppression." In *Women and the Politics of Class*, 11–49. New York: Monthly Review Press.

Brenner, Neil, Jamie Peck, and Nik Theodore. 2009. "Variegated Neoliberalization: Geographies, Modalities, Pathways." *Global Networks* 10, no. 9: 182–222.

Brenner, Neil, and Nik Theodore. 2002. "Cities and the Geographies of 'Actually Existing Neoliberalism.'" *Antipode* 34, no. 3: 341–47.

Briskin, Linda. 1989. "Socialist Feminism: From the Standpoint of Practice." *Studies in Political Economy* 30: 87–114.

– 1999. "Autonomy, Diversity, and Integration: Union Women's Separate Organizing in North America and Western Europe in the Context of Restructuring and Globalization." *Women's Studies International Forum* 22, no. 5: 543–54.

Briskin, Linda, and Lynda Yanz. 1983. *Union Sisters: Women in the Labour Movement*. Toronto: Women's Press.

British Columbia Ombudsperson. 2012. *The Best of Care: Getting It Right for Seniors in British Columbia*, Part 2. Victoria: Ombudsperson.

Broadhead, John, Jesse Darling, and Sean Mullin. 2014. "Crisis and Opportunity: Time for a National Infrastructure Plan for Canada." *Canada 2020*, 1 October.

Brodie, Janine. 1996. "New State Forms, New Political Spaces." In *States against Markets: The Limits of Globalization*, edited by Robert Boyer and Daniel Drache, 383–98. London: Routledge.

– 2007. "Reforming Social Justice in Neoliberal Times." *Studies in Social Justice* 1, no. 2: 93–107.

– 2008. "We Are All Equal Now: Contemporary Gender Politics in Canada." *Feminist Theory* 9, no. 2: 145–64.

– 2010. "Globalization, Canadian Family Policy and the Omissions of Neoliberalism." *North Carolina Law Review* 88, no. 5: 1559–92.

Brodie, Janine, and Isabella Bakker. 2007. *Canada's Social Policy Regime and Women: An Assessment of the Last Decade*. Ottawa: Status of Women Canada.

Brodie, Janine, and Linda Trimble. 2003. "Reinventing Canada." In *Reinventing Canada*, edited by Janine Brodie and Linda Trimble, 1–15. Toronto: Prentice Hall.

Brody, Hugh. 2002. *The Other Side of Eden: Hunters, Farmers, and the Shaping of the World*. CITY: Macmillan.

Brohm, Jean-Marie. 1979. *Sport: A Prison of Measured Time*. New York, NY: Humanities Press International.

Brookman, Catherine, Margaret Denton, Isik Zeytinoglu, Sharon Davies, Susan VanderBent. 2016. "Worklife and Quality of Care from the Perspectives of Community Based PSWs." Home Care Ontario Symposium, 23 June. http://www.pswshaveasay.ca/assets/ohcpresentation_2016_finalv3.pdf.

Brophy, Enda, and Greig de Peuter. 2014. "Labours of Mobility: Communicative Capitalism and the Smartphone Cybertariat." In *Theories of the Mobile Internet: Materialities and Imaginaries*, edited by Andrew Herman, Jan Hadlaw, and Thom Swiss, 60–84. New York: Routledge.

Brown, Jennifer. 1980. *Strangers in Blood: Fur Trade Company Families in Indian Country*. Vancouver: University of British Columbia Press.

Bryan, Dick. 1995. *The Chase Across the Globe: International Accumulation and the Contradictions for Nation States*. Boulder: Westview.

Bureau du vérificateur général de Montréal. 2010. Report of the Auditor General of the Ville de Montréal to the City Council and to the Urban Agglomeration Council For the Year Ended, 31 December.

– 2013. Report of the Auditor General of the Ville de Montréal to the City Council and to the Urban Agglomeration Council For the Year Ended, 31 December.

Burgess, William. 2002. "Canada's Location in the World System: Reworking the Debate in Canadian Political Economy." PhD diss., University of British Columbia.

– 2007. "Canada: Imperialist or Imperialized?" Paper presented to IX Encuentro International de Economistas, Globalización y Problemas del Desarrollo, La Habana, 5–9 February.

Burke, David. 2016. "Heritage Minister Mélanie Joly Says Investing in Arts Will Help Grow the Economy." CBC, 15 March 2016. http://www.cbc.ca/news/canada/nova-scotia/melanie-joly-economy-heritage-minister-arts-and-culture-nova-scotia-1.3408932.

Bush, David, and Rawan Abdelbaki. 2016. *Fight for $15 and Fairness*. Global Labour Research Centre Working Paper #1, April. Toronto: Global Labour Research Centre. Accessed 16 May 2016. http://glrc.apps01.yorku.ca/glrc-working-paper-series/.

Calgary Economic Development. 2012. *Calgary: A Hub for Creativity and Innovation*. www.calgaryeconomicdevelopment.com/dmsdocument/33.

Cameron, Barbara. 2006. "Social Reproduction and Canadian Federalism." In *Social Reproduction: Feminist Political Economy Challenges Neoliberalism*, edited by Kate Bezanson and Meg Luxton, 45–74. Montreal and Kingston: McGill-Queen's University Press.

Camfield, David. 2006. "Neoliberalism and Working-Class Resistance in British Columbia: The Hospital Employees' Union Struggle 2002–2004." *Labour/Le Travail* 57 (Spring): 9–41.

– 2009. "Sympathy for the Teacher: Labour Law and Transgressive Workers' Collective Action in British Columbia, 2005." *Capital & Class* 33, no. 3: 81–107.

– 2011. *Canadian Labour in Crisis: Reinventing the Workers' Movement*. Halifax: Fernwood.

– 2016. "Theoretical Foundations of an Anti-racist Queer Feminist Historical Materialism." *Critical Sociology* 42, no. 2: 289–306.

Campbell, Bruce. 2009. *The Global Economic Crisis and its Canadian Dimension*. Ottawa: Canadian Centre for Policy Alternatives.
– 2013. *The Petro-Path Not Taken: Comparing Norway with Canada and Alberta's Management of Petroleum Wealth*. Ottawa: Canadian Centre for Policy Alternatives.
Campbell, Will. 2014. "Ontario Liberals Pushed Film and TV Subsidies Despite Internal Concern." *Globe and Mail*, 8 June. http://www.theglobeandmail.com/news/politics/ontario-liberals-pushed-film-and-tv-subsidies-despite-internal-concern/article19062248/.
Canada. 1876. *The Indian Act*. Ottawa: Parliament of Canada.
– 1945. Department of Reconstruction. White Paper on Employment and Income. Ottawa.
– 1985. Consolidation. *Canada Health Act* R.S.C., 1985, c. C-6.
– 2014. *Canadian Trade and Investment Activity. Northwest Territories' Merchandise Trade with the World*. Ottawa: Parliament of Canada.
Canada Mortgage Housing Corporation. 2015. *Rental Market Report: Vancouver and Abbotsford-Mission* CMAS, Fall.
– 2016. *Housing Now Tables – Vancouver and Abbotsford* CMAS, January.
Canada West Foundation. 2013. *At the Intersection: The Case for Sustained and Strategic Public Infrastructure Investment*. Calgary: CWF.
Canadian Broadcasting Corporation (CBC). "Waitlists for Long-term Care Growing: Report." CBC News video, 3:14. 22 November 2011. http://www.cbc.ca/news/canada/nova- scotia/wait-lists-for-long-term-care-growing-report-1.981595.
Canadian Centre for Policy Alternatives. 2013. *Canada's Infrastructure Gap: Where It Came From and Why It Will Cost So Much To Close*. Ottawa: CCPA.
Canadian Chamber of Commerce. 2013. *The Foundations of a Competitive Canada: The Need for Strategic Infrastructure Investment*. Ottawa: CCC.
Canadian Health Services Research Foundation. 2002. "Myth: The Aging Population Will Overwhelm the Healthcare System." *Mythbusters*.
Canadian Heritage. 2013. *The Creative Economy: Key Concepts and Literature Review Highlights*. Ottawa, ON. https://cch.novascotia.ca/sites/default/files/inline/documents/creative-economy-synthesis_201305.pdf.
Canadian Hockey League. 2014. "Statement from the Commissioners of the Canadian Hockey League." Canadian Hockey League, 20 October. http://chl.ca/statement-from-the-commissioners-of-the-canadian-hockey-league.
Canadian Institute for Health Information (CIHI). 2014a. Health Spending – Nursing Homes. Ottawa: CIHI.
– 2014b. *National Health Expenditures*.
– 2015. LTC *Financial Data Tables*.
Canadian Press. 2009. "Feds Offer Farmers $300M to Quit Growing Tobacco." CBC, August 1, 2009. http://www.cbc.ca/news/canada/feds-offer-farmers-300m-to-quit-growing-tobacco-1.748489.

– 2015. "'Canada is Back,' says Trudeau in Paris. 'We're Here to Help.'"
  Toronto Star, 30 November 2015.

Cantelon, Hart, and Gruneau, Richard, eds. 1982. *Sport, Culture and the
  Modern State.* Toronto, ON: University of Toronto Press.

Carr, Nicholas. 2014. *The Glass Cage: Automation and Us.* New York: W.W.
  Norton and Company.

Carrington, Ben. 2009. "Sport without Final Guarantees: Cultural Studies/
  Marxism/Sport." In *Marxism, Cultural Studies and Sport,* edited by Ben
  Carrington and Ian McDonald, 15–31. London: Routledge.

Carroll, William. 1986. *Corporate Power and Canadian Capitalism.*
  Vancouver: University of British Columbia Press.

– 2004. *Corporate Power in a Globalizing World.* Toronto: Oxford University
  Press.

Carroll, William, and Elaine Coburn. 2003. "Social Movements and
  Transformation." In *Changing Canada: Political Economy as
  Transformation,* edited by Wallace Clement and Leah Vosko, 79–105.
  Montreal: McGill-Queen's University Press.

Carroll, William, and Robert Hackett. 2006. "Democratic Media Activism
  through the Lens of Social Movement Theory. *Media, Culture and Society*
  28, no. 1: 83–104.

Carroll, William, and Robert Ratner. 1996. "Master Frames and Counter-
  Hegemony: Political Sensibilities in Contemporary Social Movements."
  Canadian Review of Sociology/Revue canadienne de sociologie 33: 407–35.

Carson, Jenny, and Myer Siemiatyki. 2014. "Resisting Precarity in Toronto's
  Municipal Sector: The Justice and Dignity for Cleaners Campaign." *Just
  Labour: A Canadian Journal of Work and Society* 22: 168–85.

Cashore, Benjamin, Graeme Auld, James Lawson, and Deanna Newsom. 2008.
  "The Future of Non-State Authority in Canadian Staples Industries:
  Assessing the Emergence of Forest Certification." In *Canada's Resource
  Economy in Transition: The Past, Present, and Future of Canadian Staples
  Industries,* edited by Michael Howlett and Keith Brownsey, 209–30.
  Toronto: Emond Montgomery Publications.

Castells, Manuel. 1977. *The Urban Question.* Cambridge: MIT Press.

CB Staff. 2017. "Canada's Richest People: The Complete Top 100 Ranking."
  Canadian Business, 9 Nov 2017.https://www.canadianbusiness.com/lists-
  and-rankings/richest-people/100-richest-canadians-complete-list/.

CBC News. 2016. "Netflix Now Has More than 5.2 Million Customers in
  Canada, Report Suggests." CBC, 15 June 2016. http://www.cbc.ca/news/
  business/netflix-streaming-cord-cutting-1.3636305.

– 2017. "Everyday Racism: Canadian Artists Discuss Minority Representation
  in Film and Media." CBC, 3 June 2017. https://www.cbc.ca/news/canada/
  british-columbia/everyday-racism-canadian-artists-discuss-minority-
  representation-in-film-and-media-1.4144038.

Chandler, Andrea. 2009. "Gender, Political Discourse and Social Welfare in Russia: Three Case Studies." *Canadian Slavonic Papers* 51, no. 1: 3–24.

Chernova, Zhanna. 2012. "New Pronatalism? Family Policy in Post-Soviet Russia." REGION: *Regional Studies of Russia, Eastern Europe, and Central Asia* 1, no. 1: 75–92.

Chomsky, Noam. 2002. *Understanding Power: The Indispensable Chomsky.* New York, NY: The New Press.

Choudry, Aziz. 2015. *Learning Activism: The Intellectual Life of Contemporary Social Movements.* Toronto: University of Toronto Press.

Choudry, Aziz, and Dip Kapoor. 2010. *Learning from the Ground Up: Global Perspectives on Social Movements and Knowledge Production.* Palgrave McMillan.

Choudry, Aziz, and Adrian A. Smith. 2016. *Unfree Labour: Struggles of Migrant and Immigrant Workers in Canada.* Oakland: PM Press.

Choudry, Aziz, and Mark Thomas. 2012. "Organizing Migrant and Immigrant Workers in Canada." In *The Politics of Labour in Canada,* edited by Stephanie Ross and Larry Savage, 171–83. Halifax and Winnipeg: Fernwood.

Chouinard, Vera, and Valorie Crooks. 2005. "'Because They Have All the Power and I Have None': State Restructuring of Income and Employment Supports and Disabled Women's Lives in Ontario, Canada." *Disability & Society* 20, no. 1: 19–32.

Chisholm, Sharon. 2003. *Affordable Housing in Canada's Urban Communities: A Literature Review.* Ottawa: MCHC.

Christensen, Julia. 2014. "Our Home, Our Way of Life: Spiritual Homelessness and the Sociocultural Dimensions of Indigenous homeless in the Northwest Territories (NWT), Canada." *Social & Cultural Geography* 14, no. 7: 804–28.

City of Toronto Minutes. 1983. Executive Committee Report Number 11.22, *Mayor's Action Task Force on Discharged Psychiatric Patients.* 1782–5.

– 1984. Executive Committee Report Number 11.1. *Final Report of the Mayor's Action Task Force on Discharged Psychiatric Patients.* 3479–586.

Clarke, Harold D., Jane Jenson, Lawrence LeDuc, and Jon Pammett. 1996. *Absent Mandate: Canadian Electoral Politics in an Era of Restructuring.* Toronto: Gage.

Clarke, John. 2008. "Living with/in and without Neo-Liberalism." *Focaal* 51: 135–47.

Clarke, Tony, Diana Gibson, Brendan Haley, and Jim Stanford. 2013. *Bitumen Cliff: Lessons and Challenges of Bitumen Mega-Developments for Canada's Economy in an Age of Climate Change.* Ottawa: Canadian Centre for Policy Alternatives.

Clark-Jones, Melissa. 1987. *A Staple State: Canadian Industrial Resources in Cold War.* Toronto: University of Toronto Press.

Clarkson, Stephen. 1985. *Canada and the Reagan Challenge.* Toronto: Lorimer.

– 2005. *The Big Red Machine: How the Liberal Party Dominates Canadian Politics.* Vancouver: University of British Columbia Press.

Clement, Andrew, and Jonathan A. Obar. 2015. "Canadian Internet 'Boomerang' Traffic and Mass NSA Surveillance: Responding to Privacy and Network Sovereignty Challenges." In *Law, Privacy and Surveillance in the Post-Snowden Era*, edited by Michael Geist and Wesley Wark, 13–44. Ottawa: University of Ottawa Press.

Clement, Wallace. 1977. *Continental Corporate Power: Economic Elite Linkages between Canada and the United States.* Toronto: McClelland and Stewart.

– 1981. *Hardrock Mining: Industrial Relations and Technological Changes at Inco.* Toronto: McClelland and Stewart Limited.

– 1982. "Sports, Sports Violence and the State." In *Sport, Culture and the Modern State*, edited by Hart Cantelon and Richard Gruneau. Toronto: University of Toronto Press.

– 1983a. *Class, Power and Property: Essays on Canadian Society.* Toronto: Methuen.

– 1983b. "Transformations in Mining: A Critique of H.A. Innis." In *Class, Power and Property: Essays on Canadian Society.* Toronto: Methuen.

– 1983c. "The Subordination of Labour in Canadian Mining." In *Class, Power and Property: Essays on Canadian Society.* Toronto: Methuen.

– 1988a. *The Challenge of Class Analysis.* Ottawa: Carleton University Press.

– 1988b. "Labour in Exposed Sectors: Canada's Resource Economy." In *The Challenge of Class Analysis.* Ottawa: Carleton University Press.

– 1989. "Debates and Directions: A Political Economy of Resources." In *The New Canadian Political Economy*, edited by Clement and Williams, 36–53. Kingston and Montreal: McGill-Queen's University Press.

– ed. 1997. *Understanding Canada: Building on the New Canadian Political Economy.* Montreal and Kingston: McGill-Queen's University Press.

– 2001a. "Canadian Political Economy's Legacy for Sociology." *Canadian Journal of Sociology/Cahiers canadiens ce sociologie* 26, no. 3: 405–20.

– 2001b. "Who Works: Comparing Labour Market Practices." In *Reconfigurations of Class and Gender*, edited by Janeen Baxter and Mark Western, 55–80. Stanford, CA: Stanford University Press.

– 2003. "Revealing the Class-Gender Connection: Social Policy, Labour Markets and Households." *Just Labour* 4 (Summer): 42–52.

– 2006. "Introduction: Mel Watkins and the Foundations of the New Canadian Political Economy." In *Staples and Beyond: Selected Writings of Mel Watkins, edited by Hugh Grant and David Wolfe*, xii–xxv. Montreal: McGill-Queen's University Press.

Clement, Wallace, and Daniel Drache. 1978. *A Practical Guide to Canadian Political Economy.* Toronto: J. Lorimer.

– 1985. *The New Practice Guide to Canadian Political Economy.* Toronto: J. Lorimer.

Clement, Wallace, Sophie Mathieu, Steven Prus, and Emre Uckardesler. 2009. "Precarious Lives in the New Economy: Comparative Intersectional Analysis." In *Gender and the Contours of Precarious Employment,* edited by Leah F. Vosko, Martha MacDonald, and Iain Campbell. London New York: Routledge.

– 2010. "Restructuring Work and Labour Markets in the New Economy: Four Processes." In *Interrogating the New Economy: Restructuring Work in the 21st Century,* edited by Nora Pupo and Mark Thomas. Toronto: University of Toronto Press.

Clement, Wallace, and John Myles. 1994. *Relations of Ruling: Class and Gender in Postindustrial Societies.* Montreal and Kingston: McGill-Queen's University Press.

Clement, Wallace, and Leah F. Vosko, eds. 2003. *Changing Canada: Political Economy as Transformation.* Montreal: McGill-Queen's University Press.

Clement, Wallace, and Glenn Williams, eds. 1989. *The New Canadian Political Economy.* Kingston and Montreal: McGill-Queen's University Press.

Coates, Kenneth. 1985. *Canada's Colonies: A History of the Yukon and Northwest Territories.* Toronto: James Lorimer and Company.

Coburn, Judi. 1987. "'I See and I Am Silent': A Short History of Nursing in Ontario, 1850–1930." In *Health and Canadian Society,* edited by David Coburn, Carl D'Arcy, and George Murray, 441–62. Richmond Hill: Fitzhenry and Whiteside.

Cohen, Marcy, Janice M. Murphy, and Kelsey Nutland. 2005. *Continuing Care Renewal or Retreat? BC Residential and Home Health Care Restructuring 2001–2004.* Vancouver: Canadian Centre for Policy Alternatives.

Cohen, Marjorie. 1991. "Exports, Unemployment and Regional Inequality: Economic Policy and Trade Theory." In *The New Era of Global Competition: State Policy and Market Power,* edited by Daniel Drache and Meric S. Gertler, 83–110. Montreal: McGill-Queens University Press.

– 2007. "The Shifts in Gender Norms through Globalization: Gender on the Semi-periphery of Power." In *Remapping Gender in the New Global Order,* edited by Marjorie Griffin Cohen and Janine Brodie, 15–43. London: Routledge.

Cohen, Marjorie Griffin, and Marcia Cohen. 2004. *A Return to Wage Discrimination: Pay Equity Losses through the Privatization of Healthcare.* Vancouver: Canadian Centre for Policy Alternatives.

Cohen, Nicole S. 2008. "The Valorization of Surveillance: Toward a Political Economy of Facebook." *Democratic Communiqué* 22, no. 1: 5–22.

– 2012. "Cultural Work as a Site of Struggle." *tripleC* 10, no. 2: 141–55.

– 2015a. "Entrepreneurial Journalism and the Precarious State of Media Work." *South Atlantic Quarterly* 114, no. 3: 513–33.

– 2015b. "From Pink Slips to Pink Slime: Transforming Media Labour in a Digital Age." *Communication Review* 18, no. 2: 98–122.

– 2016a. *Writers' Rights: Freelance Journalism in a Digital Age*. Montreal and Kingston: McGill-Queen's University Press.

– 2016b. "Why the Study of Work and Labour in the Cultural Industries Matters." Personal communication with author.

Coleman, William D. 1984. "The Class Bases of Language Policy in Quebec, 1949–1983." In *Quebec: State and Society*, edited by Alain-G. Gagnon, 388–409. Toronto: Methuen.

– 1989. "The Political Economy of Quebec." In *The New Canadian Political Economy*, edited by Wallace Clement and Glen Williams, 160–79. Kingston and Montreal: McGill-Queen's University Press.

Coleman, William D., and Timothy Mau. 2002. "French–English Relations in Business Interest Associations: 1965–2002." *Canadian Public Administration* 45, no. 4: 490–511.

Coleman, William, and Tony Porter. 2003. "'Playin' Along': Canada and Global Finance." In *Changing Canada: Political Economy as Transformation*, edited by Wallace Clement, 241–64. Montreal: McGill-Queen's University Press.

College Athletics Players Association (CAPA). 2015. "NLRB: Northwester Football Players Cannot Unionize For Now." CAPA, August 17.

Comack, Elizabeth. 2006. "Theoretical Approaches in the Sociology of Law: Theoretical Excursions." In *Locating Law: Race/Class/Gender/Sexuality Connections*, edited by Elizabeth Comack, 18–67. Halifax: Fernwood.

Conference Board of Canada. 2008. *Valuing Culture: Measuring and Understanding Canada's Creative Economy*. http://www.creativecity.ca/database/files/library/valuingculture.pdf.

Connelly, Patricia. 1983. "On Marxism and Feminism." *Studies in Political Economy* 12 (Fall): 153–61.

Conway, Janet. 2004. *Identity, Place, Knowledge: Social Movements Contesting Globalization*. Vancouver: Fernwood.

– 2013. *Praxis and Politics: Knowledge Production in Social Movements*. New York: Routledge.

Coole, Diana, and Samantha Frost. 2010. "Introducing the New Materialism." In *New Materialisms: Ontology, Agency, and Politics*, edited by Diana Coole and Samantha Frost, 1–43. London: Duke.

Cook, Linda. 2011. "Russia's Welfare Regime: The Shift toward Statism." In *Gazing at Welfare, Gender and Agency in Post-Socialist Countries*, edited by Maija Jappinen, Meri Kulmala, and Aino Saarinen, 13–45. Newcastle upon Tyne: Cambridge Scholars Publishing.

Corman, June, and Meg Luxton. 2007. "Social Reproduction and the Changing Dynamics of Unpaid Household and Caregiving Work." In *Work in Tumultuous Times: Critical Perspectives*, edited by Vivian Shalla and

Wallace Clement, 262–88. Montreal and Kingston: McGill-Queen's University Press.

Cossman, Brenda. 2002. "Family Feuds: Neo-Liberal and Neo-Conservative Visions of the Reprivatization Project." In *Privatization, Law, and the Challenge to Feminism*, edited by Brenda Cossman and Judy Fudge, 169–217. Toronto: University of Toronto Press.

Cossman, Brenda, and Judy Fudge. 2002. *Privatization, The Law and the Challenge to Feminism*. Toronto: University of Toronto Press.

Costa, Lucy, Jijian Voronka, Danielle Landry, Jenna Reid, Becky McFarlane, David Reville, and Kathryn Church. 2012. "Recovering Our Stories: A Small Act of Resistance." *Studies in Social Justice* 6, no. 1: 85–101.

Cote, Andre, and Michael Fenn. 2014. *Approaching an Inflection Point in Ontario's Provincial-Municipal Relations*. Toronto: Institute on Municipal Finance and Governance.

Coulthard, Glen. 2010. "Place against Empire: Understanding Indigenous Anti-colonialism." *Affinities: A Journal of Radical Theory, Culture, and Action* 4, no. 2: 79–83.

– 2014. *Red Skin, White Masks: Rejecting the Colonial Politics of Recognition*. Minneapolis: University of Minnesota Press.

Council of Canadian Academies. 2013. *The State of Industrial Research and Development in Canada*. Ottawa: Council of Canadian Academies.

Couturier, Eve-Lyne, and Bertrand Schepper. 2010. *Who is Getting Richer, Who is Getting Poorer: Quebec 1976–2006*. Ottawa: CCPA.

Cowan, Edgar. 2015. "Canada's Creative Industries Can Lead the Economic Charge." *Globe and Mail*, 3 July. http://www.theglobeandmail.com/report-on-business/rob-commentary/canadas-creative-industries-can-lead-the-economic-charge/article25236146/.

Cox, Laurence, and Alf Nilsen. 2014. *We Make Our Own History: Marxism and Social Movements in the Twilight of Neoliberalism*. Chicago: University of Chicago Press.

Cranford, Cynthia J., Judy Fudge, Eric Tucker, and Leah. F. Vosko. 2005. *Self-Employed Workers Organize: Law, Policy, And Unions*. Montreal and Kingston: McGill-Queen's University Press.

Cranford, Cynthia, and Deena Ladd. 2003. "Community Unionism: Organizing for Fair Employment in Canada." *Just Labour: A Canadian Journal of Work and Society* 3 (Fall): 46–59.

Cranford, Cynthia J., and Leah. F. Vosko. 2006. "Conceptualizing Precarious Employment: Mapping Wage Work across Social Location and Occupational Context." In *Precarious Employment: Understanding Labour Market Insecurity in Canada*, edited by Leah F. Vosko, 43–66. Montreal: McGill-Queen's University Press.

Creighton, Donald. 1937. *The Empire of the St Lawrence, 1760–1850*. Toronto: Ryerson Press.

Creese, Gillian, and Daiva Stasiulis. 1996. "Introduction: Intersections of Gender, Race, Class, and Sexuality." *Studies in Political Economy* 51 (Fall): 5–14.

Cribb, Robert. 2015. "Star Investigation: CHL Claims Questioned." *Toronto Star*, 17 February. https://www.thestar.com/sports/hockey/2015/02/17/star-investigation-chl-claims-questioned.html.

Cross, Philip. 2013. "The Logic Cliff." *Financial Post*, 25 February.

Crouch, Colin. 2011. *The Strange Non-Death of Neoliberalism*. Cambridge: Polity Press.

Curtis, Christopher. 2009. "Chasing the NHL Dream." *Montreal Gazette*, 3 October.

Czyzewski, Karina, Frank Tester, Nadia Aaruaq, and Sylvie Blangy. 2015. *The Impact of Resource Extraction on Inuit Women and Families in Qamani'tuaq, Nunavut Territory*. Vancouver: Pauktuutit Inuit Women of Canada.

Daly, Tamara. 2015. "Dancing the Two-Step in Ontario's Long-Term Care Sector: Deterrence Regulation = Consolidation." *Studies in Political Economy* 95: 29–58.

Daly, Tamara, Pat Armstrong, and Ruth Lowndes. 2015. "Liminality in Ontario Long-term Care Facilities. Private Companions Work in the Space 'Betwixt and Between.'" *Competition and Change* 9, no. 3: 246–63.

Daniszewski, Hank. 2011. "Ontario Tobacco Farmers Still Growing Crop after Buyout: Health Watchdog." *London Free Press*, 31 May.

Dansereau, Suzanne. 2006. "Globalization and Mining Labour: Wages, Skills, and Mobility." *Minerals and Energy* 21: 8–22.

Das, Gupta Tanya. 1996. *Racism and Paid Work*. Toronto: Garamond Press.

Das, Gupta Tanya, and Franca Iocavetta. 2000. "Whose Canada Is It? Immigrant Women, Women of Colour and Feminist Critiques of 'Multiculturalism.'" *Atlantis* 24, no. 2: 1–4.

Davidson, Mark, and Kevin Ward. 2014. "Picking Up the Pieces: Austerity Urbanism, California and Fiscal Crisis." *Cambridge Journal of Regions, Economy and Society* 7: 81–97.

Deakin, Simon. 1986. "Labour Law and the Developing Employment Relationship in the UK." *Cambridge Journal of Economics* 10: 225–46.

– 1998. "The Evolution of the Contract of Employment 1900–1950: The Influence of the Welfare State." In *Governance, Industry and Labour Markets in Britain and France: The Modernizing State in the Mid-20th Century*, edited by Noel Whiteside and Robert Salais, 212–30. London: Routledge.

Dear, Michael J., and Jennifer R. Wolch. 1987. *Landscapes of Despair: From Deinstitutionalization to Homelessness*. Princeton: Princeton University Press.

Deerchild, Rosanna. 2003. "Tribal Feminism Is a Drum Song." In *Strong Women Stories: Native Vision and Community Survival*, edited by Kim Anderson and Bonita Lawrence, 97–105. Toronto: Sumach Press.

DeLint, Willem, and Alan Hall. 2009. *Intelligent Control: Developments in Public Order Policing*. Toronto: University of Toronto Press.

Della Porta, Donatella. 2015. *Social Movements in Times of Austerity: Bringing Capitalism Back into Protest Analysis*. Cambridge: Polity Press.

de los Reyes, Julie A. 2017. "Mining Shareholder Value: Institutional Shareholders, Transnational Corporations and the Geography of Gold Mining." *Geoforum* 84: 251–64.

Demarais, Annette Aurelie. 2007. *La Via Campesina: Globalization and the Power of Peasants*. London: Pluto Press.

Deneulin, Severine, 2008. "Beyond Individual Freedom and Agency: Structures of Living Together in Sen's Capability Approach to Development." In *The Capability Approach: Concepts, Measures and Application*, edited by Flavlo Comim, Mozaffar Qizilbash, and Salbine Alkire, 105–24. Cambridge: Cambridge University Press.

de Peuter, Greig, and Nicole S. Cohen. 2015. "Emerging Labour Politics in Creative Industries." In *Routledge Companion to the Cultural Industries*, edited by Kate Oakley and Justin O'Connor, 305–18. New York: Routledge.

de Peuter, Greig, Nicole S. Cohen, and Enda Brophy, eds. 2015. "Interrogating Internships: Unpaid Work, Creative Industries, and Higher Education." *tripleC: Communication, Capitalism and Critique* 13, no. 2: 329–605.

Desfor, Gene, Roger Keil, Stefan Kipfer, and Derda Wekerle. 2006. "From Surf to Turf: No Limits to Growth in Toronto?" *Studies in Political Economy* 77: 131–55.

Deuze, M. 2006. *Media Work*. Cambridge, MA: Polity Press.

Dewing, Michael, William Young, and Erin Tolley. 2006. *Municipalities, the Constitution, and the Canadian Federal System*. Ottawa: Library of Parliament.

Donald, Betsy. 2005. "The Politics of Local Economic Development in Canada's City-Regions." *Space and Polity* 9, no. 3: 261–81.

Donnelly, Peter. 2007. "Sport as Work." In *The Blackwell Encyclopedia of Sociology*, edited by George Ritzer, 4716–18. Oxford: Blackwell Publishing.

Dorland, Michael. 1996. *The Cultural Industries in Canada: Problems, Policies and Prospects*. Toronto: Lorimer.

Drache, Daniel. 1982. "Harold Innis and Canadian Capitalist Development." *Canadian Journal of Political and Social Theory/Revue canadienne de théorie politique et sociale* 6, nos 1–2: 35–60.

– ed. 1995. *Staples, Markets, and Cultural Change: The Centenary Edition of Harold Innis' Collected Essays*. Montreal and Kingston: McGill-Queen's University Press.

Druick, Zoë. 2012. "Continuity and Change in the Discourse of Canada's Cultural Industries." In *Cultural industries.ca*, edited by Ira Wagman and Peter Urquhart, 131–46. Toronto: Lorimer.

D'Souza, Radha. 2011. "Imperial Agendas, Global Solidarities, and Third World Socio-legal Studies: Methodological Reflections." *Osgoode Hall Law Journal* 49, no. 3: 409–44.

Dua, Enakshi and Angela Robertson. 1999. *Scratching the Surface: Canadian, Anti-Racist, Feminist Thought.* Toronto: Women's Press.

Duckett, Stephen. 2012. *Where to From Here? Keeping Medicare Sustainable.* Kingston: McGill-Queen's University Press.

Duffy, Ann, Daniel Glenday, and Norene Pupo. 2010. *The Shifting Landscape of Work.* Toronto: Nelson Education.

Dufour, Pascale. 2004. "L'adoption du projet de loi 112 au Québec: le produit d'une mobilisation ou une simple question de conjoncture politique?" *Politique et sociétés* 23, nos 2–3: 159–82.

– 2008. "Des femmes en marche: vers un féminisme transnational?" In *Québec en mouvements: Idées et pratiques militantes contemporaines,* edited by Francis Dupuis- Déri, 57–70. Montreal: Lux.

– 2009. "From Protest to Partisan Politics: When and How Collective Actors Cross the Line. Sociological Perspectives on Québec Solidaire." *Canadian Journal of Sociology* 34, no. 1: 55–81.

– 2013. *Trois espaces de contestation: France, Canada, Québec.* Montreal: Presses de l'Université de Montréal.

Dufour, Pascale, and Louis-Philippe Savoie. 2014. "Quand les mouvements sociaux changent le politique. Le cas du mouvement étudiant de 2012 au Québec." *Canadian Journal of Political Science* 47, no. 3: 475–502.

Dufour, Pascale, and Christophe Traisnel. 2014. "Nationalism and Protest: The Sovereignist Movement in Quebec." In *Group Politics and Social Movements in Canada* second edition, edited by Miriam Smith, 255–81. Toronto: University of Toronto Press.

Dunk, Thomas W. 1991. *It's A Working Man's Town: Male Working-Class Culture in Northwestern Ontario.* Montreal: McGill-Queen's University Press.

Dylan, Arielle, Bartholemew Smallboy, and Ernie Lightman. 2013. "'Saying No to Resource Development Is Not An Option': Economic Development in Moose Cree First Nation." *Journal of Canadian Studies/Revue d'etudes canadiennes* 47: 59–90.

Eagleton, Terry. 2007. *The Meaning of Life: A Very Short Introduction.* Oxford, UK: Oxford University Press.

Economic Development Winnipeg. 2013. *Winnipeg: Creative Industries – Grow Brighter, Artistic and Clever.* http://www.economicdevelopment winnipeg.com/uploads/document_file/winnipeg_creative_industries. pdf?t=1397601473.

Edwards, Jason. 2010. "The Materialism of Historical Materialism." In *New Materialisms: Ontology, Agency, and Politics,* edited by Diana Coole and Samantha Frost, 281–98. London: Duke.

Edwardson, Ryan. 2008. *Canadian Content: Culture and the Quest for Nationhood*. Toronto: University of Toronto Press.

Ehrcke, Tara. 2015. "The Fight for $15 Wage in B.C. and Beyond." *Canadian Dimension* 49, no. 3 (May–June): 11–14.

Eidelson, Josh. 2013. "Alt-Labor." *American Prospect* 24, no. 1: 15–18.

Einhorn, Barbara. 1993. *Cinderella Goes to Market: Citizenship, Gender and Women's Movements in East Central Europe*. Oxford: Verso.

Eley, Geoff. 2002. *Forging Democracy: The History of the Left in Europe, 1850–2000*. New York: Oxford University Press.

Elias, Peter Douglas, 1997. "Models of Aboriginal Communities in Canada's North." *International Journal of Social Economics* 24, no. 11: 1241–55.

Employment Standards Act. RSO 1990. c E.14.

English, John. 2009. *Just Watch Me: The Life of Pierre Elliott Trudeau 1968–2000*. Toronto: Alfred A. Knopf.

Environment Canada. 2013. *Canada's Emissions Trends*. Ottawa: Minister of the Environment, October.

Ericsson, Magnus. 2012. "Mining Industry Corporate Actors Analysis." POLINARES: EU *Policy on Natural Resources*. Working Paper 16. http://www.eisourcebook.org/cms/Mining%20industry%20corporate%20actors%20analysis.pdf.

Esping-Andersen, Gosta. 1990. *Three Worlds of Welfare Capitalism*. Cambridge: Polity Press.

Evans, Bryan. 2014. "Social Democracy in the New Age of Austerity." In *Orchestrating Austerity: Impacts and Resistance*, edited by Donna Baines and Stephen McBride, 79–90. Halifax: Fernwood.

Evans, Julie, Patricia Grimshaw, David Philips, and Shurlee Swain. 2003. *Equal Subjects, Unequal Rights: Indigenous Peoples in British Settler Colonies, 1830–1910*. New York: Manchester University Press.

Evans-Lacko, Sara. and Martin Knapp. 2016. "Global Patterns of Workplace Productivity for People with Depression: Absenteeism and Presenteeism Costs across Eight Diverse Countries." *Social Psychiatry and Psychiatric Epidemiology* 51, no. 11: 1525–37.

Ewick, Patricia, and Susan S. Silbey. 1992. "Conformity, Contestation, and Resistance: An Account of Legal Consciousness." *New England Law Review* 26 (Spring): 731–49.

– 1998. *The Common Place of Law: Stories from Everyday Life*. Chicago: University of Chicago.

Ewick, Patricia, and Susan S. Silbey. 2002. "The Structure of Legality: The Cultural Contradictions of Social Institutions." In *Legality and Community: On the Intellectual Legacy of Philip Selznick*, edited by Robert A. Kagan, Martin Krygier, and Kenneth Winston, 149–65. Lanham: Rowman & Littlefield.

Fabris, Erick. 2013. "What Could Go Wrong When Psychiatry Employs Us as Peers?" In *Mad Matters: A Critical Reader in Canadian Mad Studies*, edited by Brenda LeFrançois, Robert Menzies, and Geoffrey Reaume, 130–40. Toronto, ON: Canadian Scholars Inc. Press.

Fairey, David. 2007. "New 'Flexible' Employment Standards Regulation in British Columbia." *Journal of Law and Social Policy* 21: 91–113.

Fairey, David, and Simone McCallum. 2007. *Negotiating without a Floor: Unionized Worker Exclusion from BC Employment Standards.* Canadian Centre for Policy Alternatives. SBN: 978-0-88627-548-8. Vancouver, BC: Canadian Centre for Policy Alternatives Office.

Fanelli, Carlo. 2016. *Megacity Malaise: Neoliberalism, Labour and Public Services in Toronto.* Halifax, NS: Fernwood Publishing.

Fanelli, Carlo, and Mark Thomas. 2011. "Austerity, Competitiveness and Neoliberalism Redux: Ontario Responds to the Great Recession." *Socialist Studies* 7, nos 1–2: 141–70.

Fanon, Frantz. 1963. *The Wretched of the Earth.* New York: Grove.

Fast, Travis. 2014 "Stapled to the Front Door: Neoliberal Extractivism in Canada." *Studies in Political Economy* 94 (Fall): 31–60.

Faucher, Albert, and Maurice Lamontagne. 1953. "History of Industrial Development." In *Essais sur le Québec Contemporain,* edited by Jean-Charles Falardeau, 15–37. Quebec: Presses de l'Université Laval.

Featherstone, David. 2012. *Solidarity: Hidden Histories and Geographies of Internationalism.* London: Zed Books.

Federal Labour Standards Review Commission (FLSRC). 2006. Fairness at Work: Federal Labour Standards for the 21st Century (Arthurs Commission). Government of Canada. http://www.hrsdc.gc.ca/eng/labour/employment_standards/fls/index.shtml.

Federation of Canadian Municipalities. 2012. *The State of Canada's Cities and Communities.* Ottawa: FCM.

Federici, Silvia. 2004. *Caliban and the Witch: Women, The Body and Primitive Accumulation.* Brooklyn, NY: Autonomedia.

– 2014a. "The Reproduction of Labour Power in the Global Economy and the Unfinished Feminist Revolution." In *Workers and Labour in a Globalized Capitalism,* edited by Maurizio Atzeni, 85–107. Houndmills, Basingstoke, Hampshire: Palgrave Macmillan.

– 2014b. "From Commoning to Debt: Financialization, Microcredit, and the Changing Architecture of Capital Accumulation." *South Atlantic Quarterly* 113, no. 2: 231–44.

Feenan, Dermot. 2013. "Exploring the 'Socio' of Socio-Legal Studies." In *Exploring the "Socio" of Socio-Legal Studies,* edited by Dermot Feenan, 2–19. London: Palgrave MacMillan.

Ferguson, Susan. 2008. "Canadian Contributions to Social Reproduction Feminism, Race and Embodied Labor." *Race, Gender & Class* 15, nos 1–2: 42–57.

Ferland, Marc, and Yves Vaillancourt. 1981. *Socialisme et Indépendance au Québec: pistes pour le mouvement ouvrier et populaire*. Laval: Éditions coopératives Albert St-Martin.

Ferree, Myra Marx. 1995. "Patriarchies and Feminisms: The Two Women's Movements of Post-Unification Germany." *Social Politics: International Studies in Gender, State and Society* 2, no. 1: 10–24.

Ferree, Myra Marx, and Brigitte Young. 1993. "Three Steps Back for Women: German Unification, Gender, and University 'Reform.'" *Political Science and Politics* 26, no. 2: 199–205.

Filion, Pierre, and Anna Kramer. 2012. "Metropolitan-Scale Planning in Neoliberal Times." *Space and Polity* 15, no. 3: 197–212.

Filion, Pierre, Anna Kramer, and Gary Sands. 2016. "Recentralization as an Alternative to Urban Dispersion: Transformative Planning in a Neoliberal Societal Context." *International Journal of Urban and Regional Research* 40, no. 3: 658–78.

Findlay, Sue. 1988. "Feminist Struggles within the Canadian State." *Resources for Feminist Research* 17, no. 3: 3–35.

Findlay, Tammy. 2012. "Feminist Institutionalism and Feminist Political Economy: A Dialogue on Gender, the State and Representation." Paper Presented at the 2012 Annual Meeting of the Canadian Political Science Association, University of Alberta, 13 June.

– 2015. *Femocratic Administration: Gender, Governance, and Democracy in Ontario*. Toronto: University of Toronto Press.

Fine, Ben, and Alfredo Saad-Filho. 2004. *Marx's Capital*. 4th edition. London: Pluto.

Fine, Janice. 2006. *Worker Centers: Organizing Communities at the Edge of the Dream*. Ithaca: ILR Press.

Flew, Terry, and Stuart Cunningham. 2010. "Creative Industries after the First Decade of Debate." *Information Society: An International Journal* 26, no. 2: 113–23.

Foley, Tadhg. 2011. "'An Unknown and Feeble Body': How Settler Colonialism Was Theorized in the Nineteenth Century." In *Studies in Settler Colonialism: Politics, Identity and Culture*, edited by Fiona Bateman and Lionel Pilkington, 10–27. London: Palgrave MacMillan.

Fonow, Mary Margaret, and Judith A. Cook. 2005. "Feminist Methodology: New Applications in the Academy and Public Policy." *Signs* 30, no. 4: 2211–36.

Forbes. 2018. "Global 2000: The World's Largest Public Companies." *Forbes*, 6 June 2018. https://www.forbes.com/global2000/#48d68398335d.

Forest Ethics Advocacy. 2012. *Who Benefits?* Vancouver: Forest Ethics Advocacy.

Fournier, François, and Daniel Villeneuve. 1981. "Capital, référendum, et perspectives post-référendaires." In *Capitalisme et politique au Québec*, edited by Pierre Fournier, 216–26. Montreal: Éditions Coopératives Albert St-Martin.

Fournier, Pierre. 1976. *The Quebec Establishment: The Ruling Class and the State*. Montreal: Black Rose Books.

– 1978. "Les nouveaux paramètres de la bourgeoisie québécoise." In *Le capitalisme au Québec*, edited by Pierre Fournier, 135–81. Montreal: Éditions Coopératives Albert St-Martin.

Fournier, Pierre, Yves Bélanger, and Claude Painchaud. 1981. "L'enjeu économique et la question nationale au Québec." In *Capitalisme et politique au Québec*, edited by Pierre Fournier, 53–76. Montreal: Éditions Coopératives Albert St-Martin.

Fowke, Vernon. 1957. *The National Policy and the Wheat Economy*. Toronto: University of Toronto Press.

Fox, Bonnie. 1980. *Hidden in the Household: Women's Domestic Labour Under Capitalism*. Toronto: The Women's Press.

Frampton, Caelie, Gary Kinsman, A.K. Thompson, and Kate Tilleczek, eds. 2006. *Sociology for Changing the World*. Halifax: Fernwood.

Frank, Andre Gunder. 1966. *The Development of Underdevelopment*. New York: Monthly Review Press.

Fraser Health. 2011. *Options for Residential Care*.

Fraser, Nancy. 2009. "Feminism, Capitalism and the Cunning of History." In *New Left Review* 56 (March–April): 97–117.

– 2016. "Contradictions of Capital and Care." *New Left Review* 100: 99–117.

Fraser, Nancy, and Linda Gordon. 1992. "Contract versus Charity: Why Is there no Social Citizenship in the United States." *Socialist Review* 22: 45–67.

Freedman, Des, Jonathan Obar, Cheryl Martens, and Robert McChesney, eds. 2016. *Strategies for Media Reform: International Perspectives*. Bronx, NY: Fordham University Press.

Fries, Brant E., and Charles J. Fahey. 2003. "Introduction: Lessons Learned from Eight Case Studies." In *Implementing the Resident Assessment Instrument: Case Studies of Policymaking for Long-Term Care in Eight Countries*, edited by Brant E. Fries and Charles J. Fahey, 1–5. New York: Milbank Memorial Fund.

Fuchs, Christien. 2011. "Web 2.0, Prosumption, and Surveillance." *Surveillance & Society* 8, no. 3: 288–309.

Fudge, Judy. 1991a. *Labour Law's Little Sister: The Employment Standards Act and the Feminization of Labour*. Ottawa: Canadian Centre for Policy Alternatives.

– 1991b. "Marx's Theory of History and a Marxist Analysis of Law." In *Canadian Perspectives on Legal Theory*, edited by Richard Devlin, 151–75. Toronto: Emond Publications.

– 1993. "The Gendered Dimension of Labour Law: Why Women Need Inclusive Unionism and Broader-Based Bargaining." In *Women Challenging*

Unions: Feminism, Democracy and Militancy, edited by Linda Briskin and Patricia McDermott, 231–48. Toronto: University of Toronto Press.

– 2011. *The Precarious Migrant Status and Precarious Employment: The Paradox of International Rights for Migrant Workers*. Vancouver, BC: Metropolis British Columbia.

– 2012. "Precarious Migrant Status and Precarious Employment: The Paradox of International Rights for Migrant Workers." *Comparative Labour Law and Policy Journal* 34: 95–132.

– 2014. "Feminist Reflections on the Scope of Labour Law: Domestic Work, Social Reproduction, and Jurisdiction." *Feminist Legal Studies* 22, no. 1: 1–23.

Fudge, Judy, and Brenda Cossman. 2002. "Introduction: Privatization, Law, and the Challenge to Feminism." In *Privatization, Law, and the Challenge to Feminism*, edited by Brenda Cossman and Judy Fudge, 3–38. Toronto: University of Toronto.

Fudge, Judy, and Eric Tucker. 2001. *Labour before the Law: The Regulation of Workers' Collective Action in Canada, 1900–1948*. Toronto: Oxford University Press.

Fudge, Judy, and Leah. F. Vosko. 2001a. "Gender, Segmentation and the Standard Employment Relationship in Canadian Labour Law, Legislation and Policy." *Economic and Industrial Democracy* 2: 271–310.

– 2001b. "By Whose Standards? Re-Regulating the Canadian Labour Market." *Economic and Industrial Democracy* 3: 327–56.

– 2003. "Gendered Paradoxes and the Rise of Contingent Work: Towards a Transformative Feminist Political Economy of the Labour Market." In *Changing Canada: Political Economy as Transformation*, edited by Wallace Clement, 183–211. Montreal and Kingston: McGill-Queen's University Press.

Fujita, Kuniko, ed. 2013. *Cities in the Crisis*. London: Sage.

Fumaz, Ramon Ribera, and Greig Charnock. 2017. *Socialist Register 2018: Rethinking Democracy*, edited by Leo Panitch and Greg Albo, 188–201. London: Merlin.

Fuqua, Michelle V. 1996. *The Politics of the Domestic Sphere: The Zhenotdely, Women's Liberation, and the Search for a Novyi Byt in Early Soviet Russia*. Seattle: Henry M. Jackson School of International Studies, University of Washington.

Gabriel, Christina. 1996. "One or the Other: 'Race,' Gender and the Limits of Official Multiculturalism." In *Women and Canadian Public Policy*, edited by Janine Brodie, 173–95. Toronto: Harcourt, Brace and Co.

Gabriel, Christina, and Laura Macdonald. "Beyond the Continentalist/ Nationalist Divide: Politics in a North America 'without Borders.'" In *Changing Canada: Political Economy as Transformation*, edited by Wallace Clement and Leah F. Vosko, 213–40. Montreal and Kingston: McGill-Queen's University Press.

Gagnon, Alain G., and Mary Beth Montcalm. 1990. *Quebec: Beyond the Quiet Revolution*. Scarborough: Nelson.

Galer, Dustin. 2018. *Working towards Equity: Disability Rights Activism and Employment in Late Twentieth-Century Canada*. Toronto: University of Toronto Press.

Galtung, Johan. 1971. "Structural Theory of Imperialism." *Journal of Peace Research* 8: 81–117.

Garnham, Nicholas. 1987. "Concepts of Culture: Public Policy and the Cultural Industries. *Cultural Studies* 1: 23–37.

Garcia, David. 2018. "'I Want to Play in Europe': Exploiting African Football." *Monde Diplomatique*, July 2018. https://mondediplo.com/2018/07/13football.

Garon, Francis, and Pascale Dufour. 2010. "Comprendre la mise en oeuvre différenciée d'une politique publique: Le cas d'une politique de gouvernance au Québec." *Canadian Journal of Political Science* 43, no. 3: 607–31.

Gehl, Lynn. 2000. "'The Queen and I': Discrimination against Women in the 'Indian Act' Continues." *Canadian Woman Studies* 20, no. 2: 64–9.

Geist, Michael. 2016. "The TPP's Impact on Canadian Culture Emerging as Political Issue." *Michael Geist*, 8 June. http://www.michaelgeist.ca/2016/06/the-tpps-impact-on-canadian-culture-emerging-as-political-issue/.

Gerber, Theodore, and Michael Hout. 1998. "More Shock than Therapy: Market Transition, Employment, and Income in Russia, 1991–1995." *American Journal of Sociology* 104, no. 1: 1–50.

Gibson, Diana, and Regan Boychuk. 2012. "The Spoils of the Tar Sands: Profits, Work and Labour in Alberta." In *Boom, Bust and Crisis: Labour, Corporate Power and Politics in Canada*, edited by John Peters, 55–67. Halifax: Fernwood.

Gibson, Ginger, and Jason Klinck. 2005. "Canada's Resilient North: The Impact of Mining on Aboriginal Communities." *Pimatisiwin: A Journal of Aboriginal and Indigenous Community Health* 3: 115–39.

Gindin, Sam. 2013. "Beyond the Economic Crisis: The Crisis in Trade Unionism." *Alternate Routes* 24: 236–45.

Gindin, Sam, and Jim Stanford. 2003. "Canadian Labour and the Political Economy of Transformation." In *Changing Canada: Political Economy as Transformation*, edited by Wallace Clement and Leah F. Vosko, 422–42. Montreal and Kingston: McGill-Queen's University Press.

Gitlin, Todd. 1980. *The Whole World Is Watching: Mass Media in the Making and Unmaking of the New Left*. Los Angeles: University of California Press.

Gleeson, Shannon. 2016. *Precarious Claims: The Promise and Failure of Workplace Protections in the United States*. California: University of California Press.

Glenn, Evelyn Nakano. 1992. "From Servitude to Service Work: Historical Continuities in the Racial Division of Paid Reproductive Labor." *Signs* 18, no. 1: 1–43.

Glenn, Jane Matthews, and José Otero. 2013. "Canada and the Kyoto Protocol: An Aesop Fable." In *Climate Change and the Law*, edited by Erkki J. Hollo, Kati Kulovesi, and Mehling Michael, 489–508. New York and London: Springer Dordrecht Heidelberg.

Global Affairs. 2016. *Culture*. http://www.international.gc.ca/trade-agreements-accords-commerciaux/topics-domaines/ip-pi/culture.aspx?lang=eng.

Godard, John. 2017. *Industrial Relations, the Economy and Society*. 5th edition. Concord, ON: Captus Press.

Goldenberg, Suzanne. 2015. "Trudeau Victory May Not Signal a U-turn in Canada's Climate Policy." *Guardian*, 20 October. http://www.theguardian.com/politics/2015/oct/20/trudeau-victory-not-signal-u-turn-canadas-climate-policy.

Goldring, Luin, Carolina Berinstein, and Judith K. Bernhard. 2009. "Institutionalizing Precarious Migratory Status in Canada." *Citizenship Studies* 13, no. 3: 239–65.

Goldstein, Robert Justin, ed. 2014. *Little "Red Scares": Anticommunism and Political Repression in the United States, 1921–1946*. Burlington, VT: Ashgate.

Gonick, Cy. 2006. "Is Canada an Imperialist State?" *Canadian Dimension*, 29 October.

Gordon, Ian. 2013. "Inside Major League Baseball's Dominican Sweatshop System." *Mother Jones*, March/April, 2013. https://www.motherjones.com/politics/2013/03/baseball-dominican-system-yewri-guillen/.

Gordon, Todd. 2007. "Towards An Anti-Racist Marxist State Theory: A Canadian Case Study." *Capital and Class* 31, no. 91: 1–30.

– 2010. *Imperialist Canada*. Winnipeg: Arbeiter Ring Publishing.

Gordon, Todd, and Jeffery Webber. 2007. "Imperialism and Resistance: Canadian Mining Companies in Latin America." *Third World Quarterly* 29, no. 1: 63–87.

Gough, Jamie. 2014. "The Difference between Local and National Capitalism, and Why Local Capitalisms Differ from One Another: A Marxist Approach." *Capital and Class* 38, no. 1: 197–210.

Government of Canada. 1968. *Foreign Ownership and the Structure of Canadian Industry* (popularly called "The Watkins Report"). Ottawa: Privy Council Office.

– 2016. "Strengthening Canadian Content, Discovery and Export in a Digital World." http://canada.pch.gc.ca/eng/1460743.

Government of the Northwest Territories. 2015. *Bureau of Statistics*. http://www.statsnwt.ca/.

– 2014. *Communities and Diamonds*. Yellowknife: Departments of Industry, Tourism and Investment; Education, Culture and Employment; Finance; Health and Social Services; Justice; Statistics; NWT Housing Corporation.

Government of the Northwest Territories Legacy and Hope Foundation. 2013. *The Residential School System in Canada: Understanding the Past, Seeking*

Reconciliation, Building Hope for Tomorrow, Yellowknife, Northwest Territories.

Graefe, Peter. 2007. "Political Economy and Canadian Public Policy." In *Critical Policy Studies*, edited by Miriam Smith and Michael Orsini, 19–40. Vancouver: UBC Press.

– 2012. "Whither the Quebec Model? Boom, Bust and Quebec Labour." In *Boom, Bust and Crisis: Labour, Corporate Power and Politics in Canada*, edited by John Peters, 125–41. Halifax: Fernwood.

– 2016. "The Politics of Economic and Social Development in Quebec." In *Quebec Questions*, edited by Stéphan Gervais, Christopher Kirkey, and Jarrett Rudy, 372–86. Toronto: Oxford.

Graefe, Peter, and Hubert Rioux. 2017. "Austerity of Imagination: Quebec's Struggles in Translating Resistance into Alternatives." In *Austerity: The Lived Experience*, edited by Bryan M. Evans and Stephen McBride, 272–92. Toronto: University of Toronto Press.

Grant, Karen R., Carol Amaratunga, Pat Armstrong, Madeline Boscoe, Ann Pederson, and Kay Willson. 2004. *Caring For/Caring About: Women, Home Care and Unpaid Caregiving*. Aurora, ON: Garamond Press.

Gray, Herb Peter et al. 1971. *Foreign Direct Investment in Canada (Gray Report)*. Ottawa: Supply and Services Canada.

Green, Joyce. 2003. "Decolonization and Recolonization in Canada." In *Changing Canada: Political Economy as Transformation*, edited by Wallace Clement and Leah Vosko, 51–78. Montreal: McGill-Queen's University Press.

– 2007. "Taking Account of Aboriginal Feminism." In *Making Space for Indigenous Feminism*, 20–32. New York: Zed Books.

Grignon, Michael. 2013. "The Health Care Aging Tsunami Myth." *National Post*, 30 October.

Grinspun, Ricardo, and Robert Kreklewich. 1994. "Consolidating Neoliberal Reforms: 'Free Trade' as a Conditioning Framework." *Studies in Political Economy* 43: 33–61.

Grundy, John, Andrea M. Noack, Leah F. Vosko, Rebecca Casey, and Rebecca Hill. 2017. "Enforcement of Ontario's Employment Standards Act: The Impact of Reforms." *Canadian Public Policy* 43, no. 3: 190–201.

Gruneau, Richard. 1981. "Elites, Class and Corporate Power in Canadian Sport." In *Sport, Culture and Society*, edited by John W. Loy Jr., Gerald S. Kenyon, and Barry D. McPherson, 348–71. Philadelphia, PA: Lea and Febiger.

– 1983. *Class, Sports and Social Development*. Amherst, MA: University of Massachusetts Press.

Gruneau, Richard, and David Whitson. 1994. *Hockey Night In Canada: Sports, Identities, and Cultural Politics*. Toronto, ON: University of Toronto Press.

Guard, Julie, and Wayne Antony, eds. 2009. *Bankruptcies and Bailouts*. Halifax: Fernwood Publishing.

Gunton, Thomas. 2014. "Staples Theory and the New Staple Boom." In *The Staples Theory @50: Reflections on the Lasting Significance of Mel Watkins' "A Staple Theory of Economic Growth,"* edited by Jim Stanford, 43–53. Ottawa: Canadian Centre for Policy Alternatives.

Haan, Michael, Deatra Walsh, and Barbara Neis. 2014. "At the Crossroads: Geography, Gender and Occupational Sector in Employment-Related Geographical Mobility." *Canadian Studies in Population* 41, nos 3–4: 6–21.

Hackett, Robert. 2008. "Why Media Reform Should Be a Democratic Priority." *Canadian Dimension,* 12 January. https://canadiandimension.com/articles/view/why-media-reform-should-be-a-democratic-priority.

Hackett, Robert, and Carroll, William. 2006. *Remaking Media: The Struggle to Democratize Public Communication.* New York: Routledge.

Hackworth, Jason, and Abigail Moriah. 2006. "Neoliberalism, Contingency and Urban Policy: The Case of Social Housing in Ontario." *International Journal of Urban and Regional Research* 30, no. 3: 510–27.

Haddow, Rodney. 2015. *Comparing Quebec and Ontario: Political Economy and Public Policy at the Turn of the Millennium.* Toronto: University of Toronto Press.

Haley, Brendan. 2011. "From Staples Trap to Carbon Trap: Canada's Peculiar Form of Carbon Lock-in." *Studies in Political Economy* 88: 97–132.

– 2014. "The Staple Theory and the Carbon Trap." In *The Staples Theory @ 50: Reflections on the Lasting Significance of Mel Watkins' 'A Staple Theory of Economic Growth,'* edited by Jim Stanford, 75–80. Ottawa: Canadian Centre for Policy Alternatives.

Haley, Tobin LeBlanc. 2017. "Intimate Constraints: A Feminist Political Economy Analysis of Biological Reproduction and Parenting in High-Support Housing in Ontario." *Special Issue on Geographies of Emotional Labour and Care* 3, no. 50: 1–12.

– 2018. "Resident Work in High-Support Housing: A Feminist Political Economy Analysis." *Canadian Journal of Disability Studies* 7, no. 2: 33–59.

Hall, Edward, and Robert Wilton. 2011. "Alternative Spaces of 'Work' and Inclusion for Disabled People." *Disability & Society* 26, no. 7: 867–80.

Hall, Peter, and David D. Soskice. 2003. *Varieties of Capitalism: the Institutional Foundations of Comparative Advantage.* Oxford: Oxford University Press.

Hall, Rebecca. 2013. "Diamond Mining in Canada's Northwest Territories: A Colonial Continuity." *Antipode* 45, no. 2: 376–93.

Haluza-Delay, Randolph. 2014. "Assembling Consent in Alberta: Hegemony and the Tar Sands." In *A Line in the Tar Sands: Struggles for Environmental Justice,* edited by Toban Black, Tony Weis, Stephen D'Arcy, Joshua Kahn Russell, 36–44. Toronto: PM Press/Between the Lines.

Hamilton Economic Development. 2010. *Hamilton Economic Development Strategy, 2010–2015.* http://www.investinhamilton.ca/wp-content/uploads/2011/06/Hamilton-EcDev-Strategy2010.pdf.

Hamilton, Roberta, and Michèle Barrett. 1986. *The Politics of Diversity: Feminism, Marxism and Nationalism*. Montreal: Book Centre Inc.

Hanson, Ginger C., Nancy A Perrin, Helen Moss, Naima Laharnar, and Nancy Glass. 2015. "Workplace Violence against Homecare Workers and Its Relationship with Workers Health Outcomes: A Cross-Sectional Study." B M C *Public Health* 15, no. 11: 1–13.

Hardy, Jonathan. 2014a. "Critical Political Economy of Communications: A Mid-term Review." *International Journal of Media & Cultural Politics* 10, no. 2: 189–202.

– 2014b. *Critical Political Economy of the Media: An Introduction*. New York: Routledge.

Harnum, Betty, Joseph Hanlon, Tee Lim, Jane Modeste, Deborah Simmons, and Andres Spring. 2014. *Best of Both Worlds: Sahtú Goné nę T'áadets'enų ǫ – Depending on the Land in the Sahtú Region*. Tulita: Pembina Institute.

Harris, Cole. 2004. "How Did Colonialism Dispossess? Comments from an Edge of Empire." *Annals of the Association of American Geographers* 94, no. 1: 165–82.

Hartford, Kathleen, Ted Schrecker, Mary Wiktorowicz, Jeffrey S. Hoch, and Crystal Sharp. 2011. "Report: Four Decades of Mental Health Policy in Ontario, Canada." *Administration and Policy in Mental Health* 31, no. 1: 65–73.

Harvey, David. 1973. *Social Justice and the City*. Baltimore: John Hopkins University Press.

– 1989a. "From Managerialism to Entrepreneurialism: The Transformation of Urban Governance in Late Capitalism." *Geografiska Annaler, Series B, Human Geography* 71, no. 1: 3–17.

– 1989b. *The Urban Experience*. Baltimore: John Hopkins University Press.

– 1990. *The Condition of Postmodernity: An Enquiry into the Origins of Cultural Change*. Oxford: Blackwell.

– 2003. *The New Imperialism*. Oxford: Oxford University Press.

– 2005. *A Brief History of Neoliberalism*. New York: Oxford University Press.

– 2006. *Limits to Capital*. London: Verso.

– 2010a. *A Companion to Marx's Capital*. London and New York: Verso.

– 2010b. *The Enigma of Capital and the Crisis of Capitalism*. Oxford: Oxford University Press.

– 2012. *Rebel Cities*. London: Verso.

Haslam McKenzie, Fiona M., and Aileen Hoath. 2014. "The Socio-Economic Impact of Mine Industry Commuting Labour Force on Source Communities." *Resources Policy* 42: 45–52.

Hay, Colin, and Michael Lister. 2006. "Introduction: Theories of the State." In *The State: Theories and Issues*, edited by Colin Hay, Michael Lister, and David Marsh, 1–20. New York: Palgrave Macmillan.

Hay, Douglas. 1975. *Albion's Fatal Tree: Crime and Society in Eighteenth-Century England*. New York: Pantheon Books.

Hayter, Roger. 2003. "'The War in the Woods': Post-Fordist Restructuring, Globalization, and the Contested Remapping of British Columbia's Forest Economy." *Annals of the Association of American Geographers* 93, no. 3: 706–29.

Hayter, Roger, and Trevor Barnes. 1990. "Innis' Staple Theory, Exports, and Recession: British Columbia, 1981–86." *Economic Geography* 66, no. 2: 156–73.

– 1997. "The Restructuring of British Columbia's Coastal Forest Sector: Flexibility Perspectives." *BC Studies* 113: 7–37.

Health Quality Ontario. 2014. *Measuring Up: A Yearly Report on How Ontario's Health System Is Performing.* Toronto: Ministry of Health and Long-Term Care.

Heinen, Jacqueline. 1990. "Inequalities at Work: The Gender Division of Labour in the Soviet Union." *Studies in Political Economy* 33: 39–61.

Heitlinger, Alena. 1987. "Maternity Leaves, Protective Legislation and Sex Equality: Eastern European and Canadian Perspectives." In *Feminism and Political Economy: Women's Work, Women's Struggles*, edited by Heather Jon Maroney and Meg Luxton, 247–61. Toronto: Methuen Publications.

Hele, C., Naomi Sayers, and Jessica Wood. 2015. "What's Missing from the Conversation on Missing and Murdered Indigenous Women and Girls." *Toast*, 14 September. http://the-toast.net/2015/09/14/whats-missing-from-the-conversation-on-missing-and-murdered-indigenous-women/.

Helleiner, Eric. 1994. *States and the Re-Emergence of Global Finance.* Ithaca: Cornell University Press.

Helleiner, Eric. 2003. "Toward a North American Common Currency." In *Changing Canada: Political Economy as Transformation*, edited by Wallace Clement and Leah F. Vosko, 265–86. Montreal and Kingston: McGill-Queen's University Press.

– 2014. *The Status Quo Crisis: Global Financial Governance after the 2008 Meltdown.* Oxford: Oxford University Press.

"Help Wanted: Salaries, Affordability and the Exodus of Labour from Metro Vancouver." 2015. *VanCity*, May. https://www.vancity.com/SharedContent/documents/News/Help_Wanted_May_2015.pdf.

Henderson, James (Sákéj) Youngblood. 2002. "Postcolonial Indigenous-Legal Consciousness" *Indigenous Law Journal* 1, no. 1: 2–56.

Hennebry, Jenna. 2012. *Permanently Temporary? Agricultural Migrant Workers and Their Integration in Canada.* Montreal: Institute for Research on Public Policy.

Hesmondhalgh, David. 2007. *The Cultural Industries.* London: Sage.

– 2008. "Cultural and Creative Industries." In *The Sage Handbook of Cultural Analysis*, edited by Tony Bennett and John Frow, 552–69. London: Sage.

– 2010. "User-Generated Content, Free Labor and the Cultural Industries." *Ephemera: Theory and Politics in Organization* 10, nos 3–4: 267–84.

Hetland, Gabriel. 2015. "The Labour of Learning: Overcoming the Obstacles Facing Union-Worker Centre Collaborations." *Work, Employment and Society* 29, no. 6: 932–49.

Hetland, Gabriel, and Jeff Goodwin. 2013. "The Strange Disappearance of Capitalism from Social Movement Studies." *Marxism and Social Movements* 46: 86–98.

Hill-Collins, Patricia. 2000. *Black Feminist Thought: Knowledge, Consciousness, and the Politics of Empowerment.* New York: Routledge.

– 2006. "New Commodities, New Consumers: Selling Blackness in a Global Marketplace." *Ethnicities* 6, no. 3: 297–317.

Hoffman, Steven. 2008. "Engineering Poverty: Colonialism and Hydroelectric Development in Northern Manitoba." In *Power Struggles: Hydro Development and First Nations in Manitoba and Quebec,* edited by Martin Thibault and Steven Hoffman, 103–28. Winnipeg: University of Manitoba Press.

Home Care Ontario. 2015. *Submission to Ministry of Labour Consultations: Changing Workplaces Review.* http://www.homecareontario.ca/docs/default-source/ohca-submissions/revised-home-care-ontario-submission--mol-changing-workplaces-review-sept-2015.pdf?sfvrsn=9.

Horkheimer, Max, and Theodor Adorno. 1995. *The Dialectic of the Enlightenment.* New York: Continuum.

Hoskyns, Catherine, and Shirin M. Rai. 2007. "Recasting the Global Political Economy: Counting Women's Unpaid Work." *New Political Economy* 12, no. 3: 297–317.

Howe, Jeff. 2006. The Rise of Crowdsourcing. *Wired,* 1 June. http://www.wired.com/2006/06/crowds/.

Howell, Allison, and Jijian Voronka. 2012. "Introduction: The Politics of Resilience and Recovery in Mental Health Care." *Studies in Social Justice* 6, no. 1: 1–7.

Howlett, Michael, and Keith Brownsey, eds. 2008. *Canada's Resource Economy in Transition: The Past, Present, and Future of Canadian Staples Industries.* Toronto: Emond Montgomery Publications.

Hughes, Karen. 2003. "Pushed or Pulled? Women's Entry into Self-Employment and Small Business Ownership." In *Gender, Work and Organization* 10, no. 4: 433–54.

Hulchanski, David. 2007. "Canada's Dual Housing Policy: Assisting Owners, Neglecting Renters." *Centre for Urban and Community Studies,* September.

Human Resources Development Canada (HRDC). 1997. Evaluation of Federal Labour Standards (Phase I). Final Report. Ottawa.

Huque, Ahmed Shafiqul, and Nathan Watton. 2010. "Federalism and the Implementation of Environmental Policy: Changing Trends in Canada and the United States." *Public Organization Review* 10, no. 1: 71–88.

Hurl, Chris, and Benjamin Christensen. 2015. "Building the New Canadian Political Economy." *Studies in Political Economy* 96: 167–93.

Hurteau, Philippe, and Francis Fortier. 2015 "État québécois, crise et néo-libéralisme." *Interventions économiques* 52: 2–14.

Huskey, Lee, and Chris Southcott. 2018. "Resource Revenue Regimes around the Circumpolar North: A Gap Analysis." In *Resources and Sustainable Development in the Arctic*.

Hussain, Yadullah. 2012. "Oil Explorers' New Challenges." *Financial Post*, 3 May.

Huws, Ursula. 2003. *The Making of a Cybertariat: Virtual Work in a Real World*. New York: Monthly Review Press.

– 2007. "The Creative Spark in the Engine." *Work, Organisation, Labour & Globalization* 1: 1–12.

– 2010. "Expression and Expropriation: The Dialectics of Autonomy and Control in Creative Labor." *Ephemera: Theory & Politics in Organization* 10, nos 3–4: 504–21.

– 2014. *Labour in the Digital Economy*. New York: Monthly Review Press.

ILGWU and INTERCEDE. 1993. Meeting the Needs of Vulnerable Workers: Proposals for Improved Employment Legislation and Access to Collective Bargaining for Domestic Workers and Industrial Homeworkers. Toronto: ILGWU and INTERCEDE.

Indigenous Law Research Unit. 2012. *Accessing Justice and Reconciliation Project*. Online: http://www.indigenousbar.ca/indigenouslaw/.

Innis, Harold. 1930. *The Fur Trade in Canada: An Introduction to Canadian Economic History*. New Haven: Yale University Press.

– 1946. *Political Economy in the Modern State*. Toronto: Ryerson.

– 1956. *Essays in Canadian Economic History*. Toronto: University of Toronto Press.

International Monetary Fund. 2013. "Article 4 Consultation, Country Report 13/40" Washington: International Monetary Fund, February.

Interview 2018a. Interview with Olena Lyubchenko. 25 May.

Interview 2018b. Interview with Olena Lyubchenko. 26 May.

Interview 2018c. Interview with Olena Lyubchenko. 28 May.

Interview 2018d. Interview with Olena Lyubchenko. 29 May.

Interview 2018e. Interview with Olena Lyubchenko. 30 May.

Interview 2018f. Interview with Olena Lyubchenko. 2 June.

Interview 2018g. Interview with Olena Lyubchenko. 5 June.

Interview 2018h. Interview with Olena Lyubchenko. 14 June.

Interview 2018i. Interview with Olena Lyubchenko. 25 June.

Interview 2018j. Interview with Olena Lyubchenko. 5 July.

Interview 2018k. Interview with Olena Lyubchenko. 26 July.

Inwood, Gregory J. 2005. *Continentalizing Canada: The Politics and Legacy of the Macdonald Royal Commission*. Toronto: University of Toronto Press.

Ireland, Derek, and Kernaghan Webb. 2010. "The Canadian Escape from Subprime Crisis? Comparing the US and Canadian Approaches." In *How Ottawa Spends 2010–2011: Recession, Realignment, and the New Deficit Era*, edited by G. Bruce Doern and Christopher Stoney, 87–108. Montreal: McGill-Queen's University Press.

Irlbacher-Fox, Stephanie. 2009. *Finding Dahshaa: Self-Government, Social Suffering, and Aboriginal Policy in Canada*. Vancouver: University of British Columbia Press.

Isitt, Benjamin. 2008. "Housing for All: The Social Economy and Homelessness in British Columbia's Capital Region." *Canadian Social Economy Research Partnerships: Occasional Paper Series 6*, October.

Jackson, Andrew. 1999. "The Free Trade Agreement – A Decade Later." *Studies in Political Economy* 58 (Spring): 141–60.

Jackson, Andrew, and Mark P. Thomas. 2017. *Work and Labour in Canada: Critical Issues*. 3rd edition. Toronto: Canadian Scholars Press.

James, C.L.R. 1963. *Beyond a Boundary*. London: Stanley Paul.

Jenson, Jane. 1986. "Gender and Reproduction or Babies and the State." *Studies in Political Economy* 20: 9–46.

Jenson, Jane, Elizabeth Hagen, and Ceallaigh Reddy, eds. 1988. *Feminization of the Labor Force: Paradoxes and Promises*. New York: Oxford University Press.

Jenson, Jane, and Martin Papillon. 2000. "Challenging the Citizenship Regime: The James Bay Cree and Transnational Action." *Politics and Society* 28, no. 2: 245–64.

Jetté, Christian. 2008. *Les organismes communautaires et la transformation de l'État-providence*. Quebec: Presses de l'Université du Québec.

Jin, Dal Yong. 2013. "The Construction of Platform Imperialism in the Globalization Era." *tripleC: Communication, Capitalism and Critique* 11, no. 1: 145–72.

Johnston, Anna. 2015. Track Record on Environmental Laws 2011–2015. *West Coast Environmental Law Association and Centre Quebecois du Droit de l'Environment*. https://d3n8a8pro7vhmx.cloudfront.net/envirolawsmatter/pages/281/attachments/original/1444781049/WCEL_EnviroLaw_report_med1pg_fnl2_%28small%29.pdf?1444781049.

Joly, Mélanie. 2016. "Canada's Culture Dividend: The Creative Sector As Economic Driver." Speech at Economic Club of Canada, 9 June. http://www.economicclub.ca/events/display/canadas-culture-dividend-the-creative-sector-as-economic-driver.

Kakfwi, Stephen, and B. Overvold. 1977. "The Schools." In *Dene Nation: The Colony Within*, edited by Mel Watkins, 142–8. Toronto: University of Toronto Press.

Kalb, Don, and Massimiliano Mollona, eds. 2018. *Worldwide Mobilizations: Class Struggles and Urban Commoning*. New York: Berghahn.

Kalman-Lamb, Gideon. 2017. "The Financialization of Housing in Canada: Intensifying Contradictions of Neoliberal Accumulation." *Studies in Political Economy* 98, no. 3: 298–323.

Kaminsky, Lauren. 2011. "Utopian Visions of Family Life in the Stalin-Era Soviet Union." *Central European History* 44: 63–91.

Katz, Cindi. 2011. "Vagabond Capitalism and the Necessity of Social Reproduction." *Antipode* 33, no. 4: 709–28.

Kazimi, Ali. 2012. *Undesirables: White Canada and the Komagata Maru, An Illustrated History*. Berkeley: Douglas and McIntyre.

Keil, Roger. 1994. "Green Work Alliances: The Political Economy of Social Ecology." *Studies in Political Economy* 44: 7–38.

– 2018. *Suburban Planet: Making the World Urban from the Outside In*. Cambridge: Polity.

Keil, Roger, and Stefan Kipfer. 2003. "The Urban Experience and Globalization." In *Changing Canada: Political Canada as Transformation*, edited by Wallace Clement and Leah Vosko, 335–62. Montreal: McGill-Queen's University Press.

Keil, Roger, Melissa Ollevier, and Erica Tsang. 2009. "Why Is There No Environmental Justice in Toronto? Or Is There?" In *Speaking for Ourselves: Environmental Justice in Canada*, edited by Julian Agyeman, Peter Cole, Randolph Haluza-DeLay, and Pat O'Riley, 65–80. Vancouver: UBC Press.

Kellner, Douglas. 1995. *Media Culture*. New York: Routledge.

Kellogg, Paul. 2015. *Escape from the Staple Trap: Canadian Political Economy after Left Nationalism*. Toronto: University of Toronto Press.

Kennedy, Brendan. 2015a. "OHL's Flint Firebirds Get Their Coaches Back; Show the Power of Unity." *Hockey News*, 9 November 2015.

– 2015b. "Baseball's Minor-League Wage Lawsuit Goes Class Action." *Toronto Star*, 13 December.

Khmelnitskaya, Marina. 2014. "Russian Housing Finance Policy: State-Led Institutional Evolution." *Post-Communist Economies* 26, no. 2: 149–75.

Kidd, Bruce. 1979. *The Political Economy of Sport*. Calgary, AB: Canadian Association for Health, Physical Education, and Recreation.

– 1982. "Sport, Dependency, and the Canadian State." In *Sport, Culture, and the Modern State*, edited by Hart Cantelon and Richard Gruneau, 281–303. Toronto, ON: University of Toronto Press.

Kipfer, Stefan, and Roger Keil. 2002. "Toronto Inc.? Planning the Competitive City in the New Toronto." *Antipode* 34, no. 2: 227–64.

Kipfer, Stefan, and Parastou Saberi. 2015. "The Times and Spaces of Right Populism: From Paris to Toronto." In *The Socialist Register: The Politics of the Right*, edited by Leo Panitch and Greg Albo, 312–32. London: Merlin.

Klassen, Jerome. 2009. "Canada and the New Imperialism: The Economics of a Secondary Power." *Studies in Political Economy* 83: 163–90.

Klein, Jeff. 2014. "Lawsuits Target Canadian Junior Hockey System." *New York Times*, 20 December.

Klein, Naomi. 2002. "Farewell to the 'End of History': Organisation and Vision in Anti-Corporate Movements." In *Socialist Register 2002: A World of Contradictions*, edited by Leo Panitch and Collin Leys, 1–14. London: Merlin Press.

Knox, Robert. 2009. "Marxism, International Law, and Political Strategy." *Leiden Journal of International Law* 22, no. 3: 413–36.

– 2009–10. "Strategy and Tactics." *Finnish Yearbook of International Law* 21: 193–230.

Kontos, Pia, Karen-Lee Miller, and Gail J. Mitchell. 2009. "Neglecting the Importance of the Decision Making and Care Regimes of Personal Support Workers: A Critique of Standardization of Care Planning through the RAI/ MDS." *Gerontologist* 30, no. 3: 352–62.

Kravchenko, Zhanna. 2012. "Everyday Continuity and Change: Family and Family Policy in Russia." In *And They Lived Happily Ever After: Norms and Everyday Practices of Family and Parenthood in Russia and Eastern Europe*, edited by Helene Carlback, Yulia Gradskova, and Zhanna Kravchenko, 185–206. Budapest: Central European University Press.

– 2014. "Policy Discourse and Biography: Scripting Adulthood into Housing Policies in Comparative Perspective." *GeoJournal* 79: 513–25.

Kroeger, Arthur. 1996. "Changing Course: The Federal Government's Program Review of 1994–1995." In *Hard Choices or No Choices: Assessing Program Review*, edited by Amelita Armit and Jacques Bourgault, 21–8. Toronto: Institute of Public Administration of Canada.

Kulchyski, Peter. 2005. *Like the Sound of a Drum: Aboriginal Cultural Politics in Denendeh and Nunavut*. Winnipeg: University of Manitoba Press.

Kuokkanen, Rauna. 2008. "Globalization as Racialized, Sexualized Violence: The Case of Indigenous Women." *International Feminist Journal of Politics* 10, no. 2: 216–33.

– 2011a. "From Indigenous Economies to Market-Based Self-Governance: A Feminist Political Economy Analysis." *Canadian Journal of Political Science* 44, no. 2: 275–97.

– 2011b. "Indigenous Economies, Theories of Subsistence, and Women." *American Indian Quarterly* 35, no. 2: 215–40.

Kurasawa, Fuyuki. 2003. "Finding Godot? Bringing Popular Culture into Canadian Political Economy." In *Changing Canada: Political Economy as Transformation*, edited by Wallace Clement and Leah F. Vosko, 467–92. Montreal and Kingston: McGill-Queen's University Press.

Labour Program, Workplace Information and Research Division (WIRD). 2014. *Union Coverage in Canada, 2013*. Ottawa: Employment and Social Development Canada.

Laforest, Rachel. 2007. "The Politics of State-Civil Society Relations in Quebec." In *Canada: The State of the Federation 2005*, edited by Michael Murphy, 177–98. Montreal and Kingston: McGill-Queen's University Press.

Lan, Pei-Chia. 2008. "New Global Politics of Reproductive Labor: Gendered
    Labor and Marriage Migration." *Sociology Compass* 2, no. 6: 1801–15.
Landau, Ingrid, and John Howe. 2016. "Trade Union Ambivalence Toward
    Enforcement of Employment Standards as an Organizing Strategy."
    Theoretical Inquiries in Law 17: 201–27.
Langille, David. 1987. "The Business Council on National Issues and the
    Canadian State." *Studies in Political Economy* 24 (Autumn): 41–85.
Laslett, Barbara, and Johanna Brenner. 1989. "Gender and Social
    Reproduction: Historical Perspectives." *Annual Review of Sociology* 15:
    381–404.
Lavinas, Lena. 2013. "21st Century Welfare." *New Left Review* 84: 5–40.
– 2017. *The Takeover of Social Policy by Financialization: The Brazilian
    Paradox*. New York: Palgrave Macmillan.
Law Commission of Ontario. 2012. Vulnerable Workers and Precarious Work.
    Final Report. http://www.lco-cdo.org/en/vulnerable-workers-final-report.
    Accessed 29 September 2014.
Laxer, Gordon. 1989. *Open for Business: The Roots of Foreign Ownership in
    Canada*. Toronto: Oxford University Press.
– 2014. "Alberta's Sands, Staples and Traps." In *The Staples Theory @ 50:
    Reflections on the Lasting Significance of Mel Watkins' 'A Staple Theory of
    Economic Growth,'* edited by Jim Stanford, 53–8. Ottawa: Canadian Centre
    for Policy Alternatives.
– 2015b. *After the Sands: Energy and Ecological Security for Canadians*.
    Toronto: Douglas and McIntyre.
– 2015a. "NDP Climate Plan for Alberta Might Make Things Tough for
    Canada." *Rabble*, 4 December.
Laxer, Kate. 2015. "Who Cares in Care? Gender, Power and Aging
    Perspectives." In *Women's Health: Intersections of Policy, Research and
    Practice*, edited by Pat Armstrong and Ann Pederson, 215–37. Toronto:
    Women's Press.
Leach, Andrew. 2014. "How the Oil Sands Could Very Quickly Become
    Unviable." *Maclean's*, 20 March 2014.
Leblanc, Daniel. 2016. "Everything's on the Table." *Globe and Mail*, 25 April.
    http://www.theglobeandmail.com/news/national/exclusive-canadian-heri-
    tage-announces-sweeping-canconreview/article29722581/.
Leckenby, Denise, and Sharlene Nagy Hesse-Biber. 2007. "Feminist Approaches
    to Mixed-Methods Research." In *Feminist Research Practice: A Primer*,
    249–92. Thousand Oaks: Sage.
Lefebvre, Henri. 1991. *The Production of Space*. Oxford: Blackwell.
LeFrancois, Brenda, Robert Menzies, and Geoffrey Reaume. 2013. "Introducing
    Mad Studies." In *Mad Matters: A Critical Reader in Canadian Mad Studies*,
    edited by Brenda LeFrancois, Robert Menzies, and Geoffrey Reaume, 1–22.
    Toronto, ON: Canadian ScholarsInc. Press.

Lemphers, Nathan, and Dan Woynillowicz. 2012. *In the Shadow of the Boom: How Oilsands Development is Reshaping Canada's Economy.* Drayton Valley: Pembina Institute.

Léonard, Jean-François, ed. 1978. *La chance au coureur: Bilan de l'action du gouvernement du Parti québécois.* Montreal: Éditions Nouvelle Optique.

Levitt, Kari. 1970. *Silent Surrender: The Multinational Corporation in Canada* (revised 2003). Montreal: McGill-Queen's University Press.

Levitt, Peggy, and Nadya Jaworsky. 2007. "Transnational Migration Studies: Past Developments and Future Trends." *Annual Review of Sociology* 33: 129–56.

Lewchuk, Wayne et al. 2013. *It's More than Poverty: Employment Precarity and Household Well-Being.* Toronto: Poverty and Employment Precarity in Southern Ontario.

Lewis, Jane. 1992. "Gender and the Development of Welfare Regimes." *Journal of European Social Policy* 2, no. 3: 159–173.

Liberal Party of Canada. 2015. "Real Change: Investing in Culture and Middle Class Jobs." https://www.liberal.ca/files/2015/09/Investing-in-Canadian-culture-and-middle-class-jobs.pdf.

Linebaugh, Peter, and Marcus Rediker. 2000. *The Many-Headed Hydra: Sailors, Slaves, Commoners, and the Hidden History of the Revolutionary Atlantic.* Boston: Beacon Press.

Lloyd, Liz, Albert Banerjee, Charlene Harrington, Frode F. Jacobsen, and Marta Szebehely. 2014. "Comparing the Causes and Consequences of Nursing Home Media Scandals in Five Countries." *International Journal of Sociology and Social Policy* 34, nos 1–2: 2–18.

Loxley, John. 2009. "Financial Dimensions: Origins and State Responses." In *Bankruptcies and Bailouts*, edited by Julie Guard and Wayne Antony, 62–76. Winnipeg: Fernwood Publishing.

Lum, Janet, Jennifer Sladek, and Alvin Ying. 2010. *Focus Backgrounder: Ontario Personal Support Workers in Home and Community Care: CRNCC/ PSNO Survey Results.* Toronto: Ryerson University, December.https://www. ryerson.ca/content/dam/crncc/knowledge/infocus/factsheets/InFocus-Ontario%20PSWs%20in%20Home%20and%20Community%20Care.pdf.

Lum, Ryan. 2015. "Attack on CHL Players' Rights Expands into Washington State." *Rank and File*, 10 March.

Lumsden, Ian, ed. 1970. *Close the 49th parallel etc.: The Americanization of Canada.* Toronto: University of Toronto Press.

Luxton, Meg. 1980. *More Than a Labour of Love.* Toronto: The Women's Press.

– 1988. "Two Hands for the Clock: Changing Patterns in the Gendered Division of Labour in the Home." *Sociology of the Family*, edited by Bonnie Fox, 403–20. Toronto: Canadian Scholars Press, Inc.

– 2006a. "Friends, Neighbours, And Community: A Case Study of the Role of Informal Caregiving in Social Reproduction." In *Social Reproduction:*

Feminist Political Economy Challenges Neo-Liberalism, edited by Kate Bezanson and Meg Luxton, 263–92. Montreal: McGill-Queen's University Press.

– 2006b. "Feminist Political Economy in Canada and the Politics of Social Reproduction." In *Social Reproduction: Feminist Political Economy Challenges Neoliberalism*, edited by Kate Bezanson and Meg Luxton, 11–44. Montreal: McGill-Queen's University Press.

Luxton, Meg, and June Corman. 2001. *Getting by in Hard Times: Gendered Labour at Home and on the Job*. Toronto: University of Toronto Press.

Luxton, Meg, and Harriet Gale Rosenberg. 1986. *Through the Kitchen Window: The Politics of Home and Family*. Toronto: Garamond Press.

MacDonald, Ian Thomas. 2017. *Unions and the City: Negotiating Urban Change*. Ithaca: Cornell University Press.

MacDonald, Martha. 1991. "Post-Fordism and the Flexibility Debate." *Studies in Political Economy* 36: 177–201.

– 2015. "Regulating Individual Charges for Long-term Residential Care in Canada." *Studies in Political Economy* 95: 83–114.

Mackenzie, Hugh. 2016. *Staying Power: CEO Pay in Canada*. Canadian Centre for Policy Alternatives.

Mackintosh, William Archibald. 1964. *The Economic Background of Dominion-Provincial Relations*. Toronto: McClelland and Stewart.

– 1967. *Approaches to Economic History: Essays*. Toronto: University of Toronto Press.

Macpherson, C.B. 1978. *Property: Mainstream and Critical Positions*. Toronto: University of Toronto Press.

Magder, Ted. 1989. "Taking Culture Seriously: A Political Economy of Communications." In *The New Canadian Political Economy*, edited by Wallace Clement and Glen Williams, 278–96. Kingston: McGill-Queen's University Press.

– 1997. "Public Discourse and the Structures of Communication." In *Understanding Canada: Building on the New Canadian Political Economy*, edited by Wallace Clement, 338–59. Montreal and Kingston: McGill-Queen's University Press.

Mahon, Rianne. 1984. *The Politics of Industrial Restructuring: Canadian Textiles*. Toronto: University of Toronto Press.

– 2002. "Gender and Welfare State Restructuring: Through the Lens of Childcare." In *Introduction to Child Care at the Crossroads: Gender and Welfare State Restructuring*, edited by Sonya Michel and Rianne Mahon, 1–30. New York: Routledge.

Mahon, Rianne, and Fiona Williams. 2007. "Gender and State in Post-communist Societies: Introduction." *Social Politics* 14, no. 3: 281–3.

Malhotra, Ravi. 2009. "Tale of Marginalization: Comparing Workers with Disabilities in Canada and the United States." *Journal of Law and Social Policy* 22: 79–113.

Maltais, Alexandre. 2016. *The TPP and Cultural Diversity*. Ottawa: Canadian Centre for Policy Alternatives.

Manuel, Arthur, and Grand Chief Ronald M. Derrickson. 2015. *Unsettling Canada: A National Wake-Up Call*. Toronto: Between the Lines.

Maracle, Lee. 1988. *I Am Woman: A Native Perspective on Sociology and Feminism*. Vancouver: Write-On Press.

Maracle, Sylvia. 2003. "The Eagle Has Landed: Native Women, Leadership and Community Development." In *Strong Women Stories: Native Vision and Community Survival*, edited by Kim Anderson and Bonita Lawrence, 70–80. Toronto: Sumach Press.

Marchak, Patricia. 1985. "Canadian Political Economy." *Canadian Review of Sociology and Anthropology* 22, no. 5: 673–709.

Markey, Sean, John T. Pierce, and Kelly Vodden. 2000. "Resources, People and the Environment: A Regional Analysis of the Evolution of Resource Policy in Canada." *Canadian Journal of Regional Sciences* 23, no. 3: 427–54.

Markey, Sean, Laura Ryser, Greg Halseth, Angèle Smith. 2015. "'We're in This All Together': Community Impacts of Long-Distance Labour Commuting." *Rural Society* 24, no. 2: 131–53.

Maroney, Heather J., and Meg Luxton. 1987. *Feminism and Political Economy: Women's Work, Women's Struggles*. Toronto: University of Toronto Press.

– 1997. "Gender at Work: Canadian Feminist Political Economy since 1988." In *Understanding Canada: Building on the New Canadian Political Economy*, edited by Wallace Clement, 85–117. Montreal and Kingston: McGill-Queen's University Press.

Marshall, Brendan 2017. "Facts and Figures of the Canadian Mining Industry." *The Mining Association of Canada*. Ottawa: The Mining Association of Canada. http://mining.ca/sites/default/files/documents/Facts-and-Figures-2017.pdf.

Marshall, John. 1982. *Madness: An Indictment of the Mental Health Care System in Ontario*. Toronto: Brownstone Press.

Marx, Karl. 1976. *Capital: A Critique of Political Economy*, Volume One. Translated by Ben Fowkes. Harmondsworth: Penguin.

– 1967 [1867]. *Capital: Volume 1*. London: Penguin.

Marx, Karl, and Friedrich Engels. 1970. *The German Ideology*. New York: International Publishers.

– 1998 [1848]. *The Communist Manifesto*. London: Verso.

Martin-Hill, Dawn. 2003. "She No Speaks and other Colonial Constructs of 'The Traditional Woman.'" In *Strong Women Stories: Native Vision and Community Survival*, edited by Kim Anderson and Bonita Lawrence, 106–20. Toronto: Sumach Press.

Massey, Doreen. 1995. "Uneven Development and Spatial Structures." In *Spatial Divisions of Labour: Social Structures and the Geography of Production*, 65–120. New York: Routledge.

Masson, Dominique. 1999–2000. "Constituting 'Post-Welfare State' Welfare Arrangement: The Role of Women's Movement Service Groups in Quebec." *Resources for Feminist Research* 27, nos 3–4: 49–70.

– 2006. "Engaging with the Politics of Downward Rescaling: Representing Women in Regional Development Policymaking in Québec (Canada)." *Geojournal* 65, no. 4: 301–13.

– 2015. "Institutionalization, State Funding, and Advocacy in the Quebec Women's Movement." In *Protest and Politics: The Promise of Social Movement Societies*, edited by Howard Ramos and Kathleen Rogers, 79–99. Vancouver: UBC Press.

Maxwell, Richard, ed. 2016. *The Routledge Companion to Labor and Media*. New York: Routledge.

Mayer, Margit. 2009. "The 'Right to the City' in the Context of Shifting Mottos of Urban Social Movements." *City* 13, no. 2: 262–374.

Mazzucato, Mariana. 2013. *The Entrepreneurial State: Debunking Public vs Private Sector Myths*. London: Anthem.

McAdam, Doug, Sidney Tarrow, and Charles Tilly. 2001. *Dynamics of Contention*. New York City: Cambridge University Press.

McBride, Stephen. 1983. "Public Policy as a Determinant of Interest Group Behaviour: The Canadian Labour Congress' Corporatist Initiative, 1975–1978." *Canadian Journal of Political Science* 16, no. 3: 501–17.

– 1992. *Not Working: State, Unemployment and Neo-Conservatism in Canada*. Toronto: University of Toronto Press.

– 2001. *Paradigm Shift: Globalization and the Canadian State*. Halifax: Fernwood.

– 2005. *Paradigm Shift: Globalization and the Canadian State* (2nd edition). Halifax: Fernwood.

– 2010. "The New Constitutionalism: International and Private Rule in the New Global Order." In *Relations of Global Power: Neoliberal Order and Disorder*, edited by Gary Teeple and Stephen McBride, 19–40. Toronto: University of Toronto Press.

– 2015. "Neoliberalism in Question?" In *After '08: Social Policy and the Global Financial Crisis*, edited by Stephen McBride, Rianne Mahon, and Gerard W. Boychuk, 21–39. Vancouver: University of British Columbia Press.

McBride, Stephen, and Kathy McNutt. 2007. "Devolution and Neoliberalism in the Canadian Welfare State: Ideology, National and International Conditioning Frameworks, and Policy Change in British Columbia." *Global Social Policy* 7, no. 2: 177–201.

McBride, Stephen, and John Shields. 1997. *Dismantling a Nation: The Transition to Corporate Rule in Canada*. Halifax: Fernwood.

McBride, Stephen, and Heather Whiteside. 2011a. *Private Affluence, Public Austerity: Economic Crisis and Democratic Malaise in Canada*. Halifax: Fernwood.

– 2011b. "Austerity for Whom?" *Socialist Studies* 7, nos 1–2: 42–64.
– 2013. "The Canadian State and the Crisis: Theoretical and Historical Context." In *Canadian Labour, The Canadian State and The Crisis of Capitalism: Critical Perspectives*, edited by Tim Fowler, 23–48. Ottawa: Red Quill Books.

McCall, Leslie. 2005. "The Complexity of Intersectionality." *Signs: Journal of Women in Culture and Society* 30, no. 3: 1771–800.

McChesney, Robert W. 2008. *The Political Economy of Media: Enduring Issues, Emerging Dilemmas*. New York: Monthly Review Press.

McChesney, Robert. W., and John Nichols. 2016. *People Get Ready: The Fight against a Jobless Economy and a Citizenless Democracy*. New York: Nation Books.

McClintock, Anne. 1995. *Imperial Leather: Race, Gender and Sexuality in the Colonial Contest*. New York and London: Routledge.

McCormack, Geoffrey, and Thom Workman. 2015. *The Servant State: Overseeing Capital Accumulation in Canada*. Halifax: Fernwood.

McCormick, Robert A., and Amy C. McCormick. 2006. "The Myth of the Student-Athlete: The College Athlete as Employee." *Washington State Law Review* 81: 71–157.

McCrimmon Holdings Ltd. v. MNR, [2000] R. J. Q. 823 (Can. Tax Ct., 2000) (QL).

McDermott, Patricia. 1992. *Broader Based Bargaining and Closing the Wage Gap*. Ontario: Ministry of Labour.

McDonald, David. 2012. *The Big Banks' Big Secret*. Ottawa: CCPA.
– 2018. "Building a Pro-Public Movement in Canada." *Studies in Political Economy* 99, no. 1: 59–78.

McDonough, Terrence. 1994. "Social Structures of Accumulation: Contingent History and Stages of Capitalism." In *Social Structures of Accumulation: The Political Economy of Growth and Crisis*, edited by David M. Kotz, Terrence McDonough, and Michael Reich, 72–85. Cambridge: Cambridge University Press.

McGregor, Deborah. 2009. "Honouring Our Relations: An Anishinaabe Perspective on Environmental Justice." In *Speaking for Ourselves: Environmental Justice in Canada*, edited by Julian Agyeman, Peter Cole, Randolph Haluza-Delay, and Pat O'Riley, 27–42. Vancouver: UBC Press.

McGregor, Margaret J., and Lisa A. Ronald. 2011. "Residential Long-Term Care for Canadian Seniors. Nonprofit, For-Profit or Does It Matter?" Ottawa: IRPP.

McGregor, Margaret J., Marcy Cohen, Catherine-Rose Stocks-Rankin, Michelle B. Cox, Kia Salomons, Kimberlyn M. McGrail, Charmaine Spencer, Lisa A. Ronald, Michael Schulzer. 2006. "Care Outcomes in Long-Term Care Facilities in British Columbia, Canada: Does Ownership Matter?" *Medical Care* 44, no. 10: 929–35.

– 2010. "Staffing in Long-term Care in B.C. Canada: A Longitudinal Study of Differences in Facility Ownership, 1999–2006." *Health Reports* 21, no. 4: 1–7.

– 2012. "Complaints in For-profit, Non-profit and Public Nursing Homes in Two Canadian Provinces." *Open Medicine* 5, no. 4: 183–92.

McKay, Ian. 2000. "The Liberal Order Framework: A Prospectus for a Reconnaissance of Canadian History." *Canadian Historical Review*, 81, no. 4: 616–78.

McKay, Paul. 2003. "Taxpayers Finance Construction Boom. Ontario's Nursing Home Crisis – Part 4." *Ottawa Citizen*, 29 April 2003, A11.

McKeen, Wendy. 2007. "The National Children's Agenda: A Neoliberal Wolf in Lamb's Clothing." *Studies in Political Economy* 80: 151–73.

McKeen, Wendy, and Ann Porter. 2003. "Politics and Transformation: Welfare State Restructuring in Canada." In *Changing Canada: Political Economy as Transformation*, edited by Wallace Clement and Leah F. Vosko, 109–34. Montreal: McGill-Queen's University Press.

McKeown, Mick, Mark Cresswell, and Helen Spandler. 2014. "Deeply Engaged Relationships: Alliances between Mental Health Workers and Psychiatric Survivors in the UK." In *Psychiatry Disrupted: Theorizing Resistance and Crafting the (R)evolution*, edited by Bonnie Burstow, Brenda LeFrancois, and Shaindl Diamond, 145–62. Montreal and Kingston: McGill-Queen's University Press.

McKiven, Jamie. 2014. "The Time is Right for a Major Junior Hockey Players' Association." *When in Doubt Glass and Out*, 15 July 2014.

McNally, David. 1981. "Staple Theory as Commodity Fetishism: Marx, Innis and Canadian Political Economy." *Studies in Political Economy* 6 (Autumn): 35–63.

– 2001. *Bodies of Meaning: Studies on Language, Labour, and Liberation*. Albany, NY: State University of New York.

McQuarrie, Jonathan. 2014. "'Tobacco Has Blossomed Like the Rose in the Desert': Technology, Trees, and Tobacco in the Norfolk Sand Plain, c. 1920–1940." *Journal of the Canadian Historical Association* 25, no. 1: 33–62.

Meehan, Eileen, and Janet Wasko. 2013. "In Defense of a Political Economy of the Media." *Javnost – The Public* 20, no. 1: 39–53.

Miller, James. 1996. *Shingwauk's Vision: A History of Native Residential Schools*. Toronto:University of Toronto Press.

Miller, Marvin. 1991. *A Whole Different Ball Game: The Inside Story of the Baseball Revolution*. Chicago, IL: Ivan R. Dee.

Miller, Toby, Nitin Govil, John McMurria, Richard Maxwell, and Ting Wang. 2005. *Global Hollywood 2*. London: British Film Institute.

Milloy, John S. 1999. *A National Crime: The Canadian Government and the Residential School System, 1879 to 1986*. Vol. 11. Winnipeg: University of Manitoba Press.

Mills, Sean. 2010. *The Empire Within: Postcolonial Thought and Political Activism in Sixties Montreal*. Montreal: McGill-Queen's University Press.

Mills, Suzanne E. 2006. "Segregation of Women and Aboriginal People within Canada's Forest Sector by Industry and Occupation." *Canadian Journal of Native Studies* 26, no. 1: 147–71.

– 2012. "Restructuring in the Forest Sector and the Re-Shaping of Women's Work Identities." *Canadian Geographer* 56, no. 1: 39–57.

Mills, Suzanne, and Brendan Sweeney. 2013. "Employment Relations in the Neo-Staples Resource Economy: IBAS and Aboriginal Governance in Canada's Nickel Mining Industry." *Studies in Political Economy* 91 (Spring): 7–33.

Milner, Brian. 2013. "Think Markets Raise Capital? Think Again." *Globe and Mail*, 24 March.https://www.theglobeandmail.com/globe-investor/investment-ideas/think-markets-raise-capital-think-again/article10266997/.

Milz, Sabine. 2007. "Canadian Cultural Policy-making at a Time of Neoliberal Globalization." *ESC: English Studies in Canada* 33, nos 1–2: 85–107.

Ministry of Community and Social Services – Development Services. 2015. *Spotlight on Transformation: Embracing Inclusion* 51. http://www.mcss. gov.on.ca/documents/en/mcss/publications/spotlight/DS-Spotlight_issue51_ en.pdf.

Ministry of Health. 1999. *Making it Happen: Implementation Plan for Mental Health Reform*. http://ontario.cmha.ca/files/2011/06/makingithappen1999. pdf.

– 2000. *Making it Work: Policy Framework for Employment Supports for People with Serious Mental Illness*. http://ontario.cmha.ca/files/2011/06/ makingitwork.pdf.

Ministry of Health, Ontario. 2011. *Putting People First: The Reform of Mental Health Services in Ontario*. http://ontario.cmha.ca/files/2011/06/ puttingpeoplefirst.pdf.

Ministry of Health and Long-Term Care. 2011. *Open Minds, Healthy Minds: Ontario's Comprehensive Mental Health and Addictions Strategy*. http:// www.health.gov.on.ca/en/common/ministry/publications/reports/mental_ health2011/mentalhealth_rep2011.pdf.

Ministry of Labour, Ontario. 2017. *ESA Exemptions Toolkit: Homemakers, Domestic Workers and Residential Care Workers* Toronto: Ontario Ministry of Labour. http://files.constantcontact.com/70a2e0c3401/9b479dfa-ee87-4df9-bb0a-c3ba825b9675.pdf.

Ministry of Tourism and Culture. 2010. *Ontario's Entertainment & Creative Cluster: A Framework for Growth*. http://www.mtc.gov.on.ca/en/ publications/Creative_Cluster_Report.pdf.

Mirrlees, Tanner. 2013. *Global Entertainment Media: Between Cultural Imperialism and Cultural Globalization*. New York: Routledge.

– 2016a. *Hearts and Mines: The US Empire's Culture Industry*. Vancouver: UBC Press.

– 2016b. "The US Empire's Culture Industry, At Large." *Socialist Project*, E-Bulletin No. 1253. http://www.socialistproject.ca/bullet/1253.php.

Mitchell, Michael C., and John C. Murray. 2016. "Changing Workplaces Review: Special Advisors Interim Report." *Ministry of Labour*. https://www.labour.gov.on.ca/english/about/pdf/cwr_interim.pdf.

Mohanty, Chandra. 2003. "*Under Western Eyes* Revisited: Feminist Solidarity through Anticapitalist Struggles." *Signs* 28, no. 2: 499–535.

Mongia, Radhika V. 1999. "Race, Nationality, Mobility: A History of the Passport." *Public Culture* 11, no. 3: 527–56.

– 2007. "Historicizing State Sovereignty: Inequality and the Form of Equivalence." *Comparative Studies in Society and History* 49, no. 2: 384–411.

– 2018. *Indian Migration and Empire: A Colonial Genealogy of the Modern State*. Durham: Duke University Press.

"Montreal Mayor Wants Infrastructure Funding." 2011. CBC, 2 May. http://www.cbc.ca/news/canada/montreal/montreal-mayor-wants-infrastructure-funding1.1067637.

Moody, Kim. 1988. *An Injury to All: The Decline of American Unionism*. New York: Verso.

– 1997. *Workers in a Lean World: Unions in the International Economy*. London and New York: Verso.

Moore, Jason W. 2015. *Capitalism in the Web of Life: Ecology and the Accumulation of Capital*. London and New York: Verso.

Morneau, Francis William. 2016. *Growing the Middle Class*. Tabled in the House of Commons. Ottawa, ON. http://www.budget.gc.ca/2016/docs/plan/budget2016-en.pdf.

Mosco, Vincent. 2003. "The Transformation of Communication in Canada." In *Changing Canada: Political Economy as Transformation*, edited by Wallace Clement and Leah F. Vosko, 287–308. Montreal and Kingston: McGill-Queen's University Press.

– 2009. *The Political Economy of Communication*. London: Sage Publications.

Mosco, Vincent, and Catherine McKercher. 2008. *The Laboring of Communication: Will Knowledge Workers of the World Unite?* Lanham, MD: Lexington Books.

Muckenberger, Ulrich. 1989. "Non-standard Forms of Employment in the Federal Republic of Germany: The Role and Effectiveness of the State." In *Precarious Employment in Labour Market Regulation: The Growth of Atypical Employment in Western Europe*, edited by Gerry Rodgers and Janine Rodgers, 267–85. Belgium: International Institute for Labour Studies.

Murray, Deborah, and Chantal Sundaram. 2015. "May Day in Quebec: Dress Rehearsal for the Fight against Austerity?" *Socialist.ca*, 5 May. http://www.socialist.ca/node/2752.

Nahanni, Phoebe. 1992. *Dene Women in the Traditional and Modern Northern Economy in Denendeh, Northwest Territories Canada.* Master's thesis, McGill University.

Neis, Barbara, and Susan Williams. 1997. "The New Right, Gender and the Fisheries Crisis: Local and Global Dimensions." *Atlantis: Critical Studies in Gender, Culture and Social Justice* 21, no. 2: 47–62.

NESTA. 2016. *Creative Economy Employment in the US, Canada and the UK.* http://www.nesta.org.uk/publications/creative-economy-employment-us-canada-and-uk.

Netzke, Claudia. 1994. *Aboriginal Peoples and Natural Resources in Canada.* Concord, ON: Captus.

New Politics Initiative. 2001. "Comment: A Discussion Paper on the New Politics Initiative." *Studies in Political Economy* 66 (Autumn): 143–56.

Ng, Roxana. 1989. "Sexism, Racism, and Canadian Nationalism." In *Race, Class, Gender: Bonds and Barriers*, 39–63. Toronto: Between the Lines.

Nielsen. 2015. "Top 10 List for Prime Broadcast Network TV – United States." *Nielsen Company.* Accessed 30 July 2018. http://www.nielsen.com/us/en/top10s.html.

Niewójt, Lawrence. 2007. "From Waste Land to Canada's Tobacco Production Heartland: Landscape Change in Norfolk County, Ontario." *Landscape Research* 32, no. 3: 355–77.

Niosi, Jorge. 1985. "Continental Nationalism: The Strategy of the Canadian Bourgeoisie." In *The Structure of the Canadian Capitalist Class*, edited by Robert J. Brym, 53–66. Toronto: Garamond.

Noël, Alain. 2013. "Quebec's New Politics of Redistribution." In *Inequality and the Fading of Redistributive Politics*, edited by Keith Banting and John Myles, 256–82. Vancouver: UBC Press.

Noiseux, Yanick. 2014. *Transformations des marchés du travail et innovations syndicales au Québec.* Quebec: Presses de l'Université du Québec.

Nordicity. 2016. Canadian Media in a Digital Universe. http://www.actra.ca/wp-content/uploads/CanadianMediaDigitalUniverse.pdf.Obeng-Odoom, Franklin. 2016. *Reconstructing Urban Economics: Towards a Political Economy of the Built Environment.* London: Zed Books.

O'Connor, James. 1973. *The Fiscal Crisis of the State.* New York: St Martin's Press.

O'Hara, Philip Anthony. 2006. *Growth and Development in the Global Political Economy: Social Structures of Accumulation and Modes of Regulation.* London: Routledge.

Office of the Auditor General of Canada. 2014. *Report of the Auditor General of Canada to the Northwest Territories Legislative Assembly, Child and Family Services.* Yellowknife, GNWT.

Ontario Common Front (OCF). 2015. *Backslide: Labour Force Restructuring, Austerity, and Widening Inequality in Ontario.* Toronto: OCF.

*Open for Business Act (*OBA*), Bill 68.* 2010. Legislative Assembly of Ontario. http://www.ontla.on.ca/bills/bills-files/39_Parliament/Session2/b068ra.pdf.

Organization for Economic Cooperation and Development (OECD). 2011. *Health at a Glance 2011:* OECD *Indicators.* Paris: OECD.

– 2012. OECD *Economic Surveys: Canada.* Paris: Organization for Economic Cooperation and Development.

Orloff, Anna Shola. 1993. "Gender and the Social Rights of Citizenship: The Comparative Analysis of Gender Relations and Welfare States." *American Sociological Review* 58, no. 3: 303–28.

Paehlke, Robert. 2000. "Environmentalism in One Country: Canadian Environmental Policy in an Era of Globalization." *Policy Studies Journal* 28: 160–75.

Palmer, Bryan. 2013. "Reconsiderations of Class: Precariousness as Proletarianization." In *Socialist Register 2014: Registering Class,* edited by Leo Panitch, Greg Albo, and Viveck Chibber, 40–62. London: Merlin Press.

Palmer, Bryan D., and Joan Sangster. 2017. "The Distinctive Heritage of 1917: Resuscitating Revolution's Longue Durée." *Socialist Register* 53: 1–31

Panitch, Leo. 1977a. *The Canadian State: Political Economy and Political Power.* Toronto: University of Toronto Press.

– 1977b. "The Role and Nature of the Canadian State." In *The Canadian State,* edited by Leo Panitch, 3–27. Toronto: University of Toronto Press.

– 1981. "Dependency and Class in Canadian Political Economy." *Studies in Political Economy* 6 (Autumn): 7–33.

Panitch, Leo, and Sam Gindin. 2003–04. "American Imperialism and EuroCapitalism: The Making of Neoliberal Globalization." *Studies in Political Economy* 71/72: 7–38.

– 2012. *The Making of Global Capitalism: The Political Economy of American Empire.* London: Verso.

Panitch, Leo, and Donald Swartz. 2008. *From Consent to Coercion: The Assault on Trade Union Freedoms,* 3rd ed. Toronto: Garamond.

– 2013. "The Continuing Assault on Public Sector Unions." In *Public Sector Unions in the Age of Austerity,* edited by Stephanie Ross and Larry Savage, 31–45. Halifax and Winnipeg: Fernwood.

Paquette, Pierre. 1978. "Histoire et caractéristiques de l'impérialisme canadien." *Interventions critiques en économie politique* 2: 47–75.

Parkinson, David. 2016. "Beyond Hewers of Wood and Drawers of Oil." *Globe and Mail,* 2 July.

Parkland Institute. 2013. *From Bad to Worse: Residential Elder Care in Alberta.* Edmonton: Parkland.

Parlee, Brenda. 2015. "Avoiding the Resource Curse: Indigenous Communities and Canada's Oil Sands." *World Development* 74: 425–36.

Pasternack, Shiri. 2011. "Occupy(ed) Canada: The Political Economy of Indigenous Dispossession in Canada." *Rabble*, 20 October.http://rabble.ca/news/2011/10/occupyed-canada-political-economy-indigenous-dispossession-canada.

– 2014. "Jurisdiction and Settler Colonialism: Where Do Laws Meet?" *Canadian Journal of Law and Society* 29, no. 2: 145–61.

Patch, Nick. 2016. "Canada Council for the Arts Getting Fund Infusion." *Toronto Star*, 22 March. https://www.thestar.com/news/canada/federal budget/2016/03/22/canada-council-for-the-arts-getting-fund-infusion.html.

Paul, Darel. 2004. "World Cities as Hegemonic Projects: The Politics of Global Imagineering in Montreal." *Political Geography* 23: 571–96.

Paun, Ashim, Zoe Knight, and Wai-Shin Chan. 2015. *Stranded Assets: What Next?* London: HSBC Global Research.

Pearson, Chad. 2014. "Fighting the 'Red Danger': Employers and Anti-Communism." In *Little "Red Scares": Anticommunism and Political Repression in the United States, 1921–1946*, edited by Robert Justin Goldstein, 135–64. Burlington, VT: Ashgate.

Peck, Jamie. 1996. *Work-Place: The Social Regulation of Labor Markets*. New York: Guildford Press.

– 2005. "Economic Sociologies in Space." *Economic Geography* 81, no. 2: 129–75.

– 2012. "Austerity Urbanism." *City* 16, no. 6: 626–55.

– 2013. "Explaining (with) Neoliberalism." *Territory, Politics and Governance* 1, no. 2: 132–57.

– 2014. "Pushing Austerity: State Failure, Municipal Bankruptcy and the Crises of Fiscal Federalism in the USA." *Cambridge Journal of Regions, Economy and Society* 7: 17–44.

Peck, Jamie, and Adam Tickell. 2002. "Neoliberalizing space." *Antipode* 34, no. 3: 380–404.

Peck, Jamie, Nik Theodore, and Neil Brenner. 2009a. "Postneoliberalism and its Malcontents." *Antipode* 41, no. S1: 94–116.

– 2009b. "Neoliberal Urbanism: Models, Moments, Mutations." *SAIS Review* 29, no. 1: 49–66.

Pennee, Donna. 1999. "Culture as Security: Canadian Foreign Policy and International Relations from the Cold War to the Market Wars." *International Journal of Canadian Studies* 20, no. 1: 191–213.

Pension Fund of Russian Federation. 2018. "Maternity Capital: What's New in 2018." *Press-center*. 15 March. http://www.pfrf.ru/en/press_center/~2018/03/15/155166.

Pentland, H. Claire. 1981. *Labour and Capital in Canada 1650–1860*. Toronto: James Lorimer.

Perelman, Marc. 2012. *Barbaric Sport: A Global Plague*. London, UK: Verso.

Perlin, Ross. 2012. *Intern Nation: How to Earn Nothing and Earn Little in the Brave New Economy*. New York: Verso.

Petras, James, and Henry Veltmeyer. 2014. *Extractive Imperialism in the Americas: Capitalism's New Frontier*. Leiden and Boston: Brill.

Phillips-Fein, Kim. 2017. *Fear City: New York's Fiscal Crisis and the Rise of Austerity Politics*. New York: Metropolitan Books.

Phillips, Paul. 1989. "Through Different Lenses: The Political Economy of Labour." In *The New Canadian Political Economy*, edited by Wallace Clement and Glen Williams, 77–98. Kingston and Montreal: McGill-Queen's University Press.

– 1997. "Labour in the New Canadian Political Economy." In *Understanding Canada: Building on the New Canadian Political Economy*, edited by Wallace Clement, 64–84. Montreal and Kingston: McGill-Queen's University Press.

Picchio, Anton Ella. 1981. "Social Reproduction and the Basic Structure of Labour Markets." In *The Dynamics of Labour Market Segmentation*, edited by Frank Wilkinson, 193–209. London: Academic Press.

– 1992. *Social Reproduction: The Political Economy of the Labour Market*. Cambridge: Cambridge University Press.

– 2003. *Unpaid Work and the Economy: A Gender Analysis of the Standards of Living*. London and New York: Routledge.

Pineault, Eric. 2012. "Quebec's Red Spring: An Essay on Ideology and Social Conflict at the End of Neoliberalism." *Studies in Political Economy* 90: 29–56.

– 2014. "Neoliberalism and Austerity as Class Struggle." In *Orchestrating Austerity: Impacts and Resistance*, edited by Donna Baines and Stephen McBride, 91–104. Halifax: Fernwood.

Piotte, Jean-Marc. 1998. *Du combat au partenariat*. Montreal: Nota Bene.

Plourde, Andre. 2010. "On Properties of Royalty and Tax Regimes in Alberta's Oil Sands." *Energy Policy* 38: 4652–62.

Polanyi, Karl. 1944. *The Great Transformation: The Political Economic Origins of Our Time*. Boston: Beacon Press.

Pollert, Anna. 2009. "Varieties of Collectivism among Britain's Low-Paid Unorganised Workers with Problems at Work." Working Paper. University of the West of England, Bristol. http://eprints.uwe.ac.uk/7489.

Pomeroy, Steve, and Nick Falvo. 2014. "Housing Policy in Canada under the Harper Regime." Paper presented to the European Network for Housing Research, Ottawa, Carleton University, June.

Popova, Daria. 2016. "Distributional Impacts of Cash Allowances for Children: A Microsimulation Analysis for Russia and Europe." *Journal of European Social Policy* 26, no. 3: 248–67.

Porter, Ann. 2003. *Gendered States: Women, Unemployment Insurance, and the Political Economy of the Welfare State in Canada, 1945–1997*. Toronto: University of Toronto Press.

Porter, Tony, ed. 2014. *Transnational Financial Regulation After the Crisis.* New York: Routledge.

Potts, Lydia. 1990. *The World Market For Labour Power: A History of Migration.* London: Zed Books.

Poverty and Employment Precarity in Southern Ontario (PEPSO). 2013. *It's More than Poverty: Employment Precarity and Household Well-Being.* Toronto: United Way.

Power, Michael. 2003. "Evaluating the Audit Explosion." *Law & Policy* 25, no. 3 (July): 185–202.

– 1999. *The Audit Society: Rituals of Verification.* Oxford: Oxford University Press.

Preibisch, Kerry. 2010. "Pick-Your-Own Labor: Migrant Workers and Flexibility in Canadian Agriculture." *International Migration Review* 44, no. 2: 404–41.

Price, Ray. 1974. *Yellowknife.* Markham: P. Martin Associates.

Prince, Michael. 2016. *Inclusive Employment for Canadians with Disabilities: Toward a New Policy Framework and Agenda.* Montreal: Institute for Research on Public Policy, 2016. http://irpp.org/research-studies/inclusive-employment-for-canadians-with-disabilities/.

Provincial Community Mental Health Committee. 2011. *Building Community Support for People: A Plan for Mental Health in Ontario.* http://ontario.cmha.ca/files/2011/06/grahamreport.pdf.

Puar, Jasbir K. 2017. *The Right to Maim: Debility, Capacity, Disability.* Duke University Press.

Pulkingham, Jane, and Tanya Van Der Gaag. 2004. "Maternity/Parental Leave Provision in Canada: We've Come a Long Way, But There's further to Go." *Canadian Woman Studies* 23, nos 3–4: 116–25.

Pupo, Norene, and Mark Thomas. 2010. *Interrogating the New Economy: Restructuring Work in the 21st Century.* Toronto: University of Toronto Press.

Putin, Vladimir. 2006. "Annual Address to the Federal Assembly." Marble Hall, the Kremlin, Moscow, 10 May. http://en.kremlin.ru/events/president/transcripts/23577.

PWC. 2015. "The Global Entertainment and Media Outlook 2015–2019: Global and Canadian Highlights." *The Global Entertainment and Media Outlook 2015–2019.* https://www.pwc.com/ca/en/entertainment-media/publications/pwc-global-em-outlook-2015-2019-canadian-highlights-2015-09-en.pdf.

Racioppi Linda, and Katherine O'Sullivan See, eds. 2009. *Gender Politics in Post-Communist Eurasia.* Michigan: Michigan State University Press.

Rankin, Jennifer. 2018. "Online Streaming Services Face '30% Made in Europe' Law." *Guardian,* 26 April. https://www.theguardian.com/technology/2018/apr/26/eu-third-party-trader-amazon-google-ebay.

Reaume, Geoffrey. 2004. "No Profits, Just a Pittance: Work, Compensation, and People Defined as Mentally Disabled in Ontario, 1964–1990." In *Mental Retardation in America: A Historical Reader*, edited by Steven Knoll and James Trent, 466–93. New York: New York University Press.

– 2009. *Remembrance of Patients Past: Patient Life at the Toronto Hospital for the Insane, 1870–1940*. Toronto: University of Toronto Press.

Reid-Musson, Emily. 2014. "Historicizing Precarity: A Labour Geography of 'Transient' Migrant Workers in Ontario Tobacco." *Geoforum* 56: 161–71.

Reitan, Ruth. 2008. "Review of La Via Campesina: Globalization and the Power of Peasants." *Studies in Social Justice Volume* 2, no. 1: 102–18.

Ricardo, David. 1871. *On the Principles of Political Economy and Taxation*. London: John Murray Publishing.

Richardson, Jack. 1992. "Free Trade: Why Did it Happen?" *Canadian Review of Sociology and Anthropology* 29, no. 3: 307–28.

Ricoeur, Paul. 1992. *Oneself as Another*. Chicago: University of Chicago Press.

Riga, Andy. 2014. "Super Beams and Sinkholes: Montreal's Year in Infrastructure." *Montreal Gazette*, 24 December.

Rigauer, Bero. 1981. *Sport and Work*. New York, NY: Columbia University Press.

Rioux, Ouimet Hubert. 2012. "Entre réingénierie et continuité: réforme libérale des sociétés d'État québécoises et nationalisme économique (2003–2012)." *Interventions économiques* 44: 2–18.

– 2017. *The New Sponsor States: Economic Nationalism and Venture Capital in Quebec and Scotland 1990–2017*. PhD diss., McMaster University.

Rioux, Sebastian. 2015. "Embodied Contradictions: Capitalism, Social Reproduction and Body Formation." *Women's Studies International Forum* 48: 194–202.

Rivkin-Fish, Michele. 2010. "Pronatalism, Gender Politics, and the Renewal of Family Support in Russia: Toward a Feminist Anthropology of 'Maternity Capital.'" *Slavic Review* 69, no. 3: 701–24.

Robidoux, Michael A. 2001. *Men at Play: A Working Understanding of Professional Hockey*. Montreal: McGill-Queen's University Press.

Roediger, David. 1991. *The Wages of Whiteness: Race and the Making of the American/Working Class*. London: Verso.

Romanow, Roy. 2002. *Building on Values: The Future of Health Care in Canada*. Ottawa: Commission on the Future of Health Care in Canada.

Rose, Albert. 1980. *Canadian Housing Policies: 1935–1980*. Toronto: Butterworth and Company.

Rose, Nick. 2015. "A Dispatch From Montreal's Raucous, Tear Gas-Filled May Day Protest." *Vice Magazine*, 2 May. http://www.vice.com/en_ca/read/a-dispatch-from-montreals-raucous-tear-gas-filled-may-day-protest-141.

Ross, Stephanie A. 2003. "Is this What Democracy Looks Like? The Politics of the Anti-Globalization Movement in North America." In *Socialist Register*

2003: *Fighting Identities*, edited by Leo Panitch and Collin Leys, 281–304. London: Merlin Press.

– 2008. "Anti-Statism in the Global Justice Movement: Strategic Implications." *Labour, Capital and Society* 41, no. 1: 6–32.

Ross, Stephanie, and Jason Russell. 2018. "'Caterpillar Hates Unions More Than It Loves Profits': The Electro-Motive Closure and the Dilemmas of Union Strategy." *Labour/Le Travail* 81 (Spring): 53–85.

Ross, Stephanie, and Larry Savage. 2013. *Public Sector Unions in the Age of Austerity*. Halifax and Winnipeg: Fernwood.

Ross, Andrew. 2004. *No-Collar: The Humane Workplace and Its Hidden Consequences*. Philadelphia, PA: Temple University Press.

– 2009. *Nice Work If You Can Get It: Life and Labor in Precarious Times*. New York and London: New York University Press.

– 2013. "In Search of the Lost Paycheck." In *Digital Labor: The Internet as Playground and Factory*, edited by Trebor Scholz, 13–32. New York: Routledge.

Rothwell, Neil, and Ray Bollman. 2011. "Manufacturing Firms in Rural and Small Town Canada." *Rural and Small Town Canada Analysis Bulletin* 21-006-X, 8: 6. Ottawa, Statistics Canada.

Rotkirch, Anna, Anna Temkina, and Elena Zdravomyslova. 2007. "Who Helps the Degraded Housewife? Comments on Vladimir Putin's Demographic Speech." *European Journal of Women's Studies* 14, no. 4: 349–57.

Rousseau, Julie. 2008. "Partager une même rivière sans pour autant partager le même canot." In *Québec en mouvements: Idées et pratiques militantes contemporaines*, edited by Francis Dupuis-Déri, 231–48. Montreal: Lux.

Ruas da Fonseca, Rhaysa S. n.d. "Social Policy Potentializing Inequalities? A Case Study on the Bolsa Família Program from a Social Reproduction Perspective." Working Paper. Rio de Janeiro State University.

Rude, Christopher. 2005. "The Role of Financial Discipline in Imperial Strategy." In *Socialist Register*, edited by Leo Panitch and Colin Leys, 82–107. London: Merlin.

Ruggie, John. 1983. "International Regimes, Transactions, and Change: Embedded in the Postwar Economic Order." In *International Regimes*, edited by Stephen Krasner, 195–232. Ithaca: Cornell University Press.

Russell, Bob. 1999. *More with Less: Work Reorganization in the Canadian Mining Industry*. Toronto: University of Toronto Press.

Rutland, Peter. 2013. "Neoliberalism and the Russian Transition." *Review of International Political Economy* 20, no. 2: 332–62.

Ryerson, Stanley. 1973. *Unequal Union: Roots of Crisis in the Canadas, 1815–1873*. Toronto: Progress Books.

Salée, Daniel. 1999. "Innis and Quebec: The Paradigm That Would Not Be." In *Harold Innis in the New Century: Reflections and Refractions*, edited by

Charles Acland and William Buxton, 196–208. Montreal: McGill-Queen's University Press.

– 2003. "Transformative Politics, The State, and the Politics of Social Change in Quebec." In *Changing Canada: Political Economy as Transformation*, edited by Wallace Clement and Leah Vosko, 25–50. Montreal: McGill-Queen's University Press.

– 2013. "L'évolution des rapports politiques entre la société québécoise et les peuples autochtones depuis la crise d'Oka." In *Les Autochtones et le Québec. Des premiers contacts au Plan Nord*, edited by Alain Beaulieu, Stéphan Gervais, and Martin Papillon, 323–42. Montreal: Presses de l'Université de Montréal.

Salée, Daniel, and William D. Coleman. 1996. "The Challenges of the Quebec Question: Paradigm, Counterparadigm and ... ?" In *Understanding Canada: Building on the New Canadian Political Economy*, edited by Wallace Clement, 262–85. Montreal: McGill-Queen's University Press.

Sandberg, Anders, and Sandberg Tor, eds. 2010. *Climate Change: Who's Carrying the Burden?: The Chilly Climates of the Global Environment Dilemma*. Toronto: CCPA.

Sangster, Joan. 1989. *Dreams of Equality: Women on the Canadian Left, 1920–1950*. Toronto: McClelland and Stewart.

– 2005. "*Robitnystia* and the Porcupinism Debate: Reassessing Ethnicity, Gender and Class in Early Canadian Communism." *Labour/Le Travail* 56 (Fall): 51–89.

Satzewich, Vic. 1989. "Unfree Labour and Canadian Capitalism: The Incorporation of Polish War Veterans." *Studies in Political Economy* 28 (Spring): 89–110.

– 1991. *Racism and the Incorporation of Foreign Labour: Farm Labour Migration to Canada since 1945*. London: Routledge.

Savage, Larry. 2012. "Organized Labour and the Politics of Strategic Voting." In *Rethinking the Politics of Labour in Canada*, edited by Stephanie Ross and Larry Savage, 75–87. Halifax: Fernwood.

Schmidt, Vivien. 2011. "Ideas and Discourse in Transformational Political Economic Change in Europe." In *Policy Paradigms, Transnationalism, and Domestic Politics*, edited by Grace Skogstad, 36–63. Toronto: University of Toronto Press.

Scholz, Trebor. 2013. *Digital Labor: The Internet as Playground and Factory*. New York: Routledge.

Sears, Alan. 2014. *The Next New Left: A History of the Future*. Halifax: Fernwood.

Seccombe, Wally. 1974. "The Housewife and Her Labour under Capitalism." *New Left Review* 1, no. 83: 3–24.

– 1980. "Domestic Labour and the Working-Class Household." In *Hidden in the Household: Women's Domestic Labour Under Capitalism*, edited by Bonnie Fox, 25–100. Toronto: The Women's Press.

Sharma, Nandita. 2006. *Home Economics: Nationalism and the Making of "Migrant Workers" in Canada*. Toronto: University of Toronto Press.

Sharma, Nandita, and Cynthia Wright. 2009. "Decolonizing Resistance, Challenging Colonial States." *Social Justice* 35, no. 3: 120–38.

Sharpe, Andrew. 2013. "What Do We Know About Productivity and What Is the Best Focus for Future Research?" Paper Presented to Ontario Ministry of Finance, Centre for the Study of Living Standards, 30 September. http://www.csls.ca/news/presentations/OntarioMinistryFinance.pdf.

Shewell, Hugh. 2004. *"Enough to Keep Them Alive": Indian Welfare in Canada, 1873–1965*. Toronto: University of Toronto Press.

Silbey, Susan S. 2005a. "After Legal Consciousness." *Annual Review of Law and Social Sciences* 1: 323–68.

– 2005b "Everyday Life and the Constitution of Legality." In *The Blackwell Companion to the Sociology of Culture*, edited by Mark D. Jacobs and Nancy Weiss Hanrahan, 332–45. Hoboken: Blackwell Publishing.

– 2013. "What Makes a Social Science of Law? Doubling the Social in Socio-Legal Studies." In *Exploring the "Socio" of Socio-Legal Studies*, edited by Dermot Feenan, 20–36. New York: Palgrave Macmillan.

Simmons, Harvey. 1990. *Unbalanced: Mental Health Policy in Ontario, 1930–1989*. Toronto: Wall and Thompson.

Simonpillai, Radheyan. 2017a. "Diversity in Canadian Film Isn't An Obligation, It's An Opportunity." *Huffington Post*, 31 June. https://www.huffingtonpost.ca/radheyan-simonpillai/representation-and-diversity-canadian-film_b_16883452.html.

– 2017b. "Canadian Film Industry Is Narrowing the Gender Gap." NOW, 2 November. https://nowtoronto.com/movies/features/telefilm-canadian-film-industry-narrows-gender-gap/.

Simpson, Audra. 2014. "The Chiefs Two Bodies: Theresa Spence and the Gender of Settler Sovereignty." Keynote Address at *Annual Critical Race and Anticolonial Studies Conference*. Edmonton: Athabasca University.

Simpson, Leanne. 2008. *Lighting the Eighth Fire: The Liberation, Resurgence, and Protection of Indigenous Nations*. Winnipeg: Arbeiter Ring Publishers.

– 2011. *Dancing on Our Turtle's Back: Stories of Nishnaabeg Re-creation, Resurgence and a New Emergence*. Winnipeg: Arbeiter Ring Publishers.

Sisters in Spirit. 2010. *What Their Stories Tell Us: Research Findings from the Sisters in Spirit Initiative*. Native Women's Association of Canada. http://www.nwac.ca/sisters-spirit-research-report-2010.

Slack, Enid, and Richard M. Bird. 2013. *Merging Municipalities: Is Bigger Better?* IMFG Paper 14. Toronto: University of Toronto Institute on Municipal Finance and Governance.

Slawson, Devin. 2016. "The 3 Best and Worst CHL Attendances." *Hockey Writers*, 18 January.

Smiley, Donald. 1975. "Canada and the Quest for a National Policy."
    Canadian Journal of Political Science 8, no. 1: 40–62.
Smith, Adam. 2003. *The Wealth of Nations.* New York: Bantam.
– 2008. *An Inquiry into the Nature and Causes of the Wealth of Nations.*
    Chicago: University of Chicago Press.
– 2010. *A Theory of Moral Sentiments.* New York: Penguin Books.
Smith, Adrian A. 2005 "Legal Consciousness and Resistance in Caribbean
    Seasonal Agricultural Workers." *Canadian Journal of Law and Society* 20,
    no. 2: 95–122.
– 2013. "Pacifying the 'Armies of Offshore Labour' in Canada." *Socialist
    Studies/Études socialistes* 9, no. 2: 78–93.
– 2015a. "The Bunk House Rules: A Materialist Approach to Legal
    Consciousness in the Context of Migrant Workers' Housing in Ontario."
    Osgoode Hall Law Journal 52, no. 3: 863–904.
– 2015b. "Racism and the Regulation of Migrant Labour." In *Research
    Handbook on Transnational Labour Law,* edited by Adelle Blackett and
    Anne Trebilcock, 138–49. Cheltenham: Edward Elgar.
– 2015c. "Troubling 'Project Canada': The Caribbean and the Making of
    'Unfree Migrant Labour.'" *Canadian Journal of Latin American and
    Caribbean Studies/Revue canadienne des études latino-américaines et
    caraïbes* 40, no. 2: 274–93.
Smith, Andrea. 2005. *Conquest: Sexual Violence and American Indian
    Genocide.* Cambridge: South End Press.
Smith, Dale. 2014. "The Smell O' Jobs." *Blacklocks Reporter,* 19 March.
Smith, Linda Tuhiwai. 1999. *Decolonizing Methodologies: Research and
    Indigenous Peoples.* London and New York: Zed Books.
Smith, Miriam, ed. 2014. *Group Politics and Social Movements in Canada.*
    Toronto: University of Toronto Press.
Smith, Murray E.G. 2000. "Political Economy and the Canadian Working
    Class: Marxism or Nationalist Reformism?" *Labour/Le Travail* 46 (Fall):
    343–68.
Smith, Neil. 2008. *Uneven Development: Nature, Capital, and the Production
    of Space.* Athens: University of Georgia Press.
Smythe, Dallas. 1981. *Dependency Road: Communications, Capitalism,
    Consciousness, and Canada.* Norwood, NJ: Ablex.
SNC-Lavalin. 2002. *Étude comportant la collecte d'informations et la portrait
    technique des infrastructures de la gestion publique de l'eau – Rapport final.*
Social Housing BC. 2014. Ending the Housing Crisis in BC. http://www.social
    housingbc.com/wpcontent/uploads/2014/05/STANDS4social_housing_
    grey2.pdf.
Southcott, Chris, Francis Abele, David Natcher, and Parlee B, eds. 2018.
    Resources and Sustainable Development in the Arctic. New York:
    Routledge.

Southcott, Chris, and Valloree Walker. 2009. "A Portrait of the Social Economy in Northern Canada." *Northern Review* 30 (Spring): 13–36.

SPARC. 2009. *Municipal Strategies to Address Homelessness in British Columbia*. Burnaby: Social Planning and Research Council of British Columbia.

Standing, Guy. 1999. *Global Labour Flexibility: Seeking Distributive Justice*. London: MacMillan.

– 2011. *The Precariat: The New Dangerous Class*. London and New York: Bloomsbury Academic.

Stanford, Jim. 2008. "Staples, Deindustrialization and Canadian Foreign Investment: Canada's Journey Back to the Future." *Studies in Political Economy* 82 (Autumn): 7–34.

– 2011. "Canada's Productivity and Innovation Failures: Questioning the Conventional View." *The Canada We Want in 2020: Towards a Strategic Policy Roadmap for the Federal Government*. Ottawa: Canada 2020.

– 2012. *A Cure for Dutch Disease: Active Sector Strategies for Canada's Economy*. Ottawa: Canadian Centre for Policy Alternatives.

– ed. 2014a. *The Staples Theory @ 50: Reflections on the Lasting Significance of Mel Watkins' "A Staple Theory of Economic Growth."* Ottawa: Canadian Centre for Policy Alternatives.

– 2014b. "Adding Value to Canada's Petroleum Wealth: A National Economic and Environmental Priority." In *Canada: Becoming a Sustainable Energy Powerhouse*, edited by Clement Bowman and Richard Marceau, 25–46. Ottawa: Canadian Academy of Engineering.

– 2014c. "Why Linkages Matter." In *The Staples Theory @ 50: Reflections on the Lasting Significance of Mel Watkins' "A Staple Theory of Economic Growth."* Ottawa: Canadian Centre for Policy Alternatives.

Stanford, Jim, and Sam Gindin. 2003. "Canadian Labour and the Political Economy of Transformation." In *Changing Canada: Political Economy as Transformation*, edited by Wallace Clement and Leah F. Vosko, 422–42. Montreal and Kingston: McGill-Queen's University Press.

Stasiulis, Daiva, and Nira Yuval-Davis. 1995. "Beyond Dichotomies: Gender, Race, Ethnicity and Class in Settler Societies." In *Unsettling Settler Societies: Articulations of Gender, Race, Ethnicity and Class*, edited by Daiva Stasiulis and Nira Yuval-Davis, 1–39. London: SAGE.

Statistics Canada. 2009. "Local General Government Revenue and Expenditures, Current and Capital Accounts, Annual (dollars)." CANSIM, Table 385-0024. http://www5.statcan.gc.ca/.

– 2012. "Canadian Survey on Disability, 2012." http://www23.statcan.gc.ca/imdb/p2SV.pl?Function=getSurvey&SDDS=3251.

– 2013a. "Government Finance Statistics, Statement of Government Operations and Balance Sheet, Quarterly (dollars) March 1990 to March 2016." CANSIM, Table 385-0032. http://www5.statcan.gc.ca/cansim/a26?lang=eng&id=3850032.

- 2013b. "Gross Domestic Product, Income-based, Quarterly (Dollars), March 1981 to March 2016." CANSIM, Table 380-0063. http://www.statcan.gc.ca/tables-tableaux/sum-som/l01/cst01/gdps01a-eng.htm
- 2013c. *Long Term Trends in Unionization*. Ottawa: Statistics Canada.
- 2013d. "Survey of Employment, Payrolls and Hours, Average Weekly Earnings by Type of Employee, Overtime Status and Detailed North American Industry Classification System, Annual (current dollars), 2001 to 2015." CANSIM, Table 281-0027. http://www5.statcan.gc.ca/cansim/a26?lang=eng&id=2810027.
- 2015a. "Canadian Classification of Functions of Government (CCOFOG) by General Government Component, Annual (dollars)." CANSIM, Table 385-0040. http://www5.statcan.gc.ca/.
- 2015b. "Canadian Government Finance Statistics, Statement of Operations and Balance Sheet for Municipalities and Other Local Public Administrations, Annual (dollars)." CANSIM, Table 385-0037. http://www5.statcan.gc.ca/.
- 2015c. "Compensation of Employees, Annual (dollars x 1,000,000)." CANSIM, Table 380-0074. http://www5.statcan.gc.ca/.
- 2015d. "Gross Domestic Product, Expenditure-based, Provincial and Territorial, Annual (dollars)." CANSIM, Table 384-0038. http://www5.statcan.gc.ca/.
- 2015e. "Estimates of Population by Census Metropolitan Area, Sex and Age Group for July 1, based on the Standard Geographical Classification (SGC) 2011, Annual (persons)." CANSIM, Table 051-0056. http://www5.statcan.gc.ca/.
- 2016a. "Consumer Price Index, Seasonally Adjusted, Annual (2002=100)." CANSIM, Table 326-0022. http://www5.statcan.gc.ca/.
- 2016b. "Estimates of Population, Canada, Provinces and Territories, Quarterly (persons)." CANSIM, Table 051-0005. http://www5.statcan.gc.ca/.
- 2017a. *Labour Force* Survey, August 2017. Accessed 8 August 2018 at: https://www150.statcan.gc.ca/n1/daily-quotidien/170908/dq170908a-eng.htm.
- 2017b. *Labour Force Survey* (database). CHASS (distributor). Last updated 3 February 2017. Accessed 26 July 2018 at:http://sda.chass.utoronto.ca/sdaweb/html/lfs.htm.
Steans, Jill, and Danielle Tepe. 2010. "Introduction: Social Reproduction in International Political Economy: Theoretical Insights and International, Transnational and Local Sightings." *Review of International Political Economy* 17, no. 5: 807–15.
Steiner, Christopher. 2012. *Automate This: How Algorithms Came to Rule Our World*. New York: Penguin.
Stevens, Andrew, and Doug Nesbitt. 2014. "An Era of Wildcats and Sick-outs in Canada? The Continued Decline of Industrial Pluralism and the Case of Air Canada." *Labor Studies Journal* 39, no. 2: 118–39.

Stevis, Dmitris, and Stephen Mumme. 2000. "Rules and Politics in International Integration: Environmental Regulation in NAFTA and the EU." *Environmental Politics* 9, no. 4: 20–42.

Stone, Alan. 1985. "The Place of Law in the Marxian Structure-Superstructure Archetype." *Law and Society Review* 19, no. 1: 39–67.

Storey, Keith. 2001. "Fly-In/Fly-Out and Fly-Over: Mining and Regional Development in Western Australia." *Australian Geographer* 32, no. 2: 133–48.

– 2010. "Fly-in/Fly-out: Implications for Community Sustainability." *Sustainability* 2: 1161–81.

Struthers, James. 1997. "Reluctant Partners: State Regulation of Private Nursing Homes in Ontario, 1941–72." In *The Welfare State in Canada: Past, Present and Future*, edited by Raymond B. Blake, Penny E. Bryden, J. Frank Strain, 171–92. Concord: Irwin Publishers.

Sun Life Financial. 2012. *What Does Long-term Care Cost?*

Supreme Court of Canada. 2007. Health Services and Support – Facilities Subsector Bargaining Assn. *v.* British Columbia, [2007] 2 S.C.R. 391, 2007 SCC 27.

Suttor, Greg. 2016. "Taking Stock of Supportive Housing for Mental Health and Addictions in Ontario." Wellesley Institute. http://www.wellesley institute.com/publications/taking-stock-of-supportive-housing-for-mental-health-and-addictions-in-ontario/.

Swartz, Donald. 1977. "The Politics of Reform: Conflict and Accommodation in Canadian Health Policy." In *The Canadian State: Political Economy and Political Power*, edited by Leo Panitch, 311–43. Toronto: University of Toronto Press.

Swartz, Donald, and Rosemary Warskett. 2012. "Canadian Labour and the Crisis of Solidarity." In *Rethinking the Politics of Labour in Canada*, edited by Stephanie Ross and Larry Savage, 18–32. Halifax: Fernwood.

Tanuseputro, Peter, Mathieu Chalifoux, Carol Bennett, Andrea Gruneir, Susan E. Bronskill, Peter Walkeri, and Douglas Manueli. 2015. "Hospitalization and Mortality Rates in Long-Term Care Facilities: Does For-Profit Status Matter?" JAMDA 16: 874–83.

Tarrow, Sydney. 1967. *Peasant Communism in Southern Italy*. New Haven, CT: Yale University Press.

Taylor, Harriet. 2016. "Google (and Facebook) Are Getting Almost All Digital Ad Money." CNBC, 28 July. http://www.cnbc.com/2016/07/28/google-and-facebook-are-getting-almost-all-digital-ad-money.html.

Taylor, Kate. 2017. "Mélanie Joly's Netflix Deal Fails to Address the Real Issues for Canadian Content Creators." *Globe and Mail*, 4 October. https://www.theglobeandmail.com/opinion/melanie-jolys-netflix-deal-fails-to-address-the-real-issues-for-canadian-content-creators/article3642856o/.

Teeple, Gary. 1972. *Capitalism and the National Question in Canada*. Toronto: University of Toronto Press.

– 1995. *Globalization and the Decline of Social Reform.* Toronto: Garamond
  Press.
Temple Newhook, Julia, Barbara Neis, Lois Jackson, Sharon R. Roseman,
  Paula Romanow, and Chrissy Vincent. 2011. "Employment-Related
  Mobility and the Health of Workers, Families, and Communities: The
  Canadian Context." *Labour/Le Travail* 67: 121–56.
Tenuta, Eleni, and Laura Heath Potter. 2015. "What Canadians Watched in
  2015." *Bell Media,* 21 December. http://www.bellmedia.ca/pr/press/tv-top-
  10-canadians-watched-2015/.
Teplova, Tatyana. 2007. "Welfare State Transformation, Childcare, and
  Women's Work in Russia." *Social Politics* 14, no. 3: 284–322.
Thobani, Sunera. 2007. *Exalted Subjects: Studies in the Making of Race and
  Nation in Canada.* Toronto: University of Toronto Press.
Thomas, Mark. 2009. *Regulating Flexibility: The Political Economy of
  Employment Standards.* Montreal and Kingston: McGill-Queen's University
  Press.
– 2010. "Neoliberalism, Racialization, and the Regulation of Employment
  Standards." In *Neoliberalism and Everyday Life,* edited by Susan Braedley
  and Meg Luxton, 68–89. Montreal and Kingston: McGill-Queen's
  University Press.
– 2011. "Global Unions, Local Labour, and the Regulation of International
  Labour Standards: Mapping ITF Labour Rights Strategies." In *Trade Union
  and the Global Crisis: Labour's Visions, Strategies and Responses,* edited by
  M. Fichter, M. Serrano, and E. Xhafa, 81–95. Geneva: International Labour
  Organization.
– 2016. "Producing and Contesting 'Unfree Labour' through the Seasonal
  Agricultural Workers Program." In *Unfree Labour? Struggles of Migrant
  and Immigrant Workers in Canada,* edited by Aziz Choudry and Adrian
  Smith, 21–6. Oakland: PM Press.
Thomas, Mark, and Steven Tufts. 2016a. "Austerity, Right Populism and the
  Crisis of Labour in Canada." *Antipode* 48, no.1 (January): 212–30.
– 2016b. "'Enabling Dissent': Contesting Austerity and Right-Wing Populism
  in Toronto, Canada." *Economic and Labour Relations Review* 27, no. 1:
  29–45.
Tomiak, Julie. 2016. "Unsettling Ottawa: Settler Colonialism, Indigenous
  Resistance, and the Politics of Scale." *Canadian Journal of Urban and
  Regional Research* 25, no. 1: 8–21.
Thompson, E.P. 1968. *The Making of the English Working Class.*
  Harmondsworth: Penguin.
Thompson, Paul, and David McHugh. 2002. *Work Organizations: A Critical
  Introduction.* 3rd edition. Houndmills, Basingstoke, Hampshire: Palgrave.
Thompson, Shona M. 1999. *Mother's Taxi: Sport and Women's Labor.*
  Albany, NY: State University of New York Press.

Tilly, Charles. 1964. *The Vendée: A Sociological Analysis of the Counter-Revolution of 1793*. Cambridge: Harvard University Press.

- 1992. *Coercion, Capital, and European States*, AD 990–1992. Cambridge: B. Blackwell.

- 1995. *Popular Contention in Great Britain, 1758–1834*. Cambridge: Harvard University Press.

Tombe, Trevor. 2015. "Better off Dead: 'Value Added' in Economic Policy Debates." *University of Calgary School of Public Policy Research Papers* 8, no. 9: 1–23.

Tomlins, Christopher. 2007. "How Autonomous Is Law?" *Annual Review of Law and Social Science* 3, no. 1: 45–68.

- 2010. *Freedom Bound: Law, Labour, and Civic Identity in Colonizing English America, 1580–1865*. Cambridge and New York: Cambridge University Press.

Tough, Frank. 1996. *Their Natural Resources Fail: Native Peoples and the Economic History of Northern Manitoba 1870–1930*. Vancouver: UBC Press.

Tronto, Joan. 1993. "Care." In *Moral Boundaries: A Political Argument for an Ethic of Care*, 101–24. New York: Routledge.

Trumbull, Nathaniel. 2014. "Restructuring Socialist Housing Estates and its Impact on Residents' Perceptions: 'Renovatsiia' of Khrushchevki in St Petersburg, Russia." *GeoJournal* 79, no. 4: 495–511.

Tuck, Eve, and K. Wayne Yang. 2012. "Decolonization Is Not a Metaphor." *Decolonization: Indigeneity, Education and Society* 1, no. 1: 1–40.

Tucker, Eric. 1984. "The Law of Employers' Liability in Ontario 1861–1900: The Search for a Theory." *Osgoode Hall Law Journal* 22, no. 2: 213–80.

- 2014. "Shall Wagnerism Have No Dominion?" *Just Labour: A Canadian Journal of Work and Society* 21: 1–27.

Tufts, Steven. 2014. "The Hotel Sector in an Age of Uncertainty: A Labour Perspective." In *A Hospitable World? Organizing Work and Workers in Hotels and Tourist Resorts*, edited by David Jordhus-Lier and Anders Underthus, 52–66. London: Routledge.

Tufts, Steven, and Mark Thomas. 2014. "Populist Unionism Confronts Austerity in Canada." *Labor Studies Journal* 39, no. 1: 60–82.

Tuohy, Carolyn Hughes. 2003. "Agency, Contract, and Governance: Shifting Shapes of Accountability in the Health Care Arena." *Journal of Health Politics, Policy and Law* 28, nos 2–3: 195–216.

UN-Habitat. 2016. *World Cities Report 2016: Urbanization and Development – Emerging Futures*. Nairobi: UN-Habitat.

United Food and Commercial Workers (UFCW). 2011. *The Status of Migrant Farmworkers in Canada, 2010–11*. Toronto: UFCW.

Ursel, Jane. 1992. *Private Lives, Public Policy: 100 Years of State Intervention in the Family*. Toronto: Women's Press.

Usher, Peter, Gérard Duhaime, and Edmund Searles. 2003. "The Household as an Economic Unit in Arctic Aboriginal Communities, and Its Measurement by Means of a Comprehensive Survey." *Social Indicators Research* 61, no. 2: 175–202.

Usher, Peter, and George Wenzel. 1987. "Native Harvest Surveys and Statistics: A Critique of Their Construction and Use." *Arctic*: 145–60.

Valentine, John, and Simon Darnell. 2012. "Football and 'Tolerance': Black Football Players in 20th-Century Canada." In *Race and Sport in Canada: Intersecting Inequalities*, edited by Janelle Joseph, Simon Darnell, and Yuka Nakamura, 57–80. Toronto, ON: Canadian Scholars Press.

"Vancouver Housing Affordability Drops Despite City Efforts." 2013. *Huffington Post*, 8 March.

"Vancouver Housing Market World's 2nd Least Affordable: Study." 2015. *Huffington Post*, 20 January.

Van den Berg, Axel, Charles Plante, Hicham Raïq, Christine Proulx, and Samuel Faustmann. 2017. *Combating Poverty: Quebec's Pursuit of a Distinctive Welfare State*. Montreal: McGill-Queen's University Press.

Van Kirk, Sylvia. 1980. *Many Tender Ties: Women in Fur-Trade Society, 1670–1870.* Winnipeg: Watson and Dwyer.

Veall, Michael R. 2012. "Top Income Shares in Canada: Recent Trends and Policy Implications." *Canadian Journal of Economics/Revue canadienne d'économique* 45, no. 4: 1247–72.

Veracini, Lorenzo. 2010. *Settler Colonialism: A Theoretical Overview*. London: Palgrave Macmillan.

– 2013a. "'Settler Colonialism': Career of a Concept." *Journal of Imperial and Commonwealth History* 41, no. 2: 313–33.

– 2013b. "Settler Migration and Colonies." In *The Encyclopedia of Global Human Migration*, edited by Immanuel Ness, 2732–6. Malden, MA: Wiley-Blackwell.

Vermette, Katharina, 2014. "River Woman." In *Kwe: Standing With Our Sisters*, edited by Joseph Boyden, 6–9. Toronto: Penguin Books.

Vert, P. 2005. "Housing in Vancouver Under Neoliberal Urbanism." Master's thesis, University of British Columbia.

Vosko, Leah F. 2000. *Temporary Work: The Gendered Rise of a Precarious Employment Relationship*. Toronto: University of Toronto Press.

– 2002. "The Pasts (and Futures) of Feminist Political Economy in Canada: Reviving the Debate." *Studies in Political Economy* 68: 55–83.

– 2006a. "Crisis Tendencies in Social Reproduction: The Case of Ontario's Early Years Plan." In *Social Reproduction: Feminist Political Economy Challenges Neoliberalism*, edited by Kate Bezanson and Meg Luxton, 145–72. Montreal and Kingston: McGill-Queen's University Press.

– ed. 2006b. *Precarious Employment: Understanding Labour Market Insecurity in Canada*. Montreal and Kingston: McGill-Queen's University Press.

- 2010. *Managing the Margins: Gender, Citizenship, and the International Regulation of Precarious Employment.* Oxford: Oxford University Press.
- 2016. "Blacklisting as a Modality of Deportability: Mexico's Response to Circular Migrant Agricultural Workers' Pursuit of Collective Bargaining Rights in British Columbia, Canada." *Journal of Ethnic and Migration Studies* 42, no. 8: 1371–87.

Vosko, Leah F., et al. 2019. *Closing the Enforcement Gap: Improving Protections for People in Precarious Jobs.* Toronto: University of Toronto Press.

Vosko, Leah F., John Grundy, and Mark P. Thomas. 2014. "Challenging New Governance: Evaluating New Approaches to Employment Standards Enforcement in Common Law Jurisdictions." *Economic and Industrial Democracy.* doi:10.1177/0143831X14546237.

Vosko, Leah F., Martha MacDonald, and Iain Campbell. 2009. *Gender and the Contours of Precarious Employment.* London; New York: Routledge.

Vosko, Leah F., Andrea Noack, John Grundy, Azar Masoumi, and Jennifer Mussell. 2014. "Who's Covered by the Ontario *Employment Standards Act*? Assessing the Relationships between Workers' Characteristics and Levels of Protection." Paper presented at the annual meeting of the Canadian Political Science Association, Brock University, Canada, 25 May.

Vosko, Leah F., Andrea Noack, and Mark. P. Thomas. 2016. "Employment Standards ('ES') Coverage and Enforcement: How Far Does the *Employment Standards Act, 2000* ('ESA') Extend and What Are the Gaps in Coverage?" In *Ontario Ministry of Labour Changing Workplaces Review.*

Vosko, Leah F., Andrea Noack, and Eric Tucker. 2016. "Employment Standards ('ES') Coverage and Enforcement: A Scan of Employment Standards Complaints and Their Resolution under the *Employment Standards Act, 2000* ('ESA')." In *Ontario Ministry of Labour Changing Workplaces Review.*

Vosko, Leah F., John Grundy, Eric Tucker, Mark P. Thomas, Andrea M. Noack, Rebecca Casey, Mary Gellatly, and Jennifer Mussell. 2017. "The Compliance Model of Employment Standards Enforcement: An Evidence-Based Assessment of Its Efficacy in Instances of Wage Theft." *Industrial Relations Journal* 48, no. 3: 256–73.

Vosko, Leah F., John Grundy, Rebecca Casey, Andrea M. Noack, and Mark P. Thomas. Forthcoming. "A Tattered Quilt: Exemptions and Special Rules under Ontario's *Employment Standards Act* (2000)." *Canadian Labour and Employment Law Journal.*

Vosko, Leah F., and Mark Thomas. 2014. "Confronting the Employment Standards Enforcement Gap: Exploring the Potential for Union Engagement with Employment Law in Ontario, Canada." *Journal of Industrial Relations* 56, no. 5: 631–52.

Vosko, Leah F., Nancy Zukewich, and Cynthia Cranford. 2003. "Precarious Jobs: A New Typology of Employment." *Perspectives on Labour and Income* 4, no. 10: 6–26.

Wacquant, Loic. 2010. "Crafting the Neoliberal State: Workfare, Prisonfare and Social Insecurity." *Sociological Forum* 25, no. 2: 197–220.

Wagman, Ira, and Peter Urquhart. 2012. *Cultural Industries.ca.* Toronto: Lorimer.

Walker, Richard. 2016. "Why Cities?" *International Journal of Urban and Regional Research* 40, no. 1: 164–180.

Walter, Lukas v. Lewiston Maineiacs Hockey Club, Inc and John Doe Corporation "A" operating as Les Saqueneens Chicoutimi [2014] Superior Court. Motion to Authorize the Bringing of a Class Action and to Obtain the Status of Representative.

Warskett, Rosemary. 1998. "Bank Worker Unionization and the Law." *Studies in Political Economy* 25: 41–73.

Wasko, Janet, Graham Murdock, and Helena Sousa. 2011. "Introduction: The Political Economy of Communications – Core Concerns and Issues." In *The Handbook of Political Economy of Communications*, edited by Janet Wasko, Graham Murdock, and Helena Sousa, 1–10. Malden, MA: Blackwell.

Wasko, Janet. 2014. "The Study of the Political Economy of the Media in the Twenty-First Century." *International Journal of Media & Cultural Politics* 10, no. 3: 259–71.

Watkins, Mel. 1963. "A Staple Theory of Economic Growth." *Canadian Journal of Economics and Political Science* 29, no. 2: 141–58.

– 1968. *Foreign Ownership and the Structure of Canadian Industry.* Ottawa: Supply and Services Canada.

– ed. 1977a. *Dene Nation: The Colony Within.* Toronto: University of Toronto Press.

– 1977b. "From Underdevelopment to Development." In *Dene Nation.* 84–99. Toronto: University of Toronto Press.

– 1982. "The Innis Tradition in Canadian Political Economy." *Canadian Journal of Political and Social Theory/Revue Canadienne de theorie politique et sociale* 6, nos 1–2: 12–34.

– 1989. "The Political Economy of Growth." In *New Canadian Political Economy*, edited by Wallace Clement and Glen Williams, 16–35. Kingston and Montreal: McGill-Queen's University Press.

– 1997. "Canadian Capitalism in Transition." In *Understanding Canada: Building on New Canadian Political Economy*, edited by Wallace Clement, 19–42. Montreal: McGill-Queen's University Press.

– 2003. "Politics in the Time and Space of Globalization." In *Changing Canada: Political Economy as Transformation*, edited by Wallace Clement and Leah Vosko, 79–105. Montreal: McGill-Queen's University Press.

– 2006. *Staples and Beyond: Selected Writings of Mel Watkins*, edited by Hugh Grant and David Wolfe. Montreal: McGill-Queen's University Press.
– 2007. "Comment: Staples Redux." *Studies in Political Economy* 79 (Spring): 213–26.
– 2015. "A Tribute to Abe Rotstein: A Giant of Canadian Political Economy." *The Broadbent Blog*, 4 May. http://www.broadbentinstitute. ca/a_tribute_to_abe_rotstein_a_giant_of_canadian_political_economy.
Weeks, Kathi. 2011. *The Problem with Work: Feminism, Marxism, Antiwork Politics, and Postwork Imaginaries*. Durham: Duke University.
Wellstead, Adam. 2008. "The (Post) Staples Economy and the (Post) Staples State in Historical Perspective." In *Canada's Resource Economy in Transition: The Past, Present, and Future of Canadian Staples Industries*, edited by Michael Howlett and Keith Brownsey, 19–37. Toronto: Emond Montgomery Publication.
Weil, David. 2014. *The Fissured Workplace: Why Work Became So Bad for So Many and What Can Be Done to Improve It*. Cambridge: Harvard University Press.
Weiner, Elaine. 2009. "Eastern Houses, Western Bricks? (Re)Constructing Gender Sensibilities in the European Union's Eastward Enlargement." *Social Politics: International Studies in Gender, State & Society* 16, no. 3: 1–24.
Westhead, Rick. 2014. "Twin Lawsuits Filed against WHL, QMJHL over Working Conditions." TSN, 31 October.
– 2015a. "'Flawed' WHL Law Passed against Legal Advice." TSN, 13 August.
– 2015b. "Union Alleges Intimidation after Minister Orders OHL Examination." TSN, 22 April.
Westhead, Rick, and Robert Cribb. 2014. "Major Junior Hockey Gets New Push to Unionize." *Toronto Star*, 7 July 2014.
White, Graham. 2006. "Cultures in Collision: Traditional Knowledge and Euro-Canadian Governance Processes in Northern Land-Claim Boards." *Arctic*: 401–14.
Whiteside, Heather. 2015. *Purchase for Profit: Public-Private Partnerships and Canada's Public Health Care System*. Toronto: University of Toronto Press.
Whitson, David. 1984. "Sport and Hegemony: On the Construction of the Dominant Culture." *Dialectics and Humanism* 11, no. 1: 5–19.
Whitson, David, and Richard Gruneau. 1997. "The (Real) Integrated Circus: Political Economy, Popular Culture, and Major League Sport." In *Understanding Canada: Building on the New Canadian Political Economy*, edited by Wallace Clement, 359–85. Montreal: McGill-Queen's University Press.
– 2006. *Artificial Ice: Hockey, Culture, and Commerce*. Toronto: University of Toronto Press.
Williams, Fiona. 2011. "Towards a Transnational Analysis of the Political Economy of Care." In *Feminist Ethics and Social Policy: Towards a New*

Global Political Economy of Care, edited by Rianne Mahon and Fiona
Williams, 21–38. Vancouver: UBC Press.

Wilson, Carter. 2000. "Policy Regimes and Policy Change." *Journal of Public
Policy* 20:247–74.

Wimmer, Andreas, and Nina Glick Schiller. 2002. "Methodological
Nationalism and Beyond: Nation-State Building, Migration and the Social
Sciences." *Global Networks* 2: 301–34.

Winseck, Dwayne. 2008. "The State of Media Ownership and Media Markets:
Competition or Concentration and Why Should We Care?" *Sociology
Compass* 2, no. 1: 34–47.

– 2011. "Introductory Essay: The Political Economies of Media and the
Transformation of the Global Media Industries. In *The Political Economies
of Media: The Transformation of the Global Media Industries*, edited by
Dwayne Winseck and Dal Yong Jin, 3–48. London and New York:
Bloomsbury Academic.

– 2015. "Media and Internet Concentration in Canada Report, 1984–2014."
The Canadian Media Concentration Research Project (CMCRP). http://
www.cmcrp.org/media-and-internet-concentration-in-canada-report-1984-
2014/.

– 2016a. "Why Media Concentration Matters." Personal Correspondence
with author.

– 2016b. "A Radical Broadband Internet and Cultural Policy for Canada."
https://dwmw.wordpress.com/2016/04/27/a-radical-broadband-internet-
cultural-policy-for-canada/.

Wolfe, David. 1984. "The Rise and Demise of the Keynesian Era in Canada:
Economic Policy, 1930–1982." In *Modern Canada, 1930s to 1980s*, edited
by Michael S. Cross and Gregory S. Kealey. Toronto: McClelland and
Stewart.

Wolfe, David, and Matthew Lucas, eds. 2005. *Global Networks and Local
Linkages: The Paradox of Cluster Development in an Open Economy*.
Montreal and Kingston: McGill-Queen's University Press.

Wolfe, Patrick. 1999. *Settler Colonialism and the Transformation of
Anthropology: The Politics and Poetics of an Ethnographic Event*. London:
Cassell.

– 2006. "Settler Colonialism and the Elimination of the Native." *Journal of
Genocide Research* 8, no. 4: 387–409.

– 2008. "Structure and Event: Settler Colonialism, Time, and the Question
of Genocide." In *Empire, Colony, Genocide: Conquest, Occupation, and
Subaltern Resistance in World History*, edited by Dirk Moses, 102–32.
New York and Oxford: Berghahn.

Wood, Ellen Meiksins. 1995. *Democracy Against Capitalism: Renewing
Historical Materialism* Cambridge: Cambridge University Press.

– 2002. *The Origin of Capitalism: A Longer View*. London: Verso.

Wood, Lesley. 2014. *Crisis and Control: The Militarization of Protest Policing.* London: Pluto Press.

Woolford, Andrew, and Amanda Nelund. 2013. "The Responsibilities of the Poor: Performing Neoliberal Citizenship within the Bureaucratic Field." *Social Service Review* 87, no. 2: 292–318.

Workers' Action Centre (WAC). 2015. *Still Working on the Edge: Building Decent Jobs from the Ground Up.* Toronto: WAC.

Wyonch, Rosalie. 2017. "Canada Needs to Follow Quebec Lead on Taxing Netflix." *Toronto Star*, 23 October. https://www.thestar.com/opinion/commentary/2017/10/23/canada-needs-to-follow-quebec-lead-on-taxing-netflix.html.

Yakabuski, Konrad. 2017. "Joly Barely Moves the Dial on Cultural Policy." *Globe and Mail*, 28 September. https://www.theglobeandmail.com/opinion/joly-barely-moves-the-dial-on-cultural-policy/article36414543/.

YK Dene First Nation Advisory Council. 1997. *Weledeh Yellowknives Dene: A History.* Dettah: Yellowknives Dene First Nations Council.

Young, Brigitte. 2000. "Disciplinary Neoliberalism in the European Union and Gender Politics." *New Political Economy* 5, no. 1: 77–98.

Young, Ian. 2015. "Vancouver's Housing Crisis: No, Not Like Before, and Not Like Anywhere Else (except Hong Kong)." *South China Morning Post*, 3 June. http://www.scmp.com/comment/blogs/article/1815597/vancouvers-housing-crisis-no-not-and-not-anywhere-else-except-hong.

Young, Robert, and Martin Horak, eds. 2012. *Sites of Governance: Multilevel Governance and Policy Making in Canada's Big Cities.* Montreal and Kingston: McGill-Queen's University Press.

Young, T.R. 1986. "The Sociology of Sport: Structural Marxist and Cultural Marxist Approaches." *Sociological Perspectives* 29: 3–28.

Zhurzhenko, Tatiana Iu. 2001. "Social Reproduction as a Problem in Feminist Theory." *Russian Studies in History* 40, no. 3: 70–90.

Zirin, Dave. 2014. "The Northwester University Football Union and the NCAA's Death Spiral." *Nation*, 27 March.

Zoe, John B. 2005. "Tlicho History." *The Tlicho History Project*, 2014. https://tlichohistory.ca/en/timeline.

Contributors

GREG ALBO is a professor of political economy with the Department of Political Science, York University, Toronto. He is currently co-editor of the *Socialist Register*, co-author of *In and Out of Crisis: The Global Financial Meltdown and Left Alternatives*, co-editor of *A Different Kind of State: Popular Power and Democratic Administration*, and author of numerous articles in journals such as *Studies in Political Economy*, *Socialist Register*, *Canadian Dimension*, and *Monthly Review*. Professor Albo's research interests are the political economy of contemporary capitalism, labour market policies in Canada, and democratization.

HUGH ARMSTRONG is a distinguished research professor, professor emeritus of social work and political economy at Carleton University in Ottawa, Ontario. Dr Armstrong's major research interests include long-term care, the political economy of health care, unions and public policy, the organization of work, and family and household structures. He has published widely on the political economy of health care, and is co-author of *Critical to Care: the Invisible Women in Health Services* (University of Toronto Press), *Wasting Away: The Undermining of Canadian Health Care* (Oxford University Press), and *The Double Ghetto: Canadian Women and Their Segregated Work* (Oxford University Press).

PAT ARMSTRONG is a distinguished research professor in sociology and Fellow of the Royal Society of Canada, cross-appointed to gender, feminist and women's studies at York University, Toronto. She held a ten-year Canada Health Services Research Foundation/Canadian Institute of Health Research chair in health services. For over a decade, Armstrong chaired Women and Health Care Reform, a group funded by Health

Canada. Focusing on the fields of social policy, women, work, feminist theory, and health and social services, she has published widely, co-authoring more than a dozen books and co-editing another dozen, as well as popular pieces and journal articles. Her first book, *The Double Ghetto: Canadian Women and Their Segregated Work*, was published in 1978 and her most recent are *Wash, Wear and Care: Clothing and Laundry in Long-Term Residential Care*, published in 2017, followed by *Creative Team Work: Rapid, Site Switching Ethnography* in 2018. She is currently principal investigator of a seven-year SSHRC-funded project on "Reimagining Long-Term Residential Care: An International Study of Promising Practices" and coordinator of a smaller one on "Healthy Aging in Residential Places," as well as a PI on "Changing Places: Unpaid Work in Public Places" and co-investigator on the "Invisible Women: Gender and the Shifting Division of Labour in Long-Term Residential Care" and "Seniors – Adding Life to Years: Late Life Issues." Framed by feminist political economy and focused on making change for social justice, her research has long been collaborative and partnered with community and union groups.

SIMON BLACK is an assistant professor of labour studies at Brock University where he teaches "The Labour of Sport." Since 2006, Black has written a sports column, from a radical's perspective, for *Canadian Dimension* magazine. His scholarly research has been published in journals including *Labour, Capital and Society*, *Labor Studies Journal*, and *International Journal of Urban and Regional Research*. He is a former NCAA student-athlete, having played Division I soccer for the University at Buffalo Bulls.

JACQUELINE CHOINIERE is an associate professor in the School of Nursing, York University. Since coming to York in 2008, her research has focused on the influence of political, economic, and social forces on the quality of care and the quality of work and life for nurses and other health care providers. Her work critically examines the influence of current reform directions on women's work in general, and on nursing and health care workers in particular. Most recently Choiniere has been exploring the intimate connections between conditions of work and conditions of care in settings where older adults reside.

WALLACE CLEMENT is a professor of sociology at Carleton University and was director of Carleton's Institute of Political Economy from 1993 to 2001. He is former Dean of the Faculty of Arts and Social Sciences and of the Faculty of Graduate and Postdoctoral Affairs. In 2002, Clement was appointed as Chancellor's Professor of Sociology. His work is formative in the Canadian political economy tradition and he has edited or co-edited three definitive volumes in the field. His co-authored book with John Myles, *Relations of Ruling: Class and Gender in Postindustrial Societies*, was awarded the 1994–95 Harold Adams Innis Prize by the Federation for the Humanities and Social Sciences. As a researcher and teacher, he is interested in political economy, Canadian society, social stratification, and the labour process; case studies of class formation and the labour process in mining and fishing; national surveys of class structure and gender in Canada, with a comparison to Finland, Norway, Sweden, and the United States; class and the state in Canada, Australia, Sweden, Japan, Germany, and the United Kingdom; and comparative labour market policies and practices. He has lived, taught, and researched in Sweden, Germany, and Japan.

TAMARA DALY is a professor of health policy and director of the York University Centre for Aging Research and Education. Daly also directs a SSHRC partnership grant entitled "Age-Friendly Communities within Communities: International Promising Practices." She recently completed a five-year CIHR research chair in gender, work, and health. Author of numerous publications focused on the political economy of health and social care, Daly is internationally recognized as a health policy researcher committed to applied research that advances the health of seniors and those who provide their care. She investigates health equity for older adults through interdisciplinary lenses that address aging and long-term care, health and social care policy, formal and informal care systems, conditions of care and care work, and how gender and ethnicity shape access to health and social care.

CARLO FANELLI is an assistant professor and coordinator of work and labour studies in the Department of Social Science at York University, and is also appointed to the graduate program in sociology. He is the author of *Megacity Malaise: Neoliberalism, Public Services and Labour in Toronto*, and co-editor (with Bryan Evans) of *The Public Sector in an Age of Austerity: Perspectives from Canada's Provinces and Territories*. Since 2009, Fanelli has served as editor-in-chief of *Alternate Routes: A Journal of Critical Social Research*.

PETER GRAEFE is an associate professor of political science at McMaster University. He has published on Quebec political economy and public policy, including recent chapters on comparing development policy in Ontario and Quebec (in *Comparing Canada*, UBC Press, 2014), and on economic and labour market trends in Quebec (in *Boom, Bust and Crisis*, Fernwood, 2012). He has also worked on Canadian intergovernmental relations and social policy, recently co-editing the volume *Overpromising and Underperforming: Understanding and Evaluating New Intergovernmental Accountability Regimes*.

REBECCA JANE HALL is an assistant professor in the Department of Global Development Studies at Queen's University. Her scholarly publications have examined multiple sites of contemporary de/colonizing struggle in Canada, including resource extraction, property relations, caring labours, and interpersonal violence. Her dissertation, awarded a Governor General's Gold Medal and the Mary McEwan Memorial Award for feminist research, examines the impact of the northern diamond mining industry on Indigenous women.

TOBIN LEBLANC HALEY is an assistant professor (LTF) of sociology at Ryerson University and formerly the Ethel Louise Armstrong Postdoctoral Fellow in the School of Disability Studies at Ryerson University. She obtained a PhD in Political Science (2017) from York University specializing in Canadian politics, gender politics, social and public policy, and disability politics. Her research interrogates the implications of social policy making in Canada's provinces and territories for people living with disabilities. Her analytical approach sits firmly at the intersection of feminist political economy and disability studies.

OLENA LYUBCHENKO is a doctoral candidate in the Department of Politics at York University. Her research interests include neoliberal restructuring, gender order transformations, and labour market insecurity in former Soviet and Eastern Bloc countries; social reproduction under Soviet state-command economy; as well as comparative welfare state and family policy.

STEPHEN MCBRIDE is a professor of political science and Canada Research Chair in public policy and globalization at McMaster University, where he is also a member of the Institute of Globalization and the Human Condition and an associate member of the School of Labour Studies. He has published widely on issues of global and Canadian political economy and public policy. His book *Not Working: State,*

Unemployment and Neo-Conservatism in Canada won the Canadian Political Science Association's 1994 Smiley prize for the best book on Canadian politics. Recent books include: *Working: Employment Policy in Canada, The Austerity State* (co-edited with Bryan Evans), and *Austerity: The Lived Experience* (co-edited with Bryan Evans).

SUZANNE MILLS is an associate professor in labour studies and geography and earth sciences at McMaster University. She has published widely in the area of work and employment in Canada's provincial and territorial norths. In her work, Mills has partnered with Indigenous communities and labour unions to critically examine Indigenous employment programs on resource development projects and to explore the role of unions and Indigenous governments in the regulation of northern work. Her present research examines the work experiences of sexual and gender minorities living in northern and southwestern Ontario.

TANNER MIRRLEES is an associate professor in the Communication and Digital Media Studies Program at the University of Ontario Institute of Technology (UOIT) and the vice-president of the Canadian Communication Association (CCA). A critical political economist of the ICT and cultural industries, his research centres on US Empire and communications, the nexus of right-wing extremism and social media, and cultural work and labour. Mirrlees is the author of *Hearts and Mines: The U.S. Empire's Culture Industry* (University of British Columbia Press, 2015) and *Global Entertainment Media: Between Cultural Imperialism and Cultural Globalization* (Routledge, 2013).

STEPHANIE ROSS is an associate professor in the School of Labour Studies at McMaster University. Her research and teaching focus on democracy in working-class and social movement organizations, union renewal, union politics and strategy, public sector unionism, and the links between social justice organizing inside and outside of the workplace. She is the co-editor of three books (with L. Savage): *Rethinking the Politics of Labour in Canada* (Fernwood, 2012), *Public Sector Unions in the Age of Austerity* (Fernwood, 2013), and *Labour Under Attack: Anti-Unionism in Canada* (Fernwood, 2018), and co-author of the third edition of *Building a Better World: An Introduction to the Labour Movement in Canada* (Fernwood, 2015). Her work has been published in journals including *Labour/Le Travail, Studies in Political Economy, Labor Studies Journal, The Socialist Register,* and *Just Labour.* Current areas of research include the effectiveness of different strategies used by unions to make political change and the conditions that shape job quality for contract academic faculty.

NANDITA SHARMA is the director of the International Cultural Studies Program and an associate professor in the Department of Sociology at the University of Hawaii at Manoa. She has published extensively on the political economy of immigration, migration, and citizenship. She is an activist scholar whose research is shaped by the social movements she is active in, including No Borders movements and those struggling for the commons. She is the author of *Home Economics: Nationalism and the Making of "Migrant Workers" in Canada* (University of Toronto Press, 2006).

ADRIAN A. SMITH is an associate professor at Osgoode Hall Law School and the academic director of Parkdale Community Legal Services. He was previously cross-appointed to the Institute of Political Economy and the Institute of African Studies at Carleton University. Smith's research interests include labour studies and the global economy, migration, the political economy of development, social movements, and visual legal studies. His research projects have taken him to Northern Africa, Western Europe, South America, the Caribbean, and throughout the US and Canada. He is co-editor of *Unfree Labour? Struggles of Migrant and Immigrant Workers in Canada* (PM Press, 2016).

JIM STANFORD is economist and director of the Centre for Future Work in Sydney, Australia, and Harold Innis Industry Professor of Economics at McMaster University. Previously, he worked as economist and director of policy with Unifor (and before that the Canadian Auto Workers). He is the author of *Economics for Everyone*, 2nd edition (2015), which has been translated into six languages.

MARK P. THOMAS is an associate professor in the Department of Sociology at York University. He is the author of *Regulating Flexibility: The Political Economy of Employment Standards* (McGill-Queen's University Press, 2009), co-author of *Work and Labour in Canada: Critical Issues*, 3rd edition (Canadian Scholars Press, 2017) and *Closing the Employment Standards Enforcement Gap: Improving Protections for People in Precarious Jobs* (University of Toronto Press, forthcoming), and co-editor of *Interrogating the New Economy: Restructuring Work in the 21st Century* (University of Toronto Press, 2010) and *Power and*

Everyday Practices, 2nd edition (University of Toronto Press, 2019). His work has also been published in journals including *Antipode, Economic & Industrial Democracy, Economic & Labour Relations Review, Journal of Industrial Relations, Labor Studies Journal, Labour/Le Travail*, and *Studies in Political Economy*.

STEVEN TUFTS is an associate professor in the Department of Geography at York University. His research interests are related to the geographies of work, workers, and organized labour. Current projects include the use of strategic research by labour unions and labour union renewal in Canada, the integration of immigrants in urban labour markets, labour market adjustment in the hospitality sector, the impact of climate change on hospitality work, and the intersection between labour and growing populism. He has recently published in *Antipode, Labor Studies Journal*, and *The Economic and Labour Relations Review*.

LEAH F. VOSKO is a professor of political science and Canada Research Chair (Tier 1) in the political economy of gender and work at York University. Vosko is the author of *Temporary Work: The Gendered Rise of a Precarious Employment Relationship* (University of Toronto Press, 2000), *Managing the Margins: Gender, Citizenship and the International Regulation of Precarious Employment* (Oxford University Press, 2010), and co-author of *Closing the Employment Standards Enforcement Gap: Improving Protections for People in Precarious Jobs* (University of Toronto Press, forthcoming) and *Self-Employed Workers Organize: Law, Policy, and Unions* (McGill-Queen's University Press, 2005). She is the editor and co-editor of seven books including *Liberating Temporariness?: Migration, Work and Citizenship in an Age of Insecurity* (McGill-Queen's University Press, 2014). She also oversees the collaborative Gender and Work, Comparative Perspectives on Precarious Employment, and Employment Standards Database projects.

LESLEY J. WOOD is an associate professor of sociology at York University. She is author of *Direct Action, Deliberation and Diffusion: Collective Action after the World Trade Organization (WTO) Protests in Seattle* (Cambridge University Press, 2012), which won the John Porter Tradition of Excellence Book Award, *Crisis and Control: The Militarization of Protest Policing* (Pluto/Between the Lines, 2014), and co-author of *Social Movements, 1768–2012*, 3rd edition (Routledge, 2016). Her research interests are social movements, political sociology, globalization, diffusion, transnational movements, repression, internationalism, and deliberation.

Index

Tables and figures indicated by page numbers in italics